'During my many visits to Timor-Leste as a pro-bono adviser to Prime Minister Xanana Gusmão, I occasionally heard talk of the "helium rip-off".

I was aware there was a helium plant in Darwin, one of only a dozen or so in the world.

I was also aware that under the treaty between Australia and Timor-Leste signed in early 2006 (the treaty known as CMATS that is now subject to allegations of spying by Australia during its negotiation), Timor-Leste was entitled to 90 percent of revenue from the Bayu Undan gas field.

What I did not realise, until I read *Oil Under Troubled Water*, was that the helium processed in the plant in Darwin was from the Bayu Undan gas field, and the Australian government had, in Bernard Collaery's words, "connived to hide from the United Nations and the Timorese the presence of massive quantities of helium gas", produced as a by-product of processing the Bayu Undan gas in Darwin.

With the forensic eye of a highly skilled lawyer, Bernard Collaery delves into the detail of the helium rip-off and exposes the secret deals orchestrated by the Australian Department of Foreign Affairs, and its Minister Alexander Downer, that benefitted multinational oil companies at the expense of the desperately poor Timorese and, as it turns out, Australian citizens.

As a proud Australian it is devastating to learn of the extent of our betrayal of the Timorese in the years following independence in 1999. While our army was on the ground bravely bringing peace to a shattered land, in Canberra our Department of Foreign Affairs was scheming to deny Timor-Leste billions of dollars of desperately needed revenue.

Oil Under Troubled Water is essential, if difficult, reading for all Australians.'

STEVE BRACKS

'Bernard Collaery has devoted much of his legal life to advancing the welfare of the people of East Timor—against Indonesian brutality, Australian chicanery and oil company greed. Now the government and its unintelligent intelligence service is persecuting him, but he refuses to be silenced—this book expertly analyses the foreign policy failures, over the past 70 years, by which Australia has sold out and then cheated its impoverished neighbour. East Timor is the country on our conscience.'

GEOFFREY ROBERTSON

'That one of the richest countries in the world would betray and rip off one of the poorest is shameful in the extreme. Bernard Collaery's meticulous account of this unconscionable misconduct is an important record. But more importantly his fight for those treated unjustly, and courage standing up to those who betray their positions of trust, is an inspiration to us all.'

ANDREW WILKIE

Bernard Collaery is an Australian solicitor and barrister who specialises in litigation in high-profile catastrophic personal injury cases. He has acted for families of victims of the Thredbo landslide, the Royal Canberra Hospital demolition tragedy, the Glenbrook rail disaster in the Blue Mountains, the fire aboard HMAS *Westralia*, the tragic loss of an RAAF F111 in the South China Sea and an RAF Special Forces aircraft and crew in Iraq. He has appeared as counsel in many criminal jury trials.

Throughout his career as a solicitor, advocate and politician Bernard has been a fearless advocate for human rights. During his tenure as Attorney-General for the Australian Capital Territory, he introduced an independent law reform process that culminated in the drafting of human rights legislation, including anti-discrimination legislation.

Bernard Collaery advised the East Timor Resistance for more than thirty years, providing advice on international law and other matters during the United Nations Transitional Administration from 1999. He acted for East Timor at the International Court of Justice in relation to a maritime sea boundary dispute with Australia.

Currently Bernard Collaery is patron and honorary solicitor of various charitable and non-profit organisations serving Indigenous Australians and marginalised sectors of the community. For some years he assisted in the work of the Sydney-based St James Ethics Centre.

OIL UNDER TROUBLED WATER

AUSTRALIA'S TIMOR SEA INTRIGUE

BERNARD COLLAERY

MELBOURNE UNIVERSITY PRESS

MELBOURNE UNIVERSITY PRESS
An imprint of Melbourne University Publishing Limited
Level 1, 715 Swanston Street, Carlton, Victoria 3053, Australia
mup-contact@unimelb.edu.au
www.mup.com.au

First published 2020
Text © Bernard Collaery, 2020
Map on page 362 © Alain Murphy, 2019
Design and typography © Melbourne University Publishing Limited, 2020

National Security Series edited by Professor Clinton Fernandes

This book is copyright. Apart from any use permitted under the *Copyright Act 1968* and subsequent amendments, no part may be reproduced, stored in a retrieval system or transmitted by any means or process whatsoever without the prior written permission of the publishers.

Every attempt has been made to locate the copyright holders for material quoted in this book. Any person or organisation that may have been overlooked or misattributed may contact the publisher.

Cover design by Philip Campbell Design
Cover images courtesy Getty Images and iStock
Typeset in Bembo 11.5/14.5pt by Cannon Typesetting
Printed in Australia by McPherson's Printing Group

A catalogue record for this book is available from the National Library of Australia

9780522876499 (paperback)
9780522876505 (ebook)

CONTENTS

Preface and Acknowledgements	ix
A Note on Sources and the Limitations of Archival Research	xix
Introduction	1
1 The Atlantic Charter—'Whither Thou Goest'	15
2 The Allies, Australia and Portuguese Timor	27
3 After the War—The Vision Fades	62
4 Australia and Portuguese Timor	77
5 The Australian Continental Shelf—Declaring Boundaries	109
6 Post-Colonial Abandonment—Australia and the Indonesian Occupation of Timor-Leste	133
7 Timor-Leste Edges Towards Independence	174
8 Transition in Timor-Leste and the Timor Gap Treaty	198
9 The Transitional Government Negotiates a New Treaty	226
10 'Independence' for Timor-Leste	247
11 The FALINTIL Tragedy	259
12 Australian Opportunism	274
13 Lighter Than Air—The Helium Escapes	281
14 A Matter for Inquiry	319
15 Australian Gameplay	325
16 Export Trade *Versus* Defence	339
17 Determining Maritime Boundaries	359
18 Timor-Leste Complains	373
19 The Universal Relevance of the Rule of Law	385
Notes	390
Index	452

PREFACE AND ACKNOWLEDGEMENTS

Recalling a childhood spent immediately after World War II, perhaps the only thing that made sense was the nobility of Australian sentiment in support of the values Britain and its Allies had fought for during that war. Many of my generation were marked by that great struggle and the stories and literature that emerged from it. Against that upbringing there is no wonder about my reaction when life led me to bear witness to the long duel within public conscience in Australia over Timor-Leste.[1] It was a duel between rule of law and opportunistic greed, with all the usual actors—politicians of foresight, foreign entanglements, decent and dissimulating diplomats, devious petroleum corporations and their political lackeys, muffled scientists, and, off stage but always in the wings, the intelligence services.

This book is as much about the history of events affecting East Timor as it is lament about the moral decay in Australian political leadership. In this study of the modern history of Australia–Timor-Leste relations I have attempted to cast some light on how Australia through its leaders, some of noble intent and others of shameful moral weakness, played a role in the lives of ordinary Timorese through the darkness of World War II and during Timor-Leste's painful progression to independence. There were turning points in Timor-Leste's history, some shaped by collateral events far away of great moment during World War II and the Cold War and others by an opportunism that some see as peculiarly Australian.

Hopefully, the reader may form a view as to when key Australian players abandoned the conviction so often expressed by Australia's wartime and post-war leaders that Australia would be an exemplary society. I have sought to illustrate an important concern to all who hold democracy and rule of law dear, namely, why, in the federal sphere in Australia, did the Westminster system of government fail the Timorese? In the second half of the 20th century, and so far in the 21st, both sides of Australian national politics have, with some notable individual exceptions, abandoned a rules-based order to support the exploitation of the sovereign petroleum assets of a poor neighbour.

Philosopher and anthropologist Professor James Laidlaw sought to submit to empirical analysis dimensions of human conduct that may have been sidestepped or denied in social analysis. His reviewer says that Laidlaw believes ethics is a meaningful and irreducible part of human life.[2] If you agree, the reader may wonder how we allowed our leaders' decisions on Timor to sidestep ethics. Receiving comment in the street after a controversial hearing is often the lot of a trial lawyer; not once in all my years of public advocacy for the Timorese has anyone in the street—the ordinary reader—upbraided me. From whom do our elected leaders believe they derive their support for their exploitation of the Timorese? That is a question to bear in mind while turning these pages. I share the hope that most Australians would not support their leaders' misconduct towards the Timorese were the truth revealed. This book is my attempt at that task—a task that will, I expect, be corrected and supplemented by those who both know more and have the courage to tell.

In finding a want of character in certain Australian leaders and institutionalised deceit in Australian foreign policy, this book records events of wider significance than the travail the Timorese were subjected to by Australia and Indonesia for 25 years. The Timor–Australia story may confront the reader not only with the ethics of petroleum diplomacy but also with the ongoing damage to Australia's long-term security interests by a foreign policy based on dominating smaller neighbours rather than living with them.

Pushing Indonesia, peacefully in boundary negotiations, as far north as possible on the Australian Continental Shelf after the Indonesia-Malaysia Confrontation (*Konfrontasi*) is understandable, but the opportunistic moves by the McMahon and Whitlam Governments to avoid cooperation with Portugal as the colonial power in Timor-Leste around the time of the 1972 OPEC crisis does some of that generation of Australian politicians and their advisers little credit. Later, the connivance with Indonesia led to genocide.[3] Although many Australian ears refuse to hear the word 'genocide', Australia was complicit for many years in a breach by Indonesia of fundamental legal norms not much different from the Armenian genocide 90 years earlier or the reckless starvations of occupied nations by Hitler's Germany during World War II.[4]

The refusal by the Australian Executive, on spurious grounds of 'national security', to release documents evidencing that complicity compounds that guilt.[5] It is too easily forgotten that after the military tribunals in 1945, the 12 Nuremberg successor trials embraced corporate executives, judges and lawyers, and Foreign Ministry diplomats.[6] The trials before the International Military Tribunal of the German public servants who directed the expropriation of Jewish assets in occupied territories should be read carefully in Canberra. Not enough of this reckoning appears to have had salutary effect. I hope this book may help. As Professor Grayling says, 'If anyone should be expected to uphold the rule of law, it is the law's own servants'.[7]

The moral world order sought by Prime Minister John Curtin and the indefatigable H.V. (Bert) Evatt stands in stark contrast to the unforgivable conduct 30 years later of Gough Whitlam and his advisers on East Timor. The beneficiaries of the state-sponsored larceny of Timorese assets are now spread wide in the Australian corporate sector. In common purpose with a secretive unit at Australia's premier geoscience agency that lent scientific credibility to a questionable 'two shelves' claim in the Timor Sea, Australia has now stripped the poor peoples of Timor of a significant proportion of their non-renewable sovereign assets. Hopelessly enmeshed in living a lie, both of Australia's main political groupings, negotiating with a liberated Timor-Leste, continued to regard the threat of economic hardship as a legitimate instrument of diplomatic persuasion.

When the Timorese, who still lose a high proportion of their infants before they reach the age of five, began to show some fight, Australia resorted to the tactics of a grubby cheat. When found out, the Australian Government raided the home of a retired Australian Secret Intelligence Service (ASIS) senior officer who, without any compromise of names or techniques, was prepared to give evidence in camera of unlawful conduct. In absolute contempt of the Permanent Court of Arbitration, the Abbott Government cancelled the witness's passport and harassed him with threatened prosecution.

Not stopping there, the Federal Attorney-General of the day issued his own warrant under national security laws introduced to combat terrorism to allow the seizure of legally privileged documents from the author's chambers. The Australian Government then successfully edged the Timorese out of pursuing an eminently winnable case and into a 'conciliation process' under the auspices of the United Nations out of which Australia has again emerged a winner. This book throws light on the role of the United Nations and Australia in depriving future generations of Timorese of their sovereign birthright.

As the Timor–Australia story emerged first-hand and from government archives, mostly in the UK, Portugal and Holland, and scattered documentary sources, it seemed that in rolling out such a large canvas the best one might hope to produce from such a grand illustration of Australian bad faith would be to illuminate the evil that was done and the pressing need to call to account those responsible. For events long ago the task may fall to the professional historian, but for those wrongdoers still in our midst, the task relies on the objectivity of independent judicial enquiry and trial. Some within the Australian legal profession, including Australian public service lawyers, must also face scrutiny.

Before I commenced much of the research for this book I held to the view that Professor Philip Allott was somewhat harsh in his judgement on the role of diplomacy that he had once practised. So far as the Australia–Timor-Leste story is concerned, the reader may understand why I have come around to the view Philip expressed in such memorable words:

> Diplomacy is an education in deceit. It sets before the people an example of practical amorality, the pursuit of any profitable end by any practical means. The public imagination is caught by the world of espionage, lying and cheating and stealing in the public interest. But every word and every act of diplomacy is objectively a deceit, since a government speaks and acts in relation to another government in order to produce a particular effect, and not for the sake of doing good.[8]

That amoral Australian diplomacy stands apart from other Australian institutions has been brought home to me repeatedly over the years by the staunch support for the East Timorese, albeit discreet at times, from within Australian defence and intelligence circles. But for the wonderful work in Timor-Leste of many Australians in the defence services and non-government agencies, including religious orders, a half-century of corrupt Australian diplomacy to our near north has up to now avoided Australia having a hostile state on our doorstep. The chronicle of misdeeds and manipulation should shock all right-thinking Australians. We must redeem our national conscience by establishing an independent national inquiry in which the complicit, dead or alive, are identified, prosecuted or otherwise shamed and their honours stripped from them. My purpose is twofold: first, to call upon Australians to treat fairly the good people of Timor whose forbears supported our young soldiers in their hour of need; second, to influence politicians of courage and integrity to come forward and question the conduct of their colleagues.

As lawyer and witness I must admit my own subjectivity—all the more since, long after I commenced this story, Australian secret service agents placed listening devices in my home and chambers and plundered my electronic archives. On 3 December 2013, secret service agents, accompanied by a public service 'lawyer', executed a search warrant on my home and chambers, issued by Attorney-General George Brandis QC under powers given post 9/11 to combat terrorism.

My knowledge of East Timor commenced during my final years at the University of Sydney Law School when I received some specialised training from an Australian intelligence agency. One of those training us was an ex-World War II, Australian Army 'Z' Special Unit commando who spoke passionately of the Timorese people. I had little idea of where Timor Island was but what I heard from this veteran caused me to read Sir Bernard Callinan's account of his Independent Company's war behind the lines in Timor. Later, I was fortunate to learn more field-craft from my commando-turned-intelligence officer, including why Callinan concluded his story about our Timor-Leste allies so memorably: 'Money could not repay them, there is no coinage appropriate to such loyalty'.[9]

Years later it dawned on me that the role of Professor Julius Stone[10] in my student life had been beyond the jurisprudence he so passionately led us into. It was he who helped explain my absences from class, but that is another story. Stone dedicated his wartime text, *Atlantic Charter*, to an ex-student who had perished while serving as an RNZAF Pilot Officer. He spoke fondly of that student and gave me a now treasured copy of his book after he found me out at Law School, long before I was due to study jurisprudence. He was aware that, as the son of one of Australia's wartime dead, I held a Soldiers' Children's Education Board Scholarship. Few of us could have imagined that our benign professor had held senior rank in a shadowy wartime outfit about which more emerges in pages to come. In teaching us, Stone spoke of his colleague, Professor Sir Hersch Lauterpacht QC LLD. By life's great twist, my mentor and friend as I reassembled my papers in the safety of Cambridge after the raid on my chambers was that great jurist's son, Professor Sir Elihu Lauterpacht CBE QC LLD.

The Australian Department of Foreign Affairs, with an abysmal record of geostrategic blunder and compromise of values, has drawn successive Australian political leaders into error over Timor-Leste. Some, like Alexander Downer, adapted to and excelled in empty sophistry as foreign policy and ethical interest became separated. On Downer's watch during the Howard years, sensible strategy towards a new state emerging on Australia's doorstep was distorted by the lure of oil such that the world's most powerful petroleum companies held Australia's foreign policy on Timor in thrall. Downer and his close ministerial advisers on Timor-Leste were nothing better than pageboys in the Court of Royal Dutch Shell, ConocoPhillips and Woodside Petroleum. During 1999–2003 a fledgling Timor-Leste was induced to sign the 2002 Timor Sea Treaty and the International Unitization Agreement, while Australia connived to hide from the United Nations and the Timorese the presence of massive quantities of helium gas. Over the years, in their conjoint exploitation of the Timorese, a petroleum-intoxicated kleptocracy turned the Australian Parliament into a sham as it rubber-stamped treaty licences to steal.

Early in his career the former Australian Federal Minister for Resources, Energy and Northern Australia, more recently Minister for Environment and Energy and, in the Morrison Government, Treasurer and Deputy Leader of the Liberal Party, Josh Frydenberg, worked as an adviser in the Parliamentary Office of Foreign Minister Alexander Downer. Downer and Frydenberg, together with bureaucrats and industry players, have much that they might assist an inquiry with. It is unlikely that any Coalition or Labor Government would establish an inquiry, but complaints by shareholders may trigger judicial proceedings. If there is such an inquiry with immunities, when appropriate, the outcome may shake Australian democracy to its foundations.

A lot has been written about our national shame over Timor-Leste, focusing on the events of 1974–75 when invading Indonesian Special Forces murdered Australian, British and New Zealand newsmen. With the help largely of UK Foreign Office archives I have sought to delve further back into modern Australian history. Not so far back as Banjo Patterson's sturdy Timor pony in *The Man from Snowy River*,[11] but rather to a secret 1940 treaty between Britain, Portugal and Australia aimed at limiting Japanese access to oil exploration concessions in Portuguese Timor. This seems to be from where the oil slick spreads.

This record of events aims to evoke questions about a breakdown of Parliamentary and Executive conscience in Canberra rather than provide, in the absence of archival release and testimony under summons and/or immunity, a fully documented history. While the Australian story is marked by nationalists of vision and integrity like Evatt, Sir David Fairbairn and Tom Uren, the expediency practised by the likes of Sir Garfield Barwick, Gough Whitlam and Alexander Downer deserves condemnation and may bring the reader to support a national apology to the Timorese.

Over long years of my involvement with East Timor, Ann Collaery and our children Matthew, Caitlin, Lucy and Brigid often went without in a variety of ways, not least financial. In expressing my abiding gratitude, I am conscious that it has all come at a price. In recent years Eli Lauterpacht and Lady Cathy Lauterpacht gave me their steadfast support while the struggle went on at The Hague and elsewhere to bring those who breach the rule of law to account. Sadly, Sir Eli has not lived to see this book published. He taught me so much.

I acknowledge the courage of two war veterans, both intelligence officers, whom I cannot name. Their moral compass, a generation apart, showed me the light on Timor-Leste. This book took shape with the encouragement and friendship of the Master and Fellows of Trinity College, my colleagues at the Centre of South Asian Studies, University of Cambridge, the staffs of the National Archives at Kew and the Australian National Archives at Canberra, my Readership at the London School of Economics, and my courageous Australian law colleagues Jolan Draaisma, Tobias (Toby) Hanson, Carla Mazur,

Maria Gawander, Chloe Preston, Alice Bolt, and especially Amy Maree McMullen, who arrived as our receptionist and travelled many hard roads with me, studying at times for her law degree by lamplight under a mosquito net. The only unashamed tear I have ever shed in Court was when I had the privilege in 2016 to call her admission as a lawyer.

If this book, encouraged by Nathan Hollier of MUP and edited wonderfully by Rachel Salmond, succeeds in widening the debate, I must thank Ian and Margaret Melrose who, with an interest-free loan in 2015, rescued me financially after our team was pushed off the case leaving me with costly expenses in London. Now outplayed and worn down for a second time, an element of the Timor-Leste leadership gave away the strong hand we had established for them before the International Court of Justice and the Permanent Court of Arbitration, preferring another unhappy compromise with Australia that has sown the seeds of further discord across the Timor Sea.

In the aftermath of the dispersal of our litigation team while the attack by Australia continued, many Australians, including Nick Xenophon, Scott Ludlam, Andrew Wilkie, Nick McKim, Clinton Fernandes, Mark Davis and Shirley Shackleton, gave moral support. In the current retributive climate, I shall not name some Australian journalists who also worked hard to get the truth out. They amply validate that old aphorism, 'Publicity is the soul of justice'. One journalist, Amy Ripley, whom I met one day in Balibo, pushed me along to complete this book. Our London team owes a debt to Garry and Gwenda Coombe, two retired ordinary Australians for their posted Christmas cakes, Anzac biscuits, Anglican op shop woollens and constant encouragement. Without regard for what I hope becomes an illustrious career, Matilda Wall joined us as an intern when retribution loomed. I salute her young lawyer courage and the support in the best liberal democratic tradition given her by staff and colleagues at the Australian National University. Small wonder that the Josephite Sisters, whose founder Saint Mary MacKillop used her strong Scottish sense of justice to shape our early nation, taught me as a child and have come to my aid with spiritual and practical support. That congregation, along with others of equal faith, supported the Timorese through the dark years and led by the indefatigable Susan Connelly and Josephine Mitchell campaigned for justice.

I should single out a few of the many legal colleagues and friends who were supportive during the raids and pressure that followed, namely, Dennis Wheelahan QC, who, early in the morning after the raid on my chambers rang me as I looked over a cold sea at The Hague, lifting my spirits and offering immediate assistance, Bernard Gross QC, Professor Nicholas Cowdery QC, Bret Walker SC, the one and only Alan Conolly, and my Law School classmate Geoffrey Robertson QC. I look forward to my other classmate Philip Ruddock, who was Attorney-General at the time of the treaty-making misconduct at Dili, being afforded the opportunity in an appropriate forum to disown conduct I know he would not have countenanced. One must make mention of the selfless support given to me by the partners of law firm Gilbert & Tobin, Sydney, and the team of barristers instructed by them. My friends in the legal profession all deserve a medal for standing up on the issue regardless of whether Commonwealth Briefs would any longer be in the offing.

Bernard Collaery
Cambridge, June 2019

A NOTE ON SOURCES AND THE LIMITATIONS OF ARCHIVAL RESEARCH

There is an extensive literature in English and Portuguese by scholars who have examined Timorese cultural roots, Portuguese and Indonesian colonisation, and the struggle for independence. Except where indicated, I have not sought to reformulate the written history of the Timorese. In that sense, key texts such as Geoffrey Gunn's *Timor Loro Sae: 500 Years*, Clinton Fernandes' *The Independence of East Timor* and Cornell University's 2013 collection of thought-provoking essays on the future for Timor-Leste[1] stand alone for their integrity and require little supplementation beyond that from an eye witness to some events as United Nations nation-building failed and was overrun by greedy Australian neo-colonialism.

In writing this book I am constrained by self-imposed privacy issues relating to my long personal association with some of the principal actors, my formal appointment by Xanana Gusmão, President of the Conselho Nacional da Resistência Timorense (CNRT) in early 2000 as Legal Adviser to the CNRT until its disbanding in 2002, a duty of confidentiality with respect to aspects of a formal retainer by the government of Timor-Leste in 2012–14, and Australian law concerning legitimate national security interests. Advance publicity about this book, a threatening letter from the Australian Government Solicitor and the issue of a summons for conspiracy against my client known only as 'Witness K', and, myself, resulted in significant aspects of the history about what I had written being potentially subject to the *sub judice* rule. The manuscript was revised. I ask the reader to draw what inferences are now possible and to bear in mind that in different circumstances much more could be added to the debate. The present 'circumstances' include ongoing political oversight of the *Australian Archives Act 1983* that inhibits research and has a chilling effect on actors whose involvement in historic events remains part of the unreleased or redacted record.

Unlike the more effective implementation of national archives legislation in the United States and United Kingdom, the failure by successive Australian Governments to administer lawfully the *Australian Archives Act 1983* restricts historical foreign policy research, resulting in a less than authoritative historical record. This is well illustrated in respect of the dismissal of Prime Minister Gough Whitlam in 1975, about which sensational conspiracy theories persist, with one historian directing her suspicions against the British Royal Family rather than investigating issues relating to the rule of law. The limited and selective archival release of intelligence records might be borne in mind in any consideration of the author's concluded views. Motives for this veil of secrecy vary, but may include sensitivity over a long-overdue independent evaluation of Soviet and, latterly, Chinese covert influence within key Australian policy areas. At this stage, it is fair to say that, from the time the Cold War commenced, Australia remained in lockstep with British and United States intelligence assessments concerning the threat of Soviet and Chinese communism, and when those assessments were compromised they were likely also compromised in Australia.

The various 'histories' of the Australian Security Intelligence Organisation (ASIO) refer, without any real analysis, to the frequent probable compromise of counter Soviet-espionage activity by ASIO. They do not deal with inexplicable failure to deal with suspected moles and to take retaliatory measures. Actual counter-espionage steps against an aggressive Soviet role in Australia during the Vietnam War are not mentioned in any of the 'approved' histories of ASIO. Likewise, Soviet activity has not been related to the Whitlam dismissal. There should be no national security inhibitions on the archival release of historically important intelligence material that may have added, rightly or wrongly, to the material deliberations of the Governor-General in that dismissal.

Prior to the Vietnam debacle, Australia failed to develop an independent foreign policy that would allow for alliances or empathetic linkages with North and Southeast Asian states emerging with socialist or communist governments. Canberra followed Washington and Whitehall in perceiving such states as subversive threats to democracy. Until Vietnam was finally recognised as a state, albeit Communist, with a genuine independent nationalistic foreign policy, Australia naively joined the wagons drawn around Moscow and Beijing. The role of the Australian intelligence community in the reins of government in Canberra, including favoured journalists, is suspected but is as little known as are the skills of the horse whisperer. Members of Parliament arrive in Canberra naïve to the influences of the intelligence community and as they progress to the ministerial paddock they stand agog, even entranced, by the sedulous voice of the intelligence analyst. Intelligence archives worthy of release remain closed despite the lessons they may impart for future governance.

Archival releases in Washington and London of intelligence reports and foreign policy appreciations that went to the Executive at critical historical junctures in the United States and Britain have been of signal assistance in the historical review of executive and administrative action. Not so in Australia where the governing cabal of Coalition and Labor politicians and their senior bureaucratic advisers have a long-standing aversion to the disclosure of key historical records, usually under the rubric of 'protecting foreign relations'. This has been accomplished to some extent in Australia by instructing amenable former foreign policy and intelligence personnel in the archival assessment process, both within the National Australian Archives (NAA) Office and in the notorious 'pre-assessing' by key agencies before those agencies comply with statutory obligations to retain and transfer records to the NAA.[2] To cap this off, both sides of the political spectrum in Australia appoint political allies to administrative review tribunals. This has created an unfortunate perception of bias in the minds of those dealing with challenges to redactions or refusals to release that has poisoned the process.[3]

INTRODUCTION

Serious moral enquiry into the conduct of politicians with whom we identify in some way is not popular. For scandalous conduct there is an ever-ready ear, but few of us in a pluralistic society with differing values want to confront an established order even though it may be morally delinquent. This book aims to confront the reader with images of an established bipartisan delinquent political order in Australia—a delinquency that grew out of notions of national development in the 1960s and manifested itself in dispossession, genocide and corruption. While it may be fair to say that most Australians acknowledge a duty of repair to our Timorese brothers and sisters over the 1974–99 collaboration with Indonesia, Australia's main political parties offer no apology and no change to their ways. It seems right and just to shake this political complacency and to call for a return to the moral leadership in Australian federal politics that marked the challenges of the Great War, the Great Depression, World War II and National Reconstruction.

At the outset, I invite the reader to test what I say are two of the most unrepentant and self-deluded statements that have entered this debate:

> The Timor Sea Treaty and the subsequent treaties really are a model example of how two States can work together for mutual benefit …

One of Timor-Leste's arguments for dispensing with the current treaty framework is that it claims Australia has exploited Timor-Leste's vulnerability as a developing State. I hope we have demonstrated this is simply untrue.[1]

Timor Island, under a tropical sun 10 degrees south of the Equator, is one of the first of the islands that arc west to east across the top of Australia to Samoa in the Pacific Ocean. In 1914, Timor was not much more than a coaling stop for steamers plying between Asia and Australia. By the end of World War I, Timor Island was recognised as part of the island screen to Australia's north that may act as a first line of defence against any invader—articulated at that time as the 'yellow peril'. Within 60 years of the ANZAC landings at Gallipoli on 25 April 1915, the history of both world wars had been forgotten by Australian political leaders and Timor became the scene of diplomatic activity in support of perceived friendly corporate interests that ran counter to good conscience and Australia's long-term defence interests.

By the time the Paris Peace Conference ended World War I in 1919, Australia and New Zealand had been self-governing nations only for as long as many of the 80,000 ANZACs who perished in the great conflict had lived. Proposals from London that the Dominions be represented at the Conference by Britain met with a storm of protest in Canada, South Africa, Australia and New Zealand. The French soon realised that they should drop the idea of objecting to Britain having a multiple voice at the Conference for the simple reason that Britain had critical, rather than supportive, Dominion voices at the table. Confidence in British General Defence Staff ability had been shaken and Australia and New Zealand wanted to divide up the former German Pacific possessions—for New Zealand, German Samoa, and for Australia, a screen of all the German islands south of the Equator and to the north of Australia.

Pax Britannica

On 14 January 1916, as Australian Prime Minister Billy Hughes prepared to embark at Sydney for London, Defence Minister Sir George Pearce had a secret letter delivered to Hughes. Referring to their earlier discussion concerning the future of the Pacific Islands, including those captured in 1914 by Australia from Germany, Pearce advised that the islands south of the Equator containing minerals and phosphate deposits had a capacity for commercial development. They were of 'incalculable value to Australia ... their strategic value is exceedingly great to Australia as forming a shield to the Northern portions of our continent. They possess many good harbours'.[2] Pearce's papers reveal an anxiety in the Australian Cabinet about Japan's rise to power and the decline of British power in the Far East.[3]

Britain's use of the Japanese Navy to escort Australian troopship convoys to the Middle East and England was a sobering experience for White Australia. Australian strategy at the Versailles Peace Conference reflected an anxiety about the future defence of Australia. Just as Australia is now questioning the certainty of the United States umbrella, the Australian delegation at Versailles was mindful of the decline of *Pax Britannica* in the Far East. Prime Minister Hughes, aware, prophetically, of Britain's defence limitations in the antipodes, spoke of the islands to Australia's north providing better security for Australia. His Welsh compatriot, Britain's Prime Minister Lloyd George, supported the Australian request for trusteeship over most of Germany's former colonial possessions south of the Equator. Although Japan was at the table with the allied victors, Hughes and his Cabinet colleagues viewed the Rising Sun over the Pacific with concern when they sought to bolster Australia's island screen.

The Dominion Government of Australia had developed an uneasy awareness of Britain's relationship with the Japanese following the signing of the Anglo-Japanese Treaty Alliance in August 1905. The May 1907 Conference between the British and Japanese General Staffs regarding the unresolved question of mutual defence assistance in Article VII of the 1905 treaty did little to assuage Australian concerns. While the Japanese had a well-equipped Navy, Japan's lack of a troop transport capacity negated the prospect of Britain securing from the 1907 Conference a promise of early Japanese troop dispositions to assist Britain defend India, Afghanistan or Persia in the event of a Russian attack. Unlike some voices in Whitehall, Australia, aware of Japanese naval supremacy over Russia, had no desire to see Japan develop a military expeditionary capacity.[4] Australians viewed with suspicion Japanese requests at the Paris Peace Conference for island bases in Micronesia.

Portugal, a colonial power with the Dutch on Timor Island, had joined the Allies on the Western Front in 1917–18 and supported the

Australian request for trusteeship over the former German colonies adjoining the Bismarck Sea. Australia secured an island screen, albeit under trusteeship, to the northeast in the Bismarck Sea but not in the northwest Australia-facing Timor Island and the Dutch East Indies.

In an unorthodox move, US President Woodrow Wilson sent on ahead to the Paris Conference his friend and confidant, Texan Edward House, whose advice he relied on more than the State Department's. Twenty years later President Roosevelt did the same, sending personal emissaries to war-torn London, the pre-eminent one being his friend Harry Hopkins who was the President's preferred antennae.[5] Both Wilson and Roosevelt were Democrats opposed, in principle, to colonial imperialism. While Wilson could only use the Paris Peace Conference as a platform to argue for the rights of colonial peoples to self-determination, Roosevelt was in a stronger position in 1941. At his first meeting with Churchill, Roosevelt sought a *quid pro quo* on Wilsonian lines from imperial Britain by securing British War Cabinet endorsement of the Atlantic Charter. With the Charter sentiments, Roosevelt sought to extend his New Deal to the world. To the chagrin of Britain's wartime leadership, Australia's External Affairs Minister H.V. Evatt became a standard-bearer for Roosevelt.

Australian Designs on Portuguese Timor

History may have evolved differently for the Timorese peoples if Dr Evatt's suggestion in June 1943 to British Foreign Secretary Anthony Eden that Portuguese Timor should not be returned to Portugal after the war but presented to Australia had been adopted.[6] Britain and the US rejected Evatt's proposal not on principled grounds but for ephemeral wartime geostrategic reasons. Roosevelt made clear that after the defeat of Japan, the US would use the mandated League territories held by Japan in the Pacific as elements in its own defence arc. At a Pacific War Council meeting in January 1944, where business was conducted informally (much to Australian Representative Justice Owen Dixon's chagrin), Roosevelt also proposed that the US take over French New Caledonia after the war. When Evatt recorded Roosevelt's unguarded comment as a US proposal in the January 1944 Australia–New Zealand Agreement, US Secretary of State, Hull, conscious of French sensitivities, took offence and complained to Prime Minister Curtin about the breach of protocol by Evatt.

As the record shows, Australia, then without petroleum resources of its own, emerged from the war against Japan with a strategic interest in Portuguese Timor that, but for Portugal's Prime Minister Dr Salazar's early intransigence and Australian deference to Washington and London, could have been accommodated within the Atlanticist sentiments championed by Dr Evatt. Years later, when an elderly Dr Salazar challenged Australia to adopt a role in the governance and development of Portuguese Timor, Australia's then Prime Minister, Sir Robert Menzies, advised by a narrow External Affairs clique, rebuffed the proposal. This short-sighted decision marked the beginning of a great tragedy for Australia's wartime Timorese allies.

In retrospect, Dr Evatt's thwarted plans were prescient and an opportunity to better the lot of the Timorese and to further Australian strategic interest was lost. Judging by the reception given by the Timorese to Australian troops during the war and the principled post-war Australian administration of Papua New Guinea, it is not improbable that a post-war Australian UN mandate over liberated Portuguese Timor may have led to an orderly process of autonomy as an Australian overseas territory and possible self-determination as a petroleum-rich mini-state by the early 1980s. Ironically, a more visionary foreign policy may have led to earlier Australian petroleum investment in Timor-Leste, to the protection of a modern Australian-educated and trained Timorese people from Indonesian incorporation, and to an enduring Maubere–Australian relationship.[7]

Any geographer may understand why the Australian War Cabinet understood the strategic importance of Portuguese Timor. Professor Gunn introduced his topic in incomparable terms:

> Timor's location on the map, which became well known to American whalers in the nineteenth century, was also evoked by the author of Moby-Dick, who observed that, stretching south-eastwards in a continuous line from the Malacca peninsula, 'the long islands of Sumatra, Java, Bali and Timor, which, with many others, form a vast mole, or rampart, lengthwise, connecting Asia with Australia, and dividing the long unbroken Indian Ocean from the thickly studded oriental archipelagos'. While the deep and narrow straits separating these islands offered passage to the first circumnavigation of the globe—and also to Melville's migrating whales—the strategic importance of these passages for American submarines moving from the northern Pacific

to the Indian Oceans was also not lost upon Pentagon planners and their Australian counterparts at the time when Timorese clamoured for independence in 1975.

Stretching 470 kilometres along a southwest-northwest axis, 110 kilometres wide at its broadest part, the island of Timor occupies an area of 32,300 square kilometres. Lying some 430 kilometres distant from northern Australia across the Arafura and Timor Sea, the island is situated some eight to ten degrees south of the equator. While more than one observer has commented upon the crocodile-like shape of Timor, the island takes its name from the Malay term for east, reflecting its easternmost location in the archipelago.[8]

Most Timor–Australia surveys commence with insights into the World War II relationship between Portugal and Australia. Four hundred years of Christian colonial administration and intermarriage between locals and Europeans resulted in Australian troops isolated by the Japanese advance being provided with succour and support by the Timorese and their Portuguese-trained Roman Catholic priests. The rapport between the peoples of Timor-Leste and Australia was the only such population-wide rapport established by European troops in the Southeast Asian theatre of war, and it has endured thereafter.

This legacy and post-war defence preparedness influenced Australia to maintain a cooperative relationship with Portuguese colonial authorities in Timor. However, no Australian Government answered calls by war veteran organisations for Australia to assist their gallant wartime allies across the Timor Sea in post-war reconstruction. Curiously, the Australian Labor Party, outspoken on independence for the peoples of the Dutch East Indies, including West Timor, had little to say for the Timorese at the eastern end of Timor Island.

The United Nations and Decolonisation

During the post–World War II tumult of decolonisation of British, French, Spanish and Dutch possessions, Portugal's colonies remained in a time warp. Dr Salazar's adroit entry into the Atlantic Pact in 1949 gave Portugal a continuing strategic role within the North Atlantic Treaty Organisation (NATO), which muted the criticism Portugal was likely to attract from most of the Western democracies participating in the decolonisation work of the UN. Proposals at the UN to include Portuguese colonies in the examination of the conditions of life of peoples who by geographical and ethnic cultural distinctiveness were not to be considered part of the metropolitan state governing them were not enthusiastically supported by the Atlantic Pact countries.[9] When British Prime Minister Harold Macmillan gave his famous 'wind of change' speech to the South African Parliament in Cape Town on 3 February 1960 foreshadowing the end of British colonialism in Africa, he avoided direct reference to unrest in Portugal's African colonies. Nevertheless, Macmillan warned that a failure to adjust to emerging nationalism 'may imperil the precarious balance between East and West on which the peace of the world depends'.

The following year, having lost patience with Portugal, the UN General Assembly, with a membership that could now outvote the Western allies, declared all of Portugal's colonies, including Timor, and dependencies to be non-self-governing territories. The resolution requested Member States to deny Portugal 'any support and assistance which it may use for the suppression of the peoples of its Non-Self-Governing Territories'.[10]

In a more strident resolution a year later, the General Assembly condemned the attitude of Portugal as being inconsistent with the Charter of the United Nations, reaffirmed the inalienable rights of the peoples of the territories under Portuguese administration to self-determination and independence and urged Portugal to cease all acts of repression in its colonies. The resolution requested all states to refrain from providing military assistance to Portugal and urged states to continue pressure on Portugal to conform to the rights of the peoples it was repressing.[11]

Meanwhile, Indonesian President Sukarno's ambition for a Greater Indonesia was attracting attention. On 15 January 1963, the UK High Commissioner in Canberra conveyed a Foreign Office request that joint British, US, Australian and New Zealand talks take place in Washington about developments in Indonesia. Britain was concerned about Indonesian opposition to the creation of Greater Malaysia in lieu of a Greater Indonesian Malaysia. Indonesia was also seen by Britain as supporting the rebellion in Brunei and likely to take over Portuguese Timor. Despite being Britain's oldest ally, Portugal was not included in the joint talks.[12] Indonesian expansionism was already under close watch by the Australian Defence Committee and, in preparation for the talks in Washington, a series of Cabinet reviews took place. On 5 February 1963, the Australian Cabinet resolved that in relation to the current state of world opinion there was no practical alternative to eventual Indonesian sovereignty over Portuguese Timor.[13]

A contemporaneous review of Australia's strategic position by the Australian Department of Defence was coupled with a Cabinet request for the Department of External Affairs to submit a report on the position of Portuguese Timor and the Borneo territories in relation to Indonesian policies of expansion.[14] The review by the Defence Department concluded that it was likely that Indonesia would gain control of Portuguese Timor 'in consonance with an international campaign against Portuguese colonial rule'.[15] The External Affairs Minister's subsequent advice to Cabinet was that Portuguese Timor-Leste was no longer strategically important to Australia's defence.[16]

United States concern about the situation in Portuguese Timor providing scope for Indonesian intervention led Assistant Secretary of State Averell Harriman to propose during the Washington conference that Australia should take the lead in persuading Portugal to make reforms. In an opportunity lost to build on an alliance with the Timorese people forged in wartime, Australia's Minister for External Affairs Sir Garfield Barwick saw no merit in Australia taking the initiative and rejected Harriman's proposal.[17] With the Soviet Union and China at the forefront of decolonisation pressure at the UN, the work of the various committees examining the conditions of the peoples under Portugal's domination became embroiled in Cold War strategy. In a near repeat of what had occurred during World War II, NATO members moderated their criticism of Portugal as a colonial power so as not to prejudice NATO access to military bases on Portuguese territory. While Portugal had maintained ostensible neutrality throughout World War II, Dr Salazar showed little hesitation during the early frosts of the Cold War in bringing Portugal under the NATO mantle.

Although Australia had long recognised Portuguese sovereignty over Timor-Leste, there was by the early 1960s unease in Canberra with Salazar's administration of the island. Australian Cabinet papers prepared by the Department of External Affairs in 1963 and 1965 refer, misleadingly, to correspondence from Prime Minister Menzies allegedly unanswered by Dr Salazar regarding the colony's future.[18] The Cabinet papers record advice that an independent Timor-Leste would not be viable economically and might eventually be absorbed by the Republic of Indonesia.

From 1965 onwards the Australian Bureau of Mineral Resources, Geology and Geophysics oversaw seabed surveys of the Australian Continental Shelf, including large areas claimed by Portugal.[19] The world-renowned Bureau and its successor, Geoscience Australia, are yet to come to terms with the manner in which science and unethical territorial expansionism subsequently collaborated.

The OPEC Crisis and Australian Neo-Imperialism

While mouthing support at the UN for legitimate nationalist struggles and accepting that European colonialism was giving way to the 'wind of change', particularly in Africa, Australia embarked in the mid 1960s on a new imperialism that would lead Canberra to share the spoils of invasion, turn a blind eye to genocide and compromise Australia's virtue won by earlier generations of Australians who had pioneered, fought and died for a 'fair-go' social democracy. This betrayal was supported, even led, by certain senior Canberra bureaucrats who held not to the value of true public service.

In 1970, when Australia began negotiations in earnest with Indonesia over maritime boundary delimitations in the Arafura and Timor seas, Australia knew enough about the petroleum potential of the Timor Sea adjoining Portuguese Timor to review the economic assumption underpinning the earlier Cabinet appreciation that an independent Timor-Leste would not be economically viable. Instead, Australia set about a course to access the seabed resources for itself, despite earlier advice by David Fairbairn, Australia's Minister for National Development, that the claim was of doubtful legitimacy.[20]

Uncertainty after the 1972 OPEC crisis heralded a new foreign policy imperative that brought the potential petroleum resources of the Australian Continental Shelf under the Timor Sea to the surface in Canberra.[21] Thereafter, successive Australian Governments sought to exert influence over Portuguese Timor and its seabed resources. Australia and Portugal commenced issuing overlapping exploration permits, which led to protests and counter-protests between Canberra and Lisbon.

In 1971 and 1972, Australia and Indonesia signed treaties with respect to the Australia/Indonesia interface in the Arafura and Timor seas, leaving what was to become the infamous 'Timor Gap' at the Australia/Portuguese Timor interface. Meanwhile, elements of the loosely grouped independence movement in Timor-Leste were giving voice in New York to the call for independence from Portugal. On 12 December 1973, the General Assembly reaffirmed its support for the leadership of the national liberation movements in Angola, Cape Verde, Mozambique and Sao Tome by declaring those movements to be 'authentic representatives of the peoples concerned'.

The course of Timor-Leste history may have changed if a credible single voice for national unity had emerged from Dili. Instead, Timor-Leste was not included in the General Assembly's call upon all governments, specialised agencies and institutions associated with the UN to render to the peoples of four other of Portugal's overseas territories all moral and material assistance for the achievement of their national independence and the reconstruction of their countries.[22] Following the Carnation Revolution of 25 April 1974 in Lisbon the UN General Assembly noted moves in Lisbon to conform to UN Charter requirements with respect to Portuguese colonies.[23] On 27 July 1974 the Portuguese Council of State decreed an acceptance of the right to self-determination of Portugal's overseas territories and the decision to waive so much of the Portuguese Constitution of 1933 as would prevent that. Just 12 months later, on 17 July 1975, the Portuguese Council of the Revolution, citing the law passed by the revolutionary Junta on 27 July 1974, reaffirmed the right of the people of Timor to self-determination in accordance with the relevant resolutions of the UN and, 'with the strict observance of the principle of the respect of the will of the people of Timor', called upon the people of Timor by popular assembly constituted through direct, secretive universal election to decide their future.[24]

The Council of the Revolution provided for a staged process whereby all prerogatives of sovereign administration of the Portuguese republic would cease in Timor by the third Sunday of October 1978. The Revolutionary Council set up a structure for the staged devolution of power in Timor-Leste. The July law passed in Lisbon set up a transitional council with various secretariats for the staged devolution of administrative responsibility in Timor. Despite the efforts made by the Revolutionary Council in Lisbon to create a staged devolution of power to Timor-Leste that would be supported at the UN, the FRETILIN (Frente Revolucionára de Timor-Leste Independente) Party unilaterally declared independence for Timor-Leste on

28 November 1975. Two days later, in response, other factions headed by the União Democrática Timorense (UDT), Associação Popular Democrática Timorense (APODETI), Kota and Partido Trabalhista either proclaimed their version of independence or called for the immediate integration of Timor into the Republic of Indonesia. The move by FRETILIN that leapfrogged an orderly endorsement for independence by the UN General Assembly was exactly what the hawks from Canberra and Washington, now circling over Timor-Leste, were looking for.

The sorry tale of how Portuguese Timor, now a focus of concern in Washington, Canberra and Jakarta, was at this critical juncture left out of the anticipated UN endorsement of the proposals put forward by the Revolutionary Council in Lisbon is yet to be explained by the principal actors. The failure of the Timorese leadership to present a unified voice was a national tragedy in 1974 and is a timely reminder of the corrosive force in Dili of personality politics. It remains for the surviving leaders to provide the full history of the brutal internal struggle for power in Timor followed by the Indonesian invasion.

Invasion

Within a year, Australia's Labor Prime Minister Gough Whitlam had ignored principles long endorsed by his party that enshrined the rights of Portuguese Timor's peoples to self-determination. Plans by Australia, Indonesia and the US to forestall a perceived Marxist government in Dili reached fruition with a visit by President Ford and Secretary of State Kissinger to General Suharto in Jakarta. A week later Indonesia invaded Timor-Leste, landing paratroopers at Dili on 7 December 1975 and then commencing a seaborne invasion. Australia thereafter colluded with Jakarta to subjugate the Timorese people and expand international petroleum company access to petroleum resources belonging in international law to the Timorese.

Modern texts chronicle a pattern of conduct by Australia and Indonesia contrary to international law leading to the Treaty on the Zone of Cooperation in an Area between the Indonesian province of East Timor and the Northern Territory (Timor Gap Treaty) between Australia and Indonesia (also referred to as ZOCA or ZOC).[25] Portugal argued before the International Court of Justice that the 1989 treaty was based on forcible territorial acquisition and as such conferred no treaty-making rights on Australia.[26] Australia responded rather lamely that the absence of a clear condemnation by UN organs and the international community allowed Australia international recognition for its treaty with Indonesia. The Court held that since Indonesia was not a party to the litigation the matter could not be heard.[27]

It was against this background of unsettled international jurisprudence that in 1999 Timor-Leste achieved self-determination after a UN-supervised ballot, whereupon Indonesia unilaterally abrogated the 1989 Timor Gap Treaty. In response to this Australia secured during the UN mandate over Timor-Leste a 'revalidation' of the 1989 treaty such that on Independence Day, 20 May 2002, the terms of the 1989 treaty became the Timor Sea Treaty between Timor-Leste and Australia.[28]

Liberation

As will emerge later in this book, FRETILIN's uneasy commitment to democracy, which led the UN to withhold, so tragically, support for Timor-Leste's move to independence in 1974, still pertained in 1999. As the outcome of a UN-supervised autonomy or independence ballot unfolded, the UN assumed full governing power in Timor-Leste; but little had changed over the intervening 25 years. By early 2000 the same group of differing political parties reasserted their voices in Dili. The largest party, FRETILIN, with a controversial legacy, was now led by diaspora Timorese who had spent most of the years of Indonesian occupation in Angola, Mozambique and Australia. FRETILIN had also undergone a momentous change in March 1986 when Xanana Gusmão, as Commander of FALINTIL (Forças Armadas da Libertação Nacional de Timor-Leste), moved political control of the internal military resistance away from a party he could not democratise.[29]

FRETILIN, still perceived by much of the population, who were unaware of the party's true state, as the party of active resistance, retained significant albeit uninformed support. Inexplicably, UN Secretary-General Kofi Annan overlooked FRETILIN's record and Congresso Nacional da Resistência Timorense (CNRT) leader Xanana Gusmão's call for a government of national unity and allowed his Special Representative in Timor-Leste, Sergio Vieira de Mello, to fashion an ersatz self-government by placing a FRETILIN-controlled Cabinet composed largely of diaspora Timorese into power.

Australian Petroleum Diplomacy

Not content with the 2002 Timor Sea Treaty, Australia moved in 2004 to secure advantageous revenue clauses in a further treaty. By 2006 the Alkatiri Government had been chiselled into agreeing to a 50-year moratorium on maritime boundary delimitation while Australia exercised a free hand in Timor Sea areas that might otherwise belong to Timor-Leste in international law.[30]

Using laws introduced to protect national security information Australia reacted aggressively after Timor-Leste launched international law proceedings against Australia in 2013. Despite a provisional decision of the International Court of Justice against Australia's actions, Australian authorities ignored the Court's orders and sought to question Timor-Leste's legal advisers.

This book seeks to illuminate the reason or reasons why a civilised nation like Australia departed over many years both from the rule of law and from the 'fair-go' principles espoused by its founders. Incompetent and sly foreign policy together with oppressive policies at home have seen Australia lose any role it may have had in providing exemplary democratic leadership in the region in which it seeks a place. Regrettably, a full moral reckoning requires credible source information from within government archives. Awareness of who the reckoning might implicate has prompted the political order in Australia to withhold access to material that should be in the public domain.

1
THE ATLANTIC CHARTER—'WHITHER THOU GOEST'

The Australian Government's emphatic response to the Atlantic Charter is a useful starting point for the story of Australia's relations with East Timor. The Charter's drafting history tells much about a new world order insisted upon by President Franklin Roosevelt and embraced more wholeheartedly by Australia than by Britain. The Charter sentiments, widely publicised, gave promise of a more secure post-war society watched over by the United States and Britain.

After three days of talks aboard warships anchored in Placentia Bay, Newfoundland, British Prime Minister Winston Churchill and US President Franklin Roosevelt released an eight-point joint declaration on 14 August 1941, soon after captioned 'The Atlantic Charter'.[1] Among other declarations of principle, the Charter affirmed the right of all peoples 'to choose the form of governments under which they will live'. Within three years, Roosevelt's proposal at Placentia Bay of two great powers policing a post-war world evolved into a United Nations world order.

With Roosevelt's New Deal response to the Great Depression widely admired within the Australian Labor Party (ALP), the Atlantic Charter's assurance of a more egalitarian post-war world order had an immediate impact on Labor's formulation of an independent Australian foreign policy. Although there was nothing new in the exposition of principle in the Charter,[2] the timing was of great significance. President Roosevelt and sections of the US Congress were anxious that the US not be brought into a war that would restore the old order. Having formulated a statement of four basic freedoms in his annual address to Congress on 6 January 1941, Roosevelt now appeared to find common ground with Churchill for the restoration of democracy in Europe and democratic progress elsewhere.

A working concept for a declaration was discussed aboard the USS *Tuscaloosa* by Roosevelt luminary Under Secretary of State Sumner Welles and Foreign Office head Sir Alexander Cadogan on 9 August 1941,[3] after Roosevelt and Churchill had met that morning and agreed that they should issue a joint declaration of 'the aims and desires of the two governments regarding the kind of world that should be constituted after the war. It was to be regarded as a summary of the objectives of those nations opposed to the domination of the world by the Axis powers'.[4] Welles and Cadogan, to whom Churchill had assigned Britain's role in drafting the declaration, spent the afternoon at Welles' desk on the *Tuscaloosa* weaving the thoughts of the two leaders into a joint declaration of war aims.[5] Both men had preconceived notions of what each side hoped to achieve from the declaration. Cadogan was privy to discussions between Churchill and Roosevelt's adviser Harry Hopkins en route to Placentia Bay, and, according to Roosevelt's son, Welles had flown from Washington with a working draft.[6] Hopkins had crossed the Atlantic with Churchill and was empathetic to Britain's predicament. Churchill later made clear that he both anticipated and was receptive to Roosevelt's idea of a joint declaration of principles.[7]

While Churchill recognised that a joint declaration in lofty terms had to come, his unwavering purpose was to edge a supposedly neutral US further into the European war and to secure immediate support for a strong warning to Japan. On the first evening, Churchill retired to his quarters aboard HMS *Prince of Wales* and committed his thoughts to a draft, which Cadogan took to Roosevelt's wardrooms aboard the USS *Augusta* and gave to Welles. Churchill's draft opened with a statement as to why the leaders had settled on the need for such a declaration, which Welles recalled 'glowed with Churchill's genius'.[8] Although the onboard working papers and secret cables to London, Stalin and the Dominion governments referred to a proposed declaration of 'war aims', the document as released had become, for Congressional digestion, a declaration of principles 'on which they base their hopes for a better future for the world'. The second section of Churchill's draft contained the text of the declarations, which was rewritten, as Welles found Churchill's declarations 'too vague or too sweeping'.[9] From the language adopted, one may recognise that in framing the principles, Cadogan allowed Welles to adapt phrases from Roosevelt's speeches, settled American doctrine and Welles' own recent pronouncements.[10]

Under Secretary Welles had known Eleanor Roosevelt since childhood and for many years, much to Secretary of State Hull's chagrin, had enjoyed privileged access to the President. A reading of Welles' wartime speeches leaves little doubt that Welles was contributing from personal conviction to the Charter drafting.[11] Neither Hopkins nor Sumner Welles throw much light in their accounts of the Charter drafting on the consultation process, if any, with Congressional leaders on the draft before a further version was handed to Churchill around midday on 11 August 1941. Shortly afterwards, and conscious that the meeting was due to conclude the following morning, Churchill cabled his all but formally declared Deputy Prime Minister Clement Attlee, informing him that Roosevelt wanted to release a declaration of war aims after the meeting and asking Attlee to summon the full War Cabinet that evening and let him have a response to 'the Roosevelt draft ... without the slightest delay'.[12] In his cable to Attlee, Churchill proposed several wording changes to the 'free-trade' fourth paragraph and a qualified reference to the League of Nations in paragraph seven. Neither Roosevelt nor Churchill was keen on any commitment to revive the League. The Welles/Cadogan redraft that Churchill represented to Attlee as Roosevelt's draft was sent unchanged a minute later by separate cable.[13]

The full War Cabinet met immediately and responded in two cables. The first, at 4:10 am on 12 August 1941, requested two changes: first, the addition to Roosevelt's free-trade paragraph four of the words 'and to promote greatest possible expansion of markets for the interchange of goods and services throughout the world'; and second, the insertion between Roosevelt's paragraphs four and five of a new paragraph— 'Fifth. They support the fullest collaboration between nations in the economic field with the object of securing for all peoples' freedom from want, improved labour standards, economic advancement and social security'.[14] Authorship of this paragraph, later given hallowed status in British Labour Party history as 'the social security clause', was attributed to the Minister for Labour and National Service Ernest Bevin and became a Labour Party rubric.

The War Cabinet's second cable proposed the addition before the word 'promote' in paragraph four of the words, 'with due respect to their existing obligations'.[15] Later that day Churchill advised Attlee that Roosevelt had accepted all of the amendments proposed by Britain.[16] Soon afterwards Churchill took the precaution of requesting the Dominions Office to inform Dominion governments immediately that the text of a joint declaration of war aims would soon be released and that a reference to 'economic co-operation' should not be interpreted as prejudicing imperial trade preferences agreed at the 1932 Ottawa Conference.[17] After Welles returned to Washington, Secretary of State Hull berated him for not securing from Britain a clear commitment to abolish the imperial trade preferences that so offended US free-trade sentiments.[18]

Beyond the addition of the fifth paragraph concerning social security and a revised wording of the free-trade declaration, there was little substantive change to the seven-point Welles/Cadogan draft. While the final eight-article declaration was issued officially as a joint US–Britain effort, the ideology sprang from the New World[19] and was what the labour parties in Britain and Australia wanted to hear. Those working on the draft were settling on a page that would become for generations the catch-cry of US democratisation. Unsurprisingly, Attlee's papers reveal that the text of the draft Charter evoked a unanimous assent from his Labour colleagues in the War Cabinet.[20] With Churchill's astute encouragement, Attlee wasted no time in broadcasting to the world by BBC Radio the text of the Charter.[21] Jago observes that 'after persistently reassuring his party colleagues that Labour was faithful to socialist principles in its handling of the war, Attlee announced the Atlantic Charter, giving substance to his claim ... For the first time he linked the continued fighting with a tangible step towards the extension of socialism'.[22] Attlee's words fell on receptive ears in Canberra where the ALP was to take government within two months.

Roosevelt's White House confidante and Special Envoy to Britain, Harry Hopkins, returning to report to Roosevelt on a visit to Russia, accompanied Churchill aboard HMS *Prince of Wales* to the

Placentia Bay meeting. Roosevelt, like Hopkins, saw the necessity to counter isolationists within the war-wary US Congress by telling the American people there was a compelling ideological basis to justify more direct US support for Britain. From the start of his very personal role as Roosevelt's emissary to Britain, Hopkins mirrored faithfully Roosevelt's grand vision of a New Deal for democracy. The fervour with which Roosevelt and Hopkins set about this task as the Nazi grip on Europe tightened and war with Japan loomed, was unsurprising.

Hopkins' first mission to London eight months earlier had been nothing less than apocalyptic. Arriving at Waterloo Station on the evening of 9 January 1941 during a heavy air raid with incendiary bombs falling on the railway lines at Clapham Junction as his train entered London,[23] Hopkins was treated to the spectacle of a centre of democracy under fire. Before returning to Washington, he moved Churchill to tears when, during a dinner with Churchill and the Secretary of State for Scotland Tom Johnson, he said:

> I suppose you wish to know what I am going to say to President Roosevelt on my return. Well, I'm going to quote you one verse from the Book of Books in the truth of which Mr Johnson's mother and my own Scottish mother were brought up: Whither thou goest, I will go; and where thou lodgest, I will lodge; thy people shall be my people, and thy God my God. Even to the end.[24]

By March 1941 Roosevelt had secured assent to the Lend-Lease Bill,[25] which not only bolstered Britain's war effort but also accelerated US industrial preparedness for war.

Churchill had been diffident about three articles in the Roosevelt-inspired Charter. First was the right to self-determination of all peoples, which Churchill knew was a necessary ingredient to assuage neutrality-minded elements of Congress, but he was not keen to see it applied to the British Empire. Second was a post-war free-trade agreement, a concept regarded with suspicion by the Conservative Party, which supported Imperial trade preferences. Third was the reference to a world free 'from want and fear', whatever that meant to the non-New Deal minded Churchill. Churchill accepted a commitment to self-determination at the time, but later qualified Britain's intention. Roosevelt conceded a tweaking of the free-trade declaration, and, on the 'freedom from want and fear' issue Roosevelt accepted readily, in British Labour terms, a more specific commitment to 'social security'.

Reporting on his meeting with Churchill to Congress, President Roosevelt affirmed a broad application of the Charter.[26] This was certainly the interpretation of Australian Prime Minister Robert Menzies, who told the Australian Parliament that the Charter was 'a reminder to us that the new order of the world, of which we have from time to time spoken, is now in the making'.[27] In his statement to the House of Commons on 9 September 1941, Churchill referred to progress towards constitutional government in India, Burma and other parts of the British Empire and claimed that the Charter referred primarily to European States under Nazi domination.[28] He told the House of Commons that the Charter was 'a statement of certain broad views and principles which are our common guide in our march forward', adding that he would not have agreed with Roosevelt on the terms of the Charter, 'without being supported by the Cabinet'.[29]

Hopkins held a unique political role as Roosevelt's Special Adviser and lived at the White House as Roosevelt's closest non-family confidant for three years until his remarriage in 1943. Hopkins was a former New Deal social support worker who privately denounced colonialism and imperialism, and his significant influence extended not only to the drafting of the Atlantic Charter but to US strategy generally at the Tehran and Yalta wartime conferences.[30] On the colonial world, somewhat to Churchill's discomfort, Hopkins and Australia's Minister for External Affairs H.V. Evatt, a brilliant lawyer and former Australian High Court judge, sang very much to the same tune. Interestingly, both Hopkins' and Evatt's reputations have attracted innuendo about their alleged wartime pro-Soviet sympathies.[31] Hopkins, in his desire to secure the collaboration of the Soviet Union, was probably not a deliberate betrayer of secrets.[32] To attribute pro-Soviet sentiment to Hopkins may confuse sympathy with empathy. At the time of his first meeting with Stalin and subsequently in his persistence in getting huge quantities of defence materiel to Russia, Hopkins remained moved by the immense suffering of the Russian people.

Although there is general agreement that, at core, aspects of both the Roosevelt and Churchill administrations were penetrated throughout the war by Soviet intelligence, there is no evidence that Stalin had any hand in the Atlantic Charter. Indeed, less than a fortnight after the Charter was published, the Soviet Union's Ambassador to Britain, Ivan Maisky, told Foreign Secretary Sir Anthony Eden that excluding Russia from a role in the declaration of the Charter hardly won favour in Moscow.[33] Drawing on both Roosevelt's and Hopkins' records in his work on the Roosevelt years, Kennedy asserts that the Charter was initiated by Roosevelt 'partly as a way of assuaging American anxieties that a war in alliance with Soviet Russia might contaminate democratic ideals'.[34] Certainly, both leaders were conscious of the need to have the Soviet leader marching with them. Immediately the final draft of the Charter was struck, Roosevelt and Churchill each dispatched shipboard cables informing Stalin of the meeting and of the need to co-ordinate resources to combat Hitler.[35]

Publication of the Charter prompted debate worldwide about the post-war future of European colonial possessions and League of Nations trustee territories. The reaction by the leadership of the independence movements in India and Burma was immediate, prompting urgent cables from the respective Governors seeking instructions.[36] The Charter sentiments struck a ready chord with the ALP, still critical of Great Britain's treatment of Australia's national debt during the Depression years. Led at that time by the future Prime Minister John Curtin, the Australian labour movement had long advocated the progression to self-government of Britain's remaining colonies. In Washington, Australia wasted no time in subscribing on 2 January 1942 to the UN Declaration by Allied and empathetic countries that adopted the principles of the Atlantic Charter.[37] New Zealand also joined the original 26 signatories to the Declaration.[38] The Declaration adopted the Atlantic Charter and committed the parties to employ their full resources against the Axis powers and not to make a separate peace.

As debate concerning the Atlantic Charter widened internationally, President Roosevelt reasserted on 27 October 1942 that the Charter 'applies to all humanity … as the Secretary of State and I have said several times before'.[39] Thereafter, the Atlantic Charter was cited prominently in the text of the numerous Mutual Aid Agreements between the US Government and other allied nations such as Greece, Czechoslovakia and Norway.

Roosevelt had no need after the Charter was promulgated to preach to Britain's Dominions in the Far East. By then, the exigencies of war were bringing about a realignment of Britain's relationship with the Dominion governments in Australia and New Zealand. In Canberra, an awareness of Britain's fight for survival against the Nazi might and news of one military and naval disaster after another in Malaya and in the Dutch East Indies in face of advancing Japanese forces led the Cabinet to seek direct military assistance from the US. With the menace to Australia fully apparent and most of Australia's armed forces committed to Britain's defence in the air and in the Middle East, the Australian Prime Minister John Curtin handed full command of all Australian forces engaged in the immediate defence of Australia to the US. This was perhaps the first time in modern history that a sovereign power had willingly relinquished complete command of national defence forces to a foreign state. Living perpetually under the shadow of Asia, Australia has, unsurprisingly, remained in close defence compact with the US. This relationship, linked inextricably to the Democratic and Republican seesaw in Washington and to US strategic corporate interests, is central to the topic of this book.

Although the Australian conservative Prime Minister Menzies had wholeheartedly welcomed both the proposed meeting between Churchill and Roosevelt and the declaration that followed, it took little time for Menzies' opponents to seize upon the Charter sentiments to support part of the socialist agenda. Leaving no doubt that the Placentia Bay declaration had let a genie out of the bottle, Dr Evatt, by then Australia's Minister for External Affairs following the fall of the Menzies Government, declared that the future of the Pacific and Southeast Asia region would be based on Charter principles:

> [T]he name 'Atlantic Charter' ... does not refer only to the Atlantic region or to powers having interest in the Atlantic. The Charter derives its name from the place where it was signed. The 28 nations which have subscribed to it extend around the globe, and the Declaration is universal in its scope and application. It follows that the future of the regions of the Pacific and of South-East Asia are to be governed by the broad principles of the Atlantic Charter.[40]

The Roosevelt influence carried over into ALP legislative activism. In a far bolder move, Evatt, as Attorney-General, responded to the Atlantic Charter by introducing into the Australian Parliament on 1 October 1942 the Constitution Alteration (War Aims and Reconstruction) Bill. Although Evatt explained that his Bill was being introduced to empower the federal government to make laws for carrying into effect war aims and objects of the United Nations, including post-war reconstruction, the Bill was really an Atlanticist charter embracing Roosevelt's 'four freedoms'.[41]

In explaining the constitutional limitations and the need for each of the Australian states to introduce parallel legislation, Evatt observed:

> Without carefully considered constitutional amendment the result in the post-war world of Australia will be social and economical [sic] disorganisation, chaos in production, mounting unemployment, widespread social insecurity—in short, anarchy. But the problem goes even deeper. This country, like all the other United Nations, has pledged itself to the task of achieving a broad objective embodied in the Atlantic Charter and in the historic declaration for the four historic human freedoms—freedom of speech and expression, freedom of worship, freedom from want, freedom from fear—anywhere and everywhere in the world. These declarations are not legal instruments technically binding on Australia; they are far more. They are solemn pledges of our dedication as a nation to the great ends of economic security, social justice and individual freedom.[42]

Dr Evatt's initiative failed. Neither a federal referendum, if constitutionally feasible, nor state legislation to change enabling acts to allow the introduction of an Australian Bill of Rights has occurred. Professor Stuart Macintyre traverses the lukewarm support Evatt received within conservative Labor ranks and the antagonism to the Bill by Opposition Leader Robert Menzies.[43]

Meanwhile, pressure was mounting for Britain to join with the US in making a declaration on colonial policy in general. When the War Cabinet discussed the matter on 7 January 1943, both Attlee and Eden endorsed the need for a declaration of sorts: 'this will rescue us from the dangers of the Atlantic Charter'.[44] The Cabinet considered a telegram from Lord Halifax in Washington reporting Roosevelt's interest in British plans for devolution. Now that Britain had irretrievably lost its status as a colonial power in the Far East, Roosevelt had made no secret of his wish to see Britain give up its possessions. He had confided to Canadian Prime Minister Mackenzie King on 15 April 1942 that, excepting New Guinea and possibly Borneo, there were 'no possessions in the East to which self-government could not be given immediately'.[45] Churchill expressed resentment at having to take time off from War Council deliberations 'in order to find a formula to gratify the Americans'. Attlee then remarked that the original pressure had come not from either the Dominions or Washington but from calls in the Commons for a statement on colonial policy 'ever since the loss of Malaya'.[46] The War Cabinet discussed the prospect of a joint statement on policy by Britain, the US, Holland, and possibly France, but Churchill ended the discussion by reminding his colleagues that 'Cabinet had already accepted in W.P. (42) 506 my redefinition of the Atlantic Charter'.[47]

Unlike Evatt, Professor Julius Stone did not see the centrality of the Atlantic Charter, seeing it as but an element in the evolution of the UN.[48] Lamenting that Britain, unlike Canada and Australia, lacked a Constitution into which fundamental freedoms could be grafted by popular will, Professor Hersch Lauterpacht greeted Dr Evatt's constitutional amendment bill with interest. Lauterpacht, who yearned for a 'Bill of the Rights of Man', accepted that the Atlantic Charter was not the full answer, concluding that it 'was not intended as an exhaustive formulation of the rights of man to be secured by the peace settlement'.[49]

Despite Evatt's impassioned efforts, the Charter sentiments affecting the right of many of the peoples in the Asia-Pacific region to self-determination did not take hold in Canberra or, for that matter, in Lisbon from where Portuguese Timor on Australia's doorstep was ruled. Australia was not a country that offered racial equality to its own indigenous inhabitants, including those serving in the Australian Armed Forces, and the xenophobic reception, under White Australia policies, of mixed-race Dutch wartime evacuees to Australia resonates to this day.[50]

For the leadership in Britain, the Atlantic Charter failed as a humanitarian beacon. Tragic in its immensity was the active, not merely tacit approval, of the Attlee Government in the forced post-war relocation of German-speaking people from Eastern Europe, Poland, Czechoslovakia, Southern Europe and the Balkans. Estimates of this ethnic cleansing vary, but between 12 and 14 million civilians were driven, often under Allied military supervision, into Germany, some of them reoccupying former prisoner of war and concentration camps. While Soviet excesses are often cited as a cause of these population movements in which hundreds of thousands perished, Douglas echoes Lauterpacht's caution about the peace settlement and cites the indifference, even punitive stance, in Attlee's claim after the Allied victory that 'everything that brings home to the Germans the completeness and irrevocability of their defeat is worthwhile in the end'.⁵¹

Churchill's proposal at the Tehran Conference with Stalin and Roosevelt in late 1943 on war strategy is difficult to reconcile with his fine words two years earlier at Placentia Bay. To accommodate Stalin's seizure of Polish territory in the east, Churchill suggested moving Poland's borders westwards into German territory, in flagrant breach of the Charter. Foreign Secretary Eden explained to the Commons, 'we cannot admit that Germany can claim ... that any part of the Charter applies to her'.⁵²

As the Pacific War turned against Japan, Evatt's proposals for Australia to absorb Portuguese Timor and bring Dutch territory into an Australian-controlled post-war defence arc were rebuffed. Undeterred, Evatt became a prime mover in the framing of the United Nations Charter and the post-war work of the UN as third President of the General Assembly and founder of the Pacific Commission. After observing Evatt at the San Francisco Conference, reporter Carolyn Anspacher wrote in the *San Francisco Chronicle* on 14 May 1945: 'He calls forth questions from reporters as if he were conducting an orchestra in the Beethoven Seventh. The Atlantic Charter is as important to him as the Lord's Prayer and he recites it as easily and verbatim'.⁵³ Following Germany's defeat, Evatt gave an impassioned speech at the Paris Conference of Allies: 'we should adhere to our solemn undertakings in the Atlantic Charter and the UN Charter and try to ensure that the principles set in these Charters are given the fullest possible application in the Peace Treaties'.⁵⁴

Despite observance, often in the breach, the principles of the Atlantic Charter remained a catchcry for the Western democracies. In foreign policy terms, the Western allies projected the Charter as an article of faith, asserting nobility of purpose when the reverse was often the case. Thirteen years after the original Charter was promulgated, Churchill, again Britain's Prime Minister, informed the House of Commons that a communiqué, subsequently termed 'The Washington Declaration', issued by himself and President Eisenhower after talks in Washington, 'reaffirms the guiding principles of the Atlantic Charter'.⁵⁵

The mythological status of a charter of principles that unfurled a false banner at the Western masthead injected cynicism into post-war Western diplomacy at the UN. High principle became a ruse to give the anti-communist agenda a mythic truth. Myth bred an ongoing culture that allowed the removal of a government in Iran that threatened Anglo-Iranian petroleum interests, the attack on Nasser's nationalist agenda over the Suez Canal, and wide-ranging Western intelligence activities around the globe often connected to powerful corporate interests. Within this legacy the newly established Australian foreign service developed similar habits.

Although Atlanticist idealism lingered longer under Evatt and his Department Head John Burton, Australia was, by the mid-1950s and the subsequent ANZUS Treaty, a fully-pledged Western camp follower. There Australia has remained, trying its own version of neo-colonialism in harness with international petroleum companies. Like Bible-sect members living contrary to the Word, elite Canberra public servants, well-practised in surviving political vicissitudes, induced pliable politicians of both Labor and Liberal persuasion to exploit the sovereign assets of the poverty-stricken population of East Timor, all the while claiming a 'rules-based order'.

By exploiting the strategic value of Portugal's mid-Atlantic Islands, first with the Allies during World War II and then with the Atlantic Pact countries at the commencement of the Cold War, Portugal's Prime Minister Dr Salazar staved off criticism of his colonial policies such that 30 years elapsed before reform in Lisbon moved Portuguese colonies to independence. Thus, in consequence of wartime diplomatic manoeuvrings and Cold War détente, Portuguese Timor remained an undeveloped backwater in the roll call of new nations in Southeast Asia. Bypassed by the Allies in post-war reconstruction and naïve to the vast reservoirs of petroleum they were sitting on, the Good Samaritans of Timor who saved so many Australian soldiers' lives soon fell prey to petrol-sniffing corporate vultures and their political mates in Canberra.

2
THE ALLIES, AUSTRALIA AND PORTUGUESE TIMOR

As war in Europe loomed and Japan became more belligerent, the Australian Government in Canberra considered anew suggestions that Australia be more directly represented in Washington and Tokyo and, on 24 August 1939, Cabinet approved the opening of legations in Tokyo and Washington.[1] Prime Minister Robert Menzies concluded 'that a man of political experience is essential at Washington' and appointed Richard Casey who had been Treasurer under his predecessor, Joseph Lyons, to be Australia's envoy when the legation opened in Washington in March 1940.[2] Apart from Casey's personal acquaintance with Churchill and most of the British War Cabinet, his standing and connections in Britain and the United States were such that he became a key influence in developing an independent Australian foreign policy aligned, if only due to the exigencies of war, more closely to the US. By mid-1940, Casey's frequent cordial contact with Under Secretary of State Sumner Welles enabled him to convey to the Australian Government informed insights into US foreign policy.

'Descent Into Hell'
When the idea of oil sanctions against Japan arose, Casey learnt that the proposal had been 'squashed' by the State Department as

unnecessarily provocative. Following talks with the Netherlands Minister in Washington, Casey warned Canberra of Dutch concerns that the Netherlands East Indies and Portuguese Timor were in Japan's oil sights.[3] Roosevelt knew from cable decrypts that, if denied all oil, Japan would move quickly to secure oil in the Dutch East Indies. To avoid an unwanted Pacific war, Roosevelt wanted to allow Japan agreed oil tonnages.[4] At a Cabinet meeting on 18 July 1941 the President explained, 'to cut off oil altogether at this time would probably precipitate an outbreak of war in the Pacific and endanger British communications with Australia and New Zealand'.[5] Roosevelt asked Welles, who instructed State Department legal adviser Dean Acheson, to draft limited oil embargo notices. Acheson ignored his instructions and drafted sweeping embargo notices that Welles had to redraft.[6] The failure to discipline Acheson led to disaster.

Japan's brutal march southward through China and finally into French Indo-China, moved the British Government on 25 July 1941 to freeze all Japanese assets, with the US following suit the next day and closing the Panama Canal to Japan.[7] Roosevelt and Secretary of State Hull did not mean this to halt all oil shipments from the US to Japan, which relied on the US for close to 80% of its petroleum. Two days later the Netherlands also froze Japanese assets and resolved to impede any access to petroleum resources by Japan that would feed Japanese military expansionism. Further oil sales to Japan were quietly and effectively blocked by Treasury and Interior Department tactics.[8]

Undaunted by Roosevelt's edict that only himself and Hull would make decisions regarding restricting oil exports to Japan, Treasury Secretary Henry Morgenthau, Secretary of the Interior Harold Ickes and Dean Acheson, all of whom opposed any oil sales to Japan, commenced stalling the release of frozen Japanese dollars before, as Casey records on 29 July 1940, 'the State Department discovered what was afoot ... The back-kick of the whole thing ... may come on us—as Japan may well look to the NEI for her additional supplies'.[9]

On the eve of the decision to freeze Japanese assets, a frustrated Sir Alexander Cadogan, Permanent Under Secretary of the British Foreign Office, recorded that '[t]hese stupid Dominions of course get cold feet, and don't want to freeze Japanese assets without an assurance of support from the US. They must know they can't get this'.[10] Despite sour grapes in Whitehall over ANZAC reluctance to provoke Japan,

Casey, with somewhat more prudent judgement than Cadogan, saw the danger to Australia in provoking Japan into an early move, noting the 'destiny of the Netherlands East Indies as inseparable from the destiny of Australia'.[11]

Roosevelt, back from meeting Churchill at Placentia Bay, did not learn until 5 September 1941 of the deliberate undermining of his strategy not to force Japan into a corner. By then it was too late. Japanese tankers that had waited nearly two months for oil had weighed anchor in California and sailed for home. Provocation by the dissidents in Washington had destroyed the more moderate government in Tokyo of Prime Minister Konoe. Japan had to strike as withdrawal from China was unpalatable and oil reserves would run out in two years.[12]

Australia and New Zealand, now concerned about their increasing vulnerability, had not participated in the US/UK announcement. While agreeing with the British Government's view that a request by Australia for US armed support in the event of a Japanese attack might be politically embarrassing for neutral US, Menzies rejected emphatically the British view that the request should not be made.[13] On reading Menzies' robust response to Lord Cranborne, UK Secretary of State for Dominion Affairs, Casey responded, presciently, that he believed it impossible to get such an undertaking and that 'events and not logical arguments will drive the United States into belligerency'.[14]

Casey was not only at ease with his own Prime Minister, he had the confidence of Churchill. On 2 August 1941, in the company of the British Ambassador Lord Halifax, Casey informed Sumner Welles that in the event of a Japanese attack falling on British or Dutch territory, Australia attached great importance to US support. Casey suggested that the US make a clear statement to Japan of the consequences of further Japanese expansion.[15] A week later at their Placentia Bay meeting, Churchill made the same request of Roosevelt and the Atlantic Charter was released in parallel with a Joint Declaration by the US, Britain and Holland warning Japan against aggression in Indo-China or Thailand.[16] As events later unfolded, the oil embargo hastened the Japanese Cabinet's decision to secure the petroleum resources of the Dutch East Indies.

Cadogan's reaction to ANZAC reluctance to provoke Japan illustrated all that was disingenuous and blasé within the British War Cabinet about the vulnerability of Singapore and Malaya. Despite a devastating Top-Secret War Cabinet Report on 5 August 1940 on the weakness of Singapore and British arms in Southeast Asia in general, support for the oil embargo provoked Japan further when more cautious minds in Washington and Canberra were counselling a play for time to strengthen defences against Japan's southward ambitions. The War Cabinet Report acknowledged that the demands of the war in Europe and the Middle East meant that the weakness could not be rectified.[17] Despite this Churchill 'stuck to his view that Singapore should be held to the last man; and Wavell acquiesced'.[18]

To compound this ineptitude a copy of the War Cabinet Report containing a comprehensive outline of British military deficiencies was sent by surface safe-hand bag aboard the SS *Automedon*, a British merchant ship bound for Singapore. An Italian signals unit detected the vessel's route and a German merchant raider, the *Atlantis*, after its first salvo killed all on the bridge, captured the *Automedon* on 11 November 1940, and secured the British safe-hand mail including the War Cabinet Report. A month later the *Atlantis* berthed at Kobe and the valuable intelligence was passed to Tokyo.[19] By September 1941, decryption of Japanese diplomatic cables left no doubt about Japanese intentions to turn to Southeast Asia for oil and raw materials.[20]

Lacking the confidence of his colleagues, Menzies resigned on 29 August 1941. In a remarkably naïve cablegram on 8 September 1941 the stop-gap Prime Minister, Arthur Fadden, proposed to London that a contingency plan be drawn up between Britain, the Netherlands and Australia to forestall any Japanese occupation of Portuguese Timor. No suggestion was made that the Portuguese Government be consulted.[21] Australia agreed to a more sensible proposal from the Foreign Office that it consult with Dutch and Portuguese authorities:

a. His Majesty's Government in the United Kingdom agree that Japanese occupation of Portuguese Timor would constitute serious threat and that consultation with the Netherlands authorities would be desirable. It is felt however that this subject should be discussed with the Portuguese also. Before approaching either the Dutch or Portuguese we should be glad to learn whether, if the Portuguese agree in certain circumstances to accept reinforcements from outside Portuguese Timor, the Commonwealth Government would be willing to undertake this commitment in addition to their commitments in respect of Ambon and Koepang.

b. We suggest that approach to the Portuguese should be on the lines of an enquiry whether they would be prepared to accept outside help if it is found necessary by the military authorities on the spot and that the approach to both the Dutch and Portuguese should seek their agreement to Australian, Dutch and Portuguese military authorities discussing locally

    (1) the preventive action necessary

    (2) the action which should be taken if a threat should actually eventuate.

Since, however the local military authorities in Portuguese Timor may not be qualified for discussing strategic matters, we think that, as far as the Portuguese are concerned, it would be necessary to clear the ground, as far as possible, at this end first. If the Portuguese agree generally, the place and method of discussion could be settled later.[22]

Long-standing moves to close off Japanese access to petroleum resources in Portuguese Timor reached fruition with a secret accord between the Australian and UK governments. Under the Portuguese Timor Agreement of 6 October 1941,[23] Britain and Australia, acting through the British Petroleum Department, extracted an undertaking from three oil companies—D'Arcy Exploration Company Ltd., the Anglo-Saxon Co. Ltd. and the Standard Oil Co.—exploring under a joint venture registered in Portugal as Companhia Ultramarina de Petróleos (CUP), to give three months' notice to Portuguese authorities of any decision to surrender their concessionary oil exploration rights in Portuguese Timor. If such notice was given, the UK and Australia would have the opportunity to take up the oil concessions to forestall Japanese access to such rights in Portuguese Timor. At the same time, Britain was encouraging the Portuguese to extend the concessions already granted so that CUP's exploration rights would cover the whole of the colony.[24]

With war in the Far East seemingly inevitable, Prime Minister Curtin cabled Lord Cranborne on 2 December 1941, providing his government's views on the contingencies that might arise from likely Japanese attacks. In relation to an attack on Portuguese Timor, Curtin said:

> It is essential that in the event of Japanese attack ... Britain should declare war irrespective of United States attitude. Portuguese Timor is the entrance door to Australia. Secretary of State's message suggests

that Portugal expects declaration from us and that she on her part is willing, within her very limited powers, to resist Japan and declare war on her. We think a definite understanding with Portugal should now be negotiated on this footing.[25]

The vulnerability of Australia to land-based aerial attack from Timor Island, held in the east by Portugal and by the Dutch to the west, prompted the British Government to propose to Portugal on the same day as Curtin's cable, that military staff discussions between Portugal, Britain and Australia be held at Singapore.[26] The British Government also commenced exerting pressure on Lisbon to transfer Portuguese troops into Timor to forestall any occupation by the Japanese.

After Dr Salazar agreed to discreet military staff talks in Singapore, a British plane leaving Lisbon on 16 December 1941 for Cairo and the Far East was readied to carry a Portuguese representative to join talks in Singapore with the Commander Far East. The Air Ministry Movements Officer was requested by the Foreign Office to provide a seat for a passenger named 'John Smith'—the Portuguese representative Major J.C. Sá Nogueira.[27] Britain took the task of looking after Salazar's representative seriously and John Smith's odyssey shortly before and after the fall of Singapore and later Batavia included a variety of safe-passage arrangements. Nogueira eventually made it home through East Africa.

Wartime Occupation of Portuguese Timor
Before the proposed staff talks at Singapore could be held, Japan had struck on 7 December 1941 at Pearl Harbor and in Malaya. Japanese forces advanced swiftly towards the Dutch East Indies and, with Timor Island in the Japanese path, it was clear that it offered Japan the prospect of being able to use aircraft based on Dutch and Portuguese territory, at Kupang and Dili respectively, to attack Darwin and neutralise the only large naval facility left to the Allies within thousands of miles.

Recognising the danger, Britain's Resident Cabinet Minister at Singapore, Duff Cooper, cabled the War Cabinet on 10 December 1941 advising that there had been no time for staff talks with the Portuguese representative and that the Governor-General of the Netherlands East Indies had authority from his government to take necessary action to liquidate the Japanese in Portuguese Timor: 'All naval and military operations are complete, and the Dutch anticipate no difficulty but hesitate to take action which might involve Britain in difficulty with her ancient ally'.[28] The War Cabinet and Foreign Office then informed the British Ambassador to Portugal of Duff Cooper's proposal which, worryingly, sounded like a *fait accompli*.

The proposed intervention prompted an anxious exchange between the War Cabinet, the UK Foreign Office and the British Ambassador at Lisbon, Sir Ronald Campbell, lest precipitate military action in Timor jeopardise relations with Portugal. The Foreign Office canvassed the considerable complexity posed by both the proposed Dutch action and any call on the mutual defence provisions of the Anglo-Portuguese Alliance. Not least among Foreign Office concerns was the prospect that a war between Portugal and Japan might precipitate an Axis declaration against Portugal. Talks with the Portuguese had also revealed long-lasting sensitivities over territorial disputes on Timor Island between Portugal and Holland. The Foreign Office perceived the proposed intervention as palatable only to the Portuguese if it was characterised as a response under the Anglo-Portuguese Alliance and not as an occupation by the Dutch. A Foreign Office official minuted to the effect that Australian forces could be construed as British for the purposes of engaging Britain's treaty obligations. Duff Cooper was counselled to exercise care until the Foreign Office could 'get the Portuguese Government to agree to an immediate occupation of Portuguese Timor under our auspices and in virtue of the Anglo-Portuguese Alliance though it would be carried out in fact by Dutch and Australian troops'.[29]

Churchill alerted Australian Prime Minister John Curtin to the prospect of an Allied intervention in Portuguese Timor requiring Australian troops to 'augment ... even if in token numbers' a Dutch force to be deployed in defence of Portuguese Timor:

> [I]t is apparent that Portuguese Government would not agree to admit Allied troops at this stage without further evidence of Japanese designs on their territory, but we think that they might be prepared to authorise the Governor to make local request for Australian military assistance without reference to Lisbon if and when he has reason to apprehend that a Japanese attack may be threatened.[30]

Britain's offer of military assistance in the event of Japanese attack was conveyed to the Portuguese Ambassador at London on 12 December 1941. On 15 December 1941, Britain notified Portugal in formal terms, that it was, by virtue of the Anglo-Portuguese Alliance, prepared to come to the assistance of Portuguese Timor in the event of an attack.[31] The Portuguese outlook was quite definite, namely, that Japan would have to attack first before Allied troops could make an entry and that help should emanate from British forces alone; Salazar understood the 'supporting role' Australian and Dutch troops might play.[32] But Duff Cooper and General Wavell at the Far East Command in Batavia, where the pressure lay, were forcing the pace.

The Australian Government cabled the Foreign Office on 15 December 1941 advising that the Governor-General of the Netherlands East Indies had decided to act without delay to assist the Portuguese in Timor and to that end consultation was to take place at Dili on 17 December 1941 at 7 am. Noting that this was an uncommonly early hour for state to state consultations, the surprised recipients of the Australian telegram read on to learn that a combined force of Dutch and Australian troops was scheduled to land at Dili just two hours after the scheduled consultation. The Foreign Office sent an immediate response, warning the British Ambassador in Lisbon and counselling the Far East Command to allow time for a genuine consultation, but because of the time difference the force had already left Kupang.[33]

The 300-strong Australian/Dutch force that had sailed from Kupang in West Timor on 16 December 1941 landed at Dili the next day.[34] The Portuguese Governor had no means of opposing the landing and tacitly accepted the Australian occupation, but not before delivering a protest note to the Australian and Dutch Commanders of the invasion force[35] and reporting the intrusion to Lisbon. News of the landing resulted in a tense meeting in Lisbon between the British Ambassador and Salazar who asked whether local Dutch and Australian commanders had taken the law into their own hands or whether the British Government had been a full and willing participant. Knowing that the original Dutch proposal had been endorsed by Duff Cooper and the War Cabinet, Campbell was in an awkward position. Unsurprisingly, he dodged the issue of blame:

> He [Salazar] must remember, I said, that we had been at war for over two years for a large part of the time single-handed against the strongest military power the world had ever known; that just as we were beginning to pull through we found ourselves at war with another formidable and crafty enemy—a war we had not sought and had done all we could to

avoid. I then described in some detail the strategic importance of Timor and the need to take precautions before it was too late.[36]

Campbell was referring to the fact that in early December 1941, Portugal had belatedly embarked 500 troops on the *João Belo* that sailed with an escort from Lourenço Marques, Mozambique.[37] Japan had refused a Portuguese request for safe conduct, which, after the subsequent Japanese landings at Dili, left Dr Salazar in the unenviable position of choosing between confronting the Japanese or accepting the invasion as a *fait accompli*. Campbell warned Salazar that an unopposed landing by Portuguese reinforcements would not only give the impression of collaboration, but leave Portugal open to blackmail. Salazar ordered the convoy to return to Mozambique.[38] Meanwhile, in Lisbon the Japanese Ambassador was called to the Foreign Ministry to receive a note protesting Japan's violation of Portuguese sovereignty, from the Secretary-General of the Portuguese Ministry of Foreign Affairs Luís Teixeira de Sampaio. The Ambassador's response noted that the Portuguese had neither resisted, even symbolically, the Australian and Dutch landing nor demanded the release of the Japanese 'civilians' imprisoned by the Australians.[39]

With the Foreign Office now in damage control and relying upon Campbell's good offices with Dr Salazar to smooth ruffled feathers in Lisbon, Whitehall moved to disassociate Britain from the premature landing. The Foreign Office now wanted to remove any reference to the Anglo-Portuguese treaty in a communiqué to be issued by the British Government. The Portuguese wanted to inform the Japanese that they had only given way to *force majeure* and had not engaged their treaty with Britain. The Foreign Office *volte-face* attracted the ire of the Dutch Government in exile. On 17 December 1941, the Dutch Minister complained to Foreign Office Under-Secretary Sir Orme Sargent about the Foreign Office proposal that any communiqué regarding the sending of the Allied force into Timor be issued by the Dutch and make no mention of the previous proposal that the landing be characterised as a treaty response.[40] Sargent's record of the meeting is telling:

> [The Dutch Minister] accused us in effect of backing out and leaving the whole onus on the Dutch. This view of our attitude will have lost nothing in the telling when he reported to the Netherlands Minister for Foreign Affairs.

> What has happened will obviously need the most careful handling if it is not to wreck our relations with Portugal. But I feel that the other side of the picture is not yet sufficiently realised. There is in fact a definite conflict of interest between our relations with Portugal on the one hand and our relations with Australia and the Netherlands East Indies on the other.
>
> The situation in the Far East is obviously most critical and we cannot afford to be half-hearted in the prosecution of the war against Japan or to take risks which endanger the safety of the Netherlands East Indies and Australia. Portuguese Timor may be a miserable island a long way away, but it is of vital importance to Port Darwin.[41]

The Foreign Office was surprised to find on 19 December 1941 that the Dutch, despite their Minister's private protest, issued the communiqué in much the same form as suggested by the Foreign Office, thus diverting the blame away from Britain. Reflecting the dire circumstances, the British attitude was summed up succinctly by Sir Alexander Cadogan: 'Anglo-Australian-Dutch landing in Portuguese Timor has produced a crisis—Salazar (who must be rather an ass) maintaining a tiresome sanctimonious attitude'.[42]

Meanwhile British Ambassador Campbell reacted with incredulity to Canberra's reply to the Portuguese Governor's protest note given to the Australian Commander of the occupation force. It referred to the need to forestall a breach by Japan of Timor's neutrality by defending Portuguese sovereignty, adding somewhat naively that the Australian Government wanted to assist in every way possible in the administration and economic life of the Portuguese colony. Campbell, already under pressure from Salazar, voiced his concern:

> I am aghast on reading ... Commonwealth Government's message to Portuguese Governor about desire to assist regarding administrative and economic life of Timor. However well meant it will add fuel to the flame. Apart from the implication that the Portuguese cannot run their own show it will be taken as an indication of a more than passing interest.[43]

Campbell, now considerably rattled by Portuguese protest speeches in the National Assembly, continued to deal with the fallout in Lisbon, feeling bound to state his opinion that 'if no bridge is found Dr Salazar may go to the limit of breaking off relations with us'.[44]

With the Japanese now a real threat to Australia, and, learning on 22 December 1941 that Churchill was in Washington meeting

Roosevelt, Curtin instructed Casey to deliver to both leaders an assessment that, without adequate reinforcement and air support, the battle in Malaya 'will be a repetition of Greece and Crete, and Singapore will be grievously threatened'. Knowing that Britain was sorely pressed and after recalling that most of Australia's battle-trained troops were in the Middle East, Curtin's message ended with a proposal that reverberates to this day: 'It is in your power to meet the situation. Should United States desire, we would gladly accept a United States commander in Pacific area'.[45]

Curtin's proposal reflected Casey's earlier advice to Evatt that Roosevelt was contemplating the appointment of a US Commander for the Far East and the Pacific Theatres.[46] Divorced from reality or, from an Australian perspective, unsympathetic to Australia's interests, Churchill, even at this late stage, was not in favour of giving the US command over the remnants of the British navy in the Far East and the Pacific. Sensing the emotion in the former First Lord of the Admiralty's response, Roosevelt did not press his plan and the meeting wound up with little to cheer Casey. Tactfully, General Marshall advised the President to accede to the appointment of a British General, Sir Archibald Wavell, as Allied Supreme Commander, ABDACom (American-British-Dutch-Australian Command). Wavell's poisoned chalice soon overflowed.

With grim news from the embattled forces in Malaya there was little cheer for Curtin at Christmas, and on Boxing Day he struck out. Annoyed over the outcome of the expedition into Portuguese Timor and stung personally by the implied rebuke in New Zealand's protest over the incursion into neutral Portuguese territory, Curtin launched a thinly veiled attack on the British War Cabinet. Directing his criticism through the ever-resilient Lord Cranborne, Curtin complained about Australia being left with the blame for the breach of Portuguese neutrality. Nevertheless, he asked Britain not to order a troop withdrawal:

> On December 11th you indicated desire of United Kingdom that Australia should associate 'even a very small token force' with main Dutch force for the defence of Portuguese Timor against Japanese aggression or infiltration ... On December 13th you informed us that Portugal, by virtue of ancient alliance, had accepted proposal to forestall Japanese aggression and had agreed to instruct Governor either to invite assistance or acquiesce in assistance being furnished ... We

agreed to your request to send detachment, despite our very limited resources ... Subsequently plan was arranged and Dutch fixed time for landing. While acquiescing we impressed upon you desirability of getting Portuguese Government suitably informed and ready to give public explanation of operation by reference to ancient alliance ... On December 16th you approved of all arrangements and sent us draft of statement to be made by Portuguese and Netherlands Government ... At your request we agreed to amend plan so that landing should take place more than two hours after consultation with the Governor. It was only after expedition had set out that we heard from you that Portuguese Government had suddenly become hostile and lost its nerve.

... Your view was that because of the change of attitude by Portugal United Kingdom's association with operation should not be mentioned by us, although the plan was primarily yours. You suggested further that Netherlands and Commonwealth Governments might make joint statement. Before we could agree to that course, Dutch made a public statement in accordance with draft approved by you.

... Commonwealth Prime Minister received a protest direct from the Governor and in difficult circumstances and solely in order to meet your position we confined ourselves to a reply to the Governors making no reference whatsoever to your part in the enterprise and we made no public statement whatever ... Subsequently you expressed to Portugal deep regret that action was taken by Allied military authorities on the spot, the suggestion being that you were not a party to the plan ... [and repeated this explanation to the New Zealand Government when they protested] although at their request we were compelled to inform them as to how it was we came to take part in the expedition ...

We still have every desire to be helpful but we must insist that the defence of Portuguese Timor is crucial both to the Netherlands and to the whole British position in Far East and there should be no retreat. Faith of Australian public would be shaken if, having regard to what has already happened, a further withdrawal of occupying forces were to take place at the very door of Australia.[47]

A further memorandum by J.C. Sterndale Bennett reflected a Foreign Office doing its best to explain away the War Cabinet adventure into neutral Portuguese territory. Sterndale Bennett requested the War Office to advise the Far East Commander, General Wavell, that it was for him to decide whether to withdraw the Allied force, noting the bad effect it would have on UK–Portugal relations if an Allied force invited Japanese attack on Portuguese territory and then failed to defend it effectively.[48]

It was not only the Timor incident that shook Curtin's confidence in Churchill's judgement. Curtin realised it was now unrealistic to expect Australia's defence to take precedence over the immense challenges facing the Empire. The recriminations had started. With the impending disaster almost fully apparent, Curtin cabled London on 24 January 1942 leaving Churchill in no doubt that Australia had sent an army division to Singapore in the belief that Britain's outpost would be properly fortified and protected, if required, by the main fleet.[49] On 26 January 1942, General Wavell was informed that agreement had been reached in Lisbon for the withdrawal from Portuguese territory of the Australian and Dutch troops when Portuguese reinforcements arrived; subject to Salazar's prior agreement, the Australian and Dutch troops would return to Portuguese Timor immediately there was a Japanese attack.[50]

Meanwhile, news reaching Churchill and the King's Dominion Ministers heralded crises for the British Empire on many fronts, not least of which being for Australia, another apparent reverse, when Japanese forces landed at the mouth of the Comoro River near Dili on 9–10 February 1942. The thinly spread Australian and Dutch troops withdrew into the mountains and lost contact with Australia until an improvised wireless set enabled contact with Australian Army HQ two months later.[51] A week after the Australian and Dutch troops had retreated into the mountains, General Wavell, now based in Batavia and evidently out of touch with developments, informed the UK War Office that, after discussions with Salazar's representative, Major Nogueira, it was proposed that the Australian and Dutch force would withdraw to Dutch Timor and not return until the Japanese attacked the neutral colony.[52]

Understandably, Wavell was unaware of developments in the tiny Portuguese colony. Singapore had capitulated to the Japanese on 15 February 1942 and the Allied Far East Command was in disarray. The outnumbered Australian commandos of the 2/2nd Independent Company in Portuguese Timor, strengthened by remnants of a force cut off in Dutch West Timor, established hideouts in the interior and, with the assistance of the local population, conducted a guerrilla war that occupied the efforts of a Japanese Division until the main body of the Australian forces was evacuated from Timor on 19 January 1943.[53]

In June 1942, in a move that left long memories in Canberra, the Portuguese Government advised the British Ambassador at Lisbon that their Governor at Dili had raised the question of the surrender of the 'handful of Australians which, in conditions of great privation is still holding out in the hills'. The Governor hoped that, in return, the Japanese would withdraw from Portuguese territory. The Australian reply to that proposal was forthright:

> Australian Forces in Portuguese Timor number about 400, and there are about 200 Dutch with them. They are well organised, their health is satisfactory, and they are sufficiently supplied with food. There are plenty of drugs. They are conducting guerrilla warfare with the Japanese and are materially assisted by Portuguese subjects and by the natives, the majority of whom are loyal to the Allies. Secret means of communication with Australia exist.[54]

The eventual evacuation of the Australian guerrilla force from Timor followed unsuccessful attempts by the Chief of the Australian Army, General Thomas Blamey, to convince the new Supreme Commander, General Douglas MacArthur, to reinforce ground forces in Timor. Initially, MacArthur had given thought to attacking Timor with a view to reoccupation but decided a major attack was impracticable.[55] Instead, he gave priority to the threat posed to northeastern Australia by the Japanese thrust through the Bismarck Archipelago into New Guinea, approving only air and sea supply missions to the troops fighting behind the lines in Timor.[56] The anguish experienced by Curtin over the predicament of outnumbered Australian troops fighting for survival heightened his reaction to British bungling over the Timor adventure. As with the loss of the Australian 8th Division at Singapore, British ineptness was revelatory to Curtin and Evatt and hastened the move towards the US. The empathetic Timorese–Australian wartime alliance forged in the field remains a powerful factor in ordinary Australian sentiment towards Timor-Leste.[57]

Now that further archives have been released, at least in the UK, claims that Portugal came close to repudiating its Alliance with Britain and severing diplomatic relations appear exaggerated. Salazar, ever mindful that the Japanese might initiate a Nanking-style atrocity in Macau, knew he was dealing with barbarians. Likewise, in an Australian context, claims that Australian Prime Minister John Curtin purposefully breached Portuguese neutrality should be weighed against the evidence now available from the UK War Cabinet and Foreign Office archives.

In the foolhardy Timor adventure, encouraged initially by Australia and aptly summed up by Sterndale Bennett,[58] Churchill joined with Duff Cooper in a demonstrative military foray rather than a well-planned and decisive strategic action. Only good fortune, resolve and great initiative by the Australian troops saved the Timor expedition from becoming, like the campaigns on the Greek mainland, Crete and Malaya, and the Dieppe Raid, a tragic waste of Dominion arms. By all accounts, Curtin was moved deeply when informed that the 'lost'

The razor-backed ridges and mountainous terrain of Timor Island over which Australian troops and, later, FALINTIL fought against a ruthless invader, often using the topographical features for ambushing the enemy.

Australian 2/2nd Independent Company, composed largely of former station-hands, bushmen and rabbit-shooters, was in the Timorese mountains, in good order, fighting with disproportionate effect a ruthless enemy.

For those brought up on the Churchill legend it may take further historical record to comprehend how faulty some of Churchill's forays into tactical military leadership were and how close Churchill came to losing the confidence of his own War Cabinet in early 1942.[59] As the recriminations deepened over the rout in Malaya and the fall of Singapore, followed by Churchill's attempt to divert Australian troopships to Burma, Australia's High Commissioner in London, Sir Stanley Bruce, cabled Curtin on 17 February 1942 to inform him of his conversations with Sir Stafford Cripps, recently returned from his posting as British Ambassador in Moscow: 'These happenings have so shaken public confidence here in the Prime Minister that in my view if he does not face a drastic alteration in the structure and personnel of the War Cabinet there will be a considerable danger of his defeat'.[60]

The next day Cripps sent a personal telegram to Evatt advising that 'there is a strong feeling in the country that we must reorganize our Government',[61] and the War Cabinet was reorganised a day later, with Cripps becoming Lord Privy Seal and Leader of the House of Commons and Attlee taking the role of Dominions Secretary from Lord Cranborne.[62] Evatt sought a role for Australia in overall war strategy:

> At present we are informed of decisions and have little or no effective voice in their making ... the main military advisers lead us from one disaster to another. Greece, Crete, Malaya and Singapore were typical examples of the Munich mind, a combination of Conservatism, incompetence and lack of valour...We are glad that Cripps is in office and hope he will check Churchill whose attitude over this particular matter has been turbulent and peremptory.[63]

The sober account by Gavin Long describes the Syrian campaign as premature and wasteful,[64] pushed principally upon Australian arms and marked by extraordinary courage and tenacity. It joins the list of Churchillian political gestures awaiting candid historical revision. Indeed, Australian General Lavarack's reports of the botched planning and improvisation in Greece, Crete and Syria had significant effect in Canberra, where Churchill's attempt to obscure his strategic errors by finding a military scapegoat in General Wavell failed to convince the Australian political leadership.[65] Unfortunately, this realisation had not set in before Britain, with Australia in tow, embarked on the Timor adventure, again, as in Greece, Crete and Syria, with the unfortunate Wavell on the sideline. The Australian intrusion into Portuguese Timor seven months after the Syrian-Lebanon campaign was another idea developed in haste and thrust upon Australian forces that were likely to face larger and better-equipped forces. Both invasions breached international law. Although, in overall terms, the Japanese occupation of Portuguese Timor was a relatively minor event, it remains to be said, from a Timorese perspective, that the alliance forged with Australian troops was at great cost in Timorese lives—a debt Australia and Britain are yet to formally acknowledge and fully redeem.[66]

By 1943 the maritime war in the Pacific had turned against Japan, both Britain and Australia were developing plans to restore civilian rule in Japanese-occupied territories formerly held or administered by Britain and Australia.[67] Despite the rhetoric in the Atlantic Charter, Britain was not reconciled to relinquishing its colonial possessions, particularly India,[68] and, likewise, while lauding the Charter objects,[69] Australian post-war plans involved the retention of its league-mandated territories in Papua New Guinea and the inclusion of Portuguese Timor in an Australian defence plan.

The Azores and the Anglo-Portuguese Alliance

On 2 July 1943, H.V. Evatt, who was visiting London, and in consequence an *ad hoc* member of the British War Cabinet, forwarded to Prime Minister John Curtin a long cablegram together with a War Cabinet *Aide-Mémoire* informing Curtin that the War Cabinet believed the use of the Azores Islands in the Atlantic for aircraft and ships could prove a decisive factor in winning the Battle of the Atlantic. The *Aide-Mémoire* observed that the British Government had so far refrained from invoking the Anglo-Portuguese Alliance.[70] However, recent war developments had lessened the prospect of a German invasion of Portugal and the Portuguese Government was willing to consider allied access to the Azores Islands. Britain's Ambassador in Lisbon had told Dr Salazar that it would be in Portugal's ultimate interest, having regard to the post-war settlement, to honour the Alliance and meet Britain's request for a base on the Azores.

The War Cabinet noted that the approach to Salazar was after full consultation with President Roosevelt. This belied a proposal that the Azores be captured from the Portuguese. At the Third Washington (Trident) Conference, attended by Roosevelt and Churchill between 12 and 27 May 1943, US Navy Chief Admiral Ernest King had proposed that Britain should seize the islands to safeguard transatlantic communications preparatory to an invasion of France.[71] Churchill endorsed the proposal before sending it to the War Cabinet where it was not well received, as Cadogan's diary entry on Friday 21 May 1943 records: 'Attlee read out ridiculous telegram from P.M. demanding immediate (and surprise) occupation of Azores'.[72]

The matter came before the full War Cabinet on 24 May 1942 with British service chiefs backing Churchill's support for Admiral King's proposal. Sensibly, Attlee encouraged the Cabinet to adopt a more conciliatory approach. Bevin was totally against the project, recording that it 'would undo much of our progress towards world esteem'. Eden opposed the use of force and, in response to a comment that Britain's 'oldest ally hasn't played the game', Lord Cranborne replied tersely, 'But we've not been able to defend them'. Observing that the need for the Azores to support the invasion of France was, in any event, some months away, Eden's proposal that diplomatic pressure be exerted on Salazar prevailed.[73]

In subsequent negotiations for the use by the Allies of the Azores, Salazar sought a *quid pro quo*, namely, an assurance that Portuguese territories in Africa and in the Far East—Timor and Macau—would be preserved and protected. Britain was agreeable to meeting this demand; astutely, Salazar also wanted Australia to back the deal. In consequence, Evatt was prevailed upon to advise Curtin that the Portuguese Government would be glad to get a guarantee from the Australian Government that Portuguese possession of Timor would be respected. Salazar also indicated that he would wish Portugal to participate in the liberation of Portuguese Timor from Japanese occupation in due course. The *Aide-Mémoire* made available to Evatt concluded:

> In view of the vital importance to the successful and rapid prosecution of the war of obtaining in the near future the desired facilities in the Azores, His Majesty's Government in the United Kingdom feel justified in asking the Commonwealth Government to agree to associate themselves with the assurances given to the Portuguese Government on

behalf of His Majesty's Government in the United Kingdom and in the Union of South Africa and also the United States Government.[74]

Dr Evatt told Curtin that he had informed the UK Minister that Australia was prepared to agree to participate in a general guarantee of sovereignty if the Portuguese pressed it. Nevertheless, with his territorial ambition for an Australian absorption of Timor thwarted by an astute Salazar, Evatt added that the Portuguese

> should recognise Australia's fight to preserve the integrity of Timor against Japanese aggression and should indicate its readiness to enter into negotiations with Australia both in relation to the inclusion of Portuguese Timor into an Australian defence zone, and also with a view to closer transport, trade and economic relations with Australia.[75]

Soon after the end of the Pacific War, Evatt disclosed what he knew of the background to the undertaking given to Salazar:

> The occupation and use of the Azores as an air base by the United States of America and the United Kingdom were of supreme importance, and an arrangement had to be made between Great Britain and Portugal. The Portuguese asked the British Government, as part of the arrangement over the Azores, to ensure that the Government of Australia should give an undertaking that in post-war planning it would make no attempt to alter the sovereignty of Portuguese Timor.[76]

Evatt did not reveal to the Parliament that he had proposed to British Foreign Secretary Sir Anthony Eden that Portuguese Timor should not be returned to Portugal after the war but passed to Australia. British archives now reveal what Evatt evidently did not know—that at a secret session in June 1943 Eden had informed the War Cabinet of Evatt's approach. A Most Secret–No Circulation War Cabinet Minute records the conclusion:

> The Foreign Secretary said that Dr Evatt ... said that Australia thought that Portuguese Timor should not be returned to Portugal after the war, but that Australia ought to have it. This put him in the awkward position that it was necessary either to inform Dr Evatt of the steps proposed in regard to Operation Lifebelt [codename for Admiral King's proposal for Britain to secure the use of the Azores by force], or that we should run the risk, by non-disclosure of the proposed guarantee to Portugal of her overseas Empire, of giving offence to Australia ... The Prime Minister said that he had no doubt, in the circumstances,

that the right course was not to disclose the action in hand in regard to Operation Lifebelt.[77]

Evatt had flown to London via Washington where he met again with President Roosevelt and Administration officials. Although Roosevelt had agreed to leave Britain to negotiate all Allied relations with Portugal, Evatt had impressed upon the President the need for Australia to secure permanently, post-war, the Portuguese and Dutch portion of Australia's northwest flank. Within days Roosevelt wrote to Churchill suggesting that Portugal could be moved to sell Portuguese Timor to Australia.[78]

Having successfully mollified Portuguese pride after the Timor debacle in 1941, the reaction at the Foreign Office was understandably caustic. Frank Kenyon Roberts minuted to Under-Secretary Sir William Strang that, in light of the assurances given to Salazar, 'the Portuguese would obviously resent and regard as sharp practice any suggestion that they should sell Timor to Australia. If, as we now hope, they become our allies, they can themselves be brought into the defence system of the South West Pacific in some suitable form'. Kenyon then added, somewhat unfairly, 'The President might also be reminded that it was the high-handed action of the Australians in sending troops to Timor without prior consultation with the Portuguese in December 1941, which subjected our relations with Portugal to possibly the worst strain they have ever suffered'. Not to be outdone, Strang added, 'The President's fingers are always itching to dispose of other peoples' territory. Better tell him that we agree that such questions should be left till after the war'.[79]

The papers were forwarded to the Foreign Secretary, who, aware of the way the War Cabinet, anxious about Portuguese lethargy, had induced the Australians to intervene, noted on 23 June 1943: 'I entirely agree (I am only a little disturbed that we have not approached the Australian Govt. over Timor)', adding, perhaps with a twinge of conscience, 'PM would not allow'.[80] Churchill replied to Roosevelt agreeing that the issue be left until after the war and advising the President that in return for Portuguese help (over the Azores) Britain had given an assurance regarding maintenance of Portuguese sovereignty over all Portuguese colonies.[81]

Ultimately, the proposal that Britain should, if necessary, secure the Azores by force was overtaken by diplomacy and, on 12 October

1943, Churchill announced that by virtue of the Anglo-Portuguese Alliance, England's oldest mutual defence treaty, and later agreements, Portugal had granted certain facilities in the Azores for the protection of merchant shipping in the Atlantic without prejudice to Portuguese sovereignty.[82]

Ironically, German intervention in the Azores might have thwarted Salazar's tactic of playing off the Allies. Nazi High Command documents preserved within German Naval archives reveal that from early in the war Hitler expressed an awareness of potential Allied interest in the Azores and Canary Islands. The Naval Conference records reveal that Hitler anticipated Japanese domination of North and South Asia and maritime Pacific. Hitler expressed his view that the US Administration may rethink support for Britain after the defeat of Russia and successful German occupation of the entire Mediterranean. Hitler's worldwide reach at this stage of the war was so triumphant that the German High Command notes for 22 May 1941 record, for example, that '[m]ine-laying missions in Australian waters were brilliantly executed'.[83] There seems little doubt that Evatt's participation in some British War Cabinet deliberations during this crucial period of Nazi successes explains why he put the Empire first and, contrary to ALP sentiment, effectively guaranteed the Portuguese their Timor territory post-war.

Australia's Strategic Defence Interest
Although Salazar's apprehension regarding the future of Portuguese Timor under Australian military control was not misplaced and had been resolved by guarantee brokered by Britain, his colonial administration officials remained interned under Japanese Army detention. Portuguese protests over the Japanese occupation of Portuguese Timor included requests by Lisbon to the German Foreign Ministry that the German High Command put pressure on its Axis ally Japan to withdraw forces from Portuguese Timor. Although the Japanese Foreign Ministry used the pre-emptive Australian occupation as Japan's 'self-defence' justification for entering Portuguese territory, Portugal renewed pressure on Germany after the main force of Australian troops was successfully evacuated from Timor in December 1942. The last of the troops left Timor in February 1943 after which the Japanese began full-scale pacification of the Timorese.

The minutes of a German High Command Conference with Hitler on 19–20 December 1943 record that Hitler 'showed little interest in having Germany step in to settle the Timor dispute even though he admitted that it would be in our interest to strengthen the position of Salazar, and that German intervention would accomplish this'.[84] While Salazar persisted with diplomatic pressure on Tokyo to withdraw Japanese forces from Portuguese Timor, US and follow-on Australian strategic planning did not include any early plan to liberate Portuguese and Dutch Timor. No voice appears to have been raised to respond to the plight of the Timorese upon whom the Japanese were still exacting fearful reprisals for the support given to Australian troops.

The reprisals reflected the fact that the largely Christian population of Portuguese Timor had, unlike other populations in the Southeast Asia theatre of war, generally supported the trapped Australian troops. Of all the island territories awaiting liberation from a bestial invader, close knowledge of the Timorese terrain and Salazar's belated keenness to oust the Japanese by force might have beckoned a grateful Australian Army High Command;[85] but gratitude did not come into the equation. In late 1944, General MacArthur had resolved to advance upon Japan through the Philippines and the Southwest Pacific rather than using northwest Australia as a principal staging base for a direct line of approach by US and Australian forces through the Netherlands East Indies and the Malayan Peninsula. With ample troops at his command Blamey could have argued for the occupation of Timor Island as a staging base for the defeat of the Japanese garrisons in the Netherlands East Indies.

While there is little doubt that the sending, with British War Cabinet approval, of a token Allied force to Portuguese Timor in December 1941 in the face of overwhelming Japanese arms had no strategic merit, there remains, likewise, ongoing controversy over the strategic purpose of Australian military campaigns fought elsewhere in the Pacific theatre of war in 1944–45. War historians have questioned whether some of the battles towards the end of the war for possession of islands to Australia's north were fought not on informed military strategic grounds but at the urging of the Australian Commander in Chief, General Thomas Blamey, who was influenced by a group of policy planners looking, as had their predecessors in 1916, at the anticipated post-war territorial carve-up of islands north of Australia.

Although Blamey established the policy planning group at his HQ with a remit to 'conduct research on topics as tasked by Blamey, running the gambit from Imperial and international relations through to army health and nutrition',[86] it became better known for the strategic policy role it began to play in planning for Australian and British resumption of civilian control in liberated areas. Whatever the verdict, there is persuasive opinion that the island mopping-up campaign allocated to Australian forces by General MacArthur with Blamey's approval was of doubtful military value, with certain campaigns a tragic waste of human life.[87] In this context the failure to send available forces to the immediate relief of Australia's loyal allies on Timor Island was unfortunate.

The post-war planning group, established in July 1941 at the Australian Army Land HQ, Melbourne, as the Directorate of Research and Civil Affairs (DORCA), was led by Major Alfred Austin Joseph Conlon, who had extensive personal contacts with senior ALP figures, including Prime Minister John Curtin. The intellectuals Conlon brought around him included Sydney law professor Julius Stone and a young barrister, John Kerr, later to become Australia's most controversial Governor-General.[88] External Affairs Minister Evatt's close personal contact with Conlon and other members of Blamey's team gave the wartime defence establishment an unprecedented voice in Australian foreign policy formulation.[89]

DORCA's role, ostensibly to plan military and post-military government in New Guinea and adjacent islands but suspected with good reason by the British, Dutch and Portuguese of including territorial ambitions, is given prominence in several texts. Ryan claims there is evidence that it is probable that the campaigns of late 1944 and 1945 were fought 'because General Blamey wanted to continue in command of a large army in the field' and because Curtin and some of his Cabinet felt that a continued active role would strengthen their position in peace treaty negotiations. Ryan also suggests that 'both Curtin and Blamey were at least partly under the influence of a small but persuasive group of Australia intellectuals who foresaw, or thought they foresaw, a wider and more powerful Australian presence in the Pacific in the coming peace'.[90] Support for this contention may be drawn from Curtin's speech in May 1944 at the Dominion Prime Ministers London Conference:

I emphasized both in London and Washington, that as the Australian people wish to have a say in how the Pacific Area is to be managed, they realize that the extent of their say will be in proportion not to the amount of wheat, meat, or clothes they produce to support the forces of the other nations, but to the amount of fighting they do as well.[91]

Australia's ambitions were not restricted to Portuguese Timor. Although foiled by Salazar's deft handling of Allied designs on the Azores in respect of the retention of Portuguese territory in Timor, Evatt conceived a plan to complete a defence arc above Australia by securing from the Dutch a long-term lease of West Timor and Dutch New Guinea. Evatt's letter to Sir Stanley Bruce in London asking him to sound out the Dutch Government in exile also alluded to Australian interest in the future of the Dutch East Indies,[92] but his proposal gained no traction in London. Christopher Thorne has chronicled the ups and downs in this period of Australia's relations with Britain and the US as the Australian and New Zealand Governments grappled with impending post-war geo-strategic issues.[93] There are other revealing insights into British attempts to maintain 'imperial rule' and reduce the influence on Dominions policy of Australia's brilliant but abrasive External Affairs Minister Dr Evatt.[94]

In 1943, Professor Julius Stone, adviser to DORCA while holding the rank of Lieutenant Colonel concurrently with his professorial role at the University of Sydney Law School, attempted to reconcile the aspirations behind the Atlantic Charter with the planned restoration of colonial rule in Southeast Asia and the Southwest Pacific after the defeat of Japan.[95] He concluded that the Charter was

> a very preliminary prospectus rather than a comprehensive plan, so far as post-war stability and development in East Asia and the South-West Pacific is concerned. The affirmation that it is applicable to these regions, important though it undoubtedly is, is a summons to labour rather than an invitation to rest. It is clear that the Charter ... has important meaning for these regions. To that extent it would seem unwise to call for a separate Pacific Charter: but it would be unwise to leave unresolved and unfilled the doubts and the gaps which qualify its value for South-East Asia and the South-West Pacific.[96]

Kerr, then a Lieutenant Colonel in DORCA, recalled that, as the British were not going to be able to participate with troops in the retaking of British Borneo, joint Australian–British planning was underway in 1944 for military government of civilian areas in Borneo liberated from the Japanese. The British sent an officer to DORCA 'to persuade us in advance how to organise the necessary military government unit for Borneo ... As far as I know Australia never aspired to post-war power in British Borneo, and the Directorate never engaged in the planning with any such aspiration in mind'.[97]

Charlton, with considerable evidence, including a co-authored report under Kerr's own hand, questions Kerr's claim that the Directorate did not anticipate projecting Australian power into Portuguese Timor, New Caledonia, the New Hebrides and Fiji.[98] He points out that Roosevelt told a Pacific War Council meeting on 12 January 1944 that, excepting Portuguese Timor which was tied to US access to the Azores, he was sympathetic to ANZAC ambitions of creating a forward defence line in an arc above Australia and New Zealand.[99] Whatever the verdict on the Directorate's wartime territorial ambitions, Australian post-war Defence Committee Minutes reveal that British Borneo and Portuguese Timor remained within the sphere of Australian defence strategy. The Pacific War Council meeting discussed the future of strategic bases and other places in the Pacific. Charlton and Kerr record that in May 1944, General Blamey, as Commander in Chief of Australian defence forces, accompanied Prime Minister Curtin to a Commonwealth Prime Ministers conference in London.[100] Blamey also presided over a meeting of representatives of the Colonial Office, the War Office and the Foreign Office to discuss the future of Borneo and Hong Kong.

Members of Blamey's DORCA travelled to London again in 1945 to discuss post-war strategies with the Directorate of Civil Affairs in the War Office.[101] Early post-war reconstruction planning led to tensions between Britain and the Australian and New Zealand governments over policy. Australia's Dr Evatt, a strident socialist, championed the Atlantic Charter sentiments that the British Government was reluctant to see applied to Britain's possessions in the Far East. Aldrich, in chronicling US–UK rivalry for political and economic control in the Far East, cites Office of Strategic Services founder Donovan's letter to Roosevelt on 27 October 1944 ('There can be no doubt that the British and the Dutch have arrived at an agreement with regard to the future of Southeast Asia') and Leo Amery, Secretary of State for India and Burma, in London saying that the war provides 'an opportunity for opening the door to a new era of American economic imperialism'.[102] Despatches from the British High Commissioner in Canberra and his counterpart in Wellington express concern about Britain losing the lead in post-war planning in the Far East, with particular reference to Evatt's ambitions for a move to self-government in Britain's colonies.[103]

The background to this tension relates to events early in the Pacific War. The British debacle in Malaya and Singapore that prompted the Australian War Cabinet to turn to the US was of immense historical significance. Dr Evatt's speech on 3 September 1942 in the Australian House of Representatives recounted Japanese victories throughout Southeast Asia and the Pacific, including the fall of Singapore and the bombing of Darwin:

> We were weak in air strengths; we were short of tanks and other equipment; our veteran Australian Imperial Force units had not returned. Those were dark days for Australia and New Zealand.
>
> Late in February a conference was held at Melbourne between the Advisory War Council and Messrs. Sullivan and Coates representing the New Zealand War Cabinet. Future historians may well regard that conference as of special importance. As a result, a new strategic area was planned to include both Australian and New Zealand, and it was suggested that, because of the special United States concern in the Pacific, the supreme operational command should be entrusted to a United States officer. The suggestion was a bold one. There have been few occasions in history when a self-governing nation has placed its defence, and all its military resources, under the control of an ally, no matter how powerful. The new proposal was accepted.[104]

The US 'officer' Evatt referred to was General Douglas MacArthur. Manchester links the advice to Roosevelt of the Australian Cabinet decision taken in Melbourne on Saturday 21 February 1942 that the US have operational command of all Allied forces in the Pacific to Roosevelt's subsequent order that MacArthur should escape from the Philippines.[105] Roosevelt, aware of tension developing between Australia and Britain, resolved unilaterally, according to Harry Hopkins, the following day at a White House meeting with General Marshall and Admiral King, to appoint MacArthur as Supreme Commander of the Southwest Pacific Area.[106] Roosevelt knew the background to British reluctance to release Australian troops for the defence of Australia and that Curtin was objecting to Churchill's proposal that the 6th and 7th

Divisions of the Australian army that had embarked from the Middle East for Australia should be diverted to India or Burma. Churchill had sought Roosevelt's support for diverting the Australian troopships, hoping that an offer of early US troop reinforcements being sent to Australia would resolve the issue in Britain's favour. On 22 February 1942, Churchill cabled Curtin: 'We could not contemplate that you would refuse our request, and that of the US President'.[107]

Unmoved and after an anxious night, Curtin informed Churchill by cable, drafted by Evatt, that he had informed Roosevelt of the reasons for his decision and received a sympathetic reply. The Australian troops were to come home for the defence of their country.[108] Churchill and Roosevelt had already agreed in principle that Britain would assume responsibility for the defence of India and Burma, with the US responsible for the whole of the Pacific Ocean. Australia was in imminent danger and Britain had little choice but to leave the defence of Australia and New Zealand to the US. Singapore had fallen on 15 February 1942 and Churchill's War Cabinet had been informed that if the Japanese developed major operations against Australia and New Zealand, landings 'would probably be mainly confined to coastal areas ... the Japanese will have extended their control in the South China Sea by occupying key points in the islands of the East Indian Archipelago as far as Timor, inclusive, and the islands of New Guinea, New Caledonia, Fiji and Samoan groups'.[109] A week later Harry Hopkins rang Casey in Washington to advise that the President had withdrawn his objection to sending a second US Division to Australia if Curtin also ordered the Australian 9th Division home from the Middle East.[110] In the event, the 9th Division remained in Egypt, playing a decisive role in all three battles at El Alamein.

Churchill by then was playing catch-up, cabling the Australian and New Zealand Prime Ministers on 17 March 1942 explaining that he had been awaiting advice from his Joint Defence Staff regarding 'the President's proposals for dividing the commands'. Churchill was referring to the agreement in principle between himself and Roosevelt to leave strategy and direction for the Pacific theatre of war to the US and strategy to the west of Singapore to Britain.[111] By then Roosevelt had already acted on the Australian proposal that the US take over command of Australia's defence. Churchill's effusive cable[112] may have evoked some wry smiles in Canberra where deference to British War

Cabinet strategy shown by the despatch of troops to Singapore, and later by Curtin, during the proposed allied occupation of Portuguese Timor, had cooled. This was evident from two significant events in Canberra on 26 December 1941 and the following day. Curtin started the day by cabling London, saying there must be no further retreat, adding a strongly worded personal complaint over the Timor invasion bungle, referring specifically to assurances of Portuguese agreement to the landing of troops Australia could ill afford to commit, and then leaving Australia to take the blame for apparent unilateral Australian action.[113]

Later in the day, in a national radio broadcast, Curtin exhorted Australians to exert themselves more in service to their country. In a lengthy opinion piece in a Melbourne newspaper Curtin declared, 'Australia looks to America, free of any pangs as to our traditional links or kinship with the United Kingdom'.[114] Churchill, still in Washington, reacted angrily and cabled Curtin saying that such a statement would be resented within the Empire. Roosevelt reportedly summoned Casey to tell him that Curtin's statement, if intended to ingratiate, would have the opposite effect in America and 'tasted of panic and disloyalty'.[115] Lloyd Ross says that most of the article was a call to Australians for sacrifice, work and cooperation and was not deliberately timed to impact upon the Roosevelt–Churchill conference in Washington, the typescript having lain for some days in the *Herald* office before the news editor realised the news value of Curtin's piece, 'which summarized a truth that too many were unwilling to face'.[116] Curtin had responded to the *Herald* editor's invitation to write the piece before learning on 22 December 1941 of the Churchill–Roosevelt meeting and before receiving Churchill's Christmas message.

The Cairo Conference—the ANZAC Reaction

If the Christmas 1941 episode was not enough indication, it soon became clear that it was not all plain sailing for Australia and New Zealand with the US. Despite close involvement with US war strategy in the Pacific, Australia's long-term interests were not represented in the 'Big Four' post-war planning tent. On 3 December 1943, Curtin and Evatt learnt from press reports that Roosevelt, Churchill and Chinese leader Chiang Kai-Shek had met at Cairo to discuss what Evatt believed to be post-war territorial arrangements for the Asia-Pacific area.[117]

Evatt suspected that the Big Three had discussed the distribution of Pacific territory held by conquest or trusteeship by Japan. Although the communiqué issued on 2 December 1943, later known as the Cairo Declaration, included an express disavowal of any territorial ambitions, it was silent as to what would become of the islands and territories from which Japan as League Trustee was to be expelled at the end of the war.[118] To take up that issue, and as a rebuff to the US and Britain, the ANZAC partners, Australia and New Zealand, set about expanding the agenda for a conference, already planned and signalled by Evatt in a speech to the House of Representatives, to discuss the handling of 'problems of security, post-war development and native welfare' in the Southwest Pacific.[119] To the alarm of Britain and the US, the conference now grew into a strategic ANZAC plan for the future of all colonial-held and League trustee territories in near Southeast Asia, the Southwest Pacific and Oceania.

The British High Commissioner reported upon the Australia and New Zealand conference held in Canberra on 17–18 January 1944. Although the conference was hailed publicly as a meeting to discuss Pacific affairs, British concerns were aroused when the Australian and New Zealand leaders announced on 21 January 1944 that they had signed a 'comprehensive post-war planning agreement'. The Australian and New Zealand Prime Ministers sent a cablegram to the UK Secretary of State for Dominion Affairs asserting, somewhat defensively, that their conference and any resulting discussions and decisions were in line with principles of free consultation between members of the British Commonwealth:

> We are in agreement that our interests should be protected by representation at highest level on all armistices planning and executive bodies and that we should actively participate in any armistices commission to be set up. So far as Europe is concerned and in explanation of the desire to be associated with armistice arrangements in that theatre both Governments base their attitude on the fact that twice within our generation we have been involved in wars as a result of hostilities arising in Europe. While we look forward to exchanging with United Kingdom Government the fullest information as to armistice and subsequent arrangements in connection with the war in the Pacific, we feel that no time should be lost in undertaking detailed preparations in this sphere and that Australia

and New Zealand should be directly associated with this work at the earliest possible date.[120]

In a final communiqué, Australia and New Zealand proposed the establishment of a regional organisation comprising Australia, New Zealand, Great Britain, France and the US with advisory powers, known as the South Sea Regional Commission. Earlier, during the conference Curtin issued a separate statement asserting that 'the best way to defend Australia and New Zealand was by a system based on the island screen to the north', which he claimed would involve cooperation with Great Britain, the Netherlands, Portugal, France and the US.[121] There is no record as to why mention of Portugal dropped out of the final communiqué. An explanation reflecting Australian intentions towards Portuguese Timor from which Australian forces had withdrawn in 1943 emerges in a confidential report of the Conference sent by Australia to the UK Secretary of State for Dominion Affairs.[122]

The Australian Sphere of Influence—Portuguese Timor

The historic cablegram from Canberra to the Dominions Office was drafted by Evatt with an eye to Curtin's long-awaited visit to London. The proposed trans-Tasman compact rankled Whitehall in that it reflected not only an assumption by Australia of a significant post-war US strategic role in the Pacific but also the decision, evident from the ANZAC communiqué, by Australia to itself 'police' a huge northern island arc stretching from Timor far across to the Solomon Islands:

> Our vital interest in this matter is obvious. The future security of both our nations is dependent, subject to a general system of world security, on the arrangements to be made for the control and defence of the South West and South Pacific areas and these arrangements will inevitably be affected by the interim arrangements immediately following the reconquest of the Netherlands Indies and contiguous territories. Australia and New Zealand feel that they must be closely associated with all decisions and measures taken in this important formative stage and desire—subject always to consultation and agreement with other Governments concerned (a) *that Australia have full responsibility for the policing of Portuguese Timor, Australian New Guinea and the Solomon Islands Protectorate*, and (b) that Australia have a share in the responsibility for the policing of the Netherlands Indies, particularly Java, Dutch New Guinea and also New Hebrides. As regards Pacific Islands in general

south of the Equator we believe that responsibility for policing should primarily be with the United Kingdom, Australia and New Zealand, though it is realised that regard must be paid to the position of the United States, which already has a naval base in Tutuila. We assume, however, that the United States will wish to undertake a substantial share of the responsibility for policing the islands north of the Equator. We regard it as essential that such arrangements should be made as part of a general scheme and not piecemeal. We have already closely examined the means of providing a permanent instrument [emphasis added].[123]

US Secretary of State Cordell Hull responded swiftly to the Australian and New Zealand Agreement by saying that the proposals were premature, it being 'necessary to agree on arrangements for a general international security system before attempting to deal with problems of regional security'.[124] Curtin's response to Hull's rebuke was to suggest to Evatt that, as Britain, France, Portugal and Holland, not being in effective control of their territories, could hardly participate at that stage of the war, Hull's caution was reasonable. Reflecting his Atlanticist sentiments and still annoyed by the Cairo Conference and Declaration, Evatt suggested to Hull that the prosecution of the war in the Pacific might be aided, '[i]f it appeared that the powers with territorial interests in the South Pacific were determined to safeguard the future welfare and good Government of all the native peoples'.[125] The upshot was a lengthy trip in April–May 1944 by air-travel-shy Curtin to Washington, London and Washington again to press Australia's voice on strategic war and post-war issues and to mollify US and British concerns over the January ANZAC Agreement.[126]

Hull recorded the meeting between Roosevelt and Curtin, who had not met before, on, prophetically, ANZAC Day, 25 April 1944:

> Curtin promptly commenced by saying that so far as the two countries were concerned, 'the American government entered the war against Germany to defend certain principles, and that our countries should be able to co-operate in mutually satisfactory manner'. Australia had a special interest in the islands adjacent to Australia, including the Dutch East Indies and New Caledonia.
>
> ... I said that naturally we were almost flabbergasted at certain provisions in the Australia–New Zealand Agreement, especially the declaration that nothing must be done about territory anywhere in the Pacific except by agreement with Australia and New Zealand. I said

this agreement would seem to show that Australia and New Zealand have in their minds the whole question of territorial settlement in the Pacific with special reference to New Caledonia and other areas ... I once more said that we frankly do not appreciate the attitude of Dr Evatt on this and on other matters; and I referred particularly to Dr Evatt's actions in recording in a formal document private conversations with the President.[127]

Hull was referring to opening comments Roosevelt had made at a Pacific War Council meeting on 12 January 1944. Roosevelt, after mentioning the Cairo Conference, had discussed the future of 'strategic bases and other places in the Pacific':

Perhaps it would be possible to make some arrangement in the allocation of those islands. Timor is another thing we should discuss. It is a thing which it would be necessary for Churchill to talk about also in London. Then there is the question what we should do with the French islands. He, President Roosevelt, had said to Winston Churchill that the French should not have New Caledonia back under any conditions and that he believed that in this view Australia and New Zealand would back him up.[128]

In London, Evatt's struggle as External Affairs Minister to give Australia an independent voice in world affairs continued to cast a shadow over Curtin's trip. Conscious of the blow to British prestige occasioned by Australian reliance for its defence on the US and of past disputes with the Australian Prime Minister, Churchill used the Dominion Prime Ministers Conference, at which he met Curtin for the first time, to establish some rapport with the Australian leader. On 18 May 1944, at a luncheon in honour of Curtin and at which Curtin was granted the freedom of the City of London, Churchill made oblique reference to Evatt's constitution alteration ambitions, including Evatt's suspected republican sympathies. He extolled the significance of King George VI's brother, the Duke of Gloucester, being sent to Australia as Governor-General and in a smooth rewrite of history asserted that Australia's reliance on the US stemmed from the division of responsibilities early in 1942.[129] Curtin's historic response left few in doubt as to the ideals by which Curtin's Australia would steer a path in the post-war settlement:

The freedom of this City cannot but mean much to the mind of a man whom you have already had described to you as indicating, at least some part of the sort of man I have been. Yes, I was a printer's devil and I, of course, like many others of my fellow countrymen and countrywomen, have had what has been described as 'humble origins'. Yes the poor have a stake in this struggle, the very, very poor equally with the very, very rich. The rich may have that which they now possess to maintain, but the poor will have all their hopes of betterment and of improvement ... There was once an indication of complete antagonism between the conception of life as held by the aggressor and the conception of life which is the very foundation of life upon which this great Empire has been evolved—the right of people to quarrel with their own government, to criticize it, to defeat it, to provide an alternative to it, one which would undertake, as it were, some legislation after their own heart's desire.

These things may not be related intimately to the material world, but they are inherently part of the true dignity of man. They have in themselves, at any rate, the ingredients upon which the very essentials of liberty find subsistence. With all the diversities of political parties and practices and the like, nevertheless out of that discussion, that distinctiveness, that variation in the point of view, a unity emerges as a result of all that, and because it comes out of that form, it is the more permanent and effective than as the abuse of a dictator and the fears of those who must yield to his demands. It is the unity born of the supremacy of persuasion. It is the unity that emerges to give triumph to conviction rather than either cowardice or weakness. It is the strength of the triumph of reason.[130]

Post-War Australian Defence Strategy

On 10 March 1944, the Duke of Palmela, Portugal's Ambassador to the UK, conveyed to the British Foreign Office Dr Salazar's request that Portuguese troops participate in the recapture of Timor from the Japanese. Although British Under-Secretary Cadogan recorded the proposal as 'sheer pantomime',[131] discussions between the UK, US, Australian and Portuguese governments led to an agreement for the participation of a Portuguese expeditionary force 'in such operations as might be conducted eventually to expel the Japanese from Portuguese Timor'.[132] Australian Brigadier A.W. Wardell attended Staff talks at Lisbon in September 1944 and, after further liaison with Portuguese military staff, his report to Prime Minister Curtin on the likely effectiveness of the Portuguese troops was not encouraging.[133]

Although Australian defence planning continued for the participation of Portugal in the liberation of Portuguese Timor, the war ended before arrangements to base 4,000 Portuguese troops in Australia were complete.[134] The Australian Government had greeted the proposal that emerged from the Lisbon Conference of Allies with Portugal in late 1944 with little enthusiasm. Evatt's response from Washington to his Department summed up his Labor-imbued attitude to colonialism: '[I] think it would be unwise to have Portuguese troops in Australia. I do not see why we should pull their chestnuts out of the fire'.[135] This is to be compared with the Deputy Leader of the Country Party John McEwen's earlier advice to the Advisory War Council that, 'in view of the importance of Portuguese Timor in relation to the security of Australia, in the post-war period consideration should be given to the adoption of economic measures to ensure the predominance of Australian influence there as soon as Portuguese Timor was liberated'.[136] As with Prime Minister Whitlam a generation later, Evatt's dislike of Portuguese colonialism obscured his strategic vision.

Portuguese troops had last fought alongside Australian troops in France close to the end of hostilities in 1918. But history did not repeat itself and the surrender of Japanese troops in Portuguese Timor took place at Dili on 24 September 1945 under Australian supervision.[137] Soon afterwards the Portuguese civil administration was restored, with the bulk of Australian troops departing on 19 March 1946. Australian consular interests including war crimes investigators remained. Australia was reminded, somewhat ungraciously, by Portuguese authorities that further army investigation teams would require visas.[138] This met with no protest by General Blamey who had his own ghosts to bury.

A war crimes investigation unit, TIMFORCE, had been established to investigate the fate of missing Australian military personnel, including members of the highly secret Australian Army Services Reconnaissance Department (SRD) who over a long period of successful Japanese double-cross activity had been captured, in some cases turned and used by Japanese Intelligence to lure further teams to their capture, torture and death. The investigation of the SRD deaths in Timor, attributable to appalling command deficiencies within Australian Military Intelligence HQ in Melbourne, led to a cover-up on the orders of General Blamey. Blamey achieved this by issuing a directive on 6 December 1945 that no member of the Z Special Unit was to give witness evidence at war crimes trials. Eventually, only three half-hearted Timor-related war crimes trials took place at Darwin.[139] Australia's failure to apologise to the families and honour properly the young men, including loyal Australian Army Portuguese recruits who perished during the highly successful Japanese double-cross operation, is shameful. At war's end, the triumphant Japanese Unit in Timor, using the SRD secret code, radioed a thank-you message to SRD, which should have been pinned on Blamey's chest as he strutted the stage post-war. Echoes of this disaster are audible in intelligence circles to this day. As John Fahey has recently concluded, 'The whole series of operations stand as a warning against mixing intelligence collection and direct action. And against underestimating an opponent'.[140]

Blamey's refusal to allow Z Special Unit members to testify at war crimes trials and give evidence of the command cover-up bears a strange echo with the attempt in 2013 by the Australian Coalition Government to prevent the giving of evidence before an international arbitration tribunal concerning past revenue treaty negotiations in East Timor.

3
AFTER THE WAR—THE VISION FADES

Following the Japanese defeat, nationalism and anti-colonial sentiment echoed throughout liberated North and Southeast Asia. While moves to self-government were a natural progression, former United States Under Secretary of State Sumner Welles recognised that 'the fetish of white supremacy cultivated by the big colonial powers … could only exist so long as the white race actually proved to be supreme'.[1] With Prime Minister Attlee and his Labour colleagues committed, ostensibly, to Atlantic Charter sentiments, the Foreign Office faced difficult choices with respect to the re-occupation of former colonial territories, not the least of which being the Netherlands East Indies. Faced with a vacuum left by an absent Dutch Administration, Vice-Admiral Lord Louis Mountbatten, now Supreme Allied Commander SE Asia, ordered British Indian Army troops into Java without first exploring the prospect of negotiations with Indonesian nationalists.

By the time troops commenced landing on 28 September 1945, Sukarno and Mohammad Hatta had, on 17 August 1945, declared Indonesian independence. In an all too familiar refrain of improvisation and leadership foolhardiness the British Commander, Brigadier Aubertin Mallaby, was killed on 30 October 1945 and his forces forced into an ignominious withdrawal by nationalist forces well-armed by surrendering Japanese army and naval commands empathetic to nationalist fervour. A subsequent British punitive expedition that laid waste to Surabaya attracted worldwide condemnation amid allegations of British contempt for both the Atlantic Charter and the United Nations Charter.[2]

In the aftermath of Mallaby's death Attlee cabled his Australian Labor colleague, Prime Minister Ben Chifley, explaining that in balancing Anglo-Dutch relations Britain had to be careful to do nothing that could be construed as an attempt to impede resumption of Dutch control.[3] In an analysis that reflected Evatt's view of British reluctance to decolonise, Springhall summed up the situation confronting Australian foreign policy *vis-à-vis* Britain immediately after the war: 'The far-reaching events of the autumn of 1945 in both British-occupied Indochina and the NEI exemplify the temporizing, even hostile, reaction of Britain's Labour Government towards anti-colonial nationalisms in SE Asia. The impact of socialist ideology on British imperial policy-making was not very profound'.[4]

In contrast to Attlee's compromise, Chifley and Evatt held to the faith. While maintaining a close strategic defence interest in post-war developments in Southeast Asia and the Southwest Pacific, External Affairs Minister Evatt adopted a lead role in the representation of the small powers at the founding conference of the UN that began at San Francisco on 25 April 1945. Evatt rankled Britain and the US by opposing a Big Five veto power, and, seeking to widen the power and role of the General Assembly, he argued, presciently, how the Great Power veto could paralyse the UN peacekeeping role. The Australian role at the San Francisco Conference heralded, albeit in somewhat abrasive terms, a more independent voice post-war in international affairs for Canberra. Gaining the confidence to formulate strategy required a commensurate ability to monitor and react effectively in Australia's interests to world events, particularly in the region. Evatt offered that prospect but, as debate concerning the end of colonialism commenced at the UN, the Australian Government's failure post-Evatt and Chifley to develop a strategy by which each of Australia, the Netherlands, France and Portugal as regional colonial powers might 'develop' a common aspirational outlook reflected a preoccupation in Canberra with British and US policymaking.

As Paul Hasluck observed in 1980, Australian foreign policy under Evatt was for a post-war UN peace in the region, not one maintained by Britain or the US.⁵ As the Cold War deepened, Evatt's belief in a world order sustained by a UN peace created friction with Washington and Whitehall.⁶ The redoubtable Foreign Office correspondents Hoyer Miller and Strang recorded from the British Embassy in Washington that in July 1949, senior State Department official Dean Rusk had explained the US embargo of June 1948 on further secret defence liaison information exchanges with Australia as attributable partly to the way Evatt as President of the UN General Assembly had adopted a role as conciliator between the Soviet Bloc and the US and Britain.⁷ As UNGA President, Evatt remained closely identified with the Chifley Labor Government which endorsed UN peace initiatives. Unfortunately for Australia, Evatt's private meetings from time to time with the UN Soviet Representative Andrei Gromyko may have deepened intelligence concerns in Washington and London. Ironically, there is every likelihood that British suspicion regarding Evatt and his close Australian External Affairs colleagues of assisting, wittingly or unwittingly, Soviet strategy may have been misplaced. The Soviet Union had, from the traitors it had cultivated in the older democracies, far more dedicated sources of information on British and US policy.

Following Labor's defeat at the December 1949 general election, Menzies appointed Percy Spender as his Minister for External Affairs. For most of the next 10 years Australia's Department of External Affairs held witness to Spender's determination, as Minister responsible for the ANZUS Treaty negotiations and as Australian Ambassador at Washington, to get the US to accept responsibility for the security of Southeast Asia. During these years, as the future of Portuguese Timor on Australia's doorstep fell below the radar, Spender expended great effort on Australia–US ties, while a somewhat diffident Menzies clung to hopes of ongoing British responsibility for security in the region.⁸ The failure to progress Evatt's go-it-alone wartime vision of an Australian organised defence arc from Timor Island in the east to the Solomon Islands in the west, consolidated by interim 'arrangements' with Portugal and Holland and linked with a self-determined East Timor, West Papua and Australian trust territory in Papua New Guinea and the Pacific, is a subject ripe for further post-mortem.

Former Australian Prime Minister Malcolm Fraser attributes the failure of Evatt's post-war efforts to establish a defence arc based on multilateral agreements between Australia and Pacific and Southeast

Asian States to a lack of sympathy by Britain and by Australia being rebuffed by the US 'on all sides'. He notes that, although Spender and later Casey, endorsed Evatt's vision of a 'Pacific Pact', Menzies adopted a softer line, sharing US unease about the stability of some Asian states.⁹ Allan Gyngell, a former Director-General of Australia's national intelligence assessments agency, relying almost entirely on secondary sources, adopts a similar explanation, but neither Fraser nor Gyngell, like the author, could, despite past access to unreleased material, lawfully provide a more detailed narrative.¹⁰

Portugal Retains its Timor Colony

With the wartime Great Powers starting to quarrel, events in Europe were shaping both the future of Portuguese Timor and Australian post-war diplomacy. Commenting on Portuguese 'Atlanticism', Henrique Martins de Carvalho traced both the continued post-war geostrategic significance of the Azores Islands as the doorstep to the North Atlantic and Europe and Salazar's Catholic-driven abhorrence of Warsaw Bloc communism.¹¹ Carvalho sees the signing by the US and Portugal of the Azores Bases Agreement on 2 February 1948 as a preliminary move for Portugal's eventual inclusion in the Atlantic Pact. Empowered by the Vandenberg Resolution,¹² the US Administration was moving to further strengthen regional and collective security measures in Europe. By working with the key Brussels Pact members,¹³ the US sought an expansion of the Pact to embrace a mutual defence line against the Warsaw Bloc stretching from Iceland in the north to Italy in the south, with Portugal an indispensable element on the Atlantic flank.¹⁴ The air bases in the Azores Islands, so vital in tipping the balance during the Battle of the Atlantic, now facilitated the monitoring of Soviet naval traffic.

In a move reminiscent of the Allied wartime Azores arrangement, Britain took charge of negotiations with its ancient ally Portugal on behalf of the Pact. Salazar sought an assurance that the terms of entry would embrace the protection of Portugal's colonies. This was promptly rejected by Pact members on the basis that no other signatory had secured such an accommodation. Despite this apparent setback, Portugal signed the Atlantic Pact at Washington on 4 April 1949. Upon ratification a few months later, Portugal, as a fully-fledged NATO player, effectively secured a level of passive non-intervention by the major Western democracies in its colonial affairs.[15] NATO-assisted modernisation of Portugal's armed forces bolstered the suppression of unrest in Portugal's far-flung empire. Probably unknown at the time to so many of Portugal's colonial subjects in Africa and the Far East but now known to history, Salazar's astute move from neutrality to alignment was a decisive factor in delaying their emancipation.

Collective Security Measures in Southeast Asia and the Southwest Pacific

Attlee met with Dominion Prime Ministers for close to a fortnight in May 1946. International cooperation goals embracing collective security measures led Evatt, as Australian Minister for External Affairs and speaking for Prime Minister Chifley on 3 May 1946, to enlarge on the controversial 1944 ANZAC Agreement concerning regional security in Southeast Asia and the Pacific. Evatt recalled the proposal to establish a regional organisation with advisory powers: 'it might be useful to have meetings from time to time with representatives of the United Kingdom and, perhaps later, of France and the United States to discuss their common affairs ... a similar organisation for South-East Asia would similarly serve a useful purpose'.[16] Evatt worked assiduously throughout 1946 in London, Washington, Wellington, Paris and The Hague to set up an opening conference in Canberra of the six wartime-allied colonial (or trustee) powers in the Pacific—Australia, New Zealand, France, the Netherlands, UK and US. Evatt told the Australian Parliament that 'we must make positive efforts to direct and control developments in this part of the world'.[17] Neither the UK nor the US warmed to the idea of including defence, security or political matters in the role of the proposed South Seas Commission. The French Government, anxious to retain its South Pacific possessions as part of Metropolitan France, was interested in participating so long as there was no suggestion that the Commission would be involved with decolonisation issues embraced by the UN Charter.

On 26 September 1946, the Australian and New Zealand governments announced that the UK, US, France and the Netherlands had been invited to attend a conference in early 1947 to discuss 'questions of welfare and economic development'. The territories to be included in the activities of the Commission would be those 'lying generally south of the Equator and eastwards from New Guinea' with Dutch

New Guinea as the only Dutch territory.[18] The records of the first meeting of the Commission at Canberra in February 1947 contain no suggestion that Portugal, in respect of Portuguese Timor, might be invited to join the proceedings, which were largely taken up with assuring London and Washington that the ANZACs would not be turning the Commission into a regional political entity.[19] It was not until September 1951 that Portugal, urged by France, enquired about membership of the South Pacific Commission.[20] By comparison, there is little doubt that in the European context Britain saw very early the need to include Portugal in a post-war Western Alliance to counter the Soviet threat.[21]

Although Professor Stone chronicles Evatt-inspired wartime proposals to include Portuguese Timor in a post-war 'confederation' of Southeast Asia and Pacific countries, Portugal did not participate in allied discussions.[22] In concluding that the US and Britain saw little to gain by Portugal becoming a last-minute belligerent against Japan, Tarling draws extensively on Foreign Office archives.[23] While the Chiefs of Staff were apprehensive that Britain might end up being requested under the Anglo-Portuguese Alliance to provide more military logistic support than Britain could easily muster in the Far East, both Churchill and Eden were fearful that thousands of European refugees sheltering in Macau might, in response to a Portuguese declaration of war, be massacred by the Japanese. The Foreign Office also warned that Salazar's *quid pro quo* policy of making further concessions to the US in the Azores in return for further guarantees that the US, Australian or Dutch governments would not execute designs on Portuguese Timor might involve Britain in an awkward balancing act considering the Alliance.

Tarling also throws light on Dutch fears of Australian designs on the Netherlands East Indies. The Dutch had taken to heart statements by Evatt that Australia would want for the future a stable defence arc of the islands to Australia's north. The situation became further complicated when word of a possible Portuguese army contingent being landed to liberate the eastern end of the island of Timor reached Dutch ears. The Dutch Minister in London asked with concern whether Portuguese troops might take it upon themselves to go on to liberate the Dutch portion of the Island. In the event, the Australian Government stalled plans to house and train Portuguese and Dutch contingents.[24]

Further, Canberra found that the appointment of a Portuguese Chargé in Canberra was not 'timely' as Australia, bound to reciprocate, was already 'heavily' committed in establishing other Missions abroad. Tarling draws the reasonable conclusion that Australia wanted to limit the role of returning colonial powers and boost its own, and that procrastination and delay were part of the strategy.[25]

The successful edging of the Portuguese out of military planning for the final push against the Japanese—a strategy made redundant by the bombing of Hiroshima and Nagasaki—resulted in a further imbroglio involving Lisbon, London and Canberra following Salazar's request that Portugal take the formal surrender of the Japanese in Portuguese Timor. Portugal's Ambassador in London, the Duke of Palmela, visited Australian High Commissioner Bruce to get his help in ensuring that the Japanese surrender it to Portugal. Having given Palmela his assurance of support, Bruce asked him privately 'how he thought his government would react to the suggestion for a lease of Portuguese Timor to Australia for a hundred years ... his reply was that such a suggestion would touch Portugal in its most sensitive spot, namely her prestige'.[26]

Bruce then rang Hoyer Miller at the Foreign Office to inform him of the exchange. Bruce's confidence that he could secure the agreement of Canberra for Portugal to take the surrender was misplaced. Canberra had cabled the Dominions Office indicating in quite trenchant terms that Australian forces had earned the right to take the surrender:

> This territory in hostile hands can always provide very real menace to Australia, as was shown by fact that many Japanese air attacks on Northern Australia were based on or staged through Timor ...
>
> Portuguese failed us completely in arrangement made for defence of Timor with their concurrence, and as a result our forces were left to sustain singlehanded in Timor for long period an epic guerrilla warfare which had important effect on area. Now we learn that Portuguese are trying capitalise at once on Allied successes by despatch of two sloops referred to in your telegram. It is obvious that surrender of this territory should be made to Australian forces, who alone defended it.[27]

Hoyer Miller arranged for Anthony Eden to speak to Bruce,[28] and the Foreign Office found some middle ground by suggesting that Australian forces take the surrender in the presence of the Portuguese Governor and then withdraw from Portuguese territory:

> The United Kingdom Government regard the maintenance of good relations with Portugal as of great importance at the present time for economic and financial reasons and on account of the facilities which we still enjoy under the Azores Agreement ... Besides whatever may have happened in Timor in 1941, the United Kingdom cannot overlook the very considerable services subsequently rendered to the Allied cause by Portugal through grant of bases in the Azores, which have been of assistance to both the European and Far Eastern theatres of war, and through provision of credit facilities.[29]

If there was any ambition within the corridors of Australia's fledgling Department of External Affairs to emulate in the Southern Hemisphere British and US strategy of inclusiveness for post-war Western Europe, it was certainly not executed. Canberra's failure to secure for the Portuguese a role in regional planning may have reflected anti-colonial sentiment and an irresolute decision by Australia to police directly its northern approaches. Within 10 years, as the great confederation of Indonesia stirred, it became clear that post-Evatt Australian foreign policy in the Southern Hemisphere lacked the breadth of Duff Cooper's vision of a post-war Western Europe balanced by regional alliances. In describing Australia's post-war foreign policy in the region as an attempt to lead the small nations of the Pacific in a UN peace, embracing Atlantic Charter values rather than a cooperative foreign policy role supporting a regional balance dominated by American and British strategy, Hasluck explains in effect why Australia saw no role for colonial Portugal.[30]

While Australia's defence planners recognised the challenges facing Australia and the need to include the Dutch, Portuguese and French in Australia's defence arc, Australian diplomacy was antipathetic to any regional collaboration with Portugal and, soon, with the Dutch. The frequent inability of Australian defence and foreign affairs interests in Canberra to devise cohesive strategies for the region persisted for the rest of the 20th century and into the 21st, with the disastrous Howard–Downer epoch a prime example. The concerns now being expressed regarding the People's Republic of China's expanding foothold in Timor-Leste were anticipated by Australian defence and intelligence analysts, yet foreign policy and national development advisers embarked on a short-sighted attempt to duchess the petroleum industry. Treating a new nation on Australia's doorstep with contempt was bound to antagonise the future leadership in Dili of a strategically important near neighbour. Strategists like Evatt and Richard Casey, though worlds apart in personality and politics, had a knowledge of history and would not have taken their eyes off the main game pursued since 1916.

Signs of the chasm between ephemeral issues and true national interest became evident in the early post-war years. Echoing wartime sentiment, an Australian Defence Committee meeting on 13 June 1947 resolved that:

> [it] regards it as of the highest importance that a potential aggressor be denied the opportunity to establish himself in areas from which he can menace our interests. One such area is the N.E.I. of which Portuguese Timor is, by geographical considerations, virtually a part.
>
> The establishment of first-class naval and air bases in this region would enable a strong and hostile power to threaten our sea communications and to menace industrial areas in the South East of Australia by air action even in the present state of development of air power ...
>
> However, the strategic situation in the Pacific, as it affects Australia, would have to deteriorate considerably before bases in Portuguese Timor acquire a special strategic significance. Notwithstanding their limited value to us, any action by a power ill-disposed towards Australia to secure airfield facilities in Portuguese Timor would be a matter of concern to this country.

The Committee's conclusion, reached in the aftermath of the Pacific War, holds good to this day:

> Whilst the Commonwealth had no immediate military interest in Portuguese Timor ..., it is strategically important that Portuguese Timor should remain friendly to Australia, so that, if possible, not only would such facilities as she possesses be available to Australia in war, but they would be denied to other powers, whose motives conflict with Australian interests. It is, therefore, highly desirable that every endeavour should be made to promote closer relationship between Australia and Portuguese Timor.[31]

John Burton wasted no time, following his appointment by Evatt to head the Department of External Affairs, in seeking a Chiefs of Staff role in the formulation of defence strategy that would be consistent with foreign policy. Burton wrote to Evatt on 15 April 1948 taking issue with Chiefs of Staff appreciations based on the assumption that Australia would undertake commitments in accordance with British defence policy, then likely to be military action in the Middle East against the Soviet Union. Faithful, like Evatt, to the UN mission, Burton advocated a policy that emphasised the protection of Australia as a final defence if the UN had not managed to resolve the conflict. As a first step in resolving the issue, Burton had his department complete a survey of political events and trends in Southeast Asia which, in Evatt's absence while President of the UN General Assembly, Chifley as acting External Affairs Minister forwarded to the Minister for Defence, John Dedman, who was also Minister for Post-War Reconstruction. Chifley laid bare Burton's concerns:

> This survey proceeds from the principle that Australia's predominant political interest and defence preoccupation must be in the South-East Asia area, and sets out an active political programme which might be developed by the Australian Government for closer relations with countries in South-East Asia. The development of such a programme would be a practical means of stabilising this potentially dangerous area.[32]

Seemingly impervious to Burton's views on the need to consolidate foreign policy and defence strategy, the Joint Intelligence Committee (JIC) in Melbourne produced an Appreciation, dated 24 November 1948, aimed at joining Britain in combating Russian moves in the Middle East that might cut sea and air links to the UK. The anglophile Defence view did not anticipate an offensive in Asia or the Middle East south of India, Japan and Korea. As for nationalist movements south of this line, the Staff Appreciation saw unrest in French Indo-China, Burma and Malaya as pro-Soviet and that in the Netherlands East Indies as 'nationalist only'.[33] Burton's representative on the JIC sent a laconic note: 'You'll see that there are many things out of line with us'.[34] Over the next 12 months, the Defence Committee considered the External Affairs viewpoints in a series of updated JIC Appreciations without resolving Burton's wish for an overall Australian defence strategy. Defence had conceded, however, that 'appropriate political and economic measures should be taken to arrest the spread of, and ultimately eliminate, Communism throughout South-East Asian countries'.[35]

On 8 September 1949, the Australian Defence Committee noted that strategic planning for defence in the Southwest Pacific was the subject of discussions with the UK and New Zealand at a defence level and that it was premature to undertake any discussion of defence arrangements between Portuguese Timor and Australia until British Commonwealth defence planning in the area reached a more advanced stage. Although the Committee's observations were made against a backdrop of civil unrest in Borneo and the Dutch East Indies, the Chiefs of Staff appeared content to await the outcome of British deliberations.[36] On the formulation of a uniquely Australian defence strategy Evatt and Burton appeared to be getting nowhere.

Eventually, at Evatt's request, Burton wrote to Sir Frederick Shedden, Secretary of the Department of Defence and Chair of the Defence Committee, proposing a round-table conference of Defence and External Affairs officials, together with British and New Zealand representatives, including the head of the UK Foreign Office, Far Eastern Department. Australian diplomats from posts in North and South Asia also joined the conference, which commenced on 14 November 1949.[37]

The conference produced the desired outcome for Burton. There was agreement for the expansion of Australia's diplomatic representation in Southeast Asia, including the posting of Defence intelligence personnel to Australian Missions, and a concentration of political and economic efforts in Indonesia, including the training of Indonesian military staff in Australia. In one exchange, Burton mentioned the External Affairs interest in the possible development of Portuguese Timor. He asked the Defence representative at the conference, Brigadier Rourke, what the Defence view was of the strategic importance of Timor. Rourke said that the Services were more interested in the Cocos Islands and Morotai; 'If it came to a matter of an agreement with the Portuguese Government over Timor, the Defence view would be that no base rights should be given to any power, but if any power sought to use Timor bases Australia should have the right to do so also'.[38]

The JIC Appreciations[39] were shared with the British Defence Attaché in Canberra and found their way to the UK Joint Intelligence Committee. Guy Burgess, perhaps the Soviet Union's greatest British spy, had been passing thousands of documents over to his Russian handler since his arrival in the British Foreign Office Far East Department in November 1948, where he had 'regular access to intelligence from the Joint Intelligence Committee, the War Office, Far Eastern Command and MacArthur's HQ at Supreme Allied Command in Tokyo ... the various service departments, and liaising with British diplomatic posts in the region'.[40] Lownie's research also reveals that Moscow may have known that Canberra was unaware of the Top-Secret UK decision in August 1949 that regional allies in the Far East could not count on Britain for any direct intervention in an anti-communist struggle.[41] Closer than Canberra to the UK, Melbourne's Defence HQ was waiting for a British lead that did not come. Contemporary Australian Defence Committee minutes and JIC analyses make no reference to the decision by Britain in August 1949 to leave it to the US, Australia and any regional partners to commit troops to combat communist subversion.

While Britain subsequently committed troops to Korea in a UN role and later, after a policy change, to Malaya, Canberra's lack of awareness of the British decision in 1949 not to take any lead military role in combating communist subversion in the region left Australia hanging onto empty coat-tails when it should have been out much earlier looking for a broader regional defence alliance structure. The failure to engage with Portugal over Timor contrasted with the keen watch maintained by Canberra over the future of the Dutch East Indies, including West Timor.

Oil Exploration in Portuguese Timor

Although British, Dutch and Australian companies had been exploring for oil in Portuguese Timor for some years, only limited discoveries had been made onshore prior to the outbreak of World War II. In March 1940, the Portuguese Ambassador in London alerted both the Foreign Office and Australian's High Commissioner Stanley Bruce to attempts by Japan to gain control of oil exploration in Portuguese Timor. Japan was demanding that Portuguese authorities should grant an unallocated concession to Japanese interests and declare null and void an existing oil exploration concession granted to a Sydney-based syndicate Dodson Oil Concession Pty Limited. Portugal's Ambassador asked for an assurance of full support from Britain and Australia in resisting any attack upon Portugal's rights by Japan. The Ambassador explained that the pressure from Tokyo included a demand, despite Portuguese protests, that Portugal evacuate two islands near Macau that Japanese troops had occupied in 1937.[42]

Canberra was already aware of Japanese designs on exploration rights in Portuguese Timor. Bruce had been instructed some weeks earlier to inform Whitehall that the Australian Government had reviewed the issue, including the suggestion of cooperation with the Netherlands. Canberra had resolved to encourage Portugal to grant a concession for the whole of Portuguese Timor to the Dodson Oil Concession, with Dodson Oil exploiting the concession with its own capital. Failing that, Australia would prefer the UK and Australia to financially support Dodson Oil to stay in place. A fall-back position could be the formation of an operating company comprised of Dodson Oil, Anglo-Iranian and Commonwealth Refineries, with the prospect of Royal Dutch Shell joining in as a last resort.

As was his habit, Bruce had provided the Foreign Office with a copy of his instructions from Prime Minister Menzies.[43] This element of the broader Australian and British strategic gameplay against Japan, seen to be provocative by the more extreme elements in the Konoe Cabinet in Tokyo, played out in the context of British economic intelligence concerning the prospect of commercial oil discoveries in Portuguese Timor. Britain was closely monitoring strategic petroleum production issues and had informed Australia in April 1940 of earlier explorations by Anglo-Iranian Oil Company's geologists in Timor, who found that prospects of finding oil in commercially exploitable quantities were not favourable. Their conclusions were confirmed by enquiries made from the Shell Group.[44]

Under concessions eventually granted by Portugal, exploration in Portuguese Timor by petroleum geologists from oil production facilities in Batavia was underway shortly before the Pacific War. The UK Petroleum Department, then located close to Whitehall at Millbank, was monitoring the strategic oil situation and events in Timor. Two days after the Allied 'occupation' of Portuguese Timor, the Petroleum Department Under-Secretary advised the Foreign Office that an exploration party previously evacuated from Timor would return.[45] As events would show, this was rather premature as the Allied 'occupation force' of 300-odd troops could not oppose a large-scale Japanese landing. Likewise, there appears no record that a request by the Australian Department of External Affairs representative in London for the UK Petroleum Department to secure a map of the joint-venture oil exploration concessions in Portuguese Timor was actioned in time before Batavia, where the maps were held, was overrun.[46]

There was nothing new in 1940 for Australian defence policy about the diplomatic and military oil strategy emanating from the Admiralty and the Foreign Office. After his appointment in October 1911 as First Lord of the Admiralty, Churchill accelerated the conversion of the British naval fleet to fuel oil. Britain had already begun to formulate an oil-supply policy that embraced the Dominions. One of Churchill's early moves was to negotiate huge long-term contracts with Shell Oil. Gibson's recent study suggests that, initially, the

> focus was on ownership of oilfields and companies rather than control of territory. Little oil had been found in the then British Empire ... the rising use of oil fuel by the Royal Navy meant that as early as 1905 the Committee of Imperial Defence considered it vital that the Burmah Company should remain entirely British. In 1912 the government invested in the Anglo-Persian Oil Company.[47]

Shortly before the outbreak of war in 1914 the British Government secured a controlling 51% share in Anglo-Persian.[48] Ironically, at least for the Churchill legend, forcing the Dardanelles in 1915 would have guaranteed Russian oil supplies from the Black Sea. During the Naval Estimates debates in the House of Commons in 1917 Churchill laid down principles upon which the Admiralty's oil supply policy was based that were still effective in 1940 as Britain and Australia dealt with Japanese oil ambitions in the Netherlands East Indies and Portuguese Timor. The principles were that supplies should be widely spread geographically, sources should be kept open and independent competition maintained, and where possible sources should be under British control with secure transport.[49]

In the inter-war years Australian participation in imperial defence issues included the monitoring of oil supply and strategic fuel oil storage so as to facilitate any wide-ranging naval fleet activity. Australia's dependence on Admiralty oil strategy came to nought with the fall of Singapore and the loss of the main Allied naval fuel oil reserves in Britain's Far East. Australia became dependent upon supplies from the United States. While Australian strategic petroleum planning ceased after World War II to have an imperial focus, close corporate global involvement in diplomatic and defence petroleum strategy became an integral aspect of the new world economic order for the Western powers, with particular effect upon successive Australian governments.

At its meeting on 10 June 1947, the Australian Defence Committee had concluded that 'Australia would be interested in the development of oil production in Portuguese Timor from the aspect that if supplies are available from that source, our dependence upon our present supplies, which require to be shipped over longer lines of communication, would be reduced'.[50] It may be wrong to conclude from the Committee's observation that the Australian geostrategic interest in Portuguese Timor was focused on petroleum. The Defence Committee referred only to onshore petroleum potential. There is no evidence that petroleum resources were in policy contemplation when, for example, the Australian Parliament passed the *Fisheries Act 1952* and its cohort *Pearl Fisheries Act 1952*. The focus of debate concerned the regulation of Japanese pearl fisheries principally to restrict access to other sea-bed resources.[51]

With the *Pearl Fisheries Act (No. 2) 1953* went a proclamation that Australia claimed jurisdiction over its continental shelf out to a depth of 100 fathoms. This 600-foot (182.82 metre) depth limit fell far short of areas of the Timor Sea close to Portuguese Timor where the water depth plunges to 4,000 metres. Timor was not mentioned during the parliamentary debates. In introducing an amending Pearl Fisheries Bill, the Australian Minister for Commerce and Industry and Deputy Prime Minister explained the limits of Australia's territorial claim in somewhat ambiguous terms:

[T]he Australian Government intends to exercise Australia's rights to ensure both the conservation of pearl-shell resources on its continental shelf, and the preservation and orderly development of the pearl-shell industry ... the Government intends to proclaim sovereignty over our continental shelf. It will enforce a system of licensing and control of pearl fishing in waters over our continental shelf; and this system will be applied irrespective of nationality. It is clear that the waters beyond the continental shelf, that is beyond the 100-fathoms depth, are not waters in which pearl-shell occurs.[52]

In line with the decision to lay claim to the entire Australian Continental Shelf, the Northern Territory Administration began issuing mineral exploration permits for areas of the Arafura and Timor seas over the Australian Continental Shelf west of longitude 133°14'E. By this move Australia signalled to the world a claim out to the Shelf's then identified edge at the Timor Trough. Australia was conscious that this claim might attract Portuguese interest.

4
AUSTRALIA AND PORTUGUESE TIMOR

Ben Chifley's vision of an inclusive Australian foreign policy[1] was not matched by his successors. Failure to apply to the Australian situation Duff Cooper's far-sighted post-war vision of a United Kingdom linked by regional alliances in Western Europe, referred to in chapter 3, reflected a Cabinet led by Menzies and fearful of nationalist movements to Australia's north. The dynamic leadership within the Department of External Affairs during the Evatt years faltered under a conservative government deferential largely in foreign policy to Britain and the US. The post-war External Affairs bureaucracy had worked well under Department Head John Burton, who shared Labor's antipathetic outlook on European colonialism. Looking back, the outstanding and principled role senior Australian diplomats played both at the United Nations and in strife-torn Indonesia during the nationalist struggle for independence represented Australian diplomacy at its high-water mark. After Chifley's defeat in 1949 the dysfunction between a conservative Cabinet and an ascending External Affairs elite with more experience of world affairs than their political masters grew. Little changed over the years. The archives leave little doubt that, in dealing with what faced Australia in the Asia-Pacific region, the post-Chifley generation of External Affairs bureaucrats were muted by Ministers more secure in the slipstream of Britain and the US.

The 'Light on the Hill' Goes Out

As Menzies distanced himself from the vision of Evatt and Chifley, some of the key bureaucrats with wartime policy experience who stayed on under Menzies progressed to mandarin status across key departments in Canberra. There, most held to a limited vision that led Australia further under the US umbrella and away from developing pragmatic links with genuine nationalist movements in Southeast and North Asia. Eventually, the narrow focus, based on a belief that Communist China was moving south, led to Australian involvement in the Vietnam War. Edwards has chronicled the events by which Sir Arthur Tange, a more cautious bureaucrat, was sidelined and the Defence Committee sidestepped by the Chiefs of Staff Committee when Cabinet sought advice in relation to the US request in December 1964 for assistance in Vietnam.[2]

Well into the 1960s, compliance by a traditional public service with the conservatism of Menzies, Hasluck, and Labor Opposition Leader Arthur Calwell in maintaining the White Australia policy for far too long illustrated the absence of any agenda-changing 'young Turks' either in Cabinet or the top level of the bureaucracy. Although the Department of External Affairs had long recognised White Australia as a great hurdle to effective regional diplomatic relations,[3] the post-Chifley archives throw up no evidence that the senior members of the federal bureaucracy, by then an established clique in Canberra, took up the baton on the need for a dramatic change. In this era Burton's vision for a more inclusive role for Australia in North and Southeast Asia was abandoned. The post-1970s Australian archives record the Foreign Affairs elite passing the baton, and with it the same US–Australia focus, regardless of the reaction in Asia, to their tutored 'Class of '69'.

It was not just a failure by Menzies to adapt to the Australian region the geostrategic vision for Britain in post-war Europe expounded by Duff-Cooper in 1944. After the Cairo Declaration in 1944, Evatt began to express concern about US territorial and political ambitions in the Southwest Pacific and Oceania. While Evatt did not oppose US involvement, particularly in the Pacific region, he saw the need to balance it with other linkages. After Evatt's influence moved from Canberra to the UN, there were lessons in history as to why more thought might have been given to the effect on the emerging Asian leaders of such an overt alliance by Australia with the US.

At the outset, Menzies took few steps to expand effective contact Evatt's diplomats had developed with nationalist movements within the colonial world to Australia's north.[4] With Britain stumbling under the weight of wartime debt and discredited as a Great Power in the region, Australia, with a voice of intellectual integrity at the UN far above its weight, failed under Menzies to develop an independent foreign policy that would accommodate a post-colonial era and Australian development assistance in Indonesia, Indo-China and other non-British heritage countries with genuine nationalist movements.

The failure to link Australia across the Pacific with the South American republics, particularly lusophone Brazil, a wartime ally, was an early example of myopic Australian foreign policy. Evatt was at fault here too. He should have recognised that Washington's emphasis, after the Japanese attack on Pearl Harbor, on securing declarations of war by the South American republics against the Axis powers reflected not only continental strategy in the Americas but recognition of geostrategic defence issues in the Pacific affecting Australia. Immediately after the surprise attack in December 1941 that secured blue-water naval supremacy in the Pacific temporarily for Japan, Roosevelt convened a meeting of all South American foreign ministers at Rio de Janeiro and sent Welles on a resoundingly successful mission to secure their solidarity with the US. Failing to implement the lessons of history, Australia has done little since in the defence sphere to accommodate with the South American republics a joint strategy towards a growing Chinese blue-water navy presence in the Pacific, leaving policy once again to the United States.

Portugal–Australia Relations

At war's end, Australia and Brazil had shared, in some respects, a common experience with the US; yet Canberra, preoccupied with high-stakes strategy regarding the expanding UN world role including the independence movement in the Dutch East Indies, failed to develop a wider Pacific strategy. Such a strategy, with Brazilian support, might have assisted Canberra to propose to Portugal a special good neighbour relationship with Portuguese Timor and Australia's veterans' organisations may have supported such an initiative. While the Australian defence services maintained effective liaison with Portuguese authorities in Dili such that air-force planes and navy vessels supporting

Australian diplomatic initiatives during the Indonesian independence struggle were, despite Dutch sensitivities, accorded transit facilities, Australia's Department of External Affairs practically shunned the colonial relic. There is little doubt that, having failed in 1943 to secure control of Portuguese Timor, Evatt had little time for Portugal's maintenance of a colony on Australia's doorstep and his political antipathy to Portugal overcame strategic good sense, a weakness he rarely displayed. Evatt chose not to take up two invitations to Lisbon for talks in 1947 and his successor, Spender, neither followed through on a planned visit there in 1950 nor acted upon subsequent invitations to Lisbon in 1951 and 1952.[5]

When Portugal established a Consulate at Sydney in 1943, the Consul's role was largely taken with the interests of displaced nationals from Japanese-occupied Portuguese Timor. Although Portuguese Timor had been bypassed by US and Australian troops as the war moved closer to the Japanese mainland, Lisbon was anticipating Allied assistance in the recovery of Macau and Timor. The mood in Canberra towards Portugal reflected a narrow-minded antipathy to the restoration of colonialism, a prejudice Evatt himself demonstrated on occasion,[6] together with a mistaken sense of grievance that Portugal had left the fight against the Axis, particularly against the Japanese, to Australia.

As Britain's oldest ally, and possessed of a vital strategic mineral, wolframite, Portugal's precarious circumstance during the years of rampant Nazi might in Europe was too often overlooked in Canberra. Foreign Office archives reveal consistent though cautious support for the Allies by Salazar until the threat of invasion by Germany eased. Thereafter, Portugal remained supportive, though neutral, with tacit support from Churchill who did not want a war front developing on the Iberian Peninsula. The leadership in Lisbon, London and Washington, if not Canberra, was aware throughout the Pacific War of the dire risk to thousands of refugees sheltering in Macau should Portugal declare war on Japan.

On 26 February 1945, the Duke of Palmela, Portugal's Ambassador to Britain, called on the Australian High Commissioner Sir Stanley Bruce and, referring to a 'shared interest in Pacific affairs', asked whether Canberra was ready to accept a Portuguese Chargé d'Affaires. The Duke's reference to a 'shared interest' was appropriate, but unfortunate given the prejudiced outlook in Canberra. Canberra advised

Bruce in a terse instruction that an upgrade in diplomatic relations was out of the question at least until there was some clarification of the military and political position of Portuguese Timor. Bruce was told to let the Ambassador know that Australia would feel guilty of discourtesy if it did not reciprocate and there was no reasonable prospect that it had the logistical capacity to do so.[7]

When Bruce called on the Duke on 7 June 1945 he explained the Australian rebuff on the basis that Australia had been requested by other European allies to open full diplomatic relations and to accept Portugal's request and deny others could be counter-productive. This disingenuous explanation had worn thin by 1960, when Australia finally consented to full diplomatic links with Portugal. The way a lingering distaste for colonialism overshadowed the development of a pragmatic relationship with the potentially self-governing peoples of Portuguese Timor is illustrated by an early exchange between the two countries. On 10 September 1951, the Portuguese Consul visited the Australian External Affairs departmental head, Alan Watt, and asked for Australia's views on the value of Portuguese participation were Portugal to join the South Pacific Commission. Watt was non-committal.[8] Although at odds with a sensible defence strategy, Watt's negative response reflected the attitude adopted and pursued within the Department of External Affairs that Australia's regional foreign policy needs could be best met without cooperation with Portugal. At diplomatic level throughout the 1950s and 1960s Australia remained keen not to be seen to be in any lockstep with Portugal in relation to Portuguese Timor. Australian sensitivities about colonialism were foundationally historic, stirred by the Atlantic Charter and referenced at San Francisco by Evatt's preoccupation with the drafting of Chapter XI of the UN Charter, wherein Articles 73 and 74 lauded the 'sacred trust' of States 'administering' territories 'whose peoples have not yet attained a full measure of self-government'.

When Portugal acceded to the UN Charter in 1955, it gave Chapter XI a wide berth, declaring that it did not regard its overseas provinces as non-self-governing territories within the purview of Chapter XI. Nevertheless, Lisbon indicated that it would cooperate by providing 'information' regarding developments in 'metropolitan' provinces. Later that year Spain also acceded and made a similar declaration. Subtleties of outlook by Member States were inherent in the drafting of Articles 73 and 74, particularly the absence of the terms, 'colonial' and 'colonialism'. Portugal and Spain were not alone in their interpretation of Chapter XI. Both the UK and France had adopted the stance that Chapter XI was a declaration of noble intent and saw no role for the UN in international supervision of colonial rule.[9] By 1960 this was all to change irreversibly when 14 new countries, almost all in Africa, were admitted to the UN in one day, followed soon after by two more former French colonies and Nigeria.[10]

On 14 December 1960, 89 member states of the General Assembly adopted Resolution 1514, being The Declaration on the Granting of Independence to Colonial Countries and Peoples. No country opposed the resolution, but of the nine countries that abstained—Australia, Belgium, Dominican Republic, France, Portugal, Spain, South Africa, UK and US—only the Dominican Republic was not a colonial power. The power-play had changed dramatically and Australia had become a fellow colonial power with Portugal in the region. Soon, both Portugal and Australia were reporting regularly to the emboldened General Assembly via a Chapter XI UN Committee of 24 nations overseeing decolonisation in Timor and Papua New Guinea respectively, and elsewhere. Portugal in right of her African colonies was having a much harder time before the Committee than Australia, although both countries were being harried by Eastern Bloc Committee members and China.

Indonesian Expansionism
By the mid-1950s, President Sukarno of Indonesia had turned his attention to the rebellions against British rule in Borneo. His expansionist ambitions and antipathy to the proposed Malaysian Federation caused the Western allies to consider the strategic balance in Asia. While Australian Cabinet papers of that era foreshadow the long-lasting influence of Indonesian domestic politics on Australian foreign policy formulation,[11] recent studies of US policy approaches suggest that Australia was very much on the sidelines of strategic gamesmanship over Indonesia being played in Cold War and corporate terms within London and Washington with Moscow and Beijing.[12]

As with Vietnam and East Timor a generation later, the failure of conservative Australian foreign policy-makers to differentiate nationalism from communism played out again in the sell-out of the West

Papuan people. In the early years of Indonesian nationalism, to the chagrin of the US and Britain, it was Australia, followed by India, that mobilised the UN on behalf of the Indonesian independence movement. The leadership of the self-proclaimed Indonesian Republic was deeply appreciative of Australian foreign policy initiatives. Professor Macmahon Ball, leader of an Australian Goodwill Mission to East Asia in mid-1948, reported, '[Sukarno] was most friendly and sincere, like Hatta, referred with gratitude and admiration to Dr Evatt's work on the Security Council, and his general policy towards Indonesia ... I feel that Australia has a singular opportunity to give some intellectual leadership to the Republic'.[13] External Affairs Head John Burton moved ahead with a plan to improve social conditions and thereby combat the attraction of communism by an 'early and determined' program of economic and technological assistance and extension of consular posts to Borneo, Sumatra, French Indo-China and Burma.[14] Ironically, Portuguese Timor was not viewed within the ambit of Burton's foreign policy objective for the very fact that conditions in the colony were so primitive that organised moves towards independence had not emerged.

The foreign policy emphasis was to change following the defeat of the Chifley Labor Government in December 1949. Prime Minister Menzies was not prepared to offend either Whitehall or Washington on issues where Evatt had pressed principle ahead of Western power sensitivity. Menzies saw Southeast Asia in terms of where a threat to Australia's security might emerge, rather than the opportunity Evatt and Burton had identified. As late as 1962, Menzies reaction to Sukarno's agitation for West Papua to become Indonesia's West Irian province included reference to the prospect of communist infiltrators crossing the 'indefensible' frontier into Australian-administered Papua New Guinea.[15]

Despite real difficulties in the relationship during the independence struggle in the Dutch East Indies, Australia and the Netherlands agreed to work together on a low-key basis in their respective administration of the two halves of New Guinea. In 1957, Australia's Territories Minister Paul Hasluck met officials in the Dutch territory. Later, Hasluck participated with Menzies and External Affairs Minister Casey in discussions with the Dutch in Canberra about joint UN policy and development goals. Further meetings at The Hague in 1960 took place against a backdrop of the US and Britain bowing to the 'wind of change' and pressure from within the General Assembly for a devolution of power in West Papua. Both Washington and London wanted to avoid any process that might lead to West Papua being abandoned to perceived pro-communist liberation.

By December 1957, Australian concerns over the expulsion of Dutch citizens from Indonesia and the expropriation of Dutch assets led Prime Minister Menzies to request the US Administration to exert pressure on Indonesia at the highest level. In a message to US Secretary of State John Foster Dulles, Menzies noted, as a close neighbour of Indonesia and a somewhat exposed Western democracy, Australia was apprehensive about Russian or Chinese intervention in the region and about Indonesia's persistent violation of personal freedom and property rights.[16] A submission to the Menzies Cabinet noted that:

> On 14 December, the Indonesian Government proclaimed sovereignty over 'all waters around, between, and connecting the islands or parts of the islands belonging to the Indonesian State'. This proclamation, if enforced, would have the effect of extending Indonesian jurisdiction over large areas of the high seas, including the Java Sea and over such important waterways as the Sunda Straits and the Straits of Malacca and Macassar. In addition to extending territorial limits beyond three miles, and also a possible arbitrary application of the 'base line' principle, the waters between the islands (including the Java Sea) would become 'internal waters' (where other powers presumably could be denied the rights customarily accorded in territorial waters). Written protests have been made by Australia, the United States, the United Kingdom, France, the Netherlands, New Zealand, and Japan. The United Kingdom is at present encouraging other Powers (principally European ones) to lodge protests.[17]

On 18 December 1959, Australia's Consul in Dili reported a Portuguese request for Australian assistance in training Portuguese garrison troops in Timor in jungle warfare.[18] External Affairs advice was that this might leave Australia open to criticism, given Portugal's ongoing colonial rule. Over many years, Portuguese and Australian army and navy personnel based in Timor and Darwin had been making unofficial exchange visits. The Australian Department of External Affairs was keen to keep all such liaison at an unofficial level, leaving, for example, the question of dealing with Portuguese naval deserters to the Immigration Department, unlike the official process under visiting forces agreements with other allied countries. It seems probable that conversation in officers' messes in Darwin and Dili would have included reference to Indonesian expansionism. Unfortunately, the destiny of the East Timorese lay more in the hands of the Australian Department of External Affairs, with its largely unwitting sycophancy with Washington, than of the Australian Defence Department. Consequently, the Portuguese request for military training was not progressed.

On 11 January 1962, the Chargé d'Affaires of Portugal's new embassy in Canberra, Dr Coutinho, went so far as to make an official request regarding Australia's position in the event of aggression against Portuguese interests in Timor. Coincidentally, the following day, in what became a precursor to a similar 1963 Cabinet position on Portuguese Timor, External Affairs Minister Garfield Barwick presented a Cabinet Submission arguing that early self-determination for West Papua could lead to instability in the region and that Indonesian accession was in Australia's interests, if not inevitable.[19] Against such appeasement over West New Guinea, the Timorese had little to hope for. Menzies appears not to have supported Barwick's sell-out proposal for West New Guinea, issuing instead a statement applauding the peaceful settlement of disputes under UN guidance.[20] Despite Menzies' principled approach to the future of West New Guinea, the Department of External Affairs persisted in its approach. In his despatch of 16 March 1962 to his departmental head, Sir Arthur Tange, Australia's Ambassador to Indonesia, Patrick Shaw, laid bare External Affairs policy regarding the future of West Papua: 'Unity means a great deal to all Indonesian Political leaders ... [E]mphasis on self-determination for West New Guinea has dangerous overtones for Indonesians. A united Indonesia which is non-communist is our major objective in this part of the world, and on present indications one which we can reasonably hope to attain'.[21]

A month later, in a Cabinet Submission dealing with Portuguese Timor, Barwick, now in a formidable duo with Tange, recorded the response to Dr Coutinho's request:

> [T]he Australian Government would naturally take a serious view of any Indonesian aggression. The steps to be taken in such an event would be decided in the light of all the relevant circumstances at the time. Subject to that general proviso it could be expected that political

action by the Australian Government would include support of proposals in the United Nations for a cease fire and for a withdrawal of Indonesian forces.[22]

To the evident satisfaction of Canberra's strategists at the Department of External Affairs, the incorporation of West Papua into Indonesia was 'resolved' in 1962 in a three-step process by the very powers voicing support at the UN for genuine acts of self-determination. As a first step the Dutch flag came down on 15 August 1962—the outcome of negotiations a lonely Netherlands Foreign Ministry, deserted by the major Western powers, conducted with Jakarta. The territory was to be placed under UN Administration, followed in May 1963 by transfer of administration to Indonesia with the promise of a plebiscite within five years. In the event, the 1969 plebiscite was little more than a simulated UN-supervised ballot to formalise the 1962 takeover. As we shall see, the UN lent itself again, 40 years later, to a similar tactic by which a powerful neighbour, this time Australia, placed the FRETILIN Party into power in Timor-Leste over unsophisticated peoples without a genuine ballot.

While Canberra went along in accordance with Big Power diplomacy with a *faux* self-determination in West Papua, unease in the Menzies Government led Cabinet on 7 September 1962 to request the Defence Committee to reassess Australia's strategic defence position *vis-à-vis* Indonesia, having regard to the utility of Australia's defence base in Malaya. Noting the steadily declining British defence capacity in Southeast Asia, an Australian diplomat recorded the view of his Ministry:

> The Secretary again reiterated his view that Australia should make a conscious endeavour to secure a capacity for independent action. There may be a time when this could become important, for example, in connection with a difference of opinion about international waters. A greater capacity for independent military action could have a direct bearing on our relations with the United States. We must not assume that the United States will do all our soldiering for us. The Netherlands New Guinea episode demonstrated clearly that the United States simply will not let certain kinds of situations develop to the point where their obligations under ANZUS and SEATO are attracted.[23]

While noting that in Timor some build-up of Indonesian forces and propaganda on alleged border incidents and treatment of the Timorese by Portugal was to be expected, Indonesia alone was unlikely to constitute a major threat to Australia as long as Australia and its allies retained a forward military posture in Southeast Asia.[24] If Indonesia, presently neutral, succumbed to encroaching communism, Australia would be subject to the combined threat of Communist China and a Communist Indonesia.[25]

Meanwhile, Allen Dulles was fostering anti-communist sentiment within the Indonesian Army command, while tolerating large-scale arms purchases from Moscow by the Indonesian Air Force and Navy. He saw *Konfrontasi* as a sabre-rattling phase in building a nationalistic and centralised Indonesian Army command rather than a serious threat to the West. Properly influenced and 'educated' at residential officer-training schools in the US, some 2,800 future Indonesian army leaders would be oriented to the West and likely to control a non-communist Indonesia.[26] The eventual reliance by the US on Indonesian army suppression of the Timorese FRETILIN party was consistent with this strategy.

One would expect the CIA program in Indonesia to have been monitored closely by MO9 (predecessor of the Australian Secret Intelligence Service (ASIS)), staffed largely out of Melbourne by officers with a military intelligence or civilian analyst Defence Department background. MO9's first Director, Alfred Deakin Brookes, had cultivated a close relationship with CIA Director Allen Dulles.[27] Brookes had also served in Batavia as Australia's Acting Political Representative while on temporary assignment from a post in Singapore to the Department of External Affairs. It was primarily through his personal contact with leading republican dissidents that Australia secured a working relationship with the Indonesian leadership that British Foreign Office archives reveal was to hold Australian security intelligence interests close to the pulse in the Presidential Palace for many years to come, including through the dark period of the Balibo killings, recounted in chapter 6.

Brookes' reports from March to June 1946 displayed his opposition to Dutch colonial interests and his sympathy for the nationalist cause. His close contact with the Minister for Foreign Affairs in the Provisional Government, Dr Sutan Sjahrir, one of the principal architects of Indonesian independence, worried External Affairs Department Secretary William Dunk, such that Brookes' recall was mooted. Evatt quashed the proposal, commending Brookes for his ability and integrity.²⁸ While Brookes' reports stand out for his awareness of Evatt's agenda, their significance lies in the cautious pre-Burton departmental reaction to them. After the ASIS role was transferred out of the Defence Department in Melbourne to a base in Canberra, intelligence reports embracing contact with the anti-communist-oriented Indonesian military hierarchy during the build-up of the Indonesian central army command had a less circuitous route to Casey and his successor, Barwick.

As history records Australia built up a significant post in Jakarta that worked closely with Indonesian national security and strategic agencies, as well as with British and US intelligence complements.²⁹ After the elimination of Partai Komunis Indonesia (PKI) influence, the removal of Sukarno, and the installation of General Suharto in 1967, in which Western intelligence services played a significant role,³⁰ Canberra adopted a more sanguine approach towards Indonesia. There seemed a real prospect of Australia acquiring a strong and powerful neighbour with which it could develop effective relations.

Meanwhile, Australia's counter-espionage agency, the Australian Security Intelligence Organisation (ASIO), together with British and US colleagues were not focused entirely on the Soviet threat at home. By the mid-1960s, China, where Australia lacked diplomatic representation, was allowing increasing numbers of diaspora Chinese to travel within China. Both MO9 and ASIO lacked executive powers of arrest and search. Operations at home against organised Chinese 'malpractice' acquired no teeth until Sir Peter Heydon, who had established the Australian Legation at Kuibyshev in January 1943 and endured both Evatt's social prejudices³¹ and the wiles of Soviet intelligence, established in 1967–68, with Cabinet approval following United States and British reviews, a Special Reports Branch (SRB) within the Department of Immigration, with wide powers of entry, search and seizure under the *Migration Act 1958*. The SRB, led by British veterans, commenced examining issues at home and abroad. Heydon was still building the SRB, of which the author was a member, when he died suddenly on 13 May 1971.

Prior to these capacity-building developments in Australia and shortly before President Kennedy moved him on from the CIA, Allen Dulles had visited Canberra in 1961, spending time with Barwick. While Dulles is unlikely to have shared all with Barwick, both were fellow corporate lawyers aware of the mineral riches of West Papua. Within five years US mining giant Freeport, encouraged by Australian visa concessions, was operating an exploration program in West Papua out of Cairns in North Queensland. Both Washington and Canberra deflected criticism of the Freeport Mine operation with pious references to the economic potential it offered the people of 'West Irian'. Nothing was said about the effective expropriation of the original landholders' rights.[32]

Barwick's department was not new to such corporate liaison. The Australian Government was also monitoring, and later assisted, negotiations for Rio Tinto's access to the rich gold, copper and zinc deposits on Bougainville Island. Rio Tinto Board member Dick Austin, a gifted linguist and former senior Department of Foreign Affairs and Military Intelligence Officer, maintained close links with Tange and ASIS.[33] In one respect at least, the well-connected British/Australian mining major was more generous than its US counterpart in West Papua. With astounding effrontery, the Australian Government and Rio Tinto announced that landowners in Bougainville were to receive a 5% royalty over the 42-year lease while the rich deposits were worked out and the profits repatriated. A compliant new legislature in Port Moresby went along with the machinations in Canberra. Twenty years later much the same occurred over the petroleum resources of the Timor Sea. This time a new generation of Australian diplomats, referred to in some quarters by their intake year as, 'the Class of '69', took out their predecessors' manual, and Darwin, as Cairns had been for Freeport, became the safer place from which to run the enterprise with Dili, under Mari Alkatiri, agreeing to a joint-venture.

Not averse to exploiting racist sentiment against ethnic Chinese Indonesians, Dulles was relentless in a bloody intrigue that might now be labelled 'Deep State'.[34] Dulles, given the opportunity to brief presidential candidate John F. Kennedy on the CIA operation to overthrow Fidel Castro, now at a late stage, refrained. After his election Kennedy was to be presented with an almost *fait accompli*. The subsequent debacle mirrored a similar disaster for Dulles four years earlier in Indonesia when a shrewd Sukarno foiled a CIA-sponsored rebellion.[35] Poulgrain notes that Barwick was briefed by the CIA when in Washington in September 1962. Kennedy had by then 'retired' Dulles from the CIA, although Dulles' influence persisted in West Papua mining for decades to come. In retirement, Barwick expressed regret over his own role in contributing to the outcome in West Papua.[36]

In November 1962, an attempted rebellion against British rule in Brunei raised questions again in London, Canberra, Washington and Lisbon about Indonesian territorial ambitions. An initiative to bring the Western alliance together in relation to Indonesia was taken by the British Foreign Secretary.[37] The British Foreign Office, anxious not to have Britain's ancient defence alliance with Portugal called upon in defence of Portuguese Timor, proposed to the US that tripartite talks be held between the UK, Australia and the US. The proposal was later extended to include New Zealand. The British, ever sensitive with Lisbon over access rights in the Azores and overflight rights in Africa as it juggled the relics of its colonial empire, continued careful diplomatic exchange with Portugal.

On 15 January 1963, the UK Government advised Canberra that it had instructed its Ambassador to the US to convey 'to the Americans the Foreign Secretary's concern about developments in Indonesia and to discuss with them the question of policy towards Indonesia'. The Foreign Secretary's Briefing Note listed British concern about: Sukarno's territorial ambitions reaching beyond West Irian; Indonesian involvement in the Brunei rebellion and its effects; indications of Indonesia's plans to incorporate Portuguese Timor; Sukarno's opposition to the formation of Malaysia and his wishes for a Greater Indonesian Malaysia; the likelihood of an expansionist regime pushing on to the Philippines; the possibility of that regime wanting to move into the other half of New Guinea and eventually into Melanesia; Indonesia's reliance on the Communist Bloc for arms and backing; and the fact that a large amount of American aid will be used by Indonesia to subsidise the purchase of arms from and to service its debts to the Communist powers. The Note then sought the US Administration's analysis:

> It is, of course, fully understood that American policy has been to try and keep Indonesia from becoming completely dependent on Russia and China and to support the Armed Forces in Indonesia as a counter balance to the Communist Party. But the further problem is how to contain Indonesian expansion. We are doing so in Brunei, but have the Americans any idea how they can help? As a first step we would like to know whether the United States Administration share this analysis and what are their own views about the dangers ahead of us.[38]

In response to the British proposal for talks in Washington, the Menzies Cabinet requested relevant ministers to submit policy appreciations, which, together with the records of the Washington Conference, are of considerable significance.[39] A lengthy assessment of Australia's strategic position by the Defence Committee included reference to Timor:

> There is no doubt that Indonesia's activities in relation to Portuguese Timor, Brunei and the other Borneo Territories are in part inspired by her anti-colonial convictions and the background of her struggle for independence. Her real aims, however, which will be pursued with persistence by Sukarno, must be regarded as directed towards the ultimate incorporation of these territories into Indonesia, or at least the creation there of regimes closely bound to Indonesia.[40]

The outcome of the various submissions was that Cabinet noted Indonesia's growth as a military power, her declared opposition to the Malayan Federation and her use of power in respect of diplomatic aims. The Australian Cabinet agreed to an increase in the scale of defence programming, 'not only to ensure the security of the Australian mainland and East New Guinea but also to allow us to make an effective and sustained contribution in South-East Asia and to present a deterrent to possible activities by Indonesia inimical to our strategic interests'.[41] It concluded that the government should consider both the risk of military involvement with Indonesia and the fact that Australia's military strategy was based on a forward position in Southeast Asia and resolved to continue supporting the creation of Malaysia and to accept the risk of tension in Australian and Indonesian relations.

The Washington Conference on Indonesian Threat

The discussions proposed by the UK took place at Washington on 11–12 February 1963. The Department of External Affairs recorded the agreed outcome for the four governments involved in the talks (US, UK, Australia and New Zealand) as:

a. It was agreed that the problem of Portuguese Timor was one for Governments to keep under continuing discussion and that there should be further consultations between parties in Washington about United Nations tactics.

b. There was agreement on the need for concerted action well in advance of any Indonesian moves.

c. No agreed course of action emerged during discussions although it was generally felt that the United Nations involvement with Timor would remain unacceptable to Portugal because of the precedent which would be created with regard to Angola and Mozambique.

d. The United States delegate suggested that there might be some possibility of influencing the Portuguese Government to take a realistic view of the situation of the territory and to make changes in its present policy to take account of world opinion on colonial matters. He had in mind a ten-year reform programme of education and welfare to be followed by a plebiscite in which the Timorese were to decide their own future. The Australian representatives referred to contact with the Portuguese which showed no alteration to policies. (In addition, it seems unlikely that major reform programmes could succeed without substantial changes in the Portuguese administration).[42]

The UK Foreign Office recorded the outcome of the consideration of the threat to Timor from Indonesia somewhat differently:

At these talks all four delegations accepted:

a. that Timor would inevitably go to Indonesia in the end;
b. that there was little hope of persuading the Portuguese to make progress to self-government;
c. that the best protection for Western interests would be to ensure that the United Nations should take charge of the problem sooner or later.

It was also agreed to recommend to the four governments that a continuing Quadripartite Committee be set up in Washington to keep the Timor question under review and to make recommendations about the timing and nature of action in the UN.[43]

The 1963 Cabinet Decision on Portuguese Timor

The position adopted by Australia at the Washington Conference followed an extraordinary Australian Cabinet Minute outlining the Australian government's attitude to Portuguese Timor. Referred to subsequently as the '1963 decision on Portuguese Timor', it was to remain for years the *leitmotif* of Australian policy affecting Portuguese Timor:

[T]he Cabinet accepted the view that in the current state of world opinion, no practicable alternative to eventual Indonesian sovereignty over Portuguese Timor presented itself. It would not be acceptable to Australia or the West for Indonesia to proceed against Portuguese Timor with arms, and this must be brought home to Indonesia. But otherwise the course which it seemed best to follow is for Australia to bring such quiet pressure as it can upon Portugal to cede peacefully and in addition to explore ways by which the community might bring pressure on Portugal.[44]

Two weeks later the colonial administration of Timor was criticised in a further Cabinet Minute which relied on reports by the Australian Consul at Dili, James (Jim) Dunn, that 'it was difficult to see how Portuguese Timor could exist as a viable economic state without substantial financial aid and technical assistance from outside'. Dunn, who later supported the cause of independence for the East Timorese, also reported that 'if the people were given the opportunity there would be some pressure towards setting up an independent state but the majority would probably favour Indonesian rule as the alternative to the continuation of Portuguese rule'.[45] Dunn's advice neither addressed the basis for his assertion nor the probable opposition of the Vatican to the absorption of the many Roman Catholic Timorese by an overwhelmingly Muslim Indonesia. More importantly, perhaps, Dunn failed to emphasise the mineral and petroleum potential of the island. Tragically, as we shall see, the subsequent External Affairs Cabinet Minute emphasised the negativity in Dunn's report and also failed to address the prospect of economic self-sufficiency based on mineral and petroleum resources. In 1999, in evidence before a parliamentary committee, former Prime Minister Gough Whitlam emphasised the role Dunn had played in the 1963 Cabinet Decision:

> The analysis that Barwick put to the Menzies cabinet was mainly based on information given by our consul, Jim Dunn, who was there for a year and a half. You will notice that Barwick's analysis, and the analysis which I got from all the departmental secretaries whom I inherited, was exactly what Salazar said to Menzies and what the Menzies government believed: that East Timor was non-viable politically and economically. That was my view.[46]

The Department of External Affairs' long-standing aversion to engagement with Portugal was reflected in the claim in the Cabinet Submission that Australia had been unable to develop an effective dialogue with the Salazar regime in Lisbon. In noting the Australian position, the Cabinet Submission by the Minister for External Affairs recorded:

> During the 1939–45 war and for some years thereafter, it was Australian policy to regard Portuguese Timor as being of strategic importance to Australia. In consequence, it was felt desirable to keep a friendly Portuguese administration in control of the island. From the time of a message being conveyed to Dr Salazar in September 1943, through to at least 1950, we envisaged an increase in commercial ties and consultations on 'matters of mutual security interest'. There is no record of any positive response by the Portuguese Government to our approaches. More recently our policy on the future of the territory has been influenced by –
> 1. A new defence assessment that—
>   a. whether controlled by Portugal or Indonesia, Portuguese Timor has no military importance to Australia, and
>   b. the acquisition of the territory by Indonesia would not significantly affect any threat to Australia.
> 2. Our public advocacy of the principle of self-determination. This has brought us to direct criticism of Portuguese colonial theory in the United Nations. The Prime Minister wrote to Dr. Salazar in October 1961 and again on 8th February 1963. In the first instance, he gave clear notice of Australia's support for the principle of self-determination and referred in particular to Portuguese position with respect to its African colonies. In his second letter the Prime Minister warned Dr Salazar that the United Nations Special Committee on Colonialism, of which Australia is a member, would again be paying attention to Portuguese African territories in 1963 and may also discuss the future of Portuguese Timor. The Prime Minister said that it would be difficult for Australia to refrain entirely from taking part in such a debate. He concluded by pointing out that the Australian Government is concerned that in the absence of any intention of allowing the Timorese people to express a choice as to the international relationships and status which they desire, there will arise a serious threat to the peace of the territory.
> 3. Portuguese Timor is an anachronism in this part of the world and there is no evidence that an improvement of the living conditions or social status of the Timorese is possible under Portuguese rule. It is not capable of political independence, even if Indonesian Timor

by some means was united with it. Thus, if Indonesia seeks to incorporate Portuguese Timor by genuinely peaceful means and providing that this was in accordance with the freely expressed wishes of the Timorese, Australia would have little alternative but to acquiesce. Indeed, such an arrangement might have the advantages over other possibilities.

4. While Australia—or for that matter any other country—would not assist the Portuguese in resistance to a military takeover by Indonesia, the Government will be forced by regard for our responsibilities in East New Guinea as well as by respect for Australian public sentiment, to play a leading role in bringing the matter before the United Nations.

5. In reply to a Portuguese enquiry in February 1962, the Secretary of the Department of External Affairs, with my approval, told the Portuguese Chargé d'Affaires, that the Australian Government would naturally take a serious view of any Indonesian aggression. The steps to be taken in such an event would be decided in the light of all the relevant circumstances at the time. Subject to that general proviso it could be expected that political action by the Australian Government would include support of proposals in the United Nations for a cease fire and for a withdrawal of Indonesian forces. We also asked what objectives Portugal had for the eventual political status of the territory and advancement towards these objectives. No reply has ever been received.[47]

To digress, relevantly, more than 10 years later, Dunn, with David McLennan, Head of the Department of Foreign Affairs' Indonesia Section, visited Timor. In their subsequent report, Dunn and McLennan revived the possibility of integration with Indonesia, which Dunn had suggested in 1963 from Dili when Consul and upon which Barwick had then relied. In a remarkable twist, Dunn, in his post-Foreign Affairs role as Director of the Parliamentary Library Foreign Affairs Group, passed to the British High Commission a copy of a report on East Timor he had prepared dated 27 August 1974.[48] The British, who relied on Australia for word of developments in East Timor, were somewhat puzzled. They had secured in Jakarta from Australian Embassy sources a copy of Dunn and McLennan's earlier report, which was at the time the most up-to-date on-the-spot assessment available to the Department of Foreign Affairs. In that report, prepared after their visit to East Timor between 17 and 27 June 1974, the authors asserted:

> Today the Portuguese have good relations with the Indonesian authorities in Western Timor and their past fears have relaxed. But the old attitude persists among Timorese. At the same time, it is said that many Timorese might be sympathetic to the idea of association with Indonesia if they felt free to express their opinion. But they are fearful that the Portuguese might return to Timor after decolonization as they did after the Pacific war … It is hard to gauge the real character of Timorese opinion about Indonesia and the relative strength of different attitudes. Present opinion could change with increasing political maturity.[49]

The extraordinary assessment that it was 'hard to gauge the real character of Timorese opinion about Indonesia' suggests that neither Dunn nor McLennan put their head inside a Catholic church in Timor or spoke to any of the nationalist elements. Given McLennan's senior role in the Department of Foreign Affairs, it appears probable that the report by Dunn and McLennan influenced the Department to adopt the view that the Timorese could be brought around to accepting a merger with Indonesia. This is consistent with the view ascribed around the same time to the Department of Foreign Affairs by the British Foreign Office: 'The Department of Foreign Affairs have been nursing the hope that Indonesian military intervention would not be necessary to achieve this end—and that the people of Portuguese Timor would resolve the dilemma by a free vote for merger'.[50] In his Parliamentary Library report, open to public scrutiny, Dunn backed completely away from the outlook he and McLennan had presented within the cloisters a month earlier: 'the option of integration with Indonesia … has attracted very little support in Timor and it seems inconceivable that the Timorese would freely choose this solution to their future'.[51] Tragically, this was not the official message he and McLennan had conveyed to the government.

Australia Rejects US Proposal for Staged Self-Determination

Returning to the events of 1963, one could be kind and say that it was disingenuous of Barwick to inform the Cabinet on 21 February 1963 that Portugal had failed to respond. Menzies had only written via diplomatic valise to Salazar a fortnight earlier. In opening, Menzies had thanked Salazar for his lengthy reply to Menzies' earlier letter of 18 October 1961. Further, Salazar did respond by 1 March 1963, again at length and this time constructively. Barwick's failure to await Salazar's response and to justify his stated reliance upon a defence assessment that, whether controlled by Portugal or Indonesia, Portuguese Timor had no military importance to Australia may have contributed to the ultimate tragedy.

None of the major Australian strategic defence review papers available to Cabinet in 1962 and 1963 contain any suggestion that Portuguese Timor had 'no military importance to Australia'; the diplomatic record suggested the contrary. In his report of the Washington Conference, Barwick refers to the views of Sir Arthur Tange, who had accompanied him to Washington. Tange's record of his 11 February 1963 meeting with US Secretary of State Dean Rusk and Assistant Secretary Averell Harriman indicates that Washington wanted Australia to 'assume the defence burdens' arising in the Australian region and that Malaysia was to be a British Commonwealth defence responsibility. Undoubtedly, the US regarded Portuguese Timor as within the area it wanted Australia to assume military responsibility for. Tange records the fateful conversation about the future of Portuguese Timor:

> Harriman described the repressive policies of the Portuguese Administrators and the low level of literacy and public health. We told them that Portuguese Timor represented a potential embarrassment to the Australian Government with a difficult Parliamentary situation. The Prime Minister had written to Dr Salazar a strong letter about the threat to the peace which might arise if Portugal failed to grant some political freedom to the Timorese. This was the real question and it was not one of raising their standard of living. We did not see that Australia could go any further than this.[52]

Writing in 2008 of his 11 years as Secretary of the Department of External Affairs from 1954, including most of the Barwick years, Tange recorded that Australian diplomacy was dominated by concern for the nation's security: 'After a long period of nursing our relations with Indonesia ... we in External Affairs (criticised as we only later learned for being too conciliatory) accepted that a military response might be necessary to curb Sukarno, while we could still hope for internal restraints on him'.[53]

The 'internal restraints' were a mixture of internal political party and military pressures building up against Sukarno, encouraged in certain respects by US and British intelligence, including 'black ops' out of Singapore that led to Suharto's move to power.[54] Overall, Tange's recollections lend weight to the conclusion that Barwick's concern to maintain good relations with Indonesia and an expectation that Sukarno's excesses would soon be reined in by the generals were the dominant factors in assessing where the future of West New Guinea and Portuguese Timor best lay for Australia. Tange's expectation that Sukarno's Moscow leanings might soon be 'corrected' was well founded. It appears likely that Tange was receiving 'feed' from US, UK and Australian intelligence agencies during the Suharto phase, when an alleged attempted coup against President Sukarno on 1 October 1965 failed and was followed by the elimination of hundreds of thousands of PKI members, supposedly under direction from Suharto. Robinson asserts that the botched coup was merely the pretext for a carefully planned anti-communist campaign of annihilation.[55]

Despite Averell Harriman's offer to lend US support for a 10-year staged self-determination development program for Portuguese Timor, provided Australia took the lead role, Barwick rejected the proposal in unconvincing terms:

> Harriman ... appears attached to the idea that Portugal should be induced (and assisted) to bring in a 10-year development programme which would be linked to an act of self-determination by the Timorese at the end of the period...[I]n his view, Australia should take the lead in persuading Portugal to make reforms. I am convinced Harriman's idea has no future in it and both Sir Arthur Tange and Sir Howard Beale ... have indicated our lack of enthusiasm for the idea ... We have made it clear to the United States that through the Prime Minister's letters to Salazar, we have made some practical effort to have the Portuguese see the cold facts of the situation. I do not think that we will make much impression in Lisbon unless there is change of Government.[56]

Barwick's conclusion was deceptive. While civil war between the groups calling for independence or autonomy from Portugal or for union with Indonesia took another 11 years to surface, it is difficult to understand how the Australian delegation reconciled a potential liberation struggle close to Australia's shores as something Australia could go no further with. Australia's strategic defence and intelligence reviews emphasised the need to adopt policies to deal with communist influence during colonial devolution in Southeast Asia. The US was offering Australia the means to diminish the threat of communist-assisted civil insurgency recognised by Menzies in his first letter to Salazar and accepted by him as an issue Portugal already faced in its African colonies.

Whether Barwick and Tange were moved by a quiet consensus in Canberra that Australia wanted no truck with liberation movements in West Papua and Portuguese Timor is difficult to tell. The answer may come when further archives are released. The evidence so far suggests that a takeover of West Papua and Portuguese Timor by Indonesia with a now well-identified anti-communist military hierarchy was seen by Barwick and his advisers as a safer route to stability in the region to Australia's immediate north than Harriman-style development assistance to democracy movements. More than 20 years later, it was obvious that stability had not been secured in West Papua. On 26 June 1985, five West Papuans arrived on Australian territory at Thursday Island in the Torres Strait. Initially, they sought political asylum, stating that they were from the Merauke area of West Papua fleeing from persecution by the Indonesian military. Represented by the author, one was lodged at the island hospital while receiving treatment for a bayonet wound. The Australian government quickly downplayed the issue, eventually avoiding Federal Court proceedings by allowing the five to remain in Australia without further contest regarding their claims to be fleeing persecution.[57]

In the absence of any sensible Australian foreign policy initiative, the US resolved in 1974 to deal with the threat of a perceived communist-aligned East Timor by proxy through Indonesia's President Suharto, whom the CIA, particularly during the Allen Dulles years, had long cultivated in a quest to establish a strong centrally commanded Indonesian army as a bulwark against communism.[58]

Barwick's extraordinary claim in the 1963 Cabinet paper prepared by his Department that there had not been any positive response by the Portuguese Government (meaning, in context, Dr Salazar) to Australian encouragement for self-determination in Portuguese Timor requires critical examination. This assertion by Barwick and his advisers has perpetuated a belief in some quarters that Salazar refused to consider self-determination in Timor, but the correspondence between Menzies and Salazar belies this assertion. The letters now represent a poignant chronicle of lost opportunity and all too familiar myopic foreign policy by Australia.[59] Salazar's responses were constructive, erudite and far from dismissive. Barwick's claim does insufficient justice to the Portuguese leader who, in his quandary as to what to do with the colony on Australia's doorstep, even offered it, if only rhetorically, to Australia to administer. In his reply on 1 March 1963 to Menzies' second letter of 8 February 1963, Salazar noted Australia's desire for good relations with a non-communist Indonesia and, taking a leaf out of Australian defence strategy, reminded Menzies of Australia's wartime interest in a common defence strategy for Portuguese Timor:

> [A] Portuguese Timor seems incomparably safer and more attentive to the interests of Australia than the same Timor integrated in that Republic. We continue to see the problem in the light of our relations and of the official statements made by the Australian Government during the Second World War. In fact, the Minister of Foreign Affairs stated in Parliament on 27th November 1941 that Australia had a very direct interest in preserving the complete independence of Timor. In the Note of the British Embassy in Lisbon, dated 14th of September 1943, we were told that His Majesty's Government in the Commonwealth of Australia trusted that the Portuguese Government would share the view that the two Governments should concert between them measures for the common defence of Timor and Australia. This was the line of thought of the Australian Government of those days, and it does not appear that the world situation enables it now to think differently.[60]

Salazar then developed a new theme—the prospect of Australia assuming some or all responsibility for Portuguese Timor. Aware that Australia was itself a colonial power in the region and capable, as asserted by Australia's Representative at the UN, of delivering a good outcome for the peoples of Papua New Guinea, Salazar asked rhetorically whether Portuguese Timor could secure a similar place under the Australian umbrella:

> Given the fact that Timor cannot be an independent State it either continues as an autonomous province or is annexed; there does not seem to be any foreseeable hypothesis of an Australian dominion or condominium ... But, then if an Australian dominion is impossible, if the independence of Timor (fed with large sums of money given annually out of the metropolitan budget) is impossible, if Portuguese sovereignty is the only safe one for Australia, what does the latter think of doing, or what can it do to maintain the status quo?[61]

The Cabinet Submission distribution list was remarkably short considering the issues raised; it did not include Defence Minister and former Territories Minister Paul Hasluck, and no meetings were organised by the Department of External Affairs either with the Department of Territories, responsible for Papua New Guinea, or with the Defence Department or Treasury to consider Salazar's offer. Hasluck's known antipathy to Indonesia during the West Papuan imbroglio and his success in administering the undeveloped peoples of Papua New Guinea may have given the Cabinet an informed voice on Salazar's offer. Salazar's proposal for a direct role by Australia in the future of Portuguese Timor ran counter to the External Affairs policy that the integration of Portuguese Timor into Indonesia was inevitable.

Available External Affairs files bear no evidence that the Salazar correspondence was shared either in or outside the Cabinet process with relevant Ministers and policy-making Departments. It was widely known that Tange's working relationship with Barwick was close,[62] but less so with Menzies.[63] A 'mandarin supremo', Tange, like Hasluck, had played a supporting role in London, Washington and San Francisco in the major events of Evatt's diplomacy, but Tange had an uneasy relationship with Hasluck, who had hoped to succeed Richard Casey in the External Affairs portfolio. Bolton reminds of the oft-quoted rumour in Canberra that Tange, consulted by Menzies about Casey's replacement as Minister for External Affairs, told Menzies he would have difficulty working with Hasluck.[64] Whether it was antipathy to Hasluck or Tange's close-to-the-chest style of policy decision-making or both, few would doubt that Hasluck, in his cautious enquiring manner, would have asked to see the Salazar correspondence and, crucially, US and British intelligence assessments.

All parties to the 1963 Quadripartite Talks in Washington had agreed to set up a joint working group of officials in Washington to monitor developments, but it did not eventuate. Upon his return to Canberra, Tange set up an internal departmental working group on Timor, whose report of 4 April 1963 said that Australia wanted 'to find peaceful and legitimate processes to end Portuguese rule in Portuguese Timor ... Portugal, on the other hand, would probably prefer Portuguese Timor to be speedily and forcibly annexed rather than enter into agreements'.[65] The working group considered that a West New Guinea type of arrangement might work and that Australia should discuss the future of Timor with Indonesia and cause the issue to be brought before the UN. Not a word in the working group's report touches on Salazar's rhetorical query as to whether Australia could take on a direct role in East Timor's future; nor did the group seek advice concerning the now recognised mineral and petroleum potential of Portuguese Timor. More than seven months later, Menzies' response to Salazar's letter was courteous and direct: 'Your Excellency's letter discusses the question of an Australian dominion or condominium in Portuguese Timor. Let me say that this is not a solution which we have ever contemplated. It is a solution which in my view would appeal neither to the Timorese nor the Australian people'.[66]

Considering the great tragedy that followed for the Timorese peoples, it is truly lamentable that nation-builders like Barwick's predecessor Richard Casey and successor Paul Hasluck, who led Papua New Guinea to independence and, if consulted, as Minister for Defence may have advised Menzies not to send his fateful reply. More to the point, if the Department of External Affairs had developed any form of effective dialogue with Salazar and shared that dialogue with the Departments of Defence and External Territories, Salazar's disposition to permit Australia to assume a direct role in administering Timor may have been further explored.

Salazar's final letter on 5 March 1964 was prophetic. Predicting Australian policy to come, the Portuguese leader referred to Indonesia being 'appeased' with West New Guinea and that the UN had failed to deliver self-determination to the peoples of West New Guinea. The Department of External Affairs resolved that nothing could be achieved by replying further to Dr Salazar. Barwick's rejection of the US State Department proposal for a staged devolution of power in Portugal's Timor colony appears contrary to settled Australian defence strategy of encouraging democratic processes in Southeast Asia. There have been fulcrum points to the fractured defence and foreign policy debate in Canberra affecting East Timor. Barwick's and Tange's report to Cabinet following the Washington Conference of February 1963 was an early example of myopic and deceitful Australian foreign policy advice from the whisperers in the External Affairs Department.

At the second round of Quadripartite Talks in Washington in October 1963, Barwick again acknowledged Indonesia's expansionist aims, arguing that a determined diplomatic and anti-guerrilla stance would let Jakarta know that the West would not tolerate further attempts to undermine Malaysia.[67] Australia spurned the apparent willingness of the Kennedy Administration to contribute indirectly to substantial development assistance for the Timorese. Concrete assistance for a staged withdrawal of the Portuguese colonial administration in East Timor in areas of municipal facilities, health, education, policing trade, sport and tourism required little adaptation from Australia's role in Papua New Guinea.

In early 1963, the US Administration was riding high in Western Europe on an anti-Soviet agenda close to Salazar's visceral loathing of communism. With the US Administration in empathy with Lisbon, it may be reasonable to conclude that Barwick and his advisers were aware that Harriman's offer of support may have provided the impetus for a receptive Salazar to support a joint Australian–Portuguese effort to bring about a staged devolution of power in Dili. While this may have entailed a Papua New Guinea-style ten-year plan, the challenge may have been no greater in magnitude than that facing the equally non-economically self-sufficient but far more diverse peoples of Papua New Guinea. Barwick was aware that such a process aimed at suppressing communism and supported elsewhere in Southeast Asia through Australian development assistance programs would entail the exploration of development goals for the Timorese, including economic self-sufficiency. But by this time, as we shall see in the following chapter, Barwick and his Department had no interest whatsoever in allowing the Timorese to develop their own resources.

Australia's successful Casey-inspired Colombo Plan to educate and train future leaders in the region, particularly in post-colonial Malaysia, was adaptable to the Timor context. Successive Australian Defence White Papers still maintain, in effect, the World War II and post-war assessment of Timor's geostrategic importance to Australia. While the assessment provided for the Washington Conference by the Australian Department of Defence conceded that Indonesia might inevitably absorb Portuguese Timor, Defence maintained that any such Indonesian objective would have to be secured by peaceful means after an act of self-determination.

There is no evidence that the Menzies–Salazar correspondence was shared with the Australian defence and intelligence community and opened for debate. The author has not located any contemporary defence intelligence reports that supported Barwick's claim that Timor had no strategic defence value; all the evidence points the other way. Australia lacks protected deep-water anchorages along most northern and northwest approaches; the tidal problems at Darwin were legendary. The necessity to base World War II submarine operations thousands of miles to the south, at Fremantle near Perth, was lesson enough in pointing to the need for deep-water anchorages closer to international shipping lanes. Portuguese Timor offered such facilities, both for an entrenched foreign power in Timor and for friendly operations.

Barwick's claim that Portuguese Timor was in defence terms strategically unimportant to Australia appeared necessary to fortify the Cabinet decision he had earlier sponsored that accepted the inevitability of an Indonesian takeover. Implicit in Barwick's formulation was that an Indonesian encroachment into Portuguese territory was not such a threat to Australia as would merit any strong opposition by Australia. Barwick's lack of empathy for an independent Timorese nation is apparent in his report of the Washington Conference. This was a precursor to the sell-out that his Department would eventually go along with. Lisbon, by now preoccupied with the challenge of perceived communist-inspired insurgencies in its African territories, did not revive Salazar's offer of a bilateral Portuguese–Australian effort to bring Timor into the 20th century. There is persuasive evidence that the policy adopted by Barwick towards Portuguese Timor was part of another strategy at odds, ultimately, with Australia's national interest.

It may be asked whether the prospect of Australia having to share its continental shelf with Portugal and with a future independent Timorese nation was an unstated reason for Barwick's curt and ultimately tragic rejection of Washington's proposal that Australia actively assist self-determination for the East Timorese. Government Cabinet discussions do not proceed in isolation. At the time of his February 1963 visit to Washington, Barwick was engaged in policy issues at Cabinet level affecting competing claims by Portugal, Indonesia and Australia to the Australian Continental Shelf extending almost to the shorelines of East and West Timor. US and Australian oil exploration companies were seeking exploration permits for the areas in likely dispute and Barwick had participated in Cabinet and Treasury discussions concerning extending petroleum search subsidies and taxation concessions. Barwick and his advisers were aware that the petroleum exploration subsidies were interlinked with Australia's compliance with the 1958 Geneva Convention on the Continental Shelf, which restricted outer shelf sovereign claims to the limits of exploitability. With an unrivalled insight into the riches of the Timor Sea, Barwick, a former corporate lawyer holding both the Attorney-General and External Affairs portfolios, was immensely influential in Cabinet.

Remarkably, but perhaps predictably considering the Barwick objective, the papers prepared for the Washington Conference by External Affairs contain not a word about the appreciation held by the Australian Treasury and Australia's Department of National Development of the petroleum potential of the Timor Sea.[68] Significantly, in his Federal Election Policy Speech on 12 November 1963, Menzies claimed that complete success in Australia's petroleum search would 'revolutionise' the Australian economy.[69]

While the Australian Minister for National Development was not on the Cabinet distribution list for the Top-Secret defence papers, Barwick with his two portfolios was an active participant in Cabinet discussions concerning tax concessions for petroleum exploration companies mooted by the Minister for National Development. The *Petroleum Search Subsidy Act 1959* (Cth) made provision for the payment of subsidies in respect of petroleum search operations in 'Australia' as defined. In an amending Act No. 57 of 1964, following earlier Cabinet approval, Parliament inserted section 3(2) to read: 'In this Act ... a reference to "Australia" shall be read as including a reference to the sea-bed and subsoil of the continental shelf contiguous to any part of the coasts of Australia or the coasts of a Territory ... [as defined]'.

In so far as the coasts of Australia and Portuguese Timor were opposite and adjacent to a common continental shelf, this definition sat uneasily with Article 6 of the 1958 Geneva Convention on the Continental Shelf (entered into force 10 June 1964) to which Australia was a signatory. Article 6 declared the boundary between the two states to be, in the absence of agreement or 'special circumstances', to be the median line. The significance of the 1964 amendment to the *Petroleum Search Subsidy Act 1959* is, in the definition of 'Australia', an implicit 'special circumstances' claim made to the sea-bed of the Timor Sea to coincide with the Continental Shelf convention coming into effect.

For 60 years Australia has clung to an argument of 'special circumstances' without providing a detailed geomorphological exposition of the claimed 'special circumstances'.

By the time of the 1963 Washington Conference, planning had already commenced at the Australian Bureau of Mineral Resources for a seismic survey of the Timor Sea. By 1965 that survey had established the petroleum potential of the sea-bed close to Portuguese Timor. The facts establish quite clearly that Barwick had a comprehensive oversight of the petroleum potential of the Timor Sea. The prospect of Australia solving its reliance on petroleum imports was a far more strategically important issue than self-determination for the peoples of Portuguese Timor. Accordingly, despite Australian platitudes at the UN, no effective foreign policy was developed other than to secure for Australian and foreign companies the riches of the Timorese sea-bed.

In consequence, although Southeast Asia was brimming with nationalist ferment, Portuguese Timor remained a backwater attracting little public attention. It took close to another 40 years and a lost generation of Timorese for Australia to commence, belatedly, the nation-building training and developmental assistance to its near neighbour, mooted so sensibly in February 1963 by the Atlanticist relic, Averell Harriman. Evatt, then frail, had barely three more years to live when Barwick presided over two of Australia's most unprincipled foreign policy decisions that led to so much suffering in West Papua and Portuguese Timor. Evatt's lonely gravestone at the Woden Valley Cemetery, Canberra, is a black granite boulder chiselled simply, 'Herb Vere Evatt Son of Australia'. In terms of standing for Australian values, albeit abrasively at times, few Australian foreign policy-makers in the post-war era can match the claim made for Evatt. As we shall see, the tragic history of East Timor is for Barwick, Whitlam and Downer, their millstone in history, not their monument.

After his time in the Menzies Government, in an extraordinary further chapter in his life, Barwick, as Chief Justice of Australia, advised extrajudicially on the dismissal of Prime Minister Whitlam[70] and delivered the key High Court judgement that extinguished the extra-territorial sea-bed claims of the Australian states and consolidated Canberra's power over the Timor Sea resources.[71] Only later, with the release of archives, has Barwick's significant role in diverting the riches of the Timor Sea to the corporate boardrooms of Australia and the

US been revealed. Barwick's failure to implement the Atlantic Charter values pressed upon him by Averell Harriman was a contributing factor in the ultimate tragedy that befell the Timorese peoples—a tragedy as great as, if not greater than, Whitlam's shallow deal with the corrupt General Suharto ten years later.

While providing foreign policy advice to Senator Don Willesee, Whitlam's long-suffering Foreign Minister, Nancy Viviani, who went on to become a distinguished academic, gained an informed insight into Whitlam's dictatorial foreign policy-making style. After Whitlam's dismissal and with the advantage of contemporaneity, Viviani recalled of Whitlam:

> He conceived a new role for Australia in international relations, and he wanted Australia to emerge from the shackles of past fears and parochialism and share his vision. He delighted in the untrammelled nature of the power involved in foreign policy making—he would not consult his cabinet on foreign policy issues generally, and did not on Timor, and he was loath to have such issues raised in Caucus.[72]

There are attempts, understandable perhaps, to gloss over the colossal foreign policy blunders within the region by two generations of Canberra foreign policy-makers. Gyngell's *apologia* is a recent example:

> [A]n emerging Australian foreign policy would have to embrace three broad responses to address the nation's fear of abandonment. First, Australia could continue ... to embed itself with what Robert Menzies famously called 'our great and powerful friends'. Second, it could seek to shape the region around it to create a more benign environment. Another prime minister, Paul Keating, would explain that as seeking Australia's security 'in and not from Asia'. Finally, as a state with weight in the world but not enough of it to determine outcomes through its own power, it could support and try to influence, in its own interests, the organisations, rules and norms—the generally accepted standards of behaviour that most states apply to themselves and others—which together make up a rules-based international order.[73]

Gyngell then claims that elements 'of all three responses have been woven into the fabric of the foreign policies of every Australian Government since'. Later chapters of this book illustrate how self-deluded Gyngell's 'rules-based order' is. It is sobering to consider that Gyngell, a member of the high-achieving 1969 diplomatic trainee intake, finished his career as a leading Australian foreign policy and intelligence adviser. Gyngell unashamedly acknowledges the lack of effective rules-based control over Australian foreign policy in his summary of post-war foreign policy. This 'free for all' is quite unlike other Western democracies governed either by constitutional instruments and/or human rights legislation, with effective parliamentary oversight. In language reminiscent of the confidence that international law could be ignored, shown by his predecessor Richard Woolcott in 1974, Gyngell asserts:

> Most Australian prime ministers take to international policy questions with a sense of exhilaration and relief. The exhilaration comes from the subject matter—the world—which is important and interesting. The relief stems from the fact that, for the most part, this area of government policy is free of the grinding slog of developing and passing legislation and the frustration of dealing with state governments and domestic stakeholders. The constitution is refreshingly unambiguous regarding the Commonwealth government's responsibility for external affairs, providing prime ministers and their foreign ministers with an opportunity to play on a large stage and to influence great causes.[74]

Gyngell does no more than emphasise the problem in a democracy when maverick foreign policy is emboldened by government and opposition sharing a common outlook that is contrary to rules-based order. Tange's memoir of the policy tension between himself and Prime Minister Menzies related to Menzies' belief that the US would defend Australia from any threats in the region. In an assessment that resonates today, Tange and Australian defence strategists believed that 'the reaction of the Americans could not be predicted'. This was at odds with Menzies' outlook that Australia could not stand alone without a military alliance with the US.[75]

Unquestioningly, Gyngell accepts the Menzies outlook as the first of the three strands of Australia's 'enduring' foreign policy. But in an observation apposite to this day, Tange reveals the lack of parliamentary oversight over the tension between the Menzies focus on nationalism as a communist threat and his own more considered view: '[M]y assessment of Australia's best interests in respect of nationalist struggles against colonialism, and the antipathy of some Asian leaders to Australia's military alignments, had sometimes differed markedly from [Menzies'] view when he encountered these issues in the Commonwealth and read reports of their treatment in the United Nations'.[76]

5
THE AUSTRALIAN CONTINENTAL SHELF—DECLARING BOUNDARIES

The loss of intellectual integrity in Australian foreign policy-making became evident during Sir Garfield Barwick's years as Minister for External Affairs. Australia's devious abandonment of its historical purpose as a new democracy so that it could secure access to petroleum resources that might rightly belong to a likely emerging state an hour's flight from Darwin was a profound breach of trust to the Australian people. Shrewdly, Barwick did not articulate why he saw no merit in a staged devolution of power in Portuguese Timor. The United States recognised the need to bring Salazar around to a more enlightened outlook, but, because of NATO sensitivities, wanted Australia to take the lead. It is not difficult to find a reason why Barwick, in contrast to other US–Australia bilateral issues, was driving in a different direction from that of the US Administration.

A reason appears to lie in an awareness of Barwick and his advisers of the petroleum potential of the Australian Continental Shelf. Before entering the Australian Parliament and becoming Attorney-General in October 1958, Garfield Barwick QC had a leading commercial practice at the Sydney Bar and was well connected to Australian mineral and petroleum prospecting boardrooms. As Attorney-General and Minister for External Affairs, he had chaired the Standing Committee of the Commonwealth and State Attorneys-General, whose agenda from 1962 included the regulation of offshore petroleum exploration. Barwick knew that the Portuguese had failed since 1963 to protest the granting by Australia of exploration permits for areas of the Continental Shelf in the Timor Sea beyond the limit of exploitability formula set by the 1958 Geneva Convention on the Continental Shelf.[1]

Reflecting a consciousness of unresolved federal/state offshore territorial issues and competing Portuguese and Australian claims of sovereignty over areas of the Australian Continental Shelf in the Timor Sea, Australian mineral and petroleum exploration companies had begun seeking assurances as to their legal right to prospect offshore. As Attorney-General, Barwick had endorsed advice by former Solicitor-General Sir Kenneth Bailey that Australia should lay claim out to the extremity of the Australian Continental Shelf, arguably within Portuguese waters. As there had been no resolution since Australian Federation in 1901 of the question whether the states or the federal government had offshore territorial jurisdiction past the three-mile limit, exploration companies were seeking reassurance on both constitutional and international legal grounds of their prospecting rights.

On 29 May 1964, the Australian Cabinet authorised the Minister for National Development to write to assure Woodside (Lakes Entrance) Oil Company N.L.[2] in regard to 'the outcome of the Cabinet discussion on 14 April 1964 on their joint submission dealing with offshore minerals' and 'the importance of encouraging the companies to go ahead with their exploration programmes'.[3] The background to this decision concerned approaches made to the federal government by oil-prospecting consortia granted permits in 1963 by the Northern Territory Administration to explore areas of the Timor Sea adjacent to Timor out to which the Australian Continental Shelf extended. Since the Northern Territory was governed from Canberra, the issue was for the federal Cabinet.[4]

Oil Companies Seek Sea Boundary Assurances

An earlier Cabinet submission dated 10 April 1964, dealing with exploration for petroleum on the Australian Continental Shelf adjoining Portuguese Timor, records an enquiry about exploration rights from Woodside (Lakes Entrance) Oil Co. N.L. and its associate company, Mid-Eastern Oil N.L., which makes clear Barwick's early role in the Timor Sea petroleum prospecting issue. The Cabinet Minute records that:

> These two Australian companies have recently arranged for The Burmah Co. Ltd and Shell Development to become partners in exploring these areas, which are in the Timor Sea near the W.A./N.T. border. The areas covered by the permits issued by the Northern Territory extend beyond the 100-fathom line into deeper waters of the Timor Trough between Timor and the North-Western coast of Western Australia. I have been advised by our colleague, Sir Garfield Barwick, as Attorney-General, that this aspect was considered at the time the permits were issued. The conclusion then reached, with which Sir Garfield agrees, was that the areas covered by the permits are part of the continental shelf of Australia.
>
> Woodside asks for re-assurance from the Commonwealth Government that, in the event that it is determined that the Commonwealth has jurisdictions over these off-shore areas of the companies, that the Commonwealth would not vary the terms laid down by the State Government on the issue of such permits, to the detriment of the permit holder.[5]

The submission by the Minister for National Development W.H. Spooner continues: 'I feel strongly that some re-assurance to Woodside and its associate company are called for and that we should go as far as we possibly can to remove any air of uncertainty so that the companies concerned may be encouraged to go ahead with their programme'.[6] It indicates that a joint submission was to be prepared for Cabinet from related ministries, but 18 months elapsed before the historic joint submission reached the federal Cabinet.

The 1965 Cabinet Decision on Maritime Boundaries

On 25 November 1965, the Minister for National Development Senator David Fairbairn, Minister for Territories Charles Barnes, and Attorney-General Billy Snedden, made a joint submission to the Australian Cabinet concerning Australia's maritime boundaries. Two of the ministers sought Cabinet approval for a recommendation that the issuing of exploration licences for areas that were arguably outside Australia's territorial jurisdiction should continue.[7] The Ministers advised the Cabinet that they were not in agreement on the Timor Sea issue. As both the Commonwealth and the Western Australian governments had been issuing exploration licences for the preceding two years in the Timor Sea area, the Ministers sought from Cabinet a decision whether 'Australia would continue to assert a legal right over certain areas to the north-west of Australia in the general direction of Portuguese Timor'.[8]

This submission from the three ministers appears to be the seminal Australian Cabinet document concerning the Timor Sea maritime boundary delimitation issue. It sought a decision with respect to international boundaries, especially in the Timor area, and domestic boundaries between the Northern Territory and Queensland and between Papua and Queensland.[9] The Cabinet debate is illuminating for the crosscurrents disclosed. The Attorney-General said that the 1958 Geneva Convention on the Continental Shelf provided that, where the same continental shelf is adjacent to the coast of opposite countries, the boundary could be determined by agreement or, in the absence of an agreement and unless another boundary was justified by special circumstances, the boundary was the median line.[10] The Australian Cabinet was told that the Convention did not define 'continental shelf with precision',[11] saying only:

> the sea bed and subsoil of submarine areas adjacent to the coast but outside the area of the territorial sea (12 nautical miles), to a depth of 200 metres or, beyond that limit, to where the depth of the superjacent waters admits of the exploitation of the natural resources of the said areas.[12]

Fairbairn acknowledged that 'special circumstances' in the Convention allowed Australia to define the limit of its continental shelf in accordance with the development of exploration technology.[13] However, the submarine area of the Timor Trough was an area of very great depth, and he acknowledged that technology at that time might not justify a claim under the Convention to areas within the depths of the Timor Trough,[14] then arguing that:

> The time will almost certainly come (and probably quite soon) when depths as great as those of the Timor Trough will be exploitable. *It will then be possible to argue that there is here a common continental shelf between Australia and Timor and that therefore the applicable international rule is the median line* [emphasis added].[15]

The Attorney-General informed the Cabinet that in the past, acting upon advice received from Sir Kenneth Bailey, Solicitor-General at the time, Australia had issued exploration permits that went beyond the 200-metre depth line on the basis that the permit areas were a prolongation of the Australian Continental Shelf. He added that his predecessor, Sir Garfield Barwick, had expressed the view that, from an international standpoint, the areas were part of the continental shelf of Australia and 'that nothing should be done to encourage operators to lodge an application with Indonesia'.[16]

It is revealing to stray briefly from the Cabinet discussion and examine the background to the comments attributed to Barwick. Barwick's opinion sat oddly with Australia's accession to the Convention on the Continental Shelf establishing that shelf prolongation alone did not confer exclusive jurisdiction on a coastal state when two countries shared a common shelf. Bailey, a long-time law professor at the University of Melbourne, had, as Solicitor-General, supported the Australian delegation to the United Nations conferences on the Law of the Sea that culminated in the 1958 suite of international maritime conventions on the Continental Shelf, on the Territorial Sea and the Contiguous Zone, on the High Seas, and on Fisheries and the Natural Resources of the Sea.[17]

A principal working document for the Geneva Conference was the *Report on the Regime of the High Seas* by the International Law Commission (ILC) of the UN. The Commission at first considered defining the 'continental shelf' in terms of shelf at a depth to the limit of exploitability. The United Kingdom argued that this introduced an element of vagueness and that a fixed depth would provide certainty. Having considered the views of member states, the ILC adopted a fixed depth of 200 metres, while acknowledging that a limit then sufficient for all practical needs 'has been fixed because it is at that depth that the continental shelf, in the geological sense, generally comes to an end'. It went on to recognise that it had adopted 'a geographical test of the continental shelf as the basis of the juridical concept of the term' and had departed from the 'strict geological connotation of the term'.[18] As we shall see, there was, with the adoption of the 'limit of exploitability' test in the 1958 Convention on the Continental Shelf, a return to the geological concept of the 'continental shelf'.

The ILC's August 1953 report to the UN General Assembly led immediately to two proclamations on 11 September 1953 by the Australian Governor-General, both of which adopted the exact wording of Article 2 of the Draft Articles on the continental shelf in the ILC Report.[19] The first proclamation asserted, in similar terms to the Truman proclamation of 28 September 1945, that, in accordance with international law, Australia had sovereign rights over the sea-bed and subsoil of the continental shelf contiguous to the Australian coastline and the coasts of any Australian overseas territory. The second proclamation replicated the first claim on behalf of the Australian Territory of New Guinea.

The urgency associated with the Australian proclamations related to public opposition, evident from parliamentary debates of that period, to the resumption of unregulated Japanese pearl fishing off the northern coasts of Australia. The *Pearl Fisheries (No. 2) Act* was enacted on 17 September 1953, six days after the two proclamations. A further proclamation issued on 25 September 1953 fixed the limits of the continental shelf, for the purposes of the Act, being all the Australian Continental Shelf north of the parallel 27°S latitude, effectively all shelf to a 200-metre depth north of a Carnarvon–Brisbane line.

It was against this background that the 1965 Cabinet was reminded that Indonesia and Portugal had not made any protest in relation to Australia's adoption of the 200-metre contour line when it passed the *Pearl Fisheries Act 1952* (Cth), followed by the 1953 amended Act and proclamation of 25 September 1953 to define pearl fishing areas.[20] While the passage of the Acts might have engaged Papuan and New Guinean, Dutch and Indonesian interests from the Torres Strait across to the uniformly shallow Arafura Sea, the reference to Portugal failing to protest was disingenuous, as Indonesian traditional fishing was for shallow-water *trepang* in the uniformly 200-metre Arafura Sea, and the depths of the Timor Sea across the Timor Trough over which Portugal might contemplate jurisdiction were far deeper than 200 metres. The pearl-fishing legislation and the proclamation of 25 September 1953 were both intended to regulate the resumption of Japanese pearl diving down to 100 fathoms in waters directly north of Australia and not in the Timor Sea, but the Portuguese Consulate in Sydney monitoring parliamentary debates may have perceived Australian intentions as such. Moreover, during the debates on the Bill the 100-fathom limit was acknowledged as the extent of Australia's claimed jurisdiction.[21]

The Minister for National Development acknowledged that exploration companies required certainty of title as exploration costs were significant. The Cabinet was reminded that the Commonwealth was providing subsidies to assist petroleum companies to conduct exploration in the Timor Sea. Nevertheless, Senator Fairbairn maintained the view that a median line should be adopted, beyond which Australia should abandon all claims.[22] His Department pointed out that, in early 1965, Britain and Norway concluded an agreement that adopted a median line between the two countries as a boundary for their shared continental shelf. Fairbairn noted UK Foreign Office advice that 'the whole of the submarine area between the two countries, including the channel deeper than 200 metres, was treated as "continental shelf" as defined in the Convention' and that the Foreign Office had stated that Britain had suggested 'division on median line principles partly because of the clear preference for this method shown in the Continental Shelf Convention and partly because it seemed that in the absence of "special circumstances" (whether of an historical or geographical nature) division on median line principles was fair to both parties'.[23]

Snedden and Barnes were of a contrary view, arguing that, unlike Britain and Norway, special (Convention) circumstances were available to Australia, because the continental shelf between Indonesia, Portuguese Timor and Australia was arguably broken by the Timor Trough. Despite this argument by Attorney-General Snedden, Fairbairn, after illustrating the way Norway and Britain had resolved their boundary on equitable principles, submitted that a median line should be adopted. The Attorney-General, supported by Barnes, argued that Australia should claim the whole of the continental shelf down to the foot of the trough, although they did not support their proposal by reference to expert geological opinion. Foreshadowing a prior occupation without protest claim, the Attorney-General argued further that all existing permits that crossed the median line in the Timor Sea should be endorsed with maximum publicity.

The Cabinet Submission asserted that Australia and Timor 'did not have a common continental shelf'.[24] The Cabinet resolved to 'confirm existing permits and claim jurisdiction over areas covered by these permits without prejudice to such rights as Australia may possess over areas beyond'. The expression 'areas beyond' suggests that, despite international treaty law, the Attorney-General still believed Australia to have scope for a shelf prolongation claim.

Although the Australian Bureau of Mineral Resources, Geology and Geophysics (BMR) had conducted a reconnaissance survey of the Australian Continental Shelf in 1965, a full gravity, seismic and magnetic survey was not undertaken until 1967.[25] Before the 1967 survey, the position adopted by the BMR was:

> Knowledge of the geology of the north-western continental shelf of Australia is restricted to inferences drawn from geophysical and bathymetric data, extrapolation from onshore geological knowledge (particularly structural trends, stratigraphy, and nature of the basement), and from one stratigraphic well: Ashmore Reef No. 1 ...
>
> In the Timor Sea area, the continental shelf extends 200 to 300 miles out from the coast, and geophysical results show that it contains depths of 20,000 feet or more of relatively young sediments, probably mainly Tertiary and Mesozoic ... The shelf is terminated to the north-west by the Timor Trough ... a north-east elongated feature which is up to 10,000 feet deep and which separates the Australian continent from the young orogen of the Timor-East Celebes Geosyncline ...
>
> Audley-Charles ... has concluded, after a study of the Permian and Mesozoic systems of Timor and north-western Australia (the Canning and Bonaparte Gulf Basins), that the spatial relation of these two land masses has remained relatively constant through the Permian and Mesozoic. Mineralogical considerations and evidence of large-scale slumping indicate that the autochthonous Permian rocks of Timor were probably derived as detritus from the Kimberley region, Timor occupying a shallow shelf area. During most of the Mesozoic, the paleo-geographic evidence is interpreted by Audley-Charles as indicating that Timor and Australia were separated by a wide, shallow sea.
>
> Crustal down-warping in the Upper Cretaceous resulted in the formation of a major geosyncline centred on Timor. The area between Timor and Australia ... would have become an infra-neritic zone at this time. The Timor Trough was formed, according to Audley-Charles ... during the lower Eocene, when this deep-water zone contracted and moved south and Timor emerged as an island.[26]

The Ministers' submission noted the view of the Department of External Affairs that 'it would be undesirable to pursue the negotiation of an agreement with either Indonesia or Portugal'. Indonesia was considered unlikely to envisage any solution other than a median line. On the other hand, negotiations with Portugal were regarded as 'quite feasible', but the Department saw a difficulty in Australia dealing with Portugal as this could be interpreted as accepting Portugal's right as a colonial power to 'share in decisions permanently affecting the future of the area', which might discourage Indonesia from engaging in negotiations with Australia: 'Cabinet in February 1963, expressed the view that no practical alternative to eventual Indonesian sovereignty over Portuguese Timor presented itself. As a consequence, it would seem preferable not to seek negotiations with Portugal'.[27]

The 1963 and 1965 Cabinet Submissions were turning points on the Timor Sea issue. Geostrategic considerations affecting Indonesia were persuasive, as was the Attorney-General's view that jurisdiction 'asserted without challenge constitutes a powerful claim in international law'.[28] The 1965 Submission noted that Australian exploration permits had been issued outside the median line and beyond the 200-metre depth line for more than two years, 'with adequate publicity and without challenge'.[29] The submission implicitly recognised the limit of exploitability test in the 1958 Continental Shelf Convention that bound Australia as it did Portugal. No exploitation of the sea-bed in any of the areas disputed subsequently by Portugal and Australia took place prior to 1974 when the first Troubadour Well was sunk, long after Portugal had officially protested.

As Senator Fairbairn's Department administered the BMR (later Geoscience Australia), some significance may be attributed to his advice to Cabinet that there would be a time when the Timor Trough would be exploitable and it would then be possible for Australia, Portugal and Indonesia to argue that there was a common continental shelf between Australia and Timor.[30] Fairbairn's advisers were well aware that drilling technology had advanced considerably since the 1958 Convention had been drafted. Just a week after the 1965 Cabinet submission it was revealed that Shell had drilled core holes as deep as 3790 feet, with sedimentary penetration going more than 750 feet below the sea-bed. The limit of exploitability test in the 1958 Convention on the Continental Shelf was, through technological advances, allowing Australia to justify the granting of permits in deeper water over the Australian Continental Shelf. It was, as Senator Fairbairn observed, only a matter of time before Australia's claimed jurisdiction approached the coast of Timor Island.

While it must be assumed that the Australian Cabinet was conscious of the potential hydrocarbon resources of the Australian

Continental Shelf, described succinctly in the BMR's 1967 Report,[31] Senator Fairbairn was sounding an early and prophetic warning that the 'two shelves' argument might not resonate in informed scientific circles or with Indonesia and Portugal. The submission warned that 'confrontation' could arise if Indonesia commenced issuing permits and authorities to foreign search organisations and that such a situation could present 'a decision to go to war with Indonesia over a doubtful claim (possibly for the benefit of a foreign oil company) or whether to repudiate our responsibilities to the people [exploration companies] who had taken action and incurred great expenditure in good faith under our [Australian] grant'.[32]

At the time David Fairbairn, a war veteran, and Barnes and Snedden made their submission, Australian forces were deployed in Malaysia and Borneo against Indonesia. Fairbairn appears to have viewed a median line as more equitable and less provocative. The opinion of former Solicitor-General Sir Kenneth Bailey, unsupported by reference to geological advice, was that to concede a median line would erode Australia's 'broken shelf' position under the Convention on the Continental Shelf and that, as Australia had to date asserted jurisdiction without challenge, this constituted 'a powerful claim in international law'.[33]

The Minister for Territories, however, supported the Attorney-General and, thus, the opportunity for Australia to adopt a principled approach was missed.[34] Despite the clear terms of international law, successive Australian Governments maintained a claim to areas of the Timor Sea that are outside Australia's territorial jurisdiction. As recently as 2014, Australian Attorney-General Senator George Brandis stated:

> You are also wrong, Senator Xenophon, in the suggestion that a median line is the only applicable principle. One thing your question ignores is the fact that the Australian continental shelf to the northwest of Western Australia runs beneath the Timor Sea very close to the southern coastline of East Timor. The median line principle, or the equidistance principle as it is sometimes referred to...may be displaced by other circumstances.[35]

A recent summary of the scientific literature on the Timor Trough cites geological surveys that leave the 'two shelves' Australian position in doubt.[36] The 1965 Cabinet decision nevertheless appears to be the genesis of the acceptance in 1971 of a median line in most of the Arafura Sea between Australia and Indonesia.[37] The 1965 Cabinet submission observed that the Arafura Sea was mostly at a depth of 200 metres or less and that a median line with Indonesia would be appropriate under the Convention on the Continental Shelf. This formed the basis of the Australian negotiation position for the eventual treaty in 1971 with Indonesia affecting the Arafura Sea.

The position reached shortly after the 1965 Cabinet decision included the staged adoption in domestic legislation of the 1958 Convention on the Continental Shelf and the 1958 Convention on Territorial Sea and the Contiguous Zone, both of which were favourable to Australian continental shelf ambitions.[38] Sections 7 and 12 of the *Seas and Submerged Lands Act 1973* authorised the Governor-General to declare by proclamation the limits of the whole or any part of the territorial sea, or of the continental shelf of Australia. After its accession to the 1982 UN Convention on the Law of the Sea (UNCLOS), Australia formally repealed the two 1958 Conventions it had brought into domestic law.[39]

Despite the failure by Portugal in the early years to formally protest implied Australian encroachments arising from the grant of exploration permits, international law does not support the notion that Australia somehow acquired territory while Lisbon slept. The second limb of any such argument by Australia would be that, upon independence, Timor-Leste became the successor to and is bound by the territorial concessions made during the colonial period by Portugal. International customary law supports the notion of restraint by states in undelimited maritime areas, particularly if the area is in dispute between states.[40]

In the late 1960s and early 1970s issues concerning Australia's claimed maritime domain attracted widespread commentary, including that from public servants and Australian academics. Harders observed in 1968 that Commonwealth and state legislation relating to offshore petroleum adopted the definition of 'continental shelf' from the Convention on the Continental Shelf. In the *Petroleum (Submerged Lands) Act 1967–1968* the Commonwealth delineated areas of the North-West Australian Continental Shelf that 'have or during the period of the operation of the Act will have, the character of continental shelf within the meaning of the Convention'. The Act was accompanied by a map depicting 'adjacent areas' within which 'as technology expands' the sea-bed could fit the definition of 'continental shelf' within the 1958 Convention. A perusal of the map annexed to the Act suggests that Australia's legislative claim went no further than the 200-metre line.[41] While the 200-metre line in areas of common shelf between states less than 400 nautical miles apart was subsequently displaced by the 1982 Convention on the Law of the Sea, nothing in the 1967–68 Australian legislation put the Portuguese Government on notice of any claim exceeding that permitted by the 1958 Shelf Convention.

Although the debate about the Australian Continental Shelf maritime boundary elicited no formal *démarche* by the Portuguese, the record shows that by the early 1960s Lisbon sought, through the Portuguese Embassy in Canberra, to monitor the grant of exploration permits in areas known by Australia to be claimed and open to claim by Portugal. Australia had acquired a knowledge of Portugal's position on the Timor Sea issue during the *travaux préparatoires* on the 1958 conventions, but sought to differentiate Australia's claim by reliance on the alleged exercise of jurisdiction without challenge and on suspect geomorphology.[42] Later, in 1974–75, knowing that Portugal would likely challenge the Australian claims, Canberra joined with Indonesian President Suharto and cut short that prospect.

Portugal did not have a full diplomatic mission in Australia before 1960, but it seems clear that by 1967 Portugal was on notice of the Australian enlarged claim out to the limits of the continental shelf in the Timor Sea. Sir Kenneth Bailey's advice some years earlier, if quoted correctly,[43] that jurisdiction claimed by Australia without challenge (by Portugal) constituted a powerful argument in law appears to inform the Australian claim to this day. This 'squatter's rights' assertion, so emblematic of the Australian colonial condition, may overlook the specific exclusion of territorial waters already claimed by states from the ambit of Australia's original 1953 proclamation and the effect of the 1958 Convention on the Continental Shelf and the Convention on the High Seas made the same year.

Moreover, Portugal's claim that Timor Island is an uplift on the Australian Plate, and thus sharing to the south in the Timor Sea the same continental shelf as Australia, appears to pre-date the grant of exploration permits by Australian authorities. The record shows that Australia actively sought for many years to limit Portugal's diplomatic presence in Australia. Soon after Portugal opened a full diplomatic mission at Canberra, Lisbon began to seek information, including maps concerning exploration permits issued by Australian authorities.

The first of these maps for high seas remote and unpatrolled from Lisbon's far-flung colonial outpost was provided in 1968.

As Portugal and Australia had both maintained a conventional position in international law relating to territorial waters supplemented by their accession to the 1958 Conventions, Portugal may have reasonably felt secure.[44] It may be recalled that after the 1958 Convention, and to the extent to which Portuguese Timor shared the Australian Plate, territorial rights were appurtenant and, until the UNCLOS in 1982, there were no formal processes for continental shelf claims to be recognised. Neither Timor-Leste nor Australia has ever lodged a claim under UNCLOS in relation to the disputed area of the Timor Sea under which the Australian Plate moves north with Timor Island, a geological uplift from the sea-bed, on its back.[45]

Indonesian Regional Hegemony

Senator Fairbairn's reference in the 1965 Cabinet Submission to war with Indonesia was in the context of *Konfrontasi*. In a Cabinet review of the strategic basis of Australia's defence policy, the Minister for Defence, Senator Shane Paltridge, referred to Indonesia's aim to achieve 'regional hegemony and to eliminate from the area the British or any other influences inimical to her'.[46] He further submitted that 'Indonesia is likely to interfere increasingly in Papua-New Guinea. She will be encouraged in this, as Australian policies become increasingly a focus for attention from countries opposed to the continuation of colonial status for dependent territories'.[47] Paltridge advised that 'the only direct threat to Australia and its territories is from Indonesia, ... [whose] geographical location coupled with their extravagant claims to airspace and maritime waters poses a threat to Australia's defence interests, particularly our air and sea communications to South-East Asia'.[48]

Thus, by the mid-1960s Australia had developed a forward military posture to counteract perceived Indonesian territorial ambitions.[49] Military confrontation between Britain and Indonesia developed into undeclared localised warfare involving British and Australian forces. Tension with Indonesia sharpened British interest in the prospect of an Indonesian move on Portuguese Timor. Policy differences concerning relations with Indonesia and Timor's future emerge from a report to London by Britain's Deputy High Commissioner at Canberra:

> Main comment of D.E.A. [Department of External Affairs] is that Australia would not regard Portuguese Timor as being of strategic concern to her and, from this point of view would acquiesce in it passing to Indonesia. They consider the main threat to Timor is not overt aggression but Indonesian subversion. Departmentally D.E.A. are disposed to view that matter should be handed over to United Nations trusteeships for settlement. This is however reversion by D.E.A. to ideas which they had worked out following quadripartite talks on South East Asia in Washington in 1963. Prime Minister's Department then refused to take matter far with Sir Robert Menzies on that basis, as it was politically impracticable in their view for any Australian government with Indonesia behaving as she has in the last two years taking any move which could be presented as encouraging Indonesia to expand further.[50]

As *Konfrontasi* waned by the end of the 1960s, unrest in Lisbon and in various Portuguese colonies focused some attention at the UN on the future of Portuguese Timor. At the time of Australia's participation in the decolonisation work of the Fourth Committee of the UN affecting Portuguese Timor, Australia was interested in securing favourable boundaries in the Timor Sea before Indonesia sought further territory.

Portugal and Australia Issue Overlapping Exploration Licences

Australian Foreign Ministry files contain early expressions of interest by the Portuguese Government with respect to the well-publicised search for oil in the Timor Sea. On 30 October 1967, Portugal's opening gambit appears to have come from the Chargé d'Affaires in Canberra, who wrote to the Minister for National Development asking for copies of Australian laws concerning phosphate mining, advising that he was taking the opportunity to request 'any information you may have available on the search for oil off the coast of Australia particularly on the North-East coast'.[51]

On 30 June 1967, the BMR released a comprehensive map and inventory of all exploration permits issued on the Australian Continental Shelf. Relevantly, this showed a series of exploration permits covering areas of the Timor Sea past the 200-metre contour line and extending past a median line with Portuguese Timor in areas later disputed with Timor-Leste. The permit holders in the three main grants were Woodside (Lakes Entrance) Oil N.L., Mid-Eastern Oil N.L., Burmah

Oil Company of Australia Ltd, Shell (Development Australia) P/L., and in two instances BP Petroleum Division Australia Ltd.[52] The early involvement of these companies is significant and suggests an appreciation of the gas analyses; it is addressed in a later chapter dealing with the helium issue.

On 31 December 1968, a US-registered company, Oceanic Exploration, applied to the Portuguese Government for exclusive exploration rights for five years in areas of the Timor Sea north of the median line with Australia. Twelve months elapsed before the Portuguese Ambassador in Canberra called on Australian External Affairs officials and advised that he had been requested to ascertain the exact boundaries of the titles granted by Australia on the Australian Continental Shelf. In response, the Portuguese Embassy was supplied with a map entitled 'Petroleum Exploration and Development Titles, 31 December 1968' and a letter advising that they were 'granted in accord with the Geneva Convention on the Continental Shelf and their outer limits were determined by the limits of exploitability'.[53] On 25 May 1971, the Ambassador called again at the Department of Foreign Affairs and expressed his government's view that the Geneva Convention on the Continental Shelf should apply to the maritime boundary issue between Australia and Portuguese Timor. A Senior Assistant Secretary in the International Legal Division advised the Ambassador that in Australia's view there was no common continental shelf between Australia and Timor, there being two shelves separated by the Timor Trough, which constituted the boundary; there was therefore no question of negotiating a common sea-bed boundary.[54]

The Two Shelves Morphological Argument

For a reason or reasons not apparent from incomplete Foreign Ministry records at the National Archives of Australia, Sir Laurence McIntyre, former Australian Ambassador to Indonesia and then Deputy Secretary of the Department of External Affairs, requested a report on the geology of the Timor Trough from the BMR. On 5 March 1970, the BMR forwarded a report noting that the Australian Continental (Sahul) Shelf descends gently at 200-metres depth

> to a shelf edge at a depth of about 400 metres. Beyond this point an undulating continental slope occurs, underlaid by a continuation of the gently dipping Cainozoic sediments noted beneath the shelf ...

> [T]his slope merges into the undulating floor of the Timor Trough at a depth of about 2500 metres ... a sedimentary sequence of Cainozoic age can be followed from beneath the Sahul Shelf through the Timor Trough and presumably to Timor itself ... This in turn suggests that the Timor Trough was initiated in the Middle or Upper Tertiary, perhaps 15 to 20 million years ago, by down warping and subsequently by more severe structural deformation. Uplift of Timor as well as other islands of the Sunda Shelf was largely the result of structural deformation and uplift beginning about this time.[55]

Geologically, the Bureau's research concluded that the Island of Timor was a structural uplift on the same sedimentary rock of Cainozoic age that lies beneath the Australian Continental (Sahul) Shelf: 'There appears no evidence of oceanic crust in the floor of the Timor Trough and hence no evidence to suggest there is any continental margin between the Sahul Shelf and Timor'. Having established that there was no substance to the argument that two continental shelves faced each other across the Timor Trough, the BMR then proffered an alternative argument based not on geological grounds but on the superficial appearance of two shelves. Australia's diplomats readily adopted this morphological pretension. From the Bureau's 1970 report onwards, 'morphology' remained the ploy used by successive Australian political leaders.

Morphology, the study of the shape and form of things, helps us describe how things look rather than the geological substance of what is being observed. Regrettably, the BMR departed from a geological explanation and proposed a polemical argument that obscured the fact that, as two great continental plates ground into each other millions of years earlier, the unbroken Australian Plate buckled downwards at the Timor Trough, uplifted Timor Island and descended into a subduction zone north of Timor Island. Two submerged surface layers of each Plate, namely the Sahul and Sunda Shelves, were ancient superficial elements of the collision. While there was an unbroken Australian plate, being the floor of the Timor Trough beneath them, the two residual elements of the collision could be said to 'look like' two continental shelves. The enticing 'form rather than substance' proposal from a premier science institution was:

> Clear separation of the Sahul and Sunda Shelves ... by the Timor Trough should be established on morphological rather than on

geological grounds. Marked differences in structural environments on either side of the Trough and probable major structures in the trough itself provide both support and reason for the physical separation of the Sahul and Sunda Shelves in this region.[56]

There is early evidence that the Department of External Affairs seized upon the so- called 'morphological' argument to support a 'two shelves' case, without acknowledging, in terms of the Continental Shelf Convention, that the two surface shelves faced each other above the real shelf, namely, the Australian Continental Shelf. When the Portuguese Ambassador met External Affairs officials in Canberra on 24 April 1970, he advised a senior official, Laurence Corkery, that Lisbon was now aware that Australia had granted permits on the Australian Continental Shelf 'well beyond the median line'. The Ambassador sought some explanation. In his record of the conversation, Corkery noted that, after referring to the International Court's decision in 'the North Sea Case [sic]',[57] he informed the Ambassador:

> It was our contention that there are two continental shelves in the area and accordingly we never felt required to discuss with others the delimitation of the Australian Continental Shelf in that area. The position was quite different in the Arafura Sea and to the south of West Irian/Papua. Here there was a common single continental shelf and we had recently had informal and exploratory discussions with Indonesia.[58]

The Ambassador immediately proposed talks between Portugal and Australia. The kindest interpretation to place on Corkery's response is that while there are certainly 'two shelves in the area', both were riding on the top of the Australian Plate. Correctly interpreted, the BMR's advice was that the Australian Sahul Shelf is a surface feature of the Australian Plate as it descends continuously beneath the Sunda Shelf upon which Timor Island is uplifted. It was unfortunate that in introductory comments the BMR's report used the word 'intervening' in a morphological (terrain) sense rather than a geological sense, suggesting to a lay reader there was a geological break: 'Although bathymetry in the region lacks detail, the broad morphology of these continental shelves and intervening Timor Trough is clear'.[59]

In other words, while there was a deformation where the Australian Shelf buckled under the Asian (Sunda) Shelf, the geological structure of the Australian Shelf continued all the way to Timor. Geoscience Australia has had ample time to concede that the February 1970 report of its predecessor, the BMR, was, in geological terms, misinterpreted. As we shall see, the compromise of a government agency the public should be able to trust becomes worse by the 1990s when, as others suggest, state-sponsored theft of petroleum resources from beneath the Timor Sea commenced.

Unsurprisingly, with no substance to the Australian two shelves argument, the record shows that Australia did its best thereafter to avoid engagement with Portugal until petroleum prospecting companies began to press for certainty of title to their exploration licences. A proposal in August 1970 from the Australian Embassy in Lisbon that an opportunity be taken to discuss Timor Sea issues during a proposed visit by a Portuguese Minister and officials to discuss emigration matters resulted in Corkery consulting Sir Kenneth Bailey, who had been on the distribution list for the February 1970 BMR report. The Australian Chargé d'Affaires in Lisbon was told not to encourage any visit.[60] In a cable to the Australian Embassies at Jakarta and Lisbon on 11 September 1970, Canberra advised that it was probable 'that we shall propose to Indonesia pending developments in international law over the next few years we put on side for the time being any arrangement between Indonesia and Australia about submerged lands in the area between Timor and Australia'.[61] The cable concluded with advice intended for Lisbon to the effect that the same applied to Portugal. By this time arrangements were practically complete for the BMR to oversee a geophysical survey of the so-called continental margin in the Timor Sea, of which Indonesia or Portugal were not advised.

Public debate concerning the Timor Sea maritime boundary issues with Indonesia and Portugal soon meant that Australia could not lie doggo and at the same time deal with explorations requests by petroleum companies. On 23 October 1970, a geographer's endorsement of the two shelves argument, which made no reference to scientific opinion, entered the debate: 'Only along Australia's north coast does the question of a shared Continental Shelf arise … The Shelf is shared with Papua from Longitude 141°E to 145°E and with Indonesia from Longitude 133°E to 141°E … The boundary in the Torres Strait close to the Papuan coast is not drawn on median principles'.[62]

The commencement of a shared concern in Canberra and Jakarta over Portuguese exploration approvals in the Timor Sea is evident by the end of 1970 with a cabled report from the Australian Embassy in Jakarta advising that Indonesian Foreign Minister Dr Mochtar Kusamaatmadja, a law of the sea expert, had informed Embassy officials that the co-ordinates of the concession granted by Portugal to the US-registered Oceanic Exploration Company extended into areas of the continental shelf claimed by Indonesia and, apparently, by Australia having regard to the Schedule to the *Petroleum (Submerged Lands) Act 1967*. Mochtar was reported as saying that the Indonesian Government was very unwilling to enter boundary talks with Portugal because this might give implied endorsement to a colonial regime.[63]

At this stage, the shared concern was about colonial Portugal, particularly after the election of Prime Minister Whitlam in 1972, not maritime boundary delimitation.[64] On several occasions, following Prime Minister McMahon's notorious 'two shelves' claim in the Australian Parliament on 30 October 1970,[65] Dr Mochtar, in his mixed roles as Foreign Minister, Justice Minister and expert, pressed for a median line in the Timor Sea and derided the Australian 'two shelves' claim. In 1972, as Australia sought to complete boundary negotiations with Indonesia, he made Indonesia's view crystal clear to Australian reporter Peter Hastings.[66]

Hugh Wyndham, former head of the Law of the Sea Section in the Department of Foreign Affairs, recalls that on the first day of the negotiations with Indonesia in Jakarta, Australia maintained the view it had advanced in the UN Seabed Committee—that Australia enjoyed sovereign rights to the edge of the continental margin and that in the Timor Sea the margin ended in the Timor Trough.[67] On the second day of the negotiations, Wyndham recalls that Dr Mochtar made a counter-suggestion:

> It was close to an acceptable boundary from our point of view, but included within the area under Indonesian jurisdiction a sliver of the Australian continental shelf. We explained to the Indonesian side that, in the context of the Law of the Sea negotiations, it was important to us to retain sovereign rights to the Australian continental shelf. We suggested varying the line slightly to protect our position, in return for which we would concede to Indonesia an equal area on the continental slope. We assured the Indonesian side that we had no information as to the mineral or petroleum potential of either area.
>
> With this small adjustment, the line suggested by Indonesia was accepted and forms the basis of the treaty with Indonesia (and making

something of a mockery of Mochtar's claim, some years later, that Australia had 'taken Indonesia to the cleaners' in 1972).[68]

Wyndham's recent recollection that Australia had assured the Indonesians during negotiations, which concluded in October 1972, that it had no information as to the mineral or petroleum potential of 'either area' has long been suspected and is highly significant. That the Indonesians may have been duped about the resources issue by certain members of Australia's negotiation team appears to be the conduct Dr Mochtar was subsequently so unhappy about, not merely the positioning of the boundary line as assumed by Wyndham.[69]

In truth, the BMR had commenced in late 1970 a comprehensive marine geological and geophysical survey of the entire continental margin in the Timor Sea. Using the latest techniques and specialist international marine survey firms, the BMR, with a huge budget, began reporting to the Department of National Development and, in turn, the Law of the Sea Section of the Department of Foreign Affairs in 1971 on the mineral and petroleum potential of the surveyed areas claimed by both Indonesia and Portugal. The survey was conducted ostensibly 'on the high seas' by French consultant firms employing foreign-flagged vessels utilising for the first time, with Defence cooperation, satellite GPS technology. As neither Indonesia nor Portugal had satellite 'vision', the survey, lasting nearly three years, was untroubled by any complaints of intrusion on Indonesian and Portuguese sovereign territory. The survey, one of the first of its kind for accuracy on such a large scale, was supplemented by airborne astro-triangulation measurement systems, including the use of certain passive satellites and US global positioning satellites.

On 2 November 1970 and again on 15 April 1971, the Portuguese Ministry of Foreign Affairs delivered formal Notes to Australia's Lisbon Embassy requesting consultations with the Australian Government regarding the Timor Sea maritime boundaries. Although Australia failed to respond positively to the 1970 request, archived records reveal that officials continued to take a keen interest in the petroleum issue. This interest was not matched, at least from the records available, by any expression of like interest in verifying the Australian claim by presenting the Portuguese with the alleged strong argument based on geomorphology. Australia then, as now, kept its under-sea survey information to itself and remained reluctant to engage in informed scientific debate about the claimed two shelves.

With the comprehensive sea-bed survey well underway, Australia delivered a Note on 25 May 1971 to the Portuguese Embassy in Canberra raising, finally, the possibility of negotiations on a Timor Sea boundary between the two countries. Before responding, Portugal commenced researching the Australian position. At no stage was either Indonesia or Portugal informed of either the scale or the interim results of the BMR's Timor Sea sea-bed survey, which included deep-sea sample dredging, highly sophisticated contour surveying and magnetic resonance charting for tell-tale petroleum mineralisation. A letter sent on 23 July 1971 by the Department of Foreign Affairs to the Department of the Interior, in response to requests from the Portuguese Embassy for maps showing the areas of concession grants by Australia in the Timor Sea, is revelatory. It suggests that the Department of Foreign Affairs had not misinterpreted advice from the BMR:

> We confirm that we received from the Department of National Development on 21 July 1971 four sets of maps from which the green median line has been removed ... As discussed ... it was decided that the black dotted line showing the 200 metres bathymetric contour, which line would have been difficult to remove from the maps, did not in any case prejudice our position vis-à-vis the Portuguese. It was also decided that it was impracticable to attempt to show the outer edge of the continental margin. Not only is there a problem of definition, but we have insufficient geophysical knowledge of the area to allow a useful line to be drawn.[70]

Stonewalling the Portuguese did little to assuage concern in petroleum company boardrooms. On 24 August 1971, Shell and Burmah Oil advised the Department of National Development that they intended to drill beyond the median line between Australia and Timor, but on the Australian side of the 200-metre depth line. This advice is noted by the Department official who had sent the 23 July letter quoted above, Jonathan Thwaites, a lawyer who survived the vicissitudes of diplomatic service and surfaced again in the Timor Sea debate nearly 30 years later as Director, Sea Law, Environmental Law and Antarctic Policy, in the Australian Department of Foreign Affairs and Trade.[71]

By late 1972, following the Timor Sea boundary agreement with Indonesia on 9 October 1972 and with the Law of the Sea Conferences approaching, Australia was anxious to determine Portugal's position on maritime delimitation. Australia's mission at Lisbon was instructed to ascertain the outlook of Portugal's Law of the Sea team and reported that Portugal's delegation was still resolving issues of principle.[72] Australia then delivered a formal Note to the Portuguese Embassy referring to Australia's request two years earlier on 25 May 1971, advising that Australia had settled boundaries with Indonesia and proposing early talks, if not by June 1973.[73]

The Department of Minerals and Energy, headed by Canberra mandarin Sir Lenox Hewitt, had oversight of exploration activities in the Timor Sea and was working closely with oil majors. To 'facilitate discussions with Portugal regarding the sea-bed boundary', Hewitt's Department forwarded on 14 June 1973 'a brief assessment of the economic potential of the Northwest Shelf opposite Portuguese Timor', prepared by the BMR. Although the BMR Report adopted the same geological appraisal that had led to the finding that there was no evidence of a continental boundary between the Australian Plate and Timor, the BMR appeared to be at ease in its conclusion:

> In summary, the existence of petroleum potential and indeed specific targets to be tested indicate prime importance of continued national sovereignty over the 200 metre shelf in the area opposite to Portuguese Timor; the same petroleum potential extends beyond the 200 metre shelf beneath the continental slope and, although we have insufficient data at present to delineate specific targets, we should aim to extend national sovereignty as far as practicable down the slope.[74]

The correspondence was circulated to, among other recipients, the Australian Embassy at Jakarta, from where Australian Ambassador Richard Woolcott circulated his now notorious cable, analysed in the next chapter, urging the government to regard Indonesia as a better prospect for a negotiated solution than Portugal. Shortly afterwards the Australian Government notified Portugal through the Portuguese Ambassador in Canberra that Australia had granted overlapping rights on the continental shelf. Portugal refused to recognise Australian approvals that were north of the median line and proposed talks fell into abeyance.[75]

Meanwhile other forces were at work on Australia. Now heavily engaged in the long-running UNCLOS, the Australian delegation to the Second Committee had circulated, on 16 July 1973 during UNCLOS III, a joint working paper with Norway dealing with delimitation issues. Predictably, aware of the petroleum potential, Australia was pushing for the inclusion of a natural prolongation formula for sovereignty over the continental shelf. Japan, then about to conclude boundary negotiations with Korea, was not slow to react. On 31 July 1973, a senior member of the Japanese delegation to UNCLOS III visited Canberra and advised the Australian Government that the natural prolongation formula could lead to an inequitable situation for Japan with China, as the concept might allow China to claim sovereignty over China's shelf to a point quite close to Kyushu and Okinawa. Japan was in favour of a median line formula.[76]

By the time Indonesia had invaded Portuguese Timor in December 1975 following Whitlam's and the Ford/Kissinger meetings with General Suharto, it had settled on a median line in the Arafura Sea in 1971 but had conceded in 1972, based on other political considerations and a lack of knowledge of the petroleum potential, the Australian contention that the sea-bed boundary between the two countries could lie along the southern incline of the sea-bed in the Timor Trough, well north of a median line. In this manner, and certainly from the time Jakarta learnt that Indonesia had been duped and failed to assert mistake of fact and/or treaty-making fraud, Indonesia effectively lost any future claim to that portion of the massive Greater Sunrise Field that might lie east of a lateral sea boundary out from the south coast of Timor Island.

This conclusion could be wrong if Indonesia did complain formally that the 1972 treaty was secured unfairly by Australia concealing its knowledge of the sea-bed petroleum potential. As ever, the relevant Departmental files have not been released under the *Archives Act 1983*. If Indonesia had complained, was there an underlying motive behind negotiations with Australia over the Timor Sea petroleum resources after the Indonesian takeover of Portuguese Timor? Was a resolution of this issue premised upon Australia agreeing to share with Indonesia the resources out to the median line within the now notorious 'co-prosperity zone'? Whether negotiation of the subsequent 1989 Timor

Gap Treaty with Indonesia included settlement of a complaint by Jakarta over the 1972 treaty has not been disclosed and remains speculative.

Portugal, which had been actively involved with the drafting processes for UNCLOS, argued that the boundary between Portuguese Timor and Australia should lie along the mid-line between Australia and Portuguese Timor. This argument was consistent with broadly agreed international law with which Australia professed to agree during the UNCLOS *travaux préparatoires*, but in practice avoided by relying upon an argument based on morphology. That Australia's Department of Foreign Affairs should adopt an argument based, morphologically, on how things looked rather than how things were in substance was entirely consistent with the now settled culture of deception within that Department.

6
POST-COLONIAL ABANDONMENT—AUSTRALIA AND THE INDONESIAN OCCUPATION OF TIMOR-LESTE

By mid-1972 dissension within the Organisation of the Oil Exporting Countries (OPEC) had rung alarm bells in the West. Arab OPEC members imposed an oil embargo in October 1973 in response to United States arms supplies to Israel. The embargo lasted for close to six months, causing many countries to reassess their vulnerability to an oil shock. The governments of William McMahon (1969–72) and Gough Whitlam (1972–75) had moved to improve Australia's energy security by expanding the grant of exploration permits and providing scientific support from Commonwealth agencies. Steps were taken to strengthen Australia's claims in the Timor Sea, although the use of the word 'strengthen' is problematic; the proposition that Australia had a claim to strengthen suggests that Australia had a legitimate claim that could give rise to a dispute. No dispute had arisen regarding Australia's right to control the Australian Continental Shelf sea-bed out to a median line with Timor.

As we shall see in chapter 15, Australia had no valid basis for a claim north of the median line. Acceptance by commentators that Australia has a 'claim' tends to give legitimacy to an ambition without foundation in international law. Australia's Law of the Sea advisers, following International Court judgements on maritime claims throughout the

1960s, were aware that sooner or later Portugal was likely to put an end to Australia's exploration permit encroachments in the Timor Sea. As already noted, Australian policy towards Portuguese Timor rested on Cabinet decisions in 1963 and 1965 that regarded the colony as incapable of economic self-sufficiency and likely to be absorbed by Indonesia, provided this was preceded by an act of self-determination.

Australia succeeded in 1972 in negotiating a boundary line with Indonesia well north of the median line. Indonesia, largely unaware of the petroleum potential of the sea-bed it was conceding, wanted Australian support for an archipelagic claim to inland seas. After this favourable result,[1] a wholly different and sinister policy basis for not opposing an Indonesian takeover of Portuguese Timor had emerged. Although Prime Minister Whitlam had formed his own autocratic opinion that Portuguese Timor belonged in the Indonesia area, his dealings with Suharto were overlaid by behind-the-scenes diplomatic gameplay to induce Indonesia to take over Portuguese Timor so that Australia could negotiate another favourable maritime boundary across the Timor Gap. As we shall see, both Whitlam and certain advisers were acting contrary to more principled advice from within Whitlam's own Cabinet and from Department of Foreign Affairs head, Alan Renouf.

While Indonesia conceded a maritime boundary line in the Timor Sea east and west of Portuguese Timor well north of a median line, Australia knew that any attempt to link the gap between Indonesian territorial boundaries along the same line would be met by Portugal's claim, based on principles of international law, to a median line. Australia knew an independent Timor-Leste would likely be tutored by Portugal to adopt a similar approach. This belief was heightened when Australia became aware that Portugal had granted on 31 January 1974 a petroleum prospecting concession to the Oceanic Exploration Company. The concession comprised an area of 60,070 square kilometres, including portions of the adjoining Australian Continental Shelf Portugal was entitled to claim. In June and August 1974, Australia's Woodside Petroleum reported successive successful exploratory wells in the Troubadour area of the continental shelf north of the median line within Portugal's 200 nautical mile territory.[2] On 13 February 1975, hydrocarbon deposits were reportedly found after Portuguese-approved exploratory drilling southeast of Timor within Portuguese Timor territory.[3]

By this stage, pressed for certainty by petroleum exploration interests, Australia had become vigilant about the Timor Gap embracing the Portuguese coastline of East Timor where Australia had issued encroaching exploration permits. A view emerged in Canberra that, if Australia agreed to a median line with Portugal, Indonesia might be encouraged to seek a renegotiation of the 1972 agreed boundary with Australia.[4] Weighing up the pros and cons of whether Australia should persevere with negotiations with Portugal gave reason for Australian diplomats to follow political events in Portugal.

The Carnation Revolution

After Prime Minister Salazar was incapacitated by a stroke in 1968, his deputy, Marcelo Caetano, continued the Estado Novo (New State) dictatorship in Portugal until he was removed by a group of left-wing military officers within the Armed Forces Movement when they launched their 'Carnation Revolution' on 25 April 1974. Álvaro Cunhal, a communist, and Mario Soáres, a socialist, returned from exile to join a provisional government. Soáres became Foreign Minister on 15 May 1974 and went to London shortly after the coup where he met British Foreign Secretary James Callaghan and invited him to pay an early visit to Lisbon. Ten days earlier the subject of Portuguese Timor had come up in Canberra when Foreign Affairs Secretary Alan Renouf met with British High Commissioner Sir Morrice James. Renouf was recorded as saying that he was 'increasingly exercised by the implications of the change of regime for Timor' and had asked for a Defence Department assessment but found that they had not attempted one, but would consider it:

> Renouf was trying to counteract a tendency in his own department to assume that the best future for Timor would obviously lie with Indonesia; he saw no reason why the principle of respect for the wishes of the inhabitants should be overridden in order to 'hand over' Timor to the Indonesians who would only make a terrible mess of it. If you have any material on Communist influence in Portugal since the coup, or on the coup's implications for Timor, which we could be authorised to pass on a personal basis to Renouf, we should be most grateful.[5]

British and Australian Foreign Ministry appreciations of political events in Lisbon and Dili were subsequently shared. British archival releases throw further light on events in Canberra through the tumultuous

Whitlam Government era. While the international petroleum industry was aware of exploration prospects in the Timor Sea and British Petroleum had made its own assessment of maritime boundary issues, having retained Law of the Sea expert Sir Elihu Lauterpacht QC in 1970–71, there is no indication in contemporary UK Foreign Office archive releases that Australia shared its petroleum ambitions in the Timor Sea with the Foreign Office.

In July 1974, the Armed Forces Movement, endorsed by Soáres, had announced a proposed three-choice plebiscite for Timor-Leste, namely, mixed autonomy with Portugal, independence, or integration with Indonesia. Despite Timor-Leste's long and divisive decolonisation history at the United Nations, none of the major powers moved to have the proposed plebiscite supervised by the UN, where the West had lost the numbers. There was reason for this in Washington, London and Bonn, and generally within NATO, as Western intelligence agencies assessed the largely left-wing revolutionary movements in Portugal's colonies. Kissinger had visited London the same month to hold discussions with James Callaghan. Apart from its spies, the Soviet Union had significant intercept and eavesdropping success during this period. Such was Kissinger's belief in his own destiny, his addictive use of the telephone, particularly from his aircraft, and his recording and uplift, often in flight, to his archives of state-to-state meetings, that KGB Chairman Yuri Andropov became a Kissinger transcript junkie, even enjoying his egotistical private conversations.[6]

There is little doubt that Western intelligence reporting during the Kissinger era, as the US moved to support the Indonesian takeover of Portuguese Timor, was compromised. Fresh from Chile, such was Kissinger's zeal in supporting once again, now in the Indonesian theatre, anti-communist Generals, that Andropov had a likely box seat while contemporaneous reports to Kissinger from US Missions at Jakarta and Canberra no doubt followed the Whitlam show to its *dénouement* with the sacking of a Prime Minister. Australian intelligence reporting from Jakarta and Canberra in this period has probably never been more compromised than it was during the Australian intel-exchange feed to Secretary of State and National Security Adviser Henry Kissinger. Soviet access to any compromising Australian feed from and to Jakarta during the period of the Balibo killings, addressed further in this chapter, may have given Soviet services significant scope to entrap any officials vulnerable to exposure over the killings. Balibo records should have been reviewed once Britain's MI6 and other Western services learnt in 1992–93, following the Mitrokhin defection, of Soviet access to the Kissinger communications.

Further British reporting informed Australian services of events in Portugal. Cunhal and Soáres led an unstable coalition provisional government while the future of Portuguese Timor and other colonies hung in the balance. Cunhal had established diplomatic relations with the Soviet Union and Soáres had been entrusted to end the colonial struggles and foster self-determination in Portugal's remaining colonies. While this sent an anticipatory ripple through independence movements in the colonies and galvanised the UN General Assembly, Cunhal's links with Moscow provoked concern within NATO. British Foreign Office archives confirm that Australian services also moved into the equation in respect of the call to arms in East Timor by elements within FRETILIN (Frente Revolucionária de Timor-Leste Independente; Revolutionary Front for an Independent East Timor) including top-level liaison on the issue with the Indonesian State Intelligence Service (BAKIN). In December 1974, Whitlam visited his British counterpart Harold Wilson but appears to have learnt little from the British leader on how to handle Kissinger's preoccupation with perceived liberation communism.

Despite continuing street disturbances between communist and socialist supporters in Lisbon, Callaghan visited Lisbon on 6–7 February 1975 and was received warmly by Soáres. Callaghan briefed Soáres on East/West relations and the Middle East crisis, including an account of a recent meeting in Washington between Harold Wilson, Callaghan, President Ford and Henry Kissinger. Callaghan also met with Cunhal, who 'was at pains to emphasise that a communist-dominated Portugal would still welcome British investment; he was categorical in his forecast that the elected government would be a coalition one, and the communist party would play a part in such a coalition'.[7] Cunhal and Soáres soon split. Soáres was apprehensive that Cunhal, who during his 14-year imprisonment and exile had openly supported Soviet repression in Czechoslovakia in 1968, was planning to establish a Soviet-style communist government in Portugal.

The Stockholm Committee

Fearing a move by Cunhal, Soáres began to sound out empathetic socialist governments in Europe for support. Swedish Prime Minister Olof Palme took the running by suggesting to European Socialist leaders a meeting to discuss events in Portugal, to which the Social Democrat leaders of France, Britain, Austria, Denmark, Holland, Italy and Germany agreed. At the meeting in Stockholm on 2 August 1975, Willy Brandt, Chairman of the German Social Democratic Party and German Chancellor until he stepped down May 1974, called for the formation of a high-level friendship committee to guide the process of democratic socialism in Portugal. Harold Wilson's Labour Government in Britain, French Socialist Party Leader François Mitterand and other socialist leaders supported the proposal, which led to the establishment of the Stockholm Committee.[8]

Over time the Stockholm Committee succeeded in mollifying US concerns and helped achieve a consensus in the West on the need to support Soáres with strategic intelligence interventions, advice and funds.[9] There was some apprehension in the West that Soviet strategy towards the upheavals in Portugal was the first direct attempt by Moscow to establish a communist State in Western Europe since the outcome of the agreement with Stalin at Yalta that effectively assured the Soviet Union of a free hand in establishing a *cordon sanitaire* in the East stretching from the Baltic republics through the Ukraine, Poland and to the Crimea.[10] The Western response led to a realisation in Moscow that any attempt by Cunhal's supporters at a Soviet-style takeover in Portugal would attract a robust response by socialist governments and was doomed to fail. Kissinger provided the US assessment of communism in Western Europe,[11] while European leaders assured Washington that they could handle the situation without US provocation. Palme continued to marshal support for Soáres and within 18 months Cunhal's supporters were vanquished.

FRETILIN Seeks Power

With a measure of political naivety, FRETILIN's leaders in East Timor, including Mari Alkatiri, applauded events in Portugal and called upon other powers, including communist regimes, to support FRETILIN demands. Writing in 1986, James Mackie, then head of the Australian National University's influential Department of Political and Social

Change, claimed that a factor in the Indonesian takeover was the fear in Jakarta 'that East Timor might become a nest of communist influence, "another Cuba", on her doorstep'. His assessment continued:

> The charges that Fretilin leaders were communists or pro-Chinese may have been wildly exaggerated, but some Fretilin leaders were speaking in a way which certainly justified that suspicion. Even if the charges were false, it was obvious that an independent East Timor would have to look overseas for economic assistance and perhaps also political support from some quarter, since the economy was hardly viable and the political structure rudimentary, and China or Vietnam or Russia seemed to be the most likely candidates for such a role ... East Timor might become a haven for Indonesian communist exiles.[12]

FRETILIN's more extreme elements, either unaware of the ideological struggle in Europe or insensitive to Soáres' efforts to establish, with Western support, a socialist democracy, failed to emphasise FRETILIN's ideological difference from FRELIMO's one-party Marxist–Leninist control in Mozambique. For his part, FRETILIN's José Ramos-Horta travelled abroad widely, including to Indonesia and Australia, where the media called him 'Secretary of the Political Committee of FRETILIN– the Revolutionary Front for Independent Timor', which did little to garner conservative support for the independence cause. In December 1974, Ramos-Horta had meetings with the Australian Foreign Minister, Senator Willesee, and parliamentary committee members. In relation to Indonesian fears of a subversive communist element emerging in Timor, he vigorously denied during a meeting with Foreign Affairs officers in Canberra that his movement was communist-inspired or shared any communist aspirations.[13]

FRETILIN Executive Committee member Abílio Araújo, encouraged to visit the United Kingdom by Soáres, was the first FRETILIN leader to pay an 'official' visit to London. There he addressed a group of members of parliament and journalists in the House of Commons' Committee Room, where he was reported to have said that FRETILIN wanted 'the establishment of a transitional government in Portuguese Timor, recognised by all powers, and a negotiated timetable leading to full independence'.[14] Ramos-Horta visited Canberra again in November 1975 as FRETILIN Secretary for Foreign Affairs, and called on the Department of Foreign Affairs and diplomatic missions, including the British High Commission.

On 25 November 1975, Ramos-Horta expressed concern at the tone of caretaker Prime Minister Fraser's characterisation in a radio broadcast of FRETILIN as 'communist', noting that neither the Opposition Foreign Affairs spokesman nor acting Foreign Minister Andrew Peacock shared that view. He claimed that FRETILIN now controlled all but 1% of East Timor and that the União Democrática Timorense (UDT) and Associação Popular Democrática Timorense (APODETI) had lost the war and therefore had no place at the international negotiation table. FRETILIN was willing to talk to the Portuguese whose sovereignty in East Timor they recognised, but continued postponement of talks might result in a unilateral declaration of independence by FRETILIN. The British High Commission pointed out to the Foreign Office the 'apparent difference of emphasis between the views of the caretaker Prime Minister and his Foreign Minister about Timor and FRETILIN ... [which] echoes the dichotomy which existed between the former Prime Minister Mr Whitlam and his Foreign Minister'.[15]

Efforts by Ramos-Horta and Araújo to reassure those concerned in Jakarta, the UN and Western capitals that there would be no FRELIMO-style internal party grab for power in Timor was soon undone when a small cohort of FRETILIN Central Committee members unilaterally, in both an internal party and international sense, declared independence on 28 November 1975. Whether prompted by the defeat of FRETILIN forces at Atabae the day before or the absence from Dili of key committee members, the surprise announcement of a perceived leftist, viewed by some as communist, regime change played into the hands of FRETILIN's critics. The Australian Foreign Minister promptly issued a statement that Australia did not recognise the FRETILIN declaration.[16] Thereafter, it was all downhill for FRETILIN, both with Portugal and within the Fourth Committee at the UN, where a vote on 3 December 1975 rejected FRETILIN's attempt, with support from Mozambique, to take Timor-Leste, now claiming independence, out of the Fourth Committee remit. Predictably, Indonesia took the opportunity to argue that peace had to be restored to allow the principle of self-determination, endorsed again on Portugal's initiative, to be implemented.

By this time, FRETILIN and Australia shared at least one thing—shambolic foreign policy. The Australian diplomatic response to the situation was summed up succinctly in a Foreign Office appreciation:

> It appears ... that Mr Whitlam's inclination has been to push the Portuguese and the Indonesians towards the absorption of Portuguese Timor in Indonesia. The Department of Foreign Affairs have been nursing the hope that Indonesian military intervention would not be necessary to achieve this end and that the people of Portuguese Timor would resolve the dilemma by a free vote for merger. The DFA believe that, whereas in the early days a quick and minimal intervention by Jakarta would have been possible, an overt military intervention would now be a costly and politically provocative undertaking.[17]

Ramos-Horta's reaction to the unilateral declaration of independence (UDI) was recorded by Portugal's Ambassador in London Dr Matias who had spoken by phone to his 'old friend' on 29 November 1975. According to Matias, Ramos-Horta had been surprised and upset by the premature declaration. Matias interpreted this as a victory by the more extreme elements in FRETILIN 'over the more conservative group led by Mr Horta. Dr Matias could not understand the reasoning behind the UDI since it looked, at any rate in the United Nations, as though events were going fairly well Fretilin's way'. The Foreign Office record provides a rare insight into Portuguese appreciation of Australian policy:

> I asked Dr Matias how he thought the declaration of UDI would affect the policies of the Australian government. He thought that the Australians were now faced with a potentially embarrassing situation for defence and political reasons. They had abandoned their forward defence strategy and might therefore be apprehensive of the presence on their very doorstep of a Fretilin controlled Timor, perhaps supported by 'elements further north in South East Asia with surplus war material'. (This reference was obviously to Vietnam which, he said, could, if it so wished, supply East Timor through Bacau airport.) ... Although Fretilin had plenty of ammunition, their prospects for re-supply were not particularly good ... Anti-Fretilin forces had only to wait until the ammunition ran out.[18]

In his semi-autobiographical *Funu*, Ramos-Horta explained the efforts he made throughout 1974–75 to broaden the independence movement. Although he anticipated a declaration of independence by January 1976 the unilateral declaration on 28 November 1975 took him by surprise while he was in transit for Dili in Darwin.[19] Upon his return to Dili, Ramos-Horta learnt that he had been formally appointed

Foreign Minister for the new republic. 'JRH' as he became popularly known, was fated for the world stage as a spokesman for devolution of colonial power under United Nations processes, democratisation and rule of law. After the death of Yasser Arafat in November 2004 JRH took the mantle as the longest-serving foreign envoy of any nation. The author recalls JRH's capacity to telephone without notice almost any world or former world leader or current foreign envoy. Ramos-Horta's efforts for justice and peace on the wider world stage are yet to be adequately chronicled.

By July 1976, after almost two years of political upheaval, a stable constitutionally elected Soáres-led government had emerged in Lisbon, but not so in East Timor. By then Whitlam, lacking the political nous and conscience of his socialist colleagues in Europe, had collaborated with Suharto to end the UN-Charter-protected rights of the Timorese peoples. This was contrary to the Department of Foreign Affairs' internal advice in February 1975 that an Indonesian move to occupy Portuguese Timor 'would fall into the category of outright aggression', contrary to Article 2(3).[20] But other shrewd minds in the Australian bureaucracy knew that this might provide Australia with the opportunity to solve Australia's long-sought petroleum needs. Whitlam could have been advised by those in Canberra, who had access to British Foreign Office appreciations, to adopt the tactics of the Stockholm Committee. There existed a willing and well-disposed group of Timorese nationalists with whom Whitlam, had he been thoughtful enough, could have engaged to work through a devolution of power.

Whitlam and his apologists have never explained two critically important issues. First, Whitlam's role in triggering a war of liberation—if it was not obvious, the Australian Department of Defence had advised that an Indonesian takeover would inevitably provoke a guerrilla war.[21] Whitlam's collaboration with unprovoked aggression was a fundamental breach of Article 2 of the UN Charter and a war crime. The second unexplained issue is why he and his staff, as self-styled social democrats, perceived no duty to protect fellow activists in Portuguese Timor in the event of an Indonesian takeover. If Whitlam and ALP Secretary David Combe believed they were fit to join their political cousins in the Stockholm Committee, why was their attitude so different towards the social democratic ideals of Ramos-Horta, Araújo, and other moderate FRETILIN political activists?

Suharto's ruthless suppression of perceived leftist elements in Indonesia was common knowledge. Indeed, in evidence to a parliamentary committee after the liberation of East Timor in 1999 Whitlam admitted that '[t]he Indonesians, particularly under Soeharto, were obsessed with communism. I had to hose down the idea that the communists dominated Fretilin or that China had an interest'.[22] Labor stalwart Tom Uren had earlier reminded the committee that during the anti-communist pogrom in Indonesia that had brought Suharto to power more than half a million persons died.[23]

Although the relevant Australian intelligence records are unavailable, it is clear from the reporting held on British files that the Australian Department of Foreign Affairs perceived no significant prospect of a communist regime emerging in East Timor. The political assessment being shared between Canberra and Whitehall revealed a politically inactive Chinese merchant element in Timor, an absence of any popular left-wing movement within the population outside Dili and Bacau, and no evidence of communist agitation from Portugal.[24] Although Australia and the US were collaborating closely in Jakarta, there is no evidence that Australia took any steps to press this assessment officially with Washington. There was little evidence to support a view that the FRETILIN leadership would create the Soviet or Chinese outpost in Southeast Asia feared by President Ford and Secretary of State Henry Kissinger. What Palme, Harold Wilson and other European socialist leaders had talked Ford and Kissinger out of during the foment in Lisbon was not attempted by Whitlam or his advisers with respect to the upheaval in East Timor.

While the Whitlam Government made a half-hearted offer to broker peace talks between the rival parties in Dili, Australia played no effective role in seeking UN intervention to avoid civil war an hour's flight from Darwin. Instead, Foreign Minister Willesee issued a statement enjoining the predominantly Western-educated elite in Dili to bury their differences, suggesting that Australia would support a plebiscite.[25] Whitlam misled the UN General Assembly by declaring his unqualified support for self-determination in Portuguese Timor and, when called to account much later, affected no role in his thinking at the time of the Timor Sea petroleum potential identified by his close advisers Lenox Hewitt and Richard Woolcott.

In evidence before the 1999 parliamentary committee, Whitlam claimed that all he had done was to adopt a 1963 Coalition Cabinet decision (pushed by his then conservative arch-rival Sir Garfield Barwick) that, as Portuguese Timor could not become self-sufficient, it should be absorbed by Indonesia, subject to an act of self-determination. In his evidence to the 1999 committee Whitlam conveniently made no reference to the pre-condition expressed in the 1963 Cabinet Decision. He was not challenged as to why he believed economic self-sufficiency was a pre-condition to the right for self-determination—a right he had so eloquently supported in his UN General Assembly speech, quoted later in this chapter. In any event, Whitlam surely knew that, following the discovery in 1974 of petroleum close to Timor, the 1963 Cabinet Decision was based on an outdated premise.

In retrospect, was Whitlam's claimed reliance on the 1963 Cabinet Decision just a convenient excuse for his failure to combat Kissinger's obsessive approach to perceived communism? While outspoken on the Vietnam War and critical of the Kissinger 'domino' theory of communism, Whitlam did little closer to home to counter the US Administration's support for an Indonesian takeover. Whitlam's claim in 1999 that he had to 'hose down' the idea that the communists dominated FRETILIN, or that China was involved, is not supported by the record. Predictably, weeks after the dismissal of the Whitlam Government, Ford and Kissinger gave the green light to General Suharto for the invasion of East Timor. The Soviet strategy of edging the US and its allies into unpopular and unwinnable liberation struggles had once again succeeded. Whitlam, ever critical of flawed US policy that had gifted Moscow and Beijing with one liberation war after another in Africa, South and Central America, Indo-China and now on Australia's doorstep, remained inexplicably silent as US policy moved towards a disastrous intervention by proxy in Timor. An answer may lie in Russian and Australian intelligence agency archives.

The Australian Department of Defence saw both the liberation war coming and internal political dissension in Australia arising. Looking now at the limited archival releases, nowhere in the fervid plotting between elements in the Australian Department of Foreign Affairs and the Whitlam clique was the Defence outlook addressed. As secret appreciations suggestive of an accommodation with Indonesian ambitions flowed in from Australia's Jakarta Embassy, the Australian Minister for Defence, Lance Barnard, relying on Joint Intelligence Organisation (JIO) access to cable traffic, wrote to Foreign Minister Don Willesee and to the Prime Minister warning that he was 'deeply disturbed by the present indications that the Indonesian Government is considering military action to seize Portuguese Timor'.[26] In a comprehensive JIO analysis, Barnard advised:

> Since our intervention on behalf of the Indonesians against the Dutch effort to regain control of the former Netherlands East Indies by military force, Australia has asserted an interest and status in the affairs of the neighbouring region. The abiding strategic importance for us of the archipelago to our north, extending from Atjeh in Sumatra to the islands of the South West Pacific, requires this. We cannot be, or be perceived to be, indifferent to developments affecting the nature and distribution of political power there and, in my view, we cannot accept that any other nation has the right unilaterally to change things by force.[27]

The principled position adopted by Australia's Defence bureaucracy in a vain attempt to counter plotting by Australia's diplomats in Jakarta and Canberra was yet another lesson about the danger of leaving Australia's national interests to those who treat principle like putty. Barnard's warning to the dissemblers selling out on Australia's long-term interests resonates to this day: 'I am not unduly disturbed by the prospect of a genuinely independent Timorese state. It would be poor and weak, but no more so than some of our South Pacific neighbours, and possibly with better prospects'.[28]

Although much is yet to be revealed of Australia's diplomats working against Australia's national interests again between 1998 and 2018, the time is long past for a showdown between those who dress principle with polemic and then conceal the outcomes and those who believe history may provide an important structural lesson for the future. As we shall see, in 1998 and later, Foreign Affairs officials plotted once again, outside proper Parliamentary oversight, to both hide and outplay defence intelligence assessments. In pursuit of ephemeral corporate foreign trade goals, Australia again abandoned any semblance of an exemplary humanitarian policy or a balanced national interest role.

Returning to FRETILIN's few days of glory following its UDI on 28 November 1974, officials of the Chinese Embassy at London called on the Foreign Office two days later and advised that China supported self-determination for Portuguese Timor. The officials stressed that they did not expect their government to recognise FRETILIN as the government of East Timor. The laconic Foreign Office note ended on a touch of humour:

> I stressed also that the people of East Timor had not so far had a chance to pronounce on their own future, and we did not see any justification for FRETILIN purporting to speak on their behalf. I asked what was the Chinese attitude ... Mr Lin said that his Government supported the struggle of the Timorese people for independence, without outside interference ... Mr Lin further said that the important thing was that the two super powers should not become involved. I said that I had seen no signs so far of either of them showing any desire to be involved. This observation was greeted with much hilarity.[29]

The Chinese approached the German Foreign Ministry with a similar message.[30] It is likely that a similar *démarche* was made in other Western capitals, not that it was in the interests of those in Washington or Canberra peddling the 'new Cuba' or 'Chinese domino' line to disclose China's disavowal.

An analysis of the Australian records, if they have survived and are ever released, may have to wait. What is self-evident is that, in the result, the existing Portuguese and the inevitable post-independence claim for a median line between Timor-Leste's southern coast and Australia was frustrated by force of arms by Indonesia, shrewdly portrayed below the horizon by Australia as the avoidance of a new Cuba. Significantly, Whitlam disclosed to the 1999 parliamentary committee that he knew in 1975 that a communist takeover in Dili was not a likely prospect.[31]

Although ASIS had sources in Dili, there is no evidence that Whitlam either instructed ASIS or took any steps to allay fears in Washington and Jakarta of a communist takeover. Learning that ASIS had a 'correspondent', Frank Favaro in Dili, so well placed as to have an Australian-registered light plane for use on the island, Whitlam reacted with real or feigned fury after his Foreign Minister told Parliament that his Department, meaning ASIS, had no connection with Frank Favaro. Willesee's denial of any official connection with Favaro, co-Australian owner of the Dili Hotel where visiting Australian journalists, diplomats and defence intelligence personnel usually stayed, was inept.[32] Although the denial was motivated to protect the Favaro family, it was unnecessary, as that family's friendly relations with visiting Australians were well known to the Indonesians. Whitlam's trite claim that the Indonesian Government might have been offended by the alleged recruitment of Frank Favaro as an ASIS source was both ridiculous and obsequious.

On 21 October 1975, Whitlam summarily terminated ASIS head Bill Robertson's contract. News of the sacking soon leaked, confirming effectively the widely held suspicion that Favaro was an Australian 'asset'. By this stage, three weeks before he dismissed the Whitlam Government, Governor-General Kerr, on receiving news of the sacking of his long-time friend Bill Robertson, had queried its legality. Robertson, treated so contemptuously by Whitlam and later by Fraser for not rehabilitating him, retired quietly. Close to his death, he lodged a commentary on his dismissal with the National Archives of Australia.[33] According to Fitzgerald, the Favaro incident refreshed Whitlam's rancour over belated advice he had received from Robertson four months after the 1972 election that Australian ASIS agents were acting as proxies in Chile for US interests after CIA staff had been expelled by the Allende Government.[34]

The opportunistic way Whitlam and his key advisers followed the US in exploiting Suharto's oversensitivity to left-wing agitation is sufficiently chronicled by other authors, save for a long overdue appreciation of two issues: firstly, the naïve role played by a handful of vocal FRETILIN activists and their left-wing supporters in Australia in strengthening the views of anti-communist critics in Jakarta and Washington, which China astutely tried to counteract; and secondly, the failure of the political leadership in Dili to present a united front, at least on the steps required for self-determination, to ensure that Timor gained the support the UN General Assembly voiced at that time for other Portuguese colonies.[35] After the Indonesian invasion, FRETILIN elements in the diaspora did turn to China for support at the UN, a factor that continued to influence US policy.[36]

Although Toohey says that there are no credible suggestions that the Soviets helped Labor,[37] an evaluation of any role Soviet intelligence services, successful at that time in penetrating Kissinger's circle and active in Canberra, may have played in the Whitlam court as *agent provocateur* in provoking another war of liberation in Asia may not be available until further archives are released. Key documents in the British Foreign Office Portugal files covering the Stockholm Committee during the

Whitlam, Wilson and Callaghan years have been removed and closed for 40 years.[38] While Woolcott's role was overt, conspiracy theorists have never identified any other voice in Whitlam's ear that led to an entirely predictable liberation struggle on Australia's doorstep. Such a struggle was what the Soviet Union wanted initially in Portugal and had fostered in Portugal's former colonies, particularly Angola. Tom McNally, Callaghan's political adviser, was attuned to Soviet tactics and a voice of reason in Callaghan's ear at meetings in Lisbon, Washington and Stockholm.[39] Tragically, the same play by an equally astute adviser in Canberra, if Whitlam had listened to the right advice from Defence, may have avoided the liberation war Moscow wanted[40] and got, and the genocide and oppression to come.

While Whitlam is often cast as accepting opportunistic advice from Woolcott and his followers in the Department of Foreign Affairs who were uncaring of strategic defence concerns and less than loyal to Department head Alan Renouf, there is no objective evidence that Whitlam was petroleum-driven. Woolcott's advice to Whitlam, evident so far from selective archival releases, lacks any Defence appreciation. Securing access to potential Timor Sea petroleum resources by favourable negotiations with Indonesia was Woolcott's proposal, supported by elements within Department of Foreign Affairs and by Department of Minerals and Energy head Sir Lenox Hewitt. How Australia might deal with the prospect of a liberation struggle on Australia's doorstep is not addressed in any of the available Woolcott cable traffic from Jakarta. Around this time, the British Ambassador at Jakarta, aware from his Defence Attaché of the prospect of Timorese resistance, appeared to be wary of Woolcott's judgement.[41]

Although Woodside, Burmah Oil and British Petroleum had secured concession rights in the Timor Sea and had sought legal advice as early as 1970 regarding the maritime boundary to be negotiated between Portugal and Australia, there is no indication in British Foreign Office files covering the period and released with few redactions of any awareness of an Australian tactic, advanced by Woolcott in Jakarta, to substitute Indonesia for Portugal so to advantage Australian petroleum exploration. This conclusion gains support from a report by the British High Commission of a lengthy discussion with Jim Dunn, Director of the Foreign Affairs Group, Parliamentary Library, in which Dunn reported on his recent visit to East Timor and the attitude of the local manager of Burmah Oil, 'who seemed gloomy about the prospects for Timor'. Dunn 'ridiculed the idea that the presence of oil was regarded as a possibility simply because it had been found in Indonesian New Guinea'.[42] That Dunn's appreciation went to the British Foreign Office without comment suggests that neither Dunn nor the High Commission were aware of the discovery of commercial petroleum prospects by the petroleum consortia in June 1974 at Troubadour-1. The absence of any reference to petroleum exploration in the very frank discussions between Renouf and British High Commissioner James suggests that the maritime boundary petroleum issue, seen as the pragmatic goal by Woolcott, was not a decisive factor, at least in Renouf's mind.

The objective evidence is that, although Whitlam continued to posture both in Parliament and at the UN about the right of the Timorese to self-determination,[43] two different strategies had been developed outside Cabinet by Whitlam and Richard Woolcott. Whitlam, in supreme hypocrisy considering his long-held opposition to imperialism,[44] simply regarded East Timor as belonging to the Indonesian sphere. Woolcott, aware of Whitlam's outlook, saw a strategic opportunity for Australia. Sadly, this was entirely consistent with those in the Department of Foreign Affairs who were filing the correspondence and file notes about the future of the Timorese people on files entitled *'Negotiations on Portuguese Timor Continental Shelf'*.

On 6 September 1974, Prime Minister Whitlam met President Suharto of Indonesia at Wonosobo. Contrary to the long-established Australian policy of supporting self-determination for Timor-Leste,[45] Whitlam expressed deliberately ambiguous views. First, he believed 'that Portuguese Timor should be incorporated into Indonesia. Second, this should happen in accordance with the properly expressed wishes of the people of Portuguese Timor'. He then said he believed 'that Portuguese Timor was too small to be independent'.[46] Suharto's response is recorded as a warning that an independent Portuguese Timor 'would become a thorn in the eye of Australia and a thorn in Indonesia's back'.[47] On 16 September 1974, Britain's Ambassador in Jakarta, Sir Willis Combs, reported that the Australian Ambassador had told him 'that during Mr Whitlam's recent visit to Indonesia he told President Soeharto that Australia would prefer Timor to be incorporated into Indonesia provided this could be done in a way which would satisfy International opinion'.[48] Alan Renouf recalled the outcome of the meeting between Whitlam and Suharto:

> The departmental brief upon East Timor ... said that Australia's policy was self-determination. The brief examined the possible integration of East Timor into Indonesia. It was concluded that if this were to happen through self-determination, slow and careful political development under Portugal would be best. In his talks with Suharto, Whitlam changed the policy. He told Suharto that an independent East Timor would be unviable and a potential threat to stability in South-east Asia. Integration with Indonesia was therefore desirable but the Timorese should ultimately decide their own future. Suharto said that Indonesia's preferred solution was peaceful integration. The two leaders achieved a large measure of agreement. Whitlam had, however, changed Australia's policy; the policy was now integration of East Timor with Indonesia but only through self-determination. The policy had become two-pronged and the two prongs might be irreconcilable. What was to happen if the Timorese opted for independence? Australia's new attitude lacked clarity ... Whitlam believed that an independent East Timor, non-viable and a source of instability in South-east Asia, would legitimately concern Indonesia, a country with which Australia had to have the best possible relations. Whitlam also felt that stability was more likely in regions where there were bigger countries; he had no time for 'mini-states'. Whitlam certainly did not want any more mini-states close to Australia in South-east Asia or the South Pacific. Hence, he did not want an independent East Timor; a merger with Indonesia was the only answer.[49]

After Whitlam returned to Canberra, a Department of Foreign Affairs Policy Information Report included reference to 'Australia having no special ambitions in Portuguese Timor', evoking a discussion among senior policy officers, one of whom thought the words sounded predatory. Graham Feakes suggested a rewording: 'Australia has important particular interests in Portuguese Timor (for example, in oil exploration) but we have no ambition to achieve a special position there'. With the substitution of the words 'delineation of the continental shelf' in lieu of 'oil exploration', Feakes' further draft became the Department's public position. David McLennan recalled that the phrase 'no ambition to achieve a special position'

> stemmed from our need to placate Defence who objected to our argument in the draft brief for the PM to the effect that P. Timor was of little

intrinsic interest to Australia. Our commercial and trade interests are minor. Our only substantial interest in bilateral relations is in delineation of the continental shelf. Our special interests stem from the problem of P. Timor as a factor in our relations with Indonesia.[50]

McLennan's comment is insightful. Clearly, the Department of Foreign Affairs was still at odds with the view advanced by defence policy-makers that the Australian strategic defence interest lay in a stable self-determined East Timor. This view was aptly summarised by William Pritchett of the Defence Department: 'Without prejudice to our own concern to see Indonesian strategic interests satisfied as well as our own, we would for our part, favour the emergence of the territory through self-determination, as an independent state'.[51]

The British knew that Whitlam had surprised his senior foreign policy adviser by coming out at his meeting with Suharto in favour of incorporation into Indonesia. Renouf confided his concern candidly to Britain's High Commissioner,[52] and again after Whitlam repeated his sell-out to Suharto on 4 April 1975:

> The Australian Government were in a serious dilemma. Their official and ostensible position was that there should be self-determination in Portuguese Timor. However, at their Townsville meeting, the Prime Minister had told President Suharto that Australia would not object if Indonesia absorbed Portuguese Timor: indeed, that this was the right and natural solution.[53]

Whitlam's apologists deny that he sold out on the principle of self-determination; Hocking, with little research, is content to refer to Whitlam's 'high posture'.[54] Whitlam's speechwriter Graham Freudenberg, writing 30 years after Renouf, claims that Whitlam made 'unremitting efforts' to give effect to the principle.[55] Among contemporary evidence is a US State Department cable dated 29 November 1974, which records the candid comment to a US diplomat by Foreign Minister Don Willesee that 'he regretted the way PM Whitlam had discussed Timor when he saw Suharto in October. Australians should ... certainly not encourage the Indonesians to act in a way that might be contrary to the will of the Timorese'.[56]

The more reliable contemporary record of Whitlam's inexplicable conduct is borne out in numerous despatches to London by British diplomats in Jakarta and Canberra who, like some of their colleagues in the allied intelligence and defence community (including Governor-General John Kerr), were monitoring with growing apprehension the antics of the Whitlam court, now suspected in some corridors of being naïvely responsive to Soviet influence. Suharto's fear of a communist takeover in Portuguese Timor is reflected in a secret cablegram from the Deputy Chief of the US Mission in Jakarta reporting on discussions with Malcolm Dan, his counterpart at the Australian Embassy, on 1 March 1975:

> Dan stated that Australians have been keeping GOI [Indonesian Government] abreast of GOP [Portuguese Government] thinking through a variety of channels, including intelligence. Therefore, he does not believe present GOI campaign of depicting GOP as failing to fulfil its commitment to cooperate with GOI, and Dili Government as communist-infiltrated can be attributed primarily to GOI lack of understanding of GOP position ... Dan shared our opinion that an important element in GOI evaluation of Timor is fear that GOP is unstable, and may turn further left, this making of dubious value any engagements on Timor it might make.[57]

On 5 July 1975, General Suharto met President Ford at Camp David and explained the advantage to Western efforts at curbing communism for Indonesia to absorb Timor-Leste.[58] Suharto's visit intersected with discussions taking place between Portuguese and Indonesian officials with respect to Jakarta's plans for the plebiscite.

Lisbon Offers Timorese Self-Determination or Integration

Although the military leaders in Lisbon had resolved in 1974 to support an independence vote, the 'integration with Indonesia choice' required consultation with Jakarta. On 5 October 1974, Suharto had authorised his long-time confidante General Ali Murtopo, then Deputy Chief of BAKIN, the State Intelligence Coordinating Group, to take over negotiations with Portugal. Murtopo met with military leaders at Lisbon on 14 October 1974 and found that integration with Indonesia was, at least in the minds of some of the Portuguese leadership, a real prospect. Commencing in London on 9 March 1975, Murtopo held a series of discreet meetings with Portuguese representatives continuing in Hong Kong (May), Jakarta (August) and Rome (November). Murtopo's consultation with Portugal was but an element in the strategic plan, Operation Komodo, developed by Murtopo and Suharto's military clique to ensure the takeover of Portuguese Timor in liaison with UDT and APODETI supporters.

Suharto's military clique was not alone in wishing to subvert the proposed plebiscite in Portuguese Timor. Following the 1972 OPEC crisis, the Australian media had given prominent coverage to Australia's search for petroleum resources of its own. In July 1974, FRETILIN's José Ramos-Horta was reported in the press by Peter Hastings, then affiliated with the Australian National University's Strategic and Defence Studies Centre, as anticipating that oil would be a source of wealth for an independent East Timor.[59] Soon after, the Melbourne *Age* reported Woodside Petroleum's successful drilling for oil and gas off the Timor Coast.[60]

In August 1975, Richard Woolcott, newly appointed Australian Ambassador to Indonesia, urged his Department to brief the Foreign Minister and the Department of Minerals and Energy on the advantage to Australia's petroleum interest in the Timor Sea for Indonesia to become the negotiating party on the sea-bed boundary in lieu of Portugal. Woolcott's oft-quoted cablegram, used in later years to impugn Australia's motives, is in its concluding words of lasting significance for an additional reason:

> We are all aware of the Australian defence interest in the Portuguese Timor situation but I wonder whether the Department has ascertained the interest of the Minister or the Department of Minerals and Energy in the Timor situation. It would seem to me that this Department might well have an interest in closing the present gap in the agreed sea border and this could be much more readily negotiated with Indonesia by closing the present gap than with Portugal or independent Portuguese Timor. I know I am recommending a pragmatic rather than a principled stand but this is what national interest and foreign policy is all about.[61]

Australia's ongoing misconduct in dealings with the impoverished Timorese suggests that Woolcott's revealing *modus vivendi* holds good to this day, despite self-deluded claims of Australia's long-standing support for a 'rules-based order', noted in the closing paragraphs of chapter 4. Australia, in both foreign policy and many areas of international humanitarian and civil liberties law, is one of Western democracy's least 'rules-based' societies.[62]

Whitlam gave no indication that he had effectively acquainted the Indonesian dictator Suharto with the *modus vivendi* for a repositioning acceptable to Australia of Indonesia's interests over Timor-Leste when he addressed the UN General Assembly three weeks later. Instead, in a lengthy polemic, he emphasised the principles of self-determination long espoused by Australia, proposing no practical means of ensuring an acceptable UN-supervised act of self-determination, as contemplated by the Menzies Cabinet in February 1963. With breathtaking hypocrisy, Whitlam said:

> An attempt by any State to bring about political or economic change in another through unconstitutional, clandestine, corrupt methods, by assassination or terrorism, undermines the rule of international law, encourages adventurism and anarchy, endangers world peace and turns quite quickly against even the most powerful nations who would seek to advance their cause by such methods.[63]

As the record shows, on 13 October 1975, Indonesian Government sources informally briefed Australian Embassy officials in Jakarta of President Suharto's intention to invade Portuguese Timor-Leste.[64] Because the British Foreign Office relied heavily on Australia for intelligence on Indonesian plans, the UK National Archives once again fill in gaps in Australian National Archives records, of which those released so far on the deaths of British, Australian and New Zealand born newsmen appear to be incomplete. It has long been regarded that not all details of the proposed Operation Komodo were reported to all in the Department of Foreign Affairs in Canberra.[65] Woolcott's now notorious cable of 17 August 1975 was followed a month later by a similarly pragmatic assessment by British Ambassador Ford revealing that Australian intelligence links with the Indonesian BAKIN were at the top and immediate. A secret and ultimately poignant report by British Ambassador Ford details top-level Australian and British Embassy knowledge of clandestine Indonesian military activity in Portuguese Timor and the chilling 'hurdle to be got over' by BAKIN:

> The only limitation on clandestine activity now appears to be of its exposure. The Indonesians are clearly worried about this. According to the Australians, President Suharto this morning told General Yoga, the head of Bakin, that he would not agree, for the present, to step up clandestine activities beyond their present level. A particular hurdle to be got over is a plane load of Australian journalists and politicians

who are due to visit Timor, apparently at Fretilin request, to investigate allegations of Indonesian intervention ... The information from the Australians is sensitive and should not be played back to them or repeated to other missions.[66]

Given the history of Indonesia's ruthless suppression of media dissent at home and in West Papua, it is surprising that Australia and Britain did not give more direct warnings to the media contingents that continued to arrive at Dili in September and early October 1975 in a blaze of publicity about alleged clandestine Indonesian military activity. More damning, given the top-level intelligence liaison between Australia and Indonesia revealed by Ambassador Ford, is the apparent failure to warn Lt General Yoga Sugama of the anticipated fallout were state-sponsored harm to befall foreign journalists. Clearly, the intelligence relationship, at least between Australia and BAKIN, was robust enough for such a *démarche*. Sugama was a skilled operator. He had paid a facilitated visit to Australia five months earlier in May 1975. With the Whitlam Government on the ropes, Sugama had met with Opposition Leader Malcolm Fraser and clarified alleged diffident views on self-determination for Portuguese Timor held by Shadow Foreign Affairs Minister Andrew Peacock.[67]

Since those handling Australia's intelligence links with BAKIN knew about Indonesian clandestine activities in Portuguese Timor and this had not been revealed to the Australian public, it is axiomatic that those handling the immediate link to BAKIN and Suharto understood the significance of a plane-load of politicians and journalists being a 'hurdle to be overcome'. The situation was very tense. President Ford, his Secretary of State Kissinger and, earlier, Whitlam were tacit participants in the clandestine takeover. Such information, combined with advice that BAKIN was likely to launch a media suppression operation, would have been dynamite, so far as the left wing of the governing ALP was concerned. Both BAKIN and ASIS sources in Dili were good. News of an expedition by an experienced news crew to the frontier at Balibo–Batugarde had circulated at none other than the Favaro hotel. There seems little doubt that a direct warning to Suharto, Sugama and Moerdani may have saved the lives of the investigating media team. It is for any inquiry to determine whether those dealing with BAKIN knew the news team was headed to Balibo and shared that knowledge.

Richard Woolcott, Australia's Ambassador in Jakarta at the time, backed the conclusion reached after a 2002 review of the Balibo killings by then Inspector-General of Intelligence and Security, Bill Blick, that the Australian Government 'had no intelligence material that could have alerted it in advance to the possibility of harm to the journalists'.[68] Ambassador Ford's record is at odds with Blick's conclusion and Woolcott's claim.

Suharto, Kissinger and Whitlam were on the same page and each was vulnerable to investigative journalism. Whitlam was saying one thing at the UN and to Australians while secretly leading Suharto on with statements at odds with his public stance. Britain was an informed onlooker. This may explain Ambassador Ford's turn of phrase and his enjoinder not to reveal BAKIN's plans to other Australian diplomatic missions that might report the matter to Canberra. It is difficult not to suspect that, outside regular Australian diplomatic channels, there was a sensitive feed into Canberra from a source within the Australian Mission, Jakarta. This may gain strength from the ominous significance, considering his ruthless record, of Suharto's concern, likely interpreted as an order, that potentially compromising clandestine activities not be exposed. BAKIN was well placed in Dili and it may be assumed the Indonesian Embassy in Canberra was monitoring the Australian media. It is known that Australian Embassy sources in Jakarta were advising Canberra of Indonesian troop dispositions. This culminated in cabled advice by Ambassador Woolcott on 13 October 1975, received from Indonesian sources, that Balibo was a target. Further advice revealed a force of 800 would advance, 'via Batugade–Balibo', on 15 October 1975.[69] Stone recalls that the head of Indonesian Special Forces, Major-General Benny Moerdani, had dinner with Ambassador Woolcott on Wednesday, 15 October 1975, informing him that Balibo would be attacked the following day.[70] The same day in a policy round-up an internal DFA Minute recorded: 'We would not be doing anything physically to prevent Indonesia from doing whatever it might believe it has to do. We would simply be asking the Indonesians to allow us publicly to disassociate ourselves from Indonesian military intervention'.[71]

On 16 November 2007, Sydney coroner Dorelle Pinch delivered findings that included evidence that Moerdani was being kept informed continually by his commanders of the whereabouts of the investigating news crew. At the same inquest Woolcott stated that he had no way of knowing whether the news crew were in Balibo. Presumably, Moerdani did not tell him over dinner.

Predictably, by the afternoon of Thursday, 16 October 1975, BAKIN cleared the hurdle; the five investigative newsmen at Balibo had been butchered like many of their cousins in Suharto's Indonesia. The elimination of the news team at Balibo and the remaining Australian journalist at Dili gave the plotters in Canberra and Jakarta a breathing space. The well-traversed record shows that the Australian Mission at Jakarta adopted BAKIN's line, namely the likely death of the journalists who 'knowingly entered a war zone' in 'cross fire'.[72] No mention was made of advance knowledge within the Australian and British Missions of a secret media suppression plan by BAKIN.[73] The UK National Archives provide compelling evidence successive Australian governments have continued to hide from various inquiries, including the 2007 inquest held in Sydney.

In recent Administrative Appeals Tribunal proceedings the Director-General of ASIS asserted that the disclosure of information sought concerning any ASIS role in the lead-up to the Balibo incident would harm Australia's national security and international relations.[74] Nothing illustrates better the tension in rule of law terms between the oft-cloistered claim of 'national interest' and the 'public interest' than the ongoing saga of the Balibo deaths.

Evidently, the Director-General seems unaware that Ambassador Ford's report to the Foreign Office, almost certainly derived from ASIS sources, is in the public domain. Accordingly, candid disclosure of the ASIS role may no longer be the issue. Culpability may now be assessed. Shibboleths about mosaic intelligence analysis militating against disclosure, because seemingly isolated disclosures of historic matters may enable a foreign agency to deduce wider issues, should be summarily rejected. If anything, the facts suggest that Indonesian intelligence services have been shrewdly effective in cultivating close working relationships, both in 1974–75 and again in 1998–2000. An inquiry should establish whether there is truth to the view that the Indonesian service, being aware, certainly of the public downplaying, and necessarily of the withholding of intelligence by Australia from the United States in 1999, was in fact privy to this treatment of our trusted ally in pursuit of a joint plan to preserve the Timor Gap Treaty. Specifically, who in the Australian Embassy in Jakarta and, it may reasonably be

Balibo Square with Balibo Fort in the background after the liberation in 1999. On the left is the ruined house where the murdered Australian, New Zealand and British journalists and camera crew were based. (The author traced the traditional ownership of the land and house and, with funds secured from Victorian Premier Steve Bracks, the house was purchased and restored as a community facility.)

Shirley Shackleton, widow of murdered journalist Greg Shackleton, and the author walk towards the house in which the murdered journalists and cameramen had set themselves up. An Australian flag painted on the front wall by the journalists was just visible under faded paint.

suspected, who in Canberra was 'in-the-loop' and took no action to prevent the elimination of the news team? For reasons expressed earlier in this chapter there may be good grounds for ASIO, Australia's counter-espionage service, to determine the extent to which, if any, any Australian officials involved in what may have been a long-running cover-up remain vulnerable to pressure from Russian and Indonesian intelligence services. Contrary to the Director-General's claims, some may argue, having regard to recent concerns, that bringing truth and closure to the Balibo issue may lessen the danger to national security of compromise of an agency by sources able to exploit complicity.

Doubtless, with the government of the day advised from the same quarter, there may be no move in Canberra to investigate an issue that is fundamental to moral and principled leadership. The baton may pass to the Attorneys-General in the UK, Victoria, New South Wales and New Zealand. Whether the New South Wales inquest should be re-opened is a matter for the relatives of the deceased and judicial and prosecuting authorities in that State. Given the reforms in Jakarta that have allowed significant conciliatory disclosures of Suharto era excesses further cooperative judicial processes between prosecutors in Sydney and Jakarta including the grant of any appropriate immunities may finally settle an issue that troubles many Australians not least those who still grieve.

Civil War
By August 1975 civil war had broken out in Timor-Leste. It had been a Portuguese colony for 400 years, and three main political groups had emerged, each with separate ideals for the future of the nascent nation. APODETI campaigned for integration with Indonesia. The UDT, formed in May 1974, favoured gradual independence from Portugal. Led by João Carrascalão, scion of an old Timor-Leste family, UDT formed an alliance with FRETILIN in January 1975. FRETILIN was founded by Mari Alkatiri, José Ramos-Horta and others on 20 May 1974 as the Associação Social-Democrata Timorense (ASDT), changing its name to FRETILIN in September 1974. The party, based on Leninist–Marxist ideals,[75] sought immediate independence from Portugal. FRETILIN's alliance with UDT disintegrated, culminating in FRETILIN's refusal to participate in a conference on decolonisation hosted by Portuguese officials in Macau in March 1975.[76]

On 11 August 1975, UDT supporters launched a pre-emptive armed attack on FRETILIN, whose counter-attack on 20 August 1975 is now the commemoration date for the founding of FALINTIL (Forças Armadas de Libertação Nacional de Timor-Leste: Armed Forces for the National Liberation of East Timor).[77] In the civil war that followed, many Timorese were killed in combat, executed as political prisoners, or displaced to West Timor.[78]

Early in the struggle, after divisions emerged within FRETILIN, Ramos-Horta was briefly imprisoned in Aileu and sentenced to death by the governing cadre. In marked contrast to his British Labour colleague Prime Minister Callaghan, Whitlam turned his back on Timor's social democrats and resolved not to become hostage in Australia's relations with Indonesia to 'the self-appointed leaders of the FRETILIN faction'.[79] Britain's High Commissioner at Canberra recorded:

> I understand from my DFA contacts that the consistent line on Timor taken so far by Mr Whitlam is now being challenged by Senator Willesee, following his return from New York ... I cannot see Senator Willesee winning this battle with Mr Whitlam, particularly when the relevant Branch in the DFA has consistently stressed the need to maintain the closest relations with Indonesia for short and long-term reasons—a view shared by Mr Whitlam.[80]

Britain's Ambassador at Jakarta reported a few days earlier on the wavering Australian policy position: 'I have the impression that the Australians' influence on the situation here is waning and that the Indonesians are becoming impatient with the flabbiness of the Australian Government'.[81] Worse was to come in November when the Counsellor at the British Embassy in Jakarta reported on two conversations, the first with an unnamed Australian diplomat, who

> explained that the Embassy had tended to take its lead from the Australian Prime Minister in that the aim of Australian policy towards Portuguese Timor was to do what it could to ensure that Indonesia achieved its aim of integrating Portuguese Timor into Indonesia without this harming Australian/Indonesian relations. He said officials in the Department of External Affairs in Canberra took the same line; however, the Secretary of the Department and the Minister took a more 'moral' line and tended to put more emphasis on the self-determination aspect ... Ambassador Woolcott said he had received instructions from Canberra on 16 October to deliver a clear message to

the Indonesians that Australia could not countenance Indonesian interference in the affairs of Timor ... Woolcott said he had gone back to Canberra and had his instructions modified somewhat and that when he saw Foreign Minister Malik on 18 October he had spoken as softly as his instructions permitted.[82]

FRETILIN took *de facto* control of Timor-Leste.[83] The infiltration of Indonesian Special Forces in preparation for an invasion and the murder of the journalists at Balibo on the West Timor border brought the issue to world prominence.[84] FRETILIN petitioned the UN to call for a withdrawal of Indonesian forces.[85] As noted earlier in this chapter, on 28 November 1975, FRETILIN leaders unilaterally declared 'The Democratic Republic of Timor-Leste' and the FRETILIN flag was raised in Dili. On 4 December 1975, a FRETILIN delegation, including José Ramos-Horta, Mari Alkatiri and Rogerio Lobato, left Timor-Leste to seek support for anticipated military confrontation with Indonesia.[86]

Indonesia Invades Timor-Leste

Meanwhile President Ford and Secretary of State Kissinger paid a flying visit to Jakarta. A State Department transcript of their discussion with Suharto on 6 December 1975 lays bare the understanding, profoundly unlawful in international law, reached between the leaders:

39. I [Suharto] would like to speak to you, Mr President, about another problem, Timor. When it looked as if the Portuguese rule would end in Timor we sought to encourage the Portuguese to an orderly decolonization process. We had agreement with them on such a process and we recognized the authority of Portugal in the carrying out of decolonization and in giving people the right to express their wishes. Indonesia has no territorial ambitions. We are concerned only about the security, tranquility and peace of Asia and the southern hemisphere. In the latest Rome Agreement, the Portuguese government wanted to invite all parties to negotiate. Similar efforts were made before but Fretelin [*sic*] did not attend. After the Fretelin forces occupied certain points and other forces were unable to consolidate, Fretelin has declared its independence unilaterally. In consequence, other parties declared their intention of integrating with Indonesia. Portugal reported the situation to the United Nations but did not extend recognition to Fretelin. Portugal, however, is unable to control the situation. If this

continues it will prolong the suffering of the refugees and increase the instability in the area.

40. FORD—The four other parties have asked for integration?

41. SUHARTO—Yes. After the UDT, Indonesia found itself facing a fate [sic] accompli. It is now important to determine what we can do to establish peace and order for the present and the future in the interest of the security of the area and Indonesia. These are some of the considerations we are now contemplating. We want your understanding if we deem it necessary to take rapid or drastic action.

42. FORD—We will understand and will not press you on the issue. We understand the problem you have and the intentions you have.

43. KISSINGER—You appreciate that the use of US made arms could create problems.

44. FORD—We could have technical and legal problems. You are familiar, Mr President, with the problems we had on Cyprus although this situation is different.

45. KISSINGER—It depends on how we construe it. Whether it is in self defense or is a foreign operation. It is important that whatever you do succeeds quickly. We would be able to influence the reaction in America if whatever happens happens after we return. This way there would be less chance of people talking in an unauthorized way. The President will be back on Monday at 2:00 PM Jakarta time. We understand your problem and the need to move quickly but I am only saying that it would be better if it were done after we returned.

46. FORD—It would be more authoritative if we can do it in person.

47. KISSINGER—Whatever we do, however, we will try to handle in the best way possible.

48. FORD—We recognize that you have a time factor. We have merely expressed our view from our particular point of view.

49. KISSINGER—If you have made plans, we will do our best to keep everyone quiet until the President returns home.

50. Do you anticipate a long guerilla [sic] war there?

51. SUHARTO—There will probably be a small guerilla war. The local kings are important, however, and they are on our side. The UDT represents former government officials and Fretelin represents former soldiers. They are infected the same as is the Portuguese army with communism.[87]

The following day, on 7 December 1975, Suharto's government landed paratroopers at Dili and FRETILIN forces fled to the mountains.[88] Thus began a long period of betrayal of the Timorese people following the secret collaboration of Australia and the US with Jakarta. Although the record shows that Australian defence and intelligence agencies remained uneasy and watchful of Indonesia,[89] Australian collaboration with Indonesia reached its zenith in 1995 when the Keating Government entered into the Australia–Indonesia Defence pact.[90]

The Whitlam Government was dismissed by Australian Governor-General Sir John Kerr on 11 November 1975 and a caretaker government led by acting Prime Minister Malcolm Fraser installed. Twenty years later, in a telling memoir of Australia's betrayal of the Timorese, ALP stalwart and former minister in the Whitlam Government Tom Uren wrote:

> The Australian bureaucrats in Jakarta appeared to follow the paternalistic reasoning that an Indonesian takeover was in the long-term interests of the Timorese. There was also an undercurrent in both Australian and Indonesian justification that those who resisted incorporation into Indonesia were communists rather than nationalists seeking independence.
>
> The Department of Defence thought that incorporation would risk increasing instability close to Australia's borders because the Australian public would oppose an invasion and therefore our relationship with Indonesia would deteriorate. Consequently, it argued for the colony becoming an independent state with Australia and Indonesia co-operating to ensure that no antagonistic external influences became established.
>
> It is an important question for democracy whether developments of such importance to Australia, unfolding and being debated over a period of months within the bureaucracy, should be kept from discussion by the small elite within an elected government. Australian governments, both the political wings and the bureaucracies, have played a disgraceful role in relation to East Timor during and since 1975.[91]

Another Minister in Whitlam's government, Douglas Everingham, apologised in 1999 for his government's collaboration in the invasion: 'I apologize to the East Timorese people. I am ashamed to have belonged to the first of a series of Australian cabinets which failed to protest while our Prime Minister, unlike the world community, recognized the takeover of East Timor'.[92]

Graham Freudenberg claims that Whitlam never had to make a choice between good relations with Indonesia and the principle of self-determination for Portuguese Timor. He says that until mid-1975 the two aims were compatible and that civil war between August and November 1975 rendered any meaningful act of self-determination impossible. Whitlam was determined in the first phase not to allow Australian policy to become hostage to the Portuguese Timor issue, and in the second phase not allow it to become hostage to the self-appointed leaders of FRETILIN. Ramos-Horta cites a speech Whitlam gave at the Australian National University on 30 November 1979 as evidence of 'Whitlam's professed preference for a more racially pure Timorese leadership: "Political parties emerged there for the first time in 1974 ... they were led by mestizos ... who seemed desperate to succeed the Portuguese as rulers of the population"'.[93]

Twenty years later, in evidence before the 1999 parliamentary committee, Whitlam repeated the racist slur. In other words, Whitlam had his own set, essentially racist, views about the FRETILIN leadership, forgetting that white reformers such as the redoubtable Nugget Coombs were providing Whitlam with credibility on Aboriginal affairs in Australia. The historical fact is that Whitlam was not going to put the principle of self-determination first. Surprisingly, and without evidence, Freudenberg asserts that in both phases, Whitlam, his Ministers and Australia's senior diplomats in Jakarta, Lisbon, New York and Canberra made 'unremitting efforts to persuade the governments of Indonesia and Portugal to implement an orderly process of decolonialisation'.[94] Elsewhere, he argues that Whitlam saw that Suharto's choice would not be between incorporation and independence, but 'would, sooner or later come down to a choice of methods by which incorporation, or at the very least some form of Indonesian suzerainty, would be achieved', and concluded that 'nothing Australia could say would alter the fundamental Indonesian objective, but Australia could realistically hope to influence the means by which it would be brought about'.[95]

No doubt the Australian Government had difficult policy choices, but there is no evidence that Whitlam, a senior jurist himself, felt impelled by rule-of-law precepts or saw merit in taking a leadership role, as Dr Evatt and Casey would have before him, on alternatives such as a UN-supervised ballot and peacekeeping. Whitlam does not appear to have given weight to advice, prophetic as it turned out, from Australian defence strategists that Australian community support for the embattled Timorese may have a long-term corrosive effect on Australian–Indonesian relations. To the 1999 parliamentary committee Whitlam said:

> East Timor was cocooned. There were no contacts with West Timor, and there has been no trouble in West Timor. The point is that they both had an indigenous language, Tetum…they did have the same language…There was a possibility that if they could meet each other, as they would over a three- or five- or eight-year period, that they would learn to communicate…there was a chance, with proper preparation, that the two Timors could have got to live together.[96]

The flaw in Whitlam's recollection of his motives in 1974–75 became evident in the Committee's report when Whitlam sought to rely upon outdated economic analyses to justify his conduct:

> Mr Whitlam told the Committee that Mr Barwick's 1963 analysis, Dr Salazar's views and those of the Menzies government all came to the same conclusion, that East Timor was non-viable politically and economically. That was also his own view, which he had formed after he had taken advice from Secretary of the Prime Minister's Department, Sir John Bunting, who had also held that position at the time of the Menzies-Salazar correspondence. Sir John thought that Portuguese Timor was not viable as an independent state, and this view was shared by the Secretary of the Department of Defence, Sir Arthur Tange, the Secretary of the Treasury, Sir Frederick Wheeler, and the Secretary of the Department of Foreign Affairs, Sir Keith Waller.[97]

Whitlam uttered not a word to the Committee about any effect the successful drilling by Woodside–Burmah–British Petroleum at Troubadour-1, commencing in June 1974 near the Portuguese Timor coast, would have on the assessment of Timorese self-sufficiency as non-economic. Having asked or answered questions over the years in Parliament about Australia's shelf negotiations with Portugal, Whitlam knew about the petroleum potential of the Australian Continental Shelf and Australia's two shelves claim. Did Woolcott and Whitlam assume that any petroleum revenue from the promising oilfield on the continental shelf south of the alleged trench would go to Australia, not the Timorese? Was this why an early petroleum revenue stream was not imputed into an assessment of Portuguese Timor's future self-sufficiency? Of lesser note, but relevantly, in his diverting attacks before the Committee on Portuguese colonialism and the Catholic Church, Whitlam did not explain why Indonesia and not Australia should bear the burden of advancing the Timorese into the 20th century.

In later life Whitlam and his camp followers remained sensitive when the subject of East Timor came up. Some appeared to seek redemption in public life, casting themselves as of a humanitarian outlook. Always someone who found advice that he did not agree with uncongenial, Whitlam, with a massive belief in his own destiny, mistook his own emotions, prejudices and ambitions for principles. When asked by the 1999 parliamentary committee chairman to describe the capacity in which he gave evidence, Whitlam, far from penitent for the sufferings endured by the Timorese, replied, 'Elder Statesman'. Thereafter he slithered through the issues with half-truths and egocentric reflections, repeating an unbecoming reference to persons of part-Portuguese descent.[98] Whitlam became Prime Minister at a time of national change with much of the reform agenda set before he achieved office. Further archival releases may show that, as a claimed social democrat, Whitlam was ascribed a reputation far greater than he achieved

Response at the United Nations

After Indonesia invaded Timor-Leste on 7 December 1975, the UN General Assembly on 12 December 1975 by Resolution 3485 strongly deplored Indonesian military intervention in Portuguese Timor and called for a withdrawal.[99] Although Prime Minister Whitlam's discussions with Suharto ran counter to Australia's earlier support at the UN for self-determination for Portuguese Timor-Leste,[100] Australia maintained a hypocritical posture at the UN.

On 12 December 1975, in a statement of principle at odds with Whitlam's Wonosobo message to General Suharto in September 1974, Australia's Ambassador to the UN, Ralph Harry, supported, doubtless in personal good faith, a Special Political and Decolonization Committee (Fourth Committee) resolution on self-determination for Portuguese Timor-Leste in the following terms:

> It is indeed that the duty of the Assembly to stress the need for talks, for a peaceful solution, for an end to the strife, for orderly exercise of the right of self-determination. We also deeply regret the use of

force, whether by the political factions in the Territory or by outside Powers. We shall therefore vote for the draft resolution. We shall also seek to make some suggestion to the Security Council for prompt and appropriate action, taking into account not only the legal responsibility of Portugal and the recent history of Portuguese East Timor under its colonial regime but also the realities of the existing situation.[101]

Security Council Resolution 384 called for the withdrawal of all foreign troops in Timor-Leste and observance of Timor-Leste's territorial integrity.[102] Addressing Resolution 384, a caretaker Australian Government emphasised, as it had in supporting General Assembly Resolution 3485,[103] that underlying any action by the UN was the purpose and aim of enabling the people of Timor-Leste to freely exercise their right to self-determination.[104] A British diplomat in Jakarta reporting information from a senior Indonesian official cast a different light on Australia's breast-beating at the UN. Anticipating an adverse reaction by General Suharto, caretaker Prime Minister Fraser had arranged for Richard Woolcott to deliver a letter to Indonesian Foreign Minister Malik, probably on 8 December 1975, advising in substance 'that what was being said in Australia was only for the purposes of the forthcoming election campaign and Indonesia should not misunderstand this'. The British diplomat continued:

> Certainly, Mr Akosah [Deputy Head, Asian and Pacific Directorate of the Indonesian Foreign Affairs Department] implied to me that Indonesia was not worried about what was being said at the moment even in the UN context as far as Australia was concerned, simply because the President had had this personal reassurance from Mr Fraser. The importance which Indonesians attached to such personal contact is well known and if nothing else, Mr Fraser's message was a sensible and astute move.[105]

When Allan Taylor, Counsellor at the Australian Embassy and, later, Director-General of ASIS, became aware that Akosah had revealed to the British the message from Fraser, he asked the British not to report the matter because Fraser 'had given an assurance to the Governor-General at the time of the dismissal of the Whitlam Govt. that no foreign policy initiatives would be taken during the interregnum'. Weighing up this request the British diplomat recorded that the only substantial interest in the message, beyond Australian domestic politics, was that 'it presumably explains why the Australians feel free to take a tough line in the UN, having warned the Indonesians in advance to pay no attention'. The provenance of the alleged message from Fraser would be of interest in determining whether in fact the initiative came from the Australian Embassy in Jakarta. The letter is not with documents released subsequently by the Department of Foreign Affairs and Trade with Alexander Downer's pious foreword that there was a public right to know what had occurred.[106]

Addressing the same Resolutions, Indonesia claimed that it wanted peace and stability re-established in 'Portuguese Timor' and that the future status of Timor-Leste had to be based on an exercise of the right to self-determination.[107] Indonesia opposed both Resolutions and, thereafter, every successive resolution of the Security Council and the General Assembly relating to Timor-Leste. Likewise, in contradiction of its earlier support for Resolution 3485, the Fraser Government voted against or abstained from every successive resolution of the General Assembly relating to Timor-Leste.[108] Successive Australian governments followed suit until Security Council Resolution 1264, which authorised an international peace-keeping force for Timor-Leste in 1999.[109]

Although the response by the US at the UN to the Indonesian invasion of Timor-Leste mirrored that by Australia, the question as to who was holding the looking-glass requires other historical analysis. The US Embassy at Jakarta appears to have worked in tune with Jakarta and Canberra in relation to the core motivating issue in Jakarta—the perceived communist threat from FRETILIN. Daniel Moynihan, US Ambassador to the UN at the time, reflected on the Indonesian invasion:

> China altogether backed FRETILIN in Timor, and lost. In Spanish Sahara, Russia just as completely backed Algeria, and its front ... and lost. In both instances, the United States wished things to turn out as they did, and worked to bring this about. The Department of State desired that the United Nations prove utterly ineffective in whatever measures it undertook. This task was given to me, and I carried it forward with no inconsiderable success.[110]

On 19 July 1977, in testimony before a US House of Representatives Committee, George Aldrich, Deputy Legal Adviser, Department of State, explained the ambivalence of US policy on Timor-Leste and the importance of supporting relations with Indonesia, which under Suharto were strongly anti-communist:

> [I]t was the policy of the United States to favor a resolution of the problem of East Timor by the Timorese and other concerned parties themselves. We supported Security Council Resolution 384 as well as U.N. General Assembly Resolution 3485 of December 12, 1975, also calling for respect for the right of self-determination of the people of East Timor. We remained hopeful that the report of the special representative of the Secretary General would offer a promising course but ... it was inconclusive and again called on the parties to work out a solution. We abstained on Security Council Resolution 389 of April 22, 1976, largely because the Security Council did not accept an amendment which would have acknowledged steps taken by Indonesia to begin withdrawal of its forces from East Timor, but at the same time the U.S. Representative reaffirmed 'our support of the right of the people of East Timor ... for ... self-determination' ... The U.S. Government did not question the incorporation of East Timor into Indonesia at any time. This did not represent a legal judgment or endorsement of what took place. It was, simply, the judgment of those responsible for our policy in the area that the integration was an accomplished fact, that the realities of the situation would not be changed by our opposition to what had occurred, and that such a policy would not serve our best interests in light of the importance of our relations with Indonesia. It was for these reasons that the United States voted against UN General Assembly Resolution 31/53 of December 1, 1976, which rejected the incorporation of East Timor into Indonesia and recommended that the Security Council take immediate steps to implement its earlier resolutions to secure exercise by the people of East Timor of their rights of self-determination.[111]

Gough Whitlam's alleged 'new-age' enlightened democratic role, snuffed out by a maverick Governor-General, awaits the release of surviving archives and/or the oral history of some actors silenced by Australia's bipartisan political misuse of archives and national security laws. But fairness demands a return to the perception of Ralph Harry's speech at the UN calling for self-determination as 'hypocritical'. Harry was, of course, relying on instructions from Canberra and there is no evidence that Harry, a man of personal integrity, was an architect of Whitlam's strategy at the UN. As Ambassador to South Vietnam he had in 1972 proposed by secret cablegram a contingency plan for the evacuation of locally engaged staff including Australian intelligence 'assets'. The Department of Foreign Affairs recoiled at the proposal and promptly quelled further cable traffic, lest the US perceived any defeatist sentiment. The outcome was tragic, with long-serving staff and loyal associates abandoned as Australian diplomats scrambled out of Saigon in May 1975. A request from the French for support with the clandestine rescue through Laos of significant 'assets' they had passed on or were co-managing was rebuffed by the US and Australia. Australia not only refused aircraft but made clear that it would not accept those rescued. A similar stonewall, authorised personally by Whitlam, had gone out in a secret signal to the Commander of a Royal Australian Navy vessel in the South China Sea, instructing that an overloaded refugee boat observed to be in danger of foundering was not to be rescued.[112] Whitlam's failure as a humanitarian leader extended beyond his interventions over East Timor and South Vietnam to interventions by his office in restricting the processing, suspected to be favourably encouraged by ASIO, of perceived anti-communist refugees from Eastern Europe. The author recollects that, at the time, the compromise of the clandestine pipeline of Jewish escapees through Poland and Sweden from the Soviet Union, co-managed from Paris by Secours Catholique and allied agencies, caused rancour when suspicion fell on Australia.

Indonesian Occupation
In the immediate aftermath of the invasion, FRETILIN/FALANTIL established liberated zones and resistance bases, the last of which had fallen by February 1979. After a brutal campaign, Indonesia declared Timor-Leste pacified on 26 March 1979.[113] The years of repression, famine and genocide that followed are yet to be fully chronicled.[114] Least chronicled of all is the performance by one of Australia's spy agencies in that period. Co-located within the Australian diplomatic community since its transfer from Defence premises at Melbourne in the early 1960s, ASIS may have suffered from its proximity to enterprising diplomats vulnerable, during the mores of that era, to entrapment. History may one day reveal whether Indonesian intelligence services did have success in developing effective links within the Australian diplomatic service. Desmond Ball reports that suspicion culminated in an investigation in 1998–99 for the source of persistent leaks to Indonesia.[115]

In a recent study, Clinton Fernandes concludes that the Australian Cabinet 'not only looked away from the calamity, but participated enthusiastically in the subjugation of Timor'.[116] Malcolm Fraser, Prime Minister in the early period of famine in Timor-Leste, has acknowledged that Australia 'should have been asking for United Nations monitoring and observations to keep watch on Timor-Leste'.[117] Renouf verifies Fraser's opposition to Indonesia's use of force:

> Fraser was incensed at Indonesia's conduct but could do no more than condemn it, within the UN and without. Even after his sweeping electoral victory in December 1975 Fraser adhered to this attitude. When he visited Jakarta in October 1976 Fraser had an opportunity to change and let the past be the past but he refused so as not to antagonize the Australian media. Bitterness between Australia and Indonesia over the East Timor affair was therefore carried over from the Whitlam to the Fraser Government.[118]

Armed resistance continued throughout the intervening years. Geographer/historian Professor Durand has graphically illustrated the territory over which the struggle extended, and in a recent publication three authors have begun the mammoth task of recording, largely from oral history, the opposing campaigns.[119]

Canberra's diplomatic collaboration with Indonesia in the 1980s extended well beyond the long-drawn-out negotiations for an agreement to share the Timor Sea petroleum resources. Throughout the 1980s Australia worked in unison with Indonesia's services to monitor the activities of émigré groups and Australian sympathisers within Timorese and West Papuan communities in Australia and Papua New Guinea. Although the ALP was in government, in one celebrated operation in June 1984, intelligence agents working in liaison with Foreign Affairs officials recorded the movements and contacts with ALP parliamentarians of West Papuan leader David Joku and José Ramos-Horta, who were attending the Pacific region meeting of the World Council of Indigenous Peoples. They also monitored contact between Aboriginal leader Charles Perkins and Joku.

While open government in Canberra was wilting, more deadly battles for survival were grinding on throughout the 1980s in East Timor, with no relief in sight. Xanana Gusmão was becoming steadily more disillusioned with the FRETILIN leadership. On 7 December 1987, he resigned from FRETILIN in the face of opposition to his policy of resistance based upon national unity rather than FRETILIN partisanship.[120] The aspirations of the Timorese people for a popular democracy reflected in Gusmão's 7 December 1987 declaration were ignored by the Howard Government in Australia when it commenced an extraordinary manipulative process in 1999 of placing FRETILIN into power. A conservative Australian government was deliberately supporting a Marxist–Leninist relic leader into power.

Within four years Australia's petroleum grab led to stagnation and tragedy in Timor. Howard and Downer were aware of the potential future under Alkatiri's FRETILIN. In 2000, describing Gusmão's declaration as the 'Ideological Turnaround', Dr Sara Niner quotes Gusmão's emphatic rejection in 1987 of Marxist Central Committee governance:

> The suppression of any other political choice has created in our bosom a fatal divisiveness and a notorious resentment at all levels of the organisational structure. We have been unable to express freely opinions about the mistaken points of view of members of the Central Committee who rely on long-winded clarifications of Marxist precepts. Meanwhile, the practicalities of conducting the war were handed over to the initiative—more or less uncontrollable and inconsistent—of local military commanders. This was a drawback during the period of the support bases (1976–78). Being condemned to make a revolution, during a war we could not sustain, is a clear demonstration of political blindness.
>
> The West placed itself alongside Indonesia, while the Eastern countries did not lift a finger, calling us loudly and clearly, excessive adventurers ...
>
> 1. I publicly declare my total and wholehearted rejection of those doctrines that promote suppression of democratic freedoms in East Timor.
> 2. I publicly declare that the FALINTIL aswain will not permit the installation of a leftist regime that not only intends to provoke internal disintegration, but also to destabilise the whole area in which East Timor is situated.[121]

From early 1988, Xanana Gusmão commenced restructuring FALINTIL as the politically non-partisan Territorial Army of Timor-Leste. By year's end, Gusmão announced that FALINTIL had become the armed wing of the new Conselho Nacional da Resistência

Maubere (CNRM: National Council of Maubere Resistance), which initially included members from FRETILIN, UDT and other nationalist parties. Created following a further reorganisation of the resistance in December 1988 by Gusmão, the CNRM was intended 'as a unifying non-partisan body bringing together the Timorese political forces and all the underground Timorese political resistance operating in Timor-Leste and Indonesia'.[122]

While the years of struggle in East Timor unwound, Portugal, the responsible administrative power for Timor-Leste as a non-self-governing territory, kept the question of occupied Timor-Leste before UN General Assembly Committees. In the meantime, the Australian Government called publicly upon the Indonesian Government to exercise restraint, at the same time signalling secretly its willingness to reconvene maritime boundary discussions. The position taken by successive UN resolutions effectively endorsed Portuguese claims that Indonesia had acted unlawfully in the invasion of Portuguese Timor and that Australia from 1989 had compounded this illegality by reaching a treaty on the sharing of petroleum resources contrary, as Portugal claimed, to the inalienable right of the people of Timor-Leste to their natural resources.

7
TIMOR-LESTE EDGES TOWARDS INDEPENDENCE

On 5 September 1988, the Australian Foreign Minister, Senator Gareth Evans, announced that Australian and Indonesian officials had reached agreement in principle to establish a Zone of Cooperation in the Timor Gap. The Portuguese Foreign Minister condemned the announcement before the UN General Assembly, but in December 1989 the Australian and Indonesian Foreign Ministers signed the Timor Gap Treaty,[1] and images circulated of Evans and his Indonesian counterpart, Ali Alatas, sipping champagne in an aircraft circling over the Timor Sea. The treaty was entered into for an initial term of 40 years, with provision for successive terms, unless by the end of each term the contracting states had concluded an agreement on the permanent delimitation of the continental shelf between Australia and Timor-Leste. The Portuguese Government circulated a letter of protest at the United Nations and recalled its Ambassador from Canberra. By letter passed to Australia's Prime Minister Bob Hawke in early 1991, Xanana Gusmão, leader of the Timorese resistance, condemned the treaty as a 'total betrayal' by Australia of the Timorese people.[2]

Portugal v Australia at the International Court of Justice
Portugal filed proceedings in the International Court of Justice (ICJ) against Australia on 22 February 1991, claiming that Australia had failed

to observe 'the right of the people of Timor-Leste to self-determination and the related rights, and Article 25 of the Charter' and that the Timor Gap Treaty between Indonesia and Australia affected the rights of Timor-Leste and Portugal. The ICJ was asked to order reparation of the damage and loss to the people of Timor-Leste. In its judgement on 30 June 1995, the ICJ by a majority declined to adjudicate as Indonesia was not a party to the proceedings.[3] The case attracted widespread international interest and sharpened focus on Australia's collaboration with Indonesia.

In his dissenting opinion, Judge Weeramantry referred to the Australian contention that 'the progressively lessening vote in favour of the General Assembly resolutions cited by Portugal show that those resolutions were of a diminishing level of authority'.[4] He said that once a General Assembly resolution has been duly passed within the ambit of the UN's legal authority, 'it commands recognition and it is part of the courtesy due by one principal organ of the United Nations to another to respect that resolution, irrespective of its political history or the voting strength it reflects'.[5] Weeramantry cited a passage from the court's decision in a South-West Africa Advisory Case, where Judge Hersch Lauterpacht observed:

> Whatever may be the content of the recommendation and *whatever may be the nature and circumstances of the majority by which it has been reached*, it is nevertheless a legal act of the principal organ of the United Nations which Members of the United Nations are under a duty to treat with a degree of respect appropriate to a resolution of the General Assembly.[6]

Focusing on the Australian argument that, over time, fewer nations were supporting UN General Assembly resolutions critical of Indonesia's occupation of East Timor, Weeramantry addressed the core issue:

> Indeed, this Australian submission has grave implications in the circumstances of this case, for the resolutions which Australia would have the court ignore are resolutions affirming the important principle of self-determination which is a well-established principle of customary international law. A heavy burden would lie upon a party contending that the validity of such a resolution has been affected by declining support for it in the United Nations ... More especially is caution required from the court in regard to resolutions dealing with obligations *erga omnes* and rights such as self-determination which are fundamental to the international legal system.[7]

The Santa Cruz Massacre

The 1991 massacre of 271 people in Santa Cruz at a funeral for a youth killed by Indonesian forces (Tentara Nasional Indonesia (TNI)) solidified the resistance movement based on national unity and projected the plight of the Timorese to the world stage. In a move that brought unprecedented support from the Australian and world community, leaders of the East Timorese resistance in Sydney, including Ines Almeida, Agio Pereira, Estanislau da Silva and Harold Mucho, organised a protest and vigil outside the Indonesian Embassy in Canberra. Two hundred and seventy-one white crosses, each inscribed with the name of a victim, were planted in the grass verge outside the Embassy and blessed by Catholic, Anglican and Uniting Church leaders.

In a bizarre response, Foreign Minister Gareth Evans introduced a regulation, purportedly in accordance with Australia's statutory obligations under the Vienna Convention on Diplomatic Immunity, to ban the public display of the Christian cross in the vicinity of the Indonesian Embassy on the ground that it offended the dignity of the Mission. Canberra police, who some months earlier had been under the author's ministerial supervision,[8] obligingly gave notice of their intended uprooting of the crosses. Images of them doing so and stacking the wooden crosses reverently in a truck flashed across the world, accompanied by claims that public display of the Christian cross had not been banned for more than 400 years. The images of Evans and Alatas sipping self-congratulatory champagne above oppressed East Timor once again circulated globally too.[9]

Unedited footage of massacre scenes, captured courageously by Max Stahl at the Santa Cruz Cemetery and smuggled out of Dili, was rushed to the author's chambers.[10] Lawyers representing the Foreign Minister had the unenviable experience of having to watch the footage shown in court. Federal Court proceedings challenging the validity of the regulation were successful at first instance, with Judge Howard Olney choosing to bring judgement down on Holy Thursday 1992.[11] Police returned the crosses to the author's custody on Good Friday morning. As the hour of the crucifixion approached, a procession of East Timorese men, women and children, each carrying a cross and led by a priest, walked slowly up the road reciting the rosary. The crosses were replanted in the verge outside the Indonesian Embassy. Veteran news journalists, including camera crews for whom the Indonesian invasion of 1975 and the murder of journalists and camera crew so strongly resonated, wept. It was a defining moment in the years of public protest in Australia against the Indonesian–Australian collaboration and a worldwide public relations disaster for the Australian Government.

Not dissuaded by clear public opinion rallying around the East Timorese vigil outside the Indonesian Embassy, Evans issued a new regulation in response to further Indonesian protest and appealed the decision of Justice Olney. The crosses were again uprooted but this time returned to the author's custody by police unhappy with their task. On appeal, the Federal Court examined whether the Minister had the power to make such a regulation. If he did, the question of fact as to whether the Minister had exercised such a power properly was for another day. By a majority, the full court found that the Commonwealth Government did have power to make a regulation concerning the conduct of public events outside diplomatic missions and the objects that protesters might carry.

Nevertheless, future High Court Chief Justice, Federal Justice Robert French, in a hint that even Foreign Minister Evans could not miss, expressed the view that 'it is difficult to see how the lawful placement of a reproachful and dignified symbol on public land in the vicinity of a mission would amount to a disturbance of its peace or an

On 25 November 1992, for the second time, Federal Police remove crosses placed outside the Indonesian Embassy in Canberra to commemorate the Santa Cruz victims.

impairment of its dignity'.[12] Having lost the technical legal battle but won the war, the resistance leaders resolved not to allow the crosses, now objects of reverence, to feature further in a tug-of-war with the government. They substituted a dignified lantern, which remained a site of pilgrimage outside the Indonesian Embassy for many months. After Xanana Gusmão's capture on 20 November 1992, the Embassy refused to issue a visa to allow the author to attend Gusmão's trial in Dili and delayed the return of the author's passport for many months. Gusmão's subsequent trial and sentence of imprisonment attracted world attention, and debate concerning the future of East Timor at the UN and at other fora intensified.

Renewed Calls for Self-Determination

On 3 July 1994, 50 years after Dr Salazar first used the Azores as a bargaining chip to thwart the Atlantic Charter sentiments on self-determination for Portugal's colonial possessions, Constâncio Pinto, a Washington-based representative of the Conselho Nacional da Resistência Maubere (CNRM: National Council of Maubere Resistance), addressed the UN Special Committee on the Granting of Independence to Colonial Countries and Peoples:

> East Timor is at the crossroads of three major cultures and religions: the Melanesian, binding its people to the South Pacific; the Malay-Polynesian, as many East Timorese traced their roots to South-East Asia, and the European, a result of the four centuries of Portuguese Catholic presence. These influences give the East Timorese Nation-State a distinctive character. It could be a valuable partner for ASEAN and South Pacific Forum Member States in relations with the European Union, Africa and Latin America. The majority of East Timorese exiles are resident in Australia and Portugal. They could contribute to East Timor's role as a bridge between their adopted countries and South Pacific States ... The 'Timor Gap Treaty' will be looked at, clarification will be sought, and it will be renegotiated. The sea boundary dispute will have to be settled through an international tribunal.[13]

Four years later, in April 1998, Timorese resistance parties convened at Peniche, Portugal, and resolved to establish the Conselho Nacional da Resistência Timorense (CNRT: National Council of Timorese Resistance). The imprisoned Xanana Gusmão was named as CNRT President and 1996 Nobel Peace Prize laureate José Ramos-Horta as

Vice President. All resistance parties agreed to submerge their factional differences for the good of the struggle.[14]

In the intervening years, Australian Prime Minister Paul Keating and President Suharto had signed a mutual defence pact. The terms of the 1995 treaty reflected a new accord that rendered historic Australia's previous 'forward defence strategy' against Indonesia.

President Habibie Offers Limited Autonomy

Following President Suharto's resignation on 21 May 1998, Indonesia's new President, Bacharuddin Jusuf Habibie, a distinguished Fellow of the Australian Institute of Engineers, stated at a press interview on 9 June that he was willing to consider 'special status' for Timor-Leste.[15] The CNRT rejected this offer as not going far enough. Australia had long anticipated a future FRETILIN-dominated Timor-Leste Government and its linkage to the Timor Sea petroleum issue. The Australian Government's official response was cautiously positive, and Foreign Minister Alexander Downer welcomed the proposal as a basis for further dialogue.[16] Downer reiterated a long-standing view held by Australia's two principal political parties that any 'special status' that might compromise Australia's Timor Gap Treaty with Indonesia was neither in Australia's nor Indonesia's interest.[17] Three days after Habibie's announcement, Australian Ambassador to Indonesia John McCarthy visited Timor-Leste. Further visits to Timor-Leste a few weeks later by McCarthy's British, Dutch and Austrian Jakarta-based counterparts provided further opportunity for CNRT President Xanana Gusmão, still imprisoned in Indonesia, to explain Timor-Leste's case for independence and the legacies of conflict.

In July 1998, the European Union Ambassadors issued a report highlighting the prospect of retribution within Timor-Leste's FRETILIN party over alleged killings during the revolutionary and occupied period. The report was ignored at the UN. As plans developed for a UN-supervised ballot in which the East Timorese could determine their own future, UN Human Rights officials developed no policy approach to the report of crimes against humanity in 1974–75 by and within FRETILIN and the União Democrática Timorense (UDT). Although Gusmão had been recorded as saying that historic elements of the FRETILIN Party had much to account for, the Alkatiri-led FRETILIN leadership was, post-liberation, publicly welcomed by

United Nations Transitional Administration of East Timor (UNTAET) and the Australian Mission to the UN. Aware of the tension between Gusmão and Alkatiri, Sergio de Mello, ever the diplomat, as head of UNTAET, placed FRETILIN and the CNRT on an equal footing at consultative meetings, thus undermining Gusmão's wish that past crimes be recognised and renounced through reconciliation. Such an approach, Gusmão argued, would support an even-handed pursuit of all, including Indonesians who had participated in crimes against humanity.

As events unfolded between Jakarta and Dili, the UN undertook a similar consultative process, with the UN Special Representative meeting Xanana Gusmão. Downer, who had met with Habibie, Indonesian Foreign Minister Alatas and General Wiranto in Jakarta on 8–10 July 1998, announced that Australia was working with the EU Group and the UN on the Timor-Leste issue.[18] Throughout July and August 1998 representatives of the Australian Department of Foreign Affairs and Trade (DFAT) contacted Timorese resistance leaders at home and abroad. High on the list of issues for discussion was the future attitude of a Timorese Government to the Timor Sea petroleum reserves then being exploited unlawfully, in the view of many international observers, by Australia and Indonesia.

On 21 July 1998, CNRT Deputy President José Ramos-Horta issued a statement, endorsed by National Political Commission Members Mari Alkatiri and João Carrascalão, in response to news that oil production from the Elang Kakatua Field under the Australia–Indonesia Joint Venture was about to commence. The CNRT called upon the Australian Government and oil companies operating in the Timor Gap to 'review their past assumptions and face current realities'. They called for a review of the Timor Gap Treaty, stating that the CNRT 'supports the rights of the existing Timor Gap contractors and those of the Australian Government to jointly develop Timor-Leste's off shore oil reserves in cooperation with the people of East Timor'. While the CNRT stood firm on an internationally accepted resolution of the Timor-Leste conflict, the announcement sought to mollify Australian and investor concerns. The statement avoided reference to international maritime boundary issues but implied, by calling only for the Indonesian share of the Gap revenue to be trust-funded, that Timor-Leste, on achieving self-determination, might accommodate a joint venture with Australia.[19] This was encouraging news in Canberra.

Ambassador McCarthy visited Xanana Gusmão in prison and spoke to prominent Timorese in Jakarta, while other Australian diplomats established contact with the Timorese diaspora in Portugal, Mozambique, Macau, New York and Washington. Constâncio Pinto in Washington also reported Australian interest in the internal CNRT power balance between FRETILIN and the UDT. In anticipation of concerted action by the UN to resolve the situation in Timor-Leste, the Australian Government had implemented a strategy in 1998–99 of consulting the Timorese resistance leadership with respect to the status of both the Timor Gap Treaty and existing production-sharing contracts in the Zone of Cooperation, seeking assurances that status quo would be maintained. The CNRT indicated that, while it would not subscribe to aspects of the Timor Gap Treaty that affected maritime boundaries, it would leave existing production-sharing arrangements in place.[20]

Between 14 and 20 August 1998, DFAT officials monitored the FRETILIN National Congress at Warwick Farm, Sydney. FRETILIN leader Mari Alkatiri from Mozambique and Australian FRETILIN leader Estanislau da Silva were invited to meet Foreign Minister Alexander Downer and driven around Canberra in an official government limousine. After so many years of unfriendly surveillance of the resistance movement, Collaery Law staff were surprised when, accompanying Alkatiri and da Silva from a conference at their law offices, they recognised a young diplomat from the Timor-Leste desk standing by with car and chauffeur. (Two years later, after Timor-Leste's liberation, when Xanana Gusmão visited Canberra to thank Australia and seek help for the FALINTIL veterans, the law firm was obliged to borrow an official-looking car from a local supporter to hide the affront by DFAT to the CNRT President; Canberra was going to accord Gusmão as little official recognition as possible. The reason for this did not take long to emerge; by mid-2001 the Australian Government was supporting premature self-government through an early FRETILIN accession to power.)

Despite Alkatiri's assurance that a future FRETILIN Government of an independent Timor-Leste would maintain the status quo for Australian interests in the Timor Sea, Canberra advised Indonesian Foreign Minister Ali Alatas on 29 August 1998 that Australia would endorse 'the autonomy approach'.[21] As this would leave defence and foreign affairs, including the Timor Gap Treaty, with Jakarta and Canberra, Australia put its Timor Sea interests ahead of the almost unanimous call by the Timorese for full independence. Nevertheless, the Australian Government continued its dialogue with FRETILIN.

Now that Indonesian authorities were tolerating a level of political dissent, Bishops Carlos Belo (in Dili) and Dom Basilio do Nascimento (in Bacau) responded to the need for the various political and activist groups to consult. They organised the first Consultative Commission meeting, later known as Dare 1, held 10–11 September 1998 at the Jesuit seminary at Dare in the hills above Dili.[22] The Australian Government had provided funds to the Dili-based human rights NGO, Yayasan HAK. Joaquim Fonseca of Yayasan HAK acted as an interlocutor at the meeting, which endorsed independence. Reliable reports of the meeting reached the Timorese diaspora and the Australian Government.

Australia Supports Limited Autonomy

Although soundings within the Timorese diaspora and consultations with the imprisoned CNRT President Xanana Gusmão by Australian diplomats had revealed a unanimous desire for independence for Timor-Leste, the Australian Government remained opposed. On 19 December 1998, Prime Minister Howard wrote to President Habibie:

> It has been a long-standing Australian position that the interests of Australia, Indonesia and East Timor are best served by East Timor remaining part of Indonesia ... it might be worth considering a means of addressing the East Timorese desire for an act of self-determination in a manner that avoids an early and final decision on the future status of the province ... [This] would allow time to convince the East Timorese of the benefits of autonomy within the Indonesian republic.[23]

Howard's letter reflected DFAT's focus on Australia's mutual interest with Indonesia in the Timor Sea, aptly explained by a principal architect of the Australian–Indonesian collaboration, John Dauth, to the 1999 parliamentary committee on East Timor: 'a very important part of our thinking at the time that the Prime Minister despatched his letter was that Indonesia really only had one chance to keep East Timor as part of Indonesia'.[24] In a chapter of his autobiography entitled 'The Liberation of East Timor' John Howard recollects:

When asked to list the achievements of my prime ministership of which I am most proud, I always include the liberation of East Timor in 1999. Now years later, it stands out as one of the more noble things that Australia has done in many years. Our nation was directly responsible for the birth of a very small country whose people remain deeply grateful for what we did.[25]

There seems good reason to accord Howard the recognition he deserves for moving with the times after President Habibie proposed a solution to the Indonesia–Timor-Leste imbroglio in 1998. Habibie's lengthy private conversation with Howard in Bali on 27 April 1999 was a turning point. Howard left Bali knowing that Habibie was in serious doubt about whether keeping Timor-Leste as the troublesome 27th Province of Indonesia was worth the cost and effort. Habibie also conveyed to Howard his confidence about overcoming Indonesian military sentiment. Howard now saw the prospect of being seen to redeem the Australian conscience over Timor-Leste and securing the sea-bed resources of the Timor Sea without the prospect of confrontation with Indonesia. In executing their plan, Howard and Downer resolved to fit Jakarta and Washington into an Australian strategy without bringing either into their confidence. The reason for this was that there were strategic policy forces at work in Canberra aimed at preserving Australia's encroachment in the Timor Sea, but Howard does not address this history, particularly the extent to which Australia risked the US intelligence alliance, in his autobiography.

Australia Conceals Intelligence from the United States

Robinson reports that in February 1999 the US State Department was searching for alternatives to a referendum to determine Timor-Leste's future governance:

> [A]n official explained that it was because both Alatas and the Indonesian army opposed it. Paul Wolfowitz, who had previously served as ambassador to Indonesia … added misleadingly that the Indonesian army had been the only guarantee of peace and order in the territory, and a referendum would give rise to renewed violence among East Timorese. In seeking to avoid a popular vote, then, U.S. officials were taking their cues from the Indonesian foreign minister and the army, not from President Habibie or East Timor's political leaders.[26]

The Clinton Administration may have reacted differently if informed by Australia of the level of threat posed by top-level Indonesian army plans to thwart the independence ballot.

On 6 January 1999, the Australian Defence Intelligence Organisation (DIO) provided a secret Current Intelligence Brief reporting that the Indonesian military (ABRI) were continuing to arm local militia in East Timor and that ABRI had identified at least 440 villages where the population was sufficiently integrationist to permit militia units to be armed. A Current Intelligence Brief on 4 March 1999 asserted that ABRI personnel in East Timor were condoning the activities of pro-Indonesian militants who had threatened Australian lives and that further violence, particularly in Dili, was certain. It noted that General Wiranto's attitude to ABRI involvement was not known, but warned that, if Jakarta did not rein it in, ABRI would continue to either support intimidation and violence, or at least not prevent it. Three days later Australian Foreign Minister Alexander Downer said:

> If it is happening at all, it certainly isn't official Indonesian Government policy; it certainly isn't something that's being condoned by General Wiranto, the head of the armed forces, but there may be some rogue elements within the armed forces who are providing arms of one kind or another to pro-integrationists who have been fighting the cause of Indonesia.
>
> When I raised it [arming the militia] with Ali Alatas the other day [23 February], he said that it certainly wasn't happening, that they weren't arming paramilitaries; there was some arming of the informal police support group who are civilians in East Timor but that applies in all of the provinces of Indonesia. There is nothing different or unusual about that, so I mean, I do accept the Indonesian Government's word for it, that it's not official Indonesian policy.[27]

An examination of the evidence, some of it in the secret and confidential reporting available to Downer, suggests that his remarks were directly contradicted by intelligence summaries available to him. A substantial number of secret Australian Defence Intelligence Organisation (DIO) documents were leaked to the media in the aftermath of the 1999 events in Timor-Leste. On 30 April 1999, a carefully weighed Defence Intelligence Report had predicted conflict as 'almost certain to be bloody' and had referred to the alternative of a 'UN sponsored force agreed to by all parties'.

Given the controversy surrounding the events in Timor-Leste, it is inconceivable to suggest that neither Downer nor his close advisers were unaware of the DIO briefing material and secret intelligence available to the Minister. Downer's conduct and that of his top advisers, who would share the DIO briefing material, requires scrutiny. Downer's public statements regarding the threat of violence were made in the expectation that the briefing material was unlikely to see the light of day. The leaked DIO intelligence summaries show that Downer continued with his disingenuous statements for several months. An inquiry may confirm that he was aware of information received from an Indonesian East-Timorese defector giving credible information of high-level ABRI plans to wipe out the pro-independence movement in Timor-Leste. Indeed, the defector, Tomas Goncalves, while being debriefed by Portuguese and Australian intelligence officials in Macau, stated that he attended a meeting on 26 March 1999 in Dili organised by the Governor of Timor-Leste, Abilio Osorio Soares, who told him to '[prepare] to liquidate all the senior pro-independence people—and their parents, sons, daughters and grandchildren. If they sought shelter in the churches ... kill them all, even the priests and nuns'.[28]

Tragically, the Defence Intelligence briefings were correct. By April 1999 massacres commenced, culminating on 6 September 1999 in mass killings in Suai in which even an Indonesian Roman Catholic priest was slaughtered.[29] Despite Goncalves' testimony, which was available to Foreign Minister Downer and his advisers, Canberra continued to dissemble.[30] Australia knew that news of Habibie's intention to grant Timor-Leste autonomy, if not independence, had prompted opposition within pro-Indonesian elements in Timor-Leste supported by the Indonesian armed forces. The worst of the intimidation preceding the independence referendum was a massacre that started during Mass at the village church at Liquiçá on 6 April 1999 and continued for three days.[31] After his release by the Indonesian Government in September 1999 and return to East Timor in October, Xanana Gusmão was accorded a memorable traditional welcome to Liquiçá by the survivors. To the consternation of his SAS guards, massed armed villagers greeted Gusmão. To drumbeat, the warriors danced backwards for several hundred metres as Gusmão strode before them, past the ruined and burnt buildings and into the village square where another contingent of armed warriors stood to attention. Bob, the leader of the SAS

After returning to his beloved Timor-Leste in late 1999, Xanana Gusmão pays homage to the dead in Liquiçá amid emotional scenes.

contingent, who had developed a warm rapport with Xanana, had another story for his children as did the author.

In his testimony before the parliamentary committee on December 1999, John Dauth, then DFAT Deputy Secretary, said that in April 1999 it would have been an absurd notion to propose a peacekeeping force for Timor-Leste.[32] How Dauth, as Head of the East Timor desk, if brought before a properly constituted inquiry, would respond to the same questioning now that leaked intelligence summaries are in the public domain, is yet to be determined. The late Desmond Ball was not alone in concluding that Australia deflected the US from exercising a duty to protect—a duty that the US was known to have acknowledged in more exacting circumstances in Kosovo.

In an insightful analysis of the US–Australia bilateral dynamic of that era, Dr Kelton records 'Australia's refusal to submit all information from Indonesia' and suggests that Prime Minister Howard could have called for earlier, more direct and likely more effective pressure by Washington on Jakarta. She puts Howard's exaggerated claims in context: 'In Australia's enduring quest for middle power status and independence, its actions initially betrayed its desires. As a consequence, in the necessary resort to crisis management, the choices for Australia in mediation were circumscribed, and ultimately it was dependent on the US for assistance'.³³ An official inquiry into Australian complicity in the failure to protect Timorese civilians (and the unarmed Australian police contingent) in 1999 is another long overdue element in restoring the Australian conscience. Far from clearing the Australian conscience over East Timor, the Howard Government deepened it.

The May 5 Accord
One month after the atrocity at Liquiçá, the UN-brokered 'Agreement between the Republic of Indonesia and the Portuguese Republic on the Question of East Timor' (May 5 Accord) was signed and a UN-sponsored popular consultation was planned to determine the question of independence for Timor-Leste. Although received unfavourably by elements within the Indonesian military, the Accord laid down a framework for progress towards either autonomy under Jakarta or independence for the Timorese, which was to include a UN-supervised ballot. The UN, Indonesia and Portugal were to sort out security for the ballot, but there seems little doubt that the Accord was signed with knowledge of a real risk of violence.

Ian Martin, who as Special Representative of the UN Secretary-General (SRSG) for the East Timor Popular Consultation led the UN Assisted Mission in East Timor (UNAMET), established after the May 5 Accord, reported:

> Observers had little doubt that the Indonesian armed forces ... were responsible for forming and arming the pro-integration militia groups and for directing their activities. While this was officially denied to international critics, there was no concealment of the degree of official approval of their existence: military, police and civilian officials attended inaugural and other functions throughout the territory. The culmination was a parade ceremony in front of the governor's office in Dili on 17 April, in the presence of senior officials, at which João Tavares of Halilintar and Eurico Guterres of Aitarak spoke as commander and deputy commander respectively of the militias' umbrella organisation.³⁴

Former FALINTIL commander Mau Hodu Ran Kadalak (José de Costa), who had played a prominent role at the FRETILIN National Conference in Sydney 14–20 August 1998 and at the September 1998 Dare 1 meeting, visited Australia at a very keyed-up time in May 1999. Subsequent events suggest that Mau Hodu made a fatal error in emphasising during his visit his expectation that Gusmão would form a government of national unity, post-liberation. Unease with Mau Hodu's outspoken call for leading FRETILIN members to stop opposing Gusmão's policy of national unity embracing all elements of the resistance was long-standing.

Kiernan records events in the desperate years of resistance that led to the divide between the Leninist–Marxist, no-negotiation, 'fight-alone' outlook and unified resistance strategy of Mau Hodu and Gusmão,[35] who had been together during the epic breakout from encircling Indonesian troops in November 1978. Gusmão's beloved Taur Matan Ruak, Nino Konis Santana and Mau Hunu also survived the gauntlet and, unsurprisingly, the survivors of that intrepid band remained staunch comrades as the Indonesian occupation entered its final phase in 1999. Ironically, Gusmão attributed his survival during the murderous final months of the Australian–Indonesian collaboration, as each side eyed the likely post-ballot leadership, to his imprisonment under international gaze.

In Sydney on 19 August 1998, Mau Hodu, as Permanent Political Secretary of the FRETILIN Central Committee, in an impassioned speech stressed the 'imperative need for national unity' as the means of achieving self-determination and independence for Timor-Leste. He was flanked during this session by FRETILIN's less than enthusiastic head, Mari Alkatiri. During his visit to Canberra in May 1999, Mau Hodu commented on 'Mari's unreformed strategy' and was surprised to learn from the author that Mari Alkatiri and Estanislau da Silva had been hosted in Canberra by DFAT during discussions in August 1998 with Alexander Downer concerning Indonesian and Australian petroleum exploration in the Timor Sea. Mari Alkatiri had been appointed during the CNRT establishment conference at Peniche, Portugal, in April 1998, as one of eight members of the all-party National Political Commission (NPC), and da Silva was Alkatiri's alternate on the Committee.[36]

Mau Hodu, who was accompanied on his visit to Australia by Domingos de Sousa, a Timor-Leste-based member of the NPC,[37] made clear that continued exploitation of Timor-Leste's Timor Sea petroleum reserves would depend upon a future elected Timor-Leste Government and not the views of diaspora elements within FRETILIN who had spent most of the occupation abroad. Tragically, observers noted that Mau Hodu was emerging as a likely key player in the prospect of a post-independence, Gusmão-led unity CNRT/FRETILIN Government. Shortly before his departure, Mau Hodu gave a televised press conference at the Collaery Law Boardroom in Canberra. Clear-thinking, articulate, and no stranger to intrigue, Mau Hodu was, unlike Alkatiri, going to be a staunch political ally of CNRT leader Xanana Gusmão and, with colleagues, likely to displace the expatriate FRETILIN leadership after independence. A renowned field veteran, he had the confidence of both FALINTIL and the Church (never easy in relations with FRETILIN); like Gusmão, he had wide national standing.

On 8 September 1999, Amnesty International issued a communiqué stating that Mau Hodu had been kidnapped in Dili by TNI soldiers and militia. Other reports claim that Mau Hodu was murdered sometime after leaving his Kupang hotel whilst being escorted to Jakarta by the Indonesian military. Mau Hodu, then a member of the Peace and Justice Commission, a joint initiative between Dili and Jakarta, was allegedly travelling to Jakarta as an emissary of Bishop Belo. After the International Force for East Timor (INTERFET) occupation of Timor-Leste, Mau Hodu's body is believed to have been tentatively identified at a site within Australian patrol lines near the Timor-Leste border town of Batugade, on the other side of the island from where he was last seen alive.

So why was Mau Hodu eliminated? Although he was free to promote the CNRT cause under the new UN-brokered liberalisation, it was too late for him to be another resistance leader to perish, as he was captured mysteriously by the Indonesians during field operations. Mau Hodu's death nullified or at least weakened the prospect of a post-liberation CNRT/FRETILIN unity government, long-envisaged by Gusmão and opposed by elements within the FRETILIN Central Committee.[38]

Australian diplomacy during this intense wake-up period for DFAT included further odious and anxious collaboration with Indonesia with respect to the Department's Holy Grail—the Timor Gap Treaty. Whether those exchanges included DFAT's appreciation of the tension between the likely FRETILIN/CNRT viewpoint, as expounded by Mau Hodu and de Sousa, on the future of the treaty and the understanding Downer and his officials believed they had reached with

Alkatiri in August 1998 in the joint FRETILIN and Australian interest and Jakarta's interest is a matter long overdue for inquiry.

Ascertaining whether there was an exchange of information on official or unofficial grounds between Canberra and Jakarta concerning the FRETILIN/CNRT dynamic following Mau Hodu's visit is only one aspect of determining whether Australia played a role in the events that led to Mau Hodu's death. One may discern that the 1999–2000 period was a tumultuous time in Australia–Indonesia intelligence liaison. This period included an investigation in Canberra and elsewhere to determine the source of highly sensitive Australian intelligence appreciations believed to be reaching the hands of Australian and US-trained Indonesian Army General Hendropriyono.[39]

An independent international inquiry into Mau Hodu's death should identify the level of any collaboration between Australia and Indonesia regarding Mau's visit to Australia, and, since there is little doubt that Mau Hodu's visit was reported upon, whether diplomatic exchanges and/or successful Indonesian intelligence penetration of DFAT in the relevant period contributed to a death that may have changed the course of history. As we shall see, Australia's successful sponsorship of the Alkatiri push for power gave Australia and corporate interests the suite of treaties they wanted and extended the suffering of the Timorese people for another four years until the unelected Alkatiri Government ended in violence.

UN-Supervised Ballot

In the popular ballot, supervised by UNAMET on 30 August 1999, more than 78% of Timorese voted for full independence from Indonesia. Although the Australian Foreign Minister was aware from intelligence reports that elements of the Indonesian military had a scorched-earth contingency plan for a loss at the poll, the Australian Government made no candid disclosure at the UN or to the Commissioner of the Australian Federal Police (AFP). This may, to some extent, explain the UN failure to draw up a workable plan to protect UNAMET personnel, including AFP elements. UN Secretary-General Kofi Annan attempted to explain this failure on 10 September 1999:

> We knew it was going to be difficult, we knew about the security problems, but not the carnage and the chaos we have seen. I can assure you that if those who were putting together the deal—and we must

remember the agreement was signed by Portugal and Indonesia with the support of their leaders, unanimously endorsed by the [Security] Council—if any of us had an inkling that it was going to be this chaotic I don't think anyone would have gone forward ... We are no fools.[40]

Annan's Special Representative Ian Martin explains it somewhat differently:

Once Habibie had offered that choice, the UN and the key countries following closely the UN's negotiations were well aware of the risk. But neither they nor the East Timorese could have countenanced the opposite risk—of failing to grasp an opportunity that had been closed for twenty-four years.

It was then the responsibility of the UN and Portugal to gain the best agreements, including the strongest security guarantees, they could, and of those with influence with Indonesia to support them in this. The security agreement fell well short of the UN's proposals for disarming the militia and neutralizing the TNI, and the UN's proposals themselves never envisaged a peacekeeping force before the ballot. Perhaps more could have been obtained at the negotiating table if Portugal and the UN had been willing to risk the very prospect of the agreement that they—and the CNRT—so strongly desired and had called for more U.S. and other pressure on Jakarta. But it is impossible to believe that this could have gone as far as inducing acceptance of an international peacekeeping force; Habibie could not have accepted this and survived politically to see it implemented. And only the presence of international peacekeepers with a robust mandate and the withdrawal of most of the TNI would have prevented the violence before and after the ballot.[41]

In retrospect, the key issue is that Australia possessed the intelligence that may have galvanised earlier action at the UN, particularly by the US, the EU, Britain and Portugal to press for a TNI withdrawal and a disarming of the militia. Although President Habibie was himself isolated to some extent from the TNI, the US with its historic ties could have exerted strong pressure directly on the Indonesian military hierarchy. Instead, clashes, instigated primarily by the Indonesian military and aided by pro-Indonesia Timorese militias, escalated after the declaration of the pro-independence ballot.

Desmond Ball chronicles the way the Australian intelligence community became the almost silent witness to the unfolding tragedy, revealing that in February 1999 Dr Ashton Calvert, then DFAT Secretary, met with the US State Department's Assistant Secretary for East Asian Affairs, Stanley Roth, concerning the need for a peacekeeping force. Calvert sought to dissuade the US, preferring 'adept diplomacy'.[42] By March 1999 Roth was asking Australia for intelligence material it may have on links between the ABRI and the pro-Indonesian militia. Australia rebuffed repeated US requests, arguing, according to Ball, the need to protect sources.

As the day of the ballot approached amid claims by Downer downplaying the risk of violence, the Australian Government was invited to make clandestine operational contact with the CNRT resistance so that accurate appreciations of impending militia violence would be available. This was effected with the assistance of the author. For reasons relating to fears that any compromise of Australian SAS on-ground activity might push Australian–Indonesian relations to a flash-point, UK Special Forces were to be deployed. Atrocities by Indonesian-led militia escalated. On 26 August 1999, former Deputy Prime Minister Tim Fischer led an Australian parliamentary delegation to Timor-Leste. The delegation received a strong plea from Bishop Belo of Dili that an international peacekeeping force be deployed after a pro-independence vote. Belo had conveyed his view that such a force was needed to Australian diplomats for some months. The delegation reported to Downer on 3 September 1999 that Belo had stated

> that he believed many East Timorese had not registered to vote because of intimidation and fears about security. He indicated that the supporters of autonomy had manipulated the security situation and that the police were unable and unwilling to control the activities of the militias. The Bishop considered that the pro-independence fighters were unlikely to accept a pro-autonomy result and the war in East Timor would continue. If the independence side won there would be seven or eight days of violence and then the militia would give up. He considered that East Timor would need an international force to keep order and that it was impossible to rely on the Indonesian forces to keep order in the interim period until the People's Consultative Assembly or MPR made its decision on East Timor.[43]

The previous day, New Zealand's Foreign Minister Don McKinnon had made a similar suggestion, saying that a group of countries from the region could 'mount a support operation to prevent the country descending into chaos and halt the bloodshed'. An Australian Government spokesman was reported as responding, 'Just for everyone who has still not got the message, Australia has no intention of invading Indonesia'.[44]

UNAMET head Ian Martin places strong emphasis upon the role of the World Bank and the International Monetary Fund (IMF) in dealing with the escalating crisis. He notes Indonesia's increasing dependence on the IMF and World Bank and that East Timor had featured at a July 1999 meeting of the Consultative Group for Indonesia (CGI), 'when donors' pledges were put in the context of support for Indonesia's political transition, including "the Government's commitment to provide the security necessary for the August popular consultation on East Timor"'. The World Bank president wrote to Habibie on 8 September, reminding him of assurances given in July, and seeking swift action to restore and maintain order in East Timor. Successive IMF statements indicated that it was watching the situation in East Timor and on 9 September the IMF announced its intention to put on hold a mission to Indonesia on which the resumption of IMF lending depended.[45] Following the World Bank and IMF initiatives, the Clinton Administration made clear to Jakarta that the US might withdraw support for both World Bank and IMF loans to Indonesia and any further military cooperation.

Security Council Resolution 1264
While the Netherlands, which had the Presidency of the Security Council, organised a Security Council mission to Jakarta, Australia, ever timid, welcomed the United Kingdom taking the lead in drafting Security Council resolutions and statements on Timor-Leste.[46] As the security situation in Timor-Leste deteriorated rapidly, requests from John Howard to President Clinton for deployment of US troops to Timor-Leste were rebuffed.[47] Clinton's understandable response to the idea of the US assuming the larger burden of military intervention represented the weak-kneed end of failed Australian diplomacy. Ever tremulous in relations with those in power in Jakarta, Downer and his officials, with their 'adept diplomacy' exposed for its moral bankruptcy, moved for cover and passed the baton to men and women of action. Fortunately, at defence level, US and Australian defence commanders had been planning in advance for such a contingency.[48] As the suffering

in Timor intensified, little more was heard from those who had been dissembling while others of conscience in the Australian defence and intelligence community had urged concrete action to reel in the TNI. But, as we shall see, the whisperers behind the Howard Government were regrouping, urged on by petroleum interests.

Agio Pereira, Sydney-based CNRT strategist then in Timor-Leste as a CNRT observer, telephoned the author early on 6 September 1999 and advised that he had reliable information, allegedly from within the militia, of militia leaders' plan to kill Bishop Belo and to 'empty' the compound of hundreds of Timorese sheltering at the Bishop's house on the Dili waterfront at Lecidere. The author telephoned his long-time former Narrabundah neighbour and friend, Senator Nick Minchin, who at that moment was walking into a Cabinet Meeting in Melbourne. Minchin, with his mobile telephone cupped, conveyed the information to Prime Minister Howard, who, to his credit, acted promptly through Habibie's office. Belo was evacuated by helicopter that afternoon to Bacau shortly before his house was destroyed and those sheltering put to flight. Given the proven reliability of Pereira's source(s) in respect of other militia assassination plans,[49] it is likely that Minchin's and Howard's interventions saved Belo's life.[50]

Howard made no other decisive call, leaving it to the US to rein in General Wiranto. As already noted, World Bank President James Wolfensohn intervened on 8 September to warn Jakarta and postpone the IMF's September mission. The same day, the Commander-in-Chief of US Forces in the Pacific region, Admiral Dennis Blair, now armed with irrefutable evidence, no thanks to the Australian Foreign Ministry, informed General Wiranto that the US would not tolerate any further deterioration in the humanitarian crisis.[51] The following day in Washington, President Clinton raised the prospect of international peacekeeping intervention—a call he repeated two days later in a dramatic and forceful address at the Asia-Pacific Economic Cooperation (APEC) meeting in Auckland.[52] By calling specifically for Australia to take the lead with an international peacekeeping force, Clinton broke the paralysis in Canberra that had set in when confrontation with the Indonesian TNI appeared inevitable. Drawing strength from Clinton's threat of broad-based economic sanctions and the cessation of all military ties, President Habibie overcame further TNI-based political opposition in Jakarta. Recalling for a third time in the 20th century where US nerve-endings were, Lisbon, playing the same old card, added to the pressure on Washington by threatening to rescind landing rights in the Azores for US military flights to and from Kosovo unless action was taken to provide humanitarian relief in East Timor.

Security Council members worked out a *modus vivendi* whereby an international force would restore order in Timor-Leste during an Indonesian military withdrawal.[53] With the benefit of US support, and having finally given a decisive ear to his defence planners, Howard moved astutely to position an Australian-led multinational force for military intervention. During this mayhem, UN Secretary-General Kofi Annan issued a communiqué, grimly renamed in Dili 'Kofi's Death List', which, anticipating wrongly, a balanced outcome to the ballot, established a pro-autonomy and pro-independence Consultative Council to the UN's Special Representative in Dili. To the CNRT's astonishment, the pro-independence nominees were identified. They had to flee when pro-Indonesia militia began hunting for them.

Civil violence diminished progressively after the INTERFET commenced its military occupation of Timor-Leste on 20 September 1999, pursuant to UN Security Council Resolution 1264.[54] The occupation was complete some six weeks later as INTERFET troops, landing again by sea, expanded their perimeter in the enclave of Oecusse. The INTERFET Mission ended on 23 February 2000 with a formal handover to a UN peacekeeping force, the main elements of which remained Australian defence personnel. Contrary to Howard's assertion that he and Australia took the lead role in inducing Jakarta to accept peacekeeping forces, Gunn and Huang conclude that Indonesia ultimately allowed international intervention because of direct and indirect pressure from international actors: 'While the Secretary-General and the Security Council played the central role, other actors including the World Bank and the United States along with the international media crucially tipped the balance'.[55]

Duty to Protect

If a judgement is to be made, Australia played an ignoble role in not disclosing promptly to the UN, Washington and EU actors, particularly Portugal as the administering power, the intelligence it held regarding the likely organised mayhem after the 1999 ballot. Writing in 2001, UNAMET Head Ian Martin left open the question of the extent to which the whole chain of command of the TNI was responsible for the post-ballot violence, concluding that this 'may perhaps become clearer as investigations and judicial proceedings are pursued. UNAMET's failure fully to predict this, despite the warnings known to it and its expectation of substantial post-ballot violence, was shared by most diplomatic analysts but requires explanation if not excuse'.[56]

The late Desmond Ball's analysis of leaked Australian intelligence assessments reveals unease in the defence establishment with the timidity of Howard and Downer and points some of the way to where an effective inquiry might begin.[57] It might commence with an investigation into the decision-making in Canberra that led to the controversial restriction of intelligence information to the US and the downplaying of the risk of violence in the run-up to the ballot. There has been no such move by successive governments in Canberra, where maintenance of strong bilateral relations with Jakarta has been an article of faith, even at cost to the Australia–US alliance. The disinclination by the US in early 2014 to accept Alexander Downer as Australia's Ambassador in Washington may have been based not only on satisfaction with the incumbent Kim Beazley, but also on a reflection of the strains Downer imposed on the Clinton Administration in that tumultuous period of US–Australia relations over East Timor.

Much later Downer and his trusted adviser on East Timor, John Dauth, teamed up in London. Dauth, by all reports, had much earlier expressed an interest in being Australia's Ambassador to Jakarta, but that was not to be. Later, he was housed in London as Australian High Commissioner. After his retirement, Downer became High Commissioner in London where Dauth remained, occupied among other involvements as Chairman of the Menzies Centre's Advisory Board. In 2018, a trio became complete when former Australian Attorney-General Senator George Brandis replaced Alexander Downer in London as Australian High Commissioner.

Peace in Our Time
On 7 September 1999, Gusmão was released by Indonesian authorities from house arrest in Salemba, Central Java. He was escorted to the British Embassy in Jakarta and then onto a flight to New York, where he joined CNRT Deputy President, José Ramos-Horta. Gusmão and Ramos-Horta wasted no time in meeting Ali Alatas there.

Their discussions centred on the suppression of the rampant TNI-sponsored militia and the welfare of those suffering under the scourge of militia violence. Alatas made clear his acceptance of the need for international intervention and that Indonesia's respect for the outcome of the ballot included an early handover of Timor Sea petroleum operations. Gusmão and Ramos-Horta then flew to Darwin where, after a briefing from Alkatiri and without securing expert legal advice, the trio were ushered into a meeting with Phillips Petroleum and DFAT officials. A draft joint declaration was produced and read to Gusmão by Ramos-Horta, before the trio signed the ill-advised declaration. The text, which Australia and Woodside/Phillips swiftly exploited to the full, read:

> CNRT wishes to assure all ZOC [Zone of Cooperation] contractors of our support for continued development of the petroleum resources within this area. Working with the United Nations, Australia and Portugal it is our intent to negotiate appropriate transition arrangements and consequent changes in the current Treaty that maintain its legal authority over petroleum resource development. Without limiting our rights and interests in the Zone of Cooperation, we wish to assure all ZOC contractors operating under current Production Sharing Contracts that their legal rights will continue through the full term of those contracts and that fiscal policies applicable to production sharing and taxation will be no more onerous than current policies as they relate to the contractors share.

In burnt-out Dili, the regrouped CNRT leadership, now joined by the author, found that at almost every meeting with Australian officials, still housed in the Consulate building designed and built in Indonesian vernacular style under Australian supervision some years earlier,[58] they were being led not to measures to deal with the parlous food situation and the tens of thousands of homeless people, but to a discussion of arrangements for the Timor Gap Zone of Cooperation. Returning to Dili, the Australian Representative, James Batley, was quick to wave at his next meeting the declaration signed by Gusmão, Alkatiri and Ramos-Horta. Batley had stepped off the plane from Darwin with a copy of the joint declaration, an original of which had already been couriered to Canberra. Batley's piece of paper would come to haunt the Timorese leadership in years to come.

8
TRANSITION IN TIMOR-LESTE AND THE TIMOR GAP TREATY

With the aftermath of the scorched-earth retreat of Indonesian militia from East Timor into West Timor dominating world media, the United Nations Security Council resolved on 25 October 1999 to establish a UN Transitional Administration in East Timor (UNTAET) with a mandate to provide security and maintain law and order, establish an administration, help develop civil and social services, ensure assistance was coordinated and delivered, support capacity-building for self-government, and help establish conditions for sustainable development.[1] A month later UN Secretary-General Kofi Annan's Special Representative (SRSG), Sergio Vieira de Mello, established an office at Dili and promulgated UNTAET Regulation 1999/1 of 27 November 1999,[2] which gave him, as Transitional Administrator, complete power of governance for Timor-Leste. This was the first time the Security Council had, by Resolution pursuant to Chapter VII of the UN Charter to restore peace and security, created with close to unanimous General Assembly support, a UN Mission with full legislative, judicial and executive power over a territory. The SRSG in Timor-Leste was not a delegate of the UN Secretary-General as was the case in almost all prior UN administrations following conferral of powers by interested States and/or by self-limiting agreements such as the 1991 Paris Peace Accord regarding Cambodia. Sergio de Mello was, in law, exercising the functions of the Secretary-General.

The taking up by the UN of administering power over territories following resolutions by the General Assembly and/or the Security Council has left a controversial legacy with East Timor no exception. In his study of the legal status of territories subject to administration by international organisations, particularly the UN, Knoll deals with the manner in which, following agreement between Indonesia and the Netherlands a United Nations Temporary Executive Authority (UNTEA) was established on 21 September 1962 with, 'full authority under the direction of the Secretary-General to administer West New Guinea' only to see power transferred eight months later to Indonesia. The legal status of UN administrations in Namibia (1967) and Kosovo (1999) were both open to challenge in international law. With respect to Kosovo the assent to UN administration by the former Republic of Yugoslavia, threatened by further NATO military action, was arguably not freely made and thus void. Against this background the UN administration of East Timor was seen by many observers as a chance to see Chapter VII of the UN Charter in action finally, as drafted principally by Evatt in the aftermath of the Second World War.[3]

In an unprecedented state vacuum, de Mello faced an immense challenge as the whole of East Timor was in ruins, with tens of thousands of displaced Timorese roaming the countryside, but his task was poisoned from the start. Fresh from UN headquarters in Kosovo, Kofi Annan's appointee had other hungry petitioners pleading for attention. On the very day he established his authority in Dili, de Mello, under pressure from Australia, sought advice from UN's New York headquarters on the validity of the Timor Gap Treaty, the prospect of UNTAET renegotiating it on behalf of Timor-Leste, any linkage with maritime boundary negotiations, and the question of UNTAET 'succession' to Indonesia in respect to the treaty. Phillips Petroleum, which had a 50.29% share in the Bayu-Undan Field in the Zone of Cooperation (ZOC) established under the 1989 Timor Gap Treaty, had also written to the UN Secretary-General seeking similar advice, and de Mello had received an uncompromising briefing from the Australian Foreign Minister before assuming his post.[4]

In an opinion dated 2 December 1999 that covered the issues raised by de Mello and Phillips Petroleum, Under-Secretary-General for

Legal Affairs and Legal Counsel for the UN, Hans Corell, international lawyer and former Swedish judge and diplomat, observed:

> The illegality of the annexation ... does not necessarily invalidate the Treaty or the rights and obligations which have been acquired thereunder. When in the Namibia Case a similar question arose, the ICJ made a distinction between the illegality of the annexation and the legal acts of the unlawful occupant. It accordingly decided that where such legal acts create for the inhabitants of the territory rights and obligations, they should be respected, recognized and be given legal effect.[5]

Corell did not explain how he saw the Namibia Case as relevant when the Timor Gap Treaty did not impose any obligations on or create successor 'rights' for the peoples of East Timor. No benefits had flowed to the Timorese peoples from the treaty and the idea of any obligations was obscene. The Timorese had endured genocidal oppression while revenue from the treaty had flowed to corporate interests and into state coffers at Jakarta and Canberra. Undoubtedly, Corell was aware that treaties conflicting with a peremptory norm of general international law (*jus cogens*) are invalid. The rights of the East Timorese peoples to self-determination and sovereignty over their natural wealth were protected by that principle.[6] In 2005 the International Court of Justice (ICJ), in recognising the principle as 'a principle of customary international law', recalled instruments that Corell would have been familiar with in his role—namely, General Assembly Resolution 1803 (XVII) of 14 December 1962 on Permanent Sovereignty Over Natural Resources, further elaborated in the Declaration on the Establishment of a New International Economic Order (General Assembly Resolution 3201 (S.VI) of 1 May 1974) and the Charter of Economic Rights and Duties of States (General Assembly Resolution 3281 (XXIX) of 12 December 1974).[7]

Empowered by the Security Council to govern East Timor and backed by international law, to which Australia had subscribed, now was the time for the Secretary-General to bring Australia to the table for a reckoning. A crucial issue was the high cost UNTAET had imposed on the UN budget. Inexplicably, there was no exploration of the issue of the reparations that might be due to the East Timorese from Australia and Indonesia over a 'treaty' that divided the spoils while the rightful owners starved. Instead, as soon as the UN set about finding an early revenue stream to alleviate the financial burden on the UN, a conflict of interest arose. Knoll observes from issues arising out of the Nauru Case[8]:

> Not unlike colonial and protectorate administrations, an international fiduciary administration has to simultaneously pursue the interests of the 'metropolitan core' as well as represent the interests of the non-self-governing territorial unit. These two functions have, in the case of Mandate administration, been in conflict with each other.[9]

More puzzling was Corell's observation that, if the treaty was invalid, 'it will lead to the conclusion that all legal acts of Indonesia, including in particular Indonesian law applicable in East Timor, should be declared null and void. UNTAET Regulation No. 1999/1 for East Timor, however, which specifically upheld Indonesian law, took the opposite approach'.[10] Faced with a choice of law with which to govern, de Mello had issued UNTAET Regulation No. 1999/1 adopting, *pro tem* but nevertheless controversially, Indonesian law less some provisions such as capital punishment. The regulation had no declaratory effect on the application of Indonesian law during the unlawful occupation. In fact, it expressly stated that it could not operate to legitimise the prior acts of the Indonesian regime—namely, it could not apply *ex post facto* to the unlawful treaty. In any event, if Corell perceived a problem with the regulation, he could fix it, as it had been cleared internally by his legal secretariat.[11] The need for the Secretary-General to have secured independent legal advice becomes more apparent from the acknowledgement in Corell's opinion that the UN Secretariat had accepted the Timor Gap Treaty for registration and publication in accordance with Article 102 of the UN Charter.

Embarrassment the UN should have felt over the registration of the invalid 1989 Timor Gap Treaty, when other organs of the UN had by successive resolutions declared the occupation of Timor-Leste to be unlawful, was brushed aside when Corell recorded in his advice that 'representatives of the East Timorese have expressed their desire, in principle, to be bound by the Treaty with modifications. We also note that the Australians have agreed to renegotiate certain aspects of the Treaty for the benefit of East Timor'.[12]

Article 102 has an interesting history. Originally Article 18 in the Covenant of the League of Nations, Article 102 replicated the obligation on states to register all treaties and for their publication by the

League. How then was a brazen expropriation of the assets of an unlawfully occupied country registered by the UN as a treaty? Portugal had challenged the validity of the Timor Gap Treaty in the ICJ in 1991 and observers knew that Portugal's lack of success in that endeavour gave no legitimacy to the treaty. The ICJ's decision not to accept Portugal's case for adjudication because Indonesia was not a party to the proceedings and the hearing of argument would involve a judgement of the validity of Indonesia's annexation of Portuguese Timor[13] has been criticised as inconsistent with the ICJs earlier decision in the Nauru Case,[14] where, ironically, Australia was sued alone, despite New Zealand and Britain being co-administrators of the Island.[15]

The registration of an agreement secured after forceful invasion that offended the territorial integrity of Portugal as the administering power was incompatible with the Charter itself and peremptory principles of international law. The Timor Gap Treaty should not have been processed for registration by the Legal Secretariat, of which Corell later became head. Article 103 of the Charter makes clear that the obligations of member states to the Charter prevail over any obligations derived from treaty-making. Moreover, treaty provisions that are incompatible with *jus cogens* are void.[16] This includes all contracts, licences, permits and dealings howsoever procured under such treaty provisions. Legal advice available to Australia and the petroleum companies would have revealed this. Australia had assisted in the drafting of UN principles that specifically declared: 'Where obligations arising under international agreements are in conflict with the obligations of Members of the United Nations under the Charter of the United Nations the obligations under the Charter shall prevail'.[17]

The notion of *ordre international public* has a relatively modern history. In the Oscar Chinn Case,[18] Judge Schucking, in dissent, argued that the Court should not recognise an agreement contrary to international public policy. Dörr and Schmalenbach's commentary also adverts to Hersch Lauterpacht's precursor draft Article 15 to Article 53 of the Vienna Convention on the Law of Treaties, wherein Lauterpacht as Special Rapporteur proposed the test as to whether the object of a treaty is illegal should be not so much as inconsistency with customary international law but 'with such overriding principles of international law which may be regarded as constituting principles in international public policy (*ordre international public*)'. Fitzmaurice subsequently proposed the incorporation of the essentiality of *jus cogens* into Article 15,[19] which Article 53 of the Vienna Convention now reflects.

As the UN had assumed complete powers of governance in East Timor, the failure by the Secretary-General to engage with the parties directly affected by the unlawful Timor Gap Treaty and with the international community in relation to the legal effect of the treaty, and the question of reparations contrasts unfavourably with a multiplicity of both the League's trusteeships and the UN's prior involvement in like issues affecting emerging states.[20] Moreover, the UN Legal Secretariat of which Corell was a member was monitoring successive reports since 1988 of a Special Rapporteur and Sub-Committees on the proposed development of guidelines on the right to remedies and reparations by, *inter alia*, subjugated peoples.[21] The East Timorese were within that category.

The 1989 Timor Gap Treaty offended *jus cogens* and was invalid. The UN Security Council could not mandate the Secretary-General to undertake any act that offended *jus cogens*. Adopting the terms of such a treaty to provide an early revenue stream for East Timor offended *jus cogens* because it perpetuated the *jus cogens* violation. Australia had secured a position in the Timor Sea in breach of a peremptory norm. It was fundamentally wrong for the UN to give tacit recognition to Australia's ongoing unlawful occupation.

Ample jurisprudence would have justified the Secretary-General informing Australia and the oil majors that he required time to secure a full appreciation of where they stood in law and how the interests of the Timorese peoples should be pursued. In that task, the Secretary-General may have been assisted by a then recent decision of the Appeals Chamber of the International Criminal Tribunal for the former Yugoslavia in the Tadic Case where the court held that the Security Council could not adopt definitions of crimes that deviated from customary law.[22] Likewise, Judge Elihu Lauterpacht, echoing his late father's thesis, held in the *Genocide Case*: 'The relief which Article 103 of the Charter may give the Security Council in case of conflict between one of its decisions and an operative treaty obligation cannot—as a matter of simple hierarchy of norms—extend to a conflict between a Security Council resolution and *jus cogens*'.[23]

The apparent urgency of the situation following Phillips Petroleum's letter to the Secretary-General is puzzling. Revenue accruing could and should have been placed in an escrow account. A short delay while informed external advice was secured by the UN from petroleum consultants and industry lawyers on timing and development issues, including production-sharing contracts appurtenant to the treaty, would have been a prudent step. Nor should the Secretary-General and his adviser Corell have been swayed by the agreement, manifestly uninformed, in terms of the production-sharing contracts, by Alkatiri, Ramos-Horta and Gusmão that it was in East Timor's interest that the treaty provisions could continue in some form. It seems extraordinary that Gusmão, released into the care of the British Embassy at Jakarta after nine years in custody and flown to New York, could be expected to include in his round of meetings an informed discussion with petroleum representatives.

When the author shortly afterwards queried the origins of the 20 October 1999 CNRT Declaration signed at Darwin by Gusmão on his way home from New York, Gusmão professed no knowledge that the registration of the Timor Gap Treaty by the UN, clothing it with ostensible legality, had been improper; nor was Gusmão told that connected production-sharing contracts contained complex and oppressive clauses. There was no mention of reparations during meetings at New York, and the Secretary-General, in his protective role for the Timorese, took no initiative subsequently in that regard. The argument being pressed by Australia and corporate interests upon the three Timorese in New York, said to represent the people of Timor-Leste, was that any rupture in the existing production arrangements might cause long-term prejudice to East Timor. That argument persisted throughout the UNTAET administration. Within two years, under UN supervision and prior to any democratic election, the 2002 Timor Sea Treaty had bound the peoples of Timor-Leste to an exploitative 30-year oil and gas treaty containing a maverick definition of 'petroleum'.

After their meetings in New York and Darwin, Mari Alkatiri and José Ramos-Horta had urged early release of the October 1999 CNRT Declaration. Thus, Timor-Leste's economic development was viewed from the start through a narrow petroleum prism. The Timorese leadership should have been assisted by an independent special commission of experts convoked by the Secretary-General to determine the issue of reparations by Australia and Indonesia and the way forward in the Timor Sea, if only on an interim basis.

Following the April 1998 meeting of resistance groups at Peniche in Portugal that established the CNRT, FRETILIN delegation leader Mari Alkatiri had been given responsibility for Timor Sea oil negotiations following FRETILIN's demand that it take carriage of the Gap issue.

No evidence of the claim by Corell that Australia had agreed to renegotiate provisions of the 1989 treaty, 'for the benefit of East Timor', has emerged. Key UN consultant adviser Peter Galbraith, had from the outset assumed that a new treaty was required and that, in the interim, production-sharing contracts would be honoured.[24] This was not a circumstance where the Timorese, as claimed by Corell, were agreeing 'in principle, to be bound by the (existing) Treaty with modifications'. It appears that this was a course that Corell was anticipating, and ultimately achieved, but that was not the view expressed in Dili by the CNRT. On a visit to Canberra in November 1999 Alkatiri was reported as saying, 'we are not going to be a successor to an illegal treaty'.[25]

Although it had assumed governing functions in Timor-Leste, the UN, not being a state, lacked, arguably, the capacity to bring proceedings before the ICJ as to the legality of the continued Australian occupation of the Timor-Leste sea-bed north of any provisional median line.[26] At that time Australia's reservations could not, arguably, take effect. There was strong international support for Timor-Leste from many countries, including China, the United States, the European Union and the Lusophone world. Decisive leadership by Kofi Annan and domestic pressure within Australia might have shamed the Howard Government into submitting the legal question to the ICJ or at least into emulating Indonesia and withdrawing from unlawful occupation of Timor-Leste's sovereign territorial sea-bed.

Instead, the UN effectively stepped into the shoes Indonesia had formerly occupied in the disputed area of the Timor Sea to collective sighs of relief by interested company boards and shareholders. One eminent commentator, Professor Gillian Triggs, perhaps unintentionally, gave a semblance of legal propriety to the views of the relieved parties, referring to them as 'stakeholders':

> By continuing the terms of the Timor Gap Treaty, it has been possible to maintain the legal status quo for Australia, UNTAET and all contractors under PSCs negotiated under the Timor Gap Treaty. The rights and obligations of all stakeholders are thus preserved, except that

UNTAET, acting on behalf of the peoples of East Timor, has assumed Indonesia's sovereign rights in the ZOC.[27]

Where petroleum exploitation, or 'Black Poison',[28] is concerned, other values may apply. Sovereign risk factors for existing investor interests, albeit trespassing, appear from the record to have been of overriding concern for the UN and Australia. On one view, as this push progressed, Foreign Minister Downer and Australian Government officials, in regular contact with the industry players, adopted a manipulative path to Timor-Leste's independence.

The approach in 1999 by Corell to the 1989 Timor Gap Treaty is to be contrasted to that adopted in his advice dated 29 January 2002 to the President of the Security Council concerning the signing of contracts by Morocco for petroleum exploitation off-shore of the non-self-governing territory of Western Sahara:

> The recent State practice, though limited, is illustrative of an opinion juris on the part of both administering Powers and third States: where resource exploitation activities are concluded in Non-Self-Governing Territories for the benefit of the peoples of these territories, on their behalf, or in consultation with their representatives, they are considered compatible with the Charter obligations of the administering Power, and in conformity with the General Assembly resolutions and the principle of 'permanent sovereignty over natural resources' enshrined therein.[29]

If there was any States practice, this being doubtful, Corell in his own analysis distinguished the Nauru, Namibia, Timor-Leste and Western Sahara circumstances. Indeed, Timor-Leste's circumstance was more in keeping with the multinational corporation exploitation of Namibian resources that was condemned by the General Assembly and the Security Council.[30] In the case of occupied Timor-Leste, neither Indonesia nor Australia were 'administering Powers'; they were invader and accessory respectively, and neither was exploiting the Timor Gap for the benefit of the Timorese peoples. Both were liable to reparation claims. Moreover, it was premature, if not misleading, for Corell to assert in his Advice that 'representatives' of the Timorese people were supporting continuation of the Timor Sea Treaty. With the country in ruins and most of the population dispersed, the 'representatives' referred to were led by an unelected diaspora Timorese, Mari Alkatiri, who had returned to Dili from a career in Mozambique and assumed a representative role on an issue of profound national sovereignty without any form of plebiscite.

It is important to recall that the local FRETILIN structure had been dislocated by violent events throughout 1999 during which leaders such as Mau Hodu were liquidated in suspicious circumstances, as noted in the previous chapter. Many activist FRETILIN families were dispersed and hungry and the concept that they could be brought into the debate is absurd. The largely non-traumatised diaspora-led FRETILIN members were operating alone and, even within the CNRT, non-consultatively, as illustrated dramatically in the first vote at the CNRT National Congress in August 2000, described later in this chapter.

Australia and UN Replicate the Timor Gap Treaty

Subsequent events illustrate the all too familiar disingenuous and posturing make-believe world of the UN at New York. While the Australian military dealt on the ground with the scorched product of failed Australian foreign policy relating to Timor-Leste, Australia's diplomats wasted no time at the UN in developing an alternative strategy for preserving the status quo in the Timor Sea for international petroleum interests. Unlike Indonesia, where the People's Consultative Assembly voted on 19 November 1999 to formally renounce sovereignty over Timor-Leste and to signal an end to the Timor Gap Treaty, Canberra had other ideas. Events soon revealed that Australia had no intention of relinquishing its unlawful role in support of international petroleum exploitation of areas of the Timor Sea sovereign to Timor-Leste or offering the Timorese any more favourable status in the Timor Sea. As the early post-liberation decisions taken in relation to the Timor Sea resources will affect the economic condition of the peoples of Timor-Leste throughout the 21st century, an analysis from what records are presently available is of vital importance.

Exploration and development of the petroleum resources of the Australian Continental Shelf below the Timor Sea had a long, largely bipartisan, history in Canberra. It expanded after petroleum exploration taxation incentives were introduced during the Menzies/Barwick era, was justified by External Affairs Minister McMahon's 'two shelves' claim in 1970,[31] advanced infamously by Whitlam and aggressively under Hawke, Keating, Howard and Gillard. The somewhat apologetic or even defensive phases during the Fraser and Rudd administrations were marked by a certain diffidence—in Malcolm Fraser's case by the troubled conscience he revealed shortly before his death.[32]

In the heady years of 1998 and 1999, when autonomy or independence loomed for Timor-Leste, revenue from oil and condensate well-head sales was being divided, effectively, between Australia and Indonesia in accordance with the 'co-prosperity' formula in the Timor Gap Treaty. While Australia yearned for a gas pipeline to Darwin where liquefied natural gas (LNG) processing could provide an infrastructure boost to the local economy, Canberra had a concealed ambition—the prospect that the Bayu-Undan Field would solve Australia's total reliance on imports of helium, a strategic commodity required increasingly in the defence, nuclear, electronic and hi-tech medical industries. How Australia achieved that ambition is an extraordinary story, but first the settings had to be put in place.

After the 30 August 1999 ballot in East Timor, collaboration with Indonesia in the Timor Sea was at an end. Australian Prime Minister John Howard and his two directly engaged Ministers, Alexander Downer and Nick Minchin, sought to mould a joint-venture relationship, initially with UNTAET and later with a new government in Dili.

The 1974 and 1995–96 gas analyses from Bayu-Undan had added a policy dimension to the Timor Sea oil and gas issue for Australia—namely, the prospect of an LNG pipeline delivering infrastructure gains to Australia's Northern Territory and the chance of securing for Australia its first helium-generating plant. The logistical difficulties Australia experienced in providing land support from Darwin to the UN intervention forces in Timor-Leste after the 1999 ballot added new urgency to development in Australia's north. Plans for a rail connection from the south to Darwin were accelerated. A strategic defence assessment before the INTERFET period had revealed logistical challenges in bringing defence materiel forward, particularly munitions. If there had been a wider maverick Indonesian military response to the situation, Australia's depleted F-111 strike force had insufficient stores and munitions in Darwin for more than its short suppression.

The Howard Government's declared aim for supporting the construction of a natural gas pipeline from the Bayu-Undan Field about 40 kilometres off the Timor-Leste coast to the Australian coast about 550 kilometres away was to expand Australia's LNG export trade. No public mention was made that the Bayu-Undan gas analyses lodged with Australia's geoscience agency meant that a pipeline to Australia could satisfy a critical helium commodity need. After the 1972 OPEC crisis, Australia had commenced the construction of a mammoth national natural gas grid and, while that grid was assessed at least initially to require no augmentation from Timor Sea LNG, the need to diversify Australia's export income away from unprocessed exports of mineral ores and oil and gas condensates would be met by onshore processing of the Bayu-Undan LNG at Wickham Point, near Darwin, and immediate export. While suiting foreign corporate interests, the failure to make a connection to the national gas grid was contrary to the Australian national interest.

Against this background, the period that bears analysis leading to the controversial pipeline decision commences in early 2000 with the robust negotiating style of UNTAET Political Affairs head Peter Galbraith, a man of wide experience in Washington and internationally. As the US Ambassador to the emerging state of Croatia, he was already well known to Sergio de Mello, now responsible for governing Timor-Leste. To put the 2001–02 negotiations leading to the 2002 Timor Sea Treaty into perspective, it is necessary to recount the events following the 30 August 1999 ballot.

The ashes of burnt-out Dili were barely cold before Australia commenced importuning the surviving largely diaspora Timorese leaders and the recently freed Xanana Gusmão. It was no surprise, therefore, that in late September–early October 1999, while the INTERFET military operation to deal with the aftermath of the militia violence was still underway in the shattered 13 districts of Timor-Leste, Australia's representative in Dili, James Batley, sought a meeting with CNRT representatives to discuss the future of the Timor Gap Treaty.

Batley now had the CNRT Declaration of 20 October 1999 signed at Darwin whereby the CNRT signatories, Gusmão, Ramos-Horta, and Alkatiri, welcomed 'the opportunity to work cooperatively with contractors to capture the maximum value from petroleum development within the Zone of Cooperation'. The declaration, drafted at Alkatiri's request and urged by Ramos-Horta, was circulated and discussed at a meeting between Batley and CNRT representatives in Dili on 27 October 1999. A copy was passed promptly to Phillips Petroleum by both the UN Legal Secretariat in New York and the Australian Government. The discussions on 27 October 1999 led Alkatiri to confirm what he had said to Alexander Downer in August 1998—that FRETILIN, and he expected the CNRT, would honour so much of the treaty terms as extended to production commitments with and between the consortia. The question of maritime boundary delineation was for another day, as was the question of overall resource management.

CNRT Timor-Leste

ON THE "TIMOR GAP TREATY"

The National Council for Timorese Resistance has as it principal goal the establishment of a truly independent, democratic and self-sufficient State of East Timor. Working cooperatively with the United Nations, Portugal and others, CNRT seeks to implement policies that will achieve this goal at the earliest opportunity.

In order to create an environment that values and sustains the well being of all East Timorese people, economic development is of great importance. Responsible development of natural resources within the sovereign control of East Timor, or which may be shared with others, will provide an important contribution for our future security.

With regard to the current Timor Gap Treaty and the so-called Zone of Cooperation, CNRT wishes to assure all ZOC contractors of our support for continued development of the petroleum resources within this area. Working with the United Nations, Australia and Portugal it is our intent to negotiate appropriate transition arrangements and consequent changes in the current Treaty that maintain its legal authority over petroleum resource development. Without limiting our rights and interests in the Zone of Cooperation, we wish to assure all ZOC contractors operating under current Production Sharing Contracts that their legal rights will continue through the full term of those contracts and that fiscal policies applicable to production sharing and taxation will be no more onerous than current policies as they relate to the contractors share. In exchange for these assurances, we would expect that petroleum exploration and development within the Zone of Cooperation would continue in the both the near and long term.

CNRT welcomes the opportunity to work cooperatively with contractors to capture the maximum value from petroleum development within the Zone of Cooperation. We expect that ZOC contractors and others in the region will work closely with CNRT also to develop our human and physical resources in a timely manner so that East Timor can contribute more fully in the development of its petroleum resources and in the realization of its benefits for all East Timorese.

We look forward to a long and mutually beneficial relationship.

Kay Rala Xanana Gusmão   José Ramos-Horta   Mari Alkatiri

Darwin, 20th October 1999

The Timor Sea Treaty 1989 *became popularly known as the* Timor Gap Treaty.

Much later the Timorese would argue bitterly that ConocoPhillips had no intention of acting for the mutual benefit of its shareholders and the impoverished Timorese. Certainly, the CNRT Declaration put Phillips Petroleum on notice from the outset that the CNRT sought a *bona fide* relationship to maximise production value from the Bayu-Undan Field.

While the young men and women in the Australian Army INTERFET patrol lines converging near Com at the snout of Avo Crocodilo[33] were sweating it out in the mountains and valleys of Australia's devastated World War II ally, the Australian Department of Foreign Affairs and Trade (DFAT), unbowed by the appalling outcome of unprincipled collaboration with Indonesia, was making another foray of the kind it was good at, aimed at preserving in another form the ill-gotten Timor Gap Treaty. In a *démarche* ordered by Downer, Australia's Deputy Permanent Representative at the UN, David Stewart, and a colleague on 12 November 1999 handed over to UN Legal Counsel Hans Corell the CNRT Declaration of 20 October 1999 they had secured, together with an *Aide-Mémoire* from Canberra asserting that the CNRT had expressed a desire for the Timor Gap Treaty 'to remain in force'. The *Aide-Mémoire* went on to quote a series of statements by Gusmão, Ramos-Horta and Alkatiri allegedly supportive of the 'continuation' of the Timor Gap Treaty.

Whether Stewart was conscious of the contradiction between the *Aide-Mémoire* and the CNRT Declaration that explicitly sought 'changes to the Treaty' may await his memoirs. 'Given the urgency attached to this situation', the Australian Note proposed that UNTAET enter into a 'state succession agreement with Australia on the Timor Gap Treaty'. Stewart and his colleague then proceeded to hand over to their UN listeners, a map, the text of the Timor Gap Treaty including the four annexures, being the map coordinates, the petroleum mining code for Area A, the model production-sharing contract and a taxation code for the avoidance of double taxation.

In conclusion, Stewart suggested that an interim agreement between Australia and the UN be signed to provide for the 'continuation of the Timor Gap Treaty'. Ignoring the true words of the CNRT Declaration and the fact that the production-sharing contracts, if signed, might bind the Timorese well into the 21st century, the *Aide-Mémoire* ended with an assurance of a sunset clause:

We would expect that the Special Representative would act only if satisfied that such treaty action would be accepted by broadly representative Timorese opinion, and on the grounds that it would be completely without prejudice to any action (succession or otherwise) that the East Timorese themselves may wish to take upon independence.

Stewart then presented Corell with a draft *Note Verbale* that would constitute the basis for an exchange of letters between the UN and Australia, and a draft memorandum of understanding recording the continuation of the Timor Gap Treaty that, contrary to the *Aide-Mémoire*, contained no sunset clause operative upon independence. When the question arose as to who would be party to the proposed agreement, Stewart said that, although he understood the interest of Portugal as former Administering Power in Timor-Leste, his government considered that Portugal should not sit at the table and negotiate on the matter.[34] After Corell remarked that the UN usually dealt with States in a neutral way, but that in the case of Timor-Leste the UN was acting on behalf of Timor-Leste, he and the six senior UN officials accompanying him, including a law of the sea expert, retired to consider the Australian intervention.

Corell perceived that, while neither the UN nor Timor-Leste could be termed 'successors' to Indonesia if the CNRT wanted to adopt the Timor Gap Treaty, the question whether the Timor Gap Treaty was illegal became moot. For Corell, this was fortuitous, because the UN was in a difficult position with respect to questions concerning the legality of the Timor Gap Treaty. He observed:

> We must also recall that the United Nations Secretariat accepted the Timor Gap Treaty for registration and publication in accordance with Article 102 of the United Nations Charter (Registration No. 28462). The United Nations, or any of its organs is, therefore, not well-placed to argue the invalidity of a treaty it considered valid at the time of registration. In addition, this registration was not challenged by any Member State.[35]

As for Australia's advice that it would be 'discussing with Indonesia the modalities for Indonesian disengagement from the Treaty', Corell observed that this was properly a role for the UN not Australia. Having listened to Stewart and read the CNRT Declaration, Corell concluded that the CNRT had 'expressed their desire in principle to be bound by the Treaty with modifications'. How Corell reached the further conclusion that 'the Australians have agreed to renegotiate certain aspects of the Treaty for the benefit of East Timor' is neither evident from the text of the Australian *Aide-Mémoire* nor from subsequent reports from de Mello in Dili. If Stewart said something to that effect when delivering Australia's CNRT trump card, it appears lost to the record.

Thus, by the time Peter Galbraith arrived at Dili in January 2000 to head the Political Affairs Division of UNTAET, charged with moving Timor-Leste to independence, the Australian Government had already secured from the CNRT and the UN Legal Counsel a tacit understanding that development of the Bayu-Undan Field would continue under production-sharing contracts that had evolved in the Indonesian era. Faced with such a *fait accompli* and aware that the UN was unlikely to sponsor any challenge to the legality of the 1989 Timor Gap Treaty, Galbraith had limited room in which to manoeuvre.

UN pragmatism immediately after the Indonesian withdrawal allowed the ill-prepared Timorese leadership to squander an opportunity to seek support from a receptive world audience for the preservation of the inalienable rights of future generations of Timorese to their sovereign resources. Former Secretary-General Kofi Annan emerges from subsequent events in a poor light. With the UN compromised by the registration of the illegal Timor Gap Treaty at the very time when other organs of the UN were condemning the Indonesian–Australian encroachment, the Timorese leadership should have been given access to high-level independent advice and Portugal offered a chance to assist. On the latter point, few at the UN involved with responding to the Australian *démarche* would have been unaware of the scholarship possessed by Portugal on the illegality of the Timor Gap Treaty and the maritime boundary issues. Clearly, Australia wanted to exclude any informed oversight of the machinations underway.

By the time other advisers, including the author and Galbraith, were appointed, the CNRT was in damage control. Oppressive provisions of the lengthy and complex production contracts, endorsed unseen by the commercially naive CNRT leadership in October 1999, had come to light. Strains in the CNRT leadership, particularly after the first CNRT National Congress in August 2000, meant that FRETILIN saw itself on a path to self-government wholly dependent upon an early petroleum revenue stream. Sergio de Mello faced the challenge of keeping FRETILIN's divisive push for power in check while trying to garner support in New York as he pushed back against the Australian attempt to preserve the Timor Gap Treaty.

Meanwhile, in an insightful but extraordinary move, Indonesia handed UNTAET a Diplomatic 'Non-Paper' containing a thinly veiled warning that Timor-Leste was not up for plunder. On the afternoon of 27 January 2000, Peter Galbraith met with Harry Haryono, Director of Treaties and Legal Affairs at the Indonesian Department of Foreign Affairs. Haryono handed Galbraith a note that said in part:

> Indonesia has no specific interest on the future status of the Treaty but it is the concern of Indonesia to pursue the policy that could secure the future legitimate interest of East Timor's natural resources. Therefore, it is the view that it should be the State of East Timor (as the successor state) to determine the succession issue of the Treaty. Nevertheless, should the UNTAET determined [sic] to succeed Indonesia as the party to the Treaty, it is essential to ensure all Parties concerned that there is no legal constraints to that effect and the succession will not affect the rights of the State of East Timor over Timor Gap territory.[36]

The irony of Indonesia's concern for Timor-Leste's interests was not lost on all who read the note. The following day Sergio de Mello cabled New York:

> 1. As you can see, the non-paper raises the key issue of whether or not UNTAET's accession to the terms of the treaty is a matter of State succession. The non-paper suggests that if it is not seen as such then consideration should be given to terminating the treaty. The Australian delegation to the recent workshop had suspected that this might be the line of argument adopted in their bilateral talks scheduled to commence in Jakarta on 1 February. If Indonesia does argue that the treaty has terminated then they may argue by extension that the funds currently in the Joint Authority General Account (roughly USD 4 million) should be disbursed between the parties to the treaty—Australia and Indonesia.
>
> 2. …Our position has always been that this is not a succession issue. Accordingly, we see no reason in law why the termination of the treaty between Australia and Indonesia could not exist effectively in parallel with the establishment of a new working relationship, between UNTAET and Australia, through the memorandum of understanding.[37]

Fear that termination of the Timor Gap Treaty might lose Timor-Leste the US$4 million already on account was easily dealt with on instructions from New York. The potential revenue far outweighed any concern (ultimately unfounded) that the Indonesians might seek the release of its share of pre-ballot result revenue held by the former Joint Authority. The proposal by de Mello that a new working relationship between UNTAET and Australia evolve by way of 'the' Memorandum of Understanding underscored the absence of an UNTAET role in the draft agreement. Australia had already presented a draft Memorandum of Understanding. It was a done deal with no consultation with any wider representative Timorese or with Portugal, the former administering power.

Less than a fortnight later on 10 February 2000, to the puzzlement of the newly liberated Timorese, still picking through the ashes of their burnt-out towns and villages, it was announced that the UN SRSG Sergio de Mello and the head of the 'Australian Mission' James Batley had signed an agreement whereby 'all the rights and obligations' of Indonesia under the 1989 Indonesia–Australia Timor Gap Treaty were assumed by UNTAET 'acting on behalf of East Timor, until the date of independence of East Timor'.[38] Observers in Dili wondered what the immediate relevance of such an announcement had for those still struggling desperately to find food and locate loved ones. The announcement, heard only by those who, like the author, had battery and solar access to Radio Australia, bore all the hallmarks of a back-room process remote from the realities of everyday life and the interests of the displaced Timorese.

The author recalls those early months in burnt-out Timor while Australia's diplomats manoeuvred. In Dili there were no birds, no dogs or cats. Dust and ashes swirled in the heat. There was little food at Gusmão's headquarters. Largely without windows or doors, the rooms of looted premises in which we had slung mosquito nets over airbeds or matting had been penetrated by dust. One amusing image persists in the otherwise unforgettable discomfort—co-Nobel Peace Prize Laureate José Ramos-Horta fastidiously picking a sardine from a can with an old dagger while Xanana warned him to take care with his tongue, the resistance's great asset.

On forays into the interior with the SAS team, Xanana would give away our rations to the starving villagers. In village after village infants were carried in wicker baskets to burial, Xanana and sometimes our team holding the baskets and weeping. Diminutive nuns carried a baby on each arm—some of the babies with burns and bloodied bandages. Terrorised children gripped the nuns' skirts, with no mothers in sight. On occasion Xanana took the whole team to the beach opposite our headquarters; ten deep at arms-length we collected and bagged the hundreds of thongs, sandals, shoes that floated in from those taken out on barges to their execution, FALINTIL guards remarking grimly in Tetum, 'The crocodiles grow fat'.

By early 2000 UNTAET and the CNRT had identified some remarkably oppressive clauses in the production-sharing contracts (PSCs) not brought to the attention of FRETILIN or the CNRT by Australia or the contractors in early discussions. Sergio de Mello's first move was to inform Jakarta and Canberra that UNTAET would welcome early discussions on the question of the Timor Gap Treaty 'succession'. UNTAET and the CNRT agreed that, while the Timorese would need assistance to deal with the Australians over the Gap, talks with Indonesia were out of the equation until and if lateral boundary issues between Timor-Leste and Indonesia arose. UNTAET and the CNRT agreed, following meetings of the National Consultative Council, that goals for a planned first meeting in Canberra would be to ensure that the Timor Gap Treaty was discredited and that a new petroleum exploitation regime had to be negotiated before independence. Sadly, as we shall see, the most oppressive issue in the PSCs was not identified by or on behalf of the Timorese.

On 10 March 2000, Canberra informed Dili that it would welcome discussions. DFAT suggested that the UNTAET team meet with Downer in Adelaide on 20 March 2000 on the way to a three-day discussion in Canberra with several Australian Government departments. As for the first two items on the Draft Agenda presented by UNTAET, namely, a future Timor Gap Treaty with Timor-Leste and maritime delimitation, DFAT advised that while it would be happy to receive UNTAET's comments it would not be presenting Australia's position, as there was no government mandate in relation to the two issues and, 'moreover, we would expect these issues to be negotiated, in due course, with the future government of East Timor'.

Reporting to de Mello on the talks in Canberra, Galbraith concluded that Australia hoped to stonewall the process, to enable the old

Timor Gap Treaty regime to continue indefinitely. Galbraith recorded that, after a

> large, vinous lakeside dinner ... it became clear that: a. They know they would lose at the ICJ; b. The real issue for Australia is not the revenue but rather protecting their political claim to a seabed boundary at the outer-point of their physical continental shelf; and c. While they contemplate extreme steps to protect that boundary (including rejecting an ICJ decision), they are also prepared to pay not to have an adverse boundary decision in the Timor Gap.[39]

Sergio de Mello reported the 'true nature of the Australian position' promptly to New York.

Evidence of Australia's sensitivity on being brought to account over Australian encroachment in the Timor Sea soon emerged. In a move calculated to undermine Galbraith, who was approaching his task robustly, Australia's Director of the Law of the Sea team, Jonathan Thwaites, flew to New York. On 23 May 2000, Thwaites and a colleague met with senior UN officials. Thwaites complained that Galbraith's statements to a FRETILIN Conference, including reference to inflated figures of percentages and revenues, were counter-productive to the Timorese who were being influenced by people Australia considered unreliable. There was concern, he said, 'that UNTAET's stance could undermine investors' confidence, killing "the goose that lays the golden egg"'.[40] Thwaites said that in the long term, Australia, Timor-Leste and Indonesia would have to live together and, although he understood the UN interest in establishing a regime to be in place on Independence Day, it was not for UNTAET to set the parameters for the long-term negotiations. Evidently, for Australia the UN was qualified to open the batting but not to score any runs.

In response, a senior UN official observed that, while it was not for the UN to engage in actual boundary negotiations, the UN had an obligation to bring Timor-Leste to independence in a responsible way and renegotiation of the Timor Gap regime was part of the legitimate functions of UNTAET. Thwaites' colleague then made crystal clear the disingenuousness of the Australian approach. For Australia, the official said, the two issues, of apportionment of the proceeds and delimitation, were separate issues while Mr Galbraith believed they were interlinked.[41] Informed of the Australian complaint, Galbraith said that his figures came from Phillips Petroleum with whose CEO he was in close contact: 'We and the CNRT have assured them that, regardless of the negotiations, the new fiscal regime will be no more onerous than the existing one. They have repeatedly told me that they have no concerns about changes in the allocation of revenues between the Treaty partners'.[42]

All parties now realised that Australia was determined to leave no stone unturned in its desire to avoid any retreat on the continental shelf. If it had been genuinely concerned about investor confidence, those in Dili realised it may have sent a trade official to New York to complain. On 14 June 2000, an UNTAET delegation attended a day-long seminar on 'East Timor and its Maritime Dimensions' in Canberra, hosted by the Australian Institute of International Affairs. Australian officials present were discomforted by the contribution of a maritime geographer, who argued that the Eastern Lateral of the Zone of Cooperation might not have embraced sufficient off-set weight for the island of Jaco, off Timor-Leste's eastern tip and that a readjustment may shift the lateral up to six miles eastwards to encompass a significant slice of the Greater Sunrise-Troubadour Field.

Despite the belief, held at least by Corell, that Australia would renegotiate the treaty to provide more favourable terms for Timor-Leste, the terms of the Exchange of Letters between the UN and Australia on 10 February 2000 effectively replicated the unlawful 1989 treaty. In this manner Australia gained from the outset a crucial negotiating advantage for the petroleum consortia, namely business as usual. Unwisely, in the lead-up to the August 1999 ballot and before seeking disclosure and expert advice, both FRETILIN and the CNRT had signalled their willingness in principle to honour existing production contracts and Australia wasted no time in securing formal agreements.

On 3 August 2000, in a move welcomed by the CNRT leadership, Shadow Foreign Minister Laurie Brereton pushed through the Australian Labor Party's National Conference a Platform Resolution he took to the CNRT Conference in Dili later that month. It supported negotiation of a 'permanent maritime boundary in the Timor Gap based on lines of equidistance between Australia and East Timor. Such a settlement would see major gas and petroleum reserves within East Timor's maritime boundaries and would be a just outcome consistent with the Law of the Sea'.[43]

CNRT Proposes a Government of National Unity

At the opening of the first CNRT National Congress held in the Dili Gymnasium on 21–29 August 2000, there were signs that the FRETILIN Party, which had failed to gain the confidence of the UN General Assembly in 1974, still lacked political maturity, to the consternation of the Australian Government. The conference was planned

CNRT National Congress, Dili Gymnasium, 21 August 2000.

Sergio de Mello opens the CNRT National Congress, 21 August 2000.

in consultation with UNTAET officials who assisted many delegates from remote areas, including the Oecusse enclave, to attend. UN SRSG Sergio Vieira de Mello and Bishop Belo opened the Congress, and were followed soon after by FRETILIN leader Mari Alkatiri, flanked in the front row by 17 mostly expatriate FRETILIN members, who moved an opening dissent to the agenda of the Congress. In background discussions Alkatiri had opposed the inclusion on the agenda of a speech by CNRT Vice-President José Ramos-Horta, complaining that this over-emphasised the CNRT role.

The motion, in which Alkatiri told the restive audience that they alone should set the agenda, was greeted with a hubbub of voices. Xanana Gusmão then rose to speak to a packed throng of delegates from all 13 districts, many having walked days to get there. For many this was their first sighting of their legendary leader about whom many myths circulated throughout the Island, including a fable of his ability to turn himself into a white dog to escape detection.[44] He said that all were free to speak, that the eyes of the world were on Timor, and this was their first violence-free exercise of political will. The delegates, some wearing traditional *tais* (woven robes of a joined circle of cloth in regional patterns), lined up to cast a secret vote into one of dozens of used cardboard boxes cut with slits.

Delegates queue to vote on FRETILIN motion, CNRT National Congress, 21 August 2000.

Predictably, the motion, interpreted as a challenge to Gusmão, was defeated by 429 votes to 17, which those observing the 17-member FRETILIN delegation read as a resounding disaster for FRETILIN, especially for the sheer tactical naivety in bringing on such an unwinnable vote. Clearly, at a grass-roots level, Alkatiri, who had spent

Gusmão sits behind Alkatiri's empty chair (flanked by Lú-Olo Guterres and Harold Moucho) while the vote is taken, CNRT National Congress, 21 August 2000.

Gusmão and Agio Pereira, later to become Gusmão's key strategist for the Timor Sea issue, work on the CNRT leader's speech for the CNRT National Congress on 21 August 2000.

Gusmão calls for renunciation of violence and an apology for the past at the CNRT National Congress, while Alkatiri waits to respond negatively. Leandro Issac who had survived 'Kofi's Death List' is seated facing the camera.

José Ramos-Horta, Xanana Gusmão and Mario Carrascalão take the dais at the CNRT National Congress.

most of the occupation years abroad, could not counter the Xanana Gusmão mystique. For the Australian observers present, it was clear that if Australia was to get FRETILIN into power it would not be by popular vote, so Australia then set about a strategy of securing its objective without a democratic vote.

Calls by Xanana Gusmão and CNRT Vice-President José Ramos-Horta for delegates to renounce violence, to apologise for past excesses and to support a future government of national unity were rejected by the FRETILIN delegation. Observers from the US, UK, Portugal, Brazil, Australia and Thai Diplomatic Missions were in attendance. After the Alkatiri-led intervention, a delegate from the Eastern District said:

> We need our pride back. In history we never imported rice. When we fought the rice was not planted. When we managed to plant rice recently in Natarboro and Viqueque a brown rat with a reddish tinge ate the shoots the floods hadn't washed away. Our people are challenged enough by nature without political instability caused by people more hungry for political power than for rice.[45]

The Conference was closely monitored by the Australian Mission. After the resounding rebuff to FRETILIN, an Australian official was seen to leave the Gymnasium and heard to report the event immediately over a mobile phone.[46] The proceedings of the entire three-day Congress were videoed by a dashing young Australian attached to a local NGO that wanted to record the event 'for posterity'.[47] The history exercise was greeted with wry smiles within the CNRT leadership as the recordings were regarded as a sure way to get the message across that the people wanted genuine democracy rather than a clique of diaspora FRETILIN relics.

The largely 'diaspora elite' background of the FRETILIN leadership at the Congress presented a clear challenge to the SRSG, whose mandate required democratisation initiatives. UNTAET's opposition to a countrywide World/Asian Bank Community Empowerment Project (CEP) sustained FRETILIN's non-consultative destined-to-rule outlook. Chopra describes the UNTAET's ineptitude:

> The CEP was unable to recover from the acrimonious negotiations leading up to its establishment. It continued to be effectively rejected by UNTAET internally, with the consequence that the transitional administration never had much of a presence below the district

level, where 80 percent of the population lives ... The UN failed to create any kind of local government and lost the opportunity for introducing democratization alongside existing hierarchical paradigms. Instead, villages reverted to traditional power structures, which were manipulated—well below the radar screens of international observers— to achieve an overwhelming result in the Constituent Assembly elections of August 2001 [for FRETILIN and Alkatiri].[48]

Three days of intense discussions between UNTAET and Australia took place on 9–12 October 2000 in Dili. The UNTAET team was headed by Peter Galbraith and included Alkatiri, who was Cabinet Member for Economic Affairs in the Transitional Government, and CNRT Vice-President Mario Carrascalão. Alkatiri was accompanied by Portuguese Attorney Miguel Galvão Teles and FRETILIN's maritime boundary legal adviser Dr Nuno Antunes, a former Portuguese naval officer. Galbraith opened by saying that the question of the revenue share was inextricably linked with Timor-Leste's maritime entitlements. He said that the two issues to be addressed were Timor-Leste's sovereign entitlement north of the median line, and the nature of the area in question, including the lateral boundaries and Jaco Island. Dr Antunes reminded the Australian Delegation that the 1972 boundary treaty between Australia and Indonesia acknowledged explicitly that the lateral intersection points at each end of the Gap might have to be settled with a third state, meaning at that time Portugal or a successor State and suggested that the time had come to consider this.

Australian senior legal adviser Bill Campbell QC responded robustly, asserting that Australia was convinced there were two continental shelves and that if the issue went to litigation the court might adjust the median line northwards in Australia's favour, resulting in Australia obtaining sole control of the Bayu-Undan Field. Campbell and Australian delegation leader Michael Potts maintained that any broadening of the area under discussion would arouse Indonesia's interest. Australia did not accept that the 1989 Timor Gap Treaty was illegal and viewed the question of the boundaries as settled. The UNTAET record of the meeting includes a comment by Potts that the 'macho attitude' displayed by UNTAET and Timor-Leste meant that it might be better to take the matter to court, as the issue was beginning to register on the 'Geiger counter of sensitivity' back in Canberra.

In context, Australia's bullying approach came from what Canberra knew was a position of strength. The UN, already in dialogue with donor nations regarding the huge cost of administering a whole country, sought an early petroleum-based revenue flow for the Timorese. The UN was not likely to support Galbraith in a standoff and Alkatiri, anxious to project a well-funded FRETILIN Administration into power, had reaffirmed his view that Timor-Leste wanted an agreement to be in place by independence. The numbers were coming up for Australia and the interests of the ordinary people of Timor-Leste depended upon support for Galbraith and rational thought by the FRETILIN Party, which had effective hold over the process for Timor-Leste.

The upshot of the early period of negotiations between UNTAET and Australia was that the UN in New York failed to support Galbraith, who wished to tackle the fundamental issue concerning the unlawfulness of Australia's claimed jurisdiction in the Timor Sea, and the consequential capacity of an independent Timor-Leste to declare all production contracts void for reasons of their illegality and to seek reparations from Australia and the petroleum contractors. The petroleum companies were well aware of cogent complaints of trespass filed by successive Portuguese administrations and the long-stated position of the Timorese resistance that the maritime boundary issue would have to be settled by an international tribunal.[49]

Closely linked with Alexander Downer and his ministerial staff, petroleum interests were the unseen actors sharing the Australian strategy. Woodside and Phillips Petroleum had worked previously with skilled Indonesian negotiators, and this time they wanted to get more out of the process. In many respects, the Indonesian withdrawal advantaged the petroleum interests, as they no longer had to deal with an oil- and gas-producing state, savvy about production contracts and with a long history of maritime law involvement.

9
THE TRANSITIONAL GOVERNMENT NEGOTIATES A NEW TREATY

The first sign that Australia would try to take the Timorese to the cleaners through production-sharing contracts (PSCs) came at the October 2000 meeting in Dili between the UNTAET and Australian Government representatives. Knowing that the Australian delegation would include John Hartwell, a senior public servant with wide petroleum industry experience, including in negotiating with the Indonesians, Galbraith brought to the meeting a Norwegian gas industry legal adviser, Bjorn-Erik Leerberg. In his presentation, Leerberg commented on the PSCs arising from the 1989 Timor Gap Treaty and accepted on an interim basis under the UNTAET–Australia Memorandum of Understanding for their continuation. He pointed out that in the Norwegian model for gas production, gas was valued not at the well-head flange as the PSCs in a Zone of Cooperation Area (ZOCA) provided, but at the outlet flange of the landing terminal. All knew that Australia's management of the ZOCA with Indonesia had not involved a landed pipeline and a new valuation formula would be required if the pipeline to Darwin that Australia planned was built.

Hartwell's response was that the Norwegian model would involve a 'fundamental change from the current treaty terms' and Australia would not contemplate the extension of any Timor-Leste/Australia Joint

Authority jurisdiction into its own waters. Galbraith observed rather dryly that a pipeline does not enter Australian waters when it leaves the 'so called ZOCA', but when it enters Australia's territorial seas. In a response that suggested that FRETILIN was either unaware of or had no interest in the vital significance of flange ownership, Alkatiri observed that the issue could await further examination. Timor-Leste's future might have been better served if Alkatiri had insisted that valuation on the Norwegian model was non-negotiable and if UNTAET had commissioned a bathymetric survey to test the Australian negotiators' claim that a pipeline to Australia was the only option.

The Transitional Cabinet met on 18 October 2000 and noted that the more contentious issues for negotiation with Australia were the allocation of jurisdiction, the definition of the area or areas in question, and the gas pipeline regime. Alkatiri advised the meeting that, if the issues were not concluded in future negotiations, he was confident that an international arbitration mechanism or the International Court of Justice (ICJ) would decide in Timor-Leste's favour. The Timor-Leste Cabinet approved the immediate placement on retainer of legal counsel to prepare a case in law to support Timor-Leste's claim, stating that any decision to actually enter into litigation would not be taken by UNTAET or the Transitional Cabinet, but by the government of independent East Timor. Funds would come from the monies allocated to Timor-Leste by the Joint Authority for the Timor Gap or from states that supported Timor-Leste's position. UNTAET political staff then discussed establishing a secure filing system to deal with the Australian omnipresence in Dili and using encrypted communications on the assumption that Australia was monitoring all United Nations and CNRT communications.

The next meeting between the two countries took place in Singapore on 22–24 November 2000, with Galbraith again leading the Timor-Leste delegation and Michael Potts leading the Australians. Galbraith mused aloud, somewhat provocatively, that for Timor-Leste there was the prospect of either an ICJ case or a victory for the Australian Labor Party (ALP) in Australian federal elections, and it might therefore be difficult for Timor-Leste to give much away in negotiation.[1] Potts responded by noting that if there was no progress, his delegation would have to revert to the Australian Cabinet which would not meet again until February, so that negotiations could not resume until March 2001, a prospect Australia knew Alkatiri, as Cabinet Member for Economic Affairs, was uncomfortable with.

Galbraith touched a raw nerve when he raised the prospect of UNTAET discussions with Indonesia, drawing Potts' defensive argument that nothing would be forthcoming from the Indonesians, who would not participate at the ICJ in any event. If Timor-Leste wanted litigation, Australia would not accept any temporary agreement pending a court outcome and development would be frozen. Potts stunned the delegation by strengthening threats implied at the March 2000 meeting with Foreign Minister Downer in Adelaide (reported in chapter 8) when he said that Australia had a 'get out of jail card' it would be willing to use—of opting out of the compulsory jurisdiction of the ICJ and all tribunals.

The parties met again in Cairns on 11–12 December 2000 and the mood was subdued. The Australian Cabinet had endorsed an offer of 75% to the Timorese and 25% to Australia from the disputed zone, but any further negotiation was contingent on downstream issues. For reasons not disclosed to the Timorese delegation or their Norwegian petroleum law expert Bjorn-Erik Leerberg, Australia wanted Timor-Leste's role to finish at the well-head flange in the Timor Sea. As suggested, the Timor-Leste position should have been to investigate possible reasons for Australia's determination to value the Bayu-Undan gas at the well-head flange and have 'downstream' ownership of the pipeline and its contents. It was well known that during the Australia–Indonesia joint venture the wet gas was processed and the dry gas was pumped back underground, until a pipeline to a landed facility was built. So why was the dry gas worth recovering? The answer lay in the gas analyses, but it appears the findings were not disclosed to UNTAET.

Although helium was a known high-end component of LNG and even at that time minimal web research could have informed Alkatiri, he appeared focused on a revenue allocation from the LNG and a pipeline to Timor-Leste. He agreed that a unitisation agreement to deal with the future Greater Sunrise Field that straddled the eastern lateral boundary of the disputed zone could be put off until after independence. Once again Alkatiri failed to appreciate the crucial significance of the gas analyses of the Bayu-Undan and Greater Sunrise fields. As we now know, the analyses and a bathymetric survey may have tipped the balance on the cost issues for a short pipeline to Timor-Leste to service both fields. Once Bayu-Undan gas was piped to Timor-Leste, the outlet for Greater Sunrise might be a forgone conclusion. But Australia wanted the helium to come ashore on the Australian mainland. If Alkatiri had known the helium assay, he would have had a strong card to play. Even after receiving Norwegian advice that the LNG gas-stream could include valuable inert gases, such as helium, UNTAET failed to secure the inclusion of the helium in the economic modelling.

For Alkatiri, the immediate issues at hand appear to have been FRETILIN's need to secure an early funded base for independence and pressure from the Phillips-Woodside consortia to get production from the Bayu-Undan Field underway. One may only conclude that UNTAET and Alkatiri failed to appreciate the trap behind the oft-repeated demand by Phillips Petroleum, Woodside and the Howard Government that the future revenue regime be 'no more onerous' than the former Australia–Indonesia regime where no provision was made for the helium, which was being pumped underground. Replication of the illegal 1989 PSCs would, as we shall see, deliver a bounty for those hunting the impoverished Timorese. UNTAET recorded Alkatiri moving into the trap:

> The policy for investors was transparent and designed to be more helpful to investors than the Indonesian model. The CNRT had already made it clear that the future conditions would not be more onerous than the current regime. Any Timorese/Australian co-ordination and co-operation on the future petroleum law would be welcome from the East Timor side.[2]

Discussion then moved to the management models to be considered in place of the former Australia-Indonesia regime, which brought up the interests of the petroleum companies, represented as usual by John Hartwell.

In retrospect, if a moment is to be chosen when warning bells first sounded about the significance of valuing petroleum product at the well-head flange it was during the afternoon of 11 December 2000. Galbraith appeared cautious, unsure of what Australia was up to. UNTAET recorded the exchange:

> Galbraith commented that the Australian cabinet decision had been characterized as being contingent on downstream issues. He was aware of the pipeline but wanted to know what additional issues were at stake.

Hartwell replied that the Phillips/Woodside gas fiscal issues were crucial as well as how and where the gas would be valued. Also, the question of the pipeline jurisdiction and the administrative and regulatory regime would have to be established.

Galbraith summarized the legal situation from his point of view; the gas as it leaves the ground is subject to the East Timorese applicable fiscal law as far as the revenue collection is concerned, it then is transferred to Australia and its transport on the high seas is comparable to that of a ship until it reaches the 12 mile Australian territorial waters. Its valuation will take place on shore in Australia at the outlet flange.

Hartwell saw the valuation of the gas as similar to that of oil, instead of going into a tanker it enters the pipeline. The valuation should take place at the well head and the revenue share be determined at that stage. The companies were not interested in the revenue sharing; they wanted to know where the valuation would take place and the method.

Galbraith considered that there was a different value at the well head and at the outlet flange.

Hartwell replied that the extra price was the cost of transport that someone would have to pay in any case. The ownership changes hands at the well head and the consumer pays for the transport service. The pipeline owner wants a return on his investment. If the producer and pipeline owner is the same person in a vertically integrated structure, care has to be taken to avoid the manipulation of values. It would be better for a separate entity to own the pipeline.

Galbraith maintained that more expertise was necessary to determine the best method of valuing the gas and the matter should be left for a technical discussion.[3]

If there was to be any semblance of good faith by Australia, the helium assay should have been disclosed at this juncture as an element of good oilfield practice. The question of where the gas would be valued arose again when Galbraith observed that Australia would benefit from the economic activity resulting from the sale of gas downstream. He presumably had in mind the infrastructure boost to the Northern Territory, but any word about helium appears to have eluded him. Hartwell's reply now assumes enormous significance. He 'argued that Phillips and Woodside would not go ahead without getting the best possible price given the marginal nature of the project. *They had no downstream interests in the project* so why would they sell at a lower price if the producers and customers were different' [emphasis added].[4] This implied that the only financial interest Phillips and Woodside had was purchase from the Joint Authority at the well-head and processing of LNG.

Leerberg joined the discussions the next day by phone from Norway. He considered 'that it would be sensible to have the point of evaluation when there was a transfer of ownership to a commercial operator in the commodities market'. He pointed out that 'oil was a different question as all it had to do was enter the tanker, but for gas it would be best when it was at a commercial specification and pressure' and went on to explain that 'valuation at that point would give a higher probability of obtaining a true market price without distortion', as more entities could be partners in the off-take and there would be 'more opportunities for arms-length deals between the producer and consumer'.[5]

He explained that there had been two Supreme Court cases in Norway relating to valuation point issues and suggested the solution was to have the gas measured and valued at the contract point and each contract would specify the location as the outlet flange onshore. In reply to the Australian claim that there was no direct benefit to the Australian Government as to where the gas was valued, Leerberg said, prophetically, that the economic effort should be put into enhancing recovery from the reservoir. The UNTAET/Timor-Leste delegation did not realise the importance the Australian Government attributed to ownership of the gas passing at the well-head flange. With a free hand at the onshore flange Australia could establish by a commercial proxy its first helium production plant, meet an important strategic aim, and not share the proceeds with Timor-Leste. The gas analyses lodged with Geoscience Australia's predecessors from the first and subsequent Bayu-Undan wells were in the long-sought 0.03% helium concentration range. Australia was about to secure a 'critical commodity'—or was it?[6]

The December meeting concluded in general agreement about the urgency of the situation, with Potts observing that only an elected body could legitimise the anticipated treaty. Australia had devised a formula that would avoid a popular election that would almost certainly be won by a CNRT national unity team led by Gusmão. The approach involved convincing Gusmão that Alkatiri had negotiations about the Timor Sea capably in hand. Australia's Foreign Minister Alexander Downer was backgrounding all who would listen to his explanations that, with Timor-Leste civil society in turmoil, the first stage of self-government would be fraught with difficulty and a better long-range strategy would be to allow an 'established party', the amenable FRETILIN, to try its hand at governing the new nation. With no bathymetric survey, no disclosed gas analyses, and Alkatiri keen for FRETILIN to be in power, Australia was on a roll.

The Howard–Downer strategy was coordinated with Australian diplomatic activity in Washington. US Secretary of State Colin Powell, who had become acquainted with Gusmão, lent a hand, recommending to the CNRT President that he accept the role of President, rather than popular parliamentary leadership in any future independent structure. 'Former guerrilla leaders do not make good political leaders', were words oft-repeated in Gusmão's ear, and Gusmão was receptive to such entreaties for reasons relating to his FALINTIL oath, which he explained:

> The history of the Third World is repeating itself: the leader of the resistance will end up as President, even if he is not up to the task; guerrilla commanders will be generals and politicians will strive to become Ministers. All because we were the heroes; all because we worked hard, suffered more than others! If this were to happen, it would be an outrage to the whole meaning of our struggle, the whole meaning of the sacrifices made by our people. It would be a betrayal.[7]

After the second round of formal talks on 4–6 April 2001 in Melbourne, de Mello reported with concern to the UN that the Australian delegation was not led, as in the past, by Potts; the Australians now wanted to link the issues of the pipeline and the unitisation of Greater Sunrise and were now demanding that the pipeline be under Australian jurisdiction. De Mello, unaware of the reasons for the new tactic but intuitively concerned by the insistence of Australia and Phillips Petroleum that ownership of the gas pass to Phillips at the well-head flange, told New York that the progress made at the Singapore and Cairns discussions had been reversed. He suspected, rightly, that Australia had adopted a new tactic of pressuring a very eager FRETILIN Party by delaying production from Bayu-Undan, and thus revenue for an independent Timor-Leste, until Australia got the Greater Sunrise Field in the bag, but he too seemed unaware of Australia's hunt for helium.

The winning strategy, though not the endgame, was revealed 18 months later by a senior Department of Foreign Affairs and Trade

(DFAT) official, Geoffrey Raby, commenting on the prospective International Unitisation Agreement (IUA) between Australia and Timor-Leste relating to the Sunrise and Troubadour Fields during testimony before the Australian Parliament's Joint Standing Committee on Treaties considering the Timor Sea Treaty:

> On the first question of the relationship between the IUA and the treaty, the question, as I recall it, was: what was in Australia's national interests? As I said last time, from the government's point of view Australia's national interest will be maximised and preserved if the treaty, the IUA and all other instruments, including the PSCs, come into effect simultaneously.

In reply to Andrew Wilkie's questioning about whether Timor-Leste would benefit equally if ratification of the treaty was prior to or at the same time as unitisation, Raby said that it wouldn't, reiterating that 'The big Australian interest is with Sunrise and, as we have just heard from one of the commercial partners, we need a unitisation agreement to realise that interest'. Further pressed about the reasons for his statement about Australia's interests being maximised and preserved if the treaty, IUA and all other instruments coming into effect simultaneously, Raby replied:

> I think that gives us the comfort, if you like, that we have both elements together. The East Timorese element and interest is with the early development of Bayu-Undan. We have some interest in Bayu-Undan, but Australia's bigger interest is demonstrably with the development of Greater Sunrise. To do the treaty without having concluded an IUA for Sunrise would leave us possibly in a situation of less confidence and less certainty than at present.[8]

Galbraith and Alkatiri met with Australian Industry Minister Nick Minchin in Hobart on 9 April 2001. Alkatiri told Minchin Timor-Leste was offering a generous split of revenue from the Timor Sea resources and reminded Minchin that the Timorese considered the petroleum their right under international law. True to the Australian strategy, Minchin reminded Galbraith and Alkatiri that the major oil companies had come a long way and a revenue source for the Timorese was stalled. Australia was now in a win-win position. Outplayed, Alkatiri had little more to say. Returning to Dili where the Transitional Ministry was due to be dissolved on 15 July 2001 and a campaign for the election of a Constituent Assembly to draft a Constitution scheduled to start on

30 August 2001, Alkatiri issued a media release describing the outcome of the April Melbourne talks as a 'setback'. With the CNRT dissolved to allow for a multi-party democracy and FRETILIN chasing power without opposition from Gusmão, the Australians sensed that they had the game sewn up. Predictably, a media offensive emerged from the oil company boardrooms. The oil companies wanted the earliest possible endorsement of sales and purchase agreements.

The parties went back to the negotiating table on 3 May 2001. During informal talks at Brisbane, Australia offered an 85:15 split, with Hartwell pressing again for the gas to be valued at the well-head, emphasising that a system that was simple and perceived to be 'fair and equitable' needed to be developed. After the meeting, Australia provided draft petroleum and gas regime proposals for a follow-up meeting. Galbraith sent the proposed Petroleum Code to Bjorn-Erik Leerberg, who provided a comprehensive commentary on 11 May, covering matters that had to be addressed in any treaty, protocol, petroleum code or PSC. He emphasised the need to define the meaning of 'petroleum', suggesting the adoption of a definition from the *Norwegian Petroleum Act*: 'any naturally occurring mixture of hydrocarbons in the subsoil, whether in a gaseous, liquid, or solid state *as well as other substances produced in association with such hydrocarbons*' [emphasis added].[9]

Leerberg warned that full flow-through ownership of the petroleum deposit must be secured for Timor-Leste through the arrangements to be reached with Australia. Specifically, the terms must ensure that 'Australia may not in any way or form, permit, allow or tolerate any other entity to establish any right, claim or interest in the petroleum deposit'—prophetic words indeed. UNTAET and the Transitional Cabinet could not have been warned more explicitly that negotiations must ensure that all petroleum resource processing must be shared, with no proxy ownership of the petroleum resources. How Timor-Leste's and Australia's contractor ConocoPhillips came to 'own' the helium potentially worth more than the gas is one of the great commercial coups in Australian history.

Galbraith and two colleagues arrived in Canberra from Dili on Sunday 20 May 2001. DFAT delivered a draft memorandum of understanding to Galbraith at his hotel later that day,[10] which he faxed to Norway for Leerberg's comments. Informal talks between officials began on Monday morning. Hartwell, representing Minchin's

Department, was now pushing strongly for valuation at the well-head flange. The Australian delegation wanted their proposed memorandum of understanding to reflect the main points of a treaty to be signed later by Timor-Leste. The UNTAET delegation made clear that it could not sign an agreement that would bind a future Timor-Leste Government and that in the meantime the petroleum production would be owned by each country in accordance with the agreed percentages.

Towards the end of the second day of discussions, Galbraith agreed to meet with Ministers Downer and Minchin later that afternoon in Downer's rooms at Parliament House. Downer's adviser, Josh Frydenberg, was present. Discussion focused on the sticking point of Australia's proposal—that petroleum products not be shared as state assets but belong to the companies that extracted them. Downer made it clear that his forward plan was for Australia and Timor-Leste to take a back seat on sovereign ownership at the well-head. Having not been briefed on the gas analyses, the extent to which the UNTAET delegation realised the significance of Downer's proposal is unclear. Downer made no mention of helium recovery when he proposed that both countries effectively relinquish sovereignty over state assets. Had he mentioned helium the game would have been up.

At the follow-up meeting in Dili on 29–30 May 2001, Australian officials presented a first draft of the points of tentative agreement reached in Canberra a week before. The Australian draft contained the first recorded mention during negotiations of 'helium'; it mentioned 'helium' specifically and included the industry-accepted definition of 'petroleum activities' that would have caught helium. After Australia presented a further draft proposed definition of petroleum that listed 'natural gas, nitrogen, hydrogen and carbon dioxide', Leerberg advised on 29 May 2001 that listing 'particular substances' that may follow the petroleum stream out of the reservoir was too specific, adding presciently, 'for all we know other substances than nitrogen, hydrogen and carbon dioxide may be discovered in quantities in the new reservoir'. He again emphasised the wisdom of adopting the definition of 'petroleum' in the *Norwegian Petroleum Act 1996*.

The UNTAET/Timor-Leste delegation worked through the drafts at further meetings, commencing at Canberra on 12 June 2001. If there was any discussion about the prospect of helium recovery, identified in the Australian draft, and consistent with Leerberg's suggested generic definition of 'petroleum' that embraced helium, it was not recorded. Although, in retrospect, it might be said that UNTAET should have commissioned an independent report on the oil and gas analyses from Bayu-Undan and Greater Sunrise, reliance upon the candour of their Australian joint-venture partner was, in the author's view, a legitimate expectation.

Leerberg's warning that the terms 'oil' and 'gas' embraced a variety of recoverable products seems not to have sparked the interest of Alkatiri's team. Neither the author nor Timor-Leste's own geologist and future Minister for Petroleum and Natural Resources in the Gusmão Government, Alfredo Pires, were made privy to the negotiations. Although Leerberg's advice was shared by Timor-Leste's negotiators with DFAT and adopted by both treaty negotiation teams it remained for the separate joint-venture contractors who were dealing at direct ministerial level to implement the industry standard definition of petroleum in the PSCs. Instead the Indonesian era PSCs that excluded inert gas recovery were given to the Timorese to sign and Leerberg's advice came to nothing. Only an inquiry will determine whether the Australian treaty negotiating staff were aware that the PSCs presented to the Timorese joint-venture personnel by the contractor entities and the Australian joint-venture staff were inconsistent with the agreement reached at state-to-state (UNTAET) level.

Late on 14 June 2001, Foreign Minister Downer, with Josh Frydenberg and Industry Minister Nick Minchin, joined the talks. Both Ministers stressed that the Australian Cabinet was under pressure from the major oil companies. Minchin said that there were two main issues of concern to the oil companies—the continuation of existing PSCs and that future fiscal arrangements be in accordance with the statement the CNRT had signed on 20 October 2000, which required fiscal policies be 'no more onerous' than existing policies. Galbraith observed that on any unitisation deal both countries were gambling, as neither country knew how much gas lay on each side of the 1989 line. Minchin countered by saying that the PSCs had been entered into under the old Timor Gap Treaty and, since the 20 October 2000 CNRT Declaration, '[w]e have to deal with the companies on that basis'. Galbraith said that UNTAET/Timor-Leste was prepared to repudiate the 'no more onerous' statement, but Downer responded saying that the 'no more onerous' statement was fairly clear and repudiating it 'would not be a good idea' as the companies would 'go feral'. Again, there was no mention of helium or that the definition of 'petroleum' in the 1989 PSCs excluded helium.

With FRETILIN's rush to power underway, the structure of the joint development regime was hammered out swiftly between working parties, aided by Australian and UNTAET drafting and taxation experts. The terms of a Timor Sea Treaty only required polishing prior to 'independence'. Under Galbraith's leadership, Timor-Leste had secured a vital revenue source from Bayu-Undan without committing to a unitisation formula for Greater Sunrise. The parties acknowledged that unitisation of Greater Sunrise was inextricably linked to the positioning of the Eastern Lateral. Boundary setting, either directly or by implication, in a unitisation agreement, was a matter for sovereign governments. The helium issue was lurking unseen in the background by UNTAET, as any PSCs were to be signed separately within the Joint Authority.

Although Potts had warned during informal talks in November 2000 that Australia might contemplate withdrawing from the jurisdiction of the ICJ and associated tribunals, neither the Timor-Leste leadership nor UNTAET took any steps with donor nations or at the UN to dissuade Australia from such a move. The author has no recollection of either de Mello or Alkatiri informing the CNRT leadership of Australia's threat. There is no basis for the popular belief that Downer's announcement on 22 March 2002 of Australia's withdrawal took Timor-Leste by surprise. Alkatiri had been forewarned, but there is no evidence that he sought advice on whether steps to forestall such a move could or should be taken. Doubtless, the threat by Australia would have attracted international opprobrium and criticism at the UN.

The Transitional Cabinet approved the draft treaty on 3 July 2001, with Alkatiri indicating that it was a framework agreement with 'some issues' to be resolved outside the treaty terms. These included a decision on the pipeline issue scheduled for a meeting later in July. Galbraith noted that the draft treaty would not come into effect until it was approved by the elected government. The Memorandum of Understanding signed by Downer and Minchin for Australia and Alkatiri and Galbraith for Timor-Leste on 5 July 2001 ensured that all the ZOCA PSCs under the notorious 1989 Timor Gap Treaty between Australia and Indonesia were to continue to apply. The document was in much the same form as the draft memorandum of understanding

Stewart, as Australia's Deputy Permanent Representative at the UN, had handed to UN Legal Counsel Hans Corell in November 1999.

The UNTAET/Timor-Leste negotiation team, together with Joint Authority observer and experienced Australian petroleum explorationist Robert Mollah, met with representatives of Phillips Petroleum and Woodside at Dili on 20 July 2001. The industry representatives focused on the 'no more onerous' statement, with Phillips Petroleum saying that any other basis than the 'no more onerous' commitment was 'unacceptable'. Both companies expressed interest in where the gas stream would be valued. Woodside wanted confirmation that the pipeline owner would be free to implement any system. Australia's Department of Industry representative said that this meant a valuation at the first point of custody transfer of gas from one party to an unrelated party, bought for further value. Woodside demurred and Phillips Petroleum asked whether such a valuation method would apply to an onshore pipeline.

This exchange and the earlier Australian draft definition of 'petroleum' that mentioned helium, allow two broad possibilities. Either DFAT officials were being disingenuous as part of an elaborate plan to secure the helium, or, unaware of an intended helium plan, they had simply been instructed to secure ownership of the gas stream at sea for Phillips Petroleum and the contractor parties. While a full explanation awaits proper analysis the more plausible explanation is the latter; a plan to exclude helium from being part of the accountable resource recovery had evolved elsewhere with the contractor parties, as it was not in the interests of either the Australian or Timorese peoples.

The role of the more technically savvy industry advisers on the Joint Authority, to whom negotiators on both sides deferred for technical advice, was crucial. The UNTAET/Timor-Leste position on the valuation point was that further consideration needed to be given to the issue so that all participants could agree on a definition of an arms-length sale that was 'transparent and market-related'. Both parties acknowledged that valuation at an LNG plant was a more complex issue, but both UNTAET and FRETILIN appear not to have noticed that the model PSC prepared in Canberra during the Australia–Indonesian era contained a clause (1.3) that allowed Australia and Phillips Petroleum and Woodside to use maverick definitions of 'petroleum', 'natural-gas' and 'wet-gas' so as to exclude helium.

The evidence suggests a plan to secure the gas stream without paying Timor-Leste for the valuable inert gases, including helium, and that this plan was not shared with all officials directly involved in the negotiations. The final push to allocate petroleum at the well-head directly to the petroleum companies and not to regard the petroleum as a sovereign asset arriving on shore for processing occurred at ministerial level. The records, such as they may be, concerning any dialogue between Downer, his adviser and go-between on the issue, Josh Frydenberg, and Phillips/Woodside, as to the relinquishment of State ownership at the well-head and use of the model PSC from the Indonesian era may only be accessible in judicial and/or parliamentary proceedings.

With ownership to the gas stream passing at the well-head flange and Leerberg's advice on the definition of petroleum adopted but side-stepped, one more step would allow Phillips Petroleum, Woodside and the contractor parties to secure the helium. This was for the Joint Authority representatives to adopt the model PSC from the Indonesian era, assuming that Timor-Leste and its advisers had not noticed the import of the insidious Clause 1.3 that was incompatible with Leerberg's advice. In the result, the post-well-head flange gas worth billions of dollars was lost to the Joint Authority. Australia and Timor-Leste became the big losers.

Any 'national security' justification for cheating the Timorese can have no basis in law. There was no national interest need to give the helium away to Phillips Petroleum, Woodside and the contractor parties; quite to the contrary, it was squarely against the national interest to surrender a long listed 'critical commodity' to largely foreign corporate interests. Those in the know were aware that all through the contentious production years of the Australia–Indonesia Timor Gap Treaty the inert gases had been pumped back underground. The contractor parties and those involved with them were now savouring the prospect of bringing the valuable helium back to the surface and processing it in Australia—but would the Timorese find out in time to spike the proposed helium plant? This worry peaked by 2004 when planning for the helium plant had reached a critical stage.

Bayu-Undan to Darwin LNG Pipeline
Talks on a pipeline from the Bayu-Undan Field to Darwin had commenced informally at the meeting in Cairns on 11–12 December 2000.

The Australian position on the pipeline suggested the prospect of a single Timorese jurisdiction up to the Australian territorial (12-mile) sea and, from there, Australian jurisdiction through to the terminal. Galbraith and Hartwell both favoured a separate bilateral agreement by which Timor-Leste and Australia delegated managing the pipeline to the Joint Authority. Hartwell considered that the pipeline owner should pay taxes, as distinct from the resource tax.

Potts' suggestion that the question of a single jurisdiction and the pros and cons of valuation at the well-head or landing-point should be explored with Leerberg suggests that there was no guile at this stage in DFAT's approach to the valuation issue. Indeed, Leerberg's advice was shared with the DFAT team. Whether Downer revealed to his own officials any reason why he and his adviser Josh Frydenberg wanted the petroleum consortia to 'own' the petroleum from the well-head remains unclear. Any argument that Australia did not want a joint authority 'owning' the pipeline or controlling jointly an onshore landing flange, though plausible, contrasts with the sovereign giveaway at the well-head.

When Australia's draft memorandum of understanding was faxed to Leerberg after it was presented on 20 May 2001,[11] the parties had already reached tentative agreement that a landing pipeline would be subject to the jurisdiction of the territory it lands in from the inlet flange of the pipeline at the well-head. The records are opaque as to how this agreement evolved after Timor-Leste offered Australia jurisdiction over the pipeline from the flange for a fee—a proposal accepted by Australia. Whether the two issues are connected and what exactly was the trade-off are questions of fact, but a well-head inlet flange valuation point, contrary to the Norwegian model, was agreed to. The reason for this turnaround that allowed the contractor parties to syphon off the inert gases is not apparent from the written record. The 2002 Timor Sea Treaty subsequently fell into place along those lines.

It may be easy to say in hindsight that the former FRETILIN leadership, whose Cabinet member José Teixeira co-signed the 2003 PSCs under the 2002 Timor Sea Treaty, owe the people of Timor-Leste an explanation as to why, with good advice to hand, they failed to protect the interests of their people by ensuring that Leerberg's emphatic caveat on no proxy commercial ownership of sovereign resources was implemented. This may fail to recognise that, when signing complex

PSCs, the Timor-Leste party relied on good faith advice within the Joint Authority for the Timor Gap and an understandable assumption that Australia, as joint-venture partner, would protect a common interest.

Curiously, on another issue concerning oppressive terms in the PSCs inherited by East Timor, UNTAET had written to Prime Minister Howard in June 2001 recording that during a meeting a month earlier in May both the Australian and the East Timor, negotiating teams were 'stunned to learn that the PSCs entered into pursuant to the Timor Gap Treaty contained terms far out of line with industry standards and any sense of fair play'. UNTAET's appeal to Howard, effectively on behalf of the proposed joint venture, focused on the cost both to Australia and East Timor of adopting the PSCs from the illegal gap treaty that,

> provide contractors with an incredible 127% investment credit, meaning investors get back $2.27 for every dollar spent on capital and exploration. This is paid to the contractor before any profit is shared with the resource owner. In the case of Bayu-Undan, this will cost East Timor and Australia $1.7 billion more than under a standard Indonesian PSC.[12]

While the extraordinary investment credit issue was renegotiated by UNTAET with the contractors, Howard, Downer and their advisers consistently supported demands by Phillips Petroleum and Woodside that no other changes be made to the PSCs. Why?

In consequence, the helium was also lost to Australia. The author, then advising the CNRT President Xanana Gusmão, was informed that Dr Alkatiri was following advice. The President's office had no role in the negotiations. UNTAET did provide funds for Leerberg's advice about the petroleum and for a maritime boundary opinion to be secured from Professor Ian Brownlie QC. Against this background it is difficult to understand why, when crucial decisions were taken, Australia secured the main prize for the petroleum lobby. Australia's withdrawal from submission to the International Court and UNCLOS tribunals made it easy to keep the maritime boundary issue off the table. While there seems little doubt that, in expertise terms, the Timorese were out of their depth in the Timor Sea negotiations, Galbraith could not do it all on his own. He could not have foreseen that expert industry advisers accompanying each Australian delegation had either not put a critical eye over the PSC fine-print or were aware of the maverick definition of petroleum and said nothing. Likewise, it may be unfair to blame FRETILIN for not anticipating the unthinkable—that Australia, in advancing the proposition that sovereign ownership pass at the well-head flange, was losing the game for both itself and Timor-Leste in favour of the commercial consortia. All that remained was to use the Timor Gap era Australia–Indonesia PSC and trust FRETILIN not to notice that two crucial words—'and inerts'—worth billions were missing.

Memorandum of Understanding Between Timor-Leste and Australia

The interim arrangements reached between the UN and Australia allowed the joint-venture petroleum companies to continue with their plans to connect the Bayu-Undan reservoirs in the Timor Sea to a gas production plant at Wickham Point near Darwin. In the knowledge that these plans were already well advanced and anxious for an early revenue stream, the UNTAET negotiators appeared to accept that the first pipeline would land in Australia. As a *quid pro quo*, Article 8(c) of the interim arrangement provided that 'the country where the pipeline lands may not object or impede decisions of the Joint Commission regarding a pipeline to the other country'. Nevertheless, the Bayu-Undan project still required certainty in international law, as no agreement had been reached on territorial sovereignty.

On 5 July 2001 at Dili, FRETILIN leader Mari Alkatiri and UN Adviser Peter Galbraith, both appointed by the SRSG to their roles in a transitional cabinet within the UNTAET Administration, with Australia's Foreign Minister Alexander Downer and Minister for Industry and Research, Senator Nick Minchin, signed an interim agreement to share management of and revenue from the Timor Gap.[13] The sole term of the agreement was that 'Attachment A', being a close copy of the 1989 Timor Gap Treaty with necessary changes to terminology and management structures, would be 'suitable for adoption as an agreement between Australia and Timor-Leste upon Timor-Leste's independence'.

Having accepted Galbraith's proposal to give control of the pipeline to Australia for a fee, Downer also dated and signed on his ministerial letterhead an extraordinary note to Alkatiri and Galbraith confirming that his government would provide East Timor with $A8 million per annum in financial support additional to the new Timor Sea arrangements and with effect from the date of commencement of the operation of the proposed pipeline from the Joint Petroleum Development Area to Darwin, which is expected to be 2005, for the duration of the pipeline's operation.[14]

With this paltry deal, Australia and Phillips Petroleum had the multi-billion game sewn up.

In place of the notorious Australia–Indonesia Zone of Cooperation of the 1989 Timor Gap Treaty, the joint management area was renamed as the 'Joint Petroleum Development Area' (JPDA). Article 7 of 'Attachment A' enjoined the parties to negotiate an agreed Petroleum Mining Code to govern the exploration, development and exploitation of petroleum within the JPDA, as well as the export of petroleum from the JPDA. Article 9 required the parties to 'work expeditiously and in good-faith' to reach agreement on the method by which any reservoir of petroleum that extended across the boundary of the JPDA would be most effectively exploited and shared equitably.

Alexander Downer, with Nick Minchin seated to his right, and Mari Alkatiri sign the Agreement on 5 July 2001 in Dili, in the presence of (standing, from left to right) Louise Frechette, José Ramos-Horta, Sergio de Mello, Rosemary (unidentified) and Xanana Gusmão.

Despite all the bluster with Australia and informed advice from Leerberg concerning the industry standard definition of 'petroleum' that would embrace immensely valuable helium gas, the terms of the treaty on any reasonable view almost replicated those in the unlawful 1989 Timor Gap Treaty. The push by commercial consortia and Australia for a 550-kilometre pipeline to Darwin in preference to a short pipeline to the Timor-Leste coast from where gas could be exported was never seriously challenged. The claims made by those consortia and Australia of deep canyons and a tectonically active Timor Trough were not tested. Later, an independent Timor-Leste commissioned a bathymetric survey of relevant sea-bed areas of the Timor Trough which revealed undulations and valleys out of the trough. A pipeline to Timor-Leste's southern coast was feasible. If UNTAET was unable to research the scientific literature, it should have provided funds for a tectonic appraisal. Like the outcome of the bathymetric survey of the sea-bed, the result would have been favourable. Subsequent geological research has cast doubt on any claims that the level of tectonic activity in the Timor Trough would inhibit the laying of a pipeline.[15] Most damning of all was UNTAET's failure to factor in anticipated earnings from helium recovery. Now worth almost as much in revenue terms as LNG, helium production revenue would radically alter any economic feasibility study for a short pipeline to Timor-Leste.[16]

Proper research by the UNTAET would have allowed claims of an allegedly untraversable trough to be challenged and may have prompted a full reassessment by the UN, including the ethical pros and cons of boosting the economy of Australia's Northern Territory as against long-term infrastructure support for impoverished Timor-Leste. If the UN had accepted the Norwegian Foreign Ministry's offer to effectively take over the task of providing direct support, there is little doubt that the gas analyses would have been secured, the helium bounty recognised, and a new equation extrapolated to support the feasibility of an under-sea pipeline to Timor-Leste's southern coast.

To cap the disaster for Timor-Leste and despite expert advice from Leerberg shared by Timor-Leste with Australian officials, Timor-Leste and Australia, in one fell swoop in Alexander Downer's ministerial office in May 2001, divested their peoples of half the prize value of the Bayu-Undan Field by accepting a proposal that ownership of the gas flow should pass to the contractor entity at the well-head flange.

Not long afterwards, the contractor entity delivered the *coup de grâce* by securing the signature of the Joint Commission for the JPDA on PSCs from which two words, 'and inerts', were missing from the industry-accepted definition of 'petroleum'. The immensely valuable helium in the so-called 'waste-gas flow' escaped into largely foreign commercial hands.

If the deal done in May 2001 was not already a blow to Australia's public finances, another time-bomb for the Australian people had commenced ticking, and those who were aware of its impact in the Australian Government were either being ignored or were taking a calculated risk. With all production from the Bayu-Undan Field to be exported and no significant onshore fields to come on stream, an issue of national significance for Australia loomed. If gas from Greater Sunrise and/or the Browse Basin (north of Western Australia) was not linked to the national grid within the life of the Bayu-Undan production contracts, Australia, at predicted consumption rates, would likely face a gas shortage.

Officials from the Department of Industry, Science and Resources, which administered the Australian Geological Survey Organisation (Geoscience Australia from 2001), were at all stages supporting Australia's Timor Sea negotiation team. By 1999 those officials would have been aware of 11 comprehensive Australian Petroleum Accumulation (APA) Reports covering the Australian continent, which embraced size, development and production history and were linked to a database developed in cooperation with petroleum companies. By 2001 a significant proportion of Australia's petroleum- and gas-producing fields were regarded either as 'mature' or nearing depletion. The capacity of fields coming on stream and about to be tapped gave no confidence that Australia's predicted domestic gas needs would be met within the 15-year estimated development time span of new onshore prospects.

When a domestic gas shortage hit Australia in 2017, one of the principal advisers in the over-zealous sale of the Timor Sea LNG, Josh Frydenberg, was Australia's Minister responsible for energy policy. In May 2017, Prime Minister Turnbull raised the prospect of introducing controls on LNG exports, but Frydenberg remained silent on the obvious question of why none of the suite of long-term Timor Sea PSCs that Australia had oversight of contained national security provisions for an energy emergency. He preferred, in a bold and questionable response, to deflect criticism to the States.[17]

The sale of the entire Bayu-Undan gas output at a price that has failed to keep up with wholesale market prices stems from the single-minded pursuit of an expanded LNG export trade in 1999–2002 by the Howard Government and corporate allies without sufficient regard for Australia's national interest. Due enquiry should have revealed that both Greater Sunrise and the Bowen Basin in Central Queensland had problematic exploitation issues unlikely to be resolved easily.

10
'INDEPENDENCE' FOR TIMOR-LESTE

A United Nations Security Council delegation visited East and West Timor in November 2000 to review the implementation of Security Council Resolution 1272 (SCR1272), which had in 1999 determined the mandate of United Nations Transitional Administration in East Timor (UNTAET). The delegation noted the continuing plight of displaced persons in West Timor and that UNTAET was charged with preparing Timor-Leste for independence.[1] By this time the earlier consensus reached by most in the CNRT that a lengthy transition period of civil society-building precede independence was weakening as the UN moved to hasten independence. It appeared that the SCR1272 mandate to 'support capacity-building for self-government' was only being given lip service. The Security Council extended UNTAET's mandate to 31 January 2002.[2]

On 16 March 2001, UNTAET Regulation 2001/2 was issued, containing a controversial provision, Article 2.6: 'The Constituent Assembly shall become the legislature of an independent East Timor, if so provided in the Constitution'.[3] I had obtained a draft of the Regulation late on 31 December 2000, and, devastated by its intent, I woke CNRT President Gusmão at 8:15 am on the first day of 2001 to show him the draft. The President's wife, Kirsty Sword Gusmão, brought out coffee, which Xanana sipped, contemplating its district of origin.

| 247

Xanana's guards, alarmed at the early commotion, were anticipating a likely call-out but were waved away as we put our heads down. It was clear that the UN, by including Article 2.6 in the new Regulation was going to assist FRETILIN into power, a course favoured by the Australian Government. After so many years of struggle for a democratic Timor Lorosae (as Timor-Leste was usually referred to prior to independence), it was dispiriting to pore over the draft that morning, but Xanana reminded me that he had experienced worse treachery. We sat on in silence on Xanana's little rebuilt terrace sipping coffee as the cocks crowed in Becora and the guards, aware that something was brewing, worked their gun mechanisms. There was no need to articulate our thoughts. Would there be a dramatic *démarche*? Should we confront de Mello? After a while, Xanana resolved to play a waiting game to avoid any violence that a move to confront FRETILIN might provoke. It seemed as if unseen hands were turning a fateful page in East Timor's history.

Article 2.6 of the draft regulation could only aid FRETILIN and its backers—the Australian Government. Gusmão was not alone in his concern about whether the Timorese, given their levels of dislocation and illiteracy, could make an informed choice. This was not like a simple ballot for independence by which oppressed peoples would throw off the yoke of oppression. A working democracy required informed choice between political parties. Church and community leaders were wary of an early election, as most Timorese knew little more than the flag of FRETILIN's resistance. For Australia, however, FRETILIN offered the swifter path to petroleum. It was clear that we needed to visit the UN in New York.

Gusmão's trip to New York in March 2001 to discuss the need for a civil society awareness programme to be linked with the general election or otherwise delay the election was unproductive and failed to lift the gloom. Behind the scenes, he was working hard to secure an acknowledgement of past errors, including crimes against humanity committed by the União Democrática Timorense (UDT) and FRETILIN's old guard. If the old guard did not give account of those crimes and apologise, any pursuit of Indonesian crimes would be meaningless and damaging to reconciliation efforts.

On 24–25 April 2001, in a good-will visit to celebrate Anzac Day with Australian troops, Australian Governor-General Sir William Deane visited Timor-Leste. For his meeting with CNRT President Xanana Gusmão, Sir William was accompanied by Admiral Chris Barrie, Chief of the Australian Defence Force (CDF). The meeting took place at CNRT HQ at a critically important juncture for both countries. The CNRT President was wrestling with the daunting prospect of bringing his country into the community of nations. Gusmão's interest in defence matters extended to the prospect of an active defence relationship with Australia that would not be regarded with suspicion in Jakarta. The meeting, against a background of his own close relationship with Australian military leaders, allowed Gusmão to look past the gloom and to see a prospect of reconciliation with Indonesia and a more integrated relationship at all levels with Australia.

Deane's visit, as Commander in Chief of Australia's defence forces, together with his CDF, provided an opportunity to balance the shallow and opportunistic nature of Australian petroleum diplomacy with the solid integrity of those to be trusted in selfless service—values Gusmão well understood. The prospect opened for Gusmão, still undecided whether he would seek government, of campaigning on a platform of a closer relationship with Australia, a special category of student and worker visa concessions, early reconciliation with Indonesia, closer defence ties with Australia, and an honourable end to the bickering over maritime sovereignty.

At this time Gusmão had an Australian wife, an adept university-trained senior strategy adviser, Agio Pereira, a trained geologist adviser, Alfredo Pires, and a legal adviser, all of whom were Australian citizens. Around us at HQ were legendary men and women of the resistance years, strong with their faith in Xanana. The noise and bustle of those happy to be alive contrasted with the quiet dignity of Xanana's office. Many a time I sat as he dictated to his assistant Lourdes, while she juggled her notebook and fed a babe at her breast. Still recovering from his resistance ordeal, Xanana had developed an abiding bond with our Australian SAS guards, whose stealthy presence and field craft calmed and steadied his mind. There was hope that Australia would show some vision, and the prospect of a new era quickened our steps at CNRT HQ. Concrete steps had already been taken to ensure there could be an effective defence and intelligence relationship between Australia and the emerging new nation, and it is for this reason that I was so disheartened by the way DFAT nullified our efforts.

Gusmão's hopes of a deep and enduring relationship with Australia were dashed later that month when word came in to CNRT HQ that the FRETILIN Constitution was being backed by strong work behind the scenes by DFAT. This could only mean that Australia wanted to shoehorn in a FRETILIN Government. Once again, Australia's long-term interests, particularly with defence ties as an integral aspect of positive foreign policy, suffered directly from petroleum diplomacy. Worse was to follow as foreign policy incompetence, or worse, turned to base treachery.

Despite Gusmão's concerns, the UN backed, or perhaps followed, Australian Prime Minister Howard's lead and proclaimed the ostensible stability of FRETILIN as a majority political party. The main players seemed determined to put the unreformed FRETILIN Party with its authoritarian structure into power. Unsurprisingly, an inclusive program for prosecution of war crimes with necessary international backing did not eventuate. Any investigation of war crimes prior to the Indonesian invasion would likely focus on FRETILIN, and Australia was not going to support any undermining of its support for FRETILIN. In Dili, Sergio Vieira de Mello, anxious to maintain peace with Indonesia, failed to back his deputy, Dennis McNamara, who had sought Jakarta's support for the arrest and trial of indicted war criminals, including General Wiranto.[4]

Kirsty Sword Gusmão, the author and Rebecca Engel at Columbia University, New York, during Xanana Gusmão's trip to the UN, March 2001.

Shortly after the UN's intent behind Article 2.6 became clear, Xanana Gusmão resigned as Speaker of the National Council, citing as his reason the lack of consultation in the process of drafting a Constitution. On 7 May 2001, registration of political parties and independent candidates for an election of a Constituent Assembly commenced, and on 9 June 2001 the CNRT was dissolved. When civil registration ended on 23 June 2001, 778,989 Timorese had registered and been issued temporary identity cards.[5] Article 2.6 was not mentioned publicly. On 28 June 2001, de Mello addressed the National Council and called for a Pact of National Unity, which the FRETILIN Party rejected summarily, in the same way that it had rejected a similar call by Gusmão. Mau Hodu's ghost was walking off the stage.

The election of a Constituent Assembly proceeded on 30 August 2001. This was won by the FRETILIN Party, with 57.3% of the vote, secured as a result of a bizarre poll devised by UNTAET in which the 13 key district seats were elected on a first-past-the-post basis. The balance of seats were secured on a preferential voting system equally unsuited to an election being conducted in the absence of informed party manifesto debate. Predictably, an overall 55/88 majority was secured by FRETILIN, which had campaigned within a largely illiterate country electorate on its flag of resistance. The outcome of the poll left FRETILIN with just five more non-FRETILIN votes of the 60 required to approve a Constitution. Needing to field a local resistance figure, the diaspora FRETILIN encouraged Lú-Olo Guterres to assume the Assembly's Presidency. On 20 September 2001, the Transitional Cabinet was abolished and a Council of Ministers of the Second Transitional Government, containing three expatriate FRETILIN Ministers led by Mari Alkatiri, Rogerio Lobato and Estanislau da Silva, was sworn in.

As many commentators feared, the Constituent Assembly President on 22 October 2001 signed a resolution adopting the Constituent Assembly's recommendation that UNTAET hand over sovereignty to an 'elected' East Timorese Government on 20 May 2002. Noting that resolution, the UN Security Council on 31 October 2001 approved continuation of the UN role in Timor-Leste after independence to avoid any destabilising effect of premature withdrawal.[6] On 30 November 2001, the Constituent Assembly approved a draft Constitution, which in all significant respects replicated the FRETILIN Constitution approved at FRETILIN's National Conference in Sydney in August 1998, which had been sponsored by the Mozambique diaspora delegation led by Mari Alkatiri and another Timorese exile from Mozambique, Ana Pessoa, former wife of José Ramos-Horta.

The strategy the UN in New York and the Australian Government had developed was to put FRETILIN, which they perceived as the major political party, into power without a popular vote. Article 2.6 of the UNTAET Regulation 2001/2 was the mechanism that enabled a FRETILIN-controlled Constituent Assembly to introduce a Constitution that declared, in effect, a FRETILIN legislature. Despite the objections of many local politicians, some UNTAET advisers, Bishop Belo, Jesuit jurist Frank Brennan, John Dowd, then President of the International Commission of Jurists, and many NGO observers, independence was contrived at a time when Timor-Leste's leadership was ill-equipped to deal with the complexities of government, including international maritime law.

In the mid-1970s, while attached to the Australian Embassy in Paris, I was enlightened by my francophone maternal uncle, a Cambridge graduate and former British officer embedded within General de Gaulle's Free French HQ, on the tension between Winston Churchill, Roosevelt and de Gaulle concerning the fear that de Gaulle might establish, following the liberation, a one-party state backed by military power. Eventually, in October 1944, four months after D-Day, a provisional government led by de Gaulle was given official recognition by Britain and the United States, but only after certain understandings were reached. General de Gaulle used his authority as provisional leader to reduce chaos in liberated continental France and to establish a National Committee of Liberation that led to the founding in 1946 of the Fourth French Republic. I heard more from a former French resistance hero, then close to the Élysée Palace, who spoke often of the post-Liberation period as the French recovered from chaos. In early 2000, as I sat as an adviser to the CNRT President at meetings of Sergio de Mello's Consultative Council, tales of the tension between de Gaulle and Churchill and Roosevelt came back to me. I realised that the UN was totally unprepared for its role.[7] The UN, with no plan and no experience in running a government, could have recalled a 1944–46 historic road map in the experience of devastated France with a charismatic army leader.

At the first national conference of the CNRT in August 2000, Xanana Gusmão, the charismatic leader of a humane resistance, proposed a coherent way forward. He pressed for a provisional government of national unity, working with a national committee of liberation that embraced all political interests. He was being inclusive. His FALINTIL, led in the field by his beloved deputy Taur Matan Ruak, were under disciplined command. This fell on deaf ears. Neither the UN nor Australia supported the establishment of a provisional government. Instead, they opted for an opportunistic experiment with FRETILIN, led by a relic Leninist whom they perceived to be a more pliable route to a Timor Sea settlement. But Alkatiri was astute and aggressive and the UN and Australia failed to weigh the consequences of placing an undemocratised FRETILIN party in power, elements of which had already put feelers out to Beijing.

The need for further military intervention in Timor-Leste in 2006 left the UN to answer the question whether one aspect of the mandate handed to UNTAET by SCR 1272—'to support capacity-building for self-government'—had been discharged. Although, SCR 1272 stressed the need for UNTAET to develop local democratic institutions,[8] the UN allowed one political group, FRETILIN, to impose a constitution drafted in Mozambique. It was a deeply flawed document that did not separate legislative, judicial and executive powers adequately.

Although the FRETILIN Draft Constitution did contain some clauses consistent with an intent to govern democratically, the drafting process was irregular and undemocratic. The failure of the UN to include civil society in the constitution-building process was its most significant lapse. While the Secretary-General had reported to the Security Council that UNTAET had managed to establish general conditions of freedom of movement and personal security by January 2000,[9] the decision at the UN later that year to initiate a popularly-based constitution-drafting process seemed almost surreal to those on the ground in Timor-Leste. Randall Garrison, now a Canadian parliamentarian, addressed subsequent events comprehensively:

> It is obvious that not all Timorese were able to participate in the Constitution building process as many remained in refugee camps in West Timor. By March 2001 well over two-thirds of those who had been displaced had returned home, but still 50,000 to 80,000 refugees remained in West Timor ... This means that some 5 to 10% of the

population of Timor-Leste was excluded from the constitution building process simply as a result of their absence from the territory. It is also clear that many of those who had not supported the independence option for Timor-Leste faced significant obstacles to participation in the constitution building process. Both the United Nations High Commissioner for Human Rights and Amnesty International reported cases of violence and intimidation directed against returning refugees and those alleged to have had links with the Indonesian security forces as an ongoing problem in 2001.[10]

As Garrison's analysis continues, 'the selection of Portuguese as the working language for the constitution-drafting process did little to promote inclusion in a country where less than 10% of the population spoke Portuguese'. A final obstacle to participation in drafting the constitution was simply logistical. Timor-Leste's limited development, coupled with the destruction of transportation and communications infrastructure in 1999, made it extremely difficult for anyone outside Dili to participate. The UN's failure to listen to Gusmão and a host of informed observers was all the more reprehensible, because UNTAET knew of the significant logistical support needed to achieve the participation of the population in the CNRT National Congress of all political parties in August 2000. Furthermore, the UN and Australia knew that, far from being a 'majority party', FRETILIN was a diaspora-led urban cabal that had been comprehensively defeated on all important motions at that National Congress.

Simply put, the Timorese at the National Congress who were prepared to engage at grass-roots level in debating their future no longer wanted FRETILIN, no matter how estimable its leadership had been in the 1975–87 struggle before Gusmão moved away from FRETILIN and freed FALINTIL from political Commissar control that had extended to attempts by diaspora FRETILIN leaders to control the internal resistance. Within FRETILIN in Timor Leste, Mau Hodu's decision to accommodate Gusmão's structural reorganisation had not been received favourably by the diaspora FRETILIN leadership. Gusmão's charismatic hold over the Timorese peoples, so evident to all at the CNRT National Congress in August 2000, was met with a mixture of fear and misapprehension by the diaspora FRETILIN leadership and by the Australian Government. Rumours spread in Dili and Canberra that Gusmão was likely to lead a military-backed party into power. He was, however, an inclusive leader whose humble reluctance to assume power, strengthened by those constantly reminding him that guerrilla leaders rarely made good politicians, was exploited by those he listened to.

UNTAET's timetable specified that the Constituent Assembly would produce a draft Constitution within 90 days of its election, which gave no time for an alternative model for drafting by a broadly representative Constitutional Commission. As Garrison has noted, 'it ruled out the idea of adopting an interim Constitution to allow for more extensive civic education and consultation as some in the NGO community had suggested. It presumed adoption of the Constitution by a vote of the parties in the Constituent Assembly and not by a popular referendum'.[11] UNTAET's proposal that political parties be required to register and thus be eligible to seek representation in the Constituent Assembly was advertised for public consultation.

It was obvious to Gusmão and those close to him that 'maximum authority' would lie with the political party likely to control the Constituent Assembly. The 'minimalist' role ascribed to the UNTAET by Galbraith amounted to allowing the FRETILIN Party to secure power without any genuine democratic process. Further evidence of this emerges from the primacy of the political groupings in drafting the Constitution, such that established political parties were the key decision-makers:

> Civil society organisations and anyone else wishing to have influence would be forced to make their input known through political parties. The power of parties was reinforced by the National Council's decision to elect members to the Constituent Assembly on a system of proportional representation that strongly favours central party organisations. With only a single member of the Assembly being elected on a plurality basis in each of the 13 districts, the proportion of members able to act relatively independently of a party organisation would be small. The other 75 members of the Assembly owe their position to the party who placed their names on its list, thus reinforcing party discipline.[12]

With only 57.3% of the national vote, FRETILIN secured a clear majority (55 out of 88) of seats in the Constituent Assembly, having been advantaged by a UN-devised voting system that combined a first-past-the-post poll with proportional ballot. Aware of the strength of post-liberation patriotism under the FRETILIN flag rather than manifesto-influenced support, Xanana Gusmão asked de Mello to sponsor a widespread 'manifesto' debate, but his request fell on deaf ears. Such a debate would have allowed voters to understand why Gusmão had not been identified with FRETILIN for such a long time. (After Timor's liberation many villagers would dig out the FRETILIN flag to welcome their popular leader Xanana Gusmão as he travelled round the country, revealing that many non-urban Timorese were unaware of the 1987 schism within FRETILIN.)

When the Constituent Assembly began its work on a new Constitution, five parties submitted draft texts. As already noted, FRETILIN used the draft Constitution it had adopted at its national conference in Sydney in 1998 as the basis for discussion. Four thematic committees of the Constituent Assembly worked through the draft, but little of substance was changed in the end. The five international constitutional experts brought in by UNTAET, input from public consultations, and drafts by four other political parties resulted in no serious modification of the FRETILIN draft. The schedule was extended to allow for public consultations at the district level, with six minority parties proposing a month's extension, but the FRETILIN majority imposed a ten-day extension.[13] The district-level consultations were led by the Constituent Assembly members from 24 February to 2 March 2002, but the process was marred by the limited timeframe and by the lack of information for the public in advance of the meetings. Further disadvantaging the impact of district-level consultations was the fact that the draft constitution existed only in Portuguese until Tetum and Indonesian versions were completed late in the process and not generally available in advance of the meetings. Often the consultation meetings were more about providing information about the content of the draft constitution than about receiving any input.[14] The draft, with few changes from the FRETILIN-proposed draft, was adopted by the Constituent Assembly, with 72 members in favour and 14 against, one abstention and one absentee. Those against were from parties that alleged that the drafting process had been dominated by FRETILIN and had produced a 'FRETILIN Constitution'.

An answer to the question of whether a Constitution, rushed through so undemocratically under the eyes of a complicit UN, provided a foundation for post-conflict nation-building may be found in subsequent events. The 2002–06 Alkatiri Government has been heavily criticised for its failure or inability to develop constitutional mechanisms to provide important safeguards—for example, to either constitute or properly convoke constitutional institutions such as an appeal court and a constitutional review body. An analysis of these lapses, which triggered occasional protests, helps to explain the paralysis that set in early once the Alkatiri Government came under public siege.

The accelerated move towards independence played into the hands of those seeking an early treaty base in international law for petroleum exploitation in the disputed areas of the Timor Sea over which Australia knew it had no lawful claim under the UN Convention on the Law of the Sea. De Mello explained his cooperation with the Australian Government/FRETILIN strategy as 'the urgent need to get Timor-Leste a revenue base, not an alliance with Australia'.[15] However, there was more to favouring FRETILIN against Gusmão's wish for a government of national unity than FRETILIN's early assurance of certainty for petroleum exploitation.

Australia and the UN Deny Recognition of FALINTIL

After Gusmão was released from custody by Indonesian authorities in September 1999, he returned to Timor-Leste as the most eminent surviving hero of the national liberation struggle and resumed as Commander-in-Chief of FALINTIL, the armed wing of FRETILIN from which he had resigned in December 1987 when some FRETILIN leaders in Timor-Leste and abroad persisted in opposing his concept of a resistance based on national unity.[16] As noted in chapter 6, in 1988 Gusmão had re-established FALINTIL as the armed wing of the Conselho Nacional da Resistência Maubere (CNRM: National Council of Maubere Resistance). Thus, the charismatic resistance hero returned to Timor-Leste in 1999 as the leader of an army, which was a matter of some concern in Canberra, where Australia's Foreign Minister had in August 1998 hosted FRETILIN's leader Mari Alkatiri, obtaining from him an assurance that it would be a FRETILIN Government's policy to honour commercial petroleum production-sharing contracts in the Timor Sea.

With FALINTIL regarded by the FRETILIN leadership as Gusmão's power base, fears were expressed that an independent Timor-Leste could fall sway to army rule. While this was plausible, Gusmão's split from FRETILIN in 1987 had been founded on the concept of a politically neutral military force, a call for national unity among resistance groups, and accelerated diplomatic efforts abroad. Gusmão's demonstration of inclusiveness at the August 2000 CNRT National Congress, including his repeated calls for a government of national unity, also suggested that independent Timor-Leste would not fall sway to army rule. Tragically, for those who suffered in 2006, the alternative of FRETILIN rule was not subjected to similar levels of scrutiny by the UN and the Australian Government.

As subsequent events showed, the UN made a serious policy error in allowing FRETILIN, essentially a diaspora group, to claim an inheritance they barely deserved, thus sidelining Gusmão who had directed a humane and intelligent resistance. For Australian policy-makers in Canberra, however, it was by no means an error. Using a combination of high-level intrigue in Washington and New York the Howard Government outwitted the UN and the Timorese leadership to deliver a windfall to the petroleum consortia. A real prize for the Australian people would have been a staunch and forgiving ally at a critically important stopping point on Australia's path into Southeast Asia. Instead, the Howard Government, backed by Australian Labor Party leaders, projected a mean-spirited image of Australia to nations in the region looking on and to an embittered generation of new leaders in Timor. Were it not for the more generous image projected by Australian military forces and Australian NGOs and religious orders, the damage wrought by the enduring dishonesty of Canberra's foreign policy-makers might have been more far-reaching.

11
THE FALINTIL TRAGEDY

An inquiry into the violence in Timor-Leste in May 2006 reported on the poor foundation of the security sector in the new nation: 'The current functioning of the police service (PNTL), and the Defence Force (F-FDTL) in particular, is hampered by a perceived lack of legitimacy arising from the manner of their creation'.[1] The United Nation's treatment of FALINTIL before and after the 30 August 1999 ballot was a further aspect of the UN's failure to conceptualise and plan for post-conflict nation-building. The May 5 Accord in 1999 between the UN, Indonesia and Portugal, outlined in chapter 7, provided for the separation of the military combatants as a preliminary to the planned popular consultation. The Accord recognised the combatants as the Indonesian army (TNI) and FALINTIL, but the UN failed to recognise FALINTIL in its subsequent mission plan, which had lasting and tragic consequences.

Following the May 5 Accord a series of meetings brokered in part by the UN between the CNRT and Indonesian officials resulted in agreement by the end of June 1999 that TNI and FALINTIL would withdraw to agreed areas. In addition, the Indonesian Peace and Stability Commission sponsored a series of now notorious public displays by the militias whose leaders pledged to disarm and work towards a peaceful ballot. In a move sanctioned by Xanana Gusmão from his ongoing confinement in Indonesia, FALINTIL Deputy Commander Taur Matan Ruak announced that his troops would withdraw to self-imposed cantonments, both as a concession to and a public inducement for the TNI to do the same. While a TNI response was awaited, militia violence surged, causing Gusmão and FALINTIL regional commanders to question their orders. It was clear that the violence had been provoked by the arming of militia by the TNI as they withdrew from operations against FALINTIL. On 25 January 1999, in a seemingly co-ordinated response, the pregnant wife of a FALINTIL commander was cut down by gunfire at Galitas, near Zumalai in Covalima District. The militia commander subsequently admitted the targeted killing.[2] On 5 April 1999, a furious Gusmão, still FALINTIL Commander despite his imprisonment, revealed to the media that he had authorised FALINTIL to push back against the militias. The following day a church congregation was massacred in Liquiçá, as noted in chapter 7. Faced with this provocation, Gusmão retracted his orders after Indonesian media and some of his close advisers raised the prospect of a civil war developing in which a ballot might not take place.[3]

Meanwhile, as knowledge of the FALINTIL cantonments quickly spread, significant numbers of people moved into the FALINTIL zones for protection. Thereafter, FALINTIL troops showed admirable restraint as the militia wreaked their violence in the lead-up to the ballot.[4] The tight military discipline shown by FALINTIL avoided any confrontation with the pro-integration militia, which the TNI Command could have presented as a civil war justifying the ballot's cancellation. Throughout the militia violence following the ballot, FALINTIL troops held firm to their orders. Worldwide condemnation of the violence ultimately led President Habibie to agree to international intervention. Understandably, many Timorese, less aware of the strategic imperatives in the run-up to the ballot, criticised FALINTIL for not intervening. Many FALINTIL personnel, loyal to their orders, whose families perished during the 'stay-put' strategy became deeply traumatised.

Thus, by the time the International Force East Timor (INTERFET) troops made operational contact with FALINTIL commanders, FALINTIL troops had experienced an anti-climax in military terms to their 24-year struggle. In this context the CNRT Leader and FALINTIL Commander Xanana Gusmão and INTERFET Commander General

Peter Cosgrove commenced discussion of FALINTIL's status. Cosgrove believed, or was instructed by Canberra, that he was required to disarm all forces other than those engaged in UN policing. Although Security Council Resolution 1264 (SCR1264) provided no such express mandate, the Security Council authorisation to 'restore peace and security' authorised the disarming of those who threatened peace and security. Without conceding formally that FALINTIL did not come within such a mandate, Cosgrove's move to disarm FALINTIL was not pressed. Nevertheless, Cosgrove's restrictions on FALINTIL bearing arms outside the Aileu Valley compromised the ability of FALINTIL personnel to protect themselves when they were in districts still subject to militia attack.

Any attempt to disarm FALINTIL was directly at odds with international law. FALINTIL was an armed force under disciplined command meeting an occupation that was recognised internationally as unlawful. There was no record of FALINTIL committing atrocities in its operations, and it had never attacked vulnerable targets such as Indonesian married quarters and Indonesian Catholic clergy. Although, during the resistance years, voices urged reprisal action against Indonesian interests abroad from time to time, active operations were restricted to Timor-Leste. The CNRT legal appreciation was encapsulated in an advice provided to Gusmão:

> Resolution 1264 does not provide a mandate to disarm FALINTIL unless FALINTIL is involved directly or indirectly in any continuing or apprehended violence against any individuals. It has never been argued that the presence in East Timor of FALINTIL constitutes a threat to peace and security. Likewise, it has never been argued that FALINTIL has since the Agreement of 5 May 1999 committed any violations of International Humanitarian Laws. In my view the Commander of the multi-national force has no authority under Resolution 1264 expressly or by implication to disarm FALINTIL. Indeed, as has been stated by the Vice President of the CNRT José Ramos Horta, the continuing existence of FALINTIL is consistent with Paragraph 2 of Resolution 1264 which emphasizes, inter alia, the urgent need and importance of all parties co-operating with such humanitarian organisations so as to ensure the protection of civilians at risk, and the safe return of refugees and displaced person and the effective delivery of humanitarian aid. Whilst the FALINTIL provides a protective cordon around the

cantonments they are in fact acting to the letter with Paragraph 2 of Resolution 1264.[5]

The UN edict that all 'armed groups' be disarmed also showed ignorance of the crucial role that FALINTIL had played in outmanoeuvring the TNI Command in its attempts to thwart the ballot. Only a highly disciplined force could make such a claim and to disarm such a force in such ignominious circumstances was unthinkable. The UN instruction failed to recognise FALINTIL's status in international law as the recognised army of resistance to an unlawful occupation. As this failure could not be accidental, the UN's possible motive in its outrageous treatment of FALINTIL had to be examined.

In private conversation with the author, Sergio Vieira de Mello referred to 'a view in New York and Canberra, and even within FRETILIN, that FALINTIL is Xanana's private army'. By supporting the Australian strategy of sidelining Xanana Gusmão and his perceived army, the UN lost the opportunity to honour and encourage an influential element in any nation-building effort. Instead, in November 1999 a deeply offended and somewhat demoralised FALINTIL force reluctantly accepted cantonment in the Aileu Valley and the limitation to bear arms only in the Valley, which played into the hands of FRETILIN.

On 19 November 1999, Gusmão led an armed group of FALINTIL soldiers into Dili to the UNTAET Headquarters to lodge a protest with de Mello at the disarming of a FALINTIL convoy,[6] but the UN continued in its refusal to recognise FALINTIL or include FALINTIL soldiers in peacekeeping operations. The UN also withheld desperately needed food and medical supplies from the Aileu canton on grounds that the UN remit did not extend to assisting military forces. Bishop Belo responded by sending Church rice supplies from Dili up to Aileu. The parlous condition of the health of many FALINTIL veterans resulted in anguished scenes when Gusmão visited his troops. The imposition of these sanctions by the UN verged on the ridiculous. Even in early 2000 the financially destitute Xanana Gusmão and his staff, including the author, had meagre provisions at their makeshift headquarters on the Dili waterfront, guarded by Australian SAS, who alleviated the situation by making 'strategic visits' to quartermaster stores at the Dili wharf.

FALINTIL's treatment by the UN was a significant distraction as Gusmão hosted an almost daily stream of petitioners presenting post-liberation issues. Some of the heart-rending chronicles reduced him and his advisers to tears. One of the less oppressive interventions was the unannounced arrival at Gusmão's headquarters of a group of observers from the United States. They seated themselves on makeshift planks laid across ammunition boxes, and the visitors' spokeswoman, a US Senator, asked the CNRT President if Timor-Leste's organic coffee plantations, she believed to have been abandoned by TNI and Suharto family interests, could be protected from squatter expropriation and the use of chemicals by immediate interim management under a US aid program. Ever a coffee *aficionado*, Gusmão readily agreed to this request.

Less agreeable issues took up much of Gusmão's time. In a tactic akin to the attempt in 1944 to deny General de Gaulle's Free French troops the right to march into liberated Paris, de Mello and the INTERFET command denied FALINTIL the right to bear arms in a victory march through Dili. Resentment among FALINTIL veterans of the mistreatment of FALINTIL by the UN, which they, with good reason, believe to have been instigated by the Australian Department of Foreign Affairs and Trade (DFAT), persists to this day. To mollify that resentment, Gusmão has frequently expressed his view that the

Ever the tactician, Xanana Gusmão discusses tactics for the 2001 Arafura Games in Darwin with the national football coach, Ivan Cengic and the author. Timor-Leste won in the five-nations tournament and the team's return to Dili was a memorable sight.

unfair treatment accorded FALINTIL was neither proposed nor led by the Australian military; he had an excellent personal relationship with Cosgrove. Although Gusmão never really warmed to Cosgrove's trademark welcoming cold VB beer, considered a poor relation to the wine de Mello could offer his guests, Cosgrove frequently saved the day by projecting the generosity of the Australian spirit that Canberra's bureaucratic machinations lacked completely.

The DFAT-led strategy of promoting FRETILIN and containing Gusmão, and his perceived private army, became obvious in May 2000, when Gusmão proposed that his first overseas visit be to Canberra to thank Prime Minister Howard and Opposition Leader Kim Beazley for their support for Timor-Leste during the tumultuous period following the May 5 Accord. The author telephoned Howard's office and the proposal was accepted. Although exhausted by his interminable and often harrowing travel around devastated Timor, Gusmão boarded a UN flight to Darwin. As the plane landed, the author received a call from the Prime Minister's office saying that Mr Howard had decided that it would not be appropriate to receive President Gusmão 'at this time'; no further explanation of the rejection was given.

A call to Cabinet Minister Nick Minchin revealed that Foreign Minister Alexander Downer, acting on DFAT advice, had advised the Prime Minister that the President Elect of Indonesia, Abdurrahman Wahid, might be offended if President Gusmão preceded him in Canberra. The author told Minchin that Downer's adviser on East Timor, John Dauth, should know that Gusmão and Wahid had been on close personal terms for years and, indeed, that Gusmão and Wahid had spoken that morning when Wahid had endorsed the idea of the trip. The author told Minchin that ongoing DFAT obsequiousness to Jakarta would be highly offensive to Gusmão. Minchin said that he would raise the issue with Howard and minutes before the flight was to leave Darwin for Canberra, Howard's office informed me that the visit should continue.

No official transport awaited our arrival in Canberra on 4 May 2000, but two junior DFAT officials were at the airport to tell us that it would not be appropriate for the author to accompany Gusmão to any meetings. DFAT believed it had established an accommodation with FRETILIN leader Mari Alkatiri, and its discomfort with Gusmão's first visit to the Australian people was palpable. Anticipating that the fawning sycophancy with the Indonesian Government of DFAT's Timor Desk and the plan to embrace FRETILIN would overshadow any official reception, the author's law firm had borrowed a large black American limousine from a client; a law firm staffer acted as chauffeur. Gusmão, oblivious of the snub, was taken to the law office to meet the staff who had done so much over the years for the Timorese cause. Shortly before Gusmão left to meet Prime Minister Howard at nearby Parliament House, Downer's Press Secretary telephoned to ask if Downer could meet President Gusmão at the Ministerial Entrance 'for a quick photo opportunity'. Despite Downer's opposition to the visit and the disgraceful snub by DFAT at the airport, Gusmão, with his characteristic humility, agreed.

At dinner at the author's home on 5 May 2000, generously catered by the Akcal family, long-time supporters who owned Canberra's Ottoman Cuisine, one could not resist comparing the disgraceful treatment accorded Gusmão with Downer's wooing with transport, dinner and accommodation at Canberra's Hyatt Hotel of FRETILIN Leader Mari Alkatiri in August 1998. With customary incompetence and arrogance, DFAT was not going to hedge its bets and contemplate that Xanana Gusmão might be accommodated as a future leader of a strategically important neighbouring state. DFAT's strategic vision did not extend past its Holy Grail in the Timor Sea; fortunately, Gusmão's reception by the Australian defence hierarchy was entirely positive.

Gusmão's visit to Canberra and his discussions with the Australian Returned Services League Vice-President took place in the context of unresolved discussions with the UN on the role of FALINTIL and programs for veteran relief. Again showing forbearance with Australian intransigence, the United Kingdom had proposed at the UN that Britain fund an independent study on options for a Timor-Leste security force, which included the future of FALINTIL. The British intervention was welcomed, but the moving report by the distinguished panel of experts did little to defuse the situation.[7] By revealing the essential humanity and deadly efficiency of Gusmão's guerrilla army, the report undermined the credibility of Australia's refusal to recognise FALINTIL as a territorial army. Faced with the study's presentation of Gusmão as a man of moral and intrepid leadership, the Australian Government redoubled its efforts to ensure a man who could lead an Army and inspire a nation would not become the new nation's leader.

Howard and Downer continued to favour Mari Alkatiri, a Leninist from the Timorese diaspora in Mozambique, with whom they believed they had a better chance of achieving their strategic goals.

Released on 8 August 2000, the report recommended security force options for Timor-Leste. A close reading is instructive in understanding how the will to resist an inhuman occupation can persist without retaliatory crimes against humanity. The inspiring leadership by Gusmão and Taur Matan Ruak of a humane resistance devoid of mutual atrocity leaps from its pages, but the Australian Government was not going to engage with any such understanding. The report's authors explained the Australian-inspired UN attempt to sidestep international law by reference to a so-called 'mandate caveat':

> INTERFET and, more recently, the PKF [Peacekeeping Force] have followed self-imposed limits on their activities within the cantonment area. UN military observers ... maintain a FALINTIL Liaison Team in the cantonment with observing, monitoring and reporting functions, but the PKF operates outside the cantonment area ...
>
> UNTAET is precluded by its mandate from entering into agreements that would be understood to confer legal status on FALINTIL. FALINTIL has anyway said that it will not sign a memorandum of understanding until the issue of its future role is resolved. Where FALINTIL has proposed more formal arrangements that would, for example, allow it to take part in joint patrols with the PKF or in refugee reception committees, UNTAET has found itself constrained by its mandate from endorsing these proposals ...
>
> The combination of circumstances that has left FALINTIL in an ill-defined relationship to UNTAET/the PKF and the East Timor government, and has caused its membership to become increasingly scattered and demoralized, has encouraged a view that the UN is conspiring at the elimination of FALINTIL. This opinion was aired both by commanders and ordinary troops during the Team's visit to Aileu. Some commanders go further, taking the view that that has effectively been the thrust of UN policy since the Tripartite Agreement of 5 May 1999. It is in this context that FALINTIL and the CNRT have called for a comprehensive solution that begins with the clarification of its present and future status, and have rejected an approach that addresses the issues piecemeal. Thus, FALINTIL's position on demobilization has hardened progressively since January 1999. Then, with the apparent

encouragement of members of the FALINTIL High Command, the IOM [International Organization for Migration] drafted an initial proposal for facilitating the transition of FALINTIL members to civilian life. This proposal was further refined in March 2000 and presented at a FALINTIL Study Group. Soon after, the FALINTIL deputy commander, Taur Matan Ruak, took the position that demobilization should be part of the same process as recruitment to a new force, i.e. that there could be no question of demobilization taking place before the broader status issue had been resolved.[8]

The Study Group findings effectively backed claims that the UN was in breach of international law in refusing to provide FALINTIL with the recognition it deserved and expected under the May 5 Accord of 1999:

FALINTIL is a liberation army with a firm command structure but with no formal 'rank' structure. Within FALINTIL, there is an emphasis on collective discussion among commanders. A common distinction is made between 'veterans' and 'new recruits (novatos)' ... The highest regard is reserved for the oldest veterans, 'those who never surrendered' ... Although the majority of senior commanders are from areas east of Dili, FALINTIL as a whole is made up of soldiers from virtually every area (and every language group, large and small) in East Timor... It is FALINTIL policy, for ideological as well as strategic reasons, to have a representative force that is able to operate effectively in every local area. *As such, FALINTIL is presently the only genuinely representative institution in the territory* ... As a liberation force, FALINTIL's prestige is high throughout the country, but especially in the countryside where individual FALINTIL commanders have been called upon to intervene in disputes and reconcile opposing factions. Its intelligence networks, developed over decades, are intact and the Aileu headquarters maintains regular radio contact with most parts of East Timor [emphasis added].[9]

Throughout all negotiations Gusmão and senior FALINTIL staff queried the Secretary-General's claim that SCR 1264 prevented the recognition of FALINTIL. Representations by FRETILIN in support of diplomatic pressure by the Australian Government in Dili and New York led Kofi Annan to act on claims that recognition of FALINTIL could lead to army rule. Consequently, the Australians pressed for UNTAET control over the recruitment process for the new defence force. By this time, the Australian Mission in Dili was openly courting the FRETILIN leadership, even hosting a gathering of FRETILIN leaders and Phillips Petroleum executives, who donated several Toyota motor vehicles. The FALINTIL command remained firm; paramount in their thinking was the need to exclude an UNTAET recruitment process influenced by FRETILIN links with the UN and Australia.

On 20 August 2000, FALINTIL celebrated the 25th anniversary of its founding as the armed wing of FRETILIN at Aileu in the mountains behind Dili. Given the state of the roads and the importance of a Commander reviewing his troops one last time, UNTAET provided an ageing Russian helicopter to take Gusmão, who had chosen the occasion to step down as FALINTIL Commander, his pregnant wife, FALINTIL bodyguards and the author to Aileu. Gusmão was aware that a summary of the report of the independent British study group was to be circulated that day to the FALINTIL Command. Shortly after Gusmão addressed the assembled veterans, a senior Commander, and future President of Timor-Leste, Francisco (Lú-Olo) Guterres, announced his intention to throw his support behind FRETILIN, thus giving a huge boost to a Party that in recent years had been perceived in some quarters as stronger in Marxist–Leninist ideology in exile than in resistance activity in occupied Timor-Leste. The expatriate FRETILIN leaders soon endorsed Guterres as President of the party, which was now led, at least in a titular sense, by a hero of the local FALINTIL resistance. FRETILIN rather than FALINTIL was now to demand the fruits of victory won largely by FALINTIL and its exemplary leadership.

Xanana Gusmão addresses FALINTIL troops on 20 August 2000.

Xanana Gusmão takes a final salute on 20 August 2000 before stepping down as Commander.

FALINTIL patrol in the Aileu cantonment, 2000.

When, finally, the UN agreed to the FALINTIL conditions about the recruitment of a new defence force, demobilisation occurred on 1 February 2001 and the recruitment process for the Timor-Leste Defence Force (F-FDTL) commenced. Attempts by politically active veterans, some with FRETILIN alliances, to re-enlist caused some controversy. Undaunted, the FRETILIN leadership continued to woo disaffected FALINTIL elements. On 27 August 2001, the 'active' groups of the Sagrada Familia under legendary ex-FALINTIL fighter L7 (Cornelio Gama) paraded in Dili and swore their allegiance to Lú-Olo Guterres, now titular President of FRETILIN, and Vice-President Alkatiri, which CNRT elements considered provocative and irresponsible.

For Gusmão the real issues were that the Defence Force not be politicised and FRETILIN's belief that party-political involvement in recruitment was a legitimate response to balance the Gusmão FALINTIL legacy. Once again, de Mello, while privately expressing concern about the Australian-sponsored 'Mozambique' FRETILIN clique, neither came to Gusmão's aid nor heeded his warnings, with tragic consequences for the new nation.[10]

The FRETILIN Legacy

Within three years of FRETILIN assuming total control of newly independent Timor-Leste under Alkatiri's leadership on 20 May 2002, the legislative process was in turmoil. Alkatiri's administrative style was not consultative or inclusive, and parliamentary processes were limited by infrequent sittings, the criminalisation of dissent and the persistence of Portuguese as the language of debate. The new parliament did not debate national issues or tackle the deteriorating economy and its many consequences, thus preparing fertile ground for unrest. By February 2006 the division in the F-FDTL between junior (mostly 'westerners') and senior members (mostly 'easterners') was manifestly clear. The divide stemmed from the 2001 recruitment process and even reached back to the years of resistance of Indonesian occupying forces. Formed in 2003, in response to the demands of Interior Minister Rogerio Lobato, supported by Alkatiri, that the UN establish paramilitary units to deal with persistent militia violence, the Timor-Leste police force (PNTL) was drawn mostly from the western districts. UNTAET, seeking officers with experience, recruited approximately 340 people who had served in the Indonesian police.

Thus, during the first three years of FRETILIN government, as Luke Charles-Jones has explained, structural and political factors had combined to produce an inherently politicised military and police force, leading to the eruption of the crisis 'between loyalist F-FDTL troops, the petitioners and the PNTL. Unable to resolve differences through due process, the factional influences magnified'. Charles-Jones referred to the examples of the alarming and deteriorating political situation that the report of the UN inquiry into the crisis had identified— 'Gusmão's 23 March speech, Alkatiri's treatment of the petitioners as deserters, Lobato's arming of civilians; and the arming of civilians by the F-FDTL (with the prior knowledge of Minister of Defence Rocque Rodrigues)'.[11]

In perceiving FRETILIN as the perceived major party, the UN had made a poor choice for the peoples of Timor-Leste. With so much at stake for the tiny nation, the UN, in working with Australia to expedite self-government such that FRETILIN secured power, fell prey to notions of early self-sufficiency derived from petroleum revenue. The UN failed to use the worldwide empathy for the Timorese to encourage major donors to pressure Australia into abandoning its inequitable territorial claims. The series of seminars and round-table conferences in Dili on the maritime boundary issue in the lead-up to independence were not held in full view on the world stage as they should have been.

Advisers of Prime Minister Howard and Foreign Minister Downer knew of FRETILIN's past in the civil war of 1974–75 and of notable crimes against humanity during the Indonesian occupation. Before Xanana Gusmão was released from detention in Jakarta, European Union representatives had reported on his oft-expressed intent to deal evenly with FRETILIN and Indonesian crimes against humanity. To this day, the world has continued to avoid examination of FRETILIN's role in the massacre at Lehane in Dili District of União Democrática Timorense (UDT) prisoners, arbitrary arrest and killing of civilians, and the summary executions of internal cadre. In my view by embracing FRETILIN without qualification the UN and Australia frustrated the moral reckoning due to some survivors of the grim resistance days.

By 1979 most of the *ad-hoc* FRETILIN armed resistance had been subdued by Indonesian forces. Thereafter, diehard FRETILIN elements, who had escaped from the island, developed their liberation theology in Portugal, Mozambique and Angola, while a more composed FRETILIN element settled in Australia. Gradually, FRETILIN elements garnered endorsement, particularly in former Portuguese colonies, and a FRETILIN myth of heroic ongoing armed resistance emerged, whereas it was FALINTIL that assumed the later military burden. The FRETILIN political struggle was projected by commentators such as author John Pilger and Noam Chomsky,[12] who in their support for the Timor-Leste cause in later years could have given more emphasis to FALINTIL, not FRETILIN, carrying the armed struggle in occupied East Timor.

For the ordinary people of East Timor, 'FRETILIN' was idealised to be synonymous with resistance and the desire for freedom. While there was by the 1990s a politically driven mythography around FRETILIN, the party in East Timor was structurally underground, with no capacity for its manifesto to reach countrywide. As a political movement FRETILIN was personality-driven, both in occupied Timor and abroad. At the national conference of FRETILIN in Sydney in August–September 1998, Ana Pessoa, former wife of José Ramos-Horta, presented a FRETILIN constitution drafted in Mozambique. It was at that time that the conservative Australian Government reached out to Mari Alkatiri. Australia's implied support was extended to Alkatiri at a time when Gusmão and Ramos-Horta were the acknowledged leaders of organised resistance. After Timor-Leste's liberation, FRETILIN's 17-strong Alkatiri-led delegation made little impact at the first CNRT National Congress in August 2000, as recounted in chapter 8, after which FRETILIN withdrew from the CNRT.

Howard and Downer, with the smell of petroleum in their nostrils, claimed that Australia preferred the stability of a mainstream party in Timor-Leste over any minor parties. Howard drew on his own pre-set notions and began to position FRETILIN to govern the new nation. There is an argument to say Australia put corporate trade interests above Australia's national interests. As if they hadn't suffered enough, the Timorese were condemned to more instability, culminating in 2006 in the need for further Australian military intervention. Once again the Australian Defence Department had to step in to deal with failed Australian foreign policy.

Mari Alkatiri and Xanana Gusmão in an uneasy pose before boarding helicopter flights to Aileu on 20 August 2000. Gusmão believed elements within FRETILIN should be tried for war crimes.

Xanana Gusmão and the author, 20 August 2000. Aware that FRETILIN and the Australian Government were arguing that the leader of an army should not become leader of a democracy, Commander Gusmão was about to take leave of his beloved troops.

12
AUSTRALIAN OPPORTUNISM

Following the 1972–74 OPEC crisis and the successful drilling at Troubadour-1, Australia was a persistent predator in the Timor Sea. By 2007 Australia had secured Timor-Leste's ratification of the Treaty on Certain Maritime Arrangements in the Timor Sea (CMATS) and an Agreement relating to the Unitisation of the Sunrise and Troubadour Fields (IUA). As history now records, this came at a cost of six years of misery in an almost-failed state for the Timorese people after they had achieved independence. Further analysis suggests it would be simplistic to conclude that the Australian Government finally got what it wanted by cheating a poorly resourced FRETILIN Party in negotiations and by denying FRETILIN the only significant revenue source for its government until it got the Timor-Leste Government to ratify the treaty and agreement. The flaw in this analysis is that it was not Australia that got what it wanted, but commercial consortia who won the riches of the Timor Sea.

Australia Withdraws from UNCLOS and ICJ Jurisdiction
The pattern of Australian misconduct after 1975 continued with a lack of good faith in the making of the 2002 Timor Sea Treaty. As a preliminary strategy which had been signalled in negotiations between

UNTAET and Australian representatives in 2000 (see chapter 9), Australia, on 22 March 2002, withdrew from the jurisdiction of the International Court of Justice (ICJ) and all UN Convention on the Law of the Sea (UNCLOS) tribunals, making no mention of Timor-Leste.[1] Two months later, Australia claimed that it was entering the 2002 Timor Sea Treaty in good faith and was expecting an international unitisation agreement to be negotiated in good faith.[2] Events before and after establish that these statements of intent were purposefully untrue. Dörr and Schmalenbach see the lodging of reservations to a treaty being acts that form part of a breach of a peremptory norm, relevantly 'good faith, as attracting like invalidation effects of *jus cogens*'. They argue that 'the invalidity effect of *jus cogens* extends to conflicting unilateral statements such as reservations'.[3]

When the 2002 Timor Sea Treaty was signed by Timor-Leste on its first day of independence, the negotiation of its provisions having been done on Timor-Leste's behalf by the UN, Australia was attempting to modify its submission to law. At the time the treaty was signed, customary law extended the invalidating force of *jus cogens* to ordinary international customary law because '*jus cogens* is regarded as being at the very top of hierarchy of international laws'.[4] By 2002 Australia was remarkably vulnerable to international legal scrutiny. Although the 22 March 2002 declarations lodged by Australia did not mention Timor-Leste, the reservations demonstrated a consciousness of Australian breaches of *jus cogens* that newly independent Timor-Leste might pursue before the ICJ.

It is instructive to read the reservations that Australia lodged without formal notice, on 22 March 2002 while Timor-Leste was under UN Security Council mandate. The reservations were first in respect of Australia's acceptance of the ICJ's jurisdiction and, second, in respect of all formal UNCLOS methods of resolving maritime disputes. The terms of the reservations were:

> The Government of Australia declares that it recognises as compulsory ipso facto and without special agreement, in relation to any other State accepting the same obligation, the jurisdiction of the International Court of Justice in conformity with paragraph 2 of Article 36 of the Statute of the Court, until such time as notice may be given to the Secretary-General of the United Nations withdrawing this declaration.

This declaration is effective immediately.

This declaration does not apply to:

- Any dispute in regard to which the parties thereto have agreed or shall to have recourse to some other method of peaceful settlement;
- Any dispute concerning or relating to the delimitation of maritime zones, including the territorial sea, the exclusive economic zone and the continental shelf, or arising out of, concerning, or relating to the exploitation of any disputed area of or adjacent to any such maritime zone pending its delimitation;
- Any dispute in respect of which any other party to the dispute has accepted the compulsory jurisdiction of the Court only in relation to or for the purpose of the dispute; or where the acceptance of the Court's compulsory jurisdiction on behalf of any other party to the dispute was deposited less than 12 months prior to the filling of the application bringing the dispute before the Court.[5]

Although Timor-Leste was not mentioned, the import was clear; Australia would not submit to the very procedures in international law it had so fully participated in drafting. To make doubly sure that it had hog-tied Timor-Leste even before it achieved its independence on 20 May 2002, and in a blatant attempt to overcome the legal necessity for Australia to allow an independent Timor-Leste adequate notice before any such reservation could take effect, it nullified the new nation's access to the ICJ by declaring that it would not accept process from any petitioner state unless that state had acceded for a minimum of 12 months to the ICJ Statute. Since the Timor-Leste was still not in existence as a state, it was out of the competition before it got to the crease.[6]

UN Secretary-General Kofi Annan, who had not responded to criticism of the contrived parliamentary election in Timor-Leste in 2001, took no steps to halt the treaty process. UN legal advisers 'assisting' the provisional government had ample opportunity to bring to the attention of Australia before the Timor Sea Treaty was signed on 20 May 2002 the ICJ ruling in *Nicaragua v USA*, where the Court said of similar peremptory declarations withdrawing from the Court's jurisdiction: 'It appears from the requirement of good faith that they should be treated, by analogy, according to the law of treaties, which requires a reasonable time for withdrawal from or termination of treaties that contain no provision regarding the duration of their validity'.[7]

Formal notices of the reservations could not have been served on a non-existent Timor-Leste Government. Before independence, the peoples of Timor-Leste, without the status of a state, could not bring claims against Australia. There is no evidence that UN officials overseeing Timor-Leste's path to independence took any steps to serve notice on Australia that Timor-Leste could not be bound by the reservations until an adequate notice period had expired. Not being the state victim of the breach of the peremptory norm by Australia, the UN could not, arguably, lay claim against Australia, but Secretary-General Kofi Annan could have brought his considerable influence to bear. He failed to do so.

Timor-Leste Signs Timor Sea Treaty on 'Independence' Day
Under UN supervision an Australian/UN working party replicated the terms of the 2001 interim agreement in the draft Timor Sea Treaty, which was signed by the effectively FRETILIN-appointed Prime Minister of Timor-Leste, Mari Alkatiri, and Australian Prime Minister John Howard just hours after the Declaration of Independence on 20 May 2002. On advice, the popularly elected President Gusmão declined an invitation to attend the signing ceremony on the ground that he should not give tacit assent to a treaty, unratified by Parliament. The background to Gusmão's non-attendance played out in a dramatic week in the lead-up to the so-called 'Independence Day', during which rumours began to circulate in Dili that the Timor Gap Treaty would be 're-signed' with Australia on Independence Day.

Australia's opportunism in pressuring the UN to grant early independence to Timor-Leste, ostensibly to establish an early revenue base for the fragile nation, awaits further historical analysis. The signing of the Timor Sea Treaty by an unelected 'provisional government' of Timor-Leste, after notice of the Australian reservations, was a triumph of tactics by Australia. Few observers are aware that the first popularly elected government of Timor-Leste was that of Xanana Gusmão on 8 August 2007. Upon assuming office, the Gusmão Government began to unravel the background to the agreements reached in relation to the Timor Sea during the UN Administration and the Alkatiri Government, which had left very little documentation of events.

When access to relevant documents in UN and Australian archives for this period is eventually granted, it may come as no surprise that

Australia's motives during UNTAET 'governance' and the early independence period did not depart at all from its manipulative and misery-laden pursuit of the Timor Sea petroleum resources following the OPEC crisis of the mid-1970s. The 'Independence Day' ceremony, choreographed by the UN and Australia, reached its squalid dénouement with the signing of an oil treaty. That Timor-Leste's new leaders should be asked or even allowed to sign the Timor Sea Treaty on the morning of Independence Day, before the legislature's convocation as required by the Constitution to approve the treaty, is just another facet of the UN's now widely recognised failure to discharge its mandate to protect the interests of the Timorese people.

The extraordinary document contained a provisional application clause and bore other hallmarks of a provisional agreement:
 a. it was 'negotiated' by the UN under mandate;
 b. it was not constitutionally approved by the Timor-Leste Parliament;[8]
 c. it was described as being of a provisional nature in both the Australian Parliament and the Timor-Leste Parliament;[9]
 d. the treaty, purportedly, took effect prior to ratification;
 e. the treaty required an IUA to become a workable treaty; and
 f. 'treaty' was defined, in a novel way, to include 'any Annexes subsequently agreed between Australia and East Timor'.[10]

Business as Usual

The way Australia, with UN support and an unsophisticated new government in Timor-Leste, translated the 1989 Timor Gap Treaty into an internationally recognised document, free of the complaints made in the *Portugal v Australia* case of the early 1990s, is illustrated by the minutes of the first meeting of the Joint Commission for the Joint Petroleum Development Area.[11] They record that Timor-Leste was represented by a Norwegian adviser, Einar Risa, as Executive Director of the Joint Commission, and a young Timorese law graduate, Niny Borges, as Legal Managing Director, while Australia was represented by the experienced Australian managers of the Timor Gap Joint Authority. The meeting adopted an interim petroleum mining code (PMC) and all the regulations, directions, guidelines, procedures, work programs, expenditure approvals and administrative petroleum activities in force on 19 May 2002. The Joint Commission formally recorded that all decisions in force on 19 May 2002 and decisions made under the Indonesian/Australian authority would be deemed to be decisions of the Designated Authority.

Replicate production-sharing contracts (PSCs) JPDA 03-12, 03-19 and 03-20 were approved with the decisions deemed to have effect from 20 May 2002. It was 'business as usual'. At its next meeting on 16 May 2003, the Joint Commission agreed unanimously to approve Appendix X to PSCs 03-12 and 03-13. The Minutes were signed by Risa (formerly Norwegian Secretary of State for Development Cooperation and Executive Adviser in Norway's Statoil company) and José Teixeira (formerly a Brisbane-based solicitor and Minister for Petroleum and Resources in the new government) for Timor-Leste. Other members of the Commission representing Australian interests were petroleum managers with experience in petroleum production engineering.

It emerged later that the definition of liquid natural gas in PSC JPDA 03-12 agreed to by Risa, Borges and Teixeira was not that used in the petroleum industry at large and nor in the PMC: 'all gaseous hydrocarbons *and inerts*, including wet mineral gas, dry mineral gas, casing head gas and residue gas remaining after the extraction of liquid hydrocarbons from wet gas [emphasis added]'. The definition they had agreed to in the PSC omitted the words 'and inerts'.

In an ordered state acting under rule of law and with budgetary constraints, it may be of great concern to lawmakers that an executive Australian Government has failed to investigate the helium issue and the loss of revenue. The question now is whether federal investigative agencies will accept a multi-billion-dollar revenue loss, not only to the impoverished Timorese but also to every Australian. Lest there be any argument that Australia's negotiators were also new to helium, the Australian Government's own long-developed petroleum code and codes throughout the petroleum gas extraction world that pre-date the Timor Sea PSCs include inert gases in the definition of petroleum and/or natural gas.

The Commonwealth of Australia's *Petroleum Revenue Act 1985* and *Offshore Petroleum and Greenhouse Gas Storage Act 2006* both reflect a legislative intention to ensure that helium, that long-sought 'critical commodity', is included in the definition of 'petroleum'.[12] Just how such an eagerly awaited commodity, piped from a sea-bed that Australia had stubbornly claimed as its own, slipped out of the Australian people's hands and into those of a corporate mammoth awaits due enquiry.

The helium was subsequently piped out a side valve to a plant erected adjacent to the LNG plant at Wickham Point near Darwin. The helium plant was opened by an Australian Minister who went on to become an adviser to the petroleum industry. Helium now becomes the 'smoking gun' for both major political parties in Australia.

13
LIGHTER THAN AIR—THE HELIUM ESCAPES

The story of helium in the Timor Sea may be a lesson for those who profess to have the skill to serve in nation-building or the nerve to invest in the petroleum industry stock market. The technicality of the issues shows how easy it was to outplay the newly liberated Timorese. Why the United Nations failed to protect the Timorese is harder to understand. In broad terms Australia and Timor-Leste have so far lost half the value of the Bayu-Undan Field. The Timor Sea helium story has an extraordinary background.

Helium is an inert gas that commonly leaks into the earth's atmosphere but is often trapped under caprock that forms a natural gas reservoir. Helium in its most common isotopic form, ^{4}He, is derived from the decay over millions of years of granite rocks rich in three isotopes, Uranium-238, Uranium-235 and Thorium-232. Gas in liquid or crystalline form accumulates within the rock and is thought to be released by a variety of heat events, including volcanic and tectonic activity, to join other gases and fluids. Depending upon the nature of the earth's mantle, the resultant mix of gases either remains trapped in natural reservoirs or is vented to the atmosphere. Apart from isotopic examination of rock core samples, analysis of the nitrogen content of natural gas is used as a marker for helium.[1]

For most of the 20th century, the United States petroleum gas industry was the principal world source of helium, with helium concentration in natural gas flows in the Texas oilfields of around 0.03%. As the demand and price for helium accelerated, petroleum geologists looked for the tell-tale sign of a helium prospect—concentrations of helium-generating isotopes in drill samples, sufficient fracturing of the lower levels of isotope-bearing granite rock, and a caprock or dome solid enough to hold trapped helium. For many years, economic helium recovery from natural gas required a helium concentration of around 0.03% in the gas. Advances in cryogenic recovery techniques have reduced the required concentration for economic extraction to less than half the old benchmark. A 2014 Australian study of world sources of helium suggested that, if natural gas deposits with helium were appropriately managed, there was little likelihood of helium shortages in the short term.[2] Notwithstanding his involvement with a Norwegian helium exploration company in the discovery of helium reserves in Tanzania's Rift Valley, Professor Ballentine has warned that currently identified helium reserves may run out in 15 to 20 years.[3] Helium remains such a scarce resource that the scientific community is already rationing its usage.[4]

Any discussion within the petroleum exploration industry of the volume and geological composition of oil and gas reserves under review will include an assessment of the helium concentration in the gas stream. Oil and gas industry analysts apply internationally recognised methods to such assessment. Historically, due to US market leadership of the oil trading industry, valuation benchmarks were set in US dollars, and the US dollar continues to be commonly used as the pricing standard.

During the late 1970s and early 1980s, when stock investors were monitoring exploration results from the Timor Sea, there was no valuation benchmark in public use for the helium content value of natural gas. Monitoring the gas assays for helium required specific knowledge of the inert gas analyses that would show, for example, helium and argon gas concentrations. By the late 1980s mercantile stock exchanges had developed understandings based on widely accepted industry indices of the potential worth of oil and gas fields once data was available on estimated reserves, feasibility of recovery, and gas price projections for the type of petroleum product expected to pass from the well. Above all, investors seek an awareness of what saleable oil and gas commodities are to pass out of the pipeline into the market. Investors aware of the measured helium concentration from an anticipated gas flow will input the value of helium extraction. The Australian Stock Exchange (ASX) rules have for many years required quarterly disclosure statements by listed exploration companies.[5] Reviewing gas analyses from drilling on the Sunrise High in 1974, Woodside's own scientists conceded in 2003 that the 'inert gas content' was an important aspect of gas field economics.[6]

As the end of the 20th century approached, all helium in Australia was still imported. As noted in earlier chapters, helium has for many years been listed in Australia's national strategic interests as a 'critical commodity'.[7] The original 1974 oil and gas analyses from the continental shelf drilling on the Sunrise High close to Timor attracted Australia to the Timor Sea like a pickpocket scanning a race-day calendar. Exciting more interest in 1995/96 was analysis from a series of test wells in the Bayu-Undan Timor Sea natural gas field that revealed an abundance of helium.[8] By the mid-1990s, rather than being just a by-product of gas and oil drilling, helium had become a prime drilling target. At the common economic US extraction concentration level of 0.03% by volume, the value of helium is now, in the opinion of eminent experts, about the same as the remaining 99% of the discovered gas volume (assuming a saleable methane).[9]

Helium, a Strategic Commodity

In 1925, the US Government established a federal helium reserve by purchasing waste gas containing helium from oil rigs and injecting the gas into a relatively impermeable geologic dome at the Cliffside Field Government Reserve in Texas.[10] At that time, the US Department of Defense identified an ongoing need for helium to support the airship and air defence industry. By the 1960s, the reserve had assumed new significance in the space race as helium could provide inert gas pressure in volatile rocket fuel tanks, leading to the passing by the US Congress of the *Helium Act 1960*, which provided a financial incentive for the natural gas industry to capture the helium from waste-gas streams and sell it to the federal government, mostly to add to the federal reserve. Meanwhile, gas producers in Kansas, Oklahoma, Wyoming and Texas, who were meeting most of the world's demand for helium, developed more efficient extraction techniques and reduced its production costs. In 1971, the US Congress modified tax and subsidy benefits in the *Helium Act 1960* and began to reduce the accumulated federal helium debt. Following the passing of the *Helium Privatization Act 1996*, the US Government progressively sold down the entire helium reserve by 2015 and eliminated the federal helium debt. This process lowered the price of helium, causing gas industry suppliers competing on the open market to complain. In 2012, the US Government responded by retaining the reserve and continuing to fix the price of helium under the *Helium Stewardship Act 2013*. Controlled disposal of the remaining reserve by the US Bureau of Land Management removed any risk of dumping in the world market. Nevertheless, helium remains a strategic commodity, with the US Geological Survey (USGS) required by law to complete a regular national and international assessment of helium resources.[11]

In the second half of the 20th century, helium use in aeronautical and marine inert gas applications accelerated and the defence and nuclear power industries now require abundant helium for various purposes. Helium has also acquired a vital role in other fields, such as magnetic resonance imaging, construction, aviation safety and the space industry. In Australia, where certain commodities are of strategic national defence significance, helium is listed as a 'critical commodity'.

The Petroz Takeover
In late 1999 the UN, together with the newly liberated Timorese and their international advisers, stepped into the petroleum industry and all its complexity. As the prospect of independence for Timor-Leste became brighter throughout 1999, the price of oil, which reached a high of over US$35 per barrel in 2000, became a matter of intense interest. Petroleum exploration companies already engaged in the Timor Sea—Phillips, Royal Dutch Shell, Woodside, Santos and Australian-domiciled Petroz NL (PTZ)—were vitally interested in Timor-Leste's path towards independence, but none of them mentioned, at least publicly, the helium prize in the Sunrise High vault.

Well before the 1999 ballot in East Timor, the Bayu-Undan project outline for a pipeline to Australia had been developed by companies already holding production-sharing contracts (PSCs) under the Australia–Indonesia regime, later, effectively the Australia-UNTAET regime.[12] In late 1999, the participating companies had, as proposed joint-venture participants, approved the gas recycle phase of development and were applying pressure for an early outcome to negotiations between Australia and the UN. Watching on were other potential players, who faced an effective 'done deal' between the companies already exploiting the petroleum resources and the UN. It soon became clear that the only way in for newcomers would be the acquisition of shares in the companies already negotiating 'replacement' joint-venture rights in the Australian Government–UNTAET deal-making.

Subsequent events establish that the existing players were going to resist newcomers and that elements within the Australian Government were working with Phillips Petroleum to ensure that an onshore helium recovery plant was established. First Phillips Petroleum had to shore up its position, for which Australian oil minor, Petroz NL gave Phillips an unintended opening by announcing a recapitalisation proposal on 18 July 2000. The announcement told the stock market that Petroz wanted funds to pay for its capital contribution to the Bayu-Undan Project pipeline in which it held an 8.25% share.

On 16 October 2000, a cashed-up Australian-listed exploration company, Novus, offered scrip (its own shares) for Petroz NL shares. Novus offered one Novus share for every 3.75 Petroz shares, declaring that the offer valued Petroz shares at between A$0.48.8 and A$0.50.4 per share and that Novus had the cash to fund Petroz's share of the pipeline costs. On 3 November 2000, the Petroz Board advised shareholders to reject the offer because it fell short of a valuation by expert company and security industry valuers, Grant Samuel, of between A$0.58 and A$0.74 per share. The Novus offer was soon topped by Italian state oil company Agip-ENI, which had an interest in the Bayu-Undan project after taking over British-Borneo Oil & Gas PLC in early 2000. Agip-ENI made a cash offer for Petroz NL shares at A$0.56 per share that was conditional on Agip-ENI becoming entitled to 90% of Petroz shares on issue.

On 8 December 2000, Phillips' affiliate CPWA-248 made an assertive cash offer of A$0.70 per share to take over Petroz. Although it was not conditional on CPWA-248 securing a 90% takeover position, it was accompanied by the Petroz Board recommendation that the offer be accepted on the basis of the Grant Samuel valuation. The Board added: 'Should it be required, Phillips has agreed to provide Petroz with a US$19 million interim funding facility to ensure Petroz' Bayu-Undan obligations are met'.[13]

Since the Phillips offer required approval under the *Foreign Acquisitions and Takeovers Act 1975*, early representations were made to Federal Treasurer Peter Costello, who, despite the Christmas vacation period, approved the takeover of the Australian oil company by foreign interests without delay, and Phillips announced the approval on 2 January 2001.[14] Neither the Petroz Board nor potential sellers relying on the Grant Samuel valuation knew that Phillips had factored in an element not included in the Grant Samuel market value appraisal—a helium plant that would return a windfall to Phillips Petroleum. By the end of January 2001, Phillips Australia controlled 81.72% of the shares in Petroz. On 1 February 2001, the Petroz Board resigned and Phillips Australia appointed a new Board, which approved a contract for technical and other services to be provided by Phillips.[15] Australian-based Petroz technical and support staff were retrenched.[16]

When the takeover offer closed on 14 February 2001, CPWA-248 had acquired 85.41% of the issued Petroz shares; sellers included Fletcher Challenge Energy and Australian bank and institutional fund managers. Agip-ENI held close to 12% of the 14.59% remaining Petroz shares and other minority shareholders, including Australian-registered Batoka Pty Limited and individual investors, held the balance. Thus CPWA-248 fell short of the 90% threshold that would enable it, under Australian law, to compulsorily acquire the Petroz shares held by the minority shareholders. CPWA-248's path to full compulsory acquisition thereafter was controlled by the Australian *Corporations Act 2001*, which limited the maximum purchase to 3% of the total number of shares in the company each six months. With negotiations underway between Australia and UNTAET, now assisted by Norwegian oil experts, disclosure to the stock market of the helium extraction prospect could both delay and significantly increase the cost to Phillips of achieving a full compulsory acquisition. Belated disclosure might have precipitated other problems for Phillips with respect to potential complaints by minority shareholders.

The risk for Australia and for Phillips Petroleum and Woodside that the UN would hear of the helium prospect was profound. A proper study by the UN of the PSC proffered by Australia and Phillips to the CNRT leaders before they signed and made their 20 October 1999 declaration, being the same one handed by Stewart to Corell at the UN in New York on 12 November 1999 and later annexed to the 5 July 2001 UNTAET–Australia Agreement, would have revealed that two words 'and inerts' were missing. A finding by the UN that Australia was in collusion with Phillips over the helium would have rung alarm bells loud enough to reach the CNRT leadership. Woodside and Phillips' argument that a pipeline to Australia was more economically feasible would have been seen as part of a wider strategy to net the helium. While the initial pipeline from Bayu-Undan would serve that strategy, the presence of a 36-inch main to Darwin would be a persuasive factor in a future linkage via Bayu-Undan to the Greater Sunrise project. It remains to be determined which individuals were privy to and involved in a now evident strategy to secure the helium from Bayu-Undan and leverage the helium rich gas from Greater Sunrise. In treaty terms, Phillips was the lead contractor for Australia and Timor-Leste.

To remove outside interests in the Petroz shareholdings, the Phillips-appointed Directors of Petroz formally requested the ASX on 15 November 2001 to delist the stock in Petroz, thus rendering this pioneering Australian petroleum company an unlisted public company. An effect of the request to delist the company was to release Petroz from its ongoing obligation to make quarterly disclosure statements to the ASX. Doubtless, if the gas analyses and market appraisals drawing attention to the helium content had been disclosed, either by Petroz or the only other consortium member listed on the ASX, Santos Ltd, Petroz shares might have attracted market attention.

Batoka Director, Robert Catto, a former merchant banker and experienced investor, has said that, if the helium appraisal had been disclosed at this juncture, he would almost certainly have contacted other remaining minority shareholders regarding the CPWA-248 strategy.[17] As a Petroz shareholder watcher, Catto knew from public announcements that a world-class gas and liquids field had been successfully drilled in early 1995 at Bayu-1 located in ZOCA 91-12, followed by two more proving wells drilled in ZOCA 91-12 and 91-13 with established proven and probable reserves for Bayu-Undan straddling ZOCA 91-12 and 91-13 of approximately 256 million barrels of condensate, 182 million barrels of LPG and 3.25 trillion cubic feet of gas.

Catto recalled that, because the Bayu-Undan Field crossed two search blocks, an international consultancy firm had been retained in 1997 to determine the precise proved and probable reserves and the precise blended percentages of the defined field held by the joint-venture partners. This information was also required so that future capital expenditure could be allocated among the partners. The report of Texas consultancy firm, De Golyer & MacNaughton (D&M), was concluded in 1998 and led to a detailed announcement by Petroz to the ASX of its share of Bayu-Undan reserves as at 30 June 1997. The D&M estimate of proved, probable and possible sales of gas, condensate and LPG that Petroz provided to the ASX was based on gas and condensate take-off at sea with the residue gases containing inerts pumped back into the undersea reservoirs. As the pipeline scenario had not been advanced, the D&M estimate did not mention helium recovery.[18]

An insider's knowledge of the new Bayu-Undan gas field was that analyses following the discovery of commercial quantities of gas at the Troubadour-1 well in 1974 and progressive drilling of wells in later years on the continental shelf revealed concentrations of helium close to the 0.03% benchmark for easy cryogenic extraction. A comprehensive US Geological Survey (USGS) report in 1999 on the petroleum systems of the Bonaparte Gulf Basin, including the disputed Timor Sea area, was available to the UN.[19] The geochemical analyses of the oil and gas discoveries in the Timor Sea were not included in the report, but would almost certainly have been logged, under the terms of exploration licences, with the Australian Geological Survey Organisation (AGSO) and been available to the USGS upon request. AGSO was skilled in the geochemical assessment of helium abundance and isotopic composition and, because of helium's identification as a critical commodity, AGSO was effectively mandated to advise government of any helium recovery appraisal. If AGSO had been in any doubt about its own appraisal, the author of the USGS report, whose professional registration was in the US helium-recovery state of Wyoming, would surely have been able to help clarify that doubt.

While the plan to pipe LNG to a gas-recycling plant to be built near Darwin was public knowledge, neither the Australian and Timorese public nor the remaining minority shareholders of Petroz, who were facing CPWA-248's statutory 'creeping' takeover strategy, were aware of any plan to partner the gas recycling with a separate helium extraction plant. Catto has said that an announcement of the prospect of helium recovery from Bayu-Undan may well have attracted interest not only within the minority Petroz shareholding but also from entities that may have recently sold to CPWA-248:

> There had been no announcements about the helium analyses to shareholders regarding Petroz' 8.25% shareholding in the Timor Sea Bayu-Undan Field Joint Venture. I recall shareholders being told less exciting news in some detail as to how much it would cost Petroz to pay its share of gas pipeline processing facilities. If the Petroz Board had known of the prospect of a helium recovery plant alongside the planned LNG plant it would, presumably, have factored that into its proposal to shareholders in July 2000 to recapitalise. It was probably in similar ignorance that Fletcher Challenge Energy and some major bank and institutional shareholders sold their interests into the CPWA-248 takeover.[20]

Rodney Brown, Chairman of Petroz before the Phillips takeover until he resigned in February 2001, recalled to Robert Catto in 2018 that under the ZOCA arrangements before East Timor's liberation there was no pipeline from Bayu-Undan. While he was aware of the presence of helium in the waste gas, once the condensate was taken off to tankers at the offshore well-head the waste gas was pumped back into the undersea reservoir. The anticipated call on Petroz to contribute to the cost of a 500-kilometre pipeline to Darwin was the challenge facing the Petroz Board. When the Board recommended acceptance of the CPWA-248 takeover offer, it was unaware of any proposed onshore helium recovery plant.

As plans developed within ConocoPhillips (Phillips' parent company merger with Conoco's parent company, agreed in November 2001, was completed on 30 August 2002) for the helium recovery plant, any further takeover offer would cast, necessarily, an onus upon an earlier project manager, namely CPWA-248, to deal with the gas appraisal for Bayu-Undan. Any such disclosure might trigger a postmortem into the Petroz takeover. CPWA-248 developed a further strategy, in dialogue with Agip oil executives, to acquire progressively the large block of shares owned by Agip-ENI. This arrangement, structured successfully by Freehills solicitor Paul Evans in Perth, involved an agreement with the Italians by way of three separate purchases by CPWA-248 of Petroz shares: the first on 20 September 2002 for 6.68 million shares; the second on 11 Februrary 2003 for the same number of shares; and the final block of 10.6 million shares on 27 March 2003.

Thus, CPWA-248, having reached the 90% threshold required by Australian corporations law, was in a position to compulsorily acquire the shareholdings of other minorities. A few days later, when the FRETILIN Government on 2 April 2003 signed PSC JPDA 03-12, with the two crucial words 'and inerts' missing, the joint-venture companies were ConocoPhillips (03-12) Pty Ltd (42.4%), Santos (JPDA 91-12) Pty Ltd (21.4%), Inpex Sahul Ltd (21.2%), Petroz (Timor Sea) Pty Ltd (13.4%), and Emet Pty Ltd (1.6%). Having acquired almost the entire Petroz stock, ConocoPhillips now had a 55.8% control of the joint venture and the helium. Catto recalls that the compulsory acquisition notice served by CPWA-248 on all shareholders, including more than 1400 individuals, took the rump group of shareholders by surprise:

> We learned later that Section 665E of the Corporations Law required ConocoPhillips to notify Petroz shareholders after it had reached an 85% shareholding that it may be able to compulsorily acquire the remaining securities in the class once it reaches a 90% shareholding. It was the creep of 3% from 85.41% to say 88.41%, which I believe was not announced. If we had received a notice I would have approached Agip-ENI on my own behalf or by syndicate to query the reason for the push by CPWA-248. The leapfrogging three per cent purchases by CPWA-248 made abroad under the Freehills structure, although probably lawful, ran against the spirit of the Corporations Law. We were outplayed.[21]

'Deep State' Plans

Given the long search by geologists in Australia for helium concentration, it must be assumed that Geoscience Australia's predecessors had reported years earlier to the Minister responsible for natural resources that one of Australia's most critically important commodities had been found on the Australian Continental Shelf in recoverable quantity. Such news, quarantined even within the government scientific community, was fit only for limited circulation within Cabinet.[22] No-one, it would appear, told the UN or the Timorese about the helium, and a game-plan to outwit a country with the lowest per capita income in Asia and certain Australian equity fund shareholders began to unfold in Canberra, Houston and Perth. Adding to this extraordinary story is that Australia, having sullied its reputation worldwide by exploiting the sovereign assets of a poor neighbour, then allowed the helium to fall as an alleged waste product ultimately into the sole ownership of the contractor parties. Extraordinary as it seems, Australia's ever-expanding helium needs, particularly in the defence, research and medical spheres, are now met by repurchasing the alleged waste give-away. Most of the helium from the Bayu-Undan Field is exported to Asia by the contractors to meet the needs of foreign nuclear power and defence industries. The bigger prize by far, so long as FRETILIN did not tip the applecart, awaited Woodside Petroleum, which had secured similar PSCs for the Greater Sunrise Field.

While technological developments allow the expanding fission-based nuclear power waste stockpile to be recycled using, among other methods, large quantities of helium, a guaranteed helium supply is also important in the development of much safer fusion power. With fusion reactors free from risk of meltdown or waste that remains radioactive for thousands of years, a massive effort is underway in fusion research in Russia, the United Kingdom, Europe, North America, Japan and China. An assured supply of helium is vital for energy recovery treatment of nuclear waste.

Nick Minchin, as Minister for Industry, Science and Resources in the Howard Government, supported the development of a nuclear waste storage industry, for which a world geological survey had identified ancient sedimentary basins in South Australia as suitable sites. Having earned his place in this story as adviser to Foreign Minister Downer, Josh Frydenberg, Minister for Environment and Energy from July 2016 to August 2018, was also a proponent of a nuclear waste storage industry. As matters stand, Australia, as a uranium-exporting state, is obliged by international agreement to accept back spent fuel including plutonium, but has to date sent its own waste from the Lucas Heights Reactor to France for reprocessing, while successive Australian governments have looked to a solution for the nuclear waste-treatment cycle.[23]

Babes in the Wood
Aware of their lack of industry experience, the Timorese had agreed with Australia to the nomination of industry leader ConocoPhillips as an operator that would protect the interests of the joint venture. The choice of operator for Bayu-Undan was unsurprising; by 2000 ConocoPhillips (91-12) Pty Ltd (CP 91-12), a subsidiary of parent company Phillips Petroleum, had more than 50 years' experience in

LNG processing, including in helium recovery. Phillips had developed an optimised cascade process to liquefy natural gas which established a new model for the LNG export industry and was by 2000 used in the recovery of helium from the nitrogen stream at the Phillips Kenai LNG project in Alaska.

ConocoPhillips also had years of experience in petroleum recovery in the Timor Sea pursuant to PSCs under the Timor Gap Treaty between Australia and Indonesia. The PSCs adopted the model PSC approved by the Ministerial Council established under the treaty, which had entered Australian domestic law as the *Petroleum (Timor Gap Zone of Cooperation) Act 1990*. In a sign that Australia intended to exclude helium from being shared with Indonesia, the model PSC deleted 'and inerts' from the internationally settled definition of 'natural gas': '"natural gas" means all gaseous hydrocarbons, including wet mineral gas, dry mineral gas, casinghead gas and *residue* gas remaining after the extraction of liquid hydrocarbons from wet gas [emphasis added]'. Clearly this was deliberate. As already noted, Australia was negotiating with its Indonesian accomplice for the Australian share of the gas to be sent via a pipeline from the Timor Sea to Australia, while the inert and waste gases continued to be returned to the undersea reservoir until such time as Australia could secure a pipeline to its shores. Australia did not announce any intention of sharing the helium with Indonesia.

As the Bayu-Undan Field moved towards production capacity, the Australian–Timor-Leste Joint Venture (JPDA), through a Designated Authority (DA), entered on 2 April 2003 into PSC JPDA 03-12 with a group of companies—ConocoPhillips (03-12) Pty Ltd, the successor company to the Australia Indonesia era CP (91-12), Santos Pty Ltd, Sahul Ltd, Petroz (Timor Sea) Pty Ltd and Emet Pty Ltd ('the contractors').[24] Despite having agreed to all that the gifted and resilient Galbraith had required of the production arrangement so that other products produced in association with hydrocarbons were included in the petroleum valuation formula, Australia presented to the commercially naïve Timorese the version of PSCs prepared originally for the Indonesians. Having succeeded in 1989 in excluding helium recovery from its Timor Sea gas recovery joint venture with Indonesia, Australia, in a calculated strategy in 1999–2003, did the same to the poverty-stricken Timorese, its loyal wartime allies whom Sir Bernard Callinan said 'no coinage' could repay.[25]

In summary, JPDA 03-12 commenced on 20 May 2003 and is due to expire on 6 February 2022; authorised the contractors exclusively to conduct petroleum activities within the JPDA; provided that the contractors would bear the costs of exploration and development in exchange for a share of any resulting petroleum production; required the contractors to obtain approval from the Designated Authority in respect of any tenders for petroleum activities; and stipulated that, subject to the provisions of the Timor Sea Treaty 2002, the laws of England govern JPDA 03-12. On 16 May 2003, the parties entered into a further agreement to amend JPDA 03-12 by the insertion of Appendix X, which included a formula by which revenue relating to sales of natural gas was to be shared between the parties. With respect to sales of natural gas, Appendix X gave the Development Authority a right to 40% of the revenues from the sale of natural gas.

In June 2003, the contractors began construction of the Darwin Liquefied Natural Gas (DLNG) Plant in Australia's Northern Territory. The plant, commissioned in January 2006 and operational by March 2010, is operated by Darwin LNG Pty Ltd, which is owned by the contractors. Gas is sent to the plant from the Bayu-Undan Field via a 502-kilometre pipeline built on behalf of the contractors and is converted into LNG for sale from the plant.

Australia and the contractors, having snared the helium in the Bayu-Undan Field, then moved to secure access to helium in the Greater Sunrise Field, yet to be exploited. The Greater Sunrise Field was tied up within four petroleum titles, with Australian oil major Woodside Petroleum having a major role: Retention Leases NT/RL2 and NT/RL4, issued pursuant to the Australian *Offshore Petroleum and Greenhouse Gas Storage Act 2006*; and PSC 03-19 and PSC 03-20, allegedly issued in accordance with the provisions of the Timor Sea Treaty and the Interim Petroleum Mining Code of the JPDA, but in fact containing the contradictory clause that excluded inert gases.

Australia's First Helium Plant

In 2005, BOC Pty Ltd announced plans to open a helium plant in the Northern Territory. A holding company owned by ConocoPhillips, Santos, Petroz and Emet (DLNG) contracted to supply a nitrogen-rich feed gas stream with a helium content of approximately 3 mole % to BOC, its next-door neighbour at Wickham Point.[26] BOC, now part of the Linde Group, which had been extracting helium in the US since World War I, issued a media release on 3 June 2008 announcing the construction of a helium plant.[27] The helium plant was installed and commissioned in the second half of 2009.[28] Then one of only 14 in the world,[29] it was officially opened on 3 March 2010 by the Northern Territory Chief Minister and the Australian Minister for Resources and Energy, Martin Ferguson.[30] Days after visiting Dili in March 2013 to plead, unsuccessfully, with Alfredo Pires, his equivalent in Timor-Leste's government, not to mount an Arbitration case against Australia for misconduct in the Timor Sea (CMATS) negotiations, Ferguson resigned from the Australian Parliament. He joined an oil industry lobby group seven months later.

Although the anticipated output of the DLNG plant was estimated at 150 million cubic feet of helium each year,[31] the plant had achieved a 200 million cubic feet annual output by 2014. Crude helium prices in 2013 were estimated by some US sources at an average of US$6.13 per cubic metre. Prices rose steadily and in 2015 fixed US Government prices for crude helium were US$85 per thousand cubic foot for government users and $104 per thousand cubic feet for non-government users.[32] In Australia, the price per thousand cubic feet rose steadily from close to A$50 in 1999 (fully imported) to close to A$100 in 2015. This may value the annual production of 200 million cubic feet of helium at Darwin in 2014 at around A$2 billion.[33]

Exact production figures and sales receipts remain shrouded in mystery. A Geoscience Australia publication in 2013 reported that the Darwin helium plant, the only such plant in Australia, produces approximately 4.25 million standard cubic metres of helium a year,[34] although the US Geological Survey puts the figure at 5 million cubic metres for 2014 and 2015.[35] The helium plant exports 75% of its production, mostly to Asia, while also meeting Australia's needs for helium.

A conservative estimate, based on US source data, may put the annual value of the extraction of helium from the Bayu-Undan gas flow in the region of $AUD2.5 billion per year. Arguably a 40% share of this $20 billion gross revenue is due in equity to the Autoridade Nacional do Petróleo (ANP: National Petroleum Authority) (formerly the Timor-Leste/Australian Designated Authority). Even allowing for the $50+ million establishment cost of the helium plant, staged production increases and running costs, and tax revenues on the helium sales, the sales revenue otherwise payable to Australia and Timor-Leste, after close to ten years of operation, excluding interest, represents a mammoth revenue loss to Australia and Timor-Leste.

The terms of the 2002 Timor Sea Treaty and the 2003 International Unitisation Agreement (IUA) imposed treaty and fiduciary obligations upon both Australia and Timor-Leste as joint-venture partners to work in good faith on the projects at hand. Article 9(b) of the Timor Sea Treaty states: 'Australia and East Timor shall work expeditiously and in good faith to reach agreement on the manner in which the deposit will be most effectively exploited and on the equitable sharing of the benefits arising from such exploitation'. Article 1(h) of the IUA defines 'Marketable Petroleum Commodity' as:

(i) stabilised crude oil;
(ii) sales gas;
(iii) condensate;
(iv) liquefied petroleum gas;
(v) ethane;
(vi) any other product declared by the Regulatory Authorities to be a marketable petroleum commodity.

A marketable petroleum commodity cannot be a product produced from another product of a kind referred to in subparagraphs (i) to (vi) inclusive.

Clearly, if helium could not be a 'sales gas', it could be 'any other product' that could be declared by the regulatory authority to be a 'Marketable Petroleum Commodity'. It was never suggested to the Timor-Leste representatives that such a declaration be made, and no such declaration was requested by Australia. Although by-products are excluded by definition, helium, in context, is a product originating with petroleum.

The definition of petroleum in the Timor Sea Treaty and the IUA includes the words: 'any naturally occurring mixture of one or more hydrocarbons, whether in a gaseous, liquid or solid state, as well as other substances produced in association with such hydrocarbons'.[36] Accordingly, although not a hydrocarbon, helium may be a substance produced in association with such hydrocarbons. This definition is consistent with internationally recognised classification and nomenclature guidelines developed over many years by the Society of Petroleum Engineers and the World Petroleum Congress. Significantly, the industry-accepted definition of 'petroleum' to include 'helium' was adopted by the Australian Government and the Australian Parliament with the passage of the *Petroleum Revenue Act 1985*, seven years prior to the Timor Sea Treaty.

The definition of 'production-sharing contract' in the Timor Sea Treaty, which has itself been adopted by law in Australia, describes a contract between the Designated Authority and a limited liability corporation or entity with limited liability under which production from a specified area of the JPDA is shared between the parties to the contract.[37] Article 4 of the Timor Sea Treaty states: 'Australia and East Timor shall have title to all petroleum produced in the JPDA. Of the petroleum produced in the JPDA, ninety (90) per cent shall belong to East Timor and ten (10) per cent shall belong to Australia'. As the definition of petroleum in both the Timor Sea Treaty and the IUA includes 'other substances produced in association with such hydrocarbons', it follows that Timor-Leste may have laid claim, pursuant to Article 4 of the Timor Sea Treaty, to 90% of the petroleum, including helium produced in the JPDA.

Article 12 of the IUA required a development plan to be submitted before the production of petroleum could commence. As petroleum includes helium, the question arises whether Article 12(1) was complied with. Article 12 required development plans to be 'for the effective exploitation of the unit reservoirs'.[38] Helium was a big-ticket prize for the contractor parties. If the party submitting a development plan was aware that helium is another commercially exploitable substance produced in association with hydrocarbons, then the development plan should have included details for helium extraction. A decision may then rest with the regulatory authorities as to whether the helium should be declared a marketable petroleum commodity. There is no record of any such submission to the Timor-Leste authorities. Australia was contractually bound, strengthened by fiduciary duty, to make such a disclosure to the Joint Authority.

Even if helium, as seems most unlikely, was not recognised at the time of the first development plan as a substance that could be produced in association with hydrocarbons, Article 12(6) of the IUA required the operator to submit an amendment or addition to the development plan for prior approval of the regulatory authority. If the diversion or extraction of helium requires any change to the status or function of any Unit

Installation in the Unit Area, this requires prior approval pursuant to Article 12(8) of the IUA. Again, there is no record of any such submissions to the Timor-Leste authorities. This is inexplicable on two grounds. First, as we have seen, Australia knew that helium was a prize product under the Timor Sea. Second, Australia had long recognised in various amendments to the *Excise Act 1921*, and, indeed, had eight years earlier legislated specifically to ensure that royalty and excise revenue from petroleum from areas other than the North-West Shelf area would include helium production in the *Petroleum Revenue Act 1985* (s 3). Although a different excise regime might be necessary for a joint foreign venture offshore, the definition of 'petroleum' in the Petroleum Mining Code adopts a worldwide meaning that includes 'inerts'.

The IUA defines 'valuation point' as 'the point of the first commercial sale of Petroleum produced from the Unit Reservoirs which shall occur no later than the earlier of (i) the point where the Petroleum enters an Export Pipeline and (ii) the MPC [Marketable Petroleum Commodity] point for the Petroleum'.[39] As the MPC point means 'that point where each Marketable Petroleum Commodity is produced',[40] it follows that the MPC point for helium is where it is produced by cryogenic separation from the nitrogen stream.

Article 1(k) in both the Timor Sea Treaty and the IUA define 'petroleum activities' as 'all activities undertaken to produce petroleum, authorised or contemplated under a contract, permit or licence, and includes exploration, development, initial processing, production, transportation and marketing, as well as the planning and preparation for such activities'. While it is said that helium is not a hydrocarbon, the definition of petroleum in the Timor Sea Treaty, in the IUA, in the Petroleum Mining Code, and in the PSC JPDA 03-12 by section 1.3, includes: 'any naturally occurring mixture of one or more hydrocarbons, whether in a gaseous, liquid or solid state, *as well as other substances produced in association with such hydrocarbons* [emphasis added]'. Accordingly, although not a hydrocarbon, an inert gas, such as helium or argon (commonly marketed for use in industrial welding), may be among 'other substances' produced in association with such hydrocarbons.

The gameplay being spun around Timor-Leste becomes clear in the rewording of the same sub-clause 1.3 in PSC JPDA 03-12 from PSC ZOCA 91-12 that: 'Words and terms used in this contract shall have the same meaning as those defined in the Treaty, including the

Petroleum Mining Code, as referred to in Article 7(b) to the Treaty, *except where a new definition is expressly provided for in the contract* [emphasis added]'. Relevantly, the Petroleum Mining Code for the JPDA defined 'natural gas' as 'all gaseous hydrocarbons *and inerts*, including wet mineral gas, dry mineral gas, casing head gas and residue gas remaining after the extraction of liquid hydrocarbons from Wet Gas [emphasis added]'. Consistently with oil industry practice, 'wet gas' is defined in the Petroleum Mining Code to mean: 'a mixture of hydrocarbons, *inerts* and impurities that is recoverable from a Reservoir and is gaseous at the conditions which its volume is measured or estimated [emphasis added]'.

However, PSC JPDA 03-12 amended only one petroleum industry definition. All other definitions in the treaty, the IUA and the Petroleum Mining Code are adopted. PSC JPDA 03-12 adopted the definition of 'natural gas' that had been in the model PSC used in the Australia–Indonesia ZOCA era as ConocoPhillips PSC 91-12, namely 'all gaseous hydrocarbons, including wet mineral gas, dry mineral gas, casinghead gas and *residue* gas remaining after the extraction of liquid hydrocarbons from wet gas [emphasis added]'—a definition that omitted the words 'and inerts'. It is inconceivable that the Contract Operator, ConocoPhillips (03-12) Pty Ltd, appointed to carry out petroleum activities in accordance with good oil field practice, would have been ignorant of a definition of natural gas in PSC JPDA 03-12, signed on 2 April 2003, and Appendix X, signed by the same parties on 16 May 2003, that was at odds with the Petroleum Mining Code and the IUA.[41] It may be argued that ConocoPhillips by contract and Australia as joint-venture partners with Timor-Leste had a duty to point out the discrepancies that would deprive Timor-Leste of the helium. Subsequent events pose many questions for Australia and ConocoPhillips over the helium windfall. Section 3.2 of Appendix X to JPDA 03-12 declares: 'Natural gas shall be valued at the field export point'. Appendix X also defined 'field export point' as meaning 'the natural gas export flange in the Joint Petroleum Development Area, as identified in the Development Plan'.

The ConocoPhillips strategy appears to be for ConocoPhillips (03-12) Pty Ltd as contractor/operator to obtain its share of the natural gas defined in the PSC and Appendix X to exclude inerts as valued at the 'field export point', and then to pass the 'natural gas' on to an affiliate owned by the contractor parties to process the LNG at its Wickham Point plant. The alleged waste-gas stream with a high nitrogen content would then be processed using the Phillips optimised cascade method to recover the inert gases. Under arrangements with BOC Pty Ltd located near the LNG plant, a gas line would supply the inert gases, primarily helium, for eventual sale.

ConocoPhillips as contractor/operator and Australia have argued that, as title to the gas stream passes at the export flange, the 'waste'-gas stream containing nitrogen, inert gases and other substances diverted away by another pipeline at the Wickham Point plant, is wholly owned by the contractor parties. But polemics about alleged 'waste' and the location of flanges do not release the contractor from its obligation to pay for all 'petroleum' it is obliged to market. While the loss to Australian and Timor-Leste consolidated revenue is mammoth, the final insult is the need for the Australian Government to effectively pay for the bulk of the helium required for hospital and medical procedures, principally magnetic resonance imaging, in Australia, and for the nation's research and defence industry needs.

The Windfall
The extraordinary opportunism involved in the helium coup resonates from the preamble to PSC JPDA 03-12, which includes this statement of intent: 'WHEREAS, the Designated Authority wishes to promote petroleum activities in the contract area and the contractor desires to join and assist the Designated Authority in accelerating the exploration and development of the *potential petroleum resources* within the contract area [emphasis added]'. Section 1.1 of PSC JPDA 03-12 says:

> This contract is a production sharing contract *subject to the Treaty, including the Petroleum Mining Code*. The Designated Authority shall be responsible for the management of the activities contemplated hereunder in accordance with its management functions defined under the Treaty, including the Petroleum Mining Code. The contractor appoints and authorises ConocoPhillips (91-12) Pty Ltd, being one of the contracting corporations, to be the contract operator who, on behalf of the contractor, shall be responsible to the Designated Authority for the execution of petroleum activities in accordance with the provisions of this contract, and is hereby appointed and constituted as the exclusive corporation to conduct petroleum activities [emphasis added].

The contractor shall provide all human, financial and technical resources required for the performance of petroleum activities authorised by this contract, and shall therefore have an economic interest in the development of the petroleum pools in the contract area and be entitled to share in petroleum produced from the contract area in accordance with the provisions of Section 7 of this contract.

Section 5.2 of the PSC JPDA 03-12 says:

The contract operator shall comply with all of the obligations imposed on it by the Treaty, including the Petroleum Mining Code and the taxation code, and the regulations and directions issued under the Petroleum Mining Code and, in particular, shall:

a. provide all human, financial and technical resources required for the performance of the *petroleum activities*;
b. carry out *petroleum activities* in a proper and workmanlike manner and in accordance with good oilfield practice; ...
f. submit to the Designated Authority copies of all original geological, geophysical, drilling, well, production *and other data* (including cores, cuttings and samples taken *in connection with petroleum activities* in the area) and reports compiled during the terms of the contract ... [emphasis added].

There is likely no record in the minutes of the Joint Commission for the JPDA of the contract operator ConocoPhillips (03-12) Pty Ltd, upon which the Designated Authority depended for advice on best practice in the oil industry, drawing attention to the fact that the PSC JPDA 03-12 definition of 'natural gas' excluded inert gases. Any such exclusion was inconsistent with the definition in the Petroleum Mining Code agreed between Australia and Timor-Leste (pursuant to Article 7 of Timor Sea Treaty) and brought into Australian law by the *Petroleum (Timor Sea Treaty) Act 2003* (Cth). Likewise, there is likely no record of the contract operator disclosing to UNTAET and Timor-Leste gas stream data identifying the high helium concentration of 0.03% in the Bayu-Undan Field and the potential recovery of lucrative inert gases (helium and argon) consistent with 'good oil field practice'.

Loss of the helium to the Australian and Timorese people involved four interconnected phases with the first key phase managed at ministerial level, namely, securing Timor-Leste's agreement to a sale and valuation of the gas at the well-head flange as LNG only—the 'field export point'—contrary, in view of the helium content, to 'good oil field practice'. The second was apparent ignorance by the UN and Timor-Leste that there was a recoverable helium content in the relevant gas analyses. The third was Timor-Leste accepting a definition, contrary to 'good oil field practice', of 'natural gas' that excluded 'inerts'. The fourth phase was securing the helium from Bayu-Undan by using an 'exception clause', namely PSC Clause 1.3, not adverted to as an exception to 'good oil field practice' when Timor-Leste was dependent upon ConocoPhillips acting in accordance with 'good oil field practice', it being a practice worldwide to capture inert gases when, in like conditions, there was a readily available commercial market.[42]

At a moral level it is instructive to view Australia's collaboration with ConocoPhillips and the contractor parties in light of Australia's contribution over many years at the UN during the development of the 2011 *Guiding Principles on Business and Human Rights*, which states relevantly:

1. States must protect against human rights abuse within their territory and/or jurisdiction by third parties, including business enterprises. This requires taking appropriate steps to prevent, investigate, punish and redress such abuse through effective policies, legislation, regulations and adjudication.[43]

Depriving a poor state of such a measure of its non-renewable inalienable sovereign riches as to affect the capacity of that state to tackle poverty is an abuse of human rights. Moreover, edging the Timorese out of billions of dollars and at the same time urging Timor-Leste's leaders to stabilise their economy by reaching early agreement on a Sunrise 'deal', as the gas from Bayu-Undan would soon be depleted, was and remains shameless hypocrisy.

At a juridical level, in *Hospital Products Limited v United States Surgical Corporation & Ors*, Australian High Court Justice Anthony Mason dealt succinctly with the concept of fiduciary duty:

The critical feature of these relationships is that the fiduciary undertakes or agrees to act for or on behalf of or in the interests of another person in the exercise of a power or discretion which will affect the interests of that other person in a legal or practical sense. The relationship between the parties is therefore one which gives the fiduciary a special opportunity to exercise the power or discretion to the detriment of that other person who is accordingly vulnerable to abuse by the fiduciary of his position. The expressions 'for', 'on behalf of', and 'in the interests of' signify that the fiduciary acts in a 'representative' character in the exercise of his responsibility.[44]

Paul Finn neatly encapsulates Timor-Leste's circumstance:

> What must be shown is that the actual circumstances of a relationship are such that one party is entitled to expect that the other will act in his or her interests in and for the purposes of the relationship. Ascendency, influence, vulnerability, trust, confidence or dependence doubtless will be of importance in making this out, but they will be important only to the extent that they evidence a relationship suggesting that entitlement.[45]

Until the full facts are known the position of third parties is difficult to determine. In *Barnes v Addy* Lord Selborne LC said:

> Strangers are not to be made constructive trustees merely because they act as the agents of trustees in transactions within their legal powers, transactions, perhaps of which a Court of Equity may disapprove, unless those agents receive and become chargeable with some part of the trust property or unless they assist with knowledge in a dishonest and fraudulent design on the part of the trustees.[46]

Australian courts have dealt at length with *Barnes v Addy*. The Bench is well attuned to occasional frontier practices within Australian investment, construction, mining and petroleum sectors, particularly in Western Australia. One may only have regard to the role of the then Western Australian Government in introducing legislation so strongly criticised by the High Court in the Bell Group case to understand the accommodating relationship between the corporate sector and government in Western Australia.[47] In the *Farah* case, the High Court dwelt upon the different manifestations of accessorial liability for breach of fiduciary duty.[48] More recently, the Australian Federal Court made clear in the *Grimaldi Case* that there are no clearly mapped reefs through which those seeking to avoid accessorial liability might navigate. The law may adapt to the circumstances.[49]

ConocoPhillips' parent company had a market-leading role in developing the optimised cascade LNG process (particularly at the Kensai LNG plant in Alaska) from the late 1960s when helium recovery increased to meet demand in the nuclear, space and defence industries. Consequently, there can be little doubt that ConocoPhillips had identified the potential of the Bayu-Undan Field with 3 mole % of helium as a lucrative source of helium. Aside from gas analyses after the discoveries at Troubadour and Sunrise in June–August 1974, Australia was aware of the more detailed gas data readings from the exploratory well drillings in ZOCA 91-12 and 91-13 during 1994 and 1995. The analyses were known to the Australian members of the Joint Authority and, under licence conditions, lodged by law with AGSO, which could not have failed to recognise the significance of the helium content analyses of the exploratory gas stream. Whether Indonesian members of the then Gap Joint Authority were aware of the helium content of the gas analyses is unclear.

A 1987 report by Geoscience Australia's predecessor, the Bureau of Mineral Resources, Geology and Geophysics (BMR), highlighted the urgency of Australia's search for helium: 'As a consequence of Australia's rising helium demand, and concerns which have been expressed for long term availability of helium from overseas, the Bureau of Mineral Resources has co-operated with the Australian petroleum industry to encourage the evaluation of domestic helium resources'.[50] While the report emphasised the need for cooperation between the Australian Government and the petroleum industry in the search for commercial sources of helium, subsequent events in the Timor Sea suggest that cooperation went too far.

Section 5.5 of PSC JPDA 03-12 required the Designated Authority to 'comply with all of its obligations imposed on it by the Treaty, including the Petroleum Mining Code and, in particular, shall be responsible for the management of the petroleum activities contemplated hereunder having regard to the contract operator's responsibilities for undertaking the petroleum activities'. There is no record of the Contract Operator and the Designated Authority drawing attention to the inconsistency between the definition of 'natural gas' in the Petroleum Mining Code and PSC JPDA 03-12. It is inconceivable that the Australian representatives would not query the inconsistency.

Article 6 ('Regulatory bodies') of the Timor Sea Treaty provides:
a. A three-tiered joint administrative structure consisting of a Designated Authority, a Joint Commission and a Ministerial Council is established.
b. Designated Authority:
   i. For the first three years after this Treaty enters into force, or for a different period of time if agreed to jointly by Australia

and East Timor, the Joint Commission shall designate the Designated Authority.
ii. After the period specified in sub-paragraph (i), the Designated Authority shall be the East Timor Government Ministry responsible for petroleum activities or, if so decided by the Ministry, an East Timor statutory authority ...
c. Joint Commission:
i. ... shall consist of commissioners appointed by Australia and East Timor. There shall be one more commissioner appointed by East Timor than by Australia. The Joint Commission shall establish policies and regulations relating to petroleum activities in the JPDA and shall oversee the work of the Designated Authority.

As noted in chapter 12, at the PSC JPDA 03-12 signings in April and May 2003, the Executive Director of the Joint Commission was Einar Risa and the Legal Managing Director was Niny Borges, a young Australian law graduate of Timorese origin. Borges, who subsequently worked for Norwegian oil giant Statoil, had participated with Galbraith and Alkatiri in Timor Sea Treaty negotiations in 2001 and 2002, including at the 29–30 May 2001 negotiations, when Galbraith, acting on Bjorn-Erik Leerberg's advice, had told the Australian delegation that the definition of 'petroleum' in treaty documents must include the words 'as well as other substances produced in association with such hydrocarbons'.

At the first meeting of the Joint Commission, Robert Mollah was confirmed as expert adviser. Mollah, a Brisbane-based petroleum mining engineer, had in September 1995 been appointed Co-Chairman of the Timor Gap Australia–Indonesia Joint Authority and had been present as Timor Gap Joint Authority Observer at treaty negotiation meetings that discussed the gas valuation point and the definition, ultimately adopted, of 'petroleum'. Attendees at the second meeting of the Joint Commission, including veterans of the Timor Sea Treaty negotiations John Hartwell, Borges and Mollah, agreed unanimously, on 16 May 2003, to approve PSC JPDA 03-12 and Appendix X, both of which omitted the full definition of 'petroleum' contained in the Draft Petroleum Code and established by industry practice. The documents were then signed by Einar Risa and FRETILIN Minister José Teixeira for Timor-Leste, and by John Hartwell for Australia. This was an immensely valuable contract. It appears curious that Leerberg was not, as it seems, given the final draft PSC to vet. This is, at the least, a $20-billion-plus question for investigation.

The Petroleum Mining Code

Article 7 ('Petroleum Mining Code') of the 2002 Timor Sea Treaty says:

a. Australia and East Timor shall negotiate an agreed Petroleum Mining Code *which shall govern* the exploration, development *and exploitation* of petroleum within the JPDA, as well as *the export of petroleum* from the JPDA [emphasis added]

b. In the event Australia and East Timor are unable to conclude a Petroleum Mining Code by the date of entry into force of this Treaty, the Joint Commission shall in its inaugural meeting adopt an interim code to remain in effect until a Petroleum Mining Code is adopted in accordance with paragraph (a).

An investigation may need to consider that the Petroleum Mining Code, applicable to the Timor Sea Treaty with force of law in Australia under the *Petroleum (Timor Sea Treaty) Act 2003* (Cth), defined 'petroleum' to include 'other substances produced in association with such hydrocarbons', of which helium could be one. Accordingly, the Code (at 7.4) required any discovery of helium in association with such hydrocarbons to be disclosed:

A contractor shall notify the Designated Authority in writing within twenty four (24) hours whenever any Petroleum is discovered in its Authorised Area, and shall provide such information in regard thereto as the Designated Authority may request, including details in writing of the chemical composition and physical properties of the Petroleum, and the nature of the sub-soil in which the Petroleum occurs.

According to Einar Risa, no disclosure of helium in the Bayu-Undan gas field was given to the Timor-Leste members of the Designated Authority before the PSCs that excluded helium from the definition of 'natural gas' were presented for signature. This raises profound questions. A provision in the Petroleum Mining Code (6.2 Restrictions on Choice of a Contractor) reflects the standard of conduct anticipated by the Australian Parliament:

The Designated Authority may only make a Production Sharing Contract with a person, or group of persons, which:

i. It is satisfied has, or has access to, the financial capability, and the technical knowledge and ability, to carry on the Petroleum Operations *in a manner wholly consistent with the Treaty, the Code and the Production Sharing Contract*; and

ii. Does not have a record of non-compliance with principles of good corporate citizenship; ... [emphasis added].

The Designated Authority, composed of the Australian party and the Timor-Leste party, was obliged under the PSC JPDA 03-12 to comply with all obligations imposed on it by the treaty, including an agreed Petroleum Mining Code. In particular, Australia and Timor-Leste were responsible for the management of the petroleum activities contemplated in the PSC JPDA 03-12, having regard to the responsibility of ConocoPhillips (03-12) Pty Ltd as Contract Operator for undertaking the petroleum activities.[51] The junior parties in the co-venture (Santos Pty Ltd, Inpax Sahul Ltd, Petroz (Timor Sea) Pty Ltd and Emet Pty Ltd), as co-contractors, were reliant also upon ConocoPhillips (03-12) Pty Ltd, as operator, to conduct the petroleum activities in their mutual interest. The question arises as to what knowledge and involvement, if any, Santos, Inpax and Emet, as joint-signatories to the PSCs had in the original helium appraisal, the 'revised' definition of natural gas, and the subsequent sale of the helium from the LNG plant at Wickham Point, jointly owned by them with ConocoPhillips.

PSC JPDA 03-12 was the successor to a PSC ConocoPhillips had with the former Australia–Indonesia Authority, being Contract 91-12. Contract 91-12 related to Australia–Indonesia exploration/exploitation activities in the JPDA and did not envisage an onshore LNG plant. When PSC JPDA 03-12 was executed by the Designated Authority and the contractor parties and approved by the respective Joint Commissioners on 2 April 2003, the establishment of an LNG plant at Darwin was anticipated. When Appendix X to JPDA 03-12 was executed by the same parties six weeks later, the recovery of natural gas from the Bayu-Undan discovery area and transfer to an LNG plant at Darwin was provided for. It was at this stage that the absence of the two words missing from the definition of natural gas should have been picked up and dealt with.

Einar Risa, in semi-retirement in Norway and working as a consultant, has stated: 'We were all new to it. We relied on ConocoPhillips',[52] and that he has no recollection of any discussion with ConocoPhillips about the definition of natural gas being altered from the conventional worldwide definition in the interim Petroleum Mining Code. He does not recall helium being mentioned in discussions with his financial counterpart and fellow Norwegian, ConocoPhillips' Australia Director Jarl Ellingsen.

There is no record of Australia taking a position favourable to the Designated Authority on the helium issue. Indeed, it has supported the argument advanced by ConocoPhillips that, because natural gas is defined in the PSC JPDA 03-12 as solely a gaseous hydrocarbon, the Designated Authority has no claim over the inert gases. As the *Petroleum (Timor Sea Treaty) Act 2003* adopts the Petroleum Mining Code, Australia's failure to support the Code's definition of natural gas and its own legislated definition is puzzling.

The contractor was contractually bound to market all petroleum produced and to account for the value thereof.[53] Although the contractor parties set up a structure whereby they effectively owned upstream and downstream facilities, they nevertheless had to account for sales to third parties.[54] The Designated Authority appears to have failed to ensure that the contractor submitted all production data connected with petroleum activities; such data would include gas-feed data relating to helium and gas-feed data relating to other inert gases.[55] In consequence, the Designated Authority did not undertake a full valuation and audit of the gas stream.

Without agreement between the respective parties, the Designated Authority was stymied. Unable to secure Australia's approval to submit the helium dispute to arbitration pursuant to section 13.12 of the PSC JPDA 03-12, Timor-Leste's hands were tied. PSC JPDA 03-12 makes abundantly clear that the applicable law includes the provisions of the treaty, the Petroleum Mining Code and the law of England.[56] The apparent failure of the Australian party to take legal steps to protect the interests of the Joint Venture raises wider issues. This conduct could, under current guidelines, be examined by the Australian National Audit Office.

Restitution

The opening words of the Timor Sea Treaty and the PSC JPDA 03-12 emphasise the importance of developing petroleum resources to mutually benefit Australia and Timor-Leste. Consistent with this aim, section 7.1 of PSC JPDA 03-12 says: 'The contractor is authorised by the Designated Authority *and obliged to market all petroleum produced and saved from the contract area* [emphasis added]'. The words 'obliged to market' mean, in context, that the contractor was obliged to market all petroleum for production sharing. Not only does section 7.1 oblige the contractor to market all petroleum (including all marketable inert gases), but section 7.7 says: 'the contractor shall use its best reasonable efforts to market petroleum production to the extent markets are available'.

The incontrovertible evidence is that of all petroleum exploration companies, ConocoPhillips knew from the data release in 1995 of the Bayu 1 well analysis and the confirmatory analyses from adjoining wells in 1996/1997 that inert gases, with a helium concentration approaching 0.03% in a natural gas stream through Phillips' much vaunted optimised cascade LNG process, had an available and lucrative market.[57] The Kenai LNG Plant, which had been recovering helium for many years, had been followed in 1999 by the Atlantic LNG project in Trinidad utilising the optimised cascade process.

Section 7.8 (as amended by Appendix X) says:

Any natural gas produced from the contract area and not used in petroleum activities hereunder may be flared if the processing and utilisation of the natural gas is not considered by the Parties to be economic. *Such flaring shall be permitted to the extent that gas is not required to enable the maximum economic recovery of petroleum by secondary recovery activities, including repressuring and recycling* [emphasis added].

These provisions appear to put beyond doubt that the contractor parties to PSC JPDA 03-12 anticipated 'secondary recovery activities' and, consistent with this, that flaring of natural gas and LPG produced from Bayu-Undan should be avoided to preserve the inerts. It is highly improbable that the deletion of the two words 'and inerts' did not go unnoticed by all signatories to PSC JPDA 03-12. It remains arguable that the contractor is still caught by the 'obligation' to account for all petroleum production.

The fact that all petroleum production was not approved by the Designated Authority pursuant to a Development Plan and tender procedures, as required by section 10.2, does not release the contractor from its duty to account to the Designated Authority for all funds received from the sale of all other substances, including, primarily, helium and argon. In their recent study of worldwide helium production levels, Mohr and Ward were not sure whether to attribute the Bayu-Undan Field source to Timor-Leste or to record it as Australian. Interestingly, they report that production figures for the ConocoPhillips-fed helium plant at Darwin 'could not be sourced, either from Australian agencies, such as the Bureau of Resources and Energy Economics, the Australian Bureau of Statistics or via contacting the gas plant operator directly'. They assumed the capacity of this plant to be 941 tonnes of helium per year.[58]

It is reported that 100% of Australia's helium needs can now be met from the Linde Plant at Wickham Point.[59] But, with Bayu-Undan reserves allegedly not due to run down until 2026 and good helium gas analyses available from Greater Sunrise,[60] what was the reasoning behind ConocoPhillips' recent $350 million sale of its interest in the Timor Sea to the Timor-Leste Government?

Secrecy continues to enshroud the helium issue. I can find no mention of the helium recovery in ConocoPhillips' *2016 Annual Report*, based on audited results to 31 December 2016. What is apparent from this report is that, as at 31 December 2016, the company had a full capitalisation in the order of just US$97.484 million.[61] Any potential restitution sum dwarfs this figure. Did Timor-Leste's recent agreements to purchase ConocoPhillips' and Shell's interest in the Sunrise gas project include a release and indemnity for ConocoPhillips and Shell from any further claims? The value of such indemnities, if binding, would vastly exceed the sale prices.

Despite these ongoing disasters for Timor-Leste, there are many questions for the Australian Parliament to answer, particularly whether reparations should flow. The debate may focus on whether Australia has a constructive trust liability, either as the prime mover or as an accessory. Much may depend on the nature of the Australian Government relationship to ConocoPhillips and Woodside. Export particulars for the helium may be illuminating.

With the Chinese Government–related corporation Sinopec so heavily involved between Australia and ConocoPhillips in the massive Gladstone LNG project that has occasioned the transfer of Conoco's operations to Brisbane from Perth, one expects that the Australian Government is in ongoing dialogue with ConocoPhillips, at least through the Foreign Investment Review Board, now headed by the experienced LNG China contract negotiator and former Ambassador to China, David Irvine.[62]

Countermeasures

In 2014, as the hearing dates for both the Provisional Measures Application before the International Court of Justice (ICJ) and the international arbitration approached, outside observers knew that Timor-Leste had strong grounds in relation to both matters and needed to plan for future initiatives. Commentators worldwide, including industry representatives, speculated on the outcome of anticipated invalidity of both the treaty and all Australian exploration licences and permits issued pursuant to the Side-Letters to the CMATS Treaty, signed by Ramos-Horta and Downer, which gave Australia a free hand across vast areas of the Timor Sea.[63] Modern equity law relating to constructive trusts associated with fiduciary duty allowed Timor-Leste the prospect of instituting action to recover the 'helium windfall' from the Contract Operator and, if suspicions were well founded, from Australia as an accessory. This was a grim prospect and desperate measures were taken to push Collaery Lawyers off the case.

The Australian Government had learnt a bitter lesson after the raid on the Collaery Law Chambers in December 2013. Under the international spotlight, Collaery Law filed and Timor-Leste obtained 'provisional measures' orders against Australia from the ICJ to secure the documents seized. Australia was aware that, following a probable finding that the CMATS Treaty was invalid *ab initio*, or voidable, Timor-Leste might have scope to seek further provisional orders that Australia cease issuing permits and licences over the areas over which Australia had secured authority. Elements within the Australian Government knew that Australia was highly vulnerable in relation to treaty impropriety that might impugn both the IUA ratified as part of the CMATS negotiations and, more importantly, the PSCs signed in 2003 for both Bayu-Undan and Greater Sunrise. Australia's response to public criticism of the raid on Timor-Leste's lawyers was to attack Timor-Leste for 'complicity' in breaching Australia's 'national security'.

Obliged to withdraw from proceedings following allegations of criminality against Timor-Leste's legal team by Australia at The Hague, the Collaery Law retainer with Timor-Leste was terminated on 3 June 2014. An impending arbitration under the auspices of the Permanent

Court of Arbitration was then adjourned, without consultation with either the author or Timor-Leste's leading advocate, Sir Elihu Lauterpacht QC, and then withdrawn, and the ICJ Orders made on 3 March 2014 against, *inter alia*, interception of all communications regarding the Australia–Timor-Leste maritime boundary negotiations, unconditionally discharged.

An answer by the Office of the Inspector General of Intelligence and Security on 10 July 2015 to a Parliamentary Question on Notice by Senator Nick Xenophon on 25 May 2015 asserted that the ICJ Order had been discharged unconditionally by consent of Timor-Leste. This appears to have prompted the Australian Broadcasting Corporation (ABC) to send a film crew to Dili. Initially, Timor-Leste's Prime Minister, Rui Maria de Araújo, told the ABC's Steve Cannane that the ICJ Order preventing any interception by Australia of any communications concerning the Timor Sea Maritime boundary had not been discharged. When informed of the response Xenophon had received to his question, de Araújo maintained his understanding that the Court Order had not been discharged and that he had secured advice from the President of the Council of Ministers, Agio Pereira, who had effective executive carriage of the Timor Sea issue with Australia. The Prime Minister produced a letter addressed direct to Minister Pereira on 26 May 2015 from Australian Attorney-General George Brandis stating that 'Australia recognises the need for all States to respect the confidentiality of communications between States and their legal advisers consistent with the widely accepted principle of legal professional privilege'. This, as the judges of the ICJ accepted, is only part of the issue. The Order made by the Court was:

> Australia shall not interfere in any way in communications between Timor-Leste and its legal advisers in connection with the pending Arbitration under the Timor Sea Treaty of 20 May 2002 between Timor-Leste and Australia, with any future bilateral negotiations concerning maritime delimitation, or with any other related procedure between the two states, including the present case before the Court.

Communications concerning the Timor Sea maritime boundary are far wider than legally privileged communications, hence the all-embracing Order endorsed by all but one of the judges of the ICJ.[64]

Following the outcome in March 2018 of the UN-sponsored conciliation, Timor-Leste's lawyers, DLA Piper, acknowledged that their role to devise a different strategy started with a small team in 2013, instructed by Agio Pereira, shortly before Timor-Leste's long-term lawyers were forced to withdraw.[65] Much may now depend upon what was shared with the distinguished panel of experts during the UN-sponsored 'conciliation' and the extent to which Timor-Leste has pursued the helium issue. Timor-Leste's representatives, hopefully, sought for the Timorese people a rightful share of past and future Bayu-Undan helium revenue and of helium revenue from any upcoming Greater Sunrise production.

The Helium Files
In a study published in 2003, drawing on data acquired before Timor's liberation, geologists attest to the massive reservoirs of retrograde gas condensate trapped under a 3750-square-kilometre Sunrise/Troubadour vault. The volumetric significance of the field is estimated as containing between 10 and 16 trillion cubic feet of gas. Having been given access to data from NT/RL2, NT/P55, ZOCA 95-19 and ZOCA 96-20 joint venturers Woodside Energy, Shell Development (Australia) Pty, Phillips S TL, and Osaka Gas Aust., Woodside and Phillips geologists produced a comprehensive study that refers to the gases on the Sunrise-Troubadour high as 'sweet and paraffinic'.[66]

The study notes that the original 1974 gas samples from Troubadour-1 and neighbouring wells have 'lost volatiles during storage' and the Troubadour DST sample appears to be contaminated by diesel-based drilling mud. It also noted that the first well in the field on the Sahul Platform, Troubadour-1, had in 1974 'flowed gas at a disappointing maximum', due to a technical drilling fault and required modern reappraisal.[67] But in the same year as the original Troubadour-1 discovery, six months before the Indonesian invasion of Portuguese Timor, Sunrise-1 was also drilled, about 18 kilometres away from Troubadour-1 on the Sunrise High: 'The extensive production testing program undertaken on the Sunrise-1, Sunrise West-1 and Sunrise-2 appraisal wells proved highly successful....The many samples collected during each well test were chemically analysed. *Each test showed a high level of consistency, giving a high level of confidence in the fluid data* [emphasis added]'.[68]

In their earlier study the authors of the 2003 study had also acknowledged that the fluid properties, 'particularly CGR (Condensate

Gas Ratio), LPG (liquefied propane and butane mixture) *and inert content have a significant effect on the value of a development project* [emphasis added]'.[69] If the Woodside scientists recognised in 2000 and 2003 that the inert content of the gases, namely, the helium trapped under the Sunrise-Troubadour vault, was a significant factor relating to development economics, so too would Woodside's partners, Royal Dutch Shell and ConocoPhillips.

Some may regard the way Australia has dealt with the words in the model PSC to be like a small-town sly lawyer doing a land deal with naïve and unsophisticated traditional land-owners, to ensure the helium was landed in Australia by a corporate mate, regardless of the financial loss to the Timorese and Australian peoples. Josh Frydenberg summed up Australia's strategy shortly before Australia was pushed by Timor-Leste and the UN into a fall-back conciliation:

> We're not about to enter into these further discussions because we believe we've got the balance right. But certainly East Timor are the ones who are getting the greatest benefit ... And we think any move to go towards this compulsory arbitration or coordination actually contravenes the previous agreements that both countries voluntarily entered into.[70]

This was a ruthless strategy to present Australia as a generous partner. From a legal perspective important questions remain: When and who in the Australian government was informed of the discovery of a massive quantity of helium in the Sunrise High and why was the helium discovery not disclosed to the United Nations and Timor-Leste? Further, who in the Australian Government authorised a claimed sovereign asset giveaway of immense value to the contractor parties?

It is not commonly recognised that Timor-Leste was, prior to the CMATS Treaty negotiations in 2004–05, already a signatory to PSCs for Greater Sunrise, namely JPDA 03-19 and JPDA 03-20 (unitised), respectively the post-liberation ZOCA 95-19 and ZOCA 95-20 within the original Northern Territory Permits NT/RL2 and NT/RL4.[71] The joint-venture participant equity for Greater Sunrise is Woodside, as Operator (33.44%), ConocoPhillips (30%), Royal Dutch Shell (26.56%) and Osaka Gas (10%). The sale of the gas at the well-head ensured effectively that the party that landed the pipeline also secured the helium. As we have seen, the definition of petroleum in the PSCs for Greater Sunrise and the point of sale are of crucial importance. After Gusmão became the first democratically elected Prime Minister of Timor-Leste in 2007, his government began investigating what had gone on in the Timor Sea between Australia, the UN and ConocoPhillips. Timor-Leste's helium disaster was soon uncovered.

In late 2016, Robert Catto, former Batoka Pty Ltd director, asked the spokesperson of contractor joint-venture entity Santos Petroleum what that company's current annual earnings were from helium sales by the Bayu-Undan LNG Consortium to the BOC-Linde Group. Catto was informed that the information was commercial in confidence.[72] He received a similar answer to a subsequent question about the volume of helium sold in 2014/15 to the BOC-Linde Group. The issue is also a matter for the international petroleum industry and US lawmakers with respect to corporate compliance regimes.

The extraordinary secrecy in the lead-up to the helium coup may relate to knowledge that ownership might be challenged by Timor-Leste. When the Timorese did find out about the helium, the Australian directors of the Designated Authority refused to support the request by the Timorese directors to mount a challenge. The comprehensive nature of the Australian strategy is illustrated by the legislative drafting. The production and sale of petroleum without authority and the role of any accessories may attract criminal prosecution in Australia via Article 3 of the Timor Sea Treaty and section 7(1) and (2) of the *Petroleum (TST) Act 2003* (Cth). However, the sanction is restricted to activities not in accordance with a PSC, or without the approval of the Designated Authority. In this manner Australia has ensured that the helium taking would not constitute an offence, at least under the *Petroleum (TST) Act 2003*, section 7 of which says:

(1) A person commits an offence if the person:
    (a) undertakes activities to produce petroleum in or from the JPDA; and
    (b) does so otherwise than:
        (i) in accordance with a production sharing contract; or
        (ii) with the approval of the Designated Authority.

Maximum penalty: Imprisonment for 5 years.

(2) In subsection (1):

'activities to produce petroleum' includes exploration, development, initial processing, production, transportation, marketing, as well as planning and preparation for such activities.

Article 3 of the Timor Sea Treaty required Timor-Leste to introduce an equivalent criminal law.

Regardless of the criminal law, the inability of the FRETILIN Government once it learnt of the helium loss to institute action against Australia was the legacy it left for the 2007 Gusmão Government. It soon became apparent that the Australian Government had remained silent while the Australian and Timorese peoples were deprived of their rights to significant revenue. This evidenced a lack of good faith by Australia in observance of the Timor Sea Treaty terms, Australia's fiduciary duty to its Timor-Leste joint-venture partner, and the duty to protect the Australian taxpayer. No evidence can be found in the parliamentary debates that the crucial sub-clause 1.3 in the PSCs that allowed a maverick definition of 'natural gas' to be substituted and for billions of dollars to be lost to the Australian people was disclosed to the Australian public. Australia's response to Timor-Leste's search for the truth was to raid Timor-Leste's lawyers and embark upon further conduct, leading in 2018 to another so-called 'good-faith' treaty that must soon yield to the rule of law.

As newcomers to the petroleum industry, Timor-Leste was reliant upon the advice and the integrity of both the Australian Government and the contractor party. While the massive revenue loss to both Timor-Leste and the Australian public may attract calls for a full public inquiry, both of Australia's main political parties are likely to face embarrassing scrutiny. The prospect of the helium issue coming under US Justice Department scrutiny is now very real. Former Petroz shareholders, including institutional investors, who may believe they did not receive fair value for shares may seek an explanation from Australia's corporate watchdog, the Australian Securities and Investment Commission (ASIC), and Western Australia's justice authorities.

The 2018 Timor Sea Maritime Boundary Treaty
On 6 March 2018, the Treaty Between Australia and the Democratic Republic of Timor-Leste Establishing Their Maritime Boundaries in the Timor Sea (Maritime Border Treaty) was signed by Australian Foreign Minister Julie Bishop and her Timor-Leste equivalent

Agio Pereira at the UN in New York. The signing of the new treaty reveals that the contractor parties have won out on the Bayu-Undan helium issue. Australia and Timor-Leste have not spelt out in State Party terms ownership of the vast reserves of helium within the Sunrise High vault. Once again 'petroleum' is defined in the treaty as including 'helium'; once again there was a risk the helium may escape through the infamous Clause 1.3 in the commercial PSCs.

The 2018 Maritime Boundary Treaty acknowledges in Article 10 that neither Party shall have a claim for compensation with respect to past and ongoing activities in the former JPDA, or the inclusion of existing fields within Timor-Leste territory, or, astoundingly, the cessation in many years to come of the Greater Sunrise Special Regime to be established under the treaty in terms 'equivalent' to the former PSCs. Recalling that the 2002 Timor Sea Treaty and the 2003 IUA, both state-to-state documents, involved prefiguration of commercial production-sharing regimes, the real impact of the 2018 agreement between the sovereign governments lies in the wording of the alleged 'hands-off' commercial PSCs. The hypocritical language of Article 10 is all too familiar; the seemingly balanced term of 'neither Party' having a claim for compensation is shameless. How, remotely, could Australia have a claim for compensation from the Timorese? Elsewhere, the Maritime Boundary Treaty acknowledges that the rights and obligations that arose under the now discarded 2002 Timor Sea Treaty and the 2003 IUA remain in force.[73] There is, once again, sanctimonious reference to 'good oil field practice' and cunning clauses under the existing PSCs that effectively continue the helium exploitation until existing fields now within Timor-Leste sovereign territory are depleted.[74] No provision was made to ensure that all revenue accruing while the 2018 treaty awaited ratification went into an escrow account. Timor-Leste has paid a high price and may yet pay a far higher price to secure maritime boundaries it was entitled to in international law.

Worse still, the Greater Sunrise Special Regime established by the 2018 Maritime Boundary Treaty gives title to all petroleum produced in the Greater Sunrise Field to Australia and Timor-Leste, and then declares that, as soon as practicable, the Designated Authority representing both Parties

> shall enter into the Greater Sunrise Production Sharing Contract under conditions equivalent to those in Production Sharing Contracts JPDA

03-19 and JPDA 03-20, and to the legal rights held under Retention Leases NT/RL2 and NT/RL4 in accordance with Article 22 of The Timor Sea Treaty and Article 27 of the International Unitisation Agreement.[75]

Since the 2003 PSCs allowed the helium to fall to the contractor parties as alleged waste, what is the implication behind the words 'under conditions equivalent to' in the 2018 treaty? Ordinary commercial prudence required Australia and Timor-Leste to spell out in clear terms that helium proceeds belong to both sovereign partners. It is astounding that, with knowledge of helium reserves under the Sunrise High and with helium close to equivalent revenue value with LNG, Australia and Timor-Leste have not come to terms on the issue.

With the Southern Hemisphere's only helium purification plant at Wickham Point facing the exhaustion of feeder gas from Bayu-Undan around 2026, there seems little doubt how determined Australia, for strategic reasons, and the contractor parties will be to get the Bayu-Undan pipeline linked to another far greater windfall under the Sunrise High. Xanana Gusmão's anguished letter to the UN Conciliation Commissioners shortly before the Maritime Boundary Treaty was signed, accusing the Conciliation Commission of partiality with Australia and the contractor parties in preferring a pipeline to Darwin, is a portent of what is to come from a treaty that raises more questions than provides answers.[76]

After all that has happened, it is truly extraordinary that the Sunrise venture partners were invited to participate in the UN-sponsored conciliation process. Predictably, Australia declared that it was 'pipeline neutral' and would support the decision of the commercial venture partners. There is not a single mention of 'helium' in the Report and Recommendations of the Conciliation Commission.[77] No surprise, therefore, that an expert UK-based petroleum consulting company, Gaffney, Cline & Associates, not asked to factor in the helium windfall, found that it may cost an extra US$5.6 billion to bring the gas ashore to Timor-Leste.[78] This estimate is dwarfed by restitution Timor-Leste may seek from Australia and the contractor parties over the helium coup and fails to take into account future helium revenue.

The Conciliation Commission appears not to have tackled the differences Timor-Leste has with Australia over the helium abstraction, which, under the terms of the 2018 treaty, continues from Bayu-Undan until the field is depleted. Unless action is taken, this may represent, depending on the life of the field, another $5–10 billion loss to Australia and Timor-Leste. It was within the remit, or an expanded remit, of the Conciliation Commission for Timor-Leste and Australia to agree that a dispute has arisen in relation to whether helium falls within a substance described in both Articles 1(j)(iii) of the 2002 Timor Sea Treaty and the 2003 IUA as 'other substances produced in association with such hydrocarbons'. The parties could have agreed that Article 26 of the IUA and Article 23 of the Timor Sea Treaty may be activated in accordance with the dispute resolution processes set out in those articles and to refer the issue to the Commission.

The extent to which reparation and/or restitution issues were addressed before the Commission, if they were addressed at all, is unclear. Whether the terms of the 2018 Maritime Boundary Treaty may overcome the mirror sanctions against unaccounted petroleum proceeds established by both parties under Article 3 of the 2002 Timor Sea Treaty should have been addressed by lawmakers before either Parliament moved to ratify the 2018 treaty.

14
A MATTER FOR INQUIRY

The deletion, without explanation, of the words 'and inerts' from the standard industry code definition of 'natural gas' and 'petroleum', thus depriving the impoverished Timorese and leaving ConocoPhillips with an alleged 'waste' inert gas flow of considerable value, was not the only event that advantaged ConocoPhillips. Other losers to ConocoPhillips were the shareholders of Petroz NL (PTZ), including large institutional investors, also with no knowledge of the helium potential of the gas flow. Petroz, established in 1969 as the pioneering offshore Australian oil and gas exploration, development and production company, Offshore Oil NL, had a long history of exploration activity in the Timor Sea.[1] By 2001, as plans for a gas pipeline to Australia advanced, Petroz held an 8.25% interest in the Bayu-Undan Field. As explained in chapter 13, by 1 February 2001, Phillips affiliate CPWA-248, registered in Perth, Western Australia, had acquired a controlling interest in Petroz NL, using methods that provide an extraordinary insight into the hazards of investment in the petroleum industry and the pitfalls in the workings of Australian corporations law. The creeping purchase of Petroz shares was achieved without revealing to the remaining Petroz shareholders that the Bayu-Undan oilfield appraisal included a rich potential stream of helium.

Following the resignation of the Petroz Board of Directors on 1 February 2001, the new Petroz Board announced that the company intended to launch a share buy-back scheme.[2] Shortly afterwards the Board notified a change of auditor and applied successfully to ASIC for the company's annual general meeting to be held later in the year.[3] Meanwhile the Board pursued its campaign to buy back share parcels, notifying ASIC of buy-backs almost weekly.

CPWA-248 established its compulsory acquisition rights by further strategic share purchases in 2002 and 2003, until it had a 98.37% shareholding, when it made an offer under compulsory acquisition rules by invoking Chapter 6A(2) of the *Corporations Act 2001* to acquire the 3,629,074 Petroz shares that it did not already own. Relevantly, Australian corporations law required CPWA-248 Pty Ltd to serve an independent expert report stating in effect how the value proposed in the Notice of Acquisition reflected the assessed value for the shares. At no time did CPWA-248 reveal the anticipated windfall from the exclusion of inert gases in the model production-sharing contracts (PSCs) and appendices relating to the Bayu-Undan Field. The independent expert opinion that CPWA-248 sought from industry valuation expert analysts Grant Samuel noted that:

> The largest project in which Petroz is involved is the Bayu-Undan field in the Timor Sea JPDA. Petroz has a 14.95% interest in the JPDA 03-12 PDC, which currently equates to an 8.25% interest in the Bayu-Undan field. Bayu-Undan is a world-class gas and condensate field *that has been fully appraised*, and contains proved and probable reserves of approximately 256 MMbbl [million barrels] of condensate, 182 MMbbl of LPG and 3.25 tcf [trillion cubic feet] of natural gas [emphasis added].[4]

The Grant Samuel report also noted that in February 2001, after CPWA-248 acquired a controlling interest, Petroz entered into a service contract under which CPWA-248 provided technical and other services, resulting in the retrenchment of Petroz technical and support staff. Petroz shareholders facing compulsory acquisition then became reliant upon ConocoPhillips' technical expertise for reports on the Development Plan for the export of gas from Bayu-Undan. The Plan approved under the expert market opinion of ConocoPhillips by the Designated Authority on 15 June 2003 did not mention any planned recovery of helium gas; nor did the Grant Samuel valuation opinion, signed off on 5 August 2003.

Grant Samuel had appointed PetroVal Australasia Pty Ltd to prepare a technical specialist's report having regard to the VALMIN code issued by the Australasian Institute of Mining and Metallurgy. The report's scope encompassed a review 'of cash-flow models and advice as to whether the future production plans are reasonable based on current reserve estimates, having regard to existing production capacities *and future capital plans* [emphasis added]'.[5] Significantly, the PetroVal review noted that site works by Bechtel for the Darwin LNG plant had commenced on a 'plant design based on proven Phillips technology with precursor plants previously constructed in Alaska, Trinidad and Egypt'.[6] The PetroVal review is completely silent with respect to the parent ConocoPhillips company's then much publicly vaunted, Bechtel-built, optimised cascade LNG process for producing helium. A simple web enquiry would have revealed information about the successful operation of the Kensai helium recovery plant in Alaska. PetroVal should have been aware that helium was and remains a much sought-after prospect in cryogenic LNG processes throughout the petroleum gas extraction industry. In the Australian context, it was common knowledge within the petroleum industry that helium was fully imported and a listed 'critical commodity'.

The model PSC attached first to the 1989 Timor Gap Treaty between Australia and Indonesia and then to the 2002 Timor Sea Treaty between Australia and Timor-Leste contained a seemingly innocuous clause that remained undetected by Timor-Leste when contracts were signed—namely Clause 1.3, which said the Petroleum Mining Code definitions would apply '*except where a new definition is expressly provided for in this contract* [emphasis added]'. What followed was hardly 'express'; two words 'and inerts' disappeared from the industry definitions of 'petroleum', 'natural gas' and 'wet gas'. While any experienced LNG operator aware of gas analyses would detect the deletions, neither Timor-Leste officials nor their advisers noticed the deletion, despite Peter Galbraith's insistence that all elements produced in association with LNG were to be shared.

While the PSCs were not public documents, PetroVal was entitled—even, some may argue, mandated—to see them. Moreover, the model form of contract with the missing words had been appended by Australia to the 1989 Timor Gap Treaty and the 2002 Timor Sea Treaty, both of which were domesticated into Australian law.[7] While a reading would have revealed the non-standard definition proposed by Australia and known certainly by ConocoPhillips, unless PetroVal knew of the helium assay, it may have been none the wiser. Strictly speaking, the aberrant definitions should have alerted PetroVal to the helium issue. If alerted it may have been reasonable for PetroVal to ask why would a country that enforces the inclusion of helium in the definition of 'petroleum' when taxing companies at home leave it out for a US company bound as contractor to 'good oilfield practice' in supporting a joint-venture between Australia and Timor-Leste? It is likely that, if PetroVal had detected what was going on, the outcome of the court proceedings may have been entirely different.

During the production phase of the Australia–Indonesia Zone of Cooperation, unused gas containing the helium had been pumped back into the undersea reservoirs. In the series of exchanges between UNTAET and Australia, culminating in July 2001 with the UN and Timor-Leste's Mari Alkatiri agreeing to accept terms that almost replicated those of the 1989 Gap Treaty, Alkatiri stuck to the assurance by the Timor-Leste leadership in October 2000 of a 'no more onerous' production arrangement. In this manner the aberrant PSCs crept into the 2002 Timor Sea Treaty with no reported discussion, notification or statement by contract operator ConocoPhillips that, if the proposed pipeline to Australia, or for that matter to Timor-Leste, went ahead, helium extraction was part of 'good oilfield practice'. The ConocoPhillips takeover of Petroz occurred during these developments.

PetroVal's valuation of Petroz's share of Bayu-Undan was based on accepted principles of establishing the 'maximum cash price that could be realized for the asset in an open market over a reasonable period of time assuming buyers have full information'.[8] While the valuation report noted that, under the fiscal terms of the PSC, the gas split between the Designated Authority and the contractor was based on LNG pricing on a netback basis at the offshore flange, no mention was made of anticipated windfall profits (now approaching $5 billion) downstream at Darwin from optimised cascade LNG processes recovering inert gases. It also stands to reason that an alert petroleum industry valuer examining the relevant PSCs and Appendices would have noted that the 'revised' definition of 'petroleum' meant a lucrative income stream for helium that should have been factored into the Petroz share price.

It must be noted that CPWA-248, as a subsidiary of the Bayu-Undan contract operator, did not provide PetroVal with the parent company's economic model for the Bayu-Undan project. Extraordinary as it may seem, PetroVal developed a model that was presented to ConocoPhillips for 'verification'. Although it seems odd that experienced petroleum industry valuers would have failed to consider the prospect of helium recovery from a 0.3% helium appraisal, there is no evidence that CPWA-248 revealed to PetroVal in its 'verification' that Bechtel was to construct the optimised cascade LNG process for the recovery and sale of inerts. Certainly, CPWA-248 Directors and technical staff had every opportunity to discuss the helium prospect with PetroVal. During subsequent litigation in the Western Australian Supreme Court involving Batoka Pty Ltd, a minority Petroz shareholder that had rejected the 2001 share price offer, it was contended among other matters that PetroVal had associated too closely with a ConocoPhillips employee in preparing the economic model. Although the Court noted the association as 'unwise', the contention that PetroVal and ConocoPhillips had acted 'in concert' was rejected.[9]

Although the failure of PetroVal and Grant Samuel to raise the LNG gas industry-wide issue of helium recovery is so far unexplained, in the final analysis, the onus was on ConocoPhillips in right of itself and in right of Petroz to ensure that *all material matters* were disclosed to Grant Samuel. It is evident that Grant Samuel took care to ensure that the valuation was based on correct factual bases. On 15 July 2003, as contemplated by ASIC Practice Note 42,[10] Grant Samuel forwarded to ConocoPhillips a 97-page draft of the factual assumptions underlying the proposed valuation together with the draft PetroVal technical appreciation.[11] It is evident that ConocoPhillips took no steps to inform either Grant Samuel or PetroVal that it planned to build into its LNG Plant at Wickham Point an outlet for helium recovery to meet a world market and Australia's strategic helium needs.

It may now be said by the shareholders of Petroz, who either sold to ConocoPhillips after the 0.3% helium concentration became evident to ConocoPhillips after the Bayu 1 drilling in 1995 (including majors such as Westpac, ANZ and Agip), or who had their shareholdings compulsorily acquired after the Darwin LNG project was realised, that ConocoPhillips should have revealed the helium prospect before it commenced takeover moves for Petroz.

ConocoPhillips' letter dated 5 August 2003 certifying that the information provided to Grant Samuel was provided 'in good faith and was neither incomplete, incorrect, or misleading, whether by omission or otherwise in any material respect', was an integral step in the duty to comply with Australian corporations law relating to compulsory acquisition. In that letter ConocoPhillips/Petroz also provided the required acknowledgement that it would notify Grant Samuel immediately if it became aware of 'any information after the date of this letter which is or may become relevant to the report'.[12]

The subsequent course of events at Wickham Point in Darwin raises profound issues of compliance by ConocoPhillips with Australian corporations law and ASX rules.[13] While the Bechtel construction program started to get underway together with BOC's plans to construct a neighbouring helium recovery plant, dissatisfied minority Petroz shareholders who had rejected the Petroz/ConocoPhillips share offer of A$0.89 per share were advised that CPWA-248 Pty Ltd intended to apply in the Western Australian Supreme Court for an order that the compulsory share purchase offer by CPWA-248, by then 1.28% short of 100% ownership of Petroz, be accepted.

Ultimately, Batoka Pty Ltd, unaware of ConocoPhillips' plans to use the optimised cascade LNG process to recover the inerts that had slipped from the sharing formula with Australia and Timor-Leste, held out and became the defendant in proceedings held in May and June 2005 in the Western Australian Supreme Court before Justice Templeman. Incredibly, by then the helium plant was well underway at Wickham Point, but no word of the project reached Batoka or its own expert valuer or Grant Samuel or, evidently, PetroVal or the Supreme Court before judgement favouring ConocoPhillips was handed down on 23 August 2005. After an unsuccessful appeal and faced with significant legal costs, Batoka reached a settlement with CPWA-248 in 2006.[14]

15
AUSTRALIAN GAMEPLAY

While the 2002 Timor Sea Treaty was the umbrella document, the revenue-sharing regime for the major gas field at Greater Sunrise was to be worked out in another document annexed to the Treaty, the International Unitisation Agreement (IUA).[1] Accordingly, the Australian and Timor-Leste Prime Ministers on the morning of Independence Day, 20 May 2002, signed a Memorandum of Understanding in which they agreed to work 'expeditiously and in good faith' to conclude a unitisation agreement for Greater Sunrise field,[2] the main prize for Australia which Woodside Petroleum claimed could probably produce 10 trillion cubic feet of gas, as opposed to the 3 or 4 trillion cubic feet from Bayu-Undan.[3]

On any informed view of modern international maritime law, the already well-planned Bayu-Undan gas field was almost wholly within Timor-Leste's sea boundaries, but Timor-Leste, bereft of funds and technical expertise, needed international investment for Bayu-Undan to proceed. Australia held the key to the way forward and petroleum companies felt more assured of safe investment under the Australian umbrella. Australia understood that once the gas was flowing from Bayu-Undan, Timor-Leste would have funds to secure expert advice and commence bathymetric survey and exploration activity. Events soon showed that Australia's leverage over Timor-Leste was strengthened by delaying Bayu-Undan until favourable terms were secured for the Greater Sunrise Field.

Any doubt about this is dispelled by the candid admission by Geoffrey Raby, First Assistant Secretary of the International Organisations and Legal Division, Department of Foreign Affairs and Trade (DFAT), in his evidence before the Australian Parliamentary Joint Committee on Treaties on 14 October 2002 (quoted in chapter 9). In reply to questions from Andrew Wilkie, Raby reiterated that Australia's national interest would be 'maximised through a development of all the fields ... particularly ... of Greater Sunrise'. He agreed that Australia should hold out for simultaneous ratification of the Treaty and the IUA for Sunrise, as it would be beneficial in 'a broad national interest view'.[4] The 'broad national interest view' evidently was not of the impoverished Timorese who had the lowest per capita income in Asia and a high infant mortality rate; nor was DFAT's 'broad national interest' consistent with Australian defence policy.

On 23 July 2002, Timor-Leste's Parliament made clear in passing its maritime boundaries legislation that, in accordance with the United Nations Convention on the Law of the Sea (UNCLOS), it claimed territorial sovereignty over the Timor Sea sea-bed out to a median line with Australia, and in accordance with laterals to be settled with Indonesia.[5] Thus, Timor-Leste left open its right to lay claim to all of the area designated within the joint petroleum development area (JPDA), including most of the Greater Sunrise Field and oil and gas fields known as Buffalo, Laminaria and Corallina that lay close to the western lateral.[6] Notwithstanding this enunciation of Timor-Leste's position in Parliament, the petroleum companies, all capable of obtaining their own international law advice, made clear to Timor-Leste that they would negotiate with Timor-Leste only through the Australian Government with respect to the necessary unitisation agreement required pursuant to the 2002 Timor Sea Treaty so as to provide a formula for the distribution of revenue, royalties, excises and the imposition of taxes over the field that straddled the western boundary of the JPDA.

The Timor Sea Treaty was enacted, not without further controversy in the Australian Parliament, into Australian law as the *Petroleum (Timor Sea Treaty) Act 2003* (Cth).[7] Although Australia timed the passage of the Timor Sea Treaty with Timor-Leste's signing of the IUA, both countries had to ratify the IUA and some hard bargaining lay ahead. Negotiations for an IUA ratification continued into 2004. After Woodside Petroleum, as Project Operator for the joint venture, comprising Woodside, affiliates of ConocoPhillips, Royal Dutch Shell Group and Osaka Gas Co., suspended work and withdrew exploration staff, Timor-Leste gave in and agreed to a formula. Under the unitisation formula, Timor-Leste's entitlement was to be 90% of the 20.1% of the field said to be under the Timor-Leste sea-bed—that is, only 18.09% of the defined Unit Area reserves. Woodside Petroleum's role in putting economic pressure on Timor-Leste is apparent from back-to-back media releases issued by Foreign Minister Downer and Woodside.

Aware that international law, arguably, placed practically all of the Greater Sunrise Field within Timor-Leste jurisdiction, and consistent with his claim in the Timor-Leste Parliament when introducing National Parliament Law 7/2002, Prime Minister Alkatiri delayed Timor-Leste's ratification of the IUA while talks commenced in relation to the Timor-Leste demand for further concessions, including that the gas pipeline for Greater Sunrise be constructed to the economically depressed Timor-Leste south coast. In this dialogue between the two countries, the prospect of a revised unitisation formula (ultimately Article 5 of the 2006 CMATS Treaty) arose.

Although there is a popular misconception that the resource allocation from the Greater Sunrise Field to be shared under the IUA of 81.91% to Australia and 18.09% to Timor-Leste was changed by the CMATS Treaty to a 50:50 split, the 81.91:18.09 resource allocation stipulated in the IUA remained unchanged.[8] The CMATS Treaty provided a formula for calculating the value of upstream exploitation of petroleum lying within the Unit Area as defined in Annex I to the IUA. It is not 'a field' as depicted on one-dimensional maps of Greater Sunrise, but a three-dimensional area depicted as the cubic area of the two reservoirs located one above the other.

The formula allowed Australia to secure its revenue component by the application to 81.91% of the upstream exploitation of petroleum of an Australian tax regime incorporating petroleum resource rent tax, company tax including capital gains tax, first tranche petroleum, and profit petroleum under the Timor Sea Treaty. Australia agreed to make a payment to Timor-Leste equivalent to half the aggregate of the Australian revenue component and half the Timor-Leste revenue component, calculated according to a Timor-Leste tax regime applied to 18.09% of the upstream resource allocation. In other words, the total tax revenues were to be divided equally after the application of a formula, albeit complicated to manage, that gave the commercial consortium the assurance that roughly 80% of their tax liability would be calculated according to established Australian tax laws.

Although any non-pressure linked reservoir(s) at any other depth(s) in the Greater Sunrise Field would be subject neither to unitisation nor to the 'phoenix' clause in Article 12(3) of the CMATS Treaty,[9] the Treaty's Side-Letters ensured that such reservoirs not wholly within the JPDA would be Australia's to exploit. The issue of the Side-Letters is surprising as, at the time of the CMATS Treaty negotiations, Prime Minister Alkatiri reportedly had advice from a petroleum geologist that a large oil and gas deposit could lie beneath Greater Sunrise in the Permian layer.[10]

In a separate affront to Timor-Leste, the Australian Government had issued licences, despite protests by Timor-Leste,[11] to permit the exploitation of oilfields wholly or partly in Timor-Leste sovereign territory in the Buffalo, Laminaria and Corallina fields at a loss to the Timorese said to be A$2.5 billion by the end of 2004.[12] Australia anticipated that the Side-Letters to the 2006 CMATS Treaty would effectively absolve Australia and the various consortia from reparation payments,[13] which it eventually achieved in the Maritime Boundary Treaty in March 2018. Apart from this multi-billion let-out to the petroleum companies and the Australian Government that may have been liable for reparation payments, the Side-Letters chimed with Geoscience Australia's Offshore Energy Security Program in areas adjacent to the disputed laterals. The petroleum exploration focus of the program was explained as running from 2006 to 2011 and providing 'high-quality pre-competitive data and information to help stimulate petroleum exploration in Australia' and focusing on three offshore frontier regions. Geoscience Australia's modelling studies under the program were aimed at 'improving resource estimates and stimulating further exploration' in partnership with a number of organisations. An acreage release program offered to the market exploration areas 'in producing regions of the North-West Shelf, Otway and Gippsland basins ... As those areas continue to mature and areas are returned to market after industry relinquishment, it is essential that new information be provided to support their re-release'.[14]

The conduct by Australia has another dimension. When Timor Sea treaties were debated in the Australian Parliament in 2002–03, the Coalition Government provided no information to suggest that Australia's long-term energy security was reliant upon Timor Sea gas. Although, for example, the vast reserves of the Browse Basin had been identified, there was no suggestion when Woodside withdrew from its Browse Basin project in 2014 that Australia's national energy security was affected, yet the 2006 grant of A$75 million to further Geoscience's energy security project was predicated on a doubling of Australia's domestic energy needs beyond 2011.[15] Australia's rapidly increasing domestic gas needs were well identified by 2003, yet the issue was not addressed in the nation's Parliament. When Australia's gas shortage began to impact the domestic market in 2017, neither of Australia's major political parties that had overseen the rush to export all the Bayu-Undan and Greater Sunrise gas and the Queensland basin gas had much to say.

The national resistance leaders and successive governments of Timor-Leste held firmly to the view that the 1989 Timor Gap Treaty was unlawful. The 2002 Timor Sea Treaty between Australia and Timor-Leste, which largely replicated the 1989 arrangements, was acquiesced at a time when the nascent Timor-Leste Government was wholly dependent upon aid donors. Nevertheless, it made no concessions with respect to maritime boundary lines. All that was further agreed were the commercial production-sharing arrangements overseen by Timor-Leste and Australia under joint venture arrangements.

Despite early calls by the Timorese leadership for maritime boundary negotiations to commence, Australia refrained from entering negotiations. The Timorese leadership was caught between its need for a revenue stream and Australia's reluctance to discuss maritime boundaries. On several occasions, the Australian Foreign Minister and his officials declared a 'take it or leave it' approach to the IUA agreed in 2003, which would commence a revenue flow to Timor-Leste. If the Timorese wanted money, they declared, Timor-Leste should ratify the IUA.[16] At that time, as it is today, Timor-Leste's only significant revenue source was from gas and oil.

The CMATS Treaty

With the IUA still not ratified, the first round of talks between Australia and Timor-Leste was held at Dili, 19–22 April 2004. Peter Galbraith, who had headed the UNTAET 'negotiation' team in 2002, now led the Timor-Leste delegation. Protestors threw eggs and flour at the Australian delegation as they entered the Hotel Timor and the talks ended in acrimony. Galbraith announced that, although Timor-Leste wanted monthly meetings to negotiate the maritime boundary, the Australian Government proposed that the next meeting be held in Australia in September 2004. He explained the urgency:

> That is a matter to be negotiated both with Indonesia and with Australia, and, of course, East Timor wants to negotiate with both countries. But there's real urgency to the negotiations with Australia and there is no urgency with negotiations with Indonesia. Why is there urgency to the negotiations with Australia? Because, as we speak, Australia is pumping petroleum out of the area that is under dispute, the Government is getting $1 million a day, so that already, since 1999, $1.5 billion is gone. Every day that we delay is $1 million less for this country.[17]

Downer's response to the imbroglio was extraordinary. He now intervened in a manner that cannot be reported due to the service of court process in May 2018.

On 30 July 2004, Don Voelte, Chief Executive Officer of Woodside Petroleum and confidante of Downer, accompanied by Woodside Executive Gary Gray, flew into Dili to meet with Prime Minister Alkatiri. After the meeting, Woodside informed the media that the Timor-Leste Government had been warned that Woodside would suspend development on the Greater Sunrise Field unless Timor-Leste and Australia resolved the deadlock over ratification of the IUA.[18]

At the same time as Voelte's visit to Dili, Foreign Minister Downer indicated that Timor-Leste would get no revenue from the Bayu-Undan and Greater Sunshine gas fields if it pursued its claim for a maritime boundary set at the median point between the two countries. Timor-Leste's leadership no doubt recalled that the Australian Foreign Minister had stated in 2002 that, for technical and geophysical reasons, the land mass reserves in the Timor Sea were clearly associated with the Australian land mass and not with Timor-Leste. Downer's comments at that time were leaked to the media: 'You have to face reality. If you are going to demand that all resources are Timor-Leste's—your claim almost goes to Alice Springs—you can demand that forever for all I care, you can continue to demand, but if you want to make money, you should conclude an agreement quickly'.[19] Nevertheless, the Timor-Leste Government's financial circumstances were pressuring it to defer to the Australian Government.

In September 2004, Australia and Timor-Leste agreed to resume discussions on the boundary, with the round of negotiations held at Dili, 24–27 October 2004. At those negotiations, Australia, represented by senior DFAT officials Douglas Chester and Chris Moraitis, offered a cash gift to the Timorese in exchange for an indefinite deferral of discussions over the sea-bed boundary. Australia had a non-negotiation position in relation to the maritime boundary. After consulting Prime Minister Mari Alkatiri, the Timorese delegation leader José Teixeira rejected the offer, again asserting Timor-Leste's wish, expressed at the failed April 2004 meeting, to link the maritime boundary issue with the Greater Sunrise development, and to include a greater share of the oil royalties from Greater Sunshine together with a gas processing plant and pipeline servicing Greater Sunshine to the south coast of Timor-Leste rather than to Darwin.

This proposal put at risk the Australian Foreign Minister's strategy around the already signed PSCs that anticipated landing both the Bayu-Undan gas and the Greater Sunrise gas in Australia. This was a non-negotiation approach. Unaware of the futility of their position, Prime Minister Alkatiri and Resources Minister Teixeira outlined to their Cabinet colleagues Timor-Leste's negotiating position and the importance of the issues to poverty-stricken Timor-Leste.

As discussed in chapter 9, it is unclear whether all officials sent to Dili instructed by Foreign Minister Downer, ostensibly to negotiate and/or protect Australia's maritime boundary and pipeline issues, were aware at that time of the multi-billion-dollar significance to Phillips Petroleum and Woodside of two missing words in PSCs being combined with sale of gas at the Bayu-Undan well-head and, in future, from the Sunrise Field. Without doubt this was a matter of prime commercial interest to Phillips Petroleum, Woodside and whoever within government was supporting the commercial potential of the maverick definition of 'petroleum'.

It seems probable that anyone aware of the multi-billion-dollar helium gameplay, including the imminent construction of a helium processing plant, would likely be hanging off every word of Timor-Leste's negotiators in 2004 to ascertain whether they had detected the missing words and the true import of the 'no more onerous' demand by ConocoPhillips and Woodside—a demand supported by Prime Minister Howard and his Foreign Minister and parroted relentlessly like an article of faith at treaty negotiations.

As it turned out, those in the know must have breathed a multi-billion-dollar sigh of relief not to hear from the Timor-Leste team mention of the word 'helium'. The agreed 50:50 revenue split, despite the 450km:150km boundary disparity between Australia and Timor-Leste, was presented as a generous concession by Australia and a win by Timor-Leste. With the Bayu-Undan helium close to the value of the LNG, the outcome of the CMATS negotiation was a huge loss for Australia and Timor-Leste. Australia threw the game and the question remains as to who and how many of the players were in on the own goal. In its 2018 Treaty with Timor-Leste, in which helium again was not mentioned, Australia finally conceded the inevitable, namely, that the Bayu-Undan Field, still running until 2026 or longer under the same PSCs, lies wholly within Timor-Leste waters. The long-running gameplay worked on Timor-Leste from the first maverick definition of 'petroleum' in the 2002 Timor Sea Treaty is breathtaking in its audacity.

Throughout 2004 and into 2005, Prime Minister Alkatiri was under pressure to commence infrastructure programs that would require an oil and gas revenue base. His government, which was by early 2005 experiencing civil disturbances fomented by unemployed urban youth and was facing an election campaign in 2006–07, did not want International Monetary Fund (IMF) loans, asserting that reliance on the IMF may lead to the IMF having a role in Timor-Leste's economic governance. At the same time design and construction issues for the Bayu-Undan gas pipeline to Port Wickham included anticipatory take-off of the valuable helium content. On 9 March 2005, BOC Australia announced plans to establish a helium plant adjacent to the Port Wickham LNG plant.[20]

During discussions in Canberra on 8–10 March 2005 and resuming on 20 April and 13 May 2005 in Sydney, agreement was reached between Australia and Timor-Leste on a formula for revenue-sharing and on a deferral of maritime boundary issues. Strangely, there was no debate about BOC's announcement days earlier. Australia made an offer to draft the terms of the agreement, which the Timor-Leste negotiators, attending the meeting without international law advice to hand, accepted.

'Honour on All Sides'

On 27 April 2005, at a time when he was working closely with Woodside management, Foreign Minister Downer had claimed that the Australian strategy was underpinned by a desire to avoid change to the maritime boundaries it had set up with Indonesia:

> What Australia doesn't want is to unravel all of our maritime boundaries which have been laboriously negotiated over many years with all our neighbours. If we can find a suitable settlement that keeps our principles intact, but ensures that East Timor gets a steady flow of revenue, then there should be honour on all sides.[21]

As we shall see, the claimed risk of Australia's boundaries with Indonesia unravelling was pure theatre for the gullible. Australia could have no reasoned fear that any boundary with Indonesia would 'unravel'. Why would treating Timor-Leste equitably in accordance with UNCLOS (to which Indonesia adhered) encourage Indonesia to seek a renegotiation of the 1972 boundary line? What could be more provocative to Indonesia than the subsequent Side-Letters to the CMATS Treaty where Australia gained *carte blanche* in the Exclusive Economic Zone still claimed by Indonesia?

A combination of Article 4(2) of the CMATS Treaty and the exchange of Side-Letters, both drafted by Australia and signed by Australia and Timor-Leste on 23 February 2007, permitted Australia and Timor-Leste to continue 'activities', including the authorisation of existing and new activities involving petroleum minerals outside the JPDA and south of the line agreed between Indonesia and Australia in 1972, so long as either party had legislation in place on 19 May 2002. Prior to independence on 20 May 2002, Timor-Leste could not have legislative control of its sea-bed, but Australia did under the *Petroleum (Submerged Lands) Act 1967* (Cth) and the *Offshore Minerals Act 1994* (Cth) and successor legislation. Thus, Australia had secured all that it aimed for, including the area south of the 1972 Indonesia–Australia line and thus probable protection from reparation claims over Buffalo, Laminaria and Corallina.[22]

Although Foreign Minister Downer claimed the October 2004 negotiations with Timor-Leste were important to Australia in 'national interest' maritime-boundary terms, in reality, Australia had nothing to fear and nothing to learn. Australia and Timor-Leste both knew that the arguments in law in favour of a Timor Sea median line were not novel and, without access to the International Court, Timor-Leste was powerless to secure a median line. So far as the lateral boundaries were concerned, without Indonesia at the table little could be achieved. Although Timor-Leste wanted to commence negotiations on the median maritime boundary issue, the boundary was not on the agenda for the October meeting at which neither party was accompanied to the table by international maritime lawyers. The pipeline from the Bayu-Undan Field to Australia was already in the bag for Australia and, in value terms, not that the Timorese knew, the helium prospect dwarfed any revenue split to be agreed before the International Unitisation Agreement would be ratified by Timor-Leste. Was the helium prospect the real issue of importance at the October 2004 negotiations?

It remains to be determined what Howard and Downer really expected to get out of the October 2004 negotiations. Given the intense activity to secure the helium and the cost to construct a helium plant, some $50 million as it turned out, it is probable that the assurance ConocoPhillips and Woodside required in commercial terms regarding any foreknowledge or objection by Timor-Leste about the helium prospect was at the forefront. Significantly, Peter Galbraith, chief negotiator for Timor-Leste, said in 2015 that at the October 2004 negotiations it was apparent that ConocoPhillips and Woodside were directing the negotiations.[23] For both the Australian and Timorese peoples now deprived of billions in revenue an analysis of whether it was necessary and proper and therefore lawful to employ the functions of government in oversighting the gift of the helium from Bayu-Undan and the future Sunrise High to largely foreign owned corporate interests now awaits open court proceedings. It may be easy to determine whether Downer, who monitored the negotiations from his office, had informed his team in Dili about the helium prospect. The importance of a favourable LNG revenue split for Australia, which at 30 June 2005 had a net worth of A$4458.9 billion and GDP of A$891.524 billion,[24] was hardly a national imperative, and certainly not a concern of the contractor parties who disavowed repeatedly any involvement in the state-to-state revenue percentage negotiations.

If there was a warped notion that meeting the need for helium as a 'critical commodity' might justify cheating the Timorese, how could giving the helium away to largely foreign interests be in Australia's national interest, let alone economic well-being?

More Hypocrisy

During the *travaux preparatoires* for UNCLOS, Australia had supported the need for Article 244, to which Australia, ostensibly, adheres. Headed 'Publication and Dissemination of Information and Knowledge', it states:

1. States and competent international organizations shall, in accordance with this Convention, make available by publication and dissemination through appropriate channels information on proposed major programmes and their objectives as well as knowledge resulting from marine scientific research.
2. For this purpose, States, both individually and in cooperation with other States and with competent international organizations, shall actively promote the flow of scientific data and information and the transfer of knowledge resulting from marine scientific research, especially to developing States, as well as the strengthening of the autonomous marine scientific research capabilities of developing States through, inter alia, programmes to provide adequate education and training of their technical and scientific personnel.[25]

The Australian Government has, however, consistently put assistance to private commercial interests ahead of its obligation to implement Article 244 of UNCLOS by assisting Timor-Leste as a developing petroleum-reliant nation. Clinton Fernandes has outlined the enormous expenditure over the past 40 years by successive Australian governments on gas and petroleum exploration. Exploration results held secretively were effectively gifted to oil and gas corporations fortunate to have secured exploration licences.[26] This massive subsidy to enormously wealthy companies that have repatriated profits abroad compares unfavourably with government support in other sectors such as medical and agricultural research. As we shall see, the loss of helium revenue to Timor-Leste is just one illustration of Australia's failure—a word that may be too kind for its actions—to implement Article 244.

From the 1960s onwards, the Australian Government, as a condition of the grant of exploration licences, relevantly, in the Timor Sea, stipulated that a duplicate of all seismic and geophysical data was to be deposited with Geoscience Australia's predecessor, the Australian Bureau of Minerals, Geology and Geophysics (BMR). This BMR acquisition of exploration data was well in advance of any research being conducted by entities licensed by Indonesia or Portuguese Timor. Despite the terms of the 2002 Timor Sea Treaty establishing the JPDA on a joint-venture basis, Timor-Leste was the weaker, less-resourced party. The geological archive on the Timor Sea held by the Australian Government was by 2002 vast and greatly exceeded the knowledge held by the new Timor-Leste Government.

Gusmão Picks up the Pieces

After the general election of 2007 a coalition government headed by Xanana Gusmão took office in Timor-Leste. The new government took stock of the suite of 'petroleum' treaties between Timor-Leste and Australia inherited from the Alkatiri Government. Mild-mannered Australian-trained Timorese geologist Alfredo Pires, who had shared a room with the author at Gusmão's base in 1999–2000, was appointed Secretary of State for Natural Resources. From Pires' perspective, the CMATS Treaty, which tied Timor-Leste's hands for 50 years, rankled the most, so he set about investigating the basis upon which it had been signed. Although he was aware that Australia had exercised a degree of economic coercion against Timor-Leste during negotiations leading to the CMATS Treaty, Pires doubted that evidence of such pressure could itself justify an attempt by Timor-Leste to invalidate the CMATS Treaty—a common-sense conclusion that reflected Pires' prudent and cautious approach to issues. From an international law perspective, Pires was probably correct, although the mood might be changing.[27]

While an international court or tribunal may view a claim of unequal bargaining strength and 'economic coercion' as relevant to a pattern of conduct relating to some other alleged breach of good faith, a bare claim on its own appeared too difficult a concept upon which to base an argument as to the invalidity of a commercial treaty. Both Alkatiri and Ramos-Horta had endorsed the CMATS Treaty as a 'win' for Timor-Leste. In a cash sense it was, but ever practical, Pires had set about identifying what that 'win' was. As the CMATS Treaty stipulated a six-year time limit for the approval of production plans for the two petroleum reservoirs under the Greater Sunrise Field,

Pires began to examine his country's options. There appeared little scope to alter the menu as the game had been virtually given away in advance by the long-term production contracts for Bayu-Undan and the Greater Sunrise Field signed by the Alkatiri Government. Worse still, a stunning issue emerged from a perusal of documentation held by the Timor-Leste members of the Joint Authority; it became clear that FRETILIN had been living in denial over the helium coup by Australia and Phillips Petroleum.

Pires also found that, before entering the CMATS Treaty, the Alkatiri Government, beyond protesting in the news media, had not acted to prevent Australia and corporate entities licensed by the Australian Government extracting significant revenue from oil and gas production outside the JPDA in the Laminaria, Buffalo and Corallina Fields, which in international law lie either wholly or partially within the territorial sea-bed claimed by Timor-Leste. If the Alkatiri Government had secured informed legal advice, an application for provisional measures to the International Court of Justice (ICJ) may have been made when it became apparent that Australia was issuing further licences and permits in the disputed areas. Australia's reservations regarding maritime boundary issues may not have prevented appropriately framed applications for provisional measures. Steps taken by the author's law firm for the Gusmão Government in 2011–14 to accede to the Statute of the ICJ, the Vienna Convention on the Law of Treaties and other important instruments necessary to bringing Australia to justice at The Hague were long overdue.

Politically, the Alkatiri Government had stood to gain kudos from the cash result of the 2004–06 CMATS negotiations. After signing the CMATS Treaty at Sydney on 12 January 2006, Alkatiri and Ramos-Horta had expressed their satisfaction with the outcome. But what might they have secured for Timor-Leste, had they been better resourced and started on the front foot against Australia in The Hague with a provisional measures application and a separate challenge to the reservations lodged by Australia in March 2002?

While it may be easy to criticise the failure of Timor-Leste's first government to secure and implement specialist legal advice on Timor Sea issues, it was Australia that brought to the table eminent industry and legal advisers. Having undertaken on 20 May 2002 explicitly, sealed with a handshake between Prime Ministers Howard and Alkatiri, to act in good faith in mutual self-interest, Australia may have encouraged the Timorese leadership to let their guard down. If the Timorese had known the true moral calibre of the government they were dealing with they may have double-checked matters understood to be in mutual self-interest, such as the PSCs' fine print, and legal advisers could have been included to bolster the Alkatiri–Galbraith negotiation team. One can only imagine what the outcome might have been if, for example, eminent petroleum lawyer Bjorn-Erik Leerberg had not been 16,000 kilometres away in Norway but had been in Foreign Minister Downer's office on the fateful evening when sovereignty over the Timor Sea gas was given away for Timor-Leste and Australia to the contractor, or if he had been present when the PSCs that were missing the words 'and inerts' were presented for signature.

In context, the helium issue raises a clear case for Timor-Leste to determine whether the whole suite of treaties with Australia, including the 20 May 2002 Memorandum of Understanding and Timor Sea Treaty and the bed-rock 2003 International Unitisation Agreement, are tainted with fraud.[28] Arguably, the express 'good-faith' provision in the Memorandum of Understanding signed with the parent 2002 Timor Sea Treaty, made law in Australia via the *Petroleum (Timor Sea Treaty) Act 2003*, was breached by Australia's fraudulent conduct. If so, a properly advised Timor-Leste, free of compromise within its own ranks, may ensure that an exploitative era is brought to a close.

Although Timor-Leste was not a party to the Vienna Convention on the Law of Treaties at relevant times,[29] this 'does not mean that the requirement found in Article 31 of the Vienna Convention that a treaty is to be interpreted in accordance with the ordinary meaning to be given to its terms'[30] did not bind Australia. The terrible blot on Australia's national reputation for those who hold rule of law dear is that on 20 May 2002 Australia and Timor-Leste signed both a Memorandum of Understanding that expressly bound the parties to act 'in good-faith' in future negotiations and the *Timor Sea Treaty 2002*, which included the opening words, '*Conscious of the importance of promoting Timor-Leste's economic development.*' These undertakings were sealed by handshake between Prime Minister Howard and Prime Minister Alkatiri in front of the world media.

16
EXPORT TRADE *VERSUS* DEFENCE

The Australian oil company Petroz had sought to participate in the Timor Sea gas market but had come up against the priority Australia accorded to securing a favourable outcome for Woodside Petroleum over Greater Sunrise, the confirmation of which has been analysed in chapter 15. A first question to ask is whether there was a national economic energy imperative to justify supporting Woodside when other corporations were seeking to enter the same energy market. It is difficult to discern such an imperative. Australia was proposing the export of all the gas and the Bayu-Undan contractor parties had secured the helium from that field. Likewise, a principal economic beneficiary of petroleum exploitation of Greater Sunrise under the terms of the treaties and PSCs negotiated was the commercial consortium led by Woodside Petroleum, for which Alexander Downer accepted a consultant's retainer shortly after his retirement from Parliament. Woodside is not a national oil company, even though treated as such by successive Australian governments.

As a defence ally of Australia, a stable democratic Timor-Leste utilising naturally endowed resources to lift its people from poverty assists regional stability and offers a forward posture for defence of Australia's vital sea-lanes. Apart from the Australian public interest in

Australia's observance of the rule of law, mutual defence interests alone should have encouraged fair dealing with Timor-Leste.

Timor-Leste's President Taur Matan Ruak, a former FALANTIL Commander, referred to Australia in his inaugural address in 2012 as a long-standing ally. Australia's defence establishment has worked effectively over many years to enhance defence cooperation with Timor-Leste. A 2013 Australian *Defence White Paper* listed the Australian Defence Force's four priorities as to 'deter and defeat armed attacks on Australia ... contribute to stability and security in the South Pacific and Timor-Leste ... contribute to military contingencies in the Indo-Pacific region, with priority given to Southeast Asia; and ... contribute to military contingencies in support of global security'.[1] The 2016 Australian *Defence White Paper* reaffirmed these objectives, expanding on the second as being,

> to support the security of maritime South East Asia and support the governments of Papua New Guinea, Timor-Leste and of Pacific Island Countries to build and strengthen their security. In South East Asia, Defence will strengthen its engagement, including helping to build the effectiveness of regional operations to address shared security challenges, and the ADF will have increased capabilities to make contributions to any such operations. The Government will continue its commitment to strengthened regional security architectures that support transparency and co-operation. Australia will continue to seek to be the principal security partner for Papua New Guinea, Timor-Leste and Pacific Island Countries in the South Pacific.[2]

A corollary to Australia's strategic defence policy in the region is exemplary conduct by Australia in upholding the rule of law, including binding commercial obligations.

In managing its foreign aid programs in the Asia-Pacific region Australia places emphasis on the fight against corruption. At the time Australian Foreign Minister Alexander Downer led negotiations with Timor-Leste, Australian diplomats were engaged in preparatory work at the UN in support of a treaty against corruption, which Downer signed in 2005. The treaty enjoins all countries to bolster their laws to fight corruption, particularly corruption in public office.[3]

Former High Court Justice Michael Kirby has said, 'the control of great power in transparent and accountable ways is the ultimate genius of the system of government of liberal democracies'.[4] As helium was listed in Australia as a critical commodity, one may ask whether it was compatible with national security precepts to allow the contractor parties to secure the Bayu-Undan and Greater Sunrise helium. With respect to Bayu-Undan, the central issue for the negotiation between the joint-venture partners was the ratification of the International Unitisation Agreement (IUA), held up over Timor-Leste's dissatisfaction with the 18.09% revenue split agreed in the 2003 IUA. Australia's interest in the negotiation was explained by senior Department of Foreign Affairs and Trade (DFAT) official Geoffrey Raby during testimony before an Australian parliamentary committee in 2002, quoted in chapter 9.[5]

The potential value to the respective State tax revenues of the Greater Sunrise Field depended upon the estimated gas yield and net return after all development and production costs incurred by the commercial contractors with whom both Australia and Timor-Leste had, under the JPDA structure, subsisting production-sharing contracts (PSCs). Timor-Leste and Australia met, therefore, as existing joint-venture partners with consequent mutual fiduciary duties to renegotiate the Greater Sunrise revenue split in good faith.

The anticipated tax revenues, calculated by the Treasury,[6] were not of any dimension relative to Australia's Gross National Product to 'affect' Australia's national security. Not so for Timor-Leste, which, having no other long-term revenue source, had a vital national security concern with the negotiations, both as to revenue and an expectation, derived from Article 8 in the Exchange of Notes, in force from 10 February 2000,[7] and the replicate Article 8 in the 2002 Timor Sea Treaty, that a second gas pipeline would land in Timor-Leste and boost the local economy in a manner commensurate with the way the Bayu-Undan Pipeline had boosted the Australian Northern Territory economy.

However, the commercial contractors made clear that they wished to avoid the construction of a second pipeline and, in working closely with the Australian Government, expected Australia to keep the pipeline issue off the table in negotiations with Timor-Leste. In fact, Royal Dutch Shell as part of the contractor consortium, already favoured a Floating Liquid Natural Gas (FLNG) processing facility. Timor-Leste nevertheless remained in hope for a pipeline to land in Timor-Leste. As we now know, to secure the helium from Greater Sunrise, Australia needed to secure a pipeline to Australia, via, if practicable, the Bayu-Undan pipeline using ullage and then full capacity after the Bayu-Undan Field was depleted, or a linked processing plant at sea.

In this context, Timor-Leste's interest in securing upstream secondary industrial advantages from the piping of gas and oil to its mainland met with counter-arguments from the Australian Government and Woodside Petroleum that a pipeline to Timor-Leste traversing the Timor Trough was not feasible. Woodside published diagrams showing the trough to be steep-sided and impractical to traverse; Foreign Minister Downer endorsed Woodside's assertions on numerous occasions. Contrary to these assertions, a subsequent sea-bed survey commissioned by Timor-Leste revealed gradients in and around the trough that, according to current pipeline technology, may accommodate a gas pipeline without significant challenge.[8]

Both parties understood that the maritime boundary delimitation dispute between them would remain in abeyance, as agreed in the 2002 Timor Sea Treaty, but there was a live question as to how long the boundary dispute would remain off the table. Nevertheless, there had never been any suggestion by Australia that the maritime boundary issue between Timor-Leste and Australia had any national security implication. The area of the Timor Sea in dispute contains no natural feature that would affect Australia's national security in the accepted meaning of the words in ordinary English language, understood in the statutory context.

In terms of Australia's 'energy security', there is no provision in any of the Timor Sea suite of treaties between Timor-Leste and Australia allowing either government to requisition, in circumstances of emergency, any of the petroleum product. The PSCs are equally silent in respect of any emergency power. All the LNG flowing to Darwin via the Bayu-Undan pipeline is exported from Wickham Point, which was not connected to the national gas grid. 'Australia has vast conventional gas resources', according to Geoscience Australia:

> In 2008, Australia's EDR and sub-economic demonstrated resources (SDR) of conventional gas were estimated at 180,400 PJ (164 tcf) ... Based on the above estimate of 3 mole% helium in Australian LNG, this equates to a resource of approximately 4.92 tcf helium. Most (around 92%) of Australia's conventional gas resources are located in the Carnarvon, Browse and Bonaparte basins off the north-west coast.

There are also resources in south-east and central Australia. As well as the conventional gas resources, Australia also has large supplies of unconventional gas. Large coal seam gas (CSG) resources exist in the coal basins of Queensland and New South Wales. Tight gas accumulations are located in onshore Western Australia and South Australia, while potential shale gas resources are located in the Northern Territory ... The potential of unconventional gas resources for helium extraction is unknown.[9]

Australia's energy security program had come a long way since the 1972 OPEC crisis and was now conducted by Geoscience Australia with a focus on export trade. Multinational companies conduct exploration activities under Australian-issued permits in the areas of Timor Sea bed the subject of dispute. While helium revenue might have significantly augmented Australia's coffers, royalty income to Australia is hardly a matter of 'national security'. If solving Australia's critical commodity need for helium was in the interests of Australia's national security, giving it away to largely foreign commercial entities belies any national security imperative.

The likely conclusion is that there was no 'national security' imperative 'affected by' the Timor-Leste Cabinet to justify the maverick definition of petroleum in the PSCs. If there was any declared national security imperative *vis-à-vis* Timor-Leste, successive Australian Defence White Papers have emphasised that Australia's broad national security interests are served by a stable and prosperous Timor-Leste.[10] Indeed, trade policy objectives outlined by Downer and his officials in evidence to parliamentary committees raise the question whether the emphasis given to levering a largely foreign private commercial joint-venture consortium into an advantageous position to the detriment of Timor-Leste's long-term economic future was compatible with Australia's long-term national security interests.

While the 1986 Dibb Report commissioned by Defence Minister Kim Beazley was not free of controversy within the defence community, the report had not dislodged a notion, accepted since World War II, that Australian defence planning for a threat from the north may necessarily involve a 'layered' or 'concentric circles' response.[11] Obviously, as in 1942, such a response may extend across the Timor Sea and assume Timor-Leste to be an ally. That Timor-Leste may become an ally appeared, at least to the author, the underlying theme when

CNRT President Xanana Gusmão met Australian Governor-General Bill Deane and Defence Chief Admiral Chris Barrie at CNRT's headquarters in 2001. As defence commentator Gregory Colton has observed, 'the security of Australia's maritime approaches through the archipelagic region to the north, as well as through the island chains of the South Pacific, has been a key defence objective'.[12]

It seems likely that defence commentators may argue that ill-will towards Australia by Timor-Leste over the transfer of sovereign helium assets away from Timor-Leste to private corporate interests hardly meets Australia's defence objectives, especially if Australia might need a forward base on Timor-Leste territory. Colton also observed:

> If the ADF [Australian Defence Force] was forced to act unilaterally, it could deploy an amphibious battle-group for a RAMSI [Regional Assistance Mission to the Solomon Islands]-style intervention to stabilize a neighbouring country. It is yet to demonstrate, however, that it can successfully conduct the amphibious lodgement of a combat brigade and sustain it over the horizon for any length of time ... More concerning is the lack of air-cover which an Australian amphibious force would need in the event of an air threat ... Either Australia is going to have to develop a strategy of developing, maintaining and operating from forward airbases pre-established in friendly nations throughout the region, or it will need to rely on the United States Navy to provide air cover.[13]

During the violence following the 1999 ballot in East Timor, Australia needed assistance from the French Navy in New Caledonia for landing-ship support. The US Navy provided significant support, including stationing a cruiser in the Timor Sea to support Blackhawk helicopter operations from Australia. If trouble had developed with maverick Indonesian defence elements, Australia would have faced significant challenges in providing long-range air support from Australia's northern bases. The Royal Australian Air Force (RAAF) F-111 fleet was depleted and logistical support at Darwin limited for sustained bombing and missile operations. Against this background, it was not difficult to conclude that antagonising Timor-Leste, a potential defence ally, with unfair petroleum revenue terms was inconsistent with a defence strategy aimed at not relying solely upon the United States. Not only may it be argued that the Howard Government placed corporate interests ahead of Australia's long-term national defence interests; it is apparent that Australia's domestic gas supply needs, which *were* a matter of national security, had been similarly relegated.

Looking back over Australian foreign policy one might be forgiven for saying that Australia's defence interests had once again, as in the Barwick years, been shelved by top officials in Australia's foreign ministry. Not only had Australia's foreign trade policy antagonised a potential ally important to Australian defence strategy but, working in unison with officials of the Ministry of Industry, Science and Resources, the objective of maximising LNG exports had left the Timor Sea gas unconnected to the national gas grid. The interests of the ordinary Australian gas consumer appear not to have had priority in the minds of those running between the Parliament and the boardrooms of Woodside and ConocoPhillips.

On this thesis it seems evident that the sale of all the Bayu-Undan LNG at long-term fixed prices to foreign interests was contrary to Australia's broader national interest. Besides creating a bonanza for foreign consumers, the failure to consult domestic energy suppliers on long-term projections of gas consumption was likely to leave the growing number of gas-fed domestic electricity-generating stations with a predictable shortfall in supply. Australia is now marked in history as a pariah state that lacked even sufficient skill to benefit its own citizens with the proceeds of its plunder in the Timor Sea. Australia's Federal Energy Minister Angus Taylor is now spruiking a 'national interest' need to 'relook' at environmental limits on Bass Strait and other sensitive sea-bed potential gas/petroleum exploration.

If Australia had approached the Greater Sunrise project with national interest at the forefront, a 10 trillion cubic feet (tcf) gas flow to Australia and Timor-Leste, including helium processing, could have been under way by 2010, benefiting the ordinary peoples of Timor-Leste and Australia. While neither Australian nor foreign corporations are guardians of the Australian community interest, parliamentary office-bearers have a sworn duty to advance Australia's interests. In 2013, Timor-Leste's subsequent complaints, delivered mostly in camera at arbitral proceedings on the other side of the world, were unlikely to reach the ears of the Australian population.[14] Bringing home to ordinary Australians, lawfully, the role of their political leaders in such an apparently unbelievable story seemed a daunting task. In December 2013, the Australian Attorney-General, Senator George Brandis, solved the issue in full measure by raiding in a most public style the home and office of the author. In one fell swoop, Brandis propelled Australia's treatment of Timor-Leste into world prominence.

Less arduous working sessions in the garden outside Sir Elihu Lauterpacht's study at 7 Herschel Road, Cambridge, August 2013. From left to right: Professor Vaughan Lowe QC, Carla Mazur, Amy McMullen, Jolan Draaisma.

'Foreign Relations'

On ABC TV's *Four Corners* on 17 March 2014, former Foreign Affairs Minister Downer claimed that foreign relations with Indonesia were a factor in the CMATS negotiations. Downer was referring to treaties negotiated in 1971 for the Arafura Sea and in 1972 for the Timor Sea. The 1971 median line treaty was uncontroversial and was resolved on settled principles. In 1972, Indonesia accepted a maritime boundary line on the continental shelf between West Timor and other Indonesian islands, and Australia, significantly further north of where the median line is between the two countries.[15] Downer said:

> [I]f we had made special provisions for East Timor, then naturally enough the Indonesians would've come back to us and said, well, in that case why should we adhere to these earlier treaties? And then in that context all of our maritime boundaries and seabed agreements would unravel, and that would be diplomatic folly for Australia.[16]

He had made similar claims in 2005 (quoted in chapter 15) and while defending the Timor Sea Treaty in 2002:

> [W]e are happy to hear what they [the East Timorese] have to say but we don't want to start renegotiating all of our boundaries, not just with East Timor, but with Indonesia. It has enormous implications. As I have explained to them, our maritime boundaries with Indonesia cover several thousand kilometres ... we are not in the game of renegotiating them.[17]

Downer's reference to the boundary agreements with Indonesia being potentially unstable is misleading. The 1971 treaty that established a boundary line in the Arafura Sea between Australia and Indonesia was drawn on the principles of the Geneva Convention on the Continental Shelf endorsed by the ICJ in the North Sea Cases,[18] and since reaffirmed in the 1982 United Nations Convention on the Law of the Sea (UNCLOS). Those principles were that, as the Arafura Sea is mostly at a depth of 200 metres or less, a median line was appropriate. A declassified 1965 Australian Cabinet Submission bears that out.[19] Contrary to Downer's claim, nothing in the Arafura Sea can 'unravel', as the boundary is set in accordance with established principles.

The 1972 treaty between Australia and Indonesia concerned a sea-bed boundary issue in which Australia rejected equidistance principles and pursued a 'two shelves' approach, relating to a boundary less than 1,000 kilometres in length, and not the 'several thousand kilometres' asserted by Downer. Moreover, the area between the 1972 treaty sea-bed boundary and the median line, which might conceivably 'unravel', is minuscule when compared to Australia's 12.75 million square kilometres of continental shelf entitlement. The minuscule area in question has been almost fully explored for hydrocarbon potential, apart from Greater Sunrise to which Indonesia has made no claim on significant commercially viable petroleum deposits, between the notional median line with Australia and the 1972 agreed line, that have been identified. Indonesia is well endowed with energy resources elsewhere and has yet to develop significant identified reserves well within its sovereign boundaries. What incentive could Indonesia have to now seek a median line in a relatively barren area?

Indonesia would have to unilaterally abrogate the 1972 treaty for the line to 'unravel' after any Australian agreement with Timor-Leste. Indonesia has made no *démarches* whatsoever during the lengthy public debate between Australia and Timor-Leste over the median line claimed by Timor-Leste. It is true that, in 1977, during a period of strained relations with Australia, the Indonesian Foreign Minister Dr Mochtar Kusamaatmadja, a law of the sea expert who had been a negotiating official for Indonesia during the 1971 and 1972 negotiations with Australia, claimed that Australia had 'taken Indonesia to the cleaners' in the negotiations over the sea-bed boundary: 'The Australians were able to talk us into accepting that the Timor Trench constituted a natural boundary between the two shelves, which is not true'.[20] A more sanguine view emerged in 2004 when senior Indonesian diplomat Hashim Djalal, then participating with Indonesia in the revised economic zone sea-bed negotiations, said that the Indonesian Government was unaware of the Timor Sea's oil and gas potential at the time.[21] Djalal acknowledged that Indonesia, in negotiating its 1972 boundary, wanted to be a good neighbour to Australia after the armed confrontation in the 1960s between Indonesia and Malaysia that was supported by Britain, Australia and New Zealand.

In lodging a comprehensive continental shelf submission in 2009 at the UN, Indonesia did not signal any intent to seek to renegotiate or abrogate the 1972 Treaty.[22] Indeed, Indonesia cited in its submission both the 1971 and 1972 treaties as settled and domestic law, accepting them as exceptions to Indonesia's adherence to UNCLOS principles.[23] This was unsurprising, for at no time during the 10 years of negotiations between Australia and Indonesia in relation to the eventual 1989 Timor Gap Treaty did Indonesia seek any concession with respect to the 1972 boundary line. 1987 Cabinet papers reveal that, during the post-1979 negotiations, Indonesia indicated that it wanted an economic share of the petroleum revenue to be acquired from the areas of the eventual Zone of Cooperation in the Timor Gap up to the 200-nautical mile limit not already covered by petroleum titles granted by Australia.

Indonesia expressed the sensible view that when existing petroleum titles issued by Australia for that area expired, the vacated title area should become part of Indonesia's co-economic interest. In other words, in negotiating with the additional leverage available to it after invading Timor-Leste, Indonesia sought no concessions in relation to the 1972 boundary line, but only concessions in relation to the Timor Gap. The concession was made, and Zone A became an area of joint Australian-Indonesian co-prosperity.

If, in the context of the 1989 Timor Gap Treaty, Indonesia did not seek a concession in relation to the 1972 boundary line with Australia or in relation to the lateral close to Greater Sunrise, it is hard to comprehend the basis upon which it could be asserted that Indonesia would seek a renegotiated boundary if a median line was agreed with Timor-Leste. When speaking in 2014 to *Four Corners*, Downer would have known that the prospect of Indonesia reopening the 1972 boundary agreement was ruled out by the Australian Cabinet in 1987 and by Indonesia itself in its 2009 Continental Shelf Submission.

Moreover, the 1987 Cabinet Submission that canvassed the bases upon which Australia might reach the eventual 1989 Timor Gap Treaty with Indonesia noted that,

> [U]nder international law Australia's and Indonesia's seabed rights in the Timor Gap extend from their respective coastlines to the bathymetric axis (the deepest point) of the Timor Trough, which is the end of their respective continental shelves in this area … Indonesia's position has been that there is one shared continental shelf between Australia and Indonesia and that accordingly, a boundary equidistant between the two coasts (the median line) would be appropriate. In addition, Indonesia argues that recent developments in the law of the sea, incorporated in 1982 United Nations Convention on the Law of the Sea, conferring jurisdiction over the seabed and water column out to 200 nautical miles (the Exclusive Economic Zone—'EEZ'), regardless of geomorphology, support the median as the appropriate delimitation. No agreement on the principles for a permanent delimitation seems possible … Indonesia has not accepted and is unlikely to accept the compulsory jurisdiction of the Court because it shares the traditional antipathy of less developed countries to compulsory third party settlement of disputes.[24]

In March 2002, Australia withdrew from all Law of the Sea adjudication concerning maritime boundaries. In consequence, any concern that Indonesia might litigate any boundary issue with Australia was well gone before the 2004 treaty revenue negotiations in Dili. Indonesian Foreign Minister Hassan Wirajuda had observed on 26 February 2002 that 'in due course' Indonesia might wish to be part of a three-way process in redefining the boundaries of the Timor Gap. In this context, the Indonesian Foreign Minister was referring only to the adjustment of the lateral boundaries between what is now Timor-Leste and Indonesia out to tri-junction points in the Timor Sea.

On other bilateral fronts, Indonesia has accepted the joint maritime arrangements at sea whereby Australia has assumed responsibility out to the 1972 negotiated line. Indonesia is still resolving maritime boundaries issues elsewhere and it would seem highly unlikely for Indonesia as a democratic state to seek to abrogate a long-standing international treaty. The 1997 Exclusive Economic Zone Boundary and Certain Other Boundaries Treaty (EEZ Treaty)[25] between Indonesia and Australia reaffirmed the original 1972 line, but neither Australia nor Indonesia has ratified the EEZ Treaty.

In this submission, Downer's claim that Indonesia might renege on a treaty is more than just an unconvincing justification for his treatment of the Timorese. Downer's explanation is so far-fetched that it is suggestive of an attempt to give legitimacy to his own actions.

'National Economic Well-being'

A further issue requiring analysis is the question of whether the helium take-off was in the interests of Australia's national economic well-being. Some may say there is a short answer, namely, giving the helium away and obliging the Australian taxpayer to buy it back is entirely contrary to Australia's economic well-being. Downer's comments on 17 March 2014 were revelatory:

> We were close to all stakeholders and we would've been derelict in our duty had we not been. Galbraith was working for the United Nations, that's a different thing; the United Nations doesn't have an oil company. But of course when we're involved in negotiations we maintain contact with Australian companies. The Australian government isn't against Australian companies, or if it is it's derelict in its duty. The Australian government supports Australian business and Australian industry. The Australian government unashamedly should be trying to advance the interests of Australian companies.[26]

These comments should be viewed in light of successive statements of Australian foreign and trade policy:

> The values which Australia brings to its foreign policy are the values of a liberal democracy. These have been shaped by national experience... but reflect a predominantly European intellectual and cultural heritage. They include the rule of law, freedom of the press, the accountability of the government to an elected parliament, and a commitment to a 'fair go'.[27]

Article 5 of the CMATS Treaty required that Australia and Timor-Leste 'share equally' revenues derived from the upstream exploitation of petroleum resources within the Sunrise IUA area.[28] According to Australia, the Greater Sunrise Field contains an 'estimated 8.4 trillion cubic feet of gas and 295 million barrels of condensate'.[29] The consortium holding the rights to develop the field is led by Australian oil major Woodside Energy Ltd and the projected costs of development were approximately A$6.6 billion.[30]

Following negotiation of the CMATS Treaty, Foreign Minister Downer noted that equal sharing of the upstream revenues deriving from Greater Sunrise 'could result in Australia and Timor-Leste each receiving up to US$10 billion over the life of the project'.[31] Thus, the purely fiscal impact of the CMATS Treaty on Australia and Timor-Leste over the estimated 30-year life of the project can be assessed as between the estimated revenue from the non-risk-adjusted 8.4 tcf claimed by Australia and, in standard petroleum trade terms, a risk-adjusted estimate that might reduce field potential by 15–20%.

Timor-Leste had already secured what amounted to an 18.1% share of the reserve through the Timor Sea Treaty and IUA. The National Interest Analysis tabled in the Australian Parliament with the CMATS Treaty estimated that it would involve transfers to Timor-Leste of around A$4 billion over the expected 30-year life of the project.[32] The difference between what Timor-Leste would have received under the IUA and what was negotiated under the CMATS Treaty is up to A$6 billion.

Although Timor-Leste gained from the CMATS Treaty negotiation more than double the revenue that it would otherwise have derived under the IUA, it failed to secure the main prize. During the run-up to the negotiation of the CMATS Treaty, Timor-Leste argued for the processing facility to be located in Timor-Leste in order to provide much-needed stimulus to the local economy. Prime Minister Alkatiri noted that some estimates of the economic benefits of locating the facilities in Darwin were as much as A$22 billion. He also asserted that, given Australia was receiving the downstream benefits processing from the Baya-Undan Field, it would be fair if Timor-Leste were to benefit from the Greater Sunrise Field.[33]

In fact, Dr Alkatiri had a treaty basis for this negotiation position. Article 8 of both the 2002 Timor Sea Treaty and its precursor agreement, the Exchange of Notes between UNTAET and Australia of 10 February 2000, provided: 'In the event a pipeline is constructed from the JPDA to the territory of either Australia or East Timor, the country where the pipeline lands may not object to or impede decisions of the Joint Commission regarding a pipeline to the other country'. The silence of the CMATS Treaty on the location of processing facilities was, despite Timor-Leste's analysis lacking knowledge of the helium, a A$22 billion wildcard. On one view, the major beneficiary from the CMATS Treaty in economic terms was the Woodside consortium, as the untying of Article 8 of the Timor Sea Treaty in its application to Greater Sunrise lost Timor-Leste the right to land a pipeline in Timor-Leste. To avoid this debacle, Timor-Leste would have required a term in the CMATS Treaty that preserved Article 8 and applied it explicitly to any Greater Sunrise Development Plan and to PSCs executed in anticipation of a Greater Sunrise Development Plan being approved.[34] It was not only Timor-Leste that missed out. Australia could have required Woodside to link a pipeline from Greater Sunrise to the existing Bayu-Undan pipeline to Darwin by treaty terms.

By the CMATS Treaty Timor-Leste and Australia accepted a 50% share each of the total anticipated upstream tax revenues from Greater Sunrise without knowing what the tax-deductible cost of the most important variable in the equation would be, namely, the outstanding costs of exploration, gas recovery, delivery and processing. In not securing the right to either stipulate or maintain a veto right to influence the LNG processing method, Australia and Timor-Leste left the anticipated tax revenue return from Greater Sunrise to commercial dictates.

In a provision remarkable for its hands-off approach, the CMATS Treaty simply required the State parties to agree with the contractors within six years on a Greater Sunrise Development Plan, which included the gas processing decision.[35] By April 2010 the long-anticipated decision that the consortium favoured an FLNG as the processing and delivery method was confirmed.[36] Thus, both Timor-Leste and Australia were, as matters then stood, going to miss out on the multi-billion-dollar infrastructure and employment boost from a landed facility.

In Australia's case, and adopting an Australian argument, the loss would be all the more galling because a pipeline under Australian supervision was available from the Bayu-Undan Field to Darwin, and a sea-bed connecting line from Greater Sunrise to the Bayu-Undan flange could present no unusual engineering challenges. Once at the Bayu-Undan flange, ullage in the line to Darwin could be taken up to transport a gas stream from Greater Sunrise, and LNG and condensate sales could be made direct from the Bayu-Undan plant. As the countdown for the life of the Bayu-Undan Field approaches, estimated between 2020 and 2024, a multi-billion-dollar investment in an FLNG might become less economic.

Parliamentary Scrutiny
On 6 February 2007, the Australian Government tabled the CMATS Treaty in the federal Parliament with a *National Interest Analysis* that addressed neither the helium nor the pipeline infrastructure issues.[37] The following day the government declared the legislation implementing the IUA operative. On 22 February 2007, on the eve of the Exchange of Notes the following day in Dili between Timor-Leste and Australia to bring the IUA and the CMATS Treaty simultaneously into force, Alexander Downer informed the Chair of the Joint Standing Committee on Treaties (JSCOT) that he was invoking the national interest exemption and would proceed to ratify the CMATS Treaty before the stipulated 20-day sitting period following tabling elapses.

The Executive of the federal government of Australia has authority under section 61 of the Australian Constitution to enter into, it has to be stressed, a lawful international treaty without seeking parliamentary approval. It appears extraordinary that a treaty procured the way it was, including PSCs with the missing words, has been tabled in the Australian Parliament. This appears tantamount to our parliamentarians eating off stolen silverware in their Parliamentary Dining Room.

In practice, the treaty-making process is consultative and the more so if implementation of the treaty requires support by legislation or otherwise by State and Territory governments. The DFAT website states that 'all treaties (except those the Government decided [*sic*] are urgent or sensitive) are tabled in both Houses of Parliament for at least 15 sitting days prior to binding treaty action being taken'.[38] The so-called national interest exemption (NIE) has no statutory basis. It has been a formula employed rarely outside wartime or like emergencies by which the Executive has entered into a treaty without first tabling it in Parliament. For example, using the NIE formula in response to the downing over the Ukraine on 17 July 2014 of Malaysian Airlines Flight MH17, Australia entered into a status of forces treaty with the Netherlands on 1 August 2014, without first tabling it in Parliament, thus enabling armed Australian defence personnel, weapons and communications systems to be based in the Netherlands while providing support to the UN-endorsed Dutch/Ukrainian International Mission for Protection of Investigation.

Although the parliamentary passage of the CMATS Treaty represented a major strategic win for the petroleum consortium, the leapfrogging of the parliamentary process did not pass unnoticed. When the JSCOT met on 26 February 2007, the Acting Chair, Andrew Wilkie MP, questioned senior DFAT legal adviser Penny Richards about the invocation of the national interest exemption:

> Given this treaty was signed in January 2006 and that the minister made the statement to parliament in February last year that the treaty would be brought forward virtually as quickly as possible to the Australian parliament for consideration, why has it taken until February this year for the treaty to be tabled so that this committee can investigate it?

Ms Richards replied:

> The feeling was that both governments wished to move as closely in-step as possible through their domestic processes. As you know, the processes are somewhat different, so it is difficult to dovetail them exactly, but East Timor had requested us to arrange for synchronous entry into force of the treaty. The East Timorese processes were disrupted by domestic developments in 2006 but, towards the end of last year and the beginning of this year, the East Timor government was in a position to move quickly and had requested that Australia proceed with synchronous exchange of letters and entry into force. So the Australian government sought to meet that East Timorese request to be in a position to exchange notes on the same day.

Wilkie sought her confirmation that, in contrast to the Timor-Leste Parliament, the Australian Parliament had not followed due process. She replied:

> Mr Downer, as you know, on 22 February invoked the national interest exemption … It was felt in this case, because the treaties bring significant national benefits to both countries and because there was possibly a very narrow window of opportunity to bring them into force in the

short term, that it was important to take advantage of that window of opportunity.

In reply to Wilkie's question as to why the government hadn't asked JSCOT to consider and report on the treaty urgently rather than invoke the NIE, Richards said that the treaty had been available to the public for 12 months, but 'there was a rapidly closing window of opportunity … and in the national interest it was thought best to grab that window before it closed'. Wilkie then asked a 'rather blunt question' about whose incompetence had led to the situation and asked whether the decision not to submit the treaty to JSCOT for examination had been taken by the Minister or DFAT. Richards reiterated her point about East Timor having requested the Australian Government 'to ratify synchronously' and did not answer the questions, whereupon Wilkie expressed his outrage that JSCOT hadn't been given the opportunity to examine the treaty: 'It is a failing on behalf of both the minister and the department which I find totally unacceptable'.[39]

The suggestion that the timing was to meet a request by Timor-Leste was disingenuous to say the least. In 2002, Mr Wilkie's questioning had elicited from another DFAT official an intended *modus vivendi* whereby a revenue flow for Timor-Leste anticipated by the 2003 IUA would not commence until a deal for Greater Sunrise was agreed to by Timor-Leste.[40] In other words, the IUA would not be ratified until there were treaty rights to Greater Sunrise for commercial contractors. By 2007 the Alkatiri Government had collapsed in civil strife and an interim government, still largely reliant upon donor funds, was preparing for elections.

Downer attributed uncertainty arising from the national elections in Timor-Leste as the reason why he invoked a NIE to exclude an inquiry into the CMATS Treaty by the JSCOT.[41] Mr Wilkie's retort to this claim was:

> [B]ut could someone please explain to me why on the DFAT webpage there is a media release from the minister dated 8 February, which says the process is not the timing of the elections. It says it was agreed to move through in parallel, which has already been stated, but that it was not the timing of the elections that dictated the government's approach. That is totally the opposite of what you just said.[42]

Ultimately, the question is whether the silence of the CMATS Treaty on both the location of processing facilities and the presence of helium was a benefit to Australia's national economic well-being or primarily of commercial gain to the commercial consortium. On any current analysis of information in the public domain, abdication of government control over sovereign resource processing was to both Australia and Timor-Leste's detriment, as the upstream economic development gains of a landed processing facility would dwarf total anticipated tax revenue, stated in the National Interest Analysis to be worth up to A$10 billion each to Australia and Timor-Leste. If the Greater Sunrise Field gas is processed by an internationally moored FLNG using flown-in foreign labour, the infrastructure and employment gains to Timor-Leste and Australia of a landed facility may be largely lost. Moreover, to secure the helium Australia would be obliged to show its hand.

Alexander Downer did not spell out just what 'wealth' would accrue to Australia when he gave his recollections to Marian Wilkinson for *Four Corners*: 'Woodside is a huge Australian company and they were proposing to invest billions of dollars in Greater Sunrise to create wealth, which would inter alia have been wealth for Australians, but obviously substantially for the East Timorese as well. So I was all in favour of that'. Wilkinson raised Woodside executives lobbying the government strongly during the 2004 negotiations, and Downer acknowledged that he would have 'certainly had more than one, I should think three or four meetings with the CEO of Woodside and no doubt he had a couple of other people there and I would talk to them about how the negotiations were progressing'. He claimed that the 'Australian government was on Australia's side in the negotiations and we did our best to make sure that we were able to achieve our objective, which was particularly an objective in relation to the delineation of the maritime boundaries'.[43]

The emphasis on LNG trade expansion also unfolds in the contemporaneous evidence of DFAT's Penny Richards:

> The CMATS Treaty and the IUA are good deals for Australia and very much in our national interest. The treaty will promote further investment in Australia's offshore petroleum industry. Australia is currently the fifth largest exporter of LNG, with seven per cent of global volume. The development of Greater Sunrise has the potential to build significantly on Australia's standing in the global energy market.[44]

The principal beneficiary from this debacle was the Woodside-led consortium, which had been closely involved with Alexander Downer in the negotiations.⁴⁵ The bulk of the earnings from Bayu-Undan by the contractor entities have been repatriated to non-Australian recipients. Announcements by the Australian Government during negotiations between Australia and Timor-Leste were often preceded by or followed by similar announcements by Woodside Petroleum. During negotiations between Timor-Leste and Woodside Petroleum, an official from DFAT was 'seconded' to Woodside Petroleum's offices in Dili.

In August 2005, Ashton Calvert, having retired as DFAT Secretary in January of that year, was appointed to the Woodside Board. It was during Calvert's time as DFAT Secretary that instructions for the negotiations in Dili for CMATS were given. Gary Gray was similarly embedded in Woodside, having been employed as an adviser within a year of resigning as National Secretary of the Australian Labor Party. Gray went on to be a member of Woodside's executive board. Elected to the federal Parliament in 2007, Gray was Australia's Minister for Resources and Energy, for Tourism, and for Small Business in the last phase of the Gillard Government.

ConocoPhillips and Woodside continue to survive the vicissitudes of government in Canberra where they, especially Woodside, remain both influential and an instrument of foreign policy by proxy. In late 2014, with both parties locked in litigation at The Hague over the gas fields, it came as no surprise for an adjournment to be announced when Woodside signalled a possible change to its long-preferred option of a floating LNG plant.⁴⁶ Time and time again, the Timor-Leste negotiation teams were led on with Woodside 'initiatives', only to be disappointed at the table.

The conclusion regarding all of the Timor Sea suite of treaties with Timor-Leste is that Australia has always been in the ascendancy, outplaying Timor-Leste over the helium and, more recently, over reparations and restitution. The Australian Parliament was left uninformed as to the real significance of the pipeline issue for Timor-Leste *and* Australia.⁴⁷ Foreign Minister Downer did not inform Parliament of the helium that would satisfy Australia's critical commodity needs or that a pipeline landed in Timor-Leste had significant implications for the economic growth of Timor-Leste as a stable prosperous neighbour, thus meeting a vital element of Cabinet-endorsed defence policy.

By 2010 and 2011, well after the 2004 treaty negotiations that took place against assertions by the Woodside-led consortium backed by

Downer that it was not technically feasible to cross the Timor Trough by pipeline, Timor-Leste was able to commission and pay for an independent bathymetric survey of the sea-bed areas embracing the Timor Trough adjacent to the south coast. That survey debunked the claims of steep-sided undersea canyons throughout the trough,[48] and subsequent geological research has cast doubt on whether the level of tectonic activity in the Timor Trough would inhibit laying a pipeline.[49] It is for due enquiry of Australia's scientists to establish whether Geoscience Australia had access to bathymetric data that might contradict Woodside's claims concerning the steepness of the trough. The Parliament was not informed whether DFAT had sought verification from Geoscience Australia as to the reliability of the claims made by Woodside. Geoscience executives should have been aware of the claims made by Woodside and adopted by Downer.

After he retired from the Australian Parliament in 2008, former Australian Foreign Minister Downer visited Dili during independence anniversary celebrations in May 2011 and requested a meeting with Prime Minister Gusmão at which he suggested that Timor-Leste should drop its demand that any gas pipeline from the Greater Sunrise Field go to the south coast of Timor-Leste. Downer, by then a partner in an Adelaide-based consulting firm and accompanied by another staffer from that firm, reminded Gusmão that Woodside's technical and economic appreciation pointed overwhelmingly against a pipeline across the trough to Timor. It became apparent that Downer's visit included a consulting role on behalf of Woodside Petroleum, but Downer subsequently denied that he had lobbied on behalf of Woodside.[50] Downer should indicate whether the London-based foreign, political and commercial intelligence agency company Hakluyt, of which he became an affiliate, was also at relevant times a ConocoPhillips/Woodside/Royal Dutch Shell client.

17
DETERMINING MARITIME BOUNDARIES

The term 'Timor Gap' refers to the 480-kilometre-wide gap left in the 1972 sea-bed boundary-line Agreement between Australia and Indonesia. Although the Agreement defined what Indonesia and Australia considered the span of Portuguese Timor territory, being the eastern and western extremities of the joint petroleum development area (JPDA), the 1972 Indonesia–Australia Treaty expressly acknowledged that the points identified had yet to be settled 'between governments exercising sovereign rights', meaning the government of Portugal or its successor.[1] In August 1975, Australia's Ambassador to Indonesia, Richard Woolcott, urged the Department of Foreign Affairs to have Indonesia in mind as 'successor' rather than an 'independent Portuguese Timor'.[2]

The suggestion that Indonesia was to be preferred as a negotiation party was not based on any misapprehension as to the skill and persistence of Indonesia in maritime boundary delimitation talks. At relevant times Indonesia had the assistance of eminent experts and, in a later stage, a law of the sea expert as a Cabinet Minister. Australian negotiators knew that Indonesia was seeking an accommodation on an issue of long-standing significance to the Indonesian federation of some 18,000 islands of which a little more than 10% were inhabited. On 13 December 1957, Prime Minister Djuanda Kartadiwidjaja had proclaimed Indonesia's archipelagic baselines. Although this caused alarm among mercantile marine states concerned about rights of passage, Indonesia was following the Philippines, which had made a similar claim to its enclosed waters in 1955.

There was no novelty to such claims; international law pertaining to archipelagic maritime rights was well developed. Both Indonesia and the Philippines adopted a prominent role on the issue at the First Law of the Sea Conference at Geneva out of which the four 1958 Conventions evolved. Australia participated fully in the drafting and knew that neither the Philippines nor Indonesia had succeeded in developing an acceptable regime for archipelagic entitlements. Indonesia persisted at the Second Law of the Sea Conference in 1960 without securing what it wanted. It was against a history of attempts by Indonesia to secure recognition of its archipelagic baselines that maritime boundary negotiations commenced with Australia in 1969. By the time preparatory work for the Third Law of the Sea Conference started in 1973, Indonesia and Australia had reached boundary agreements in both the Arafura and Timor Seas. Thereafter, during the 1973–82 Law of the Sea Conference, Australia proved amenable to the Indonesian archipelagic claim. In due course a regime acceptable to Indonesia emerged as Article 47 of the 1982 United Nations Convention on the Law of the Sea (UNCLOS) Declaration. Indonesia ratified UNCLOS and invoked promptly Article 47 to secure recognition of her inland seas.

The Timor Gap

The points determined by Australia and Indonesia to be the Timor Gap, 9°28'S and 127°56'E (A16) and 10°28'S and 126°E (A17), are the points at which the 1972 Australia–Indonesia sea-bed boundary joined the infamous Zone of Cooperation (ZOC) in the 1989 Timor Gap Treaty, and subsequently the JPDA in the 2002 Timor Sea Treaty. It is at those two points, often wrongly called 'tri-points' or 'tri-junction' points, where the interests of Australia, Timor-Leste and Indonesia are said to converge. Any inference that the three-way meeting points have been settled is incorrect. The points where modern international law may say the three states' interests meet have not been resolved.[3]

Following the INTERFET occupation of Timor-Leste from September 1999 to February 2000, Royal Australian Navy hydrographic vessels commenced an intensive survey of the coastline and coastal waters of Timor-Leste. Attention was paid to the line out to sea from the mouth of the Moti Masin River. In 1914, various territorial boundary lines were fixed, and where relevant at river mouths, according to midstream (thalweg) practice following a long-running dispute between the Netherlands and Portugal resolved by international arbitration.[4] The intensive Australian surveying in 1999–2000 appeared opportunistic. Despite an excellent 1954 US Army map and other Australian survey data acquired during a cooperative whole-of-Indonesia military survey program, coastal surveying permitted by UNTAET continued for months and was said to be required to define the internationally agreed area of INTERFET maritime operations *vis-à-vis* Indonesian territory. Nevertheless, the surveying covered wide areas where potential territorial boundaries extended seaward into the high seas. In anticipation of future negotiations, Australia was compiling its own baseline data. In 2003–04, a Norwegian contractor to Timor-Leste undertook a survey of the Timor-Leste coastline to set provisional baselines.

The outstanding boundary delimitation issues in the Timor Sea for resolution involve Timor-Leste, Indonesia and Australia. As has been shown in the 2017 UN-sponsored conciliation between Timor-Leste and Australia, the delimitation issue has not been pursued by the parties in unison with Indonesia. Applying current methodology, a starting point for a three-state approach may have been the drawing of provisional boundary lines:

a. a provisional median boundary line between Timor-Leste and Australia as coastal states facing each other across less than 400 nautical miles in the Timor Sea;

b. a provisional median eastern lateral dividing boundary line between Timor-Leste and Indonesia to be drawn out to sea from, arguably, the Indonesia/Timor-Leste land boundary at the thalweg of the Moti Masin River to intersect with the Timor-Leste–Australia sea boundary line; and

c. a provisional median western lateral out to sea from Timor-Leste's lands-end from a point, arguably, equidistant between the Timor-Leste Isle d'Jaco and the Island of Leti on the Indonesian archipelago, out to the Timor-Leste-Australia sea boundary line.

In 1989, Indonesia and Australia agreed that the eastern and western laterals should be lines drawn on a modified equidistance principle from points on the Indonesian and Timor-Leste coastlines,[5] commencing respectively from a mid-point between the Timor-Leste Isle d'Jaco and the nearest Indonesian island, Leti, out to point A16, and, surprisingly, not from the thalweg but from a point east of the Moti Masin River mouth, out to point A17 on the agreed 1972 Timor Gap line as depicted in the map below.

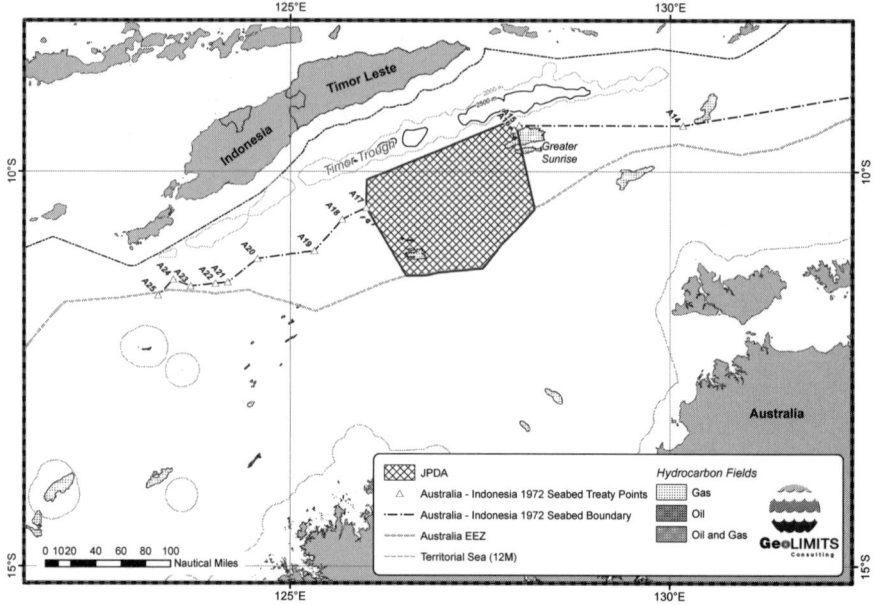

The eastern lateral made no allowance for the fact that the Indonesian island of Leti was far smaller than Timor-Leste. The laterals became the eastern and western sides of the Zone of Cooperation (ZOC) established by the illegitimate 1989 Australia–Indonesia Timor Gap Treaty and replicated in the 2002 Timor Sea Treaty as the JPDA.[6] In their opinion relating to East Timor's maritime borders (the Lowe Opinion), Vaughan Lowe, Christopher Carleton and Christopher Ward, relying upon bi-sector principles[7] projected a line from the thalweg of the Masin River to incorporate the oil and gas fields of Laminaria and Corallina to the west and, giving lesser weight to the island of Leti, skewed the line to the east and placed more of the Greater Sunrise Gas Field within Timor-Leste territory.[8]

Because the Timor Island landmass and adjacent islands facing Australia form a concave arc, lateral lines, drawn strictly in accord with equidistance, from the Indonesian archipelagic baseline and the Timor-Leste baseline points will ultimately converge.[9] The resulting 'pinch-in' effect is to Timor-Leste's detriment. No allowance was made in the

Australia–Indonesia laterals set in 1989 for the pinch-in effect, nor is explicit allowance made in the Lowe Opinion.

During the October 2002 Australian parliamentary inquiry into the making of the 2002 Timor Sea Treaty, Dean Bialek, then of the University of Melbourne and later a member of Australia's negotiation team for the CMATS Treaty, claimed that the Lowe Opinion

> fails to mention ... that Indonesia is an archipelagic state—meaning that its islands form part of its territory and it can draw base lines around the outermost points of its islands and can treat all the waters within as its own territory. You could say that makes the Indonesian archipelago, including the archipelagic waters, tantamount to a territorial continent.[10]

Indonesia has since lodged baseline data with the UN without asserting any issue associated with a maritime boundary delimitation with Timor-Leste. The application of strict equidistance principles between the relevant Indonesian baselines and Timor-Leste's provisional baselines may, in the absence of a weighing of other factors, highlight an inequity if allowance is not made either for the pinch-in effect and/or the relative size of the Timor-Leste landmass compared with the chain of Indonesian islands commencing with Leti. In evidence to the Australian Parliamentary Joint Committee on Foreign Affairs, Defence and Trade, Professor Donald Rothwell said:

> The International Court of Justice has in recent cases applied what it is calling a 'delimitation methodology' that involves three stages. The first is the establishment of a provisional delimitation line, which, in the case of adjacent coasts, will be an equidistance line, and, in the case of opposite coasts, a median line. The second is consideration as to whether there are any factors that call for an adjustment of the provisional line in order to achieve an equitable result. Finally, and after having made any adjustments to the provisional line as a result of the second stage, the International Court will seek to verify that the line does not lead to what is called an 'inequitable result' by reason of any marked disproportion between the ratio of the respective coastal lengths and the ratio between the relative maritime area of each state, by reference to the delimitation line. This process thereby ensures that there is no great disproportionality between the division of the maritime area under the limitation and the relevant coastal lengths.

> A crucial element of this methodology is the determination of the relevant area. This area will depend upon the configuration of the

relevant coasts within the geographical context, and a consideration of the seaward projections of those coasts, which will differ depending on whether a territorial sea or much larger maritime boundary, such as a continental shelf, has been delimited, and indeed the interests of any third states.[11]

In summary, to the east and west the conjunction of UN-recognised baseline data (lodged by Indonesia and Australia) and baseline data prepared for Timor-Leste in accordance with UNCLOS principles and current principles of international law may result in a moderate adjustment of both laterals such that a significant proportion of the gas and oilfields where Australian and/or JPDA licensed extraction is taking place may be identified as being within Timor-Leste sovereign territory.

Timor-Leste's position is based on established principles of international law. As noted by the International Court of Justice (ICJ) in the Tunisia–Libya Case, 'the coast of the territory of the State is the decisive factor for title to submarine areas adjacent to it'.[12] By contrast, the 1972 Treaty between Australia and Indonesia established an arbitrary boundary line based on Australia's claimed continental shelf entitlement well north of a median line. The lateral boundaries, which subsequently made up the east and west boundary lines of the JPDA, were generated from points on the occupied East Timor and the Indonesian West Timor Island landmass drawn out to points A16 and A17 on the 1972 line. Although neither the 1972 line nor the 1989 lateral lines align with modern international law embracing Article 6(1) of the 1958 Convention of the Law of the Continental Shelf and its successor, Article 15 of the 1982 UNCLOS, Australia has continued to maintain a continental shelf claim, contrary to the provisions of Article 76 of UNCLOS.

Article 76(1) provides that the continental shelf extends a distance of 200 nautical miles from the coastal baselines. As the ICJ said in the Libya/Malta Continental Shelf Case,

> [s]ince the development of the law enables a State to claim 200 miles from its coast, whatever the geological characteristics of the corresponding sea-bed and subsoil, there is no reason to ascribe any role to geological or geophysical factors within that distance either in verifying the legal title of the States concerned or proceeding to a delimitation as between their claims.[13]

Although Article 76 makes provision for a claim out to 350 nautical miles on the basis of natural prolongation, this is not applicable to the Timor-Leste/Australia circumstance as the two coasts are less than 400 nautical miles apart. In this circumstance the starting point for maritime boundary delimitation, before other factors may be taken into account, is a median line.[14]

The unredacted portions of a 1987 Australian Cabinet Submission record Australia's continued reliance on the largely discredited geomorphological argument that there are two shelves and restates Australia's and Indonesia's positions as extending 'from their respective coastlines to the bathymetric axis (the deepest point) of the Timor Trough, which is the end of their respective continental shelves in this area'.[15] The same Cabinet Submission that led to the 1989 Timor Gap Treaty with Indonesia was supported by what the submission claimed to be an assessment of the geology of the Timor Gap area by the Bureau of Mineral Resources (BMR):

1. The 'Timor Gap' area covers a portion of the northwestern continental shelf and slope of Australia opposite East Timor. Water depths range from less than 100 m in the southern part of the area to 200 m in the vicinity of the line joining the agreed boundaries either side of the Timor Gap. Water depths further north increase rapidly down the continental slope to 3000 m in the axial part of the Timor Trough.
2. It is universally accepted by geoscientists that the Australian crustal plate, with a thickness of some tens of kilometres, extends at least as far north as the bathymetric axis of the Timor Trough. BMR (and probably the majority of plate tectonic experts) believe that the weight of scientific evidence indicates that the Timor Trough *is the surface trace of an active plate convergence zone* and that the Trough marks the current northern margin of the Australian crustal plate and continental shelf.
3. The continental shelf north of the Timor Trough is considered by BMR to be part of the Asian crustal plate with which the Australian plate is slowly colliding. Thus, there are geological grounds, as well as bathymetric grounds, for concluding that the axis of the Timor Trough constitutes the dividing line between two separate continental shelves. The Timor Trough is fairly recent in geological

terms, but it has nevertheless been in existence for about 3 million years [emphasis added].[16]

The actual BMR report was not attached to the submission. The views ascribed to the BMR in the submission were contrary to BMR advice provided in February 1970 during a comprehensive survey effort: 'There appears no evidence of oceanic crust in the floor of the Timor Trough and hence no evidence to suggest there is any continental margin between the Sahul Shelf and Timor'.[17] The image projected in the Cabinet Submission of 'an active plate convergence zone' in the Timor Trough may have been scratched in a limestone cave beneath the Department of Foreign Affairs and Trade (DFAT) in Canberra millions of years ago by the submission writer's Neanderthal cousins, but is manifestly incorrect today. The claim defies the common experience of those who live along Timor's southern coast and appears to confuse the Timor Trough with the active subduction zone in the Banda Sea to the north of Timor Island. Moreover, the alleged opinion, for which no evidence was cited, of 'the majority of plate tectonic experts' is unsupported by scientific literature at the time,[18] and is certainly not the current opinion.[19] In a comprehensive review of the literature, eminent tectonic expert Audley-Charles shows that 'the Timor Trough could never have operated as a subduction ocean trench'.[20]

An issue not addressed in the 1987 Cabinet Submission is that the landmass of Indonesia could not generate entitlement to continental shelf or any maritime zone for Australia. The Indonesian coastline was not a relevant coastline from which Australian maritime boundaries are measured. The appropriate methodology was set forth five years earlier by the ICJ in the Tunisia–Libya Case, namely:

> It is not the whole of the coast of each Party which can be taken into account; the submarine extension of any part of the coast of one Party which, because of its geographic situation, cannot overlap with the extension of the coast of the other, is to be excluded from further consideration.[21]

Therefore, the delimitation between Australia and Timor-Leste in this area is a bilateral issue and does not purport to or impinge upon the established maritime entitlements of Indonesia that remain to be settled. We must assume that Australia's legal advisers knew this and were not consulted in the preparation of the 1987 Cabinet Submission. Enquiry may tell.

Avoiding a Reckoning at All Costs

As East Timor drew closer to independence, Australian policy-makers knew that the writing was on the wall regarding Australian encroachment in the Timor Sea. Once the Timorese became organised and aware, Australia's 'two shelves' would be found to be as empty as a pub with no beer. Australia knew that whatever 'historic rights' it might claim in the Timor Sea resulting from Portugal's alleged failure to protest were extinguished when Australia ratified UNCLOS. After the 1999 ballot in East Timor, Indonesia withdrew promptly from occupation of the disputed area in the Timor Sea, returning funds accrued after the ballot and abrogating the Timor Sea Treaty. Undeterred, Australia did not follow suit.

As we have seen, Australia set about a course of duplicity and intrigue in New York, Dili, Canberra and London. The Australian dimension involved an apparent belief that the Executive might place itself above the ordinary law of the land. Unable to induce the Defence Department to join its cause and already rattled by alleged defence intelligence leaks in 1999 portraying the Foreign Minister as less than candid on Indonesian military plans for a scorched-earth campaign if the vote was for independence, the government decided to 'go it alone' in an all-out effort to retain the ground it had won in 1975 with Indonesia. If Australia no longer had Indonesia as its accomplice in East Timor, it would do as much as it could to place a perceived amenable Timorese leadership into power.

While Australia's defence planners were anticipating the prospect of a new forward defence posture involving East Timor and a reconciled Indonesia, for which Gusmão, with his mutually respectful relationship with Indonesian President Abdurrahman Wahid, held the key, DFAT, in grotesque alliance with the oil majors, was developing its own candidate, while savouring the chrome and leather in corporate boardrooms. To be a loyal Australian living with and advising Xanana Gusmão in this period was to be arguing for a mutual Timor-Leste–Australian interest against sabotage by Deep State forces that knew no allegiance to the public interest of either country and no true interest in promoting regional stability through exemplary democratic leadership.

Arguably, the issue that stood between Timor-Leste and its right in international law to equitable boundary lines drawn in accordance with UNCLOS principles was the strength of the Australian public conscience concerning the reservations lodged on 22 March 2002. By 2012, there was a strong case for Timor-Leste to pursue the first case in modern times of treaty-making fraud and, if the CMATS Treaty was found to be invalid, to assess the International Unitisation Agreement for like invalidity and to secure further provisional measures against Australia and evict it from the large areas of the Timor Sea accessed by Australia pursuant to the Side-Letters to the invalid treaty.

Faced with this prospect, observers argued that Australia might be more amenable to withdrawing its March 2002 reservations and allowing the maritime boundary delimitation issue to be resolved by independent international judicial decision. Australia had consistently opposed any adjudication of the maritime boundary lines, offering an 'economic off-set' to Timor-Leste in lieu of any concession of sovereignty. Australia was in for a hiding. The case against Australia appeared indefensible and evidence of telling effect against Australia was emerging that might displace the whole suite of Timor Sea treaties. In a world first that stunned the 'Five Eyes' community, the ICJ had ordered Australia to cease intercepting not only legally privileged but all communications concerning maritime delimitation.

Surprisingly, without consultation with the leader of its international law team, Sir Elihu Lauterpacht QC, or the author, the Timor-Leste Government in Dili elected to discontinue both the Provisional Measures case before the ICJ and the arbitration over the validity of the CMATS Treaty under the aegis of the Permanent Court of Arbitration at The Hague. The ICJ orders were discharged in 2015. About the same time, a member of the Australian Labor Party (ALP) and DLA Piper alternate legal adviser to Timor-Leste, Janelle Saffin, sponsored a resolution at the ALP National Conference on 26 July 2015 that the ALP commit itself to a 'structured engagement to negotiate the settlement of maritime boundaries between Australia and Timor-Leste in accordance with international law', and to review the March 2002 reservations lodged by Australia. Timor-Leste's Ambassador to Australia, Abel Guterres, was at the Conference and publicly applauded the resolution moved by Shadow Labor Attorney-General Mark Dreyfus. If a Labor Government was elected and Australia did withdraw its reservations, Timor-Leste might have reason to evaluate the prospect of launching a successful maritime delimitation case against Australia.

It is timely to recall that in 1979, after Indonesia declared East Timor 'pacified', any prospect of the Timorese achieving independence had been crushed. Australia adopted the view that a resolution of the Timor Gap boundary now lay between itself and Indonesia as the joint occupiers of the former Portuguese sovereign sea-bed. In that false sense of security, Australia joined with the UNCLOS drafting parties to put an end by 1980, during the Third Law of the Sea Conference, to the 1958 Convention criteria on shelf prolongation and, via Articles 76 and 83, to the prospect of states in Australia's circumstance making a natural prolongation claim. By 1999, independence for Timor-Leste loomed large. Australia withdrew on 22 March 2002 from any submission to the very treaty law that it had assisted to draft. Almost certainly, under UNCLOS, Australia would have been hoist on its own petard at the ICJ were it to assert a claim to natural prolongation. By the time of the 1999 ballot, Australia knew that its morphologically inspired 'two shelves' claim might suffer the same fate as the 'rift' claim advanced for Libya in the *Libya v Malta* case. In that case the Court rejected the notion that the 'geomorphology' of the so-called 'rifts' (the Malta, Pantelleria and Linosa Troughs) could inspire any rule other than the provisions laid down in UNCLOS.[22]

The *Libya v Malta* judgement was notable for the assumption that relevant Law of the Sea provisions in UNCLOS were derived from customary law, that Articles 76 and 83 were complementary in their operation and that neither customary law nor the relevant articles in UNCLOS obligated the parties to settle on an equidistance or median line but rather that equity be done between the parties.[23] These notions were enlarged by the ICJ in the Black Sea case in 2009 into a stated methodology of approaching delimitation claims.[24] Having regard to the delimitation methodology established unanimously by the ICJ and assuming an Australian Labor Government would submit to the jurisdiction of the ICJ, the way the ICJ might approach an application by Timor-Leste could be considered with greater confidence.

First a court would have to determine the area on the global map that it will consider. The island of Timor is banana-shaped with a convex coastline facing south across the Timor Sea to Australia, approximately 281 nautical miles away. To the north, Timor Island is hemmed in by a chain of Indonesian islands within short traditional fishing distance. Issues have arisen between Timor-Leste and Indonesia in respect to access to the Oecusse enclave on the north coast. Thus, unlike either Indonesia or Australia which have large sea areas into which they may project an allowable 200-mile continental shelf and exclusive economic zone, Timor-Leste has, at best, along a large proportion of its northern coastline only a short territorial sea, barely going further in places than its 12-mile territorial sea. A court may ask whether it may deal with the application without Indonesia being a party to the action. If so, a court may be asked to look at Australia and, to the extent relevant, Indonesia, in their entire sea setting to see what nature has bestowed. However, it may not decide whether there are geo-economic factors to be taken into account until a later stage in the analysis.

The next and first methodological step is for the court to establish provisional median lines between Timor-Leste and Australia in the Timor Sea, and likewise for the laterals, if Indonesia joins or intervenes. Having applied a disproportionality test,[25] the court might re-approach the drawing of provisional median boundary lines. Using those provisional lines, the court may have regard to the ratio of the respective coastal lengths and the ratio of the respective maritime areas of the parties and adjust the provisional line.[26] Also, relevant might be: (a) the starting point, and effect of the projection seaward of lateral boundary lines from a convex coast; (b) any prior agreements between the parties; (c) geographical and geological aspects of the respective coastlines including islands, indentations, and special features; and (d) tradition and custom associated with navigation. The court may then apply a disproportionality test and examine issues that call for an equitable adjustment of the provisional median lines and, as appropriate, the Court may reset the boundary lines drawn.

Conciliation

In a move that suggested a Timor-Leste assessment that the ALP was unlikely to win government in the near future, Timor-Leste turned next to the UN Secretary-General for assistance. On 11 April 2016, pursuant to Article 298 and Annex V of UNCLOS, Timor-Leste initiated non-binding compulsory conciliation proceedings against Australia. While the Australian Foreign Minister went through the motions of expressing regret at the initiative by Timor-Leste, other indications were that Australia was unsurprised, if not relieved, by the strategy. This was the first such use of the non-binding aspect of the Convention. Each state nominated two members to the Conciliation Commission. Australia, on the advice of its Solicitor-General,[27] went through the motions of objecting to the Conciliation Commission's competence, but the objections were rejected unanimously on 19 September 2016.

On 9 January 2017, the governments of Australia and Timor-Leste and the Commission issued a joint statement announcing that Timor-Leste had notified Australia within the terms of the CMATS Treaty that it wished to terminate the treaty and that the 'phoenix' Article 12(4) of the treaty, which declared all provisions would be revived if any petroleum development took place in the treaty area, would also terminate.[28] The termination of the CMATS Treaty also restored the 2002 Timor Sea Treaty to its original terms, including its 30-year duration and, significantly, the 'supporting regulatory framework in its original form'. The poison was in the feather to the dart. The 'supporting regulatory framework' includes the production arrangements negotiated by UNTAET and Prime Minister Alkatiri. Timor-Leste's termination of CMATS represents Australia's trump card if the Greater Sunrise project proceeds. The Statement did not address the question of reparations or, explicitly, the CMATS Treaty Side-Letters and exploration permits issued thereunder by Australia. In exercising the termination provision of the CMATS Treaty, Timor-Leste accepted, implicitly, the validity of the treaty. Gone was the whole allegation that the CMATS Treaty was void *ab initio* due to treaty-making fraud. Australia was, finally, off the hook and back in business.

Close to three years had passed since Timor-Leste adjourned the arbitration on the eve of the hearing, later abandoning it. Timor-Leste now had even less time to get another source of revenue flowing as Bayu-Undan approaches depletion around 2026. The economic pressure was back on Timor-Leste. The old levers were quickly pulled in Canberra and a series of media articles appeared raising the prospect that Timor-Leste was using up its sovereign oil fund and was on borrowed time. Inexplicably, the issue of maritime boundary delimitation was to be conciliated without the protection of the ICJ order forbidding the interception of all maritime delimitation communications between the countries.

The UN Conciliation Commission held a number of hearings before adjourning to await any negotiated agreement between the parties. Procedures required the Commission to issue a report by 19 September

2017 recording any agreement(s) reached between the parties and, failing that, the Commission was obliged to issue its findings on fact and law together with recommendations. If the Commission's recommendations did not lead to a negotiated solution, further provisions of this as yet untested tract of the Convention require the parties to submit, 'by mutual consent', the unresolved boundary dispute to binding adjudication or arbitration. As we now know, Australia and Timor-Leste reached a consent agreement now termed the 2018 Maritime Boundary Treaty.

Close to eight years have passed since Timor-Leste resolved to pursue arbitration in confidential proceedings available under treaty law. Attending to the accession by Timor-Leste of vital international treaty law and awaiting, generously, the vote on Australia's quest for a seat on the Security Council took another two years. More than six further years have elapsed since Timor Leste's *démarche* to Prime Minister Gillard on 7 December 2012. In all that time, the gas, helium and condensate have flowed. Pursuant to the Side-Letters to the CMATS Treaty, Australia has issued exploration permits and there have been significant commercial shareholding shifts in the Timor Sea. Throughout, Australia clung stubbornly to an argument that an economic development formula is better for the Timorese than a line on the sea-bed. Fundamental to the Australian approach are efforts to avoid a judicial verdict and reparation payments. On 27 November 2002, when meeting Prime Minister Alkatiri at Dili, Foreign Minister Downer was recorded saying: 'We don't have to exploit the resources. They can stay there for 20, 40, 50 years. We don't like brinkmanship. We are very tough. We will not care if you give information to the media. Let me give you a tutorial in politics—not a chance'.[29]

Time and time again the leadership in Dili, almost all of whom are personally marked by the struggle for independence and, in consequence, conscious of their responsibility to lift their peoples out of poverty, have proven vulnerable to Australian pressure to get money ahead of sovereignty. The 2018 Maritime Boundary Treaty indicates that boundaries will be drawn at some stage in the future in accordance with established delimitation methodology on the basis of a trade-off by Timor-Leste of all the reparations and restitution it is due and probable acceptance of the Greater Sunrise PSCs signed by the Alkatiri Government. On a generous interpretation, Timor-Leste may be giving away something close to A$12 billion to secure boundaries it was entitled to in law.

18
TIMOR-LESTE COMPLAINS

The Timor-Leste Foreign Minister had met Prime Minister Gillard in her Parliament office on 7 December 2012 and handed her a letter from Prime Minister Gusmão, together with an *Aide-Mémoire* and requesting discussions regarding the asserted invalidity of the CMATS Treaty. It was agreed with Gillard that the issue would remain confidential between the parties. Despite this agreement between the two prime ministers, five months later Foreign Minister Bob Carr and Attorney-General Mark Dreyfus revealed to the public Timor-Leste's complaint, attributing it to 'old rumours'.[1] Their attribution could not be correct, as the information provided to Gillard had never been aired. While the Foreign Ministry's breach of the confidentiality agreement was not surprising, for some reason yet to be revealed, Australia's first law officer had joined the Foreign Minister in stonewalling the complaint and going on the offensive.

Three months after the Labor Government had been defeated in the general election of September 2013, a new Attorney-General, George Brandis QC, using powers given to ASIO to combat terrorism, authorised ASIO to conduct simultaneous search and seizure raids on the author's chambers and the home of a witness. During the search of the author's chambers, electronic data was downloaded and manipulated. Although documents taken have been returned, Timor-Leste took no steps before discharging the orders of the International Court of Justice (ICJ) to secure the return and/or deletion of all data procured during the search. Moreover, electronic data, including legally privileged correspondence with the Timor-Leste Government, on one server cannot be found. The raid occurred 24 hours after the author had left Australia for The Hague. The warrant empowered data download and included the power to conceal anything done under the warrant. Records relating to thousands of clients were laid bare in the name of powers given the Attorney to combat terrorism.

Despite ASIO's subsequent non-objection on national security grounds for a person known only as Witness K to receive a passport, Foreign Minister Bishop, using for the first time a provision in the *Passports Act* that allowed her to substitute ASIS in lieu of ASIO as a 'competent authority', denied a passport to Witness K. It emerged that this was on the advice of the then Director-General of ASIS, Nick Warner.

All lawyers, particularly those with practising certificates, are duty-bound to be vigilant in detecting signs of deceit in their instructions. The tell-tale signs of improper access to communications, which has its variant occasionally in municipal courts, cannot be ignored by international law practitioners when accepting instructions. How sure may government treaty advisers be that their instructions are not based on unlawful interception of the internal deliberations of the other party? This may be particularly important if the treaty negotiations concern existing treaty obligations and the negotiations are with that bilateral or multilateral partner. Article 26 ('*Pacta sunt servanda*') of the Vienna Convention on the Law of Treaties (VCLT) says 'Every treaty in force is binding upon the parties to it and must be performed by them in good faith'. Government lawyers holding practising certificates or as members of the Bar would do well to recall Villiger's insistence that '*Pacta sunt servanda* lies at the heart of the Convention. It applies without exception to every treaty including its annexes and appendices. The rule holds good at all stages in a treaty's life'.[2]

A common refrain by commentators is that in their sovereign international dealings 'all countries spy', so why should the circumstances of treaty-making be any different? Clearly, not the same may be said in respect of commercial dealings in the City, so where may the line be drawn? May government lawyers, particularly those holding practising

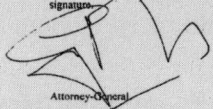

The search warrant held allegedly by the unidentified persons who entered the Collaery Law Chambers on 3 December 2013.

Timor-Leste's team at the ICJ in The Hague, 5 December 2013. From left to right: Amy McMullen, Jolan Draaisma, Sir Elihu Lauterpacht QC, Bernard Collaery.

certificates issued by professional bodies that enforce ethical standards, have one rule at home and another abroad? Is there, for instance, a qualitative difference in law, as distinct from moral turpitude, between bugging a Japanese delegation negotiating treaty issues concerned with limitations on whaling and bugging the internal deliberations of a state fiduciary during joint-venture revenue treaty negotiations?

Both customary municipal law and international law suggest not. Professor Bin Cheng identified 'good faith' as being one of the 'general principles of law recognised by civilized nations' and, as such, a principle to be applied by the ICJ, pursuant to Article 38 (1)(c) of the Statute of the ICJ.[3] Cheng declares fraud to be 'the antithesis of good faith and indeed of law, and it would be self-contradictory to admit that the effects of fraud could be recognised by law'.[4]

Good Faith and Pacta Sunt Servanda

'Good faith', as a principle, is bedrock in international law. Though the principle is found deep in early jurisprudence, it is not outmoded, as implied by those who appear to accept that all countries spy during negotiations. Robert Jennings and Arthur Watts, who steer the revision of *Oppenheim's International Law*, state: 'A principle which has … been invoked by the Court, and is of overriding importance is that of good faith. It is incorporated in Article 2 (2) of The UN Charter … The significance of this principle touches every aspect of international law'.[5] More to point for those lawyers who defend the use of espionage in treaty negotiations are the words of Professor Virally:

> [W]e cannot escape recognising that good faith is really a principle of international law, and that all actors in the international legal order are subjected to it and must endure its consequences, since good faith will serve to determine both the legal effects of their declarations and behaviour and the extent of their duties.[6]

Thirlway commenced his review of 50 years of jurisprudence at the ICJ with the principle of good faith, noting the observation that it is inextricably linked with the 'postulate', *pacta sunt servanda* (agreements must be kept).[7] A corollary of the postulate is the act of consenting to be bound that makes the agreement. Consent to an agreement must be informed and freely given and as such is, therefore, fundamental. Securing an agreement by fraud in breach of the principle of good faith is no agreement at all, and a duped party may not be bound by the agreement. Good faith is the binding substance to the willingness of the parties to enter and keep to an agreement. It 'requires respect not only for the words but also for the spirit; but to negotiate otherwise in good faith is surely not to negotiate at all'.[8]

Legal Impact of Intrusion

Whether or not treaty parties reach agreement during negotiations that have been compromised, the treaty itself is open to allegations of fraud. With respect to the CMATS Treaty, the prior declarations by the parties leave no doubt that the principle of good faith applied throughout the negotiation stages of the treaty. The Memorandum of Understanding signed by the respective Prime Ministers on 20 May 2002 contained an express undertaking by the parties to work in good faith towards a division of revenue.[9] The subsequent 2002 Timor Sea Treaty repeated this ethic and further pursued the willingness of the parties to conclude an 'equitable sharing'.[10]

By passing itself off as engaging in negotiations in good faith in accordance with prior undertakings, Australia was inducing

Timor-Leste to agree to the terms of the eventual agreement. By engaging in the sequence of unlawful actions, commencing with an unlawful common law conspiracy to defraud Timor-Leste,[11] in *jus cogens* breach of customary international law and the VCLT,[12] breaches of the Vienna Convention on Diplomatic Relations (VCDR),[13] breaches of municipal Timor-Leste laws,[14] Australia was, manifestly, in breach of both legal principle and an express undertaking to negotiate in good faith.

Whether or not agreement is reached at any bugged negotiations, the offending party has the benefit of the internal deliberations of the other party such that it might adjust its tactics accordingly. Nor is it relevant, necessarily and ultimately, whether any corruptly procured transcripts of internal deliberations of the other party assists the offending party's negotiations then or subsequently or not at all. Firstly, how may any level of admissible evidence of the effect of any eavesdropping be adjudicated? How may either party, perhaps with an entirely different government, argue *ex post facto* how it may or may not have negotiated if aware or exposed?

The United States, the United Kingdom and the Swiss delegations proposed during the drafting stage of Article 49 of the Vienna Convention that alleged fraud should be independently adjudicated; namely, that the alleged fraudulent conduct should be tested as a threshold issue. Ultimately, Article 49 was accepted unanimously by all delegations. There is, as yet, no states practice with respect to the application of Article 49. The development of procedures to introduce a threshold evidentiary step may be appropriate. Any response by an offending party to neither confirm nor deny unlawful conduct is, as much as it is an admission, an affront verging on contempt to the ICJ and a breach of the Rules of Procedure of the Permanent Court of Arbitration that enjoin all states to cooperate.

Secondly, Article 49 followed acceptance by the International Law Commission (ILC) that fraud should not be defined and the concept should evolve in practice. Clandestine eavesdropping on the deliberations of a treaty party, let alone joint-venture partner, would be a particularly repugnant breach of the principle of good faith. It appears open to assert, with reason, that proven clandestine eavesdropping on the internal deliberations of the other party vitiates, *ab initio*, the entire negotiation, irrespective of the content of the conversations captured. In which case the victim state should not have to establish injury and nor, for reasons of public policy, should the perpetrator state be permitted to argue lack of injury to the victim state and/or some other objective. Arguably, once the eavesdropping is established, both the negotiations and the outcome are irremediably tainted and any enquiry into effect moot.

Villiger cites '*Fraus omnia corrumpit.* Fraud vitiates everything. Fraud leads to a mistaken impression of reality, but unlike error ... it is the consequence of a deception by another treaty party'.[15] He says that 'Article 49 requires that, without the fraud, the other State would not have given its consent'.[16] It stands to reason that no state would conclude a treaty in the knowledge that its internal deliberations had been captured by the other state. Contributors to Dörr and Schmalenbach's commentary observe:

> The fraudulent conduct and the concomitant error must have induced the other State to conclude the treaty. Similar to Art 48 the error must accordingly have constituted an 'essential basis' of the defrauded State's consent ... The error is essential if the defrauded State would not have entered into the treaty had it known the real fact *or situation* ... The essential character of the error must be assessed against the objective yardstick of whether a third State in a similar situation would have refrained from giving its consent [emphasis added].[17]

Worldwide, in most common and civil law jurisdictions, duties, obligations and limits have been imposed on the parties to a wide category of commercial and private relationships. Within the common law and civil law jurisdictions, notions of good faith, equitable conduct and fiduciary duty have been transposed in whole or part into statutory form. For example, legislation dealing with inside trading has created new categories of criminal offences. There was a time in the mid- to late 20th century when international law and municipal (or domestic) law were regarded as somewhat separate developments. Nowadays, the infusion of international law precepts into municipal law and *vice versa* is an ongoing process.

Accepting the notion that fraud is a breach of good faith, howsoever perpetrated, a starting point is to observe that the law generally is declaratory of both the nature and the effect of fraud—hence orders for compensation, reversals of transactions, specific performance, and pecuniary and other criminal penalties. In international law, sovereign states have traditionally not been amenable to the exercise within their own jurisdiction of foreign laws, but this is changing, as exemplified in controversial foreign law enforcement measures in the as yet unratified Trans-Pacific Partnership (TPP).[18]

Nevertheless, the proscription of fraud, corruption of a representative, and coercion in the VCLT[19] is part of *ordre public international*. The provisions regulate the conduct of civilised nations upon which international order depends. In international law, fraud in treaty-making is seen, with good reason, as being at the top of the offence book—a 'capital' offence—and, in that sense, in a different category from municipal proscriptions of individual and corporate misconduct. In this context Niyungeko's observation resonates:

> It must be said that ideological considerations were not absent in all the discourse on the desirability of incorporating in the Convention specific provisions on fraud. Some delegations, in particular, were of the view that incorporating such provisions was absolutely necessary, especially to protect the Third World countries likely to fall victim to fraud on the part of western countries that have greater mastery of technology as well as more experience and expertise in diplomacy and the art of negotiation.[20]

During the drafting work of the ILC, some countries, notably, Sweden and the US, while not opposed in principle, noted that fraud in treaty-making was likely to be so rare as to question whether there needed to be separate provision in a Convention. Nevertheless, the majority of states were in favour of the provision and in the event all delegations followed suit.[21] In his report, Sir Humphrey Waldock, Special Rapporteur, had cited the ILC's earlier views: 'Fraud, when it occurs, strikes at the root of an agreement in a somewhat different way from innocent misrepresentation and error. It does not merely nullify the consent of the other party to the terms of the agreement; it destroys the whole basis of mutual confidence between the parties'.[22] Evidently, Waldock was in favour of a separate provision dealing with fraud: '"Fraud" is, as it were, an "aggravated" ground of invalidity more akin to coercion than to innocent forms of misrepresentation and mistake'.[23]

The Vienna Convention on the Law of Treaties

The work of drafting and settling the VCLT commenced in 1949, the year the author entered primary school. In 1969, some months before the author was called to the Bar at Sydney, the VCLT was laid open in Vienna for signature. The draft papers prepared over the years by the four eminent special *rapporteurs* to the ILC, Humphrey Waldock, Hersch Lauterpacht, James Brierly and Gerald Fitzmaurice, were so voluminous and illuminating that practitioners and teachers of that era, including the author's teacher, Professor Julius Stone, adopted them as substantive statements of customary international law. In consequence, few international instruments derived from customary law have such a body of extrinsic interpretive guidance as to the intention and meaning of the text than the VCLT.

Article 49 says 'If a State has been induced to conclude a treaty by the fraudulent conduct of another negotiating State, the State may invoke the fraud as invalidating its consent to be bound by the treaty'.[24] The ILC explained why a precise definition of fraud was not attempted:

> Fraud is a concept found in most systems of law, but the scope of the concept is not the same in all systems. In international law, the paucity of precedents means there is little guidance to be found either in practice or in the jurisprudence of international tribunals as to the scope to be given to the concept. In these circumstances, the Commission considered whether it should attempt to define fraud in the law of treaties … [but] concluded … that it would suffice to formulate the general concept of fraud applicable in the law of treaties and to leave its precise scope to be worked out in practice and in the decisions of international tribunals.[25]

Eminent Australian lawyers have participated in the exposition and development of international law. Successive governments in Canberra endorsed in a wide variety of statements and instruments Australia's adherence to customary international law principles. Australia also participated in and at times assumed a key role in the preparatory work of international treaty law. Relevantly, Australia endorsed principles of law and conduct enshrined in the VCLT, the VCDR and UNCLOS. Australia subsequently breached a number of those principles in its relations with Timor-Leste.

Surprisingly, Timor-Leste had not acceded to the VCLT. This was not rectified until 8 January 2013 and, since fraudulent conduct by Australia had occurred in 2004, there was no ground upon which a pleading based on Article 49 could be filed. Fortunately, the proceedings of the ILC made clear that Article 49 restated customary international law and the complaint against Australia proceeded on like ground; namely, good faith in treaty-making is a *jus cogens* element of customary international law. Relevantly, the principle that the parties to a treaty both in negotiation and performance must act in good faith is 'one of the basic principles governing the creation and performance of legal obligations'.[26]

The breach of customary international law by Australia is all the more reprehensible in light of the solemn proceedings on the morning of independence on 20 May 2002 when Prime Minister Howard and Prime Minister Alkatiri shook hands after they signed a Memorandum of Understanding recording that the parties would work 'in good faith' towards concluding a unitisation agreement for Greater Sunrise. The CMATS Treaty was the culmination of that endeavour.

On 16 December 1963, pursuant to Article 13 of the UN Charter, Australia was appointed to a UN Special Committee representative of 'the principal legal systems of the world' that would draw up a statement of principles of international law concerning friendly relations and cooperation between states.[27] A team of Australian lawyers from the Australian Attorney-General's Department and Department of External Affairs, led in part by Sir Kenneth Bailey QC, played a prominent role in developing the statement adopted by the General Assembly in 1970 as a Charter of principles, namely:

> The principles of the Charter which are embodied in this Declaration constitute basic principles of international law, and consequently appeals to all States to be guided by these principles in their international conduct and to develop their mutual relations on the basis of the strict observance of these principles.

Under the rubric that states should fulfil in good faith the obligations assumed by them, the General Assembly further proclaimed the following principles:

- Every State has the duty to fulfil in good faith the obligations assumed by it in accordance with the Charter of the United Nations.

- Every State has the duty to fulfil in good faith its obligations under the generally recognized principles and rules of international law.
- Every State has the duty to fulfil in good faith its obligations under international agreements valid under the generally recognized principles and rules of international law.[28]

The Assembly further declared that states should 'develop mutual relations on the basis of strict observance of these principles'.

In the *Nuclear Tests Case*, Australia saw fit to agitate the principle of good faith in international affairs, as reflected in the judgement of the ICJ: 'One basic principle governing the creation and performance of legal obligations, whatever their source, is the principle of good faith. Trust and confidence are inherent in international co-operation, in particular in an age where this co-operation in many fields is becoming essential'.[29]

Against this background, the role of Australia's first law officer in defending treaty-making fraud is a matter of profound concern. Much depends on who knew what and when, but the Bar Rules require reasonable diligence before allegations of impropriety or worse are levelled. Clearly, pending any judicial enquiry into Australia's activities and the advice provided to the Attorney- and/or Solicitor-General, it may be said that in relation to Timor-Leste, Australia did not live up to principles of law it helped draft and professed to support.

The Consequences

A plethora of commentators on domestic and international law relying on an almost equal number of laws, learned papers and judgements of international and municipal courts and tribunals endorse the principle that fraud practised either in the making of an agreement or in its performance may permit the offended party to claim the agreement to be void, voidable or invalidly procured. Since the misconduct by Australia during the negotiation of the CMATS Treaty went so far beyond honest behaviour as to constitute fraudulent conduct of the most palpable kind, Australia knew that the only hope of staving off the inevitable finding for the first time in modern history of treaty-making fraud and consequent invalidity of the CMATS Treaty and Side-Letters was to use any ploy to prevent the Permanent Court of Arbitration reaching a finding.

The intimidating tactics that followed, including breaching the legal professional privilege of Timor-Leste's lawyers, misleading statements relating to national security, the cancellation of Witness K's passport and ongoing refusal to grant a replacement passport, need to be weighed by police authorities to determine whether they constitute part and parcel of the original conspiracy to defraud.

The substance of the instructions given and the conduct of Australia's lawyers in the proceedings of the arbitration must also be exposed to scrutiny.[30] Any other intelligence activity aimed at preventing the exposure and prosecution of the original unlawful conduct may also be a matter for investigation.[31] Unfortunately, the prospect of a Special Prosecutor working with the Parliament in the style of enquiries conducted in Washington is remote while Australia, so far as the exploitation of the Timorese is concerned, is governed by a one-state, Liberal–Labor, commercially-oriented cabal.[32]

Few would dispute the fact that, as Timor-Leste emerged from under the yoke of Indonesian occupation, Australia acted opportunistically to continue exploitation of the Timor Sea petroleum resources. The abiding resentment of the Timorese at not securing their full sovereignty post-liberation was palpable and, for geo-strategic reasons, not in Australia's long-term national interest. Dealing with this issue in foreign policy terms required more than foreign aid and defence liaison. We have seen how, for generations, Australian foreign policy often failed to weigh the total national security implications of relations with Australia's northern neighbours. Again, with Timor-Leste, Australia has failed to weigh the ephemeral political benefit of securing for corporate shareholders ill-gotten resources, barely to the material benefit of the Australian people, with a sound and transparent foreign policy. As part of this failed foreign policy, the Howard/Downer Government, with absolutely no effective parliamentary oversight, became involved in what is now almost universally regarded in Australia as socially unacceptable behaviour towards the impoverished Timorese. If Australia continues to act as it has, this may influence other states, thereby undermining respect in international law.

19
THE UNIVERSAL RELEVANCE OF THE RULE OF LAW

The Timor-Leste story illustrates a wider malaise in Australian democracy. It makes clear that the elected Australian Parliament has little say in the machinations of the small clique of 'intelligence-fed' policy-makers supporting the Prime Minister and Foreign Minister. Cabinet members are left uninformed and there is no effective parliamentary oversight of foreign policy and intelligence. This offends the very notion of representative democracy and has resulted in repeated failure to protect Australia's real interests. The anti-communist CIA–ASIS linkage during the sell-outs of West Papua and East Timor and the perverse linkage of foreign policy and export trade throughout the governments of Bob Hawke and John Howard were not in the true interests of the Australian people.

The confessed inability of elected representatives of the Australian people, including Cabinet Ministers, to participate in Australia's foreign affairs decision-making must be remedied. Australia now faces a lonely and, to a significant extent, discredited role in the Asia-Pacific region. Australia needs policy-makers of substance. The moral integrity of politicians in the Australian Cabinet leaves a great deal to be desired, and this leads to a litmus question. Shortly put, how should the interests of the Timorese peoples be protected? Is it solely a matter of self-help for the Timorese, who may avail themselves of any legal remedies good fortune may allow? Or, should they accept that they don't need any protection? Like other post-colonial peoples, should they reconcile themselves to have missed out and simply get on with what they have left?

Has Australia's treatment of the Timorese people been such that an olive branch from the Timorese leadership during the recent UN-sponsored conciliation was an appropriate response? Does the current leadership in Timor-Leste acknowledge that the rule of law is of universal relevance and is not within a basket of choices? Offering an olive branch to an unreformed and unrepentant clique in Canberra may not have been in the interests of the rule of law and Timor-Leste's future relations with Australia.

The author has sought to examine Australia's responsibility at relevant times as a civilised nation with, as is sometimes put, the 'conscience of civilised peoples'. If Australia has acted unconscionably, should there be a remedy? If so, by what means? Much was said at the founding conferences of the United Nations in San Francisco about controlling the actions of oppressive states. Ironically, Australia adopted a prominent position arguing that the United Nations should adopt protective measures in support of emerging states.

Modern codified domestic law with extra-territorial effect may provide remedies where the misconduct falls within the global reach of prosecuting authorities, as exemplified recently by US Department of Justice enquiries into corrupt state actors in Malaysia—the very same actors DFAT was seeking to protect from exposure in court proceedings in Australia. Where codified law with extra-territorial reach is not applied against non-state actors such as petroleum corporations because the state with the capacity to prosecute will not prosecute, oppressed peoples may have to persevere with remedies available in international law against exploitative states.

The exploitation of the Timorese is a case in point. Having secured the Bayu-Undan Field in the Timor Sea during the occupation and post-liberation UNTAET years in an unequal and tainted contest, Australia set about securing the vastly more lucrative Greater Sunrise Field during the negotiation of the CMATS Treaty. Debate concerning the CMATS negotiations raises legitimate questions as to the conduct of earlier treaty negotiations. A judicial inquiry and the grant of appropriate immunities may determine the issue.

Australia's Foreign Policy Disaster

East Timor advanced into the public eye after the massacre of the investigative news team at Balibo and with it popular interest in Australian foreign policy. While East Timor has been just one casualty in the lost caravan of opportunity that has marked the tortuous route of Australian foreign policy since the Chifley Government fell in 1949, insights provided by that grim history are enduring. Complicity led to culpability in 1975 and 1999. We have seen how, with Labor given a great chance by Australian electors, the Whitlam Government seethed with discordant ambition and ended in confusion. All the while elements within the Canberra bureaucracy survive political vicissitudes, and, savouring an opportunity for the exercise of unelected ambition, secure the ear of inept and often pliable political masters. Little changed over the years in foreign policy with successive foreign ministers either falling sway to the mandarins or going their own way to their peril. Ministers, with notable exceptions such as Gareth Evans, became little but the mouthpiece of a close-knit bureaucracy as successful as ever at finding a surrogate voice to project their narrow machinations.

Criticism of Australia over East Timor is unlikely to abate until reparations are paid and sovereignty unconditionally recognised. With the 2018 Timor Sea Treaty the Timorese have again been outmanoeuvred. This may be seen in Canberra as a win. Leaving the next generation of Timorese with bitterness over exploitation is not in Australia's long-term national interest. Past negotiations between Australia and Timor-Leste have involved two long-standing leadership groups, both with much to explain to their peoples. The two-party system in Australia is said to have throttled debate and failed the Australian people. A new generation of politicians on either side of the Timor Sea may adopt a radically new outlook, but will it be too late?

After the mayhem following the 1999 ballot in Timor, which informed parties in the Defence intelligence community knew might have been suppressed if Australia had not withheld intelligence from the UN and its allies, China came into its own, supporting without hesitation UN Security Council moves and then giving practical aid in the form of agricultural equipment and police elements on the ground. Large-scale multiple aid projects followed as Dili's landscape was rebuilt, notably the Presidential Palace and the Defence and Foreign Affairs buildings. China put out early feelers, including subtle offers to Xanana Gusmão, shared with the author, and rejected.

By conniving to insert FRETILIN into power in 2002, the Australian Foreign Ministry supported Beijing's initiatives. In contrast, Gusmão had long rejected Marxist–Leninism as a form of governance. Unlike Alkatiri, Gusmão readily accepted Australian advisers and maintained a strong ideological stance on a pluralistic democracy. Prime Minister Alkatiri's leadership of FRETILIN was based on Leninist notions of party control and the very antithesis of what Gusmão had to offer. Government in Timor-Leste soon led to violence, death and disorder. That a conservative Australian Government contributed directly to this is to its eternal shame.

Australian foreign policy towards Timor-Leste remains an unmitigated disaster. Any chance of sensible Australian foreign policy sank beneath the waves of oil-greed lapping Timor's shores in the Barwick, Whitlam and Howard years and may never surface above the oil slick until the malefactors are dispersed either by trial and/or public repudiation. Australia had every chance to get to the hearts and minds of the Timorese, but the whisperers blew it as they rustled the ashes of our Australian and Timorese war dead.

A new foreign policy strategy in the Asia-Pacific region is required based on re-establishing Australia's moral standing. As with the legacy of white dealings with the first Australians, it must start with an exemplary process of recognition of past wrongs affecting East Timor, including restitution. Serving relics from the troubled Timor waters of a disgraceful era should be removed from the Australian Public Service and government funded NGO's and think-tanks. Former diplomats and intelligence personnel of integrity might be rehired to restore vision and purpose. A new foreign service must be developed with proper values instilled and competent foreign policy oversight mechanisms implemented.

ASIS and its present and past links within the Australian foreign service should be methodically reviewed. The review should include an effective process of allied agency research and positive vetting within past and current senior ranks to deal with unresolved issues. A new ASIS should be given independent statutory status and physically detached from the Foreign and Trade Ministry. ASIS operations including surrogate allied agency operations and the embedding of personnel within publicly listed corporations should be subjected to appropriate Cabinet scrutiny. Likewise, all operational activity that may substantially affect foreign and national corporate shareholder interests must be disclosed to the National Security Committee of Cabinet. Use of ASIS assets for unapproved corporate shareholder support and knowing involvement should be made specific criminal offences. These measures may cause a short-term dislocation in Australian foreign policy, but inaction is to leave Australia surrounded with a legacy of distrust and disfavour in the Asia-Pacific region—a legacy created almost entirely by secretive cabals of politicians and bureaucrats who, unchecked by any effective parliamentary scrutiny, failed so often to discern the true Australian public interest.

Notes

Preface and Acknowledgements

1 Timor-Leste is the Portuguese name for East Timor and the name adopted by the first government of the newly independent nation. In Tetum, one of Timor-Leste's two official languages, the peoples living eastwards of Dili within the districts of Manatuto, Viqueque, Bacau and Lautem referred to their country as Timor Lorosa'e (*loro* (sun) *sa'e* (easterly), in other words 'the sun rises'), and the districts west of Dili, Liquiçá, Ermera, Aileu, Ainaro, Manufahi, Cova Lima, Bobonaro, and Oecusse are known as Timor Loromonu ('the sun falls in the west'). During the resistance years much of the organised resistance used the name Timor Lorosae for East Timor, particularly in the Tetum liturgy of the Catholic Church. Throughout this text, other than in quotations and the names of publications, I have used 'East Timor' and 'Timor-Leste' in context whenever possible. For an informed commentary on Timorese socio-political identity, see David Hicks' contribution to *East-Timor: How to Build a New Nation in Southeast Asia in the 21st Century?* (Occasional paper no. 9), edited by C. Cabasset-Semedo and F. Durand, 81–94 (Bangkok: IRASEC, 2009).

2 Rachel C. Schneider, '*The Subject of Virtue: An Anthropology of Ethics and Freedom* by James Laidlaw, Cambridge: Cambridge University Press, 2014', *Religious Studies Review*, 43(1) 2017.

3 Department of Foreign Affairs, *Portuguese Timor—General*, Jakarta Embassy Papers, Part 27, 1 October 1976 to 11 February 1977 (NAA, series A10463/801/13/11/1, barcode 4185639).

4 Geoffrey C. Gunn, *Complicity in Genocide: Report to the East Timor 'Truth Commission' on International Actors* (Macau, August 2006); Clinton Fernandes, 'Ongoing Sensitivities: Australian Records about Indonesia's War Crimes in East Timor', in *Memory and Memorialization of War: Constructing Political Communities*, edited by D. Warner (Aldershot: Ashgate, 2016).

5 *Fernandes v National Archives of Australia* [2014] AATA 180; *Fernandes v National Archives of Australia* [2014] AATA 198; *National Archives of Australia v Fernandes* [2014] FCAFC 158.

6 Michael Burleigh, *Moral Combat* (London: Harper, 2010) 548.
7 A.C. Grayling, *The Challenge of Things* (London: Bloomsbury, 2015) 57.
8 Philip Allott, *Eunomia: New Order for a New World* (Oxford: Oxford University Press, 2001) 272; a former diplomat and Foreign Office lawyer, Professor Emeritus of International Law and Fellow of Trinity College, Cambridge, Allott draws on Satow's definition of diplomacy to observe that, 'Diplomacy is the application of tact and intelligence in ways which may lead to the mass murder of millions of people, the devastation of whole countries, and to social injustice of every kind locally, regionally, and globally' (Allen Roche Lecture, New College, Oxford, 2005, cited in his *Eutopia: New Philosophy and New Law for a Troubled World* (Cheltenham: Edward Elgar Publishing, 2016) 330.
9 Bernard J. Callinan, *Independent Company: The 2/2 and 2/4 Independent Companies in Portuguese Timor 1941–1943* (Melbourne: Heinemann, 1953) 203.
10 Julius Stone DCL (Oxford), SJD (Harvard), Challis Professor of International Law and Jurisprudence at the University of Sydney from 1942 to 1972.
11 Banjo Paterson, 'The Man from Snowy River', *The Bulletin*, 26 April 1890; the third stanza reads: And one was there, a stripling on a small and weedy beast, | He was something like a racehorse undersized, | With a touch of Timor pony—three parts thoroughbred at least—| And such as are by mountain horsemen prized. | He was hard and tough and wiry—just the sort that won't say die—| There was courage in his quick impatient tread; | And he bore the badge of gameness in his bright and fiery eye, | And the proud and lofty carriage of his head.

A Note on Sources and the Limitations of Archival Research
1 Geoffrey C. Gunn, *Timor Loro Sae: 500 Years* (Macau: Livros do Oriente, 1999); Clinton Fernandes, *The Independence of East Timor* (Eastbourne, UK: Sussex Academic Press, 2011); Michael Leach and Damien Kingsbury (eds), *The Politics of Timor-Leste: Democratic Consolidation after Intervention* (Studies on Southeast Asia, no. 59) (Ithaca, NY: Cornell University, Southeast Asia Program, 2013).
2 Kim McGrath, *Crossing the Line* (Carlton, Vic.: Redback, 2017) 193–197 recounts recent experiences while seeking access to certain records at the NAA.
3 Bernard Collaery, 'Creating a Just Society under Rule of Law', 1 February 2016, https://static1.squarespace.com/static/5b283d0ffcf7fd4e0101bd20/t/5b852c01562fa7a4c91d2901/1535454211207/Creating+a+Just+Society+Under+Rule+of+Law.pdf.

Introduction
1 *The Government of the Democratic Republic of Timor-Leste and the Government of Australia*, Permanent Court of Arbitration Case No. 2016-10, Transcript of Opening Session, 29 August 2016, 99 (Garry Quinlan for Australia).
2 Peter Heydon, *Quiet Decision: A Study of George Foster Pearce* (Manchester: Manchester University Press, 1965) 231.

3 Ibid., 59.
4 K.M. Wilson, 'The Anglo-Japanese Alliance of August 1905 and the Defending of India: A Case of the Worst Scenario', *Journal of Imperial and Commonwealth History*, 21(2) (1993) 334–356; for an amusing account of Hughes' contribution at the Peace Conference, see Margaret Macmillan, *Paris 1919* (New York: Random House, 2003) 44–45, 98, 101–105.
5 Michael Fullilove, *Rendezvous with Destiny* (Sydney: Penguin, 2013).
6 Conclusions of a Meeting of the War Cabinet held at 10 Downing Street London (15 June 1943) 89, [139] (NA (UK), CAB 65/34/39).
7 Outside tetum-speaking urban Dili, the Mambai people are the next largest ethnic group in Timor-Leste. Termed the 'Maubere' people by the Portuguese, Mambai speakers, some of whom adopt the 'Mau' diminutive, were often outspoken leaders of resistance during the Portuguese administration and the Indonesian occupation. After 1974, FRETILIN spokesman José Ramos-Horta commenced portraying the call to arms as a call across the political divide, a call from 'country', a call from the 'Maubere'. After his split from FRETILIN in March 1986, and his leadership of a non-political armed resistance, FALINTIL, Xanana Gusmão founded in 1988, the National Council of Maubere Resistance (CNRM) which merged in 1998 into the Conselho Nacional da Resistência Timorense (CNRT).
8 Geoffrey C. Gunn, *Timor Loro Sae: 500 Years* (Macau: Livros do Oriente, 1999) 11–12.
9 *Principles, which should guide members in determining whether or not an obligation exists to transmit the information called for under Article 73(e) of the Charter*, GA Resolution 1541(XV), UN GAOR, 948th plen. mtg, UN Doc A/RES/1541(XV) (15 December 1960). The UN General Assembly Resolution was carried by the smaller states. Ironically, the voting reflected the position of the occupied Iron Curtain states, with the USSR and entire Eastern bloc, including Albania, abstaining. Likewise, the UK, US, France, Republic of China (ROC), Australia and New Zealand abstained, while Portugal and Spain joined the minority voting against.
10 *Non-compliance of the Government of Portugal with Chapter XI of the Charter of the United Nations and with the General Assembly Resolution 1542 (XV)*, GA Resolution 1699(XVI), UN GAOR, 1083rd plen. mtg (19 December 1961).
11 *Territories under Portuguese Administration*, GA Resolution 1807(XVII), UN GAOR, 1194th plen mtg (14 December 1962).
12 Letter PCL 35/1 from UK High Commissioner G. Kimber to Secretary to the Australian Prime Minister's Department, E.J. Bunting, 15 January 1963 (NAA, series A4940, C3739).
13 Commonwealth, Minute Decision No. 632, Without Memorandum—Indonesia—Quadripartite Talks, Cabinet, 5 February 1963, 3, [4] (NAA, series A4940, C3739).
14 Cabinet Minute, Decision No. 630, Canberra, 5 February 1963 (NAA, series A4940, C3725).
15 Minister for Defence Athol Townley, Submission No. 552 to Cabinet, Australia's Strategic Position, 6 February 1963, [19] (NAA, series A5819, volume 14).

16 Commonwealth, Submission No. 575 to Cabinet, Portuguese Timor and the North Borneo Territories, 21 February 1963, [12] (NAA, series A4940, C3725).
17 Commonwealth, Submission No. 575, 21 February 1963, [15]. For a comprehensive account of this period of multilateral talks concerning the future of Portuguese Timor, see Nicholas Tarling, *Britain and Portuguese Timor* (Clayton, Vic.: Monash University Publishing, 2013) 148–167.
18 Commonwealth, Submission No. 575, 21 February 1963, [2]; David Fairbairn, C.E. Barnes and B.M. Snedden, Submission No. 1165 to Cabinet, Off-Shore Petroleum Legislation to Give Effect to Joint Commonwealth–State Legislative Arrangements, 25 November 1965. Prime Minister's Dept, Offshore Minerals—Commonwealth/State Discussions (NAA, series A4940, C3945).
19 R. Whitworth, *A Marine Geophysical Survey of the Northwest Continental Shelf of Australia 1968 (A Summary)* (Record No. 1969/137) (Canberra: Bureau of Mineral Resources, Geology and Geophysics, 1969); B.F. Jones, *Timor Sea Gravity, Magnetic and Seismic Survey 1967* (Record No. 1968/132 and 1969/40) (Canberra: Bureau of Mineral Resources, Geology and Geophysics, 1968–1969).
20 David Fairbairn, C.E. Barnes and B.M. Snedden, Submission No. 1165 to Cabinet, 25 November 1965, [25].
21 The island of Timor is asserted in most scientific literature to be riding northwards on the Australian Plate (also known as the Australian Continental Shelf) as the Plate descends under the Asian Plate creating a subduction zone to the north of the island. Thus, it is argued, Timor shares the Australian Continental Shelf with Australia. Australia has argued to the contrary that the continental shelf ends to the south of Timor leaving a trench between two separate shelves—referred to as the 'two shelves' argument.
22 *Questions of Territories under Portuguese Administration*, GA Resolution 3113(XXVIII), UN GAOR, 2198th plen mtg, 12 December 1973. Australia supported the resolution, which was opposed by the US, UK, France, Portugal, Brazil, Spain, Belgium, Bolivia and South Africa.
23 *Questions of Territories under Portuguese Administration*, GA Resolution 3113(XXVIII) 12 December 1973.
24 Heike Krieger (ed.), *East Timor and the International Community: Basic Documents* (Cambridge: Cambridge University Press, 2011) 34–36; *Council of the Revolution Constitutional Law* N. 7/75, 17 July 1975, Art. 1.
25 Treaty on the Zone of Cooperation in an Area between the Indonesian Province of East Timor and the Northern Territory, Timor-Leste–Northern Territory, signed 11 December 1989, 1654 UNTS 105 (entered into force 9 February 1991).
26 *Case concerning East Timor (Portugal v Australia)* (1965) ICJ Rep 90.
27 Ibid., 105, [34].
28 Timor Sea Treaty between the Government of East Timor and the Government of Australia, Timor-Leste–Australia, signed 20 May 2002, 2258 UNTS 3 (entered into force 2 April 2003).

29 A National Council of Revolutionary Resistance (Conselho Revolucionário da Resistência Nacional (CRRN)) was established with Gusmão as President. The external delegation of FRETILIN based in Lisbon continued to liaise with the CRRN. Gusmão remained Commander-in-Chief of FALINTIL.

30 Treaty between Australia and the Democratic Republic of Timor-Leste on Certain Maritime Arrangements in the Timor Sea, Australia–Timor-Leste, signed 12 January 2006, 2483 UNTS 359 (entered into force 27 June 2006).

1 The Atlantic Charter—'Whither Thou Goest'

1 For an account of the meeting, see Carlo D'Este, *Warlord: A Life of Churchill at War, 1874–1945* (London: Allen Lane, 2009) 575–578. Twenty-eight nations subscribed to the Charter, the full text of which is available at https://history.state.gov/historicaldocuments/frus1941v01/d372.

2 Hersch Lauterpacht, *An International Bill of the Rights of Man* (1945) (Oxford: Oxford University Press, 2013) 6, fn 3.

3 David Dilks (ed.), *The Diaries of Sir Alexander Cadogan 1938–1945* (New York: Putnam, 1971) 379.

4 Sumner Welles, *The Time for Decision* (New York: Harper, 1944) 175–176.

5 Benjamin Welles, *Sumner Welles—FDR's Global Strategist* (New York: Palgrave Macmillan, 1997) 304.

6 Elliott Roosevelt, *As He Saw It* (New York: Duell, Sloan and Pearce, 1946).

7 Winston S. Churchill, *The Grand Alliance* (Boston: Houghton Mifflin, 1950) 433.

8 Welles, *Sumner Welles*, 1997, 304.

9 Ibid., 304–307.

10 Oona A. Hathaway and Scott J. Shapiro in *The Internationalists and their Plan to Outlaw War* (London: Allen Lane, 2017) 189–191 note a textual similarity between the Charter, the Stimson Doctrine (of non-recognition, enunciated by the US in 1932) and the Welles Declaration of 23 July 1940 concerning the Soviet annexation of Estonia, Latvia and Lithuania.

11 Sumner Welles, *The World of the Four Freedoms* (London: Hutchinson, 1943).

12 War Cabinet Meetings between Mr Churchill and President Roosevelt, Joint Declaration of Peace Aims (Atlantic Charter), Cmd 6321, Cable code "Tudor", No. 15, dispatched by Prime Minister Churchill at 1:50 pm on 11 August 1941 to Lord Privy Seal (Attlee), received at 12:40 am on 12 August 1941 (NA (UK), Records of the Cabinet Office, CAB 21/4005).

13 War Cabinet Meetings between Mr Churchill and President Roosevelt, Joint Declaration of Peace Aims (Atlantic Charter), Cmd 6321, Cable code "Tudor", No. 16, dispatched at 1:51 pm on 11 August 1941, received at 10:26 am on 12 August 1941 (NA (UK), CAB 21/4005).

14 Churchill, 1950, 446–448.

15 War Cabinet Meetings between Mr Churchill and President Roosevelt, Joint Declaration of Peace Aims (Atlantic Charter), Cmd 6321, Cable code "Abbey", No. 35, dispatched at 1:41 pm on 12 August 1941 (NA (UK), CAB 21/4005).

16 War Cabinet Meetings between Mr Churchill and President Roosevelt, Joint Declaration of Peace Aims (Atlantic Charter), Cmd 6321, Cable code

"Tudor", No. 20, dispatched at 1:03 am on 12 August 1941, received at 7:35 am on 12 August 1941 (NA (UK), CAB 21/4005).
17 Cablegram from UK Secretary of State for Dominion Affairs to Robert Menzies, Prime Minister of Australia, 12 August 1941 at 1:24 pm (NAA, series A5954, 575/3, barcode 650464).
18 Welles, *Sumner Welles*, 1997, 30.
19 Joseph Lash, *Roosevelt and Churchill 1939–1941* (New York: Norton, 1976) 398–399.
20 Nicklaus Thomas-Symonds, *Attlee: A Life in Politics* (London: I.B. Tauris, 2012).
21 Records of the Cabinet Office, Text of The Lord Privy Seal's Broadcast on 14 August 1941, 94–95 (NA (UK), CAB 65/19).
22 Michael Jago, *Clement Attlee: The Inevitable Prime Minister* (London: Biteback, 2014) 125.
23 D'Este, 2009, 569.
24 Dilks, 1971, 348.
25 *An Act to Promote the Defense of the United States*, known as the *Lend-Lease Act 1941*, signed into law by President Roosevelt on 11 March 1941.
26 'President Roosevelt's Message to Congress on the Atlantic Charter', 21 August 1941, available at http://avalon.law.yale.edu/wwii/atcmess.asp.
27 Secret Cablegram from Robert Menzies, Australian Prime Minister, to Winston Churchill, United Kingdom Prime Minister, 'Atlantic Charter', Department of Defence Co-ordination, 8 August 1941 (NAA, series A5954, 575/3, barcode 650464); Commonwealth, *Parliamentary Debates*, House of Representatives, 20 August 1941 (Robert Menzies). Churchill cabled Menzies to inform him of the forthcoming meeting with Roosevelt. Menzies was seeking a warning to Japan by the US and welcomed the meeting.
28 United Kingdom, *Parliamentary Debates*, House of Commons, 9 September 1941, Vol. 374, ser 5, col 67–156.
29 Ibid., 14 July 1943, Vol. 391, cc. 189–90, col 46.
30 George T. McJimsey, *Harry Hopkins: Ally of the Poor, Defender of Democracy* (Cambridge, MA: Harvard University Press, 1987) 305.
31 M. Stanton Evans and Herbert Romerstein, *Stalin's Secret Agents: The Subversion of Roosevelt's Government* (New York: Threshold Editions, 2012) 118; see also Bill McIlvaine, 'Harry Hopkins, Franklin D. Roosevelt's Deputy President', *American History Magazine*, April 2000.
32 Max Hastings, *The Secret War: Spies, Codes and Guerrillas 1939–1945* (London: HarperCollins, 2015) 377.
33 I.M. Maiskii, *The Maisky Diaries: Red Ambassador to the Court of St James's 1932–1943*, edited by Gabriel Gorodetsky (New Haven: Yale University Press, 2015) 381.
34 David M. Kennedy, *Freedom from Fear: The American People in Depression and War 1929–1945* (Oxford: Oxford University Press, 1999) 496.
35 Dept of Defence Co-ordination, Cablegram 'Atlantic Charter' from UK Prime Minister Winston Churchill to British Embassy, Moscow, 14 August 1941 (NAA, series A5954, 575/3, barcode 650464), containing text of

message to Stalin to be delivered jointly by British and US Ambassadors on 16 August 1941.
36 Application of the Atlantic Charter to India (NA (UK), PREM 4/45/6). Burma was already in pro-independence turmoil. Reaction in Rangoon to the Charter sentiments led Churchill to invite Burma's Prime Minister U Saw to London on 18 October 1941, which achieved little. En route, U Saw visited the Japanese Consul in Lisbon seeking Japanese support to oust the British. After the Consul's report to Tokyo was decrypted U Saw and his party were arrested and interned in East Africa for the duration of the war. U Saw was executed in 1947 after being found guilty of a lead role in the assassination of his rival Aung San and Cabinet colleagues (Kin Oung, *Eliminate the Elite* (Randwick, NSW: p3 Design, 2011) 37–38 and 109).
37 Julius Stone, *The Atlantic Charter: New Worlds for Old* (Sydney: Angus & Robertson, 1943) 147.
38 Important Declarations and Agreements (NAA, series 5954, 1340/7, barcode 655535).
39 F.D. Roosevelt, Press Conference at Washington, 27 October 1942, available at http://www.fdrlibrary.marist.edu/_resources/images/pc/pc0139.pdf/.
40 Commonwealth, *Parliamentary Debates*, House of Representatives, 3 September 1942, 82 (H.V. Evatt).
41 F.D. Roosevelt, 'Address of the President of the United States', *Congressional Record* (House), 77th Congress, 6 January 1941, 46–47: 'We look forward to a world founded upon four essential human freedoms. The first is freedom of speech and expression everywhere in the world. The second is freedom of every person to worship God in his own way everywhere in the world. The third is freedom from want ... everywhere in the world. The fourth is freedom from fear ... anywhere in the world'.
42 Commonwealth, *Parliamentary Debates*, House of Representatives, 3 September 1942, 83 (H.V. Evatt).
43 Stuart Macintyre, *Australia's Boldest Experiment: War and Reconstruction in the 1940s* (Sydney: NewSouth Publishing, 2015) 253–272.
44 War Cabinet Minutes, W.M. (43) 4th Meeting, 7 January 1943 (NA (UK), CAB 195/2) 50.
45 *Diaries of Prime Minister William Lyon Mackenzie King, MG26–J13*, 15 April 1942, 315, available at http://www.bac-lac.gc.ca/eng/discover/politics-government/prime-ministers/william-lyon-mackenzie-king/Pages/item.aspx?IdNumber=24031.
46 War Cabinet Minutes, W.M. (43) 4th Meeting, 7 January 1943 (NA (UK), CAB 195/2) 49.
47 Ibid., 52. The 'redefinition' of the Charter Churchill refers to is the circulation by direction of the Prime Minister on 4 November 1942 to the War Cabinet of the text of a Statement made by Churchill in the House of Commons on 9 September 1941 following his return from meeting with Roosevelt at Placentia Bay.
48 Stone, 1943, 144–145.
49 Lauterpacht, 2013, 85.

50 Joost Coté, 'The Indisch Dutch in Post-War Australia', *Tijdschrift Voor Sociale en Economische Geschiedenis*, 7 (2) (2010) 103–125, available at https://www.tseg.nl/articles/abstract/10.18352/tseg.378/.
51 R.M. Douglas, *Orderly and Humane: The Expulsion of the Germans after the Second World War* (New Haven: Yale University Press, 2012) 80 and 177, evidencing that Attlee's view was not always shared by British occupying forces; for further analysis, see Keith Lowe, *Savage Continent: Europe in the Aftermath of World War II* (London: Viking, 2012) xv, 230–248.
52 United Kingdom, *Parliamentary Debates*, House of Commons, 23 February 1944, Vol. 397, col. 937.
53 Quoted in Kylie Tennant, *Evatt: Politics and Justice* (Sydney: Angus & Robertson, 1970) 172.
54 *Documents on Australian Foreign Policy 1937–49* (Canberra: AGPS, 1993) Document 47, External Affairs Office, London to Department of External Affairs, 31 July 1946, 83–90.
55 United Kingdom, *Parliamentary Debates*, House of Commons, 8 July 1954, Vol. 529, cc. 179–180W.

2 The Allies, Australia and Portuguese Timor

1 *Documents on Australian Foreign Policy 1937–49*. Vol. II (Canberra: AGPS, 1976) Document 148.
2 Ibid., Documents 242, 249, 259 and 309.
3 Carl Bridge (ed.), *A Delicate Mission: The Washington Diaries of R.G. Casey 1940–42* (Canberra: National Library of Australia, 2008) 44.
4 James Bradley, *The China Mirage* (New York: Little Brown, 2015) 388–389, 393–394.
5 Memorandum from Robert P. Patterson, Deputy President, to Henry L. Stimson, Secretary of War, 18 July 1941, cited in Bradley, 2015, 389, fn 41.
6 Bradley, 2015, 390–391.
7 Presidential Executive Order 8832, cited in David M. Kennedy, *Freedom from Fear: The American People in Depression and War, 1929–1945* (New York: Oxford University Press, 1999). Kennedy at 510–511 sums up the differing policy positions, noting that the US Ambassador to Japan recorded in his diary after the embargo was announced, 'Facilis descensus averni est [The descent into hell is easy]', 510–511.
8 Bradley, 2015, 390, 401–402.
9 Bridge, 2008, 84–85.
10 David Dilks (ed.), *The Diaries of Sir Alexander Cadogan 1938–1945* (New York: Putnam, 1971) 394.
11 Bridge, 2008, 77.
12 Bradley, 2015, 390, 414–419.
13 *Documents on Australian Foreign Policy 1937–49*. Vol. V (Canberra: AGPS, 1982) Document 16, Cablegram from Prime Minister R.G Menzies to Lord Cranborne, UK Secretary of State for Dominion Affairs, 25 July 1941, 24.
14 Ibid., Document 18, Cablegram from R.G. Casey, Australian Ambassador, Washington, to Dept of External Affairs, 26 July 1941, 26.

15 Ibid., Document 28, Cablegram from R.G. Casey, Australian Ambassador, Washington, to Dept of External Affairs, 3 August 1941, 47.
16 Dilks, 1971, 398.
17 Richard J, Aldrich, *Intelligence and the War Against Japan* (Cambridge: Cambridge University Press, 2000) 46.
18 Sir John Kennedy, *The Business of War* (London: Hutchinson, 1957) 196.
19 Aldrich, 2000, 46; see also Craig L. Symonds, *World War II at Sea* (New York: OUP, 2018) 128. A more detailed account from Axis records is at http://www.forcez-survivors.org.uk/automedon.html. Bryan Perrett (*Why the Japanese Lost* (Pen & Sword, Military, 2014)) says that the *Atlantis* under the command of Captain Bernhard Rogge had secured the British Merchant Navy cipher and call-signs from another British vessel and used those to plot the *Automedon*'s route and that forwarding the report by surface mail was inexplicable as the Imperial Flying Boat service to Singapore was available.
20 Aldrich, 2000, 41.
21 *Documents on Australian Foreign Policy 1937–49*. Vol. V, Document 62, Cablegram from Prime Minister A.W. Fadden to Lord Cranborne, UK Secretary of State for Dominion Affairs, 8 September 1941.
22 Ibid., Document 82, Cablegram from Lord Cranborne, UK Secretary of State for Dominion Affairs, to Commonwealth Government, 13 October 1941.
23 Defence Committee, Minute No. 128/1948, Oil Concessions in Portuguese Timor—Introduction (10 June 1948) (NAA, series A2031/1, control 128/1948, and NA (UK), PRO F7170/1290/23 and PRO F7169/1299/23).
24 Letter from Sir Ronald Campbell, UK Ambassador, Lisbon, to Sir Anthony Eden, Secretary of State for Foreign Affairs, 8 December 1941 enclosing *Aide-Mémoire* to Secretary-General, Ministry of Foreign Affairs, Lisbon, 3 December 1941 (NA (UK), Foreign Office, Far-Eastern, Portuguese Timor–Japanese Activities, FO371/27797, F13762, folios 88–89).
25 *Documents on Australian Foreign Policy 1937–49*, Vol. V, Document 153, Cablegram Commonwealth Government to Lord Cranborne, UK Secretary of State for Dominion Affairs, 2 December 1941, 261.
26 Memorandum from Foreign Office to Portuguese Embassy, London, 11 December 1941 (NA (UK), Foreign Office, Far-Eastern, Portuguese Timor–Japanese Activities, FO371/27797).
27 Letter from W.L.M. Dunlop, Far Eastern Desk, to Captain J.J.W. Herbertson, Air Ministry, 10 December 1941 (NA (UK), Foreign Office, Far-Eastern, Portuguese Timor–Japanese Activities, FO371/27797, F13468, folios 12–13).
28 Telegram from Duff Cooper, Resident Cabinet Minister, Singapore, to War Cabinet Offices, 10 December 1941 (NA (UK), Foreign Office, Far-Eastern, Portuguese Timor–Japanese Activities, FO371/27797, 13517, folios 16 and 26). The 'Japanese in Portuguese Timor' were civilian trade and other personnel believed to be fifth-column informants.
29 Telegram from Foreign Office to Duff Cooper, Resident Cabinet Minister, Singapore, 11 December 1941 (NA (UK), Foreign Office, Far-Eastern,

Portuguese Timor–Japanese Activities, FO371/27797, F13517/222/61, folio 28).
30 Telegram from Dominions Office to Australia, 10 December 1941 (NA (UK), Foreign Office, Far-Eastern, Portuguese Timor–Japanese Activities, FO371/27797, F13576, folio 34). Meanwhile, Portuguese Ambassador Armindo Monteiro had reported to Salazar that Britain was anxious to ensure that Portugal had taken steps to strengthen defences in Macau, Timor and Africa (Letter from Monteiro, London, to Salazar, 6 November 1941 (Arquivo Nacional (Portugal) AOS/CLB/T-1, pasta 1, Pt 1 AS)).
31 Oral advice on 11 December 1941 by Sir Orme Sargent, UK Foreign Office, to Monteiro, Portuguese Embassy, London (NA (UK), FO371/27797, see folio 42 and folios 35–37).
32 Telegram from Sir R. Campbell, Lisbon, to UK Foreign Office, 12 December 1941 (NA (UK), Foreign Office, Far-Eastern, Portuguese Timor–Japanese Activities, FO371/27797, F13607, folio 56).
33 Telegram 2133 from UK Foreign Office to Lisbon, 18 December 1941 (NA (UK), Foreign Office, Far-Eastern, Portuguese Timor–Japanese Activities, FCO371/27797, folio 156).
34 Bernard Callinan, *Independent Company* (Melbourne: Heinemann Australia, 1953) 13.
35 Protest note from M. d'A. Ferreira de Carvalho to Lt. Col. W.W. Leggatt and Lt. Col. W. Detiger, 17 December 1941 (NAA, series A816, 19/301/820A; translation at 142 NA (UK), FO371/49494, F14044/222/61 reads: 'The Governor of the Colony of Portuguese Timor emphatically protests against aggression, absolutely contrary to the principles of law, of which this part of Portuguese territory is a victim at the instance of Netherlands and Australian forces who state they are acting according to instructions received from the Governor of the Netherlands Indies with the agreement of the Governor-General of the Commonwealth of Australia'.
36 Note Verbale from UK Foreign Office to Portuguese Embassy in London, 15 December 1941 (NA (UK), FO371/27798, folio 9).
37 Telegram from M.d'A. Ferreira de Carvalho, Portuguese Governor, to A. de Oliveira Salazar, Portuguese Prime Minister, 3 December 1941 (Arquivo Nacional (Portugal) AOS/CLB/T-1, Pasta 1, Pt 20, AS).
38 Telegram from Sir R. Campbell, Lisbon, to UK Foreign Office, 25 February 1942 (NA (UK), General File No. 2, FO371/27798 and FO371/31732).
39 Report by Dr Luis Teixeira de Sampaio, Portuguese Secretary-General for Foreign Affairs, 19 February 1942 (Arquivo Nacional (Portugal) AOS/CLB/T-2, Pasta 4, Pts. 5 and 10, AS).
40 Telegram 6992 from UK Foreign Office to Lord Halifax, British Ambassador, Washington, 17 December 1941 (NA (UK), FCO371/27797).
41 Foreign Office Memorandum and notation from J.C. Sterndale Bennett to Sir Orme Sargent, 18 July 1941 (NA (UK), FO371/27798, F14050, 157).
42 Dilks, 1971, 425 (diary entry of 31 December 1941).
43 Telegram 1722 from Sir R. Campbell, Lisbon, to UK Foreign Office, 20 December 1941 (NA (UK), Portugal File No. 50, FO371/49494, F14004/721/61).

44 Ibid., F1408.
45 *Documents on Australian Foreign Policy 1937–49*, Vol. V, Document 214, Cablegram from John Curtin, Prime Minister, to R.G. Casey, Minister to the United States, 23 December 1941, 341.
46 Ibid., 339.
47 Cablegram 831 from John Curtin, Australian Prime Minister, to Lord Cranborne, UK Secretary of State for Dominion Affairs, 26 December 1941 (NAA, Timor (Portuguese), series A981).
48 UK Foreign Office Memorandum and notations from J.C. Sterndale Bennett to Lt. Col. Archibald M.O., 10 War Office, 19 February 1942 (NA (UK), FO371/27798, F1857/C, 29).
49 Cablegram from John Curtin, Prime Minister, to W.S. Churchill, Prime Minister, 24 January 1942 (NA (UK), WP (42) 34, CAB 66/21). Within three weeks, after hard fighting in Malaya and Singapore, 14,972 surviving Australian troops went into a brutal captivity in which about half perished. (The author was named at his father's request after Sgt Bernard Stanislaus McMahon, 2/30th Battalion, C Company, 8th Australian Division, who survived a labour camp in Thailand.)
50 Telegram from UK War Office to Supreme Commander South West Pacific, 26 January 1942 (NA (UK) CAB 121/772, folio 81).
51 Callinan, 1953, xxviii, 39.
52 *Documents on Australian Foreign Policy 1937–49*, Vol. V, Document 337, Cablegram from General Sir Archibald Wavell to UK War Office copied to Commonwealth Government, 17 February 1942, 529.
53 Callinan, 1953, 211.
54 *Documents on Australian Foreign Policy 1937–49*, Vol. V, Document 527, Cablegram from Commonwealth Government to Clement Attlee, UK Secretary of State for Dominion Affairs, 18 June 1942, 849.
55 Ibid.
56 D. Clayton James, *The Years of MacArthur*, Vol. 2 (Boston: Houghton Mifflin, 1975) 185–186; see also Walter R. Borneman, *MacArthur at War* (New York: Little Brown, 2016) 215.
57 For an excellent account, see Paul Cleary, *The Men Who Came Out of the Ground* (Sydney: Hachette Australia, 2010).
58 UK Foreign Office Memorandum and notations from J.C. Sterndale Bennett to Lt. Col. Archibald M.O., War Office, 19 February 1942 (NA (UK) FO371/27798, F1857/C, 29).
59 Andrew Roberts, *Churchill: Walking with Destiny* (London: Allen Lane, 2018), notes that General John Kennedy, Director of Operations at the War Office, recorded in his diary, after hearing Churchill's self-reproach for underestimating the Japanese during a broadcast on 15 February 1942 following the fall of Singapore, that Churchill was 'so lacking in strategical knowledge and in judgement despite his other great qualities'. Sir John Kennedy did not draw specifically upon this record in his 1957 memoir *The Business of War*, although he remained critical of Churchill, see note 18 of this chapter.
60 *Documents on Australian Foreign Policy 1937–49*, Vol. V, Document 339, Cablegram from A.T. Stirling, Australian High Commissioner, London (on

behalf of Sir Stafford Cripps), to Dr H.V. Evatt, Minister for External Affairs, 17 February 1942.
61 Ibid., Document 338, Cablegram from S.M. Bruce, Australian High Commissioner, London, to John Curtin, Australian Prime Minister, 17 February 1942.
62 Jonathan Schneer, *Ministers at War* (London: Oneworld, 2015) 122–128.
63 *Documents on Australian Foreign Policy 1937–49*, Vol. V, Document 359, Letter from Dr H.V. Evatt, Minister for External Affairs, to J.M. McMillan, Third Secretary Australian Legation, Washington, for Mr Justice Frankfurter, 22 February 1942 (to be deciphered by McMillan alone and handed by him to Mr Justice Frankfurter alone). In this controversial letter Evatt is critical of Casey's advocacy and accuses Australia's Special Representative in London, Sir Earle Page, of disobeying his instructions to oppose the deployment of Australian troops to India and Burma.
64 Gavin Long, *Greece, Crete and Syria* (Australia in the War of 1939–1945, Series 1, Army, v. 1) (Canberra: Australian War Memorial, 1953) 523–524.
65 Ibid., 326–327.
66 Estimates vary but church records suggest that up to about 40,000 Timorese perished during the Japanese occupation.
67 J.R. Kerr, *Matters for Judgement* (Melbourne: Macmillan, 1978) 97.
68 Winston Churchill, 'Prime Minister's Statement, House of Lords', 9 September 1941; United Kingdom, *Parliamentary Debates*, House of Lords, 3 December 1942, Vol. 125, col 374–421; see also letter from Sir E.E. Bridges, Cabinet Secretary, to Dominions Office, 4 November 1942, 'Extract from Prime Minister's Statement of 9 September 1941' (NA (UK), CAB 66/30/36).
69 Commonwealth, *Parliamentary Debates*, House of Representatives, 3 September 1942, 1339 (H.V. Evatt).
70 Based on a series of royal treaties, the earliest of which dates to 1294; the current alliance commences with the Anglo-Portuguese Treaty of 1373, ratified by the Treaty of Windsor on 9 May 1386.
71 Arthur Bryant, *The Turn of the Tide 1939–1943* (New York: Collins, 1957) 665–666.
72 Dilks, 1971, 532.
73 War Cabinet Minutes, WM (43), 76th Meeting, 24 May 1943 at 3 pm, *Operation LIFEBELT* (NA (UK), CAB 195/2) 204–206.
74 Secret Cablegram from H.V. Evatt, Minister for External Affairs, to John Curtin, Australian Prime Minister, 1 July 1943 (NAA, series A4764, 4, barcode 238608) 3.
75 Secret Cablegram, 1 July 1943 (NAA, series A4764, 4, barcode 238608).
76 Commonwealth, *Parliamentary Debates*, House of Representatives, 26 March 1946, 625–626 (H.V. Evatt).
77 Conclusions of a Meeting of the War Cabinet held at 10 Downing Street, 15 June 1943, 89, [139] (NA (UK), CAB 65/34/39). The War Cabinet transcripts reveal strong opposition in principle to invading the territory of an ally; see War Cabinet Minutes, W.M. (42) 156th Meeting, W.M. (43) 99th Meeting, W.M. (43) 74th Meeting, W.M. (43) 76th Meeting (NA (UK), CAB 195/2) 200–209.

78 Telegram from President Roosevelt to Prime Minister Winston Churchill, 'Personal and Most Secret', No. 292, 22 June 1943, Private Office Papers of Sir Anthony Eden, at 4B, Minute 43/184 to PM (NA (UK), FO954, Possibility of Australia purchasing Timor from Portugal).
79 Minute by F.K. Roberts, Foreign Office, dated (erroneously) 23 July 1943 (NA (UK), Anthony Eden Private Papers, FO954/21/254).
80 Notation by Anthony Eden, Foreign Secretary, on Minute by F.K. Roberts, Foreign Office, dated (erroneously) 23 July 1943 (NA (UK), Anthony Eden Private Papers, FO954/21/254).
81 Personal Telegram T 896/3 from Prime Minister Winston Churchill to US President Roosevelt, No. 331, 27 June 1943 (NA (UK), FO954/21/254, War Cabinet Minutes, and CAB 121/772, Cabinet Office: Special Secret Information Centre, Proposed Portuguese participation in defence and liberation of Timor).
82 United Kingdom, *Parliamentary Debates*, House of Commons, 12 October 1942 (Winston Churchill); see also Cadogan's record of the negotiation in Dilks, 1971, 566–567.
83 Jak P. Mallmann Showell (ed.), *Fuehrer Conferences on Naval Affairs 1939–1945* (London: Chatham, 2005) 197.
84 Showell, 2005, 374.
85 Salazar wanted Portuguese troops to undertake the liberation. In UK/Portuguese military staff conversations in Lisbon, the Portuguese requested that their military forces allocated for the reoccupation of Portuguese Timor receive training in Australia or within a reasonable distance of Timor.
86 Bruce Oswald and Jim Waddell (eds), *Justice in Arms* (Newport, NSW: Big Sky, 2014) 195.
87 Peter Charlton, *The Unnecessary War: Island Campaigns of the South-West Pacific 1944–45* (Melbourne: Macmillan, 1983); Peter Stanley, *Tarakan: An Australian Tragedy* (Sydney: Allen & Unwin, 1997) 7–25.
88 As Governor-General, Kerr dismissed Prime Minister Whitlam and his government from office in 1975; most of the group went on to make significant though less controversial contributions to public life and scholarship.
89 Graeme Sligo, *The Backroom Boys: Conlon and the Army's Directorate of Research and Civil Affairs, 1942–46* (Newport, NSW: Big Sky, 2012).
90 Peter Ryan (ed.), *Encyclopaedia of Papua and New Guinea* (Melbourne: Melbourne University Press, 1972) 23.
91 Lloyd Ross, *John Curtin: A Biography* (Melbourne: Macmillan, 1977) 360–361.
92 Letter from H.V. Evatt, Minister for External Affairs, to Sir Stanley Bruce, Australian High Commissioner, London, 20 November 1943 (NAA, series A989, 44/600/5/1/5).
93 Christopher Thorne, *Allies of a Kind: The United States, Britain and the War Against Japan, 1941–1945* (London: Hamish Hamilton, 1978) 366 and, particularly, 480–481.
94 Dilks, 1971, 609; see also P.A. Reynolds and E.J. Hughes, *The Historian as Diplomat: Charles Kingsley Webster and the United Nations 1939–1946* (London: Martin Robertson, 1976) 28 and 71.
95 Julius Stone, *The Atlantic Charter: New Worlds for Old* (Sydney: Angus & Robertson, 1943), 97–98.

96 Ibid., 239.
97 Kerr, 1978, 101–102; although he didn't mention it, Kerr was surely aware of that officer's British Special Operations Executive role and British strategy to restore imperial control in Southeast Asia.
98 Charlton, 1983, 145–147.
99 Meeting of the Pacific War Council, 12 January 1944 (NAA, series A2937/193, part 2, barcode 232340).
100 Charlton, 1983, 142 and 146; Kerr, 1978, 101.
101 Kerr, 1978, 97.
102 Aldrich, 2000, 176–177.
103 NA (UK), Foreign Office: General Correspondence, Australia and New Zealand Conference on South West Pacific, 1944, FCO 371, 40599, U687.
104 Commonwealth, *Parliamentary Debates*, House of Representatives, 3 September 1942, 78 (H.V. Evatt).
105 William Manchester, *American Caesar: Douglas MacArthur, 1880–1964* (Melbourne: Hutchinson of Australia, 1978) 251.
106 Robert E. Sherwood, *The White House Papers of Harry L. Hopkins: An Intimate History*, Vol. 2 (London: Enigma Books, 1949) 513.
107 Winston Churchill, *The Second World War*, Vol. 4 (London: Reprint Society, 1948) 143–144.
108 Ross, 1977, 261–262; Kylie Tennant, *Evatt: Politics and Justice* (Sydney: Angus & Robertson, 1970) 138.
109 War Cabinet, Report by Joint Intelligence Sub-Committee, 25 January 1942 (NA (UK), Records of Prime Minister Churchill's Office, 1942–1943, Far East (Defence of Australia), PREM 3/151/4).
110 Bridge, 2008, 241.
111 Borneman, 2016, 173–177.
112 Outward Telegram (DO) from Winston Churchill, UK Prime Minister, to John Curtin, Australian Prime Minister, 'Most Secret and Personal', No. 318 (T.H01/2), 17 March 1942 (NA (UK), Records of Prime Minister's Office 1942–1943, Far East Defence of Australia, PREM 3/151/4).
113 Cablegram 831 from John Curtin, Australian Prime Minister, to Lord Cranborne, UK Secretary of State for Dominion Affairs, 26 December 1941 (NAA, series A981, Timor (Portuguese)).
114 John Curtin, 'The Task Ahead', *Melbourne Herald*, 27 December 1941.
115 Maie Casey, *Tides and Eddies* (London: M. Joseph, 1966) 83.
116 Ross, 1977, 261–262; Tennant, 1970, 247.
117 Tennant, 1970, 157.
118 Cairo Declaration, Important Declaration and Agreements (NAA, series A5954, 1340/7, barcode 655535).
119 Commonwealth, *Parliamentary Debates*, House of Representatives, 14 October 1943, 574–575 (H.V. Evatt).
120 Inward Telegram from Australian Government to Secretary of State for Dominion Affairs, 25 January 1944 (NA (UK), FCO 371, 40599, U687).
121 Outward Telegram No. 65 from UK High Commission in Canberra to Secretary of State for Dominion Affairs, 19 January 1944 (NA (UK), U439/36/70, FC0371, 40599).

122 The disastrous attempt to continue clandestine military operations after the main force withdrew, and cover-up, that still evoked strong emotions in the author's day, is outlined in the closing paragraphs of this chapter.
123 Inward Telegram from Australian Government to Secretary of State for Dominion Affairs, 25 January 1944 (NA (UK), FCO 371, 40599, U687).
124 Ross, 1977, 342.
125 Ibid., 343–344.
126 Ibid., 344–345; Tennant, 1970, 157–158; Stuart Macintyre, *Australia's Boldest Experiment: War and Reconstruction in the 1940s* (NewSouth Publishing, 2015), 258.
127 Ross, 1977, 356–357.
128 Minutes of Meeting of Pacific War Council, 12 January 1944 (NAA, series A2937, 193, part 2).
129 Winston S. Churchill, *The War Speeches of the Rt Hon Winston S. Churchill*, Vol. 3 (London: Purnell in association with Cassell, 1970) 132–133.
130 Ross, 1977, 358–359.
131 Dilks, 1971, 609.
132 Defence Committee, Minute No. 109/1945, Portuguese participation in operations for recapture of Portuguese Timor, 27 March 1945 (NAA, series A2031, 109/1945); see also *Documents on Australian Foreign Policy 1937–49*, Vol. VIII (Canberra: AGPS, 1989) Document 55, Cablegram 72 from Lord Cranborne, UK Secretary of State for the Dominions, to Commonwealth Government, 13 March 1945.
133 *Documents on Australian Foreign Policy 1937–49*, Vol. VII (Canberra: AGPS, 1988) Document 294, 21 September 1944; Report by Brigadier A.W. Wardell to Prime Minister Curtin, 1 November 1944 (NAA, series A5954, Box 2253).
134 Defence Committee, Minute No. 181/1945, Portuguese participation in operations for recapture of Portuguese Timor, 15 May 1945 (NAA, series A2031, 181/1945).
135 *Documents on Australian Foreign Policy 1937–49*, Vol. VIII, Document 62, Cablegram E4 from Dr H.V. Evatt, Minister for External Affairs, to John Douglas Hood, Acting Secretary, Dept of External Affairs, 21 March 1945; see also, *Documents on Australian Foreign Policy 1937–49*, Vol. VII, Document 352, Cablegram from Commonwealth Government to Lord Cranborne, UK Secretary of State for the Dominions, 18 November 1944, [10].
136 *Documents on Australian Foreign Policy 1937–49*, Vol. VII, Document 294, Advisory War Council Minute 1421, 21 September 1944.
137 Ibid., Document 281, Report by W.D. Forsyth, Political Adviser attached to Commander, Australian Forces in Timor (20–27 September 1945), 1 October 1945, and Defence Committee, Minute No. 429/1945, 2 October 1945, Surrender of Japanese Forces in Portuguese Timor (NAA, series A2031/1, 429/1945).
138 Tom Hall and Lynette Ramsay Silver, *The Heroes of Rimau: Unravelling the Mystery of One of World War II's Most Daring Raids* (London: Leo Cooper, 1990) 230–248.
139 Hall and Silver, 1990, 243–245; see also Cleary, 2010, 314–319, and Michael Carrel, 'Australia's Prosecution of Japanese War Criminals: Stimuli and

Constraints', PhD thesis, University of Melbourne, 2005, 119–120. For a broader account, see Georgina Fitzpatrick, Tim McCormack and Narelle Morris (eds), *Australia's War Crimes Trials 1945–51* (Leiden: Brill Nijhoff, 2016), where the general policy of secrecy is discussed.
140 John Fahey, *Australia's First Spies* (Sydney: Allen & Unwin, 2018) 336–337.

3 After the War—The Vision Fades
1 Sumner Welles, *The Time for Decision* (New York: Harper, 1944) 297–298.
2 John O. Springhall, 'Disaster in Surabaya: the Death of Brigadier Mallaby during the British Occupation of Java, 1945–46', *Journal of Imperial and Commonwealth History*, 24(3) (1996) 422, and his *Decolonization Since 1945: The Collapse of European Overseas Empires* (London: Palgrave Macmillan, 2001).
3 Cablegram from Prime Minister Clement Attlee to Prime Minister Ben Chifley, 4 November 1945 (NA (UK), FCO 371, F99294/6398/61).
4 Springhall, 1996, 426.
5 Paul Hasluck, *Diplomatic Witness: Australian Foreign Affairs 1941–1947* (Melbourne: Melbourne University Press, 1980) 80.
6 C.W.P. Waters, 'Anglo-Australian Conflict over the Cold War: H.V. Evatt as President of the UN General Assembly, 1948–49', *Journal of Imperial and Commonwealth History*, 22(2) (1994) 294.
7 Letter from F.R. Hoyer Miller to Sir William Strang, 12 July 1949 (NA (UK), FO371/76349, W4206/2/68/G).
8 For an account of the Menzies/Spender relationship, see David Lowe, 'Mr Spender Goes to Washington: An Ambassador's Vision of Australian-American Relations, 1951–58', *Journal of Imperial and Commonwealth History* 24(2) (1996) 278.
9 Malcolm Fraser, *Dangerous Allies* (Melbourne: Melbourne University Press, 2014) 92–95.
10 Allan Gyngell, *Fear of Abandonment* (Melbourne: La Trobe University Press, 2017) 56–57. Australia's criminal law sanctions about disclosure of Commonwealth 'information' have the widest reach with respect to alleged 'national security' of any of the Western democracies.
11 Henrique Martins de Carvalho, *Portugal e o Pacto do Atlântico* (Lisbon, 1953).
12 The Vanderberg Resolution, Res 239, 80th Congress, 2nd Session (11 July 1948).
13 Signed in March 1948 by Belgium, France, Luxembourg, the Netherlands and the UK, the Treaty of Brussels was an expansion of the Treaty of Dunkirk, signed by Britain and France in March 1947. Both treaties sought primarily to prevent any resurgence of German militarism.
14 North Atlantic Treaty, signed 4 April 1949, known as the Atlantic Pact, establishing initially a 12-member, later enlarged to a 16-member, intergovernmental military alliance against communism that became known as the North Atlantic Treaty Organisation (NATO).
15 N.S. Teixeira, *From Neutrality to Alignment: Portugal in the Foundation of the Atlantic Pact* (EUI Working Paper HEC No. 91/9) (Florence: European University Institute, 1991).

16 *Documents on Australian Foreign Policy 1937–49*, Vol. IX (Canberra: AGPS, 1991) Document 229, Minutes of Meeting of Prime Ministers, London, 3 May 1946, 391.
17 Commonwealth, *Parliamentary Debates*, House of Representatives, 26 February 1947, 173 (H.V. Evatt).
18 *Documents on Australian Foreign Policy 1937–49*, Vol. X (Canberra: AGPS, 1993) Document 137, Cablegram from Department of External Affairs, Canberra to B.C. Ballard, Australian Political Representative, Allied Forces, Netherlands East Indies, 26 September 1946.
19 Kylie Tennant, *Evatt: Politics and Justice* (Sydney: Angus & Robertson, 1970) 207; J.R. Kerr, *Matters for Judgement* (Melbourne: Macmillan, 1978) 108–109.
20 Note by Alan Watt regarding visit by Portuguese Consul, Sydney to Canberra on 10 September 1951; Telegram from Australian Ambassador, Paris, 25 August 1953 (NAA, series A1838, 49/1/3, part 1, Australia–Portugal File, barcode 271655).
21 P.A. Reynolds and E.J. Hughes, *The Historian as Diplomat: Charles Kingsley Webster and the United Nations 1939–1946* (London: Martin Robertson, 1976) 37; Kerr, 1978, 113.
22 Julius Stone, *The Atlantic Charter: New Worlds for Old* (Sydney: Angus & Robertson, 1943) 225, fn 45 and 226, fn 47(ii).
23 Nicholas Tarling, *Britain and Portuguese Timor* (Clayton, Vic.: Monash University Publishing, 2013) 91–103.
24 *Documents on Australian Foreign Policy 1937–49*, Vol. VIII (Canberra: AGPS, 1989) Document 242, Letter from J.B. Chifley, Australian Prime Minster, to Beyeren van Aerssen, Netherlands Minister to Australia, 11 September 1945.
25 Tarling, 2013, 108.
26 Quoted in Tarling, 2013, 111.
27 Inward Telegram from Australian Government to Dominions Office, Far East–Portuguese Timor, Reoccupation of Timor, 28 August 1945 (NA (UK), DO35/1720 (WG773/11/6)).
28 F. Hoyer Miller, Minute of meeting, 31 August 1945 (NA (UK), Portugal— File No. 50, FO 371/49494 (Z10157/50/36)).
29 Outward Telegram from Dominions Office to Australian Government, Far East–Portuguese Timor, Reoccupation of Timor, 31 August 1945 (NA (UK), DO35/1720 (WG773/11/6)).
30 Hasluck, 1980, 80.
31 Defence Committee, Minute No. 212/1947, Portuguese Timor—Visit to Australia of Governor, 19 June 1947, 3 (NAA, series A2031).
32 *Documents on Australian Foreign Policy 1937–49*, Vol. XIV (Canberra: AGPS, 1997) Document 121, 242, Memorandum from Ben Chifley, Acting External Affairs Minister, to John Dedman, Minister for Post-War Reconstruction, 6 October 1948.
33 Ibid., Document 122, 249, Joint Intelligence Committee Appreciation 2/1948, 24 November 1948.
34 Ibid., Document 123, 253, Note from C.T. Moodie, OIC Administrative and General Division, Department of External Affairs, to John Burton, Secretary, Department of External Affairs, Canberra, 24 November 1948.

35 Ibid., Document 136, 278, Memorandum from John Burton, Secretary, Department of External Affairs, Canberra, to Sir Frederick Shedden, Secretary, Department of Defence, 30 November 1949.
36 Defence Committee, Minute No. 178/1949, Relations with Portuguese Timor, 8 September 1949, 2 (NAA, series A2031).
37 *Documents on Australian Foreign Policy 1937–49*, Vol. XIV, Document 131, 266, Memorandum from John Burton, Secretary, Department of External Affairs, Canberra, to Sir Frederick Shedden, Secretary, Department of Defence, Melbourne, 7 November 1949.
38 Ibid., Document 135, 273, Record of Discussions on South-East Asia, 14 November 1949.
39 Ibid., Document 130, fn 7 at 265, Top Secret, Joint Intelligence Committee Appreciation 5/1949, 'Strategic Implications of The Spread of Communism in China and its Effect on South-East Asia'.
40 Andrew Lownie, *Stalin's Englishman* (London: Hodder & Stoughton, 2015) 184.
41 Ibid., 186.
42 Cable 131 from Viscount Halifax, British Foreign Secretary, to Sir W. Selby, British Ambassador, Lisbon, 9 April 1940 (NA (UK), Far Eastern General, Files 6–7, 1940, FO371/24705, F2241/7/61, folio 294).
43 Secret Cablegram from Sir Robert Menzies, Prime Minister of Australia, to Sir Stanley Bruce, Australian High Commissioner, London, 18 March 1940 (NA (UK), Far Eastern-General, Files 6–7, 1940, FO371/24705, folios 276–278).
44 Letter to Sir Stanley Bruce, Australian High Commissioner, London, from Cadman, Mines Department, Millbank SW1, London, 4 April 1940 (NA (UK), Far Eastern-General, Files 6–7 1940, FO371/24705, folio 307).
45 Letter from W.A. Bridgeman, Under-Secretary to Portuguese Timor Petroleum Department, to Foreign Office, 19 December 1941 (NA (UK), FO371/27798 (F4057)).
46 Letter from W.A. Bridgeman, Under-Secretary to Portuguese Timor Petroleum Department, to Foreign Office, 13 December 1941 (NA (UK), FO371/27797 (F13720)).
47 Martin Gibson, *Britain's Quest for Oil: the First World War and the Peace Conferences* (Solihull: Helion & Company, 2017) xix.
48 Andrew Roberts, *Churchill: Walking with Destiny* (London: Allen Lane, 2018) 158–159.
49 Gibson, 2017, xix and 24; Roberts, 2018, 298 and 339, reports that in 1924, while out of Parliament, Churchill acted as a highly paid consultant for Royal Dutch Shell and Burmah Oil, successfully lobbying Prime Minister Baldwin to approve their merger with the UK Government–controlled Anglo-Persian Oil Company. He also engaged in massive buying on his own account of Shell Oil and Shell Transport & Trading Company shares.
50 Minute by Defence Committee recalling Paragraph 6(e) of Minute of Defence Committee Meeting held on 10 June 1947, 10 June 1948 (NAA, series A2031, 128/1948, barcode 9780992).

51 Commonwealth, *Parliamentary Debates*, House of Representatives, 9 September 1953, 16–18 (M. McEwen).
52 Ibid., 19 (M. McEwen).

4 Australia and Portuguese Timor

1 Expressed in his speech to the Annual Conference of the New South Wales Branch of the Australian Labor Party, 12 June 1949: 'We have a great objective—the light on the hill—which we aim to reach by working for the betterment of mankind not only here but anywhere we might give a helping hand'.
2 Peter Edwards, *Arthur Tange: Last of the Mandarins* (Sydney: Allen & Unwin, 2006) 154–155.
3 See, for example, *Documents on Australian Foreign Policy 1937–49*, Vol. XIV (Canberra: AGPS, 1997) Documents 163–169, 315–327, in which Burton remonstrates with the Immigration Dept Secretary about the need to soften the impact of the White Australia policy.
4 Arthur Tange, *Defence Policy-making: A Close-up View, 1950–1980* (Canberra: ANU E-Press, 2008) 14–15.
5 Steven Farram, *A Short-Lived Enthusiasm: The Australian Consulate in Portuguese Timor* (Darwin: Charles Darwin University Press, 2010) 64.
6 *Documents on Australian Foreign Policy 1937–49*, Vol. VIII (Canberra: AGPS, 1989) Document 62, Cablegram E4 from H.V. Evatt, Minister for External Affairs, to John Douglas Hood, Acting Secretary, Dept of External Affairs, 21 March 1945.
7 Cable from Stanley Bruce to Prime Minister John Curtin and H.V. Evatt, Minister for External Affairs, 26 February 1945; Cable from John Douglas Hood, Acting Secretary, Dept of External Affairs, to Stanley Bruce, 31 May 1945; Cable from Stanley Bruce to Prime Minister John Curtin, 7 June 1945 (NAA, series A1068, E47/38/8, Portugal Exchange of Representatives with Australia, barcode 194940).
8 Minute by Secretary, Dept of External Affairs, Alan Watt, 10 September 1951 (NAA, series A1838, 49/1/3, part 1, Australia–Portugal File, barcode 271655).
9 Bruno Simma *et al.* (eds), *The Charter of the United Nations: A Commentary*, 2nd ed. (New York: Oxford University Press, 2002) Vol. 2, 1091.
10 W. David McIntyre, *Winding up the British Empire in the Pacific Islands* (Oxford: Oxford University Press, 2014) 85; McIntyre gives a full account of British reaction to Chapter XI of the Charter in chapter 7.
11 Commonwealth, Cabinet Decision No. 630, Information on Developments in the Portuguese Timor and Borneo Territories, 5 February 1963 (NAA, series A4940, control C3739); Commonwealth, Cabinet Minute Decision No. 632, Indonesia—Quadripartite Talks, 5 February 1963 (NAA, series A4940, control C3739).
12 John Subritzky, *Confronting Sukarno* (London: Palgrave Macmillan, 2000) 12–14.
13 *Documents on Australian Foreign Policy 1937–49*, Vol. XIII, Document 167, Ball to Burton, Memorandum SINGAPORE, 7 June 1948 'Interim Notes on N.E.I.'

14 Ibid., Vol. XIV (Canberra: AGPS, 1997) xi.
15 Geoffrey Bolton, *Paul Hasluck: A Life* (Perth: University of Western Australia, 2014) 311.
16 Secret Outward Cablegram from Richard Casey, Minister for External Affairs, to Percy Spender, Ambassador to the US, 13 December 1957 (NAA, series A4940, C1943, barcode 539556).
17 Commonwealth, Cabinet Minute Decision No. 1157, Submission No. 997—Indonesia, 20 January 1958, 4 (NAA, series A4940, control C1943).
18 Telegram from Australian Consul in Dili, W.A. Luscombe to Dept of External Affairs, 18 December 1959 (NAA, series A1838, 49/1/3, part 1, Australia–Portugal File, barcode 271655).
19 Commonwealth Cabinet Submission No. 10, 12 January 1962, by Garfield Barwick, West New Guinea (NAA, A5819, Vol. 1/Agendum 10, barcode 849352).
20 Statement by the Prime Minister, the Rt. Hon. R.G. Menzies, PM No. 2/1962, 12 January 1962 (NAA, A5819, barcode 849352).
21 Despatch No. 2 from Patrick Shaw, Ambassador Jakarta to Sir Arthur Tange, Secretary, Dept of External Affairs, dated 16 March 1962 (NAA, series A1838, 3036/6/1, Part 67, West New Guinea. Developments relating to future status, barcode 584119).
22 Commonwealth, Submission No. 575 to Cabinet, Portuguese Timor and the North Borneo Territories, 21 February 1963, [12] (NAA, series A4940, C3725, barcode 1344506).
23 Minute by Keith Brennan, Dept of External Affairs, Note recording Secretary's views, Strategic Basis of Australian Defence Policy, 1 November 1962 (NAA, series A1838, TS677/3, Part 5, barcode 681375).
24 Joint Secretary Minute, Strategic Basis of Australian Defence Policy, 14 November 1962 (NAA, series A1838, TS677/3, Part 5, barcode 681375).
25 Ibid., 24 January 1963 (NAA, series A1838, TS677/3, Part 5, barcode 681375).
26 Hamish McDonald, *Demokrasi* (New York: Palgrave Macmillan, 2015) 32.
27 Edwards, 2006, 105.
28 *Documents on Australian Foreign Policy 1937–49*, Vol. IX, Documents 199, 273, 279, respectively: Cablegram from Alfred Brookes, Acting Political Representative, Batavia, to John Burton, First Secretary, Dept of External Affairs, 19 April 1946; Cablegram from W.E. Dunk, Secretary, Dept of External Affairs, to H.V. Evatt, Minister for External Affairs, 28 May 1946; Cablegram from H.V. Evatt, Minister for External Affairs to W.E. Dunk, Secretary, Dept of External Affairs, 29 May 1946.
29 Grose, *Gentleman Spy: The Life of Allen Dulles* (London: Deutsch, 1995) 452–453.
30 Ibid., 453–454; Richard J. Aldrich and Rory Cormac, *The Black Door* (London: Collins, 2016) 267–270.
31 Evatt perceived Heydon as being of the Establishment; a former staffer to Defence Minister Sir George Pearce and on the Defence Dept staff in Melbourne, Heydon, a lawyer, was an early recruit to the Dept of External Affairs.

32 Tim Flannery, *Throwim Way Leg* (Melbourne: Text Publishing, 1998) 302–303 and 308–317 is a poignant chronicle of the Freeport impact.
33 ASIS head Bill Robertson turned to his long-time colleague Dick Austin for advice following his dismissal on 21 October 1975 by Prime Minister Whitlam (see chapter 6).
34 Greg Poulgrain, *The Incubus of Intervention* (Petaling Jaya: Strategic Information and Research Development Centre, 2015) 213–247.
35 Grose, 1995, 452–453.
36 Poulgrain, 2015, 218 fn 7.
37 Nicholas Tarling, *Britain and Portuguese Timor* (Clayton, Vic.: Monash University Publishing, 2013) 139–174 deals comprehensively with British reaction to Indonesian 'confrontation'.
38 Letter POL 35/1 from G. Kimber, UK High Commissioner, to E.J. Bunting, Secretary, Prime Minister's Dept, 15 January 1963 (NAA, series A4940, C3739).
39 Commonwealth, Submission No. 552 to Cabinet, Australia's Strategic Position, 5 March 1963 (NAA, series A4940, C3739); Commonwealth, Submission No. 560 to Cabinet, The Strategic Importance to Australia's of New Guinea, 5 March 1963 (NAA, series A4940, C3739); Commonwealth, Submission No. 575 to Cabinet, Portuguese Timor and the North Borneo Territory, 5 March 1963 (NAA, series A4940, C3739); Commonwealth, Submission No. 576 to Cabinet, Quadripartite Talks on Indonesia, 5 March 1963 (NAA, series A4940, C3739).
40 Defence Committee, Minute No. 2/1963, Australia's Strategic Position, 4 February 1963, 2 (NAA, series A2031, 2/1963) 6, [17].
41 Commonwealth, Cabinet Minute Decision No. 675, 5 March 1963, [2].
42 Commonwealth, Submission No. 576 to Cabinet, Quadripartite Talks on Indonesia, 26 February 1963, 5 (NAA, series A4940, C3739).
43 Brief No. 10, Portuguese Timor, Quadripartite Talks—Second Round (Oct 1963), Foreign and Commonwealth Office (NA (UK), FO371/169909-DH1071/24).
44 Commonwealth, Cabinet Minute Decision No. 632, Without Memorandum—Indonesia—Quadripartite Talks, 5 February 1963, 3, [4] (NAA, series A4940, C3739).
45 Commonwealth, Submission No. 575 to Cabinet, Portuguese Timor and the North Borneo Territories, 21 February 1963, [12] (NAA, series A4940, C3725, barcode 1344506).
46 Commonwealth, *Parliamentary Debates*, Senate, Foreign Affairs, Defence and Trade References Committee, Hearing, Economic, Social and Political Conditions in East Timor, 6 December 1999, [50] (Gough Whitlam).
47 Commonwealth, Submission No. 575 to Cabinet, *Portuguese Timor and the North Borneo Territories*, 21 February 1963, [12] (NAA, series A4940, C3725, barcode 1344506).
48 J.S. Dunn, 'Portuguese Timor Before and After the Coup: Options for the Future', unpublished, Parliamentary Library, Canberra, 27 August 1974.
49 Letter with attachment from J.L. Beaven, British Embassy, Jakarta, to R.E. Palmer, South East Asia Dept, Foreign and Commonwealth Office, 23 July

1974 (NA (UK), Foreign and Commonwealth Office, South East Asia Dept, Political Situation in Portuguese Timor, FCO15/1956, folio 17).
50 Precis by P.J.E. Male, Private Secretary to Lord Goronwy-Roberts, 22 October 1975 (NA (UK), Foreign and Commonwealth Office, South East Asia, Portuguese Timor, FCO 15/1705, folio 139b).
51 Extract from copy of Report by Messrs McLennan and Dunn attached to Letter from Brian L. Barder, Head of Chancery, to P.G. de Courcy, South West Pacific Dept, Foreign and Commonwealth Office, 16 October 1974 (NA (UK), Foreign and Commonwealth Office, South East Asia, Political Situation in Portuguese Timor, FCO15/1956, folio 33).
52 Cable by Sir Arthur Tange, Secretary, Dept of External Affairs, from Australian Embassy, Washington to Minister and Dept EA, Defence and PM's, dated 11 February 1963, Strategic Basis of Australian Defence Policy, 222–223 (NAA, series A1838, TS677/3, part 5, barcode 681375).
53 Tange, 2008, 14.
54 McDonald, 2015, 34–43.
55 Geoffrey B. Robinson, *The Killing Season: A History of the Indonesian Massacres, 1965–66* (Princeton, NJ: Princeton University Press, 2017).
56 Commonwealth, Submission No. 575 to Cabinet, Portuguese Timor and the North Borneo Territories, 21 February 1963, [15] (NAA, series A4940, C3725).
57 Peter Hastings, 'Prospect: A State of Mind', in R.J. May (ed.), *Between Two Nations* (Bathurst, NSW: Robert Brown & Associates, 1986) 218–231.
58 Poulgrain, 2015, 48–71, especially 69.
59 Letters from Prime Minister Sir Robert Menzies to Dr António de Oliveira Salazar dated 18 October 1961 and 8 February 1963 (NAA, series A1838, 49/1/3, part 1, Australia–Portugal File, barcode 271655, folios 200 and 100 respectively).
60 Letter from Dr António de Oliveira Salazar, Prime Minister of Portugal, to Sir Robert Menzies, Prime Minister of Australia, 1 March 1963 (NAA, series A1838, 49/1/3, part 1, Australia–Portugal File, barcode 271655, folios 92–93).
61 Ibid., folio 94.
62 Edwards, 2006, 130.
63 Tange, 2008, 14–15 and 132.
64 Bolton, 2014, 321–322 and 340–341; Tange, 2008, 133.
65 Working Group of Departmental Officers. *The Future of Portuguese Timor: Report*, Canberra, 4 April 1963, available at https://dfat.gov.au/about-us/publications/historical-documents/Pages/volume-20/UnNumbered Articles-pg1-45/report-by-the-working-group-of-departmental-officers.aspx.
66 Letter from Sir Robert Menzies, Prime Minister of Australia, to Dr António de Oliveira Salazar, Prime Minister of Portugal, 15 October 1963 (NAA, series A1838, 49/1/3, part 1, Australia–Portugal File, barcode 271655).
67 Record of Meeting held in the State Dept, Washington, Quadripartite Talks, 16 October 1963 at 11:00 am (NA (UK), Foreign Office, FO371/169909, DH1071/31).

68 Strategic Basis of Australian Defence Policy, 222–223 of 279 (NAA, series A1838, TS677/3, part 5, barcode 681375).

69 Sir Robert Menzies, '1963 Federal Election ... Policy Speech', available at http://australianpolitics.com/1963/11/12/menzies-election-policy-speech.html.

70 Jenny Hocking, *Gough Whitlam: His Time* (Melbourne: Miegunyah Press, 2014) Vol. 2, 136–137.

71 *New South Wales v Commonwealth* [1975] HCA 58; (1975) 135 CLR 337 (17 December 1975).

72 Nancy Viviani, 'Australians and the Timor Issue', *Australian Outlook*, 30 (2) (1976) 197–226.

73 Allan Gyngell, *Fear of Abandonment: Australia in the World since 1942* (Melbourne: La Trobe University Press, 2017) 11.

74 Ibid., 3.

75 Tange, 2008, 14. Malcolm Turnbull's 2017 statement when he was Prime Minister, 'We are joined at the hip with the United States', is one of a plethora of such statements by Australian leaders.

76 Ibid., 15. Brian Toohey refers to Tange's 'abrasive personality' and attributes Tange's demotion to High Commissioner in New Delhi to a policy fall-out with Menzies (*Secret: The Making of Australia's Security State* (Carlton, Vic.: Melbourne University Press, 2019)).

5 The Australian Continental Shelf—Declaring Boundaries

1 David Fairbairn, C.E. Barnes and B.M. Snedden, Cabinet Submission No. 1165, Off-Shore Petroleum, Legislation to Give Effect to Joint Commonwealth–State Legislative Arrangements, 25 November 1965, [32] (Off-shore Minerals—Commonwealth/State Discussions (NAA, series A4940, C3945, barcode 1345145)).

2 The early history of Woodside and joint-venture partners in the Timor Sea emerges in the judgement of French J. in *Woodside Energy Ltd v Commissioner of Taxation (No.2)* [2007] FCA 1961 (10 December 2007) at 17–19 and 27–30.

3 Cabinet Minute Decision No. 260, Exploration for Petroleum on the Australian Continental Shelf—Request by Woodside (Lakes Entrance) Oil Co. N.L. concerning Permit Areas in the Timor Sea, 29 May 1964, 8 (NAA, series A5827, Vol. 4/Agendum 130); see also Cabinet Minute Decision No. 1062, 10 October 1963, Exploration for Petroleum on the Australian Continental Shelf—Proposals of Australian Oil & Gas Limited and Gulf Oil Corporation of America, Concerning Permit 90P issued by the Government of Queensland (NAA, A5819, Vol. 23/Agendum 912, barcode 1017523).

4 Woodside conducted an aeromagnetic survey of the North-West Australian Continental Shelf in 1964, listed in B.F. Jones, *Timor Sea Gravity, Magnetic and Seismic Survey, 1967* (Record No. 1969/40) (Canberra: Bureau of Mineral Resources, Geology and Geophysics, 1969) 56, available at http://www.ga.gov.au/corporate_data/12299/Rec1969_040.pdf.

5 W.H. Spooner, Minister for National Development, Submission No. 139 to Cabinet, Exploration for Petroleum on the Australian Continental

Shelf—Request by Woodside (Lakes Entrance) Oil Co N.L. concerning Permit Areas in the Timor Sea, 10 April 1964, 2, [3–4] (NAA, series A5827, Vol. 4/Agendum 130).
6 Spooner, Submission No. 139 to Cabinet, 10 April 1964, 2, [6] (NAA, series A5827, Vol. 4/Agendum 130).
7 Fairbairn, Barnes and Snedden, Submission No. 1165 to Cabinet, 25 November 1965.
8 Ibid., opening paragraph (a).
9 Ibid., [1].
10 Convention on the Continental Shelf, opened for signature 29 April 1958, 499 UNTS 311 (entered into force 10 June 1964) Art. 6(1).
11 Ibid., [13].
12 Convention on the Continental Shelf, Art. 1(a).
13 Ibid., Art. 6(1).
14 Fairbairn, Barnes and Snedden, Submission No. 1165 to Cabinet, 25 November 1965 [10].
15 Ibid., [25].
16 Ibid., 2.
17 For background to Australia's role in supporting a foundational rule of maritime law see Kenneth Bailey, 'Australia and the Law of the Sea', *Adelaide Law Review*, 1 (1960), 1–22.
18 International Law Commission, 'Report … to General Assembly, Document A/2456', *Yearbook of the International Law Commission* (1953) Vol. II, 212–214, available at http://legal.un.org/docs/?path=../ilc/publications/yearbooks/english/ilc_1953_v2.pdf&lang=E.
19 International Law Commission, 'Report … to General Assembly, Document A/2456', 212: 'Art. 1 … the term "continental shelf" refers to the sea-bed and subsoil of the submarine areas contiguous to the coast, but outside the area of the territorial sea, to a depth of two hundred metres. Art.2 The coastal State exercises over the continental shelf sovereign rights for the purpose of exploring and exploiting its natural resources'.
20 Fairbairn, Barnes and Snedden, Submission No. 1165 to Cabinet, 25 November 1965 [16].
21 Commonwealth, *Parliamentary Debates*, House of Representatives, 28 February 1952 (John McEwen).
22 Fairbairn, Barnes and Snedden, Submission No. 1165 to Cabinet, 25 November 1965 [25–28].
23 Ibid., [20].
24 Ibid., [21].
25 Jones, 1969.
26 Ibid., 2 and 14. This seems an early formulation of the controversial 'two shelves' argument adopted by successive Australian governments.
27 Fairbairn, Barnes and Snedden, Submission No. 1165 to Cabinet, 25 November 1965 [22].
28 Ibid., [31].
29 Ibid., [32].
30 Ibid., [25].

31 'The worldwide trend towards a change in accent from land to offshore areas in geophysical exploration for petroleum has been followed in Australia, where the volume of prospective sediments offshore is equal to that on land, while the volume of post-Palaeozoic sediments offshore is about twice as large. This trend has been given particular impetus in Australia by the discovery of large oil and gas reserves in the offshore Gippsland Basin', Jones, 1969, 1.

32 Fairbairn, Barnes and Snedden, Submission No. 1165 to Cabinet, 25 November 1965 [25].

33 Ibid., [31].

34 In a condolence motion in the Australian Parliament following Fairbairn's death on 1 June 1994, Fairbairn's colleague Ian Sinclair said that he had resigned from the Gorton Ministry over opposition to federal centralism, particularly over the attempt to assert Commonwealth control over territorial waters and the continental shelf: Commonwealth, *Parliamentary Debates*, Senate, 6 June 1994, 1417 (Condolences—Fairbairn, Hon. Sir David Eric, KBE, DFC).

35 Commonwealth, *Parliamentary Debates*, Senate, 1 September 2014 (George Brandis).

36 G.W. Tate, *et al.*, 'Australia Going Down Under: Quantifying Continental Subduction During Arc-Continent Accretion in Timor-Leste', *Geosphere* 11(6) (2015), 1–24.

37 Cabinet Minute, Decision No. 1447, 8 December 1965 (NAA, series A4940, C3945, Off-shore Minerals—Commonwealth/State Discussions (NAA, series A4940, control C3945, barcode 1345145)).

38 *Continental Shelf (Living Natural Resources) Act 1968*, repealing the *Pearl Fisheries Act (No. 2) 1953* (Cth), *Petroleum (Submerged Lands) Act 1967* (Cth), and the *Seas and Submerged Lands Act 1973* (Cth), which set out both conventions as schedules to the Act. The *Petroleum (Submerged Lands) Act 1967* was replaced by a further Act of the same title in 1976, leading to the *Offshore Petroleum Act 2006* (Cth), which was amended and renamed by the *Offshore Petroleum and Greenhouse Storage Act 2006* (Cth); for a comprehensive summary and bibliography, see Michael White, *Australian Offshore Laws* (Sydney: Federation Press, 2009) 15–74.

39 *Maritime Legislation Amendment Act 1994* (Cth).

40 See *Obligations of States in Undelimited Maritime Areas*, BICL, Report of Conference held on 22 July 2016. Articles 74(3) and 83(3) on UNCLOS adopt the same notion of restraint, viz. '(3) Pending agreement as provided for in paragraph 1, the States concerned, in a spirit of understanding and cooperation, shall make every effort to enter into provisional arrangements of a practical nature and, during this transitional period, not to jeopardize or hamper the reaching of the final agreement. Such arrangements shall be without prejudice to the final delimitation'. This enjoinder to maintain, so far as possible, the status quo ante reflects the general principle in international law of good faith: South China Sea Arbitration (The Republic of the Philippines v The People's Republic of China), Award, Permanent Court of

Arbitration, 12 July 2016, [1169]; Arbitration between Guyana and Suriname (2007) XXX RIAA 1, [485–486].
41 C.W. Harders, 'The Sea-Bed', *Federal Law Review*, 3(2) (1969) 202, 214; see also R.D. Lumb, 'The Continental Shelf', *Melbourne University Law Review*, 6 (1968) 357; A.R. Thompson, 'Australian Petroleum Legislation and the Canadian Experience', *Melbourne University Law Review* 6 (1968) 370; A.N. Dakin, 'Future Patterns of Legislation for the Petroleum Industry', *Melbourne University Law Review*, 6 (1968) 403; C.W. Harders, 'Australia's Offshore Petroleum Legislation', *Melbourne University Law Review*, 6 (1968) 415.
42 Commonwealth, *Parliamentary Debates*, House of Representatives, 30 October 1970, Vol. II, 3108 (William McMahon, Minister for External Affairs).
43 Fairbairn, Barnes and Snedden, Submission No. 1165 to Cabinet, 25 November 1965 [31].
44 Like Australia, Portugal adopted a three nautical mile territorial sea and a 12 nautical mile contiguous zone, which applied to external territories. On 11 November 1969, Portugal adopted the 200-metre contour line as the limit of all Portuguese Continental Shelf claims, consistent with the provisions of the 1958 Convention on the Continental Shelf. By this time the Australian Dept of National Development had proposed, against the Attorney-General's Dept's advice, to claim continental shelf jurisdiction out to a 2,000-metre depth line (NAA, series A1838, 756/1/4, part 1, Australia–Portugal Negotiations on Portuguese Timor Continental Shelf, barcode 558637, 756/1/4, folios 104–118).
45 For more on the geological evolution of the Indo-Australian Plate, including at the Timor Trough, see Michael Sandiford, 'Travelling with Timor-Leste', *The Conversation*, 15 April 2016, available at https://theconversation.com/travelling-with-timor-leste-57635.
46 Shane Paltridge, Minister for Defence, Submission No. 493 to Cabinet, Strategic Basis of Australian Defence Policy, 22 October 1964 [19] (NAA, seriesA4940, C3640).
47 Paltridge, Submission No. 493 to Cabinet, 1964 [23].
48 Ibid., [37–41].
49 Ibid., [43]; Cabinet Minute, Decision No. 592, Strategic Basis of Australian Defence Policy, 4 November 1964 (NAA, series A4940, C3640).
50 Telegram, Deputy High Commissioner, Canberra, G. Kimber, to Commonwealth Relations Office, 25 January 1965 (NA (UK), FO 371/180256, Foreign Office, South East Asia, Threat from Indonesia, Portuguese Timor).
51 Dept of Foreign Affairs, Australia–Portugal Negotiations on Portuguese Timor Continental Shelf (NAA, series A1838/1, 756/1/4, part 1, barcode 558637).
52 Dept of Foreign Affairs, Law of the Sea—Convention on the Continental Shelf (NAA, series A1838/392, 1592/10/5, part 2).
53 Dept of Foreign Affairs, Australia–Portugal Negotiations on Portuguese Timor Continental Shelf (NAA, series A1838/1, 756/1/4, part 1, folios 1–2, barcode 558637).

54 Note of Conversation by Keith Brennan, Senior Assistant Secretary, dated 25 May 1971 (NAA, series A1838, 49/1/3 Part 3, folio 71, barcode 591437).
55 Bureau of Mineral Resources, *The Timor Trough—A Summary of Current Geological Knowledge*, Canberra, February 1970, appended to External Affairs Memorandum from Miles Connelly to Sir Laurence McIntyre, Sir Kenneth Bailey and Mr John Corkery, 5 March 1970 (NAA, A1838, 752/1/23, Part 1, Indonesia–Australia Continental Shelf Boundary Negotiations, barcode 558528).
56 Bureau of Mineral Resources, 1970.
57 *North Sea Continental Cases (Federal Republic of Germany/Denmark; Federal Republic of Germany/Netherlands)* (Merits) [1969] ICJ Rep 3.
58 Dept of Foreign Affairs, Australia–Portugal Negotiations on Portuguese Timor Continental Shelf (NAA, series A1838/1, 756/1/4, part 1, barcode 558637, folios 3–4).
59 Bureau of Mineral Resources, 1970.
60 Dept of Foreign Affairs, Australia–Portugal Negotiations on Portuguese Timor Continental Shelf (NAA, series A1838/1, 756/1/4, part 1, barcode 558637, folios 19–20).
61 Dept of Foreign Affairs, Australia–Portugal Negotiations on Portuguese Timor Continental Shelf (NAA series A1838, 756/1/4, part 1, barcode 558637).
62 J.V. Prescott, Letter in the *Australian Financial Review*, 23 October 1970.
63 Cable from G.W. Shannon, Consul, Dili, advising limits of Oceanic Exploration concession to be between 125°42'E and 128°38'E, and, 8°29'S and 11°42'S, and Cable from Jakarta, 24 December 1970 (NAA, series A1838/1, 756/1/4, Part 1, Australia–Portugal Negotiations on Portuguese Timor Continental Shelf, barcode 558637, folios 50–52).
64 Within two weeks of his election, Whitlam instructed Australia's delegation to the UN to adopt a hard line in relation to Portugal and to support resolutions moved principally by the Eastern Bloc and emerging African states. Consequently, Australia–Portugal talks on a maritime boundary 'got nowhere' and BHP's exploration activities were 'condemned by the Australian Government' (Brian Toohey, 'Timor Test for Government', *Australian Financial Review*, 15 May 1973).
65 Commonwealth, *Parliamentary Debates*, House of Representatives, 30 October 1970, Vol. II, 3108 (William McMahon, Minister for External Affairs).
66 'If the plates collided north of Timor, then the Trough/Trench was indeed merely "an incidental depression in the sea-floor, not the definitive edge of the two shelves"' (Peter Hastings, 'Whose Riches Under the Sea?', *Sydney Morning Herald*, 3 June 1972). Mochtar repeated this view to Laws and Kraus (writing in the *Australian Petroleum Exploration Association Journal*, 14(1) 1974) and to a journalist writing in the *Far Eastern Economic Review* in 1978 and 1979.
67 The 'margin' in Law of the Sea parlance includes the floor, the slope and the rise.
68 Hugh Wyndham, 'Revisiting the 1972 Seabed Boundary Negotiations with Indonesia', *The Interpreter*, 12 January 2018, available at https://www.

lowyinstitute.org/the-interpreter/revisiting-1972-seabed-boundary-negotiations-indonesia.
69 Assuming Wyndham's recollection to be accurate, this raises the question of whether BMR assessments of the mineral and petroleum potential of the continental shelf were available to all delegation members.
70 Dept of Foreign Affairs, Australia–Portugal Negotiations on Portuguese Timor Continental Shelf (NAA, series A1838, 756/1/4, Part 2, barcode 558639, folio 95).
71 Ibid., 756/1/4, Part 1, barcode 558637, folio 118).
72 Letter from Sue Boyd, Second Secretary to The Secretary, 23 February 1973 ((NAA, series A1838/1, 756/1/4, Part 2, Australia–Portugal Negotiations on Portuguese Timor Continental Shelf, barcode 558639, folio 195).
73 Dept of Foreign Affairs (NAA, series A1838/1, 756/1/4, Part 2, Australia–Portugal Negotiations on Portuguese Timor Continental Shelf, barcode 558639, folio 198).
74 Ibid., folios 259–261).
75 Dept of Foreign Affairs (NAA, series A1838, barcode 558639, 756/1/4, Australia–Portugal Negotiations on Portuguese Timor Continental Shelf, Part 2).
76 Ibid.; Note by A.H. Loomes, First Assistant Secretary, Consular and Legal Division, Dept of Foreign Affairs, 31 July 1973 (NAA, copy from 938/17, folio 267).

6 Post-Colonial Abandonment—Australia and the Indonesian Occupation of Timor-Leste

1 Agreement Between the Government of the Commonwealth of Australia and the Government of the Republic of Indonesia Establishing Certain Seabed Boundaries, Australia–Indonesia, signed 18 May 1971, ATS 31 (entered into force 8 November 1973); Agreement Between the Government of the Commonwealth of Australia and the Government of the Republic of Indonesia Establishing Certain Seabed Boundaries in the Area of the Timor and Arafura Seas, Supplementary to the Agreement of 18 May 1971, Australia-Indonesia, signed 9 October 1972, ATS 32 (entered into force 8 November 1973); see also Treaty between the Government of Australia and the Government of the Republic of Indonesia establishing an Exclusive Economic Zone boundary and certain seabed boundaries, Australia-Indonesia, signed 14 March 1997 (not yet entered into force).
2 'Woodside Hits Gas Off Timor', *The Age*, 28 August 1974, refers to wells on the Sunrise High, later identified as Troubadour-1 and Sunrise-1.
3 *Diário de Notícias* (Lisbon, 13 February 1975). This same area later became the Zone of Cooperation between Australia and Indonesia (see Commonwealth, *Parliamentary Debates*, Joint Standing Committee on Treaties, 8 October 2002, 196 (Christopher Ward)).
4 This argument was still being peddled in Canberra in 2014. Although Australia adhered to Article 12 of the 1958 Convention on the Territorial Sea and Contiguous Zone, which stipulated a median line in an unbroken shelf situation, Indonesia had conceded a boundary well north of the median

line and its National Assembly passed two laws acknowledging the 1971 and 1972 boundary agreements with Australia. In parliamentary debate whereby Indonesia ratified UNCLOS, Indonesia specifically declared the boundary agreements with Australia to be exceptions to Indonesia's UNCLOS adherence to median line principles. In 2009, when depositing its UN Continental Shelf submission, Indonesia referred to domestic legislation accepting the Indonesia/Australia boundary agreements and declaring the boundaries as settled.

5 Letter from Brian Barder, British High Commission, Canberra, to John Hickman, South West Pacific Dept, Foreign and Commonwealth Office, 10 May 1974 (NA (UK) FCO 15/1956, folio 4, South East Asia, Political Situation in Portuguese Timor).

6 Christopher Andrew and Vassili Mitrokhin, *The Sword and the Shield: The Mitrokhin Archive and the Secret History of the KGB* (New York: Basic, 1999) 346.

7 Letter from N.C. Trench, British Ambassador, Lisbon, to James Callaghan, Foreign Secretary, 'Visit of the Secretary of State to Portugal', 12 February 1975 (NA (UK) FCO15/1704, Foreign and Commonwealth Office, South East Asia Department, Portuguese Timor); see also Keith Hamilton and Patrick Salmon (eds), *Documents on British Policy Overseas*, Series III, Vol. V, *The Southern Flank in Crisis* (Oxford: Routledge, 2006) 390.

8 In January 1976, David Combe, then National Secretary of the Australian Labor Party, wrote through Socialist International in London asking if Gough Whitlam, recently dismissed, and, by inference, himself, could participate at Stockholm Committee meetings. A decision on Combe's request was deferred for reasons not evident in unredacted material (Records of Prime Minister's Office, Portugal—Security Situation, Correspondence and Papers 1974–1979 (NA (UK), PREM 16/1053)).

9 Records of Prime Minister's Office, Portugal—Security Situation, Correspondence and Papers 1974–1979 (NA (UK), PREM 16/1053).

10 Policy Paper by Tom McNally, Political Adviser to the Foreign Secretary (NA (UK) PREM 16/1053, Records of Prime Minister's Office, Portugal—Security Situation, Correspondence and Papers 1974–1979); see also Hamilton and Salmon, 2006, 403–430.

11 Kissinger's assessment is listed by the National Archives as 'Missing' (Examiners Note, 2 May 2006, Records of Prime Minister's Office, Portugal—Security Situation, Correspondence and Papers 1974–1979 (NA (UK), PREM 16/1053)); file marking suggests that the file was recalled from the National Archives. Recent reports indicate that the Foreign Office may have recalled many sensitive documents after their archival release; see Ian Cobain, 'Government Admits "Losing" Thousands of Papers from National Archives', *The Guardian*, 26 December 2017.

12 J.A.C. Mackie, 'Does Indonesia Have Expansionist Designs on Papua New Guinea?', in R.J. May (ed.), *Between Two Nations* (Bathurst, NSW: Robert Brown & Associates, 1986) 75.

13 The Dept of Foreign Affairs report of the meeting was copied to the British Foreign Office—Letter and attachment from G.W. Hewitt to R.E. Palmer,

South-East Asia Desk, Foreign and Commonwealth Office, 20 December 1974 (NA (UK), FCO 15/1956, folio 54, Foreign and Commonwealth Office, South East Asia, Political Situation in Portuguese Timor).
14 Background Note prepared 28 October 1975 for Right Hon. The Lord Goronwy-Roberts, Parliamentary Under-Secretary of State, Foreign and Commonwealth Office (NA (UK), FCO 15/1705, folio 149, Foreign and Commonwealth Office, South East Asia, Portuguese Timor).
15 Letter from R.M. Sands, British High Commission, to J.L. Jones, South East Asian Dept, Foreign and Commonwealth Office, 28 November 1975 (NA (UK), FCO 15/1706, folio 203, Foreign and Commonwealth Office, South East Asia, Portuguese Timor).
16 Dept of Foreign Affairs, News Release M81, 'East Timor: Unilateral Declaration of Independence', 29 November 1975 (NA (UK), FCO 15/1706, folio 203, Foreign and Commonwealth Office, South East Asia, Portuguese Timor).
17 Precis by P.J.E. Male, Assistant Undersecretary of State, Foreign and Commonwealth Office, to Lord Goronwy-Roberts, Private Secretary, 22 October 1975 (NA (UK), FCO 15/1705, folio bundle, 139b, para 3, Foreign and Commonwealth Office, South East Asia, Portuguese Timor).
18 Memorandum by J.M. Hay, Foreign and Commonwealth Office, to F. Easey and Duncan Sands, House of Commons, 3 December 1975 (NA (UK), FCO 15/1707, folio 229, Foreign and Commonwealth Office, Portuguese Timor). (Arms supplies from certain departure points can reach Bacau Airport in Timor-Leste by flights from territorial airspace in Asia entering and remaining within international airspace.)
19 José Ramos-Horta, *Funu: The Unfinished Saga of East Timor* (Trenton, NJ: Red Sea Press, 1996), 97–101.
20 NAA, series A1838, 935117/3, iii, quoted in Clinton Fernandes, *Island off the Coast of Asia* (Clayton, Victoria: Monash University Publishing, 2018) 46.
21 Memorandum from William Pritchett, First Assistant Secretary, Strategic and International Policy, Department of Defence to Bill Morrison, Minister for Defence, 9 October 1975 (quoted in Senate, Foreign Affairs, Defence and Trade References Committee, *East Timor: Final Report* (Canberra, 2000) 156, available at https://www.aph.gov.au/~/media/wopapub/senate/committee/.../report_pdf.ashx).
22 Commonwealth, *Parliamentary Debates*, Senate, Foreign Affairs, Defence and Trade References Committee, Hearing, *Economic, Social and Political Conditions in East Timor*, 6 December 1999, 982 (Gough Whitlam), available at http://parlinfo.aph.gov.au/parlInfo/search/display/display.w3p;query=Id:committees%2Fcommsen%2Fe0000918.sgm%2F0003.
23 Commonwealth, *Parliamentary Debates*, Senate, Foreign Affairs, Defence and Trade References Committee, Hearing, *Economic, Social and Political Conditions in East Timor*, 4 November 1999, 763 (Tom Uren).
24 Intelligence sources were aware that a handful of alleged pro-communist activists, described disparagingly, if not in racist terms, by Whitlam in his evidence to the parliamentary committee as '*mestiços*', including one with an accompanying Portuguese spouse who had arrived in Dili from Mozambique;

see Gough Whitlam, *The Whitlam Government* (Melbourne: Viking, 1985) 112 and fn 86 to the *Interim Report of the Defence and Foreign Affairs Committee*, Committee Hansard, Parliamentary Paper; 1999, No. 200.
25 Wendy Way (ed.), *Australia and the Indonesian Incorporation of Portuguese Timor, 1974–1976* (Carlton, Vic.: Melbourne University Press, 2000) 529–532.
26 Letter from Lance Barnard to Senator D.R. Willesee, 11 February 1975, Timor—Caveat Material, NAA, series A11443, 14, barcode 4151650, folio 74.
27 Ibid., folio 72.
28 Ibid., folio 69.
29 NA (UK), FCO 15/1705, folio 206, Foreign and Commonwealth Office, South East Asia, Portuguese Timor.
30 Letter from E.J. Mitchell, British Embassy, Bonn, to L. Jones, South East Asia Department, Foreign and Commonwealth Office, London, 9 December 1975 (NA (UK), FCO 15/1707, folio 260, South East Asia Department, Portuguese Timor).
31 Commonwealth, *Parliamentary Debates*, Senate, Foreign Affairs, Defence and Trade References Committee, Hearing, *Economic, Social and Political Conditions in East Timor*, 6 December 1999, 982 (Gough Whitlam).
32 Gerald Stone, *Say It With Feeling* (Sydney: Pan Macmillan, 2011) 109–111.
33 W.T. Robertson, 'Memorandum dealing with the Termination of the Appointment of W.T. Robertson as Director ASIS by E.G. Whitlam on 21 October 1975', 20 November 2009, NAA, series M4948, 1, barcode 30819720; Max Suich, 'Spymaster Stirs Spectre of Covert Foreign Activities', *The Australian*, 20 March 2010.
34 Stephen Fitzgerald, 'At "Espionage in Australia Exhibition" at the Whitlam Institute (8 March 2019)', available at https://johnmenadue.com/stephen-fitzgerald-at-espionage-in-australia-exhibition-at-the-the-whitlam-institute-8-march-2019/.
35 UN General Assembly, Resolution 3113 (XXVIII) 'Question of Territories under Portuguese Administration', 12 December 1973. Australia supported this resolution; the US, UK, France, Portugal, Brazil, Spain, Belgium, Bolivia and South Africa opposed it. The General Assembly accepted the 'authentic representatives' of the liberation movements in Angola, Sao Tome, Cape Verde and Mozambique. Claims that FRETILIN representatives were present in New York in December 1973 and were refused status at the UN as an authentic representative body for Portuguese Timor are not documented.
36 Daniel P. Moynihan, *A Dangerous Place* (Boston: Little Brown, 1978) 247.
37 Brian Toohey, *Secret: The Making of Australia's Security State* (Carlton, Vic.: Melbourne University Press, 2019) 168.
38 Examiners Notes, 2 May 2006 (NA (UK), PREM 16/1053, Records of Prime Minister's Office, Portugal—Security Situation, Correspondence and Papers 1974–1979); Paddy Hayes makes a similar comment in *Queen of Spies: Daphne Park, Britain's Cold War Spy Master* (London: Duckworth Overlook, 2015) 257–260.
39 Tom McNally, Secret and Personal Memorandum to Secretary of State, Communism and Western European Social Democracy, Prime Minister's

Office, Portugal—Security Situation, Correspondence and Papers 1974–1979 (NA (UK), PREM 16/1053).
40 Christopher Andrew and Oleg Gordievsky (eds), *Instructions from the Centre: Top Secret Files on KGB Foreign Operations* (London: Hodder & Stoughton, 1991) xiii and 20.
41 Cablegram from J.A. Ford, British Ambassador, Jakarta, to Foreign and Commonwealth Office, 3 October 1975 (NA (UK), FCO 15/1705, folio 123, Foreign and Commonwealth Office, South East Asia, Portuguese Timor).
42 Letter from Brian L. Barder, British High Commission, Canberra, to C.W. Squire, South East Asia Dept, Foreign and Commonwealth Office, 12 July 1974 (NA (UK), FCO15/1956, folio 14, Foreign and Commonwealth Office, South East Asia, Political Situation in Portuguese Timor).
43 Commonwealth, *Parliamentary Debates*, House of Representatives, Ministerial Statement, 26 August 1975, 491–493 (Gough Whitlam); E.G. Whitlam, Address to the UN General Assembly, 30 September 1974, 279–283.
44 Commonwealth, *Parliamentary Debates*, House of Representatives, 15 September 1953, 210 (E.G. Whitlam).
45 Alan Renouf, *The Frightened Country* (Melbourne: Macmillan, 1979) 442–443.
46 Record of Meeting Between the Prime Minister and President Soeharto, State Guest House, Yogyakarta, 10 a.m., 6 September 1974, NAA, A1838/1, 756/1/4 Part 4, barcode 558643, Australia–Portugal Negotiations on Portuguese Timor Continental Shelf, folios 274–277.
47 Ibid., folio 274; the remaining half page of folio 274 is torn off and missing, as is the rest of the record; see also Way, 2000, 95, and Letter from Australian Ambassador to Indonesia Richard Woolcott to the Secretary, Dept of External Affairs, Canberra, Portuguese Timor, 24 September 1974 (NAA, series A11443, 1).
48 W. Combs, Ambassador, Jakarta, to Foreign and Commonwealth Office, Political Situation in Portuguese East Timor, 16 September 1974 (NA (UK) FCO 15/1956, folio 22).
49 Renouf, 1979, 442–443.
50 *Documents on Australian Foreign Policy*, Vol. 20. *Australia and the Indonesian Incorporation of East Timor, 1974–1976* (Canberra: AGPS, 2000) Document 34, McLennan's annotation to Minute from Feakes to Lavett and McLennan, Canberra, 20 September 1974.
51 *Documents on Australian Foreign Policy*, Vol. 20. *Australia and the Indonesian Incorporation of East Timor, 1974–1976* (Canberra: AGPS, 2000) Document 21, Memorandum to Rogers, Canberra, 15 August 1974.
52 Letter from P.G. de Courcy-Ireland South West Pacific Dept, Foreign and Commonwealth Office, to G.W. Hewitt, British High Commission, Canberra, 26 September 1974 (NA (UK), FCO 15/1956, folio 20, Foreign and Commonwealth Office, South East Asia, Political Situation in Portuguese Timor).
53 Letter and attachment from G.W. Hewitt, British High Commission, Canberra, to C.W. Squire, SEAD, Foreign and Commonwealth Office, 17 October

1975, (NA (UK), FCO 15/1705, folio 139b, Foreign and Commonwealth Office, South East Asia Department, Portuguese Timor): 'What Renouf had to say confirms our impression that considerable infighting is at present being conducted within DFA, and between Ministers and Australian posts abroad on what line Australia should take on Portuguese Timor. I know the relevant branch in the DFA do not share Mr Renouf's view that a change in policy is required'.
54 Jenny Hocking, *Gough Whitlam: His Time* (Carlton, Vic.: Miegunyah Press, 2012) Vol. 2, 394.
55 Graham Freudenberg, *A Certain Grandeur* (Ringwood, Vic.: Penguin, 2009) 419.
56 Paul Maley, 'Gough Whitlam, Don Willesee Divided on East Timor', *The Australian*, 10 April 2013.
57 Cablegram from Deputy Chief, US Embassy, Jakarta to Secretary of State, 'Timor: Discussion with Australian Chargé', 3 March 1975, available at https://www.wikileaks.org/plusd/cables/1975JAKART02589_b.html/.
58 'Exchange of Remarks between the President and General Suharto, President of Indonesia, Camp David, Maryland' (White House Press Release, 5 July 1975) available at https://www.fordlibrarymuseum.gov/library/document/0248/whpr19750705-004.pdf.
59 Peter Hastings, 'Voice for Timor Independence', *Sydney Morning Herald*, 22 July 1974.
60 'Woodside Hits Gas Off Timor', *The Age*, 28 August 1974.
61 Cablegram from R. Woolcott to Alan Renouf, Dept of Foreign Affairs, 17 August 1975 (NAA, series A11443, 13, barcode 4151649).
62 Support for this proposition is widespread; for example, in a comment by retiring Human Rights Commissioner Gillian Triggs to Jane Hutcheon, *One Plus One*, ABC TV, 22 June 2017, available at http://www.abc.net.au/news/2017-06-23/gillian-triggs-human-rights-commission-radicalised-in-the-job/8643024, and Ben Doherty, 'Australia Condemned for Trying to Make Asylum Seekers "Homeless and Destitute"', *The Guardian*, 11 September 2017.
63 E.G. Whitlam, Address to the UN General Assembly, New York, 30 September 1974, 282.
64 Desmond Ball and Hamish McDonald, *Death in Balibo, Lies in Canberra* (St Leonards, NSW: Allen & Unwin, 2000) 65–71.
65 Jill Joliffe, *Cover-up: The Inside Story of the Balibo Five* (Melbourne: Scribe, 2001); James Cotton (ed.), *East Timor and Australia: AIIA Contributions to the Policy Debate* (Canberra: Australian Defence Studies Centre, 1999).
66 Letter from Ambassador J.A. Ford to C.W. Squire, South East Asian Department, Foreign & Commonwealth Office, 15 September 1975 (NA (UK), FCO 15/1956, Foreign and Commonwealth Office, South East Asia, Political Situation in Portuguese Timor).
67 Hamish McDonald, *Suharto's Indonesia* (Melbourne: Fontana, 1980) 204.
68 Richard Woolcott, *The Hot Seat* (Sydney: HarperCollins, 2003) 153–154.
69 Submission to Minister dated 16 October 1975 by Alan Renouf, NAA, 50 series A11443, 14, barcode4151650.

70 Stone, 2011, 122. There has been little public recognition of the courageous sea voyage media tycoon Kerry Packer and Stone made to Dili in August 1975. Channel 9 cameraman Brian Peters, who travelled with them from Darwin on an old 100-foot ex-trawler, recorded their exploits. Peters, whose compelling images received world prominence, was murdered several weeks later at Balibo.
71 *Documents on Australian Foreign Policy*, Vol. 20, *Australia and the Indonesian Incorporation of East Timor, 1974–1976* (Canberra: AGPS, 2000) Document 260, Minute from Curtin to Feakes and Joseph, Canberra, 15 October 1975.
72 Joliffe, 2001, 11, 52–53, 98; Ball and McDonald, 2000, 69; John G. Taylor, *East Timor: The Price of Freedom* (Annandale, NSW: Pluto Press, 1999) 32; Paul Toohey, 'Whitlam Rejected East Timor Peace Force', *The Telegraph*, 11 April 2013, 15.
73 Geoffrey Robinson, *If You Leave Us Here, We Will Die: How Genocide Was Stopped in East Timor* (Princeton, NJ: Princeton University Press, 2010) 34–37.
74 *Dr Clinton Fernandes v Director-General NAA*, AAT Freedom of Information Division, Sydney, 2017/4836 and 2017/6606, 26–27 April 2018 (unrep); open affidavit of Paul Bruce Symon sworn 15 March 2018. Fernandes sought access to ASIS records on political developments in Portuguese Timor (1974–77) and on Indonesian views of Portuguese Timor (1974–80).
75 As explained later in this chapter, FRETILIN's espousal of these ideals was ultimately a reason why Xanana Gusmão split from FRETILIN in 1987.
76 Adam Schwarz, *A Nation in Waiting: Indonesia's Search for Stability*, 2nd ed. (Boulder, Co: Westview, 2000).
77 United Nations Independent Special Commission of Inquiry for Timor-Leste, *Report*, 2 October 2006, 16, available at http://www.ohchr.org/Documents/Countries/COITimorLeste.pdf.
78 Ibid.
79 Freudenberg, 2009, 419.
80 Letter from G.W. Hewitt, UK Deputy High Commissioner, to J.L. Jones, South East Asia Dept, Foreign and Commonwealth Office, 10 October 1975 (NA (UK), FCO 15/1705, folio 128, Foreign and Commonwealth Office, South East Asia, Portuguese Timor).
81 Cablegram from J.A. Ford, British Ambassador, Jakarta, to Foreign and Commonwealth Office, 3 October 1975 (NA (UK), FCO 15/1705, folio 123, Foreign and Commonwealth Office, South East Asia, Portuguese Timor).
82 Letter from G.A. Duggan, Counsellor, British Embassy, Jakarta, to J.L. Jones, South East Asia Department, Foreign and Commonwealth Office, 3 November 1975 (NA (UK) FCO 15/1706, folio 176, Foreign and Commonwealth Office, South East Asia, Portuguese Timor).
83 Ivan Shearer, 'A Pope, Two Presidents and a Prime Minister', *Journal of International and Comparative Law*, 7 (2) (2001) 429, 431.
84 NAA, *The 'Balibo Affair', East Timor, October 1975* (Fact sheet 238), available at http://www.naa.gov.au/collection/fact-sheets/fs238.aspx.

85 William Burr and Michael L. Evans (eds), *East Timor Revisited: Ford, Kissinger and the Indonesian Invasion, 1975–76* (National Security Archive Electronic Briefing Book No. 62), 6 December 2001, available at http://www.gwu.edu/~nsarchiv/NSAEBB/NSAEBB62/.
86 United Nations Independent Special Commission of Inquiry for Timor-Leste, 2 October 2006, 16.
87 Telegram 1579 from US Embassy Jakarta to US Secretary of State, Ford–Suharto Meeting, Jakarta, 6 December 1975, available at https://nsarchive2.gwu.edu/NSAEBB/NSAEBB242/19751206.pdf.
88 Shearer, 2001, 432.
89 Joliffe, 2001, 11, 52–53, 98; Ball and McDonald, 2000, 69; Taylor, 1999, 32; Toohey, 2013, 15
90 See, for example, Ball and McDonald, 2000, 68–71; Joliffe, 2001.
91 Tom Uren, *Straight Left* (Milsons Point, NSW: Random House, 1994) 302.
92 Douglas Everingham, Letter to *The Australian*, 24 March 1999.
93 Ramos-Horta, 1996, 77.
94 Freudenberg, 2009, 419.
95 Ibid., 423–424.
96 Commonwealth, *Parliamentary Debates*, Senate, Foreign Affairs, Defence and Trade References Committee, Hearing, *Economic, Social and Political Conditions in East Timor*, 6 December 1999, 982 (Gough Whitlam).
97 *Interim Report of the Defence and Foreign Affairs Committee*, Committee Hansard, Parliamentary Paper; 1999, No. 200.
98 Commonwealth, *Parliamentary Debates*, Senate, Foreign Affairs, Defence and Trade References Committee, Hearing, *Economic, Social and Political Conditions in East Timor*, 6 December 1999, 982 (Gough Whitlam).
99 UN General Assembly, Resolution 3485 (XXX) 'Question of Timor', 12 December 1975 (UN Doc A/RES/3485).
100 Taylor, 1999, 32; Toohey, 2013, 15.
101 UN General Assembly, agenda item 88, 12 December 1975 [54] (Mr. Harry) (UN Doc A/PV 2439).
102 UN Security Council, Resolution 384, 22 December 1975 (UN Doc S/RES/384).
103 UN General Assembly, Resolution 3485 (XXX) 'Question of Timor', 12 December 1975 (UN Doc A/RES/3485).
104 UN General Assembly, agenda item 88, 12 December 1975 [54] (Mr. Harry) (UN Doc A/PV 2439).
105 Memorandum by G.A. Duggan to Counsellor Political and Head of Mission, 12 December 1975 (NA (UK), FCO 810/29, folio 280, Foreign and Commonwealth Office, Jakarta Embassy File, Indonesia Portuguese Relations (Portuguese Timor)).
106 Way, 2000; Hocking, 2012, Vol. 2, 384, fn 58, claims that the message to Suharto stemmed from a cable from Feakes at the Dept of Foreign Affairs to Woolcott on 20 November 1975, cited as NAA, series A11443, 14 (probably barcode 4151650), recalled from NAA by the Dept of Foreign Affairs in June 2016.

107 UN General Assembly, agenda item 88, 12 December 1975 [81] (Mr Abduldjalil (Indonesia)) (UN Doc A/PV 2439).
108 Heike Krieger (ed.), *East Timor and the International Community: Basic Documents* (Cambridge: Cambridge University Press, 2011) 129–133.
109 UN Security Council, Resolution 1264, 15 September 1999 (UN Doc S/RES/1264).
110 Moynihan, 1978, 247.
111 'Human Rights in East Timor: Hearing before the Subcommittee on International Organizations of the Committee on International Relations, House of Representatives, Washington, DC, 28 June and 19 July 1977' (Washington DC: USGPO, 1977) 47–48.
112 Despite an Australian historian's comprehensive searches in the National Archives of Australia, no trace of the Fleet Signal and accompanying Dept of Foreign Affairs notation has been located.
113 United Nations Independent Special Commission of Inquiry for Timor-Leste, 2 October 2006, 17.
114 See the chronology in Taylor, 1999, and Clinton Fernandes, 'Accomplice to Mass Atrocities: The International Community and Indonesia's Invasion of East Timor', *Politics and Governance*, 3(4) (2015), 1–11.
115 Desmond Ball, 'Silent Witness: Australian Intelligence and East Timor', in R. Tanter, D. Ball and G. van Klinken (eds), *Masters of Terror: Indonesia's Military and Violence in East Timor* (Lanham, MD: Rowman & Littlefield, 2006).
116 Rose Iser, 'Cables Point to Australian Indifference to Plight of Starving Timorese Thousands,' *The Citizen*, 2 October 2013, available at https://www.thecitizen.org.au/articles/cables-point-australian-indifference-plight-starving-timorese-thousands.
117 Iser, 2013, 4; Clinton Fernandes' requests for access to records in the National Archives of Australia relating to Australia's knowledge of conditions in Timor-Leste during the 1978–79 famine have been opposed by successive governments on grounds of 'national security'.
118 Renouf, 1979, 446.
119 Frédéric Durand, *East Timor: A Country at the Crossroads of Asia and the Pacific: A Geo-Historical Atlas* (Chiang Mai: Silkworm Books, 2006) 66–90; Abílio Pires Lousada, António José Oliveira and Carlos Dias Afonso, '*A Luta Armada Timorense na Resistência à Ocupação 1975–1999* (Lisbon: Tribuna da História, 2014).
120 United Nations Independent Special Commission of Inquiry for Timor-Leste, 2006, 17.
121 Xanana Gusmão, *To Resist is to Win: The Autobiography of Xanana Gusmão*, with selected letters and speeches edited by Sarah Niner (Richmond, Vic.: Aurora, 2000) 134–135.
122 Krieger, 2011, 199.

7 Timor-Leste Edges Towards Independence

1 Treaty between Australia and the Republic of Indonesia on the Zone of Cooperation in an Area between the Indonesian Province of East Timor and

Northern Australia, opened for signature 6 December 1989, 29 ILM 469 (entered into force 9 February 1991).
2. Senate Foreign Affairs, Defence and Trade References Committee, *East Timor: Final Report* (Canberra, 2000) 165–166, available at https://www.aph.gov.au/~/media/wopapub/senate/committee/.../report_pdf.ashx).
3. *East Timor (Portugal v Australia)* (Judgement) [1995] ICJ Rep 90.
4. Ibid., 103.
5. Ibid., 103–104.
6. Ibid., 190, quoting from *Voting Procedure on Questions relating to Reports and Petitions concerning the Territory of South West Africa, Advisory Opinion, ICJ Reports 1955*, 120.
7. Ibid., 190.
8. The author was Deputy Chief Minister of the Australian Capital Territory, Attorney-General and Minister responsible for ACT policing in 1989–91.
9. 'Companion to East Timor: Gareth Evans and the Responsibility to Protect East Timor', available at https://www.unsw.adfa.edu.au/school-of-humanities-and-social-sciences/timor-companion/evans.
10. Shirley Shackleton, *The Circle of Silence* (Sydney: Murdoch Books, 2010) 263–266.
11. *Re Geraldo Magno and Ines Almeida v Gareth Evans, Minister of Foreign Affairs and Trade of the Commonwealth of Australia; Commissioner of the Australian Federal Police and Commonwealth of Australia* [1992] FCA 165 (16 April 1992).
12. *Re Minister of Foreign Affairs and Trade; the Commissioner of the Australian Federal Police and the Commonwealth of Australia v Geraldo Magno and Ines Almeida* [1992] FCA 566 (26 November 1992) [30] (French J).
13. Special Committee on the Situation with regard to the Implementation of the Declaration on the Granting of Independence to Colonial Countries and Peoples, UN Doc A/AC.109/PV.1436 (13 July 1994) 4–5.
14. CNRT Magna Carta Concerning Freedoms, Rights, Duties and Guarantees for the People of East Timor, adopted at the meeting at Peniche, 25 April 1998.
15. Australian Dept of Foreign Affairs and Trade, *East Timor in Transition 1998–2000: An Australian Policy Challenge* (Canberra, 2001) 17.
16. Ibid.
17. Ibid., 24–25.
18. Ibid., 25.
19. J. Ramos-Horta, 'CNRT statement on Timor Gap Oil', 21 July 1998.
20. Australian Dept of Foreign Affairs and Trade, 2001, 42.
21. Ibid., 27.
22. Gusmão and many of his contemporaries benefited from Jesuit tuition at Dare which, for Gusmão, opened a life-long dialogue. In his youth, Mari Alkatiri, a Muslim, also attended.
23. Prime Minister Howard to President Habibie, 19 December 1998, in David Connery, *Crisis Policymaking: Australia and the East Timor Crisis of 1999* (Canberra Papers on Strategy and Defence no. 177) (Canberra: ANU Press, 2010) 147–149, available at http://press-files.anu.edu.au/downloads/press/p501/pdf/appendix1.pdf.

24 Commonwealth, *Parliamentary Debates*, Senate, Foreign Affairs, Defence and Trade References Committee, Hearing, *Economic, Social and Political Conditions in East Timor*, 9 December 1999, 1009 (John Dauth).
25 John W. Howard, *Lazarus Rising* (Sydney: HarperCollins, 2013) 394.
26 Geoffrey Robinson, *If You Leave Us Here, We Will Die: How Genocide Was Stopped in East Timor* (Princeton, NJ: Princeton University Press, 2010) 95.
27 Desmond Ball, 'Silent Witness: Australian Intelligence and East Timor', in R. Tanter, D. Ball and G. van Klinken (eds), *Masters of Terror: Indonesia's Military and Violence in East Timor* (Lanham, MD: Rowman & Littlefield, 2006).
28 Ball, 2006, 188.
29 Robinson, 2010, 166–171.
30 Ball, 2006, 187–188; Ball quotes from informed sources, including leaked intelligence assessments.
31 Geoffrey Robinson, *East Timor 1999 Crimes against Humanity: A Report Commissioned by the United Nations Office of the High Commissioner for Human Rights* (University of California, Los Angeles, July 2003); Robinson, 2010, 107–109.
32 Commonwealth, *Parliamentary Debates*, Senate, Foreign Affairs, Defence and Trade References Committee, Hearing, *Economic, Social and Political Conditions in East Timor*, 9 December 1999, 1004 (John Dauth).
33 Maryanne Kelton, *More than an Ally?: Contemporary Australia–US Relations* (Aldershot, Hants: Ashgate, 2008) 77.
34 Ian Martin, *Self-Determination in East Timor: The United Nations, the Ballot and International Intervention* (International Peace Academy Occasional Paper) (Boulder, Col.: Lynne Rienner, 2001) 25.
35 Ben Kiernan, *Genocide and Resistance in Southeast Asia* (New Brunswick, NJ: Transaction, 2008) 172.
36 Ibid., 179–180.
37 De Sousa is one of the few non-diaspora resistance leaders to publish any form of recollection (*Colibere* (Lisbon: LIDEL 2007)).
38 Kiernan, 2008, 173–174.
39 In the Officers' Mess at the Australian Army base in Canungra, Queensland, a plaque dated 29 November 1971 records the conclusion of a course attended by Hendropriyono. In his subsequent Kopassus role, Hendropriyno also attended an intelligence course at Woodside in Western Australia. As head of the Indonesian State Intelligence Agency, Hendropriyono had extensive dealings with Australian services in 1998–99.
40 Martin, 2001, 121.
41 Ibid., 122.
42 Ball, 2006, 189–190. This included sending Australian Defence Force Deputy Chief, Air Vice-Marshal Doug Riding, on a gallant but inconclusive mission to Jakarta in June 1999 to provide senior TNI officers with evidence of TNI complicity in arming pro-Indonesian militias. The material he used had been sanitised to protect sources and was what the US had sought earlier.
43 Tim Fischer, *Seven Days in East Timor: Ballots and Bullets* (St Leonards, NSW: Allen & Unwin, 2000) 49.

44 John Aglionby and Ian Black, 'Call for International Intervention as East Timor Violence Escalates', *The Guardian*, 2 September 1999, available at https://www.theguardian.com/world/1999/sep/02/indonesia.easttimor.
45 Martin, 2001, 107–108. For the full text of the letter, see Henry Steiner and Philip Alston, *International Human Rights in Context: Law, Politics, Morals*, 2nd ed. (Oxford: Oxford University Press, 2000) 1340.
46 UN Security Council, Resolution 1264, 15 September 1999 (UN Doc S/RES/1264).
47 Kelton, 2008, 62–65.
48 Ibid., 60.
49 The lawfulness of pre-emptive targeted action against identified militia assassins was at this stage an issue within the CNRT.
50 See also Robinson, 2010, 165, and his *East Timor 1999 Crimes against Humanity* (2003) 158, 222.
51 Kelton, 2008, 63.
52 Bill Clinton, Address to APEC, 12 September 1999, available at https://www.youtube.com/watch?v=LZw7nyjekOA (accessed 23 May 2018).
53 Geoffrey C. Gunn and Reyko Huang, *New Nation: United Nations Peace-Building in East Timor* (Nagasaki-shi: Research Institute of Southeast Asia, 2004) 31–40; Martin, 2001, 113.
54 General Peter Cosgrove was appointed to lead the Australian military command of INTERFET in Timor-Leste; see Michael G. Smith, *Peacekeeping in East Timor: The Path to Independence* (Boulder, Col.: Lynne Rienner Publishers, 2003) 45–52.
55 Gunn and Huang, 2004, 46.
56 Martin, 2001, 124.
57 Desmond Ball, 'Silent Witness: Australian Intelligence and East Timor', in R. Tanter, D. Ball and G. van Klinken (eds), *Masters of Terror: Indonesia's Military and Violence in East Timor* (Lanham, MD: Rowman & Littlefield, 2006).
58 Nothing signified Australian diplomacy's arrogant insensitivity more than the Indonesian-style building standing among the ruins of Dili. It is difficult to comprehend the mentality behind an obsequious design so suggestive of Australian support for the invader.

8 Transition in Timor-Leste and the Timor Sea Treaty

1 UN Security Council, Resolution 1272, 25 October 1999 (UN Doc S/RES/1272) 2–3.
2 UNTAET, Regulation No. 1999/1 *On the Authority of the Transitional Administration in East Timor*, 27 November 1999 (UN Doc UNTAET/REG.1991/1).
3 Bernhard Knoll, *The Legal Status of Territories Subject to Administration by International Organisations* (Cambridge: Cambridge University Press, 2008) 40–42, 49 and 160, and with respect to West Papua (UNTEA), Namibia (UNCfN), Cambodia (UNTAC), Kosovo (UNMIK) at 35–36 and 40–49. Knoll also cites John Salford, *The United Nations and the Indonesian Takeover of West Papua, 1962–1969, The Anatomy of Betrayal* (London: Routledge Curzon, 2003).

4 The other contractor parties were Santos (11.83%), Inpex (11.71%), Kerr-McGee (11.2%), Petroz (8.25%), Agip (6.7%).
5 Hans Corell, Under Secretary-General for Legal Affairs, Internal memo 'Timor Gap Treaty', to Bernard Miyet, Under-Secretary-General for Peacekeeping, 2 December 1999 (United Nations, New York) [5].
6 Argued by Portugal in *East Timor (Portugal v Australia)* [1995] ICJ Rep 90.
7 *Armed Activities on the Territory of the Congo (Democratic Republic of the Congo v Uganda)* (Judgement) [2005] ICJ Rep 168 [244].
8 *Certain Phosphate Lands in Nauru (Nauru v Australia)* [1992] ICJ Rep 240.
9 Knoll, 2008, 165–166.
10 Corell, 2 December 1999, [6].
11 De Mello's UN Legal Adviser subsequently explained that the wording of section 3.1 avoided the retroactive legitimisation of the Indonesian occupation as a lawful legal regime in Timor-Leste: Hansjoerg Strohmeyer, 'Policing the Peace: Post Conflict Judicial System Reconstruction in East Timor' *University of New South Wales Law Journal*, 24(1) (2001) 173.
12 Corell, 2 December 1999, [9].
13 *East Timor (Portugal v Australia)* [1995] ICJ Rep 90, 104.
14 *Certain Phosphate Lands in Nauru (Nauru v Australia)* [1992] ICJ Rep 240, 259–260.
15 James Crawford et al. (eds), *The Law of International Responsibility* (Oxford: Oxford University Press, 2010) 663–664; see also Judge Weeramantry's dissenting opinion in *East Timor (Portugal v Australia)* (Judgement) [1995] ICJ Rep 90.
16 Vienna Convention on the Law of Treaties, opened for signature 23 May 1969, 1155 UNTS 331 (entered into force 27 January 1980) Art. 30. *Jus cogens* (literally 'compelling law') denotes a peremptory norm that is a fundamental principle of international law accepted by the international community of states as a norm from which no derogation is permitted.
17 *Declaration on Principles of International Law concerning Friendly Relations and Co-operation among States in accordance with the Charter of the United Nations*, GA Resolution 2625 (XXV), 24 October 1970.
18 *Oscar Chinn (Britain v Belgium)* (1934) PCIJ Ser A/B No. 63, 148.
19 Oliver Dörr and Kirsten Schmalenbach (eds), *Vienna Convention on the Law of Treaties: A Commentary* (Heidelberg: Springer, 2012) 901.
20 Knoll, 2008 at 161 examines the issues of trusteeship, discussing the functions of international administrations in chapter 4 and the character and function of UN administration of 'complex emergencies' at page 161.
21 This divisive process, anticipated to engage claims for compensation for historic black slavery in the US, lasted for 17 years and was eventually brought by Chile to a non-vote conclusion in the General Assembly: 'Basic Principles and Guidelines on the Right to a Remedy and Reparations for Victims of Gross Violations of International Human Rights Laws and Serious Violations of International Humanitarian Law', General Assembly Resolution 60/147, 16 December 2005.
22 *Prosecutor v Tadic* (Appeals Chamber) IT-94-1-A, 15 July 1999, [296]; see Dörr and Schmalenbach, 2012, 929–930.

23 *Application of the Convention on the Prevention of the Crime of Genocide (Bosnia and Herzegovina v Serbia and Montenegro) (Provisional Measures)* [1993] ICJ Rep 407, [100].
24 Peter Galbraith, 'The United Nations and Administration of Territory: The United Nations Transitional Authority in East Timor (UNTAET)', *Proceedings of the Annual Meeting (American Society of International Law)*, 97 (2003) 210–212.
25 Karen Polglaze, 'Timor Gap Treaty in Doubt', *The Canberra Times*, 30 November 1999, 2.
26 Knoll, 2008, at 49 claims the argument that UNTAET was exercising 'full and complete sovereignty' is untenable.
27 Gillian Triggs, 'Legal and Commercial Risks of Investment in the Timor Gap', *Melbourne Journal of International Law*, 5 (2000) 103. Apart from the Bayu-Undan shareholders referred to earlier, the stakeholders in the then Greater Sunrise Field operation by Woodside Energy at Sunrise, Troubadour and Loxton Shoals were Woodside (33.44%), Phillips Petroleum (30%), Royal Dutch Shell (26.56%), and Osaka Gas (10%).
28 As A.C. Grayling describes it in *The Challenge of Things* (London: Bloomsbury, 2015) 59.
29 Hans Corell, Under Secretary-General for Legal Affairs, Letter to President of the Security Council, 29 January 2002, available at www.arso.org/UNlegaladv.htm.
30 UN Security Council. Resolution 276, 30 January 1970 (UN Doc S/RES/276); UN General Assembly Resolution 36/51, 24 November 1981 (UN Doc A/RES/36/51); UN General Assembly, Resolution 39/42, 5 December 1984 (UN Doc A/RES/39/42).
31 Commonwealth, *Parliamentary Debates*, House of Representatives, 30 October 1970, Vol. II, 3108 (William McMahon, Minister for External Affairs).
32 Rose Iser, 'Cables Point to Australian Indifference to Plight of Starving Timorese Thousands', *The Citizen*, 2 October 2013, available at https://www.thecitizen.org.au/articles/cables-point-australian-indifference-plight-starving-timorese-thousands; Clinton Fernandes, 'Accomplice to Mass Atrocities: The International Community and Indonesia's Invasion of East Timor', *Politics and Governance*, 3(4) (2015) 1–11.
33 Grandfather Crocodile—the creation myth of the island of Timor, which when viewed at a distance from the air resembles a crocodile.
34 'Note for the File' by Juan Antonio Escudero, Associate Ocean Affairs/Law of the Sea Officer, Division for Ocean Affairs and the Law of the Sea, United Nations, 15 November 1999.
35 Corell, 2 December 1999, [7].
36 Department of Foreign Affairs, Republic of Indonesia, Non-paper, 'The Status of the Timor Gap Treaty', January 2000 (held by the author).
37 Code Cable No. 72 (Immediate) from Vieira de Mello, UNTAET, to Bernard Miyet, Under-Secretary-General for Peacekeeping, 28 January 2000, [2].
38 Exchange of Notes constituting an Agreement between the Government of Australia and the United Nations Transitional Administration in East Timor (UNTAET) concerning the continued Operation of the Treaty between

Australia and the Republic of Indonesia on the Zone of Cooperation in an Area between the Indonesian Province of East Timor and Northern Australia of 11 December 1989, Australia-UNTAET, signed 10 February 2000, [2000] ATS 9 (entered into force 10 February 2000 with effect from 25 October 1999).
39 Communications from UNTAET, March 2000 (held by the author).
40 Communications from UNTAET, May 2000 (held by the author).
41 Daphna Shaga, Note to File, 24 May 2000 (held by the author).
42 Note from Peter W. Galbraith to Hans Corell and Bernard Miyet, 30 May 2000 (held by the author).
43 On 26 July 2015, at the ALP's national conference, former parliamentarian Janelle Saffin moved a motion, seconded by Shadow Attorney-General Mark Dreyfus, which deleted the reference to median or line of equidistance in the ALP national platform. This was consistent with Timor-Leste's extraordinary backdown in the ICJ and PCA.
44 Travelling with Xanana Gusmão in a remote district in early 2000, the party was sleeping on the swept-dirt floor of a hut around a central smoking pit. In the morning Xanana was gone but, next to the author, a light-coloured dog appeared in his place, causing consternation. Xanana was out watching the sunrise and smoking a cigarette.
45 From the author's notes of the conference.
46 An Australian Mission official was overheard saying, 'Alkatiri has been completely outvoted here. It's a disaster'.
47 Australia's repressive security laws prevent a full reporting of this issue.
48 Jarat Chopra, 'Building State Failure in East Timor', *Development and Change*, 33(5) (2002) 993.
49 Constâncio Pinto, Address to the UN Special Committee the Situation with regard to the Implementation of the Declaration on the Granting of Independence to Colonial Countries and Peoples, 13 July 1994 (UN Doc A/AC.109/PV.1436) 4–5.

9 The Transitional Government Negotiates a New Treaty

1 Galbraith's comment referred to the resolution carried at the ALP National Conference on 3 August 2000, noted in chapter 8, to support settling a maritime boundary with Timor-Leste on lines of equidistance.
2 Minutes of Timor Sea Talks, Morning Session, Cairns, North Queensland, 11 December 2000 (held by the author).
3 Ibid.
4 Ibid.
5 Ibid.
6 Roger G. Skirrow, *et al., Critical Commodities for a High-tech World: Australia's Potential to Supply a Global Demand* (Canberra: Geoscience Australia, 2013) 64, available at http://www.ga.gov.au/corporate_data/76526/76526.pdf.
7 Xanana Gusmão, *To Resist is to Win: The Autobiography of Xanana Gusmão*, with selected letters and speeches edited by Sara Niner (Richmond, Vic.: Aurora, 2000), 231; see also Sara Niner, 'Maun Bot: Our Brother', *Meanjin*, 61(3) (2002) 179–185.

8 Commonwealth, *Parliamentary Debates*, Joint Standing Committee on Treaties, *Timor Sea Treaties*, 14 October 2002, 272–273.
9 *Norwegian Petroleum Act*, No. 72 relating to Petroleum Activities, 29 November 1996, ss 1–6(a), definitions of 'Petroleum'.
10 Draft Australian Text, Memorandum of Understanding between the Government of Australia and the Transitional Administration in East Timor (UNTAET), Acting on Behalf of East Timor, and The East Timor Transitional Administration on Future Arrangements for an Area of Seabed between Australia and East Timor, 18 May 2001.
11 Draft Australian Text, Memorandum of Understanding ... 18 May 2001.
12 The standard Indonesian PSC gave the contractor a 17% investment credit.
13 Memorandum of Understanding of Timor Sea Arrangement, Australia–UNTAET, signed 5 July 2001 (entered into force 5 July 2001).
14 Letter dated 5 July 2001 from Alexander Downer, Minister for Foreign Affairs, Canberra to Dr Mari Alkatiri, Cabinet Member for Economic Affairs, East Timor Transitional Administration and to Mr Peter Galbraith, Cabinet member for Political Affairs and Timor Sea, East Timor Transitional Administration (held by the author).
15 G.W. Tate, *et al.*, 'Australia Going Down Under: Quantifying Continental Subduction During Arc-Continent Accretion in Timor-Leste', *Geosphere* 11(6) (2015), 1.
16 UNTAET's role in Timor-Leste has attracted sustained criticism. Samantha Power, former UN Ambassador and foreign policy adviser to President Barack Obama and now at Harvard Law School and Harvard Kennedy School, has been strongly critical of the UN, making an unfavourable assessment of de Mello in her *Chasing the Flame: Sergio Vieira de Mello and the Fight to Save the World* (London: Penguin, 2008).
17 Josh Frydenberg, 'Power to Ease Energy Crisis Rests with the States', *The Australian*, 10 July 2017.

10 'Independence' for Timor-Leste

1 Jarat Chopra, 'Building State Failure in East Timor', *Development and Change*, 33(5) (2002) 993.
2 UN Security Council, Resolution 1338, 31 January 2001 (UN Doc S/RES/1338).
3 UNTAET Regulation 2001/2, 'On the Election of a Constituent Assembly to Prepare a Constitution for an Independent and Democratic East Timor', 16 March 2001, Art. 2.6.
4 Samantha Power, *Chasing the Flame: Sergio Vieira de Mello and the Fight to Save the World* (London: Penguin, 2008) 328.
5 United Nations Dept of Public Information, 'The United Nations and East Timor: A Chronology', available at https://peacekeeping.un.org/mission/past/etimor/Untaetchrono.html.
6 *Report of the Secretary-General on the United Nations Transitional Administration in East Timor: For the Period from 25 July to 15 October 2001*, UN SCOR, 18 October 2001 (UN Doc S/2001/983).

7 Despite the outcome of the ballot for independence, initial meetings of de Mello's Consultative Council, nominated by Kofi Annan, included a group of pro-autonomy delegates viewed by many as collaborators. Generously, it was Xanana Gusmão's edict carried far and wide that ensured the safety of the delegates. The UN writ ran nowhere. Likewise, despite the 1998 resolution creating the combined CNRT resistance, the UN provided a separate seat at the table for the UDT and for FRETILIN, despite unresolved issues relating to alleged crimes against humanity, including UDT involvement in the Balibo murders in 1974–75.
8 UN Security Council, Resolution 1272, 25 October 1999 (UN Doc S/RES/1272) Point 8.
9 *Report of the Secretary-General on the United Nations Transitional Administration in East Timor: For the Period from 27 January to 26 July 2000*, UN SCOR, 26 July 2000 (UN Doc S/2000/738) [14].
10 Randall Garrison, *The Role of Constitution-Building Processes in Democratization: Case Study, East Timor* (Stockholm: IDEA, 2005) 11, available at http://constitutionnet.org/vl/item/idea-role-constitution-building-processes-democratization-case-study-east-timor.
11 Ibid., 12.
12 Ibid.
13 Alipio Baltazar, 'An Overview of the Constitution Drafting Process in East Timor', *East Timor Law Journal* 9 (2004), available at http://easttimorlawjournal.blogspot.com/2012/05/an-overview-of-constitution-drafting.html.
14 Garrison, 2005, 20. Moves within FRETILIN by the Mudanca (Reform) Group, led by Constituent Assembly member Adérito Soares, to open up debate were blocked; Soares resigned from the Assembly in 2002, citing differences with Alkatiri.
15 Conversation between the author and Sergio de Mello SRSG, Dili, June 2001.
16 UN Independent Special Commission of Inquiry for Timor-Leste, *Report of the United Nations*, 2 October 2006, 17, available at http://www.ohchr.org/Documents/Countries/COITimorLeste.pdf.

11 The FALINTIL Tragedy

1 UN Independent Special Commission of Inquiry for Timor-Leste, *Report of the United Nations*, 2 October 2006, 18, available at http://www.ohchr.org/Documents/Countries/COITimorLeste.pdf.
2 Geoffrey Robinson, *If You Leave Us Here, We Will Die* (Princeton, NJ: Princeton University Press, 2010) 105.
3 Robinson, 2010, 107; Robinson's account differs only in emphasis.
4 Michael G. Smith, *Peacekeeping in East Timor: The Path to Independence* (Boulder, Col.: Lynne Rienner, 2003) 49.
5 Memorandum of Advice from the author to Xanana Gusmão, President CNRT, 6 October 1999.
6 Peter Cosgrove recalls this incident in *My Story* (Pymble, NSW: HarperCollins, 2007) 268–275.

7 Kings College Centre for Defence Studies, *Independent Study on Security Force Options and Security Sector Reform in East Timor* (London, 2000).
8 Ibid.
9 Ibid.
10 Sven Gunnar Simonsen, 'The Authoritarian Temptation in East Timor: Nationbuilding and the Need for Inclusive Governance', *Asian Survey*, 46(4) (2006) 575.
11 Luke Charles-Jones, *Assessing Australia's Regional Interventions: The Solomon Islands 2003 and East Timor 2006* (Shedden Papers) (Canberra: Centre for Defence and Strategic Studies, Australian Defence College, 2011) 24.
12 John Pilger, *Distant Voices* (London: Vintage, 1992); Pilger makes little mention of FALINTIL carrying on the armed struggle after 1987. Chomsky spoke at the National Press Club in Canberra on 24 January 1995 in support of the East Timorese. On the drive from the airport, Chomsky surprised the author by speaking of the ongoing 'FRETILIN' armed struggle. Confusing FRETILIN with FALINTIL was a common and understandable error. Chomsky's pithy preface for Ramos-Horta's 1986 book *Funu* is a memorable indictment of US, Australian and Western collaboration with Indonesia.

12 Australian Opportunism

1 Alexander Downer and Daryl Williams, 'Changes to International Dispute Resolution', joint media release, 21 March 2002, available at https://foreignminister.gov.au/releases/2002/fa039j_02.html.
2 Memorandum of Understanding between the Government of the Democratic Republic of East Timor and the Government of Australia Concerning an International Agreement for the Greater Sunrise Field, East Timor-Australia, signed 20 May 2002 (entered into force 20 May 2002).
3 Oliver Dörr and Kirsten Schmalenbach (eds), *Vienna Convention on the Law of Treaties: A Commentary* (Heidelberg: Springer, 2012) 927–928.
4 Ibid., 929.
5 'Declarations Recognizing as Compulsory the Jurisdiction of the International Court of Justice under Article 36(2) of the Statute of the Court', in *Multilateral Treaties Deposited with the Secretary-General: Status as at 31 December 2006*, Vol. I (UN Doc ST/LEG/SER.E/25) 12.
6 It is salutary to recollect the widely reported description by Prime Minister Gough Whitlam of France as a 'rogue' state when it took steps to withdraw from ICJ jurisdiction in January 1974.
7 *Military and Paramilitary Activities in and against Nicaragua (Nicaragua v United States of America) (Jurisdiction and Admissibility)* [1984] ICJ Rep 420, 16, [63].
8 Article 95 of the Constitution of the Democratic Republic of Timor-Leste requires prior parliamentary approval and presidential assent to treaties.
9 The Timor Sea Treaty states that it gives effect to Article 83 of UNCLOS, which requires states to make every effort to enter into provisional arrangements of a practical nature pending agreement on the final delimitation of the continental shelf between them in a manner consistent with international law: Timor Sea Treaty between the Government of East Timor and the Government of Australia, Timor-Leste-Australia, signed

20 May 2002, 2258 UNTS 3 (entered into force 2 April 2003) Art. 1(j)(iii); Agreement between the Government of Australia and the Government of the Democratic Republic of Timor-Leste relating to the Unitisation of the Sunrise and Troubadour Fields, Australia-Timor-Leste, signed 6 March 2003, 2483 UNTS 317 (entered into force on 23 February 2007) Art. 1(j)(iii) and Art. 2.

10 'The capacity of a State to provisionally apply a treaty is of such importance that it would normally be settled by the highest authoritative law of the land, the constitution' (Mahnoush H. Arsanjani and W. Michael Reisman, 'The Law of Treaties Beyond the Vienna Convention', in Enzo Cannizzaro (ed.), *The Law of Treaties: Beyond the Vienna Convention* (Oxford: Oxford University Press, 2011) 93).

11 Minutes, Timor Sea Treaty Joint Commission for the Joint Petroleum and Development Area, First Meeting, 19 May 2002.

12 *Offshore Petroleum and Greenhouse Gas Storage Act 2006*, section 7: 'petroleum' means: (a) any naturally occurring hydrocarbon, whether in a gaseous, liquid or solid state; or (b) any naturally occurring mixture of hydrocarbons, whether in a gaseous, liquid or solid state; or (c) any naturally occurring mixture of: (i) one or more hydrocarbons, whether in a gaseous, liquid or solid state; and (ii) one or more of the following, that is to say, hydrogen sulphide, nitrogen, helium and carbon dioxide'.

13 Lighter Than Air—The Helium Escapes

1 Suzanne D. Golding, Chris J. Boreham and Joan S. Esterle, 'Stable Isotope Geochemistry of Coal Bed and Shale Gas and Related: A Review', *International Journal of Coal Geology*, 120(1) (2013) 27; C.J. Boreham, D.S. Edwards, and R.J. Poreda, 'Helium Isotopic Distribution of Australian Natural Gases', 2016?, available at https://d28rz98at9flks.cloudfront.net/101684/101684_abstract.pdf.

2 Steve Mohr and James Ward, 'Helium Production and Possible Projection', *Minerals*, 4(1) (2014) 130, available at https://www.mdpi.com/2075-163X/4/1/130/htm.

3 Sarah Sedghi, 'Tanzania Helium Discovery to Boost Declining Global Supply', ABC Radio National *PM*, 29 June 2016, available at http://www.abc.net.au/pm/content/2016/s4491443.htm (accessed 31 December 2018).

4 Susan Williamson, 'Recycling Helium', *Lab+Life Scientist*, 31 July 2013, available at http://www.labonline.com.au/content/life-scientist/news/recycling-helium-271499864.

5 ASX *Listing Rules*, 'Chapter 5: Additional Reporting on Mining and Oil and gas Production and Exploration Activities', 2014, available at https://www.asx.com.au/documents/rules/Chapter05.pdf

6 R.J. Seggie, *et al.*, 'Awakening of a Sleeping Giant: Sunrise-Troubadour Gas-Condensate Field' *Australian Petroleum Production and Exploration Association Journal*, 40(1) (2000) 427.

7 Roger G. Skirrow, *et al.*, *Critical Commodities for a High-tech World: Australia's Potential to Supply a Global Demand* (Canberra: Geoscience Australia, 2013) 64, available at http://www.ga.gov.au/corporate_data/76526/76526.pdf.

8 Kathryn Waltenberg, 'Helium as a Critical Commodity: Opportunities in the Northern Territory', in *Northern Territory Geological Survey Annual Geoscience Exploration Seminar 17–18 March 2015* (Darwin: Northern Territory Government, 2015), available at https://geoscience.nt.gov.au/gemis/ntgsjspui/handle/1/82385.
9 Davina Danabalan, *et al.*, 'Helium—Hero or Houdini?', *Geoscientist Online*, 27(11) (December 2017), available at https://www.geolsoc.org.uk/Geoscientist/Archive/December-January-2017-18/Helium-Hero-or-Houdini.
10 Leslie A. Thiess, 'Managing the BLM's Helium Program', US Department of the Interior, Bureau of Land Management, 2015.
11 *Public Law 113-40*, 50 USC 167, s 16; see also US Geological Survey, 'Helium', available at https://minerals.usgs.gov/minerals/pubs/commodity/helium/mcs-2018-heliu.pdf.
12 The joint-venture participants held PSC areas known as 91-12 and 91-13 within Area A of the Australia–Indonesia Timor Gap Zone of Cooperation (ZOCA). The gas split agreed in 1997 was, respectively, 55.2% and 44.8% of the two PSC areas. By February 2000, as negotiations between Australia and UNTAET on the gas split got underway, the joint-venture participants in the Bayu-Undan Project were Phillips Petroleum (Operator) (50.29%), Santos (11.83%), Inpex (11.71%), Kerr-McGee (11.2%), Petroz (8.25%), Agip (6.7%).
13 ASX, PTZ Announcement, 8 December 2000, Document No. 138240, Part A.
14 ASX, PTZ Announcement, 2 January 2001, Document No. 138516; four months later, on 24 April 2001, Costello blocked the takeover of Woodside Petroleum by the Royal Dutch Shell Group.
15 ASX, PTZ Announcement, 1 February 2001, Document No. 138974.
16 ASX, PTZ, Announcement, 13 September 2001, Document No. 142426, Part E.
17 Interview with the author, Canberra, 12 January 2016.
18 Australian Stock Exchange (ASX) listed Disclosure Notice by Petroz, 24 February 1998.
19 Michele G. Bishop, *Total Petroleum Systems of the Bonaparte Gulf Basin Area* ... (Open-File Report 99-50-P) (US Geological Survey, 1999), available at https://pubs.usgs.gov/of/1999/ofr-99-0050/OF99-50P/.
20 Interview with the author, Canberra, 12 January 2016.
21 Ibid.
22 Australia's national security assessments regarding supply of strategic commodities such as petroleum and helium are classified documents that cannot be addressed by the author. Such information has been targeted by foreign powers. Several government departments and agencies provide advice that forms an integral aspect of defence intelligence reviews. There is no effective independent oversight in Australia of the involvement of private industry in alleged national security aspects of the supply of strategic commodities. Current national security laws prevent the author from addressing questionable aspects of foreign intelligence agency and corporate liaison within DFAT during the Timor Sea imbroglio.

23 David Wood, 'Australia Has Nowhere to Put its Shipment of French Nuclear Waste', *Vice News*, 14 July 2014, available at https://news.vice.com/article/australia-has-nowhere-to-put-its-shipment-of-french-nuclear-waste (accessed 1 January 2019).
24 Timor Sea Designated Authority for the Joint Petroleum Development Area, Production Sharing Contract JPDA 03-12, 2 April 2003, available at http://www.laohamutuk.org/Oil/PSCs/JPDA03-12.pdf.
25 Bernard Callinan, *Independent Company: The Australian Army in Portuguese Timor 1941–43* (Melbourne: Heinemann, 1953) 203.
26 Klaus Ohlig, 'The Darwin Helium Facility Operation of a Helium Purification, Liquefaction and Distribution Plant', 2010, available at https://www.laohamutuk.org/Oil/tax/LindeDarwinHeliumMay2010s.pdf.
27 BOC, 'BOC Building First Australian Helium Plant', Media Release, 3 June 2008.
28 Ohlig, 2010.
29 Williamson, 2013.
30 'BOC Opens Australia's First Helium Plant in Darwin', BOC News Release, 3 March 2010, available at http://www.laohamutuk.org/Oil/tax/RL_Darwin_Helium_opening_Australia_020310.pdf.
31 ConocoPhillips, 'ConocoPhillips in Photos—10-year Perspective' *Spirit Magazine*, first quarter 2010, 11.
32 US Geological Survey, 'Helium', *Mineral Commodity Summaries*, available at https://minerals.usgs.gov/minerals/pubs/commodity/helium/mcs-2016-heliu.pdf.
33 Waltenberg, 2015.
34 Skirrow *et al.*, 2013.
35 US Geological Survey, 'Helium'.
36 Timor Sea Treaty between the Government of East Timor and the Government of Australia, Timor-Leste-Australia, signed 20 May 2002, 2258 UNTS (entered into force 2 April 2003) Art. 1(j)(iii); Agreement between the Government of Australia and the Government of the Democratic Republic of Timor-Leste relating to the Unitisation of the Sunrise and Troubadour Fields, Australia-Timor-Leste, signed 6 March 2003, 2483 UNTS 317 (entered into force on 23 February 2007) Art. 1(j)(iii).
37 Timor Sea Treaty ..., 2002, Art. 1(j)(iii); Agreement ... relating to the Unitisation of the Sunrise and Troubadour Fields, Australia-Timor-Leste, ... 2003, Art. 1(j)(iii) and Art. 1(o).
38 Agreement ... relating to the Unitisation of the Sunrise and Troubadour Fields, ... 2003, Art. 12(1).
39 Ibid., Art. 1(t).
40 Ibid., Art. 1(i).
41 Timor Sea Designated Authority ..., 2 April 2003, s 7.6 (as amended by Appendix X).
42 'Good Oil Field Practice' is defined in the *Petroleum Mining Code for the Joint Petroleum Development Area*, 6, available at https://policy.asiapacificenergy.org/sites/default/files/PETROLEUM%20MINING%20CODE.pdf (accessed 2 January 2019).

43. United Nations, *Guiding Principles on Business and Human Rights*, 2011, 3, available at http://www.ohchr.org/Documents/Publications/Guiding PrinciplesBusinessHR_EN.pdf (accessed 2 January 2019).
44. *Hospital Products Limited v United States Surgical Corporation & Ors* (1984) 156 CLR 41, 96; for more detail, see Paul Finn, *Fiduciary Obligations: 40th Anniversary Republication* (Annandale, NSW: Federation Press, 2016); James Edelman, 'When Do Fiduciary Duties Arise', *Law Quarterly Review* 126 (2010) 302–327.
45. Finn, 2017, 372.
46. *Barnes v Addy* (1874) LR 9 Ch App 244, 251–252.
47. *Bell Group N.V. (in Liquidation) v Western Australia* [2016] HCA 21 (16 May 2016)—Justice Gageler, 'the basic problem here is that the drafter of the Bell Act either has forgotten the existence of the Tax Acts or has decided to proceed blithely in disregard of their existence. That, indeed, is the basic problem'; see also Andrew Probyn and Shane Wright, 'Christian Porter knew of WA's $1.8 billion Bell Group leapfrog', *The West Australian*, 1 December 2016, available at https://thewest.com.au/news/australia/christian-porter-knew-of-was-18-billion-bell-group-leapfrog-ng-ya-124715.
48. *Farah Constructions Pty Ltd v Say-Dee Pty Ltd* (2007) 230 CLR 89 (Gleeson CJ, Gummow, Callinan, Heydon and Crennan JJ).
49. *Grimaldi v Chameleon Mining NL (No. 2)* [2012] FCAFC 6; (2012) FCR 296 (Finn, Stone and Perram JJ); see also W. Gummow, 'Knowing Assistance', *Australian Law Journal*, 87 (2013) 311, and J. Dietrich and P. Ridge, *Accessories in Private Law* (Cambridge: Cambridge University Press, 2015) 240–242.
50. B.A. McKay, *Helium Resources and Developments in Australia: Speaking Notes Figures and Tables* (for Petroleum and Minerals Review Conference, Canberra 18–19 March 1987) (Canberra: Bureau of Minerals, Geology and Geophysics, 1987) 3, available at http://www.ga.gov.au/corporate_data/14150/Rec1987_022.pdf.
51. Timor Sea Designated Authority …, 2 April 2003, s 5.5.
52. Interview by the author with Einar Risa, Oslo, 17 January 2013.
53. Timor Sea Designated Authority …, 2 April 2003, s 7.1.
54. Ibid., s 8.3.
55. Ibid., s 5.2(f).
56. Ibid., s 15.6.
57. D.L. Andress, *The Phillips Optimized Cascade LNG Process: A Quarter Century of Improvements* (Bartlesville, OK: Phillips Petroleum Company, 1996).
58. Mohr and Ward, 2014.
59. Northern Territory Convention Bureau, 'Oil and Gas Fact Sheet', available at http://alicespringsconventioncentre.com.au/files/images/Oil_and_Gas_Fact_Sheet_FA.pdf.
60. The first Sunrise relevant gas data from the Troubadour-1 well became available to Woodside and the BMR, Canberra, in August–September 1974; that data has not been released fully.
61. ConocoPhillips, *2016 Annual Report*, 174, available at http://static.conocophillips.com/files/resources/conocophillips_2016_annualreport.pdf (accessed 2 January 2019).

62 As Australia's Ambassador in Beijing in 2000–03, Irvine had overseen significant Australian trade expansion in China, which included a A$25 billion LNG supply contract for the consortium led by Woodside Petroleum, whose executives, including Chairman Don Voelte, he had hosted during the negotiation phases in Beijing.
63 Treaty between Australia and the Democratic Republic of Timor-Leste on Certain Maritime Arrangements in the Timor Sea, Australia–Timor-Leste, signed 12 January 2006, 2483 UNTS 359 (entered into force 12 January 2006) Art. 5 (12); also Joint Standing Committee on Treaties, House of Representatives, *Treaties tabled on 6 and 7 February 2007*, Report No. 85 (2007) 46, [6.30]: 'The Committee notes that, as a consequence of Article 4, Australia will be able to continue regulating and authorizing petroleum activities outside of the JPDA and south of the 1972 Australia-Indonesia seabed treaty. This area encompasses the Laminaria-Corallina gas fields, preventing further revenue claims between the two countries in this area'.
64 The dissenting judge was Judge Ian Callinan, appointed by Brandis as Australia's *ad hoc* nominee to the ICJ. Callinan's dissent sits uneasily with his forthright reminder of 'the need for actual and apparent abstention from pre-judgement' (*Antoun v The Queen* [2006] HCA 2, 8 February 2006, [81] (Callinan J)).
65 Sol Dolor, 'DLA Piper Guides Timor-Leste to Historic Treaty with Australia', *Australasian Lawyer*, 9 March 2018, available at https://www.australasian lawyer.com.au/news/dla-piper-guides-timorleste-to-historic-treaty-with-australia-247492.aspx (accessed 2 January 2019).
66 R.J. Seggie, *et al.*, 'The Sunrise-Troubadour Gas-Condensate Fields, Timor Sea, Australasia', in M.T. Haboulty (ed.), *Giant Oil and Gas Fields of the Decade 1990–1999* (American Association of Petroleum Geologists Memoir 78) (AAPG, 2003) 189–209.
67 Seggie, *et al.*, 2003.
68 Seggie, *et al.*, 2000, 428.
69 Ibid., 427.
70 Josh Frydenberg, radio interview, 14 April 2016, cited by Robert King *The Timor Gap 1972–2017*, Submission No. 27 to the Inquiry by the Joint Standing Parliamentary Committee on Treaties into Certain Maritime Arrangements, March 2017, 82 fn 453.
71 La'o Hamutuk, a Timorese public interest NGO, reports that, despite requests, neither the Timor-Leste Government nor any other joint-venture participant will release publicly the two Sunrise PSCs, JPDA 03-19 and JPDA 03-20.
72 Interview with the author, 18 July 2017.
73 Treaty Between Australia and the Democratic Republic of Timor-Leste Establishing Their Maritime Boundaries in The Timor Sea, signed 6 March 2018 (unratified), Art. 9 (2).
74 Ibid., Art. 1, 'Valuation Point', Annex B, Art. 3(j), 'collecting revenues … prior to the Valuation Point', Art. 4 and Art. 9.
75 Treaty Between Australia and the Democratic Republic of Timor-Leste Establishing Their Maritime Boundaries in The Timor Sea, signed 6 March 2018 (unratified), Annex B, Art. 4.

76 Peter Lloyd, 'East Timor Accuses Australia of Colluding with Companies over Greater Sunrise Oil and Gas Deal', *ABC News*, 7 March 2018, available at http://www.abc.net.au/news/2018-03-06/east-timor-acuses-australia-of-collusion/9519530 (accessed 2 January 2019).
77 *Report and Recommendations of the Compulsory Conciliation Commission Between Timor-Leste and Australia on the Timor Sea*, 9 May 2018, Permanent Court of Arbitration, PCA Case No. 2016-10.
78 Ibid., Annex 27.

14 A Matter for Inquiry

1 See *Commonwealth v WMC Resources Ltd* [1998] HCA 8; 194 CLR 1; 152 ALR 1; 72 ALJR 280 (2 February 1998) for an insight into how the petroleum companies and an accommodating Australian legislature provided legitimacy to petroleum exploration activity in the disputed areas of the Timor Sea.
2 Petroz Lodgement of ASX Form 281 Notice that Company Intends to Carry Out Buy-Back, 24 May 2001.
3 ASX records indicate that the last annual general meeting to be notified was held on 24 October 1997.
4 'Independent Expert Report of Grant Samuel', 5 August 2003, 13, in *ConocoPhillips WA-248 Pty Ltd v Batoka Pty Ltd* [2005] WASC 184 (23 August 2005).
5 *ConocoPhillips WA-248 Pty Ltd v Batoka Pty Ltd* [2005] WASC 184 (23 August 2005); Report of Ian Northcott, Director, PetroVal Australasia Pty Ltd, 5 August 2003, 1.
6 Ibid., 5.
7 *Petroleum (Timor Gap Zone of Cooperation) Act 1990* and *Petroleum (Timor Sea Treaty) Act 2003* (Cth).
8 *ConocoPhillips WA-248 Pty Ltd v Batoka Pty Ltd* [2005] WASC 184 (23 August 2005); Report of Ian Northcott, Director, PetroVal Australasia Pty Ltd, 5 August 2003, 3.
9 *ConocoPhillips WA-248 Pty Ltd v Batoka Pty Ltd* [2005] WASC 184 (23 August 2005) [82].
10 ASIC, *Independence of Experts' Reports* (Practice Note 42), 8 December 1993 [23].
11 Affidavit in Support of Originating Process of Reginald Stephen Cooper, Director, Grant Samuel & Associates Pty Limited, sworn 26 October 2004 and filed in proceedings *COR 322 of 2003, Petroz NL/ConocoPhillips WA-248 Pty Ltd v Batoka Pty Ltd* as Defendant, 28 October 2004, 21.
12 Stephen R. Brand, Director, CPWA-248 Pty Ltd, to Stephen Cooper, Director, Grant Samuel & Associates Pty Limited, 5 August 2003, 1.
13 *ASX Listing Rules*, Chapter 5: Additional Reporting on Mining and Oil and Gas Production and Exploration Activities, available at http://www.asx.com.au/documents/rules/Chapter05.pdf.
14 ConocoPhillips WA lawyer, Paul D. Evans, of Freehills, was in August 2011 appointed State Solicitor for Western Australia by that state's Attorney-General, Christian Porter, during the Bell Resources issue with the Commonwealth Government.

15 Australian Gameplay

1 Agreement between the Government of Australia and the Government of the Democratic Republic of Timor-Leste relating to the Unitisation of the Sunrise and Troubadour Fields, Australia–Timor-Leste, signed 6 March 2003, 2483 UNTS 317 (entered into force on 23 February 2007); enacted into Australian law by the *Greater Sunrise Unitization Agreement Implementation Act 2004* (Cth).

2 Memorandum of Understanding between the Government of the Democratic Republic of East Timor and the Government of Australia concerning an International Unitization Agreement for the Greater Sunrise Field, Timor-Leste-Australia, signed 20 May 2002, available at http://www.un.org/Depts/los/LEGISLATIONANDTREATIES/PDFFILES/TREATIES/AUS-TLS2002SUN.PDF.

3 John Akehurst, Managing Director, Woodside Petroleum, quoted in 'Australia's Woodside Sees No Threat from Timor Gas Rivalry', *Asia Pulse*, 6 December 1999.

4 Commonwealth, *Parliamentary Debates*, Joint Standing Committee on Treaties, *Timor Sea Treaties*, 14 October 2002, 272–273.

5 Maritime Boundaries of the Territory of the Democratic Republic of Timor-Leste, National Parliament Law No. 7/2002 (Timor-Leste).

6 Northern Oil & Gas Australia Pty Limited (NOGA), a successor in title since 29 April 2016 but on notice of the Timor-Leste claims, describes the fields: 'The Laminaria and Corallina oil fields are located in in the northern Bonaparte Basin in the Timor Sea, approximately 550 km northwest of Darwin. The fields were discovered in 1994/95, with first production in November 1999. The fields are located in approximately 400m water depth. The development consists of subsea wells tied back to the FPSO through a system of subsea manifolds, flowlines, umbilicals and dynamic risers. Oil, gas and water are separated on the FPSO and stabilized oil is offloaded to trading tankers for export', http://www.northernoil.com.au/laminaria-corallina (accessed 5 January 2019).

7 Commonwealth, *Parliamentary Debates*, House of Representatives, 6 March 2003, 9371 (Bob Brown) Petroleum (Timor Sea Treaty) Bill 2003: 'I believe we are being ambushed with this legislation'.

8 Treaty between Australia and the Democratic Republic of Timor-Leste on Certain Maritime Arrangements in the Timor Sea, Australia–Timor-Leste, signed 12 January 2006, 2483 UNTS 359 (entered into force 12 January 2006) Art. 7(1)(c) and (2).

9 R. Baird and D. Rothwell (eds), *Australian Coastal and Marine Law* (Annandale, NSW: Federation Press, 2011) 114.

10 Paul Cleary, *Shakedown: Australia's Grab for Timor's Oil* (Crows Nest, NSW: Allen & Unwin, 2007).

11 John M. Miller, 'Congress Urges Expeditious Talks on Permanent Maritime Boundary for East Timor: Calls on Australia to Create Trust Fund for Disputed Revenue', *ETAN News*, 4 March 2005, available at http://www.etan.org/news/2005/03autral.htm; Guteriano Neves, Charles Scheiner and Santina Soares, *Sunrise LNG in Timor-Leste: Dreams, Realities and Challenges*

(Dili: La'o Hamutuk, 2008) 87–91, available at http://www.laohamutuk.org/Oil/LNG/LNGReportLoRes.pdf.

12 Manuel de Lemos and Nigel Wilson, 'Treaty to Pump $2.5bn to E Timor', *The Australian*, 13 January 2006.

13 Treaty between Australia and the Democratic Republic of Timor-Leste on Certain Maritime Arrangements in the Timor Sea, Australia–Timor-Leste, signed 12 January 2006, 2483 UNTS 359 (entered into force 12 January 2006) Art. 5 (12); see also Joint Standing Committee on Treaties, House of Representatives, *Treaties Tabled on 6 and 7 February 2007*, Report No. 85 (2007) 46 [6.30]: 'The Committee notes that, as a consequence of Article 4, Australia will be able to continue regulating authorizing petroleum activities outside of the JPDA and south of the 1972 Australia-Indonesia seabed treaty. This area encompasses the Laminaria-Corallina gas fields, preventing further revenue claims between the two countries in this area'.

14 Peter Southgate, 'Offshore Energy Program Underway', *AusGeo News*, 90 (June 2008), available at http://www.ga.gov.au/ausgeonews/ausgeonews200806/offshore.jsp.

15 Office of the Inspector of Transport Security, *Offshore Oil and Gas Resources, Security Sector Inquiry* (Parliamentary paper 2012, no. 172), June 2012.

16 'Alexander Downer—Pompous Colonial Git', *Crikey*, 6 March 2003, available at http://www.crikey.com.au/2003/03/06/exclusive-alexander-downer-pompous-colonial-git/.

17 Interview with Jonathan Holmes, 'Rich Man, Poor Man', ABC TV, *Four Corners*, 10 May 2004

18 Cleary, 2007, 93–97; Jane Perlez, 'U.S. Chief Pushes Oil Giant's Moves Beyond Australia', *New York Times*, 11 August 2004; Nigel Wilson, 'Australia Warns Timor On Gas Claim', *The Australian*, 30 July 2004.

19 Minutes of the Timor Sea Treaty Ministerial Meeting (Council of Ministers Meeting Room, Dili, Timor-Leste, 27 November 2002), see fn 16; Robert J. King, Submission No. 27, 'The Timor Gap, 1972–2017' to Joint Standing Committee on Treaties, 2017, 53 fn 365; Submission No. 25, 'The Timor Gap, 1972–2003' to the Joint Standing Committee on Treaties, Review of the Timor Sea Treaties, June 2003, 54; Robert J. King, Submission No. 13 to Joint Standing Committee on Foreign Affairs, Defence and Trade, Inquiry into Australia's Relationship with Timor-Leste (lapsed on Prorogation of 43rd Parliament, August 2013).

20 'BOC to Build Australian Helium Plant; Helium to Service Customers in Australia, New Zealand and Asia', *BusinessWire*, 9 March 2005, available at https://www.businesswire.com/news/home/20050309005796/en/BOC-Build-Australian-Helium-Plant-Helium-Serve (accessed 3 October 2019).

21 Mark Dodd, 'East Timor Hopes for Break in Oil Talks', *The Australian*, 27 April 2005.

22 Joint Standing Committee on Treaties, House of Representatives, *Treaties tabled on 6 and 7 February 2007*, Report No. 85 (2007) 46, [6.30] (quoted above in fn 14). If the CMATS Treaty was found to be invalid, so too would be the Side-Letters and therefore any legal basis of the Australian-approved 'activities' conferred by the CMATS Treaty.

23 'Interview: Peter Galbraith, Former US Politician and Diplomat', ABC TV, *Lateline*, 25 November 2015, available at https://www.abc.net.au/lateline/interview:-peter-galbraith,-former-us-politician/6974572 (accessed 3 October 2019).
24 Australian Bureau of Statistics, *5204.0—Australian System of Accounts, 2004–05*, available at https://www.abs.gov.au/AUSSTATS/abs@.nsf/allprimarymainfeatures/51C21550F77FDEA8CA2568A9001393E9?opendocument (accessed 3 October 2019).
25 United Nations Convention on the Law of the Sea, opened for signature 10 December 1982, 1833 UNTS (entered into force 16 November 1994) Art. 244.
26 Clinton Fernandes, *Island Off the Coast of Asia* (Lanham, MD: Lexington Books, 2018) 107–131.
27 For the interplay between the 1969 Vienna Convention on the Law of Treaties and customary international law with respect to consent to be bound and the effect of economic coercion, see Joe Verhoeven, 'Invalidity of Treaties: Anything New in/under the Vienna Conventions?', in Enzo Cannizzaro (ed.), *The Law of Treaties: Beyond the Vienna Convention* (Oxford: Oxford University Press, 2011) 304: 'It is well-known that economic coercion was, for instance, not admitted as a ground of invalidity at Vienna, despite the demands of many, mostly developing, countries. Accepting such a ground in the absence of any use of military force, however, appeared much too risky to the majority of the participants at the Vienna Conference, including almost all developed countries. Possibly, such caution was wisdom 50 years ago. Is it still? That is at least doubtful'.
28 *Thiel v Commissioner of Taxation* (1990) 171 CLR 338, Mason CJ, Brennan and Gaudron JJ at 344.
29 Timor-Leste did not ratify the Vienna Convention until 8 January 2013.
30 *Thiel v Commissioner of Taxation* (1990) 171 CLR 338, Mason CJ, McHugh, Brennan and Gaudron JJ agreeing at 356: 'because the interpretation provisions of the Vienna Convention reflect the customary rules for the interpretation of treaties, it is proper to have regard to the terms of the Convention in interpreting the Agreement, even though [the other party] is not a party to that Convention' (more recently cited in *Burton v Commissioner of Taxation* [2018] FCA 1857, Logan, Steward and Jackson JJ at 47–49.

16 Export Trade *Versus* Defence
1 Department of Defence, *Defence White Paper 2013* (Canberra, 2013) 28.
2 Department of Defence, *Defence White Paper 2016* (Canberra, 2016) 19.
3 *United Nations Convention against Corruption*, open for signature 9 December 2003, 2349 UNTS 41 (entered into force on 14 December 2005).
4 Michael Kirby, 'An Australian Charter of Rights—Answering Some of the Critics', *Law CPD*, 2015, available at http://lawcpd.com.au/online-courses/tasmania/barrister/practical-legal-ethics/australian-charter-rights-answering-some-critics.
5 Commonwealth, *Parliamentary Debates*, Joint Standing Committee on Treaties, *Timor Sea Treaties*, 14 October 2002, 271–273.

6 Commonwealth, *Parliamentary Debates*, Joint Standing Committee on Treaties, 26 February 2007, 35 (Andrew Wilkie questioning John Hartwell): 'we work together with Treasury on this one [i.e., on revenue]'.
7 Exchange of Notes Constituting an Agreement between the Government of Australia and the United Nations Transitional Administration in East Timor (UNTAET) concerning the Continued Operation of the Treaty between Australia and the Republic of Indonesia on the Zone of Cooperation in an Area between the Indonesian Province of East Timor and Northern Australia of 11 December 1989, Australia–UNTAET, signed 10 February 2000, [2000] ATS 9 (entered into force 10 February 2000, with effect from 25 October 1999).
8 Minister Alfredo Pires, interviewed by Andrew Fowler 'Taxing Times in Timor', ABC TV *Four Corners*, 1 October 2012, available at https://www.abc.net.au/4corners/taxing-times-in-timor/4291614.
9 Roger G. Skirrow et al., *Critical Commodities for a High-Tech World: Australia's Potential to Supply a Global Demand* (Canberra: Geoscience Australia, 2013) 64, available at http://www.ga.gov.au/corporate_data/76526/76526.pdf.
10 Dept of Defence, *Defence White Paper 2013* (Canberra, 2013).
11 Paul Dibb, *Review of Australia's Defence Capabilities* (Canberra: AGPS, 1986); Gregory Colton, 'Talisman Sabre 17: The Realisation of Defence Strategy', *The Interpreter*, 25 July 2017, available at https://www.lowyinstitute.org/the-interpreter/talisman-sabre-17-realisation-defence-strategy.
12 Gregory Colton, 'Australia, US and NZ Military Co-operation Augurs Well', *The Interpreter*, 3 August 2017, available at https://www.lowyinstitute.org/the-interpreter/australia-us-and-nz-military-co-operation-augurs-well.
13 Colton, 'Australia, US and NZ Military Co-operation Augurs Well', 2017.
14 Timor-Leste's senior adviser, Professor Sir Elihu Lauterpacht QC, and the author met Australia's adviser, Professor James Crawford, *ad referenda* in Cambridge on 12 November 2013. Timor-Leste proposed a hearing in camera for any national security aspects of the witness' evidence and submitted draft procedural rules to accommodate this.
15 Agreement Between the Government of the Commonwealth of Australia and the Government of the Republic of Indonesia establishing Certain Seabed Boundaries, Australia–Indonesia, signed 18 May 1971, [1973] ATS 31 (entered into force 8 November 1973); Agreement Between the Government of the Commonwealth of Australia and the Government of the Republic of Indonesia Establishing Certain Seabed Boundaries in the Area of the Timor and Arafura Seas, Supplementary to the Agreement of 18 May 1971, Australia-Indonesia, signed 9 October 1972, [1973] ATS 32 (entered into force 8 November 1973).
16 Alexander Downer, interviewed by Marian Wilkinson for 'Drawing the Line', ABC TV, *Four Corners*, 17 March 2014, available at https://www.abc.net.au/4corners/drawing-the-line/5328634.
17 Don Greenlees, 'Downer: No Change to Timor Borders', *The Australian*, 25 May 2002.
18 *North Sea Continental Shelf (Federal Republic of Germany v Denmark, Federal Republic of Germany v Netherlands)* (Judgement) [1969] ICJ Rep 3.

19 David Fairbairn, C.E. Barnes and B.M. Snedden, Cabinet Submission No. 1165, Off-Shore Petroleum, Legislation to Give Effect to Joint Commonwealth–State Legislative Arrangements, 25 November 1965, [32] (Off-shore Minerals—Commonwealth/State Discussions (NAA, series A4940, control C3945, barcode 1345145)).
20 Michael Richardson, 'Jakarta's Tough Sea Boundary Claim', *Australian Financial Review*, 20 December 1978.
21 Robert J. King, Submission No. 27, 'The Timor Gap, 1972–2017' to Joint Standing Committee on Treaties, 2017, 11–12.
22 Republic of Indonesia, 'Deposit by the Republic of Indonesia of a list of geographical coordinates of points, pursuant to article 47, paragraph 9, of the Convention', Submission to the United Nations in compliance with the deposit obligations pursuant to the United Nations Convention on the Law of the Sea (UNCLOS), 25 March 2009, available at http://www.un.org/depts/los/LEGISLATIONANDTREATIES/STATEFILES/IDN.htm.
23 Republic of Indonesia, Partial Continental Shelf Submission in respect of the area of North West of Sumatra to the United Nations Commission on the Limits of the Continental Shelf, 16 June 2008, available at http://www.un.org/Depts/los/clcs_new/submissions_files/idn08/Executive20Summary.pdf.
24 Submission No. 5261 to Cabinet, *Australia–Indonesia Maritime Delimitation Negotiations*, 6 October 1987, 2 (NAA, series A14039 barcode 31429247).
25 Treaty between the Government of Australia and the Government of the Republic of Indonesia establishing exclusive economic boundary and certain seabed boundaries, Australia-Indonesia, signed 14 March 1997, [1997] ATNIF 4 (not yet in force).
26 Alexander Downer, interviewed by Marian Wilkinson, 'Drawing the Line', ABC TV, *Four Corners*, 17 March 2014, https://www.abc.net.au/4corners/drawing-the-line/5328634.
27 Dept of Foreign Affairs and Trade, *In the National Interest: Australia's Foreign and Trade Policy: White Paper* (Canberra, 1997); see also Minister for Foreign Affairs and the Deputy Prime Minister and Minister for Trade, 'Foreign and Trade Policy White Paper', joint statement, 28 August 1997, available at http://www.foreignminister.gov.au/releases/1997/fa106_97.html.
28 Treaty between Australia and the Democratic Republic of Timor-Leste on Certain Maritime Arrangements in the Timor Sea, signed 12 January 2006, [2007] 2483 UNTS 359 (entered into force 23 February 2007) Art. 5(1) (CMATS). The remainder of Article 5 provides details on the calculation of each party's taxation revenues, while Article 6 provides the terms for appointing an assessor to review adjustments to the calculation of the revenues referred to in Article 5, if deemed necessary by either party. The 'petroleum resources' are defined in Article 7 as constituting those contained in CMATS itself, the Timor Sea Treaty, the IUA and 'any future agreement between Australia and Timor-Leste as referred to in Article 9 of the Timor Sea Treaty' (Art 7(1)(d)). With regard to 'Unit Area', Article 1 of CMATS, which is devoted to definitions, provides that the term 'Unit Area' refers to the area outlined in Attachment I to the 'Agreement between the

Government of Australia and the Government of the Democratic Republic of Timor-Leste relating to the Unitization of the Sunrise and Troubadour Fields, done at Dili on 6 March 2003' (IUA).
29 National Interest Analysis: Treaty between Australia and the Democratic Republic of Timor-Leste on Certain Maritime Arrangements in the Timor Sea, done at Sydney on 12 January 2006, [2006] ATNIA 4, [9].
30 Woodside owns 33.4% of Sunrise in partnership with ConocoPhillips (30%), Royal Dutch/Shell Group (26.6%) and Japan's Osaka Gas Co. (10%). Estimates as to the projected cost of the project vary, although US$5 billion is often quoted.
31 Minister for Foreign Affairs and Trade, 'Entry into Force of Greater Sunrise Treaties with East Timor', Media Release, 23 February 2007, available at https://foreignminister.gov.au/releases/2007/fa019_07.html.
32 National Interest Analysis: Treaty between Australia and the Democratic Republic of Timor-Leste on Certain Maritime Arrangements in the Timor Sea, done at Sydney on 12 January 2006, [2006] ATNIA 4, [10].
33 Mari Alkatiri, 'All Timor-Leste Seeks is a Fair Go', *The Age*, 3 November 2004.
34 JPDA PSC 03-12 and Appendix X, PSC 03-19, and PSC 03-20.
35 Treaty between Australia and the Democratic Republic of Timor-Leste on Certain Maritime Arrangements in the Timor Sea, signed 12 January 2006, [2007] 2483 UNTS 359 (entered-into force 23 February 2007) Art. 12(2)(a).
36 Shell Global, 'Shell Floating LNG Technology Chosen by Joint Venture for Greater Sunrise Project'. media release, 29 April 2010, available at https://www.laohamutuk.org/Oil/Sunrise/ShellfloatingLNG29Apr10.pdf.
37 National Interest Analysis: Treaty between Australia and the Democratic Republic of Timor-Leste on Certain Maritime Arrangements in the Timor Sea, done at Sydney on 12 January 2006, [2006] ATNIA 4, [10]. (A National Interest Analysis 'notes the reasons why Australia should become a party to the treaty. Where relevant, this includes a discussion of the foreseeable economic, environmental, social and cultural effects of the treaty action; the obligations imposed by the treaty; its direct financial costs to Australia; how the treaty will be implemented domestically; what consultation has occurred in relation to the treaty action and whether the treaty provides for withdrawal or denunciation', see Dept of Foreign Affairs and Trade, 'Treaty Making Process', available at http://dfat.gov.au/international-relations/treaties/treaty-making-process/pages/treaty-making-process.aspx.)
38 Dept of Foreign Affairs and Trade, 'Treaty Making Process', available at http://dfat.gov.au/international-relations/treaties/treaty-making-process/pages/treaty-making-process.aspx.
39 Commonwealth, *Parliamentary Debates*, Joint Standing Committee on Treaties, 26 February 2007, 32–33 (Treaties tabled on 6 December 2006 and 6 February 2007).
40 Commonwealth, *Parliamentary Debates*, Joint Standing Committee on Treaties, *Timor Sea Treaties*, 14 October 2002, 270–284.

41 Letter from Alexander Downer to Dr Andrew Southcott, Chair of Joint Standing Committee on Treaties, 22 February 2007: 'It is uncertain when an opportunity would arise after the Timorese election period'.
42 Commonwealth, *Parliamentary Debates*, Joint Standing Committee on Treaties, 26 February 2007, 34 (Andrew Wilkie questioning Penny Richards).
43 Alexander Downer, interviewed by Marian Wilkinson, 'Drawing the Line', ABC TV, *Four Corners*, 17 March 2014, https://www.abc.net.au/4corners/drawing-the-line/5328634.
44 Commonwealth, *Parliamentary Debates*, Joint Standing Committee on Treaties, 26 February 2007, 31 (Treaties tabled on 6 December 2006 and 6 February 2007).
45 Prior to the October 2004 negotiations between Timor-Leste and Australia expert advisers and oil executives conferred in Dili with the Timor-Leste Prime Minister. Woodside Executives had many meetings with Timor-Leste ministers and officials, such as those on 13 September 2004 when Woodside CEO Don Voelte and officials, including Gary Gray, flew into Dili by private jet, prior to discussions later that month.
46 Aaron Sheldrick, 'Woodside, East Timor in Talks for Onshore Plant for Sunrise LNG', *Rigzone*, 6 November 2014.
47 National Interest Analysis: Treaty between Australia and the Democratic Republic of Timor-Leste on Certain Maritime Arrangements in the Timor Sea, done at Sydney on 12 January 2006, [2006] ATNIA 4, [10].
48 Minister Alfredo Pires, interviewed by Andrew Fowler, 'Taxing Times in Timor', ABC TV *Four Corners*, 1 October 2012, available at https://www.abc.net.au/4corners/taxing-times-in-timor/4291614.
49 G.W. Tate, *et al.*, 'Australia Going Down Under: Quantifying Continental Subduction During Arc-Continent Accretion in Timor-Leste', *Geosphere* 11(6) (2015), 1.
50 Hagar Cohen, 'Did the Walls Have Ears?' ABC Radio National, *Background Briefing*, 23 February 2014. Downer stated: 'Well, I became a lobbyist for Woodside. I did one job for Woodside over a period of ... I've forgotten now, but three or four months, and that is all. Many years after I'd finished as the foreign minister ... I suppose this would have been around four years later. And I did one job for them, which was not to lobby anybody. I didn't lobby anyone, so to say I was a lobbyist is not right. But they asked for my advice, I was happy to give them my advice, and I did and I had some meetings with them and discussed the issues they wanted to discuss'.

17 Determining Maritime Boundaries

1 Agreement Between the Government of the Commonwealth of Australia and the Government of the Republic of Indonesia Establishing Certain Seabed Boundaries in the Area of the Timor and Arafura Seas, Supplementary to the Agreement of 18 May 1971, signed 9 October 1972, 974 UNTS 14123 (entered into force 8 November 1973) Art. 3.
2 Cablegram from Richard Woolcott to Alan Renouf, 17 August 1975 (NAA, series A11443): 'I wonder whether the Department has ascertained the interest of the Minister or the Department of Minerals and Energy in

the Timor situation. It would seem to me that this Department might well have an interest in closing the present gap in the agreed sea border and this could be much more readily negotiated with Indonesia by closing the present gap than with Portugal or independent Portuguese Timor'.

3 Technically, tri-points do not exist in the Timor Sea, as there is not yet a tripartite maritime boundary agreement between the three states. There are two sets of trilateral points; one set relates to the EEZ regime, occurring at the eastern and western ends of the south side of the JPDA, and one set relates to the continental shelf (A16 and A17).

4 *Island of Timor: Netherlands v Portugal*, Arbitral Award (Lardy), Permanent Court of Arbitration, 25 June 1914.

5 In 2009 Indonesia lodged with the UN Commission on the Limits of the Continental Shelf a declaration of coastal baselines. Timor-Leste has yet to lodge its baselines, but the Norwegian-funded survey done in 2003–04 has established reliable calculation data.

6 In evidence on 8 October 2002 before an Australian parliamentary committee, Ward said that the dimensions of ZOCA/JPDA coincided with the petroleum concession prospecting area granted by Portugal in 1974 to the Oceanic Exploration Company: Commonwealth, *Parliamentary Debates*, Joint Standing Committee on Treaties, *Timor Sea Treaties*, 8 October 2002, 196.

7 Equidistance is the favoured starting point for modern delimitation methodologies.

8 Vaughan Lowe, Christopher Carleton and Christopher Ward, *Opinion in the Matter of East Timor's Maritime Boundaries*, 11 April 2002, available at https://www.laohamutuk.org/OilWeb/Company/PetroTim/LegalOp.htm.

9 Victor Prescott, 'East Timor's Possible Boundaries with Indonesia and Australia in the Timor Sea', Exhibit No. 11, Commonwealth, *Parliamentary Debates*, Joint Standing Committee on Treaties, *Timor Sea Treaties*, 8 October 2002.

10 Commonwealth, *Parliamentary Debates*, Joint Standing Committee on Treaties, *Timor Sea Treaties*, 8 October 2002, Evidence to the Joint Standing Committee on Treaties, House of Representatives, Canberra, Transcript of Evidence, 8 October 2002, 200 (Christopher Ward).

11 Commonwealth of Australia, *Parliamentary Debates*, House of Representatives, Parliamentary Joint Committee on Foreign Affairs, Defence and Trade, 'Australia's Relationship with Timor-Leste', 21 May 2013, 42–43. It appears that Rothwell was referring to the 2009 Black Sea Case, *Maritime Delimitation in the Black Sea (Romania v Ukraine)* [2009] ICJ Rep 61, 115–122, as the current law followed in subsequent ICJ cases.

12 *Case concerning the Continental Shelf (Tunisia v Libyan Arab Jamahiriya)* [1982] ICJ Rep 18, 61, [73].

13 *Continental Shelf (Libyan Arab Jamahiriya/Malta)* [1985] ICJ Rep 13, [39].

14 *Maritime Delimitation in the Black Sea (Romania v Ukraine)* [2009] ICJ Rep 61.

15 Submission No. 5261 to Cabinet, *Australia–Indonesia Maritime Delimitation Negotiations*, 6 October 1987, 2 (NAA, series A14039 barcode 31429247), quoted in chapter 16.

16 Ibid., 8 (NAA, series A14039 barcode 31429247).

17 Bureau of Mineral Resources, *The Timor Trough—A Summary of Current Geological Knowledge*, Canberra, February 1970, appended to External Affairs Memorandum from Miles Connelly to Sir Laurence McIntyre, Sir Kenneth Bailey and Mr John Corkery, 5 March 1970, (NAA, A1838, 752/1/23, Indonesia–Australia Continental Shelf Boundary Negotiations, barcode 558528), quoted in chapter 5.
18 G.W. Tate, *et al.*, 'Australia Going Down Under: Quantifying Continental Subduction During Arc-Continent Accretion in Timor-Leste', *Geosphere*, 11(6) (2015) 1–24.
19 Michael Sandiford has called the Timor Trough 'something of a geological enigma. There is debate as to whether it constitutes a tectonic plate boundary. Maybe it did, for a short time several million years ago, but today the trough is seismically inactive—a sure sign it is now no plate boundary. Today Australia once again effectively travels with Timor as part of the Indo-Australian plate', Michael Sandiford, 'Travelling with Timor-Leste', *The Conversation*, 15 April 2016, available at https://theconversation.com/travelling-with-timor-leste-57635.
20 M.G. Audley-Charles, 'Ocean Trench Blocked and Obliterated by Banda Forearc Collision with Australian Proximal Continental Slope', *Tectonophysics*, 389(1/2) (2004) 66.
21 *Case concerning the Continental Shelf (Tunisia v Libyan Arab Jamahiriya)* [1982] ICJ Rep 18, 61, [75].
22 *Continental Shelf (Libya Arab Jamahiriya/Malta)* [1985] ICJ Rep 13, 57.
23 The ICJ followed this reasoning in *Maritime Delimitation in the Area between Greenland and Jan Mayen (Denmark v Norway)* [1993] ICJ Rep 38; *Land and Maritime Boundary between Cameroon and Nigeria (Cameroon v Nigeria; Equatorial Guinea intervening)* [2002] ICJ Rep 303.
24 *Maritime Delimitation in the Black Sea (Romania v Ukraine)* [2009] ICJ Rep 61.
25 Ibid., [210]: 'a question of remedying the disproportionality and inequitable effects produced by particular geographical configurations or features'.
26 Ibid., [211]: 'The continental shelf and exclusive economic zone allocation are not to be assigned in proportion to lengths of respective coastlines. Rather the court will check, *ex post facto*, on the equitableness of the delimitation line it has constructed'.
27 Commonwealth of Australia, *Parliamentary Debates*, Senate, Foreign Affairs, Defence and Trade Legislation Committee, Estimates, 26 October 2017, 93 (Senator Brandis).
28 Joint Statement by the Governments of Timor-Leste and Australia and the Conciliation Commission Constituted Pursuant to Annex V of the UNCLOS, 9 January 2017, available at https://foreignminister.gov.au/releases/Pages/2017/jb_mr_170109.aspx.
29 Partial unofficial transcript of Downer–Alkatiri Meeting, 27 November 2002, published 6 March 2003 at www.crikey.com.au.

18 Timor-Leste Complains

1 Senator Bob Carr and Mark Dreyfus, 'Arbitration under the Timor Sea Treaty' (Media Release, 3 May 2013), available at http://foreignminister.gov.

au/releases/2013/bc_mr_130503.html; Leo Shanahan, 'Aussie Spies Accused of Bugging Timor Cabinet', *The Australian*, 29 May 2013.

2 Mark E. Villiger, *Commentary on the 1969 Vienna Convention on the Law of Treaties* (Leiden: Martinus Nijhoff, 2009) 365.

3 Timor-Leste deposited a Declaration Recognizing the Jurisdiction of the ICJ with the UN Secretary-General on 15 October 2012. This enabled Timor-Leste to overcome, in due course, the reservation Australia had made requiring any state that may seek to litigate against Australia to have been a declarant to the jurisdiction of the ICJ for 12 prior months.

4 Bin Cheng, *General Principles of Law as Applied by International Courts and Tribunals* (Grotius Classic Reprints Series 2) (Cambridge: Cambridge University Press, 2006) 158.

5 Robert Jennings and Arthur Watts (eds), *Oppenheim's International Law*, 9th ed. (London: Longman, 2008) Vol. 1, 38.

6 Michel Virally, 'Review Essay: *Good Faith in Public International Law*', *American Journal of International Law*, 77 (1) (1983) 133.

7 Hugh Thirlway, *The Law and Procedure of the International Court of Justice* (Oxford: Oxford University Press, 2013) 9, 10–11.

8 Ibid., 23.

9 Memorandum of Understanding between the Government of the Democratic Republic of East Timor and the Government of Australia Concerning an International Agreement for the Greater Sunrise Field, East Timor-Australia, signed 20 May 2002 (entered into force 20 May 2002).

10 Timor Sea Treaty between the Government of East Timor and the Government of Australia, Timor-Leste–Australia, signed 20 May 2002, 2258 UNTS 3 (entered into force 2 April 2003) (Timor Sea Treaty), Art. 9(b).

11 Considered by the author to be a common law conspiracy to defraud. In 2014 some commentators referred to s 334 of the *Criminal Code* (ACT). The current Inspector-General of Intelligence and Security, the Hon. Margaret Stone, has observed that s 334 does not bind the Commonwealth and its agents.

12 Vienna Convention on the Law of Treaties, opened for signature 23 May 1969, 1155 UNTS 331 (entered into force 27 January 1980), Art. 49 (Clandestine interception of internal deliberations).

13 Vienna Convention on Diplomatic Relations, Arts 27(1) and (4), and 48.

14 Specifically, misrepresented immigration entry, burglary and conspiracy. In October 2004, Timor-Leste had not introduced its own criminal code. When declaring the adoption of Indonesian law in UNTAET Regulation 1/1999, the UN excluded the offences of treason and espionage. Professor Coutinho and Dr Gala mistakenly refer to the subsequent, and inapplicable Timor-Leste *Criminal Code*, Art. 200 (F.P. Coutinho and F.B. Gala, 'David and Goliath Revisited: A Tale About the Timor-Leste/Australia Timor Sea Agreements', *Texas Journal of Oil, Gas and Energy Law*, 10 (2014) 454).

15 Villiger, 2009, 615.

16 Ibid., 617 fn 20.

17 Oliver Dörr and Kirsten Schmalenbach (eds), *Vienna Convention on the Law of Treaties: A Commentary* (Heidelberg: Springer, 2012) 846.

18 Trans-Pacific Partnership Agreement, signed 4 February 2016 at Auckland, New Zealand (not yet in force).
19 Vienna Convention on the Law of Treaties, Arts 49 (Fraud), 50 (Corruption) and 51(Coercion).
20 Gérard Niyungeko, 'Article 49 Convention of 1969', in Olivier Corten and Pierre Klein (eds), *The Vienna Conventions on the Law of Treaties* (Oxford: Oxford University Press, 2011) Vol. 2, 1144.
21 *Report of the International Law Commission* ... 1966 ILC Year Book Vol. 2, 10.
22 Ibid., 245, cited in Arthur Watts (ed.), *The International Law Commission 1949–1998* (Oxford: Clarendon Press, 2000) Vol. 2, 734–735.
23 *Report of the International Law Commission* ... 1966 ILC Year Book Vol. 2, 9.
24 Vienna Convention on the Law of Treaties, Art. 49.
25 *Report of the International Law Commission* ... 1966 ILC Year Book, Vol. 2, 244.
26 *Nuclear Tests Case (Australia v France)* (Judgement) [1974] ICJ Rep 253, 268, [46].
27 *Consideration of the Principles of International Law concerning Friendly Relations and Co-operation among States in Accordance with the Charter of the United Nations*, GA Resolution 1966 (XVIII), 18th sess, 1281st plen mtg (16 December 1963).
28 *Declaration on Principles of International Law concerning Friendly Relations and Co-operation among States in accordance with the Charter of the United Nations*, GA Resolution 2625 (XXV), UN GAOR, 25th sess, 1883rd plen mtg (24 October 1970).
29 *Nuclear Tests Case (Australia v France)* (Judgement) [1974] ICJ Rep 253, 268.
30 Without leave of the parties, the proceedings of the arbitration remain confidential and cannot be addressed by the author in this book.
31 *Church of Scientology v Woodward* (1982) 154 CLR 25.
32 Jack Waterford, 'AFP Still Bloodhounds Just Sniffing Around', *Canberra Times*, 30 March 2018.

Index

Note: Page locators followed by *i* indicate an illustration

Acheson, Dean 28
Agip-ENI 285, 286, 289
aid policy 340
Alatas, Ali 174, 176, 184, 196–7
Aldrich, George 168–9
Alkatiri, Mari 89, 265, 273*i*
  as Constituent Assembly minister 251
  at first CNRT National Congress 220
  given responsibility by CNRT for Timor Sea oil negotiations 205
  joins with Gusmão and Horta in signing CNRT Declaration of 20 October 1999 197, 204, 209, 210, 211*i*
  signs Timor Sea Treaty on 20 May 2002 creating Joint Petroleum Development Authority (JPDA) 277, 278
  leadership of FRETILIN 138, 161, 172, 188, 221
  meeting with Downer 181, 265
  as Prime Minister of Timor-Leste 277
  role in Transitional Government 224
  threat of ICJ proceedings re Timor Gap treaty 227
  and Timor Gap Treaty negotiations 205, 227, 228–9, 231–2, 233–4, 242, 322
  as Vice-President of Timor-Leste 270–2
Alkatiri Government 13, 190, 257, 277, 331, 332, 336, 337–8, 351, 355, 372

Almeida, Ines 176
ALP (Australian Labor Party) 15, 21, 368
Altantic Charter 4
Andropov, Yuri 136
Angkatan Bersenjata Republik Indonesia (ABRI). *see* Indonesian military
Anglo-Iranian Oil Company 74
Anglo-Japanese Treaty Alliance 3
Anglo-Portuguese Alliance 33–4, 35–6, 40, 43–7, 67
Anglo-Saxon Co. Ltd. 31
Annan, Kofi 12, 190–1, 195, 205, 213, 267, 276, 277
ANZUS Treaty 26
APODETI (Associação Popular Democrática Timorense) 11, 140, 153, 159
Arafura Sea 76, 114, 346, 347
Araújo, Abílio 139, 140
archipelagic maritime rights 359–60
Archives Act 1983 (Cth) 131
Associação Popular Democrática Timorense (APODETI) 11, 140, 153, 159
asylum seekers, from West Papua 99
Atlantic Charter
  adoption of principles 21
  application 20
  application in Southeast Asia and Southwest Pacific 50
  drafting of 16–21
  free trade and economic cooperation 18, 19

as humanitarian beacon 24
ideology 18
impact on decolonisation movement 21
mythical status 25
and post-war Western diplomacy 25–6
publication and promotion of 15, 18
self-determination of all peoples 19
social security 18, 19
Soviet Union and 20–1
Atlantic Pact 6, 65–6
Atlee, Clement 17, 18, 23–4, 42, 44, 62, 66
Atlee Government 24
Atunes, Nuno 224
Austin, Dick 89
Australia–Indonesia Defence pact 163
Australian–New Zealand Agreement 1944 55–6, 57, 66
Australian Army
  2/2nd Independent Company 39–40, 42
  6th Division 52–3
  7th Division 52–3
  8th Division 40
  9th Division 53
  Services Reconnaissance Department (SRD) 60–1
Australian Constitution 353
Australian Continental Shelf
  competing claims by Portugal, Indonesia and Australia 104, 110
  Geneva Convention on Continental Shelf (1958) 105, 110, 112–13, 117, 119, 120, 123, 347, 364, 369
  Geneva Convention on Territorial Sea and the Contiguous Zone (1958) 119, 347
  geology 116
  history of exploration and development of petroleum resources 207–8
  initial territorial claim to 76
  maritime boundaries 111–21, 329, 342, 346–50
  mineral exploration permits 97, 110, 112, 117
  two shelves argument 118, 123–32, 364, 367

Woodside seeks sea boundary assurances 110–11
Australian Defence Force
  defence cooperation with Timor-Leste 340
  see also Australian Army; Royal Australian Navy; Royal Australian Air Force
Australian democracy, and policy-making 385–6
Australian Federal Police (AFP) 190
Australian Geological Survey Organisation (later Geoscience Australia) 245, 288
Australian neo-imperialism 9
Australian Offshore Petroleum and Greenhouse Gas Storage Act 2006 (Cth) 293
Australian Petroleum Accumulation Reports 245
Australian plate 120, 121, 124, 125
Australian Secret Intelligence Service (ASIS) 87, 88, 146–7, 157, 170, 171, 373, 374, 385, 388–9
Australian Security Intelligence Organisation (ASIO) 88, 373–4
Australia–New Zealand Agreement (1944) 4
Azores Bases Agreement 65, 195
Azores Islands, British base 43–7

Bailey, Kenneth 112, 118, 120, 382
Balibo killings 136–7, 154–9, 387
Ball, Desmond 170, 186, 191
Barnard, Lance 145
Barnes, Charles 110, 115
Barnes v Addy 302
Barrie, Chris 249, 344
Barwick, Garfield 8, 85, 88–9, 90, 97, 99, 102–5, 106–7, 109–11, 112
Batley, James 197, 209, 215
Batoka Pty Ltd 323, 324
Battle of the Atlantic 43, 65
Bayu-Undan Field 199, 208, 211, 213, 224, 237, 281, 285–90, 291, 320, 325–6, 331
Bayu-Undan to Darwin LNG pipeline 208–9, 239–42, 284–90, 293, 317, 331, 341–2
Bechtel 321, 323, 324

Bell Group case 302
Belo, Carlos 182, 192, 194, 220, 252, 262
Bevin, Ernest 18, 44
Bialek, Dean 363
Bishop, Julie 315, 374
Blair, Dennis 194
Blamey, Thomas 39–40, 48–9, 51, 60, 61
B.O.C. Pty Ltd 123, 293, 299, 324, 332
Borges, Niny 278, 279, 304
Bougainville, Rio Tinto and 89
Bowen Basin 246
BP Petroleum Division Australia Ltd 123
Bradt, Willy 138
Brandis, George 118, 196, 311, 345–6, 368
Brennan, Frank 252
Brereton, Laurie 218
Brierly, James 381
Britain. *see* United Kingdom
British Labour Party 18, 138
British Petroleum 136, 148
Brookes, Alfred Deakin 87–8
Brown, Rodney 289
Brownlie, Ian 241
Browse Basin 329
Bruce, Stanley 42, 68, 73, 74, 80–1
Brunei, rebellion against British rule 90
Brussels Pact 65
Buffalo Field 326, 328, 333, 337
Bureau of Mineral Resources, Geology and Geophysics (later Geoscience Australia) 9, 116, 117, 122, 123–4, 126, 128, 129, 130, 302, 335–6, 365–6
Burgess, Guy 72–3
Burmah Oil 129, 148
Burton, John 26, 70–1, 72, 83

Cadogan, Alexander 16–17, 28, 29, 36, 44, 59
Caetano, Marcelo 135
Cairo Conference (1943) 54, 57
Cairo Declaration 57, 78
Callaghan, James 135, 137
Calvert, Ashton 192, 357
Calwell, Arthur 78
Campbell, Bill 224

Campbell, Ronald 33, 34–5, 36
Carr, Bob 373
Carrascalão, João 159
Carrascalão, Mario 221*i*, 224
Casey, Richard 27, 29, 69, 83, 103
Catto, Robert 287, 288–9, 290, 314
Cengic, Ivan 263*i*
Chester, Douglas 331
Chiang Kai-Shek 54
Chiefs of Staff Committee 78
Chifley, Ben 63, 71, 77
Chifley Labor Government 64, 83
China, support for self-determination in Portuguese Timor 145–6
Churchill, Winston 54, 252
 and Atlantic Charter 15, 16–19, 20, 25
 on Australia's turn to the US for defence 54
 and British base in Azores 44, 47
 meeting with Curtin 58
 military strategy 30, 33, 37, 39, 40, 42–3, 52–3
 oil-supply policy 75
 support for Portuguese sovereignty over colonies 46
CIA (Central Intelligence Agency) 87, 99, 385
Clinton, Bill 194
Clinton Administration 184, 193, 196
CMATS Treaty 274, 294, 310
 economic coercion by Australia 330–1, 336
 maritime boundaries 329, 330, 331, 333–4, 368
 negotiations between Australian and Timor-Leste 330–3, 383
 outcomes 332, 334, 337, 352
 parliamentary scrutiny 353–7
 revenue sharing 351–3
 Side-Letters 328–9, 371
 termination by Timor-Leste 371
 unitisation formula 327–8
CNRM (Conselho Nacional da Resistência Maubere) 172–3, 178, 179–83, 196–7, 216–18
CNRT *see* Conselho Nacional da Resistência Timorense (CNRT); Congresso Nacional da Resistência Timorense (CNRT)

Collaery, Bernard 158*i*, 249*i*, 250*i*, 263*i*, 273*i*, 376*i*
Collaery Law 181, 189, 374
  ASIO raid on offices 310, 373–4, 375
Colombo Plan 103
Colton, Gregory 344
Combe, David 142
Companhia Ultramarina de Petróleos (CUP) 31
Congresso Nacional da Resistência Timorense (CNRT) 12
Conlon, Alfred 49
ConocoPhillips 211, 234, 289, 290, 291, 298–9, 301, 306–9, 313, 319–24, 357
Conselho Nacional da Resistência Maubere (CNRM) 172–3, 178, 179–83, 196–7, 216–18
Conselho Nacional da Resistência Timorense (CNRT) 178–9, 180–1
  concerns over clauses in Timor Gap Treaty 216
  declaration on Timor Gap Zone of Cooperation 197, 204, 209–13, 210*i*
  dissolution 234
  first National Congress 219*i*, 219–23, 220*i*, 221–2*i*, 254
  proposal for government of national unity 219–23
Constitution Alteration (War Aims and Reconstruction) Bill 1942 22–3
Cooper, Duff 32–3, 34, 40, 68, 77
Corallina Field 328, 333, 337
Corell, Hans 200, 201, 204, 205, 206, 212–13, 218
Corkery, Laurence 125
Corporations Act 2001 (Cth) 286, 290, 320
corruption 340
Cosgrove, Peter 260–1, 264
Costello, Peter 286
Coutinho, Dr 85
Covenant of the League of Nations 201
CPWA-248 285, 286, 287, 288–90, 319, 320, 322–3, 324
Cripps, Stafford 42
Cunhal, Álvaro 135, 137, 138
Curtin, John 22, 31–2, 37–8, 41, 49–50, 52–3, 54, 57–8

da Silva, Estanislau 176, 181, 188, 251
Dan, Malcolm 152
D'Arcy Exploration Company Ltd. 31
Dare 1 meeting 182
Darwin Liquefied Natural Gas (DLNG) Plant 293–9
Dauth, John 182, 186, 196, 264
de Araújo, Rui Maria 311
de Costa, José 187
de Gaulle, Charles 252
de Mello, Sergio 180, 219*i*, 220, 250, 270
  on Australian position on Timor Gap 217
  cooperation with Australian/FRETILIN strategy 257
  on FALINTIL 261–2
  negotiation of Timor Gap treaty for UNTAET 213–14, 215, 232, 243*i*
  as Transitional Administrator of Timor-Leste 198–9, 201
Deane, William 248–9, 344
Declaration on the Granting of Independence to Colonial Countries and Peoples 82
decolonisation
  impact of Atlantic Charter 21
  United Nations and 6–8, 82
Defence Committee 7, 70, 71–2, 73, 75–6, 78
Defence Intelligence Organisation (DIO) 184, 185
defence policy. *see also* regional security
  cooperation with Timor-Leste 340
  Dibb Report 343
  forward defence island arc 2–4, 50, 51, 56, 64–5
  lack of cohesion with foreign policy 69–73, 345
  move away from reliance on Britain 21–2
  post-war defence strategy 59–61
  and threat of Indonesia 86–7
  turn to US for defence 22, 52–5
Department of Defence, on likelihood of Indonesian military action in Timor 144–5
Department of External Affairs 70–1, 77, 78, 80, 89, 93–4, 96–108, 101–2, 107

Department of Foreign Affairs 95–6, 128, 132, 140–1, 145, 150–1
Department of Foreign Affairs and Trade (DFAT) 180, 250, 264–5
Department of Immigration, Special Reports Branch (SRB) 88
Department of Industry, Science and Resources 245
Department of Minerals and Energy 130
Department of National Development 128
Dibb Report 343
Directorate of Research and Civil Affairs (DORCA) 49, 50–1
Djalal, Hashim 348
DLA Piper 311–12
Dodson Oil Concession Pty Limited 73, 74
Dowd, John 252
Downer, Alexander 168, 180, 181, 193, 237, 239, 265, 272, 342, 357
　advises Howard not to meet Gusmão 264
　and CMATS Treaty 330–1, 346, 353
　downplaying threat of violence before Timorese ballot 184–5, 192
　on maritime boundaries 333
　meeting with Alkatiri 372
　meetings with Woodside 356–7
　on proposed 'special status' for Timor-Leste 179
　requests 'photo opportunity' with Gusmão 265
　support for FRETILIN as governing party 172, 231–2
　and Timor Gap Treaty 208, 211, 235, 236–7, 240, 241, 242–3, 243*i*, 347, 350
　US assessment of 196
　as Woodside consultant 339, 358
Draaisma, Jolan 346*i*, 376*i*
Dreyfus, Mark 368, 373
Dulles, Allen 87, 88–9, 99
Dunk, William 87
Dunn, James (Jim) 93, 95–6, 148–9

East Timor. *see* Portuguese Timor; Timor-Leste
Eden, Anthony 23, 25, 44, 45
Elang Kakatua Field 180
Emet Pty Ltd 290, 292, 306
energy security 133, 328–9, 339, 342–3
Engel, Rebecca 250*i*
ethnic cleansing, in post-war Europe 24–5
Evans, Gareth 174, 176, 177, 387
Evatt, H.V. 69
　alleged pro-Soviet sympathies 20, 64
　antipathy towards Portuguese colonialism 80
　and Atlantic Charter 22, 25, 63
　on British war strategy 42
　Constitution Alteration (War Aims and Reconstruction) Bill 1942 22–3
　influence 106
　on leasing West Timor and Dutch New Guinea 50
　at Paris Conference of Allies 25
　on policing of northern island arc 56–7
　on Portuguese sovereignty in Timor 44–5
　on Portuguese troops in Australia 60
　on post-war administration of Portuguese Timor 4, 44–6
　as President of UN General Assembly 64
　at San Francisco Conference (1945) 63
　on turn to US for defence 52
　and United Nations Charter 25
Everingham, Douglas 163–4
Excise Act 1921 (Cth) 298
Exclusive Economic Zone Boundary and Certain Other Boundaries Treaty (EEZ Treaty) 350

Fadden, Arthur 30
Fairburn, David 110–11, 115, 118
FALINTIL (Forças Armadas de Libertação Nacional de Timor-Leste) 12, 160, 172–3, 253, 257–8
　25th anniversary celebrations 268, 268*i*, 269*i*
　Australian refusal to recognise as territorial army 265
　cantonment in Aileu Valley 261, 262
　demobilisation 270

disarming of 261–2, 263
patrol in Aileu cantonment 269*i*
sanctions imposed by UN 262
tight military discipline throughout militia violence 260
treatment by United Nations 259, 262, 263
UN refusal to recognise as territorial army 266–8
victory march through Dili 263
withdrawal in accord with May 5 Accord 259–60
Favaro, Frank 146–7
Feakes, Graham 150
Ferguson, Martin 294
fiduciary duty 301–2, 310
Fischer, Tim 192
Fisheries Act 1952 (Cth) 76
Fitzmaurice, Gerald 381
Fonseca, Joaquim 182
Ford, Gerald 143, 144, 152, 155, 161–2
Foreign Acquisitions and Takeovers Act 1976 (Cth) 286
foreign policy
 1963 Cabinet decision on Portuguese Timor 92–7, 99
 alignment with United States 27
 antipathy towards Portugal 66–9, 80–2
 in Asia-Pacific region 388–9
 blunders in post-war era 107–8
 under Downer 69
 failure to link with South American republics 79
 and Indonesian threat to Portuguese Timor 90–2
 influence of DORCA 49
 lack of cohesion with defence policy 69–73, 345
 lack of parliamentary oversight 385–6
 legations established in Tokyo and Washington 19
 under Menzies 64, 65, 78–9
 national interest and 153
 neo-colonialism 26, 43
 post-war independence under Evatt 63–5, 69
 under Spender 64, 65
 towards Timor-Leste 387–8
France, colonial policy 66

Fraser, Malcolm 64–5, 140, 155, 167, 171, 208
Fraser Caretaker Government 167–8
Fraser Government 168
Frechette, Louise 243*i*
free trade, Atlantic Charter and 18
Freeport Mine 89
French, Robert 177–8
French Navy 344
FRETILIN (Frente Revolucionára de Timor-Leste Independente) Party 137, 271
 Australian dialogue with 181–2
 Australian support for party to govern new nation 231–2, 248, 250, 252, 253, 271, 272
 control of new Timor-Leste government 12
 crimes against humanity against and within 179, 248, 271
 de facto control of Timor-Leste 161
 declaration of independence for Timor-Leste 10–11, 140–1
 draft Timor-Leste Constitution 250, 251, 253
 electoral success 251, 255–6
 at first CNRT Nation Congress 220–4
 founding of 159
 ideology 138–40, 159
 lack of political maturity 219
 legacy of government 270–2
 myth of heroic armed resistance 272
 National Congress at Warwick Farm, Sydney 181, 252
 petition to UN re withdrawal of Indonesian forces 161
 seeking international support for independence 139–40
Freudenberg, Graham 151, 164
Frydenberg, Josh 235, 236, 239, 240, 245–6, 291, 313

Galbraith, Peter
 on Australian approach to renegotiating Timor Gap treaty 216–17
 as head of Political Affairs Division of UNTAET 213
 on LNG pipeline 240

negotiation of CMATS Treaty for Timor-Leste 330, 334
negotiation of Timor Gap treaty for UNTAET 209, 213, 214, 217–18, 224, 225, 226–8, 229–30, 233, 234–5, 236–7, 241, 242, 321
on production-sharing contracts 205
Garrison, Randall 253–4
Gascoyne-Cecil, Robert (Viscount Cranbourne) 42, 44
Geneva Convention on Territorial Sea and the Contiguous Zone (1958) 119, 347, 364
Geneva Convention on the Continental Shelf (1958) 105, 110, 112–13, 117, 119, 120, 123, 364, 369
Geneva Convention on the High Seas (1958) 120
Geoscience Australia 9, 125–6, 342–3, 358
  Offshore Energy Security Program 326–7
Gillard, Julia 373
Gillard Government 368
Goncalves, Tomas 185
good faith 230, 243, 274–5, 295, 315, 376–7, 379, 382–3
Grant Samuel 285, 286, 320, 323–4
Gray, Gary 330, 357
Greater Sunrise Field 228, 232, 233, 237, 246, 287, 291, 293, 312, 325–6, 327, 328, 330, 331, 341, 351–3
Greater Sunrise Special Regime 316–17
Greater Sunrise–Troubadour Field 218, 312–13
Grimaldi Case 302
Gromyko, Andrei 64
Guiding Principles on Business and Human Rights 301
Gusmão, Kirsty Sword 247–8, 249, 250*i*
Gusmão, Xanana 12, 264
  and Arafura Games 263*i*
  charismatic hold over Timorese people 245, 254–5
  as CNRT President 178–9, 232
  as Commander-in-Chief of FALINTIL 257, 260, 266, 268*i*, 269*i*, 273*i*
  discussions with Peter Cosgrove re FALINTIL 260–1
  at first CNRT Nation Congress 220*i*, 220–3, 221*i*, 253, 258
  forays into the interior 215–16
  hopes for enduring Timor-Leste–Australian relationship 249–50
  imprisonment 178, 188
  joint declaration on Timor Gap Zone of Cooperation 197
  meeting with Alatas 196–7
  meeting with Gillard 368
  meeting with Governor-General Deane and Admiral Barrie 249, 344
  on need for civil society awareness program 248
  paying homage to dead in Liquiçá 185–6, 186*i*
  as President of Timor-Leste 277
  on recognition of crimes against humanity 179–80, 248
  resignation as Speaker of National Council 251
  resignation from FRETILIN 171–2, 257, 258
  restructuring of FALINTIL 172–3
  and Timor Gap Treaty 174, 243*i*
  treatment in Canberra 181, 264–5
Gusmão Government 277, 314, 315, 336
Guterres, Abel 368
Guterres, Lú-Olo 221*i*, 251
Gyngell, Allan 65

Habibie, Bacharuddin Jusuf 179, 183, 191, 194
Hakluyt 358
Harriman, Averell 8, 97, 98, 106, 107
Harry, Ralph 166, 169–70
Hartwell, John 226, 229–30, 234–5, 240, 304
Haryono, Harry 214
Hasluck, Paul 83, 101, 102
Hatta, Mohammad 62, 83
Hawke Government 385
helium 182, 324
  Australia's hunt for 208, 232, 303
  as critical commodity 282–3, 291, 321
  and definition of 'natural gas' 279, 292, 298, 300, 301, 305, 306–7, 315

and definition of 'petroleum' 234, 235, 236, 238, 239, 242, 245, 279, 295–6, 297, 343
description 281
economic recovery 282
excluded from economic modelling for Timor Gap Treaty 228–9, 238, 244
first helium-generating plant in Australia 208, 280, 293–9, 324, 332, 334
first mention during Timor Gap Treaty negotiations 235
loss by Timor-Leste and Australia 299–305, 314–15
'owned' by ConocoPhillips 234
scarcity 282
sources 282
valuation benchmarks 282–3
Helium Act 1960 (US) 283–4
Helium Privatization Act 1996 (US) 284
Helium Stewardship Act 2013 (US) 284
Hewitt, Lennox 130, 144, 148
Heydon, Peter 88
Hitler, Adolf 47, 48
Hopkins, Harry 4, 16, 17, 18–19, 20, 52, 53
Hospital Products Limited v United States Surgical Corporation & Ors 301–2
House, Edward 4
Howard, John 182–3, 193, 194, 195, 208, 241, 264, 265, 272, 277, 337, 338
Howard Government 171–2, 186–7, 205, 208, 229, 245, 258, 344–5, 385
Hoyer Miller, F.R. 64, 68
Hughes, Billy, and Paris Peace Conference 2–3
Hull, Cordell 18, 28, 57–8

Ickes, Harold 28
imperial trade preferences 18, 19
Indonesia
anticommunist pogrom 143
attempted coup against Sukarno 98
CIA program 87, 99
expansionism 7–8, 82–91
independence 62, 83
Konfrontasi 87, 121–2

maritime boundaries 131, 134, 135, 346–50, 359–60
May 5 Accord on East Timor 187–90, 259
military. *see* Indonesian military
offer of limited autonomy for Timor-Leste 179–83
Peace and Stability Commission 259
regional hegemony 121–2
Seabed Boundaries Agreement with Australia (1972) 131, 134, 135, 346, 347–8, 359, 364
and Timor Gap Treaty 9, 11–12, 367
and West Papua 83–4
Indonesia–Australia relations 264, 346
Indonesian Embassy, Canberra, protest against Santa Cruz massacre 176–8, 177*i*
Indonesian military 176
anticommunism 87, 88, 99
arming of local militia in Timor-Leste 184
clandestine activities in Timor-Leste 154–5
invasion of Timor-Leste in 1975 11–12
Operation Komodo 152–3, 154
plans to wipe out pro-independence movement in Timor-Leste 185
withdrawal in accord with May 5 Accord 259
Indonesian nationalism 62–3, 83
Indonesian State Intelligence Service (BAKIN) 137, 154–7
Inpex Sahul Ltd 290, 292, 306
INTERFET Mission 195, 209, 260
International Court of Justice (ICJ), Australian withdrawal from jurisdiction 241
International Court of Justice (ICJ) Australian withdrawal from jurisdiction 228, 237, 274–7
Libya v Malta 364, 369
Namibia Case 200
Nauru Case 202
Nicaragua v USA 276
Nuclear Tests Case 383
Portugal v Australia 13, 174–5, 202, 278

Provisional Measures orders against
    Australia 310–11, 368
Tunisia–Libya Case 364, 366
International Law Commission (ILC)
    378, 380, 382
International Monetary Fund (IMF)
    193, 332
International Unitisation Agreement
    (IUA) 233, 274, 325–9, 330
Irvine, David 310
Issac, Leandro 222*i*

Japan 3, 27–30, 73–4
Joint Commission for the Joint
    Petroleum Development Area
    278–9
Joint Intelligence Committee (JIC) 71,
    72, 73
Joint Intelligence Organisation (JIO)
    145
Joint Standing Committee on Treaties
    (JSCOT) 353
Joku, David 171

Keating Government 163
Kennedy, John F. 89
Kerr, John 49, 50–1, 147, 152, 163
King, Ernest 44
King, Mackenzie 23
Kissinger, Henry 136–7, 138, 143, 144,
    155, 161–2
KOTA (Klibur Oan Timor Asuwain/
    Association of Timorese Heroes) 11

Laminaria Field 326, 328, 333, 337
Lauterpacht, Elihu 136, 311, 376*i*
Lauterpacht, Hersch 24, 175, 202, 381
Law of the Sea conferences 360
League of Nations 17, 201
Leerberg, Bjorn-Erik 226, 228, 231,
    234, 236, 240, 304, 338
Lisbon Conference of Allies 60
Lloyd George, David 3
Lobato, Rogerio 161, 251, 270
Lowe, Vaughan 346*i*, 362
Lowe Opinion 362–3

MacArthur, Douglas 40, 48, 52
Mackie, James 138–9
Macmillan, Harold 7

Malaya 22, 24, 29, 32, 51, 37, 71
Mallaby, Aubertin 62
maritime boundaries 329, 342, 346–50,
    359–60, 361–6, 368–70, 372
Maritime Boundary Treaty (2018) 372
Martin, Ian 187, 191, 193, 195–6
Mau Hodu Ran Kadalak 187–90, 254
Mazur, Carla 346*i*
McCarthy, John 179, 181
McEwen, John 60
McIntyre, Laurence 123
McKinnon, Don 192
McLennan, David 95–6, 150
McMahon Coalition Government 133
McMullen, Amy 346*i*, 376*i*
McNamara, Dennis 250
Memorandum of Understanding (2002)
    382
Menzies, Robert 5, 8, 23, 27, 108
    anticommunism 83, 84
    on Atlantic Charter 20
    attitude towards Southeast Asia 83
    correspondence with Salazar re future
        of Portuguese Timor 94, 96–7,
        99–100, 101, 102, 103
    defence and foreign policy 64, 65,
        78–9
    on requesting military support from
        US 29
    resignation 30
Mid-Eastern Oil N.L. 123
Migration Act 1958 (Cth) 88
Minchin, Nick 194, 208, 233, 236, 242,
    243*i*, 264, 291
Mitterand, François 138
MO9 87, 88
Mochtar Kusamaatmadja 127–8, 348
Moerdani, Benny 156–7
Mollah, Robert 238, 304
Moraitis, Chris 331
moral leadership 1, 385
Morgenthau, Henry 28
Moucho, Harold 221*i*
Mountbatten, Louis 62
Moynihan, Daniel 168
Mucho, Harold 176
Murtopop, Ali 152

national economic well-being 350–3,
    356

national interest 70, 145, 153, 209, 239, 326, 334, 345, 351, 353, 387
national security 340–1, 343, 345
natural gas, definition 279, 292, 298, 300, 301, 305, 306–7, 315
neo-colonialism 26, 43
Netherlands 28, 67
Netherlands East Indies (NEI) 28–9, 62–3
Netherlands–Australia relations 83–4
North Atlantic Treaty Organisation (NATO) 6–7
Northern Territory Administration, mineral exploration permits for Arafura and Timor Sea 76, 110
Norwegian Petroleum Act 1996 234, 235
Novus 285
nuclear waste storage industry 291

Oceanic Exploration Company 123, 127, 134
Offshore Minerals Act 1994 (Cth) 333
Offshore Petroleum and Greenhouse Gas Storage Act 2006 (Cth) 279
OPEC crisis 9, 133, 153, 209
Operation Komodo 152–3, 154
ordre international public 202
Osaka Gas 313

pacta sunt servanda 377
Palme, Olof 138, 143
Paltridge, Shane 121
Paris Peace Conference (1919) 2–4
Parliamentary Joint Committee on Treaties (2002) 326
Partido Trabalhista Timor-Leste (East Timor Labour Party) 11
Pax Britannica 2–4
Peacock, Andrew 140, 155
Pearce, George 2–3
Pearl Fisheries Act 1952 (Cth) 76, 114
Pearl Fisheries Act (No. 2) 1953 (Cth) 76, 114
Pereira, Agio 176, 194, 221*i*, 249, 311, 312, 316
Perkins, Charles 171
Permanent Court of Arbitration, The Hague 310–11, 362, 383
Pessoa, Ana 252, 272

petroleum, definition 234, 235, 236, 238, 239, 242, 245, 279, 295–6, 297, 343
Petroleum (Submerged Lands) Act 1967–1968 (Cth) 119–20, 127, 333
Petroleum (Timor Gap Zone of Cooperation) Act 1990 (Cth) 291
Petroleum (Timor Sea Treaty) Act 2003 (Cth) 305, 307, 314–15, 326, 338
Petroleum Mining Code 297, 298, 303, 305–7, 314
Petroleum Revenue Act 1985 (Cth) 279, 296, 298
Petroleum Search Subsidy Act 1959 (Cth) 105–6
petroleum-supply policy 75
PetroVal Australasia Pty Ltd 320–3, 324
Petroz NL 284–90, 292, 306, 319–20
Phillips Petroleum 197, 199, 209, 211, 218, 229, 230–1, 232, 238, 239, 241, 284–7
Pinto, Constâncio 178, 181
Pires, Alfredo 236, 249, 294, 336–7
Portugal
  alliance with Britain 33–4, 35–6, 40, 43–7, 67
  Armed Forces Movement 135, 136
  Azores Bases Agreement 65
  Carnation Revolution 10, 135–7
  ICJ proceedings against Australia 174–5, 202
  May 5 Accord on East Timor 187–90, 259
  and NATO 6–7, 8, 65–6
  neutrality during war 80
  offer of Timorese self-determination or integration with Indonesia 152–3
  opposition to Timor Gap Treaty 11–12
  at Paris Peace Conference 3–4
  proposed staged devolution of power in Timor-Leste 10
  proposed three-choice plebiscite for Portuguese Timor 136
  protest at Australian occupation of Portuguese Timor 34–6
  protests over Japanese occupation of Portuguese Timor 47–8
  request for assistance with military training in Timor 84–5

retention of Portuguese Timor
  following war 65–6
  and South Pacific Commission 67
  and United Nations Charter 81
  United Nations pressure regarding
    decolonisation 7–8, 10
Portugal v Australia 13, 174–5, 202, 278
Portugal–Australia relations
  and Indonesian expansionism 84–5
  in post-war era 79–82
  during World War II 6
Portuguese Timor 32. *see also* Timor-
  Leste
  Australian/Dutch occupation 34–43,
    48
  evacuation of Australian guerrilla
    force 40, 47
  guerrilla war against Japanese 39–40
  and Indonesian expansionism 7–8
  Japanese invasion and occupation 39,
    43
  oil exploration 73–6
  proposed post-war Australian UN
    mandate 4–5
  proposed staged devolution of power
    10
  strategic importance for Australia
    5–6, 8, 70, 72, 97, 103, 104, 151
  surrender of Japanese 60, 68–9
  threat of Japanese occupation 30–1
  US proposal for staged self-
    determination 98–9, 102
  war crimes investigations and trials
    60–1
Portuguese Timor Agreement (1941) 31
post-war reconstruction 51–2
Potts, Michael 224, 227–8, 231, 232,
  237, 240
Powell, Colin 232
public service, in Menzies era 78

Quadripartite Talks (Washington 1963)
  91–2, 101, 102–3

Raby, Geoffrey 233, 326, 341
Ramos-Horta, José 161, 171, 220
  call for review of Timor Gap Treaty
    180
  as CNRT Deputy President 178–9,
    180
  as Deputy President of CNRT 196–7
  at first CNRT Nation Congress 221*i*
  as foreign envoy 142
  imprisonment 160
  joint declaration on Timor Gap Zone
    of Cooperation 197, 204, 209
  meeting with Alatas 196–7
  on oil as source of wealth for East
    Timor 153
  response to FRETILIN declaration of
    independence 141–2
  and Timor Gap Treaty 243*i*
  and Timor-Leste resistance movement
    178–9
  visits to Canberra to garner support
    139–40
regional security 56–9
Renouf, Alan 134, 135, 148–9, 150,
  151, 171
Richards, Penny 354–5
Rio Tinto 89
Risa, Einar 278, 279, 304, 305, 306
Roberts, Frank Kenyon 46
Robertson, Bill 146–7
Roosevelt, Eleanor 17
Roosevelt, Franklin D. 4, 15, 17, 23,
  18–19, 46, 51, 52–4, 252
Roth, Stanley 192
Rothwell, Donald 363–4
Royal Australian Air Force 344
Royal Australian Navy 360–1
Royal Dutch Shell 313, 341
Royal Navy, oil fuel 75
rule of law 13, 157, 297, 340, 362, 386
Rusk, Dean 64

Sá Nogueira, J.C. 32, 39
Saffin, Janelle 368
Sahul Shelf 124–5
Salazar, António de Oliveira 5, 6, 32,
  34, 35, 43–5, 65–6, 101, 102, 96–7,
  103, 135
Santa Cruz massacre, protest at
  Indonesian Embassy, Canberra
  176–8, 177*i*
Santos Ltd 287, 290, 292, 306, 314
Seas and Submerged Lands Act 1973 (Cth)
  119
self-determination, Atlantic Charter
  and 19

Shackleton, Shirley 158*i*
Shaw, Patrick 85
Shell (Development Australia) P/L 123, 129
Shell Oil 74, 75
Singapore 29–30, 37–9, 40, 42, 51, 75
Sjahrir, Sutan 87
Snedden, Billy 110, 115
Soares, Abilio Osorio 185
Soáres, Mario 135, 136, 137, 138, 142
social security 142
South American republics 79
South Pacific Commission 67, 81
South Seas Regional Commission 56, 66
Southeast Asia, collective security measures 66–73
Southwest Pacific, collective security measures 66–73
Spender, Percy 64, 65, 80
Spooner, W.H. 110
Stalin, Joseph 20, 25
Standard Oil Co. 31
Sterndale Bennett, J.C. 38–9
Stewart, David 211–12
Stockholm Committee 138, 142, 147
Stone, Julius 24, 49, 50, 380
Strang, William 46, 64
Sugama, Yoga 155
Suharto 88, 98, 99, 143, 144, 149–50, 152, 179
Sukarno 7, 62, 83, 88, 89, 97–8
Sunda Shelf 124–5
Syrian–Lebanon campaign 42, 43

Tange, Arthur 78, 85, 97, 98, 101, 108
Taur Matan Ruak 253, 260, 266, 340
Taylor, Allan 167
Taylor, Angus 345
Tehran Conference 25
Teixeira, José 279, 304, 331
Tentara Nasional Indonesia (TNI). *see* Indonesian military
Third Washington (Trident) Conference 44
Thwaites, Jonathan 129, 217
TIMFORCE 60
Timor Gap 359, 360–6
Timor Gap Treaty (1989) 229
  bipartisan support for 179
  CNRT call for review 180–1
  CNRT declaration of support 197, 204, 209–13
  condemnation by Gusmão 174
  ICJ proceedings by Portugal against Australia 174–5
  illegality 199–207, 224, 329
  negotiation with Indonesia 131–2
  signing of 174
  Zone of Cooperation 197, 243
Timor Gap Treaty (2002) 182
  Australian discussions with CNRT 209–11
  Australian negotiations with UN 211–15
  Australian negotiations with UNTAET/Timor-Leste 224–5, 226–39
  Australian reservations 275–6, 277
  definition of 'natural gas' 279, 292, 298, 300, 301, 305, 306–7, 315, 321
  definition of 'petroleum' 234, 235, 236, 239, 242, 279, 295–6, 297, 321–2, 343
  definition of 'wet gas' 238, 298, 321
  draft treaty 237–8
  exclusion of helium from economic modelling 228–9, 244
  Indonesian concerns for Timor-Leste's interests 214
  interim arrangements 242–3
  International Unitisation Agreement (IUA) 233, 274, 295, 296, 297, 298, 325–9, 330
  Joint Petroleum Development Area (JPDA) 243, 326
  JPDA 03-12 290, 292–3, 297–8, 299–300
  LNG pipeline to Darwin 208–9, 239–42, 244, 285–90
  oppressive clauses in production-sharing contracts 204, 213, 216–18, 226, 236, 237, 241, 279, 286–7, 292, 321
  outcomes 244–6, 274, 345
  Petroleum Mining Code 297, 298, 303, 305–7
  plan to avoid paying Timor-Leste for inert gases 238–9, 290–1, 313–14

replication of illegality of 1989 treaty 218, 229, 244, 329
significance of well-head flange ownership 226–7, 228, 229–31, 235, 238
signing of 277–8
Timor Island 2–4, 41*i*, 243*i*
Timor Sea
Australian claims on areas outside territorial jurisdiction 118, 133–4
geological archive on mineral resources 335–6
mineral exploration permits 76, 112, 335–6
overlapping exploration licences issued by Portugal and Australia 122–3, 130
petroleum potential 105, 106
Timor Sea Maritime Boundary Treaty (2018) 315–18
Timor Sea Treaty (2018) 12, 13, 332, 387
Timor Trough 76, 112, 115, 117, 123, 124–5, 131, 244, 348, 358, 366
Timorese–Australian wartime alliance 40, 43
Timor-Leste. *see also* Portuguese Timor
arbitration case against Australia 294, 307, 310–11, 368, 371, 383–4
arming of local militia by Indonesian military 184, 260
Balibo killings 154–9, 158*i*, 387
civil war 159–61
Constituent Assembly 234–5, 247–8, 251–2, 255–6
Constitution 234–5, 250, 251–2, 253–4, 255, 256–7
Declaration of Independence 277
FRETILIN legacy 270–2
ICJ provisional measures orders against Australia 310–11
independence 247–57
Indonesian clandestine military activities 154–5
Indonesian invasion in 1975 11–12, 161–6
Indonesian occupation 170–3
INTERFET Mission 195, 209, 260–1
international law proceedings against Australia 13

limited autonomy offered by Indonesia 179–83
massacre at Liquiçá 185–6, 260
massacres preceding independence referendum 185–6, 192
Memorandum of Understanding 377–81
Memorandum of Understanding with Australia 215, 226, 234–5, 237, 240, 242, 325, 338, 382
militia violence 185–6, 192, 260
politicised military and police force 271
Santa Cruz massacre 176–8
Second Transitional Government 251
self-determination achieved by UN-supervised ballot 12
signing of Timor Gap Treaty 277–8
strategic importance for Australia 339–40, 343–4
survey of coastline and coastal waters 360–1
Transitional Government 224
unified resistance movement 178–9, 188
UN-sponsored conciliation with Australia 311, 312, 313, 317–18, 361, 370–2
UN-supervised ballot 190–3
Timor-Leste Defence Force (F-FDTL) 270, 271
Timor-Leste independence movement 10, 11
Timor-Leste police force (PNTL) 270, 271
Timor-Leste–Australia relations 344
Treaty on the Zone of Cooperation in an Area between the Indonesian province of East Timor and the Northern Territory. *see* Timor Gap Treaty (1989)
treaty-making fraud 368, 371, 377–81
treaty-making process 353–4, 374
Triggs, Gillian 205–6
Troubadour Field 233
Turnbull, Malcolm 245

União Democrática Timorense (UDT) 11, 140, 153, 159–60, 179, 248

Union of Soviet Socialist Republics
   and Atlantic Charter 20–1
   interception of Western intelligence
      reports 136–7
   and wars of liberation 144, 147–8
United Kingdom
   colonial policy 23–4, 43, 62–3
   oil-supply policy 75
   Petroleum Department 31, 74
United Nations
   advice to UNTAET re validity of
      Timor Gap Treaty 199–207
   and decolonisation 6–8
   legal status of UN administrations
      199
   support for FRETILIN to govern
      Timor-Leste 250, 253, 271
   support for self-determination in
      Portuguese Timor 252
   treatment of FALINTIL 259
United Nations Assisted Mission in East
   Timor (UNAMET) 187, 190, 196
United Nations Charter 25, 382
   Article 2 142
   Article 18 201
   Article 25 175
   Article 102 198–9
   Article 103 202, 203
   Articles 73 and 74 82
   Chapter VII 198, 199
   Chapter XI 81–2
United Nations Conciliation
   Commission 317–18, 371–2
United Nations Convention on the Law
   of the Sea (UNCLOS) 119, 120,
   121, 131, 132, 274–7, 326, 335, 347,
   360, 364–5, 367, 369, 370
United Nations General Assembly
   382–3
   and decolonisation 82
   Resolution 1803 200
   Resolution 3201 200
   Resolution 3281 200
   Resolution 3485 166, 167, 169
   response to Indonesian invasion of
      Portuguese Timor 166–70
United Nations Security Council
   authorisation of international peace-
      keeping force for Timor-Leste
      168

   call for withdrawal of foreign troops in
      Timor-Leste 167–9
   Resolution 384 167, 169
   Resolution 1264 168, 193–5, 261,
      267
   Resolution 1272 247, 253
United Nations Temporary Executive
      Authority (UNTEA) 199
United Nations Transitional
      Administration of East Timor
      (UNTAET) 180
   adoption of Indonesian law 201
   cost to UN budget 200–1, 225
   establishment and mandate 198
   extension of mandate 247
   opposition to World/Asian Bank
      Community Empowerment Project
      223–4
   Regulation No. 1999/1 198, 201, 252
   Regulation No. 2001/2, Article 2.6
      247–8, 251, 252
   and Timor Gap Treaty 211, 213–15,
      216–18
   UN advice re Timor Gap Treaty
      199–207
United States 29, 153
   Azores Bases Agreement 65
   federal helium reserve 283–4
   oil embargo and freezing of Japanese
      assets 27–9
   proposed staged self-determination for
      Portuguese Timor 98–9, 102
   support for Indonesian takeover of
      Portuguese Timor 144, 161–2,
      168–9
   territorial and political ambitions in
      Southwest Pacific and Oceania 78
   Vandenberg Resolution 65
Uren, Tom 143, 163
US Navy 344
US–Australian alliance 78–9

Vandenberg Resolution 65
Versailles Peace Conference. *see* Paris
   Peace Conference (1919)
Vieira de Mello, Sergio 12
Vienna Convention on Diplomatic
   immunity 176
Vienna Convention on Diplomatic
   Relations (VCDR) 377–81

Vienna Convention on the Law of
    Treaties (VCLT) 202–3, 338, 374,
    380, 381–3
Vietnam War 78
Viviani, Nancy 107
Voelte, Don 330

Wahid 264
Waldock, Humphrey 380, 381
Wardell, A.W. 59
Warner, Nick 374
Warsaw Bloc 65
Washington Conference (1963) 91–2,
    101, 106
Washington Declaration 25
Watt, Alan 80–1
Wavell, Archibald 30, 34, 37–8, 39, 43
Welles, Sumner 16–17, 18, 27, 62
West Papua 84–6, 89, 90, 99
West Timor, displaced persons from
    East Timor 247
White Australia policy 24, 78
Whitlam, Gough 137
  on 1963 Cabinet Decision 93, 144
  evidence to 1999 parliamentary
    committee 93, 144, 146, 164, 165,
    166
  failure as a humanitarian leader
    169–70
  foreign policy 107
  on integration of East Timor with
    Indonesia 134, 149, 150, 151
  meeting with Suharto 149–50, 151
  response to Timorese civil war
    160–1
  role in triggering war of liberation
    142–8

  sacking of ASIS head 147
  on self-determination in Portuguese
    Timor 143, 149, 154, 164
  views of FRETILIN leadership 164
Whitlam Government 133, 163, 387
Wilkie, Andrew 233, 326, 354–5
Wilkinson, Marian 356
Willesee, Don 151, 160
Wilson, Harold 143
Wilson, Woodrow 4
Wirajuda, Hassan 349
Wiranto 184, 194, 250
Witness K 374, 384
Wolfensohn, James 194
Woodside (Lakes Entrance) Oil
    Company N.L. 110–11, 123
Woodside Petroleum 134, 148, 153,
    229, 238, 239, 241, 284, 286, 287,
    291, 293, 313, 327, 330, 339, 342,
    352, 356–7
Woolcott, Richard 144, 148, 149, 153,
    156–7, 167, 359
World Bank 193, 194
World War II
  Australian campaigns in Pacific theatre
    48–50
  Australian/Dutch occupation of
    Portuguese Timor 34–43
  Battle of the Atlantic 43, 65
  division of Allied commands 53
  Japanese invasion and occupation of
    Portuguese Timor 39, 43
  Japanese surrender in Portuguese
    Timor 50, 68–9
Wyndham, Hugh 127–8

Yayasan HAK 182